HTML, XHTML, and CSS Bible

Fifth Edition

HTML, XHTML, AND CSS BIBLE

Fifth Edition

Steven M. Schafer

Wiley Publishing, Inc.

HTML, XHTML, and CSS Bible, Fifth Edition

Published by
Wiley Publishing, Inc.
10475 Crosspoint Boulevard
Indianapolis, IN 46256
www.wiley.com

Published simultaneously in Canada

ISBN: 978-0-470-52396-4

Manufactured in the United States of America

10 9 8 7 6 5 4 3 2 1

For general information on our other products and services please contact our Customer Care Department within the United States at (877) 762-2974, outside the United States at (317) 572-3993 or fax (317) 572-4002.

Wiley also publishes its books in a variety of electronic formats. Some content that appears in print may not be available in electronic books.

Library of Congress Control Number: 2009940878

For my good friend RD, for being just that.

Also for Mother, whose faith in her son never wavered.
We all love and miss you.

About the Author

Steven M. Schafer is a broad technologist and a veteran of publishing. He's been in and around technology as a programmer, an editor, a product specialist, a technical manager, and a Web developer. Steve employs both open-source and proprietary technologies and has worked with the Internet since the mid-1990s. He can be reached by e-mail at `sschafer@synergy-tech.com`.

Credits

Executive Editor
Carol Long

Senior Project Editor
Adaobi Obi Tulton

Technical Editor
Shawn Kessel

Production Editor
Rebecca Anderson

Copy Editor
Luann Rouff

Editorial Director
Robyn B. Siesky

Editorial Manager
Mary Beth Wakefield

Marketing Manager
Ashley Zurcher

Production Manager
Tim Tate

Vice President and Executive Group Publisher
Richard Swadley

Vice President and Executive Publisher
Barry Pruett

Associate Publisher
Jim Minatel

Project Coordinator, Cover
Lynsey Stanford

Proofreaders
Scott Klemp and Sheilah Ledwidge, Word One

Indexer
Robert Swanson

Cover Image
Joyce Haughey

Cover Designer
Michael E. Trent

Acknowledgments

A book like this requires a lot of hard work from a lot of talented people. This talent and hard work deserves recognition and thanks. As such, the author would like to thank the following:

The management team at Wiley Publishing for continuing to support large, tutorial reference books so folks like you (the reader) can benefit.

Jenny Watson, acquisitions editor, for getting the ball rolling on this edition.

Carol A. Long, executive acquisitions editor, for picking up the rolling ball, keeping the project on track, and keeping this author both responsible and happy.

Adaobi Obi Tulton, senior project editor and the best developer I've had the pleasure to work with. Adaobi simultaneously kept everything on track and provided crucial insights and feedback throughout the process — all while treating everyone else as valuable team members.

Shawn Kessel, technical editor, for ensuring that the information provided is accurate as well as pertinent, and for providing many useful insights.

Rebecca Anderson, production editor, for making sure each element was ushered through the editing process, maintaining the high quality of writing found within.

Luann Rouff, copy editor, who proved to be another in the "best of" class. Luann helped make my gibberish legible, ironed out the organizational rough spots, and otherwise finely crafted the text.

Wiley's production department, for ensuring that the text was consistent, well organized, and legible, and made it through the production process intact.

John Daily, friend and markup guru, whose hard work is still paying dividends today.

Contents at a Glance

Contents

Introduction

Welcome to *HTML, XHTML, and CSS Bible, Fifth Edition*. This book was conceived, designed, and written to provide a comprehensive overview of the two largest Web technologies, HyperText Markup Language (HTML) and Cascading Style Sheets (CSS).

This book serves as an introduction and reference to the information you need to create documents — simple and complex — for the World Wide Web.

A Brief History of the Internet and the World Wide Web

The World Wide Web is omnipresent in our lives today, and most computers and computerized devices are connected to it. However, the Web and its underlying Internet infrastructure had a very different childhood that betrays the consumer and commercial base it has today.

The Internet has its roots in the U.S. Department of Defense Advanced Research Project Agency (ARPA) project begun in or around 1960. Among the project's goals was the ability to network computers quickly and across great distances. The network was to be designed to be almost fail-safe, enabling connected computers to continue communicating even if assorted routes between them were to fail.

In 1969, the ARPANet was born, connecting several key universities. The network continued to grow, with more and more universities coming online. One of the goals of the initial project — robust, nearly fail-safe performance — was realized via the Internet Protocol (IP). This protocol enabled communication packets to find various routes to a destination in case one or more of the routes became unstable. This communication protocol became the backbone of today's Internet, and is how the Internet got its name.

The Transmission Control Protocol was joined with the IP to provide a robust transmission suite, a marriage of two protocols to offer more flexibility and the ability to create better communications applications for the Internet.

In the 1980s, the Internet went through several transitions. Although it was highly populated by educational institutions, the U.S. military hadn't forgotten its original project. Other government agencies also took notice and joined the crowd online; and the military decided to create its own network, MILNET, lessening the load slightly.

By 1992, the Internet was far and away the most popular network in the world. During this time, Tim Berners-Lee, a British software engineer and computer scientist, created HyperText Markup Language to create documents, a protocol — HyperText Transfer Protocol (HTTP) — to send such documents, and the first browser editor, called the World Wide Web. The "Web" soon came to the attention of the National Center for Supercomputing Applications (NCSA), where a programming team decided to create a better browser. Thus was Mosaic born, the first browser to support a high degree of multimedia. Mosaic helped usher in the crop of modern browsers we use today.

As the Web continued to be adopted outside of the government and educational sectors, it became more consumer-savvy. Many companies began using the Web infrastructure for marketing and support purposes, while many Web developers began to target a wider, nontechnical, audience.

By the early 2000s, the Web was accessible by almost any network-connected computer, many electronic devices, and some unlikely consumer devices such as automobiles. Each of these connected devices uses the same type of connection, the same languages to define documents, and the same protocols to send the information.

As more and more nontechnical users began using the Web, web "pages" began to look more like high-quality printed documents — resembling newspapers, brochures, magazines, and the like. This movement in content signaled how far the Web had come from its inception — from technical, text-only pages to full-color, heavily designed documents.

During the entire evolution of the World Wide Web, and especially in the last few years, standards, tools, and related applications have changed and evolved, sometimes at a very rapid pace. This gives Internet books a wide realm to cover.

What This Book Covers

What exactly is covered in this book? The easy answer is HTML and CSS, just as the title suggests; but with four plus notable versions of HTML, three plus notable versions of CSS, and a bevy of connected technologies, the answer is not so cut and dried.

The more exact answer is as follows:

- HTML 4.01/XHTML 1.1
- CSS 2.1
- JavaScript
- A few supporting applications to create and troubleshoot Web documents
- A few multimedia formats (graphics, video, and so on) and supporting applications

The following sections explain how these diverse sets of applications converge.

HTML 4.01/XHTML 1.1

HTML 4.01 is the latest version of HTML. This version is very stable, having been released in December 1999. Although HTML version 5 (HTML5) is in draft stage as of this writing, the specification is probably a good year (or so) away from actual release.

Note, however, that this book promotes and uses XHTML 1.1 standards. This includes standards such as the following:

- Every tag needs to be explicitly closed, whether by a matching closing tag or a slash at the end of a tag (if it has no matching closing tag).
- Every tag must be in lowercase; in other words, use `<p>` instead of `<P>`.
- Every tag attribute needs to be enclosed in quotes.
- Every tag attribute must have a value — for example, the attribute `selected` should be `selected ="selected"` instead.

Although these standards are not a mandatory part of HTML 4.01, they are covered in this book because the XHTML standards are stricter, don't hamper HTML, and prepare you for authoring documents in other XML-based languages.

Note

Future versions of HTML are to be based on XHTML coding standards. ■

Cross-Ref

Chapter 18 provides a glimpse inside HTML5. ■

CSS 2.1

The latest CSS version is 2.1. Although version 3.0 is in development, its release might still be years away. Therefore, this book concentrates on CSS 2.1 due to its maturity. CSS version 2.0 has been around for almost a decade, is used for millions of Web pages, and is well understood by most Web designers. CSS version 2.1 combines some bug fixes, exact specifications where there was some ambiguity, and a few more properties and values. At its core, however, it is very much like version 2.0.

Although the CSS version 3.0 specification exists in draft form and has certain features adopted into certain user agents, it is far from being viable for a wide audience. As such, it is safer to stick with the existing 2.1 standard.

Cross-Ref

Chapter 38 provides a glimpse inside CSS3. ■

User Agent (Browser) Coverage

As mentioned earlier in this introduction, in 1993 Mosaic was the first widely used browser for effectively browsing the Internet. Over the years many other browsers were developed — the list is long and varied. For example, the text-only browser Lynx was developed mostly for Unix/Linux use when graphics were scarce. Other browsers such as Opera were developed to remain a pure environment, rigidly supporting the current HTML and CSS standards.

The two staples of browser-dom, IE and Firefox, continue to dominate today's market but also continue to adopt their own standards in various ways that frustrate even the most seasoned Web developer.

Over the last few years, Mac users have had Safari, a Mac-native browser. Safari hasn't been known for its speed or adherence to standards, but it does give Mac users an alternative to Microsoft Internet Explorer.

In 2009, Google's Chrome browser was released, adding yet another platform to the mix. Chrome provides many enticing features, such as a robust security framework and decent compatibility, although it is still in its infancy despite being the fourth most widely used browser. As it matures it will no doubt go through its own growing pains, including support of standard XHMTL and CSS.

So, with all these browser options, which browser(s) are specifically covered in this book? Specifically, none of the above. Rather than cover the technology of any particular browser(s), this book concentrates on the current standards of XHTML and CSS. The technologies are presented in their ratified standard form. Browser support is mentioned where appropriate, but browser-specific hacks or workarounds are not covered.

Note

Although most of the figures in this book were produced with Microsoft's Internet Explorer, it is only a matter of publishing practicality, not favoritism. ■

This decision regarding what to include keeps the book content from being too confusing while trying to cover the various quirks of various browsers, and keeps the book a manageable size.

Web 2.0

In 2004, a new World Wide Web was heralded: "Web 2.0." This new age of the Web was to facilitate interactive information sharing, interoperability, user-centered design, and collaboration.

In the next few years several outlets for this new frontier were born. They included blogs, web-based communities, hosted services, and a bevy of social-networking and collaborative sites. It seemed as though the new Web was coming into its own. Except, this new Web was nothing new.

Web 2.0 is built on the same technologies as the original and normal Web: (X)HTML, CSS, JavaScript, etc. The only difference was that the new application of the technology was much more focused on social and collaborative features. If one were to follow the evolution of the web — from academia, through business marketing, through personal use — social uses would be the next step of the evolution of the Web. This step would be a natural evolution, not the technical revolution foretold. This book takes the position that Web 2.0, as defined back in 2004, never actually took root. Instead the spirit of the use of technology on the Web reached a natural point in its evolution, using the same tools and technologies that created the Web. As such, you will not find any specific Web 2.0 coverage within this book, but will be able to employ the building blocks that are covered for a wide range of purposes, including social and collaborative online tools.

Terminology

To stay progressive with the evolution of the Web and its direction today, this book uses less technical and more progressive terminology.

For example, you will seldom, if ever, see the words "page" or "Web page" used to refer to Web content in this book. That's because as the Web has matured as a publishing medium, words such as "document" are much more apt for describing content on the Web.

Similarly, the word "browser" is a bit passé, and is therefore rarely used. In the past, applications such as Mosaic, Mozilla, Firefox, Opera, and Internet Explorer were the only game in town when it came to accessing the Web. Such applications, which were primarily used to "browse" content on the Web, were aptly dubbed "browsers."

However, the devices and applications used to access Web content today are much broader:

- Personal electronic devices
- Onboard vehicle systems
- Entertainment system controllers
- Mall kiosks

Many of these Web-enabled applications are not like traditional browsers. They may access data differently, present data differently, and might be controlled differently than a browser. A better term for these applications is user agent, which basically means "something that enables a user to access data," which is what each of these does. For that reason, get used to seeing *user agent* instead of *browser*.

Who Should Read This Book?

This book is geared toward a wide audience. Readers who are just getting started with HTML and Web content will benefit the most, as this book provides both a solid learning foundation as well as ample reference material for later perusal. Experienced users will find the chapters covering new standards and technologies to be the most useful, but also will appreciate having a comprehensive reference for consultation.

Although the Web is technical in nature, this book boils down the technology into simple and straightforward terms. Whether you qualify as a computer scientist or as a computer neophyte, you will be able to understand, adopt, and deploy the information throughout this book.

This Is Not a Web Design Book

This book teaches the basics of HTML elements, how to integrate said elements, and finally how to layer CSS over the top. Design books generally skimp on the building-block detail, only covering how to best use the elements to achieve cosmetically pleasing results. While each type of book does cover principles of the other, the cross-over content is not comprehensive.

Typically, both approaches do not appear in the same book due to size constraints. The other reason why the two approaches are different has to do with the separation of content and design. This book concentrates on the content portion of Web design, whereas other design-centric books cover the design (visible attributes).

Tip

Wiley publishes many Web design books that can be paired with this book to provide a wide range of skills and techniques for creating technically correct and visually pleasing documents.

Two such recommendations include:

- ***Creating Web Sites Bible,* Third Edition, by Philip Crowder and David A. Crowder (2008).**
- ***Beginning CSS Cascading Style Sheets for Web Design,* 2nd Edition, by Richard York (Wrox, 2007).**

Visit the Wiley website (`www.wiley.com`) and search on "web design" to find other books applicable to your needs. ■

What Is Contained in This Book?

This book is divided into four major sections, plus five appendixes.

Part I: Creating Content with HTML

This part of the book covers the basics of HTML — the tags, attributes, and structure that make up the language. You learn how to structure a document, format text, and incorporate multimedia. You also learn basic and advanced scripting to lend a dynamic edge to your documents.

Part II: HTML Tools and Variants

This part of the book covers utilities to help you author, validate, and troubleshoot your documents. A few useful HTML variants and extensions — including XML and XHTML Basic — are also covered.

Part III: Controlling Presentation with CSS

This part of the book covers the basics of CSS, the syntax of CSS selectors, valid properties and values, and how to use CSS properties to effectively format the various portions of your document. You will also learn how to format a document for printing using CSS media types.

Part IV: Additional CSS Tools

The last part of this book covers additional CSS topics, including advanced layout, user interface styles, testing and validating CSS, and some CSS tips and tricks.

Reference Appendixes

The appendixes provide a quick reference to the material covered in detail throughout the rest of the book.

Tip

See the Table of Contents for a breakdown of chapter topics in each part. ■

How to Use This Book

This book can be used in a variety of ways depending upon your skill level and intent.

The sequential read

If you need to learn HTML and CSS from beginning to end, then a sequential read — reading the chapters in order from beginning to end — is for you. The chapters are designed to introduce topics in a particular order to get you started and build toward more advanced topics.

For a tutorial approach, choose a sequential read.

A targeted or random read

If you need only a refresher of certain material or want to learn in a different order than the chapters provide, then a targeted or random read — finding a topic in the table of contents or index to read, or reading chapters in a different order than numbered — is for you. Although the chapters were written to build on one another, they also are topical and encapsulate individual subjects. Find a chapter with information you need to learn and read it, or find a section within a chapter and read it alone.

For a referential approach, choose a targeted or random read.

Conventions and Features

Many different organizational and typographical features are used throughout this book to help you get the most from the information contained within.

Tips, Notes, and Cross-References

Whenever the author wants to bring something important to your attention, the information appears in a Tip, Note, or Cross-Reference. These elements are formatted as follows:

Tip

This information is important and is set off in a separate paragraph with a distinct look. ■

Tips generally are used to provide information that can make your work easier — special shortcuts or methods for doing something more easily than the norm.

Notes provide additional, ancillary information that is helpful but somewhat outside the scope of the material presented.

Cross-references indicate other places in the book you'll find information pertinent to the topic at hand.

Code

It is often necessary to display code (HTML tags, JavaScript commands, script listings) within the text. This book uses two distinct conventions, depending on where the code appears.

Code in text

A special font is used to indicate code within normal text. For example: `<body id="COMPONENT-body-0001" onLoad = “displaygraphics();">`.

Code listings

This code is set apart and indented from regular text, as follows:

```
 Code listings appear in specially formatted listings, in a different
font, similar to these lines.***
```

Companion Website

A companion website has been created to help support this book. It contains code from the book and examples within, as well as extra material not contained in this book. The website can be found at www.wiley.com/go/htmlbible5e.

Part I

Creating Content with HTML

IN THIS PART

CHAPTER

1

What Is a Markup Language?

IN THIS CHAPTER

The World Wide Web is a technology beast. If you have read this book's introduction, you should have at least a passing familiarity with how the Web started — its humble beginnings to bring cross-referenced textual documents to the masses via the connectivity of the Internet.

You are reading this book, so it's a good assumption that you are familiar with what the Web has become today — a collection of technologies capable of transporting numerous media across the Internet for consumption directly on your desktop.

However, it's important not to forget the Web's humble beginnings because the technologies used for the very first simple documents are still in use today, and must be understood. This chapter helps frame the reasons why.

What Are We Doing Here?

Why are we diving into technical topics instead of talking about how to create Web documents? Well, technically we are talking about how to create Web documents. The more you know about the technology behind the Web, the better prepared you will be to use the technology to your benefit, and the easier it will be to create Web documents.

Note

If you really do want to just dive into creating documents, check out Chapter 19, "Web Development Software," which covers tools you can use to quickly create documents without knowing the underlying technology behind it all. However, keep in mind that such tools do not always accomplish the goal you desire and sometimes their results need manual tweaking — tweaking that you will learn to perform throughout the other chapters in this book. ■

So back to the question: What are we doing here?

Answer: Web documents are created using several different technologies. The main technology is Hypertext Markup Language (HTML). HTML is responsible for telling a Web browser (e.g., Microsoft Internet Explorer, Mozilla Firefox, Opera, Mac Safari, Google Chrome, and so on) how text and other objects in a Web document should appear. Whether the text should be small, large, bold, underlined, or right or left justified is largely determined by the HTML embedded in a Web page.

As a consumer of Web pages, you rarely experience HTML directly; it's hidden from the end user by the browser. However, as a creator of content, you need to be intimately familiar with HTML and its uses, which is why we are starting from scratch and covering some basics first. Don't worry, the good stuff is right around the corner and we will get started creating actual content soon enough.

Understanding Hypertext

By its very nature, the Web and its content overcome many of the limitations of standard, linear text. This concept is best illustrated by a comparison of a book (in particular, a reference book) to the Web. For example, consider a cross-reference in a book. Accessing the cross-reference requires *you* to look up the page number, textual reference, or other object being referred to. On the Web, the reference is (usually) a single mouse click away.

Also, documents on the Web can be designed to vary depending on the user accessing them. Books, conversely, remain static objects no matter who is reading them.

The word "Hypertext" was created along with other Internet terms and technologies during the evolution of the Web. It was coined to describe documents that could change, redirect, and otherwise overcome the linearity of normal text. In short, "Hypertext" describes text on the World Wide Web.

Understanding Markup Instructions

Markup languages are not a difficult concept to grasp; most of you have "marked something up" at one point or another. For example, suppose you wanted someone to highlight a paragraph in this book. It would be fairly easy for you to instruct that person to do what you wanted — you could simply hand the person a highlighting pen, point to the paragraph, and ask the person to highlight it.

Note

Highlighting is only an example of what you might want to happen to a piece of text. You might want some text to be larger, bolder, underlined, or otherwise changed. Highlighting is used in this chapter as a simple, real-world example. ■

Consider the paragraph shown in Figure 1-1, highlighted in Figure 1-2.

FIGURE 1-1

A simple paragraph

Welcome to On Target Games, the online home of the best-selling game, Vanguard Odyssey. Enjoy browsing the site and don't forget to check out the updates section.

FIGURE 1-2

The same paragraph, highlighted

Welcome to On Target Games, the online home of the best-selling game, Vanguard Odyssey. Enjoy browsing the site and don't forget to check out the updates section.

This is a relatively easy task to ask of someone and have executed, because you, and most other people, understand the concept of paragraphs. You point to a paragraph and the person doing the highlighting knows the boundaries — the beginning and the end of the text to be highlighted. If the individual were really dense or needed more explicit instructions, you could write the instructions on or near the paragraph, as shown in Figure 1-3.

Note

Writing explicit editing instructions in or around text is generally known as *marking up* text. ■

Notice how the instructions "bookend" the portion you want affected. In other words, the "begin" instruction appears before the text to be highlighted, while the "end" instruction appears afterward. This is an important concept in text markup.

FIGURE 1-3

Explicitly designating the area to be highlighted by marking up the paragraph

Begin highlight here

Welcome to On Target Games, the online home of the best-selling game, Vanguard Odyssey. Enjoy browsing the site and don't forget to check out the updates section.

End highlight here

You might want more formatting to be done to the text. For example, suppose you wanted "Vanguard Odyssey" underlined. Specifying that additional formatting could resemble the paragraph shown in Figure 1-4.

FIGURE 1-4

Multiple formatting instructions might appear close to one another, or even nested within one another.

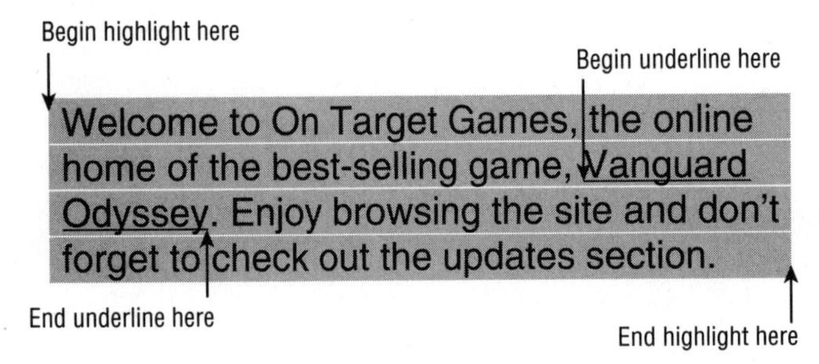
Begin highlight here
Begin underline here
Welcome to On Target Games, the online home of the best-selling game, Vanguard Odyssey. Enjoy browsing the site and don't forget to check out the updates section.
End underline here
End highlight here

Understanding Markup Language

On the Web, you aren't dealing with humans; you are dealing with computers and software — namely, Web browsers. You create content specifying how the browser should display it (highlighting certain pieces of text, and so on). When the browser displays the page, it applies the appropriate formatting accordingly so the user sees the text and document as you intended. You need a way to mark up the text so the browser understands it.

In the early 1990s, a new programming-like language was created, Hypertext Markup Language, or HTML. Don't let the word programming scare you — it is used here to put the word "language" in context; it's not really programming, as you will see. The language was created to provide a way for users to mark up documents so Web browsers could display certain elements of the document in italics, underlined, and so on.

Several requirements must be considered when telling a computer how to format text. A short list of the requirements includes the following:

- The instructions should follow a stringent set of guidelines.
- The instructions should be included in the textual document.
- The instructions should be invisible to the end user.

- The instructions should tell the display device (usually a Web browser) where to start and end, and how to apply the formatting specified.

Note

The first item in the preceding list, requiring a "stringent set of guidelines," is very important. As with most programming languages, a strict set of guidelines and syntax is necessary to ensure that the programmers (Web designers) create programs (Web pages) that the computers (Web browsers) can understand. Throughout this book, I will continually stress the standards created by organizations such as the World Wide Web Consortium (W3C), the folks behind the World Wide Web and its related standards. ■

Essentially, a *markup language* is a systematized and standardized markup instruction set.

Consider how such a language would work. As in the earlier example about highlighting, instructions could be appended to the paragraph similar to that shown in Figure 1-3. However, because the Web page needs to be in electronic text form only (no handwriting allowed!), the document would end up resembling something like this:

```
Begin Highlight Here Welcome to On Target Games, the online home of
the best-selling game, Begin Underline Here Vanguard Odyssey End
Underline Here. Enjoy browsing the site and don't forget to check out
the updates section.  End Highlight Here
```

It's difficult to tell where the text and markup begin and end when the markup is used in this way. It would be much better if the markup instructions were delimited by something so that you, and the Web browser, could tell where and what they were.

Thankfully, in HTML the markup instructions are indeed delimited. They are enclosed in angle brackets — more commonly known as "less than" and "greater than" signs (< and >). Furthermore, the directives don't need the words "begin" or "end." The beginning marks simply contain a keyword corresponding to what the markup should accomplish, and the ending marks include a slash (/). For example, the underlining markup directive is simply "u" (for underline) and it appears as shown in the following text:

```
Welcome to On Target Games, the online home of the best-selling game,
<u>Vanguard Odyssey</u>. Enjoy browsing the site and don't for-
get to check out the updates section.
```

The <u> designates the beginning of the underline and the </u> designates the end. This paragraph rendered in a Web browser would resemble what is shown in Figure 1-5.

Similarly, in HTML, bold is represented by "b" (<b> and </b>), italic by "i" (<i> and </i>), and so on. Other markup instructions and directives have similar tags. These tags are inserted into Web pages, and the Web browser reads the page and uses the tags to properly format the text and other items on the page.

FIGURE 1-5

The paragraph in a Web browser

Summary

What does all this mean? There are some basic technologies underneath the surface of the Web to which you must pay attention. HTML is the backbone of these technologies, and knowing it is the key to successful Web design. Understanding markup concepts is key to understanding proper HTML use.

CHAPTER

HTML Values and Units

IN THIS CHAPTER

In the previous chapter you learned what markup language is and how it relates to HTML and the Web. Expanding on these basics, you can add attributes to your HTML tags to further control their effect on your documents.

Basic Tag Attribute Format

Most HTML tags support one or more attributes. These attributes are included in the opening tag using a standard format, as follows:

```
attribute_name="attribute_value"
```

For example, the `border` attribute is used with the `<table>` tag to control the width of the border in and around a table in the document. The border attribute resembles the following when actually included in the `<table>` tag:

```
<table border="1">
```

Pay close attention to the following rules regarding attributes:

- Any attributes in an HTML tag need to appear after the HTML tag name.
- The attribute name must be followed immediately by an equal sign (=).
- The attribute value needs to come immediately after the equal sign.
- The attribute value must always be enclosed in quotes, either single or double.

Note

In previous versions of HTML, some attributes — namely, those with default values — did not need to have a value associated with them. However, in HTML all attributes must have a value included inside the tag with their declaration. In short, you should always provide a value with tag attributes. ■

Several different types of values can be used as values for attributes:

- Text (single words, no spaces)
- Numbers (unsigned)
- Color values (color names or color values)

In the case of color values, several options can be used to specify a particular color:

- Color names (blue, black, red, and so on)
- Color values (in hexadecimal)
- Color values (in decimal)

The color name method is very straightforward; you simply specify a color as the value of the attribute. For example, in the following color attribute snippet, the color is set simply to `"blue"`:

```
color="blue"
```

This method accepts only a preset number of colors defined by HTML — approximately 147 different colors that can be found listed on sites such as `www.w3schools.com/html/html_colornames.asp`.

The hexadecimal and decimal methods of specifying colors are slightly more complex because they allow you to actually mix colors by specifying custom amounts of the primary colors: red, green, and blue. The correct hexadecimal format follows:

```
"#RRGGBB"
```

The color specification must begin with a pound sign (#) and be followed by six digits — the first two digits corresponding to the value of red, the second green, and the third blue. Again, keep in mind that these values are hexadecimal, *not* decimal. Consider the following codes and corresponding values:

```
#FF0000          Red
#00FF00          Green
#0000FF          Blue
#FF00FF          Purple (Red and Blue)
#000000          Black
#FFFFFF          White
```

For example, to set a color attribute to purple, you could use the following code:

```
color="#FF00FF"
```

This allows more control over the actual color, but requires you to compute the value of the color in hexadecimal. Thankfully, most graphic editing programs contain features to display or convert color values in hexadecimal format. For example, Figure 2-1 shows the color selection dialog in Adobe Photoshop, which includes a hexadecimal value of the current color.

FIGURE 2-1

Most graphic editing programs, like Adobe Photoshop shown here, include methods to specify colors in both decimal and hexadecimal values.

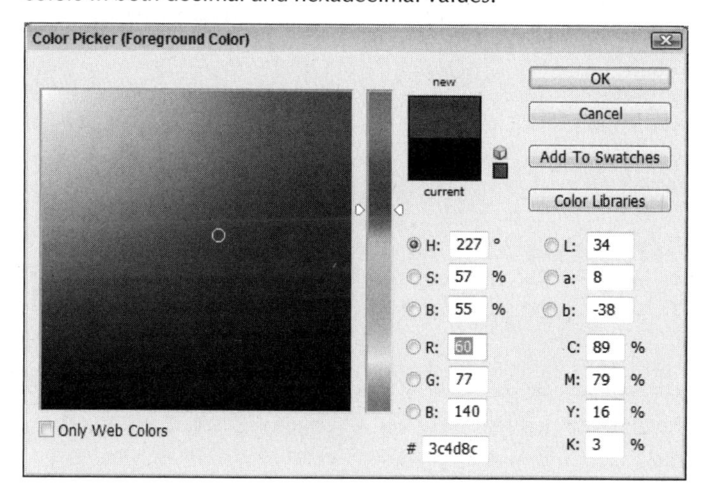

The other format supported by the color attribute is the color's RGB (red, green, blue) value in decimal format. Instead of being prefixed by a pound sign, the RGB decimal format uses the following format:

```
color="rgb(R,G,B)"
```

In this case, the values of the colors are specified as values between 0 and 255, or percentages (values between 0% and 100%). For example, to set the color to purple (max red, no green, max blue), you would use either of the following codes:

```
color="rgb(255,0,255)"
color="rgb(100,0,100)"
```

Throughout this book, the applicable attributes are discussed along with the tags to which they apply.

Note

See the next section, "Common Attributes," for attributes common to most tags. ■

Common Attributes

Several attributes are available and applicable to most tags in HTML. These attributes serve the same general purpose regardless of the tag with which they are used. The following sections describe these tags and the purpose they serve when you apply them.

Tag identifiers – IDs and classes

As you will learn in the style and scripting sections of this book, sometimes it is advantageous to identify particular tags so you can refer to them by other methods in the document.

IDs

The `id` attribute effectively assigns a unique identifier to a tag. For example, if you use a `<table>` to contain inventory data, you might use the `id` attribute to name the table `inventory`:

```
<table id="inventory">
 ...
</table>
```

Note

When using the `id` attribute, keep in mind that each tag should have a unique value for its `id` attribute. ■

Locally — that is, within the tag — the `id` attribute has no real effect. However, scripts can access and manipulate tags based on their `id` attribute.

Cross-Ref

For more information on how scripts can access tags based on their `id` attribute, see Chapters 16 and 17. ■

As you design your pages, consider whether you will need to reference any of your tags by outside means (scripts and so on).

Classes

Classes are similar to IDs in that they help identify tags in the document for use by other methods. However, unlike IDs, which should be unique, classes can (and should) be applied across several tags in your document.

Applying classes to tags is similar to applying IDs and other attributes. For example, to apply a class `"emphasis"` to a `table` tag, you would use code similar to the following:

```
<table class="emphasis">
```

As with the `id` attribute, the `class` attribute doesn't directly affect the tag to which it is added. What the `class` attribute does do is link the tag to CSS styles that also reference that specific class. To completely understand the link between the two — HTML tags using classes, and styles referencing those classes — you must understand CSS and its methods for accessing class-coded styles. However, keep classes in mind as you code your basic HTML so you can adequately incorporate them.

Cross-Ref

To get a better idea of how CSS styles work with class-coded HTML tags, see Chapters 25 through 38. ■

Besides linking styles via the `class` attribute, you can also embed specific styles into the individual tag itself using the `style` attribute. The `style` attribute has the following format:

```
style="style-definition; style-definition; style-definition;...
```

This format allows you to specify as many styles as necessary, as long as you separate them with semicolons, as shown in the preceding example.

Text and Comments

Including text that isn't processed by the user agent in your documents can be beneficial for a couple of reasons. The first reason is simple documentation — that is, to make your documents more legible and easy to follow should you need to edit them later. The second is to include more information within the document for later access or inclusion by features supported in upcoming browsers.

Comments

HTML comments are fairly simple to include in your document, as they have a simple format. A comment in your document might resemble the following:

```
<!--     This is a comment  -->
```

Notice that the HTML comment tag is a bit odd, given the dashes and exclamation point in the mix. For clarity, the tag breaks down as follows:

- The tag starts with the standard left angle bracket (<).
- The next character is an exclamation point (!).
- Two hyphens (- -) follow the exclamation point.
- The text of the comment is next.
- The tag starts to close with another set of two dashes (- -).
- The tag closes with a standard right angle bracket (>).

Note

You cannot nest comments within one another. ■

Comments are best used for short text, not for commenting out large sections of HTML code.

CDATA sections

Larger comments can make use of CDATA structures — structures created for other markup specifications but enabled in most user agents for XML, as well as HTML (XHTML), rendering. Hence, CDATA is used often for commenting large sections of code in HTML documents.

The format of the CDATA tag is as follows:

```
<![CDATA[     Commented text goes here    ]]>
```

The CDATA tag has vaguely familiar syntax:

- The tag begins with an angle bracket (<).
- The next character is an exclamation point (!).
- The next few characters define the XML tag ([CDATA[).
- The text of the comment is next.
- The tag begins to close with the two brackets (]]).
- The tag closes with the right angle bracket (>).

Like the comment tag, you cannot nest CDATA tags within each other.

Tip

The text within a comment or CDATA section is still delivered to the browser and can be seen if the user chooses to reveal the source of the page. The data in these sections is just not rendered as visible text. ■

Uniform Resource Indicators

Uniform resource indicators (URIs) are highly structured lines of text that refer to other resources — locally or on the Internet. In short, URIs are what make the Web the Web — giving pages the ability to provide a link to another page on the Internet. For example, an automobile manufacturer's website may contain links to the different models of cars the manufacturer makes, links to dealerships around the nation, or links to documents of specifications for different vehicle models.

Note

The phrase uniform resource indicator (URI) is the preferred name for a link on the Internet. Previously, such a link was commonly referred to as a uniform resource locator (URL). ■

The format of the URI is shown in Figure 2-2.

Notice how the URI includes the protocol that should be used to reach the URI resource. This is typically Hypertext Transfer Protocol (HTTP, transferring HTML documents), but it can be other protocols such as File Transfer Protocol (FTP), which transfers all manner of files.

FIGURE 2-2

The format of a URI

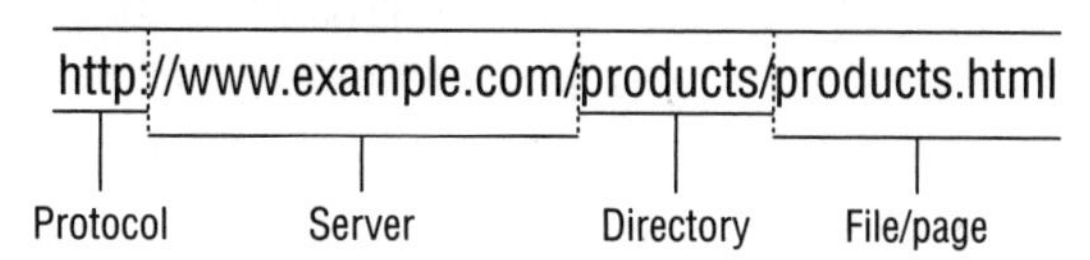

URIs are used as values for attributes in several different tags, including anchors (used for links to other documents) and images (used to insert images in a document). Consider these two examples, where the URI is underlined for emphasis:

```
<a href="http://www.example.com/detailspecs.html">Details</a>
<img src="http://www.example.com/detail.jpg" alt="details" />
```

When you construct a URI for tags in your documents, keep the various pieces of the URI in mind and always try to provide as much detail in your URIs as possible.

Cross-Ref

For more information on URIs and links, see Chapter 8. ■

Language and International Options

Several tag attributes can be used to specify language and international options for your documents and individual tags within your documents. The following sections describe those attributes.

Language code

Most tags support the `lang` attribute, which defines the language in which the content of the tag should be displayed. For example, specifying `en` corresponds to English; `en-US` specifies the United States version of English (as opposed to UK). This attribute has the same format as the rest of the attributes:

```
lang="en-US"
```

Tip

Valid language codes can be found in RFC1766, a copy of which is online at `www.ietf.org/rfc/rfc1766.txt`. ■

Text direction

Along with language specification is text direction. You can specify the direction as right to left (rtl) or left to right (ltr). The actual direction is specified using the `dir` attribute in whichever tag you want or need to specify it.

Tip

The Unicode specification, available online at `www.unicode.org/unicode/standard/versions/`, provides more details on the direction of text in different languages and conditions. ■

Summary

This chapter covered the basics of supplying attributes to HTML tags, including using proper attribute syntax in your HTML, adding identifiers and class attributes, inserting text and comments in your HTML documents, using a URI, and placing international attributes in your document's tags. Subsequent chapters cover individual tags, their formatting, and specific usage.

CHAPTER

3

What Goes into a Web Document?

IN THIS CHAPTER

HTML has come a long way from its humble beginnings. However, despite the fact that you can use HTML (and its derivatives) for much more than serving up static text documents, the basic organization and structure of the HTML document remains the same.

Before we dive into the specifics of various elements of HTML, it is important to summarize what each element is, what it is used for, and how it affects other elements in the document. This chapter provides a high-level overview of a standard HTML document and its elements. Subsequent chapters cover each element and technology in detail.

Specifying Document Type

One attribute of HTML documents that is frequently overlooked is the <!DOCTYPE> tag, used to specify a Document Type Definition (DTD). This definition precedes any document tags and exists to inform HTML clients of the format of the content that follows — what tags to expect, methods to support, and so forth.

You can think of the DTD as a packing list of sorts that tells the user agent and other clients that read the document what to expect (and not expect) in the document, enabling the client to act more intelligently, anticipating formatting and such. Validation systems use DTDs to actually perform the validation, using the DTD contents as a road map and a syntax guide. HTML editing programs can use the DTD to provide tag auto-completion tools and while-you-type syntax checking.

The <!DOCTYPE> tag is used to specify an existing DTD. It resembles the following:

```
<!DOCTYPE HTML PUBLIC "-//W3C//DTD HTML 4.01//EN"
   "http://www.w3.org/TR/html4/strict.dtd">
```

This tag specifies the following information:

- The document's top tag level is HTML (`html`).
- The document adheres to the formal public identifier (FPI) "W3C HTML 4.01 Strict English" standards (`PUBLIC "-// W3C//DTD HTML 4.01//EN"`).
- The full DTD can be found at the URL `www.w3.org/TR/html401/strict.dtd`.

Note

The DTD concept might be new to even some of the more seasoned Web developers. However, it should be a priority to include an appropriate <DOCTYPE> tag in every Web document you produce. Doing so can save you more work in the long run and helps ensure that your documents are rendered as you intend them to be. ■

Overall Document Structure: HTML, Head, and Body

All HTML documents have three document-level tags in common. These tags, <html>, <head>, and <body>, delimit certain sections of the HTML document.

The <html> tag

The <html> tag surrounds the entire HTML document. This tag tells the user agent where the document begins and ends. You can think of the <html> tag as the virtual top and bottom of your page, as shown in the following:

```
<html>
... document contents ...
</html>
```

Additional language attributes can also be declared within the <html> tag. Such options, notably `lang` and `dir` (the language and directional information, respectively) are routinely contained in the document type definition (<!DOCTYPE>). However, many experts strongly suggest including the attributes in the <html> tag. The `lang` attribute typically takes a two-letter language abbreviation as its value, such as `lang = "en"` for English. The `dir` attribute supports one of two values: `LTR` to specify the text flows left-to-right, or `RTL` to specify the text flows right-to-left.

The <head> tag

The <head> tag delimits the HTML document's heading section. The document's title, meta information, and, in most cases, document scripts are all contained in the <head> section.

Picture the <head> section of the document as the information commonly found in the letterhead or opening section of a printed document. The difference on the Web is that a good portion of the header information is not visible to the end user.

A typical <head> section could resemble the following:

```
<head>
<link rel="stylesheet" type="text/css" href="/styles.css" />
<title>On Target Games Home Page</title>
<meta name="description" content="On Target Home Page" />
<meta name="keywords" content="On, Target, Games, Videos" />
<script language="JavaScript">
function NewWindow(url){
fin=window.open(url," ",
"width=800,height=600,scrollbars=yes,resizable=yes");
}
</script>
</head>
```

Cross-Ref

Most <head>-level tags are covered in detail in Chapter 4. JavaScript scripting is covered in more detail in Chapters 16 and 17. ■

The `title` element determines what the user agent displays as the page title. Most user agents display the document title in their title bar, as shown in Figure 3-1.

The <body> tag

The HTML document's main visual content is contained within <body> tags. That's not to say that *everything* appearing between the <body> tags will be visible, but, like a printed document, this is where the main body of the document is placed and appears.

Note

With HTML version 4.01, most presentation attributes of the <body> tag have been deprecated in favor of specifying these attributes as styles. In previous versions of HTML, you could specify a bevy of options, including the document background, text, and link colors. The <body> tag's `onload` and `onunload` attributes, as well as global attributes such as `style`, are still valid. However, you should specify the other attributes in styles instead, as in the following example:

```
<!DOCTYPE HTML PUBLIC "-//W3C//DTD HTML 4.01//EN"
  "http://www.w3.org/TR/html4/strict.dtd">
<html>
  <head>
    <title>Document Title</title>
    <style type="text/css">
      body { background: black; color: white}
      a:link { color: red }
```

```
        a:visited { color: blue }
        a:active { color: yellow }
      </style>
    </head>
    <body>
  ... document body...
    </body>
  </html> ■
```

FIGURE 3-1

In most user agents, the document's <title> ("Introducing the Oasis of Tranquility") appears in the user agent's title bar.

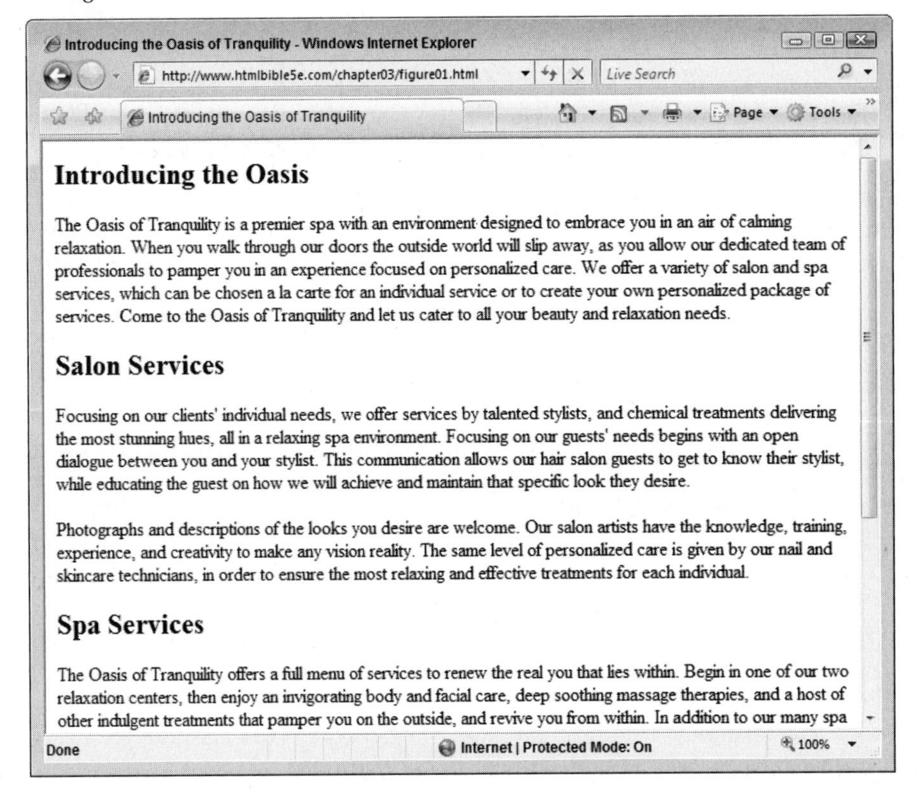

Style Definitions

Styles have revolutionized how HTML documents are coded and rendered, and they are a technology that should not be neglected when creating Web documents.

Style definitions appear in the head section of a document, linked from a separate file, or are included in individual tags via the `style` attribute.

At their root, styles are simply an aggregation of display attributes combined to achieve a particular result. Those familiar with styles in word processing will have little trouble understanding HTML styles. The important point about styles is that they enable you to radically change a document's appearance by simply applying new styles. This enables you to display the document differently for different uses — different display or output devices, for example — or to provide a different look and feel for different audiences.

It also enables you to make global formatting changes — change one style and every element using that style changes too; there's no need to change every occurrence of the styled element in every document in which it appears.

Cross-Ref

Styles are covered extensively in the third part of this book, Chapters 25 through 38. ■

Block Elements: Markup for Paragraphs and Other Blocks of Content

As with most word processors, HTML includes several tags to format blocks of text. These tags include the following:

- `<p>` — Formatted paragraphs
- `<h1>` through `<h6>` — Headings
- `<blockquote>` — Quoted text
- `<pre>` — Preformatted text
- `<ul>`, `<ol>`, `<dl>` — Unnumbered, ordered, and definition lists
- `<center>` — Centered text
- `<div>` — A division of the document

It helps to picture each one of these elements formatting paragraph-size chunks of text. Each of the block elements results in a line break and noticeable space padding after the closing tag. As such, the block elements work only on blocks of text — they cannot be used to format characters or words inside blocks of text.

Cross-Ref

You'll find more details on block elements and their formatting in Chapter 5. ■

Formatted paragraphs

The paragraph tag (`<p>`) is used to delimit entire paragraphs of text. For example, the following HTML code results in the output shown in Figure 3-2:

```
<p>Welcome to On Target games, the online home of the best-selling
game, Vanguard Odyssey. Enjoy browsing the site and don't forget
to check out the updates section.</p>
```

```
<p>If you have not yet played Vangard Odyssey, visit the download
section, download, install, and play the demo version.</p>
```

FIGURE 3-2

Paragraph tags break text into distinct paragraphs.

Cross-Ref

Paragraph tags are covered in more detail in Chapter 5. ■

Headings

HTML supports six levels of headings. Each heading uses a large, usually bold character-formatting style to identify itself as a heading. The following HTML example produces the output shown in Figure 3-3:

```
<!DOCTYPE HTML PUBLIC "-//W3C//DTD HTML 4.01//EN"
   "http://www.w3.org/TR/html4/strict.dtd">
<html>
<body>
<h1>Heading 1</h1>
<h2>Heading 2</h2>
<h3>Heading 3</h3>
```

```
<h4>Heading 4</h4>
<h5>Heading 5</h5>
<h6>Heading 6</h6>
<p>Plain body text.</p>
</body>
</html>
```

FIGURE 3-3

HTML supports six levels of headings.

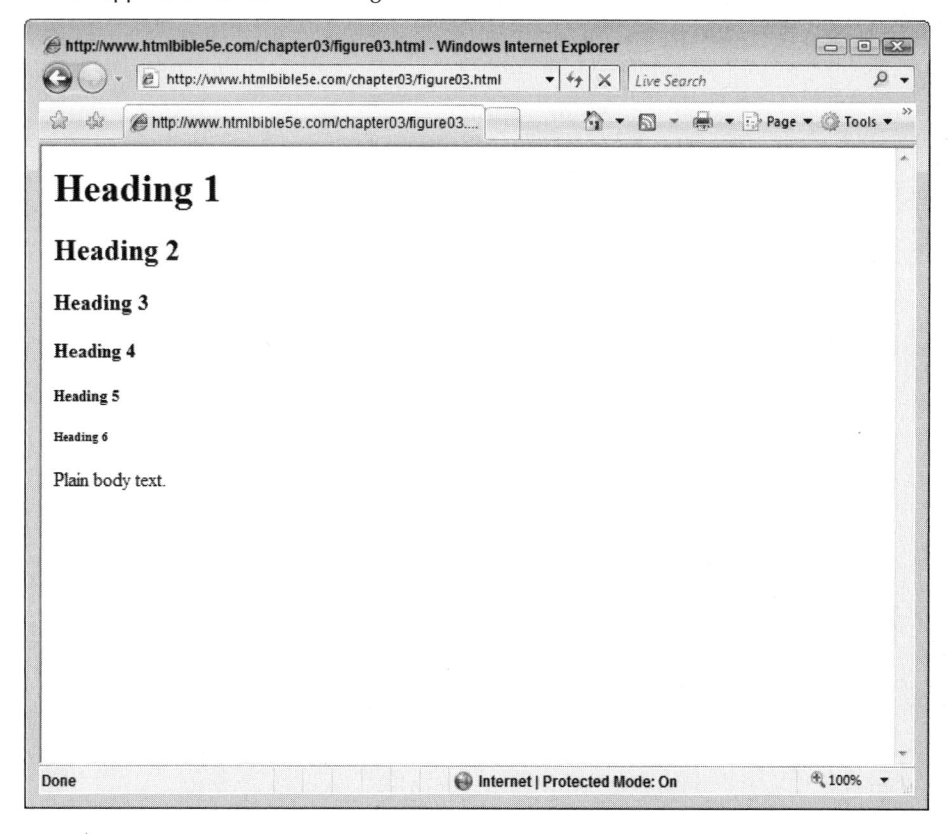

The six levels begin with Level 1, considered highest or most important, and go to Level 6, the lowest, least important. Although there are six predefined levels of headings, you probably will find yourself using only three or four levels in your documents. There are no restrictions regarding specific levels. You can pick and choose which levels you use; for example, you don't have to use <h1> and <h2> in order to be able to use <h3>. Also, keep in mind that you can tailor the formatting imposed by each level by using styles.

That said, it's a good idea to use the headings the way they were intended — to show the relative importance of one heading to another, and to organize the material. Simply picking a heading based on its size is a bad idea because you can't always be certain the heading will be rendered in that exact size on every user agent. However, you can be sure the headings will retain their relative size to one another.

Quoted text

The <blockquote> tag delimits blocks of quoted text. For example, the following code sets the review snippet off as a quote:

```
<p>Don't trust us regarding the merits of our game, listen to what
others have to say:</p>
<blockquote>
I'm impressed by the depth of Vanguard Odyssey and its near perfect
blend of the RPG, shooter, and strategic genres. I give it a hearty
10 out of 10. - Acme Game Reviews
</blockquote>
```

The <blockquote> tag indents the paragraph to offset it from surrounding text, as shown in Figure 3-4.

List elements

HTML specifies three different types of lists:

- Ordered lists (usually numbered)
- Unordered lists (usually bulleted)
- Definition lists (list items with integrated definitions)

The ordered and unordered lists both use a list item element (li) for each of the items in the list. The definition list has two tags: one for list items (<dt>) and another for the definition of the item (<dd>).

The following HTML code results in the output shown in Figure 3-5:

```
<ol>To reboot the router, follow these steps:
  <li>Press and hold the reset button
  <li>Wait for the power LED to turn red
  <li>Release the reset button and wait for the power LED to return
  to green
</ol>
<ul>Your new router has these new features:
  <li>Stateful packet inspection
  <li>Passthrough VPN support
  <li>Four gigabit ethernet ports
</ul>
<dl>Popular gaming genres:
  <dt>Action games
  <dd>Action games are usually "run and gun" games where you run
```

```
    around shooting at things. Lots of "action" here.
    <dt>Adventure games
    <dd>Adventure games are played at a much slower pace. Generally
    you follow a storyline that progresses slowly as your character
    travels and unravels puzzles.
    <dt>Role playing games (RPG)
    <dd>Role playing games are very similar to adventure games, except
    that the game enforces more investment in your character. The
    character advances in capabilities as the game continues allowing
    you to "role play" the character instead of simply controlling it.
</dl>
```

FIGURE 3-4

The <blockquote> tag indents the paragraph.

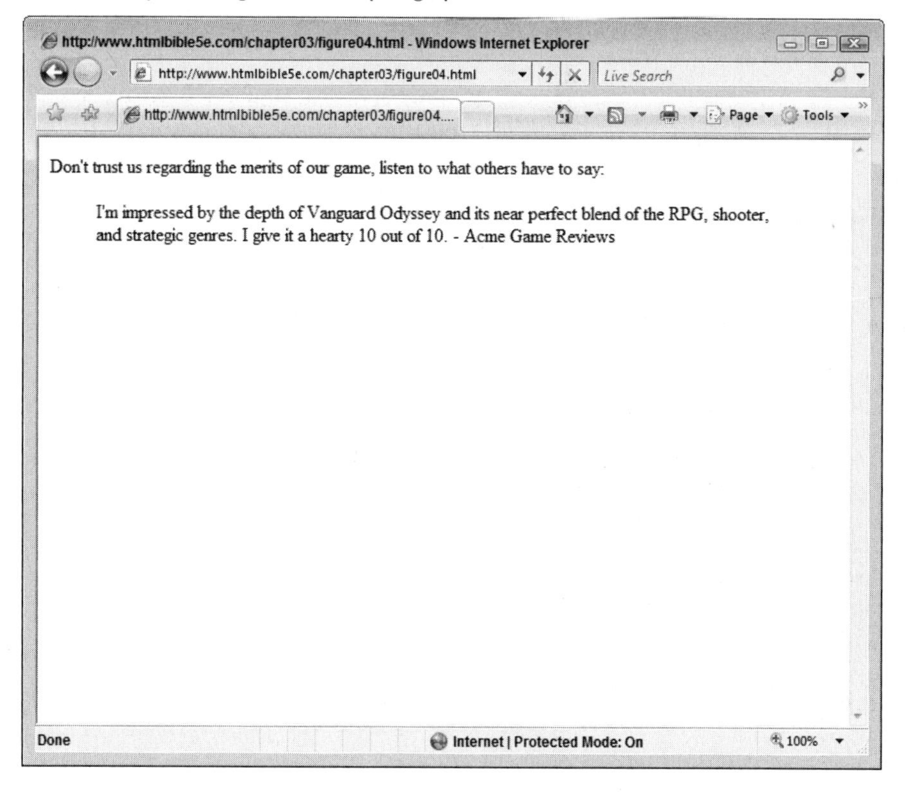

Because of the amount of customization allowed for each type of list, you can create many styles of each list type. For example, you can specify that an ordered list be ordered by letters instead of numbers.

Cross-Ref

Lists are covered in more detail in Chapter 7. ■

FIGURE 3-5

A sample list in HTML

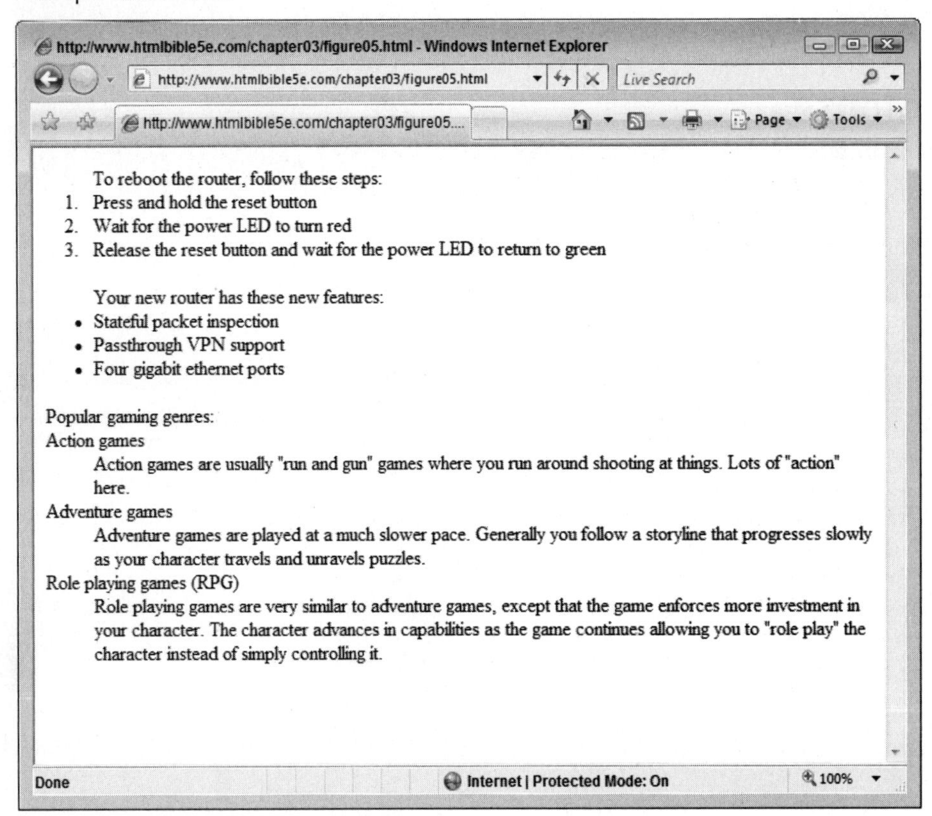

Preformatted text

Occasionally, you will want to hand-format text in your document or maintain the formatting already present in particular text. Typically, the text comes from another source — cut and pasted into the document — and can be formatted with spaces, tabs, and so on. The preformatted tag (<pre>) causes the HTML client to treat white space literally and not condense it as it usually would.

For example, the following table will be rendered just as shown:

```
<pre>
+---------------+-----------------+
| name          | value           |
+---------------+-----------------+
| update        | 1069009013      |
| date          | Wed, 8/28, 8:18pm|
```

```
| status        | 0                |
| feedupdate    | 1069009861       |
+---------------+------------------+
</pre>
```

Divisions

Divisions are a higher level of block formatting, usually reserved for groups of related paragraphs, entire pages, or sometimes just a single paragraph. The division tag (`<div>`) provides a simple solution for formatting sections of a document. Basically, if you need to collect various objects into a larger container, `<div>` is your tool.

For example, if you need a particular document section outlined with a border, you can define an appropriate style and delimit that part of the document with `<div>` tags, as in the following example:

```
<!DOCTYPE HTML PUBLIC "-//W3C//DTD HTML 4.01//EN"
  "http://www.w3.org/TR/html4/strict.dtd">
<html>
<head>
<title>Introducing the Oasis of Tranquility</title>
  <style>
    .bordered {
      border-style: solid;
      width: 60%;
      padding: 20px;
      margin-left: auto;
      margin-right: auto;}
    .centered {
      text-align: center;}
  </style>
</head>
<body>
<h2>Introducing the Oasis</h2>
<p>The Oasis of Tranquility is a premier spa with an environment
designed to embrace you in an air of calming relaxation. When you
walk through our doors the outside world will slip away, as you
allow our dedicated team of professionals to pamper you in an
experience focused on personalized care. We offer a variety of salon
and spa services, which can be chosen a la carte for an individual
service or to create your own personalized package of services.
Come to the Oasis of Tranquility and let us cater to all your beauty
and relaxation needs. </p>
<div class="bordered">
<h2class="centered">Some of Our Specific Services Include</h2>
<h2>Salon Services</h2>
<p>Focusing on our clients' individual needs, we offer services by
talented stylists, and chemical treatments delivering the most
stunning hues, all in a relaxing spa environment. Focusing on our
guests' needs begins with an open dialogue between you and your
```

```
stylist. This communication allows our hair salon guests to get to
know their stylist, while educating the guest on how we will achieve
and maintain that specific look they desire.</p>
<p>Photographs and descriptions of the looks you desire are welcome.
Our salon artists have the knowledge, training, experience, and
creativity to make any vision reality. The same level of
personalized care is given by our nail and skincare technicians, in
order to ensure the most relaxing and effective treatments for each
individual.</p>
<h2>Spa Services</h2>
<p>The Oasis of Tranquility offers a full menu of services to renew
the real you that lies within. Begin in one of our two relaxation
centers, then enjoy an invigorating body and facial care, deep
soothing massage therapies, and a host of other indulgent treatments
that pamper you on the outside, and revive you from within. In
addition to our many spa services, take a refreshing dip in the
swimming pool, melt in one of our whirlpool spas, or rejuvenate
in the sauna.  </p>
</div>
<h2>Give the Gift of Tranquility</h2>
<p>All services at the Oasis of Tranquility can be experienced
individually, or selected a la carte to create you own personalized
day of pampering.  Gift certificates are excellent for surprising
your loved ones with an hour or a day of pampering and
rejuvenation.</p>
<h2>In Summary...</h2>
<p>So when you are looking for an experience that will relax,
rejuvenate, and free you from the weight and stress of everyday
life and leave you looking and feeling like the person you really
are, come to the Oasis of Tranquility.</p>
</body>
</html>
```

This code results in the output shown in Figure 3-6.

Cross-Ref

For more information on how to format blocks of text with the `<div>` tag, see Chapter 5. ■

Inline Elements: Markup for Characters

The finest level of markup possible in HTML is at the character level; as in a word processor, you can affect formatting on individual characters. This section covers inline formatting basics.

FIGURE 3-6

<div> tags delimit sections of text and/or collections of objects.

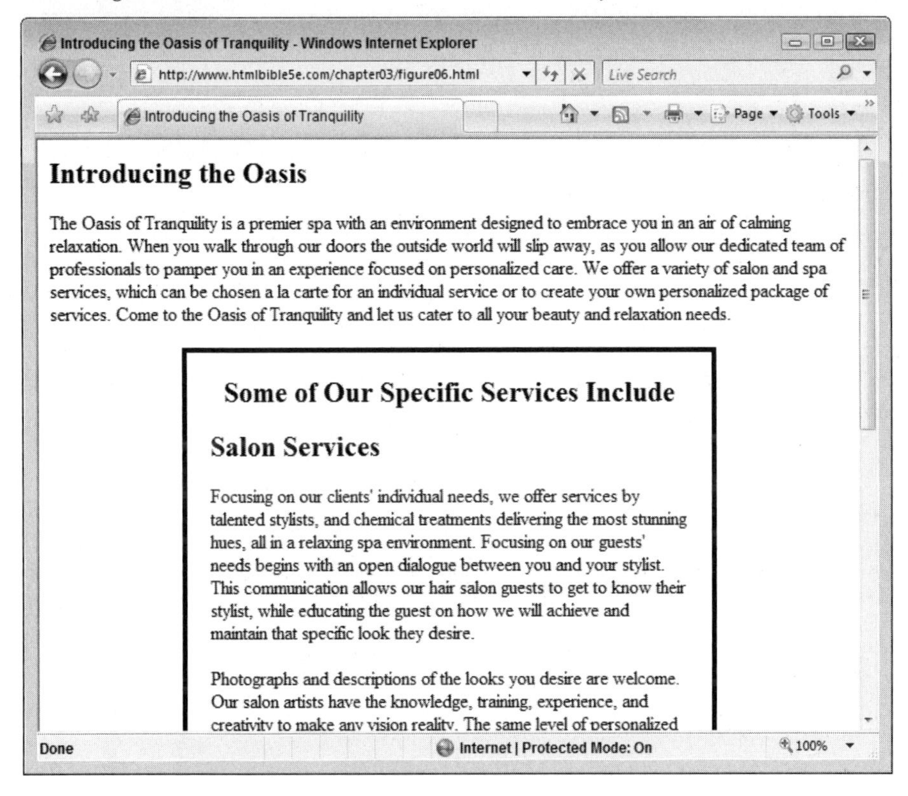

Basic inline tags

Inline formatting elements include the following:

- Bold (`b`)
- Italic (`i`)
- Big text (`big`)
- Small text (`small`)
- Emphasized text (`em`)
- Strong text (`strong`)
- Teletype (monospaced) text (`tt`)

For example, consider the following sample paragraph, the output of which is shown in Figure 3-7:

```
<!DOCTYPE HTML PUBLIC "-//W3C//DTD HTML 4.01//EN"
  "http://www.w3.org/TR/html4/strict.dtd">
<html>
<body>
<p>This paragraph shows the various inline styles, such as
<b>bold</b>, <i>italic</i>, <big>big text</big>, <small>small
text</small>, <em>emphasized text</em>, <strong>strong text</strong>,
and <tt>teletype text</tt>.</p>
</body>
</html>
```

FIGURE 3-7

Inline elements can affect words or even individual characters.

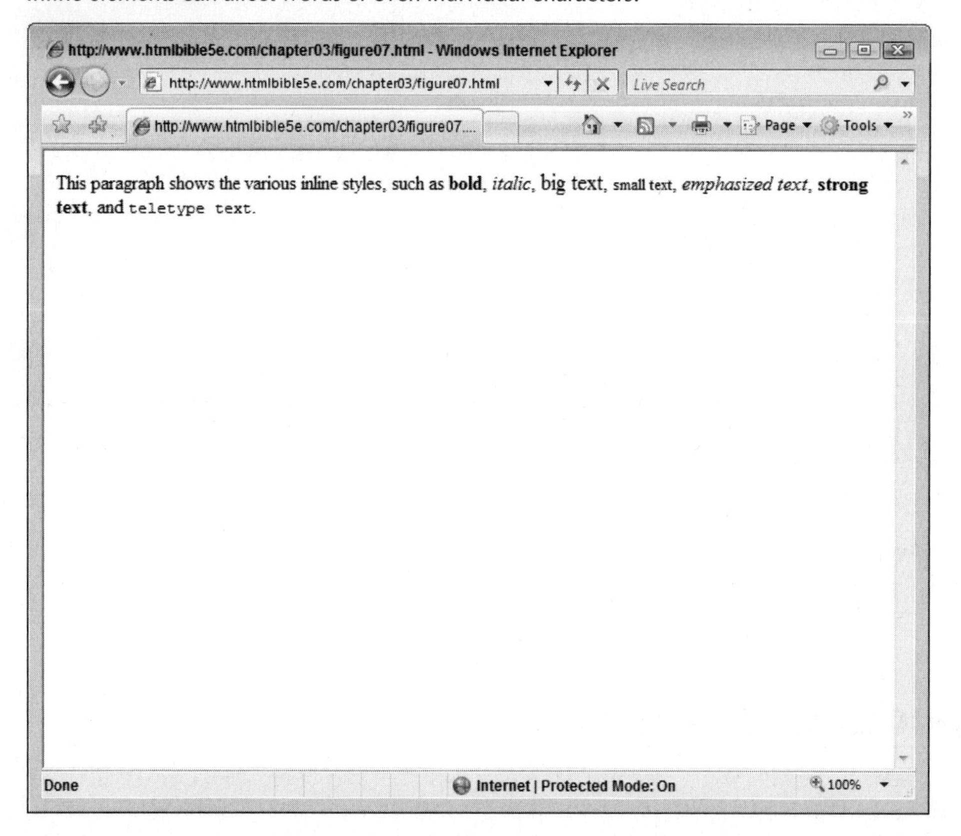

Note that several inline tags, such as strikethrough (<strike>) and underline (<u>) tags, have been deprecated in the current HTML specifications. Even the font tag (<font>) has been deprecated in favor of styles. As for the strikethrough and underline tags, they have been replaced by delete (<del>) and insert (<ins>), which are used for revisions (delete for deleted text, insert for inserted text).

Although it seems counterintuitive, most Web experts recommend using `strong` instead of `bold`, and `emphasized` instead of `italic`, when formatting text. The reasoning has to do with what the styling is supposed to accomplish — strengthen or emphasize text — not how it looks (bold or italic). If you use the appearance styles, most user agents will strive to achieve that particular appearance, even if the representation is different.

Cross-Ref

Chapter 6 contains more information on inline elements. ■

Spanning text

Span tags (<span>) are used to span styles across one or more inline characters or words. In effect, the <span> tag enables you to apply your own inline styles. For example, if you need to specify text that is bold, red, and underlined, you could use code similar to the following:

```
<!DOCTYPE HTML PUBLIC "-//W3C//DTD HTML 4.01//EN"
  "http://www.w3.org/TR/html4/strict.dtd"><html>
<head>
<style>
  .emphasis { color: red; text-decoration: underline;
      font-weight: bold;}
</style>
</head>
<body>
<p><span class="emphasis">This text is emphasized as red, bold, and
underlined</span>, while this text is not.</p>
</body>
</html>
```

The <span> tag enables you to apply the stylistic formatting inline, exactly where you want it. Without any stylistic additions, the <span> tag has no effect on the text it surrounds.

Special Characters (Entities)

Some special characters must be referenced directly instead of simply typed into the document, and some of these characters cannot be typed on a standard keyboard, such as the trademark symbol (™) or the copyright symbol (©). Others could cause the HTML client confusion (such as the angle brackets,< and >). These specially coded characters are commonly referred to as *character entities*.

Entities are referenced by using a particular code in your documents. This code always begins with an ampersand (&) and ends with a semicolon (;). Three different ways to specify an entity exist:

- mnemonic code (such as `copy` for the copyright symbol)
- decimal value corresponding to the character (such as `#169` for the copyright symbol)
- hexadecimal value corresponding to the character (such as `#xA9` for the copyright symbol)

Note that if you use the decimal or hexadecimal methods of specifying entities, you need to prefix the numeric value with a number sign (#).

The following are all examples of valid entities:

- ` ` — A nonbreaking space (used to keep words together)
- `<` — The less-than symbol, or left-angle bracket (<)
- `©` — The copyright symbol (©)
- `&` — An ampersand (&)
- `—` — An em dash (—)

Cross-Ref

You'll find more information on entities in Chapter 14. ■

Organizational Elements

Two HTML elements help organize information in a document: tables and forms.

Tables enable you to present data in column and row format, much like a spreadsheet.

Forms enable you to present (and retrieve) data using elements common to GUI interfaces, such as text boxes, check boxes, and lists.

The following sections describe these elements.

Tables

HTML tables are very basic but can be very powerful when used correctly. At their base level, tables can organize data into rows and columns. At their highest level, tables can provide complicated page design, much like a page in a magazine or newspaper, providing columns for text and sections for graphics, menus, and so on.

Tables have three basic elements and, hence, three basic tags:

- The table definition itself is defined and delimited by `<table>` tags.
- Rows of data are defined and delimited by `<tr>` (table row) tags.
- Table cells (individual pieces of data) are defined and delimited by `<td>` (table data) tags. Alternatively, `<th>` tags can be used for cells in header rows. Table cells, when stacked in even rows, create table columns.

For example, consider the following simple table code, which results in the output shown in Figure 3-8:

```
<table border="1">
  <tr><th>Upgrade</th><th>Unit Cost</th></tr>
  <tr><td>Cargo Container</td><td>300</td></tr>
  <tr><td>Extended Range Radar</td><td>1000</td></tr>
  <tr><td>Redundant Computers</td><td>4000</td></tr>
  <tr><td>Turret Auto-Target</td><td>500</td></tr>
  <tr><td>Zeno Hyperdrive</td><td>10000</td></tr>
</table>
```

FIGURE 3-8

Simple tables can be used to display data in rows and columns, as in a spreadsheet.

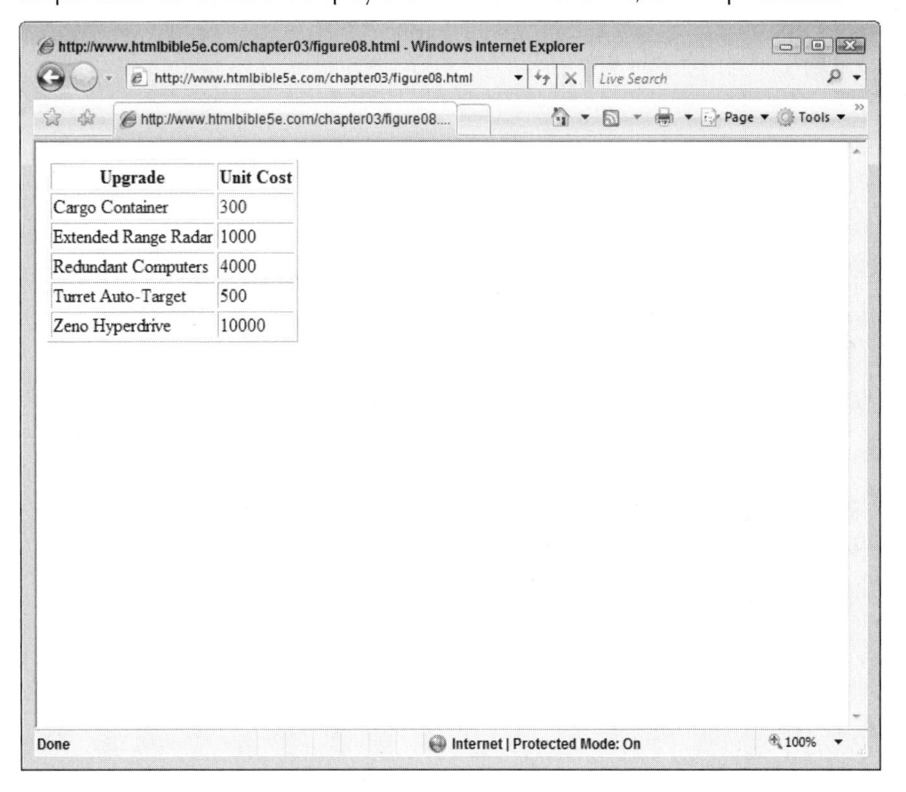

This example is straightforward because the table is simple. However, because you can both use a number of options in formatting table elements and nest tables within tables, the tables in your HTML documents can become very complicated (and very powerful).

Tables have long been used to control page layout using similar methods to those used for displaying columnar data. Figure 3-9 shows a Web page that uses tables for its layout; the table borders are displayed to illustrate how the tables enforce the page layout.

FIGURE 3-9

Complex tables can be used for complex, custom formatting jobs.

Cross-Ref

Tables are covered in detail in Chapter 9. ■

Forms

HTML forms provide a method to use standard GUI elements to display and collect data. HTML forms offer the standard litany of GUI elements, including text boxes, check boxes, pull down (also referred to as drop-down) lists, and more. HTML forms provide a rudimentary method of collecting data and passing that data to a data handler for validation, storage, comparison, or other tasks.

A typical HTML form resembles the following code, the output of which is shown in Figure 3-10:

```
<form>
  <!-- Text field -->
  <b>Name:</b> <input type="text" name="name" size="40">
  <br><br>
```

```
<!-- Radio buttons -->
<b>Age:</b>
      <input type="radio" name="age"> < 20
      <input type="radio" name="age"> 21 -- 30
      <input type="radio" name="age"> 31 -- 40
      <input type="radio" name="age"> 41+
<br><br>
<!-- Select list -->
<b>What is your favorite type of game?</b>
  <select name="game">
    <option name="action">Action
    <option name="adventure">Adventure
    <option name="rpg">RPG
  </select>
<br><br>
<!-- Check boxes -->
<b>How may we contact you for more information?</b><br>
<input type="checkbox" name="phone">Phone<br>
<input type="checkbox" name="mail">Mail<br>
<input type="checkbox" name="email">Email<br>
<input type="checkbox" name="no">Do not contact me<br>
<p><input type="submit" value="Submit" />
<input type="reset" /></p>
</form>
```

Note

The preceding example form is very simple; it shows only some basic elements, and has no handler to process the data collected by the form. Real-world forms can be quite complex and usually require validation scripts to ensure that the data collected is valid. However, this simple form illustrates the amount of control you can assert over data and format using HTML. ■

Cross-Ref

Forms are covered in detail in Chapter 11. ■

Linking to Other Pages

The main advantage to the World Wide Web is the ability to link to other documents on the Web. For example, if you had a page that detailed local zoning laws, you might want to include a link to a local government site where additional information could be found. A link typically appears as underlined text and is often rendered in a different color than normal text.

For example, a link might appear in a user agent as follows:

```
More information can be found here.
```

The word `here` is linked to the other document; when the user clicks the word, the user agent displays the specified page.

FIGURE 3-10

Form elements provide standard GUI controls for displaying and collecting data.

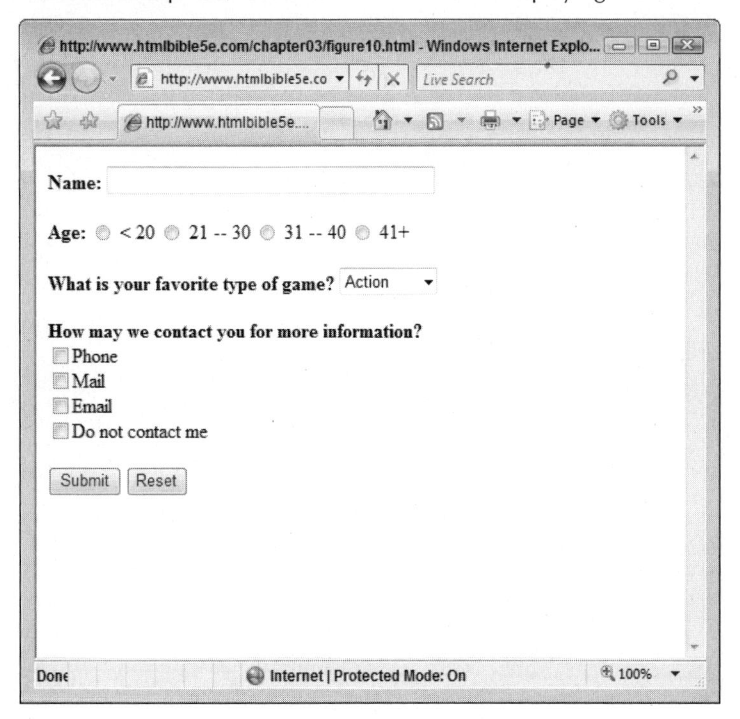

Links are created by use of the anchor tag, `<a>`. At its simplest level, this tag takes one argument — the page to link to — and surrounds the text to be linked. The preceding example could be created with the following code:

```
More information can be found
<a href="http://www.whitehouse.gov">here</a>
```

The anchor tag's `href`, or Hypertext REFerence attribute, specifies the protocol and destination of the link. The example specifies `http://` because the destination is a document to be delivered via the HTTP protocol. Other protocols (such as `ftp://` or `mailto:`) can also be used where appropriate.

Additional attributes can be used with the anchor tag to specify such things as where the new document should be opened (for example, in a new window), the relationship between the documents, and the character set used in the linked document.

You can also use a variant of the anchor tag to mark specific places in the current document — a bookmark of sorts. A link can then be placed elsewhere in the document that can take the user to the specific place. For example, consider this HTML code:

```
For more information see <a href="#Chapt2">Chapter 2</a>
. . . More HTML . . .
<a name="Chapt2">Chapter 2</a>
```

In this example, the user can click the Chapter 2 link to move to the location of the Chapter 2 anchor. Note that the `href` link must include the hash, or pound, symbol (#), which specifies that the link is an anchor instead of a separate page.

Cross-Ref

More information on links and anchors can be found in Chapter 8. ■

Images

One of the great innovations the World Wide Web and HTTP brought to the Internet was the ability to serve up multimedia to clients. The precursors to full-motion video and CD-quality sound were graphical images in the Web-friendly Graphics Interchange Format (GIF) and Joint Photographic Experts Group (JPEG) format.

You can include images in HTML documents by using the image tag (`<img>`). The image tag includes a link to the image file as well as pertinent information used to display the image (for example, the image's size). A typical image tag resembles the following:

```
<img src="/images/tmoore.jpg" alt="A picture of Terri"
width="100" height="200" />
```

The preceding example would result in the image `tmoore.jpg` being displayed at the location in the document where the tag appears. In this case, the image is in the `images` directory of the current server and will be displayed without a border, 100 pixels wide by 200 pixels high. The `alt` attribute provides a textual alternative for the visually impaired, or user agents that cannot display graphics (or whose users have configured them not to). The attribute can also be used to display additional information about the image, as most user agents will show the attribute's value as a tooltip when the mouse is hovered over the image.

Images can also be navigation aids, enabling the user to click certain parts of an image to perform an action, display another document, and so on. For example, a map of the United States could be used to help users select their state — clicking a state would bring up the applicable page for that state. Navigational images are commonly referred to as *image maps* and require a separate map of coordinates and geometric shapes to define the clickable areas.

Cross-Ref

You'll find more information on images in Chapter 12. ■

Comments

Although HTML documents tend to be fairly legible all on their own, there are several advantages to adding comments to your HTML code. Some typical uses for comments include aiding in document organization and document-specific code choices, or marking particular document sections for later reference.

HTML uses the tag `<!--` to begin a comment, and the tag `-->` to end a comment. Note that the comment can span multiple lines, but the user agent ignores anything between the comment tags. For example, the following two comments will both be ignored by the user agent:

```
<!-- This section needs better organization. -->
and
<!-- The following table needs to include these columns:
  Age
  Marital Status
  Employment Date
-->
```

Scripts

HTML is a static method of deploying content; the content is sent out to a user agent where it is rendered and read, but it typically doesn't change once it is delivered. However, there is a need in HTML documents for such things as decision-making ability, form validation, and, in the case of Dynamic HTML (DHTML), dynamic object attribute changes. In those cases (and more), client-side scripting can be used.

Cross-Ref

For more information on client-side scripting, see Chapters 16 and 17. ■

Client-side scripting languages, such as JavaScript, have their code passed to the user agent inside the HTML document. It is the client's responsibility to interpret the code and act accordingly. Most client-side scripts are contained in the HTML document's `<head>` section within `<script>` tags, similar to the following example:

```
<!DOCTYPE HTML PUBLIC "-//W3C//DTD HTML 4.01//EN"
  "http://www.w3.org/TR/html4/strict.dtd">
<html>
<head>
  <script language="JavaScript">
    function MiscWindow(w,h,url){
      opts = "width="+w+",height="+h;
      opts += ",scrollbars=no,resizable=yes";
      fin = window.open(url,"",opts);
    }
  </script>
</head>...
```

You can also include the JavaScript in an external file and use the <script> tag's src attribute to reference it. For example, the following script section references the external script file utility.js:

```
<script type="text/JavaScript" src="utlity.js"></script>
```

Note that the <script> section still includes an opening and closing tag. When would you want to place your code in an external file? When the scripts are used by multiple documents, placing the code in an external file enables you to reference the one copy from multiple documents and to maintain one copy of the code, not one copy per document.

In many cases, the document uses events as triggers to call the script(s). Events can be connected to scripts via HTML event-handler attributes. These attributes can be included in links (onclick), forms (onchange), and elements such as the body tag (onload, onunload).

Putting It All Together

As you can see, the standard HTML document is a fairly complex beast. However, when taken piece by piece, the document is really just like any other document.

The following HTML listing shows how all of these pieces fit together:

```
<!DOCTYPE HTML PUBLIC "-//W3C//DTD HTML 4.01//EN"
   "http://www.w3.org/TR/html4/strict.dtd">
<html>
<head>
  <meta ... meta tags go here ... >
  <title> ... title of the page/document goes here< .../title>
  <link rel="stylesheet" href=" ...external style sheet name ..."
     type="text/css">
  <style>
   ... any document specific styles go here ...
  </style>
  <script>
   ... client-side scripts go here ...
  </script>
<body>
 ... body of document goes here ...
</body>
</html>
```

All HTML documents should have a <DOCTYPE> declaration, <html> and <body> tags, and at least a <title> within the <head> section. The rest of the elements are strictly optional, but they help define a document's purpose, style, and ultimately its usability, as you will see in subsequent chapters.

Summary

This chapter covered the basic elements that make up a Web document — the frame of the document, the heading, and the basic markup for the content. You learned what a document type definition is and why it's important to specify one for your documents. You read about framing tags `<html>`, `<head>`, and `<body>`, including styles in your documents, tag elements used for marking up blocks of content, and those for marking up inline pieces of text. In addition, this chapter discussed placing character entities in your content, tag elements used to organize content, linking to other documents and sections, as well as including images, comments, and scripts in your documents.

CHAPTER

The HEAD Elements

IN THIS CHAPTER

You have seen what various pieces make up HTML documents and how they all fit together. In Chapters 5 through 14 you will see how each individual piece is formatted and placed in the document. This specific chapter deals with the elements in the head section of the document.

Specifying the Document Title

The <head> element of an HTML document contains several other elements, including the document title. The document title is delimited between <title> tags and can include any character or entity. For example, consider the following <head> section, which includes a registration mark:

```
<title>Welcome to On Target Games &reg;</title>
```

This title shows in the title bar of Internet Explorer, as shown in Figure 4-1.

While it is useful to have the title of your document in the title bar of the client's browser, the title is used in several other locations as well. It is used as the default shortcut/favorite name in most browsers, linked to in most search engines, and so on. As such, you should always include a title for your documents, and make it as descriptive (but concise) as possible.

Providing Information to Search Engines

Your document's <head> section can also include <meta> tags. These tags are not rendered as visible text in the document; they are used to pass information and commands to the client browser.

FIGURE 4-1

Entities are rendered correctly in document titles.

As its name implies, the <meta> tag contains *meta information* for the document. Meta information is data about the document itself, instead of information about the document's contents. Most of a document's meta information is generated by the Web server that delivers the document. However, using meta tags you can supply different or additional information about the document.

The amount of information you can specify with <meta> tags is extensive. If you use the HTTP-EQUIV parameter in the <meta> tag, you can supply or replace HTTP header information. For example, the following <meta> tag defines the content type of the document as HTML with the Latin character set (ISO-8859-1):

```
<meta http-equiv="Content-Type" content="text/html;
charset=ISO-8859-1" />
```

In addition, you can control some aspects of how the client browser treats the document. You can specify how long the document should be cached (if cached at all), refresh the browser with a different page after a delay, and so forth. For example, the following two <meta> tags tell the browser not to cache the current page (pragma, no-cache) and to refresh the browser window with a different page after three seconds (refresh):

```
<meta http-equiv="pragma" content="no-cache" />
<meta http-equiv="refresh"
content="3;URL=http://www.example.com/newpage.html" />
```

Note

For a comprehensive list of HTTP 1.1 headers, see the HTTP 1.1 definition on the W3C website: `www.w3.org/Protocols/rfc2616/rfc2616.html`. ■

A bevy of supplemental data can be included using `<meta>` tags. Many Web authoring tools embed their name, version, and assorted authoring information, for example. In addition, you can include categorization information and assorted short notes.

Most search engines have stopped using the meta description and meta keywords as the sole source of indexing a document, relying instead on their own, proprietary indexing methods. However, several smaller robots still use these fields and the majors sometimes reference them.

The description and keywords data is provided by the following two `<meta>` tags:

```
<meta name="description" content="The affordable day spa" />
<meta name="keywords" content="facial treatments, hair,
manicures, pedicures, relaxation, spa, pools, sauna" />
```

Setting the Default Path

When defining links and references in your HTML document, be as exact as possible with your references. For example, when referencing a graphic with an `<img>` tag, you should make a habit of including the protocol and the full path to the graphic, as shown here:

```
<img src=http://www.example.com/images/spacescene.gif />
```

However, it isn't very practical to type the full path to every local element referenced in your document. As such, a document residing on the `example.com` server could reference the same graphic with the following code:

```
<img src="images/spacescene.gif" />
```

What if the document is relocated? The images directory might no longer be a subdirectory of the directory where the document resides. The image might be on a separate server altogether.

To solve these problems, you could use the `<base>` tag. The `<base>` tag sets the default document base — that is, the default location for the document. Using the preceding example, a document in the root directory of the `example.com` server would have a `<base>` tag similar to the following:

```
<base href="http://www.on-target-games.com/images/" />
```

Any absolute references in the document (those with full protocol and path) will continue to point to their absolute targets. Any relative references (those without full protocol and path) will be referenced against the path in the `<base>` tag. Meta tags can also be used to refresh a document's content or redirect a client browser to another page. Refreshing a document is useful if it includes timely, dynamic data, such as stock prices. Redirection comes in handy when a document moves, as you can use a redirect to automatically send a visitor to the new document.

To refresh or redirect a document, use the `http-equiv "refresh"` option in a `<meta>` tag. This option has the following form:

```
<meta http-equiv="refresh" content="seconds_to_wait; url" />
```

For example, suppose that a page on your site (`on-target-games.com`) has moved. The page used to be on the server's root as `listing.html`, but now the page is in an `oldpage` directory as `listing.html` (`/oldpage/listing.html`). You want visitors who previously bookmarked the old page to be able to get to the new page. Placing the following document in the server's root (as `bio.html`) would cause visitors to automatically be redirected to the new page after a three-second wait:

```
<!DOCTYPE HTML PUBLIC "-//W3C//DTD HTML 4.01//EN"
   "http://www.w3.org/TR/html4/strict.dtd">
<html>
<head>
  <title>This Page Has Moved!</title>
  <meta http-equiv="pragma" content="no-cache" />
  <meta http-equiv="refresh" content="3;
     URL=http://www.on-target-games.com/oldpage/listing.html" />
</head>
<body>
<p>This page has moved. You will be redirected to the new page
in 3 seconds, or you can click the link below.</p>
<a href="http://www.on-target-games.com/oldpage/listing.html" >
The new page.</a>
</body>
</html>
```

To refresh the current page every three seconds, use the following:

```
<meta http-equiv="refresh" content="3" />
```

Tip

Using the `pragma no-cache` meta tag along with the `refresh` meta tag is always a good idea. This helps keep the browser from caching the document and displaying the cached copy of the document instead of the updated document. Because different browsers treat `no-cache` differently, it is also wise to add an `expires` meta tag, as shown here:

```
<meta http-equiv="expires" content="0" />
```

This tag causes the document to be immediately expired in the cache and, hence, not cached at all. ■

The refresh technique is especially useful on pages that show timely information. By forcing the page to reload at certain intervals, you can help ensure that site visitors see current information.

Script Sections

HTML documents can include scripting sections. Such sections typically contain JavaScript scripts, but other types of scripting (for example, VBScripting) can also be used.

All scripting in a document should appear between `<script>` tags. These `<script>` sections can be placed in the document head section or anywhere in the body. The `<script>` tags should adhere to the following format:

```
<script type="text/javascript">
  ...scripting code...
</script>
```

Note that the MIME type of the code (in this case `text/javascript`) is included as a `type` attribute.

Note

The exception to where code should appear in a document is within event attributes within specific tags. For more information, see Chapters 16 and 17. ■

Style Sections

Style blocks are another large section that can appear in the head section of the document. Style blocks are formatted as shown in the following listing:

```
<style type="text/css">
...style definitions...
</style>
```

Note

As with scripts, styles can also be used as attributes of HTML tags (the `style` attribute). More information on styles can be found in Chapters 25 through 38. ■

Specifying Profiles

Profiles are an interesting concept, allowing XML-based data structures to be attached to HTML documents. These profiles enable compatible readers to return the profile information, specifying items such as the document's author, last modification date, and more.

A profile document is a properly formatted HTML document consisting of a definition list containing terms and data of the profile itself. Consider the following document:

```
<!DOCTYPE html PUBLIC "-//W3C//DTD XHTML 1.0 Strict//EN"
 "http://www.w3.org/TR/xhtml1/DTD/xhtml1-strict.dtd">
<html xmlns="http://www.w3.org/1999/xhtml"
  xml:lang="en" lang="en" >
```

```
<head><title>HTML Profile Document</title></head>
<body>
 <dl class="profile">
  <dt id='author'>author</dt>
   <dd>Author of the document</dd>
  <dt id='keywords'>keywords</dt>
   <dd>A list of the keywords for the document.</dd>
  <dt id='copyright'>copyright</dt>
   <dd>Copyright information for the document</dd>
  <dt id='date'>date</dt>
   <dd>The date that the document was last updated.</dd>
 </dl>

</body>
</html>
```

Additional information can be added to the profile as additional definitions, as required.

To tie the profile to a document, you use the profile attribute in the document's `<head>` tag. For example, suppose the profile document were at the following address:

```
http://www.example.com/profiles/profile1.html
```

You would use the following `<head>` tag:

```
<head profile="http://www.example.com/profiles/profile1.html">
```

Applicable readers and browsers can use this information to access the profile appropriately.

Background Color and Background Images

One of the easiest changes you can effect on your Web pages is to alter the background color of your document. Most browsers use a white background, so specifying a different background color or a background image can easily make your document distinct.

Specifying the document background color

If you code your HTML against the transitional format of HTML, you can use the `bgcolor` attribute in the `<body>` tag. However, using that attribute is not recommended for the following reasons:

- The attribute is not valid for strict HTML and might impair the validation of your document.
- If you want to change your documents' background color, you must change each individual body tag in each document.

A better practice is to use appropriate styles, typically in an external style sheet.

The document background color is set using the `background-color` property. For example, to set the background color to blue, you would use the following style definition:

```
<style type="text/css">
  body { background-color: blue;}
</style>
```

Cross-Ref

For more information on styles, refer to Chapters 25 through 38. ■

Specifying the document background image

Besides setting the document's background to a solid color, you can also specify an image to use as the background. As with the background color attribute for the body tag, there is also a background image attribute (`bgimage`) for the body tag. However, as with the background color attribute, it is not a good idea to use that attribute.

Instead, use the `background-image` property as a body style, as shown here:

```
<style>
  body { background-image: url(<char:Variable>path_to_image</char:Variable>);}
</style>
```

For example, the following style results in `grid.jpg` being placed as the document's background:

```
<style type="text/css">
  body { background-image: url(images/grid.jpg);}
</style>
```

The effect is shown in Figure 4-2.

Note

When you change the background color to a dark color or use a dark image, you should also change the text color so it will contrast with the background. For example, the following style sets the body background color to black, and the body text color to white:

```
<style>
  body { background-color: black; color: white;}
</style> ■
```

FIGURE 4-2

The grid in the document's background is courtesy of an image, grid.jpg.

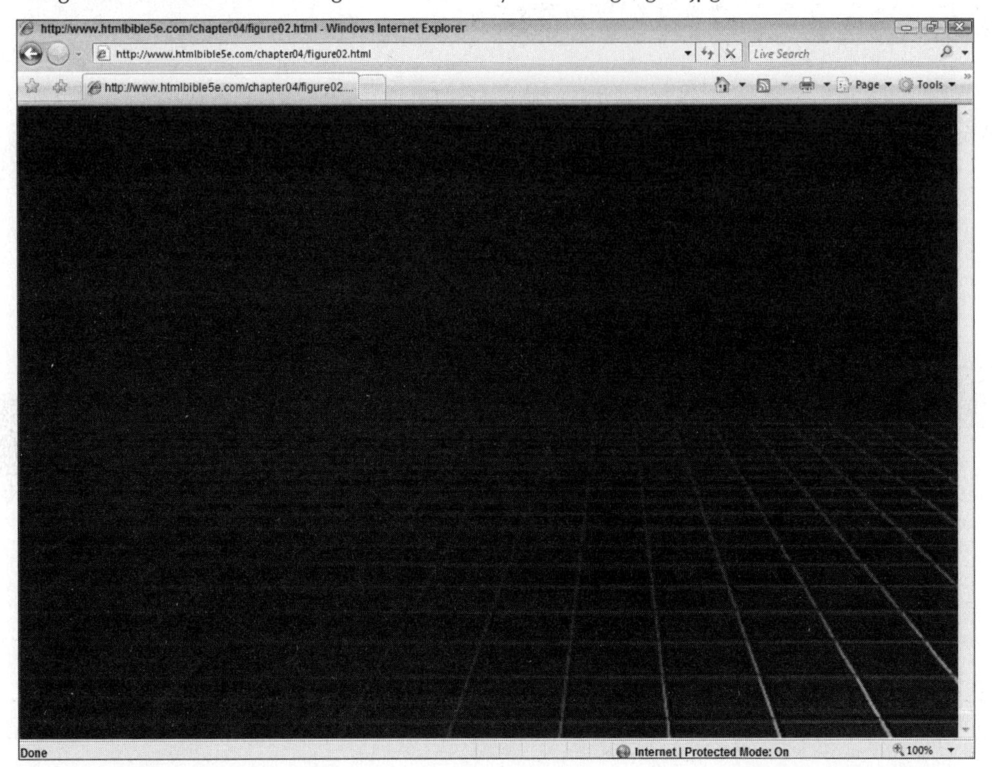

Summary

This chapter described the basic elements you need in all of your HTML documents. You learned how to set the document's title, how to include supplemental information in your documents using `<meta>` tags, how to use the `<base>` tag to set a default path for your document's URIs, and how to automatically refresh or redirect a document after a timed delay. The chapter also covered embedding scripts in HTML documents, placing style sections in a document, using profiles, and setting your document's background color and/or using an image as your background.

The next few chapters cover various formatting elements in more detail.

CHAPTER

Text Structuring Essentials

The Web is used to transfer information in a variety of formats, but text is still the main form of communication across the Internet and even on the multimedia-rich World Wide Web. As such, it is important to understand the methods you can employ with HTML to format text.

This chapter covers the big picture — that is, text at the division and paragraph level. The next chapter delves into character formatting and other inline formatting concepts.

IN THIS CHAPTER

Formatting Paragraphs

The most basic form to fit text within, whether in a book or on a Web page, is the paragraph. As you might have guessed, HTML supplies a specific tag to format text into discrete paragraphs.

The paragraph tags, `<p>` and `</p>`, provide the most basic block formatting for Web page text. Their use is straightforward: Place the opening tag (`<p>`) at the start of the paragraph and the ending tag (`</p>`) at the end of the paragraph. The user agent will format the paragraphs appropriately, usually by placing a blank line between them.

As an example, consider the following HTML code. Figure 5-1 shows the result of running this code in a browser.

```
<p>Welcome to The Oasis of Tranquility -- your source of day
spa services at hair salon prices. Come visit us for that
deep tissue or relaxing massage, facial, manicure, or
hair coloring you have been putting off.</p>
<p>Our concept is simple -- provide luxurious service affordable
to most consumers. So stop in and let our experts please and
pamper you today.</p>
```

FIGURE 5-1

Most user agents format paragraphs by placing a blank line between them.

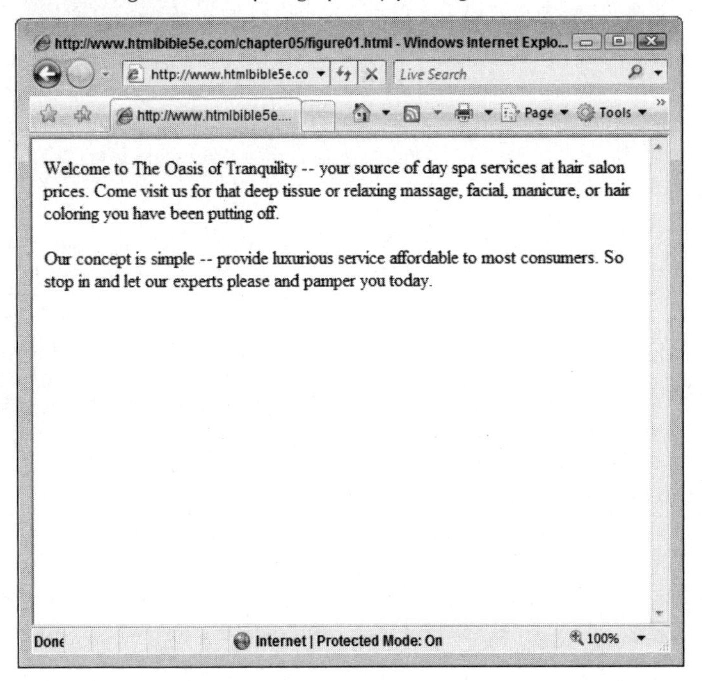

You can, and typically should, use paragraph tags to encapsulate text even when the text is within a higher-level block tag. For example, note how the paragraph in the following code is placed within paragraph tags even though it is already within table data (<td>) tags:

```
<td>
  <p>Games with an "E" rating (Everyone) are suitable for
  consumers age 6 and older. These games may contain a
  minimal amount of mild violence (typically animated) and/or
  mild language.</p>
</td>
```

Cross-Ref

The <td> and other table tags are discussed in detail in Chapter 9. ■

Other objects besides textual paragraphs can appear between paragraph tags also. For example, you might want an image to be vertically spaced evenly between two paragraphs. Placing the image tag within its own set of paragraph tags accomplishes that feat, as shown by the following code and corresponding rendering in the browser in Figure 5-2:

```
<p>Welcome to The Oasis of Tranquility -- your source of day
spa services at hair salon prices. Come visit us for that
deep tissue or relaxing massage, facial, manicure, or
hair coloring you have been putting off.</p>
```

```
<p><img src="images/massage.jpg" width="328px" height="232"
  alt="Massage" /></p>
<p>Our concept is simple -- provide luxurious service affordable
to most consumers. So stop in and let our experts please and
pamper you today.</p>
```

FIGURE 5-2

Paragraph tags aren't just for text; they can lend their block element encapsulation to any nonblock element.

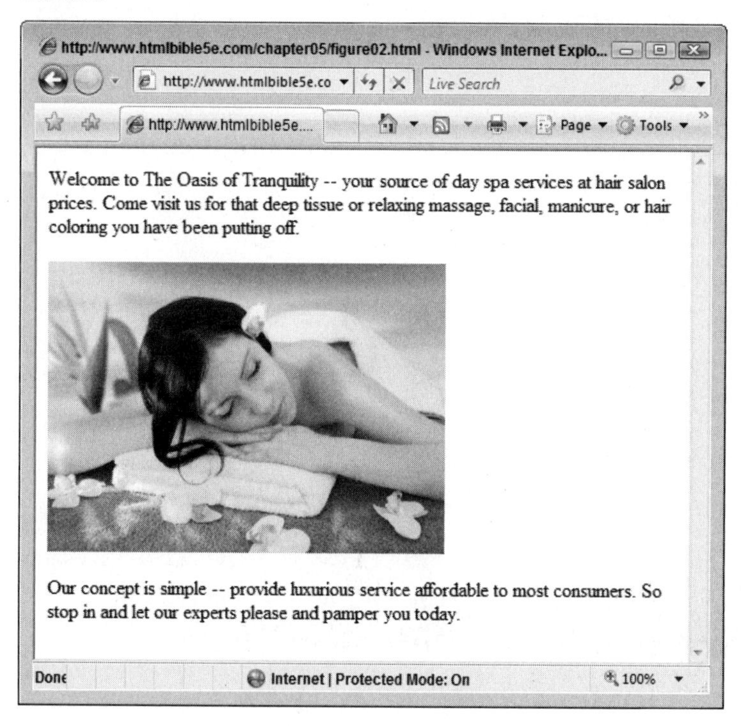

Line Breaks

Occasionally, you will want to break a line of text without ending the paragraph in which it appears. Reasons for doing so will vary, but typically the goal is to avoid the blank line that would result when the user agent displays your text.

For those times when you want to prematurely end a line but not the paragraph, use the line break tag (`<br />`).

An address block provides a good example of where to use the line break tag. Consider the following two address blocks and how they render in the browser shown in Figure 5-3:

```
<p>On Target Games</p>
<p>1 Target Place</p>
```

```
<p>Fishers, IN 46038</p>
<p>On Target Games<br />
1 Target Place<br />
Fishers, IN 46038</p>
```

FIGURE 5-3

Using the line break tag enables you to keep your text tight while still being able to prematurely break lines.

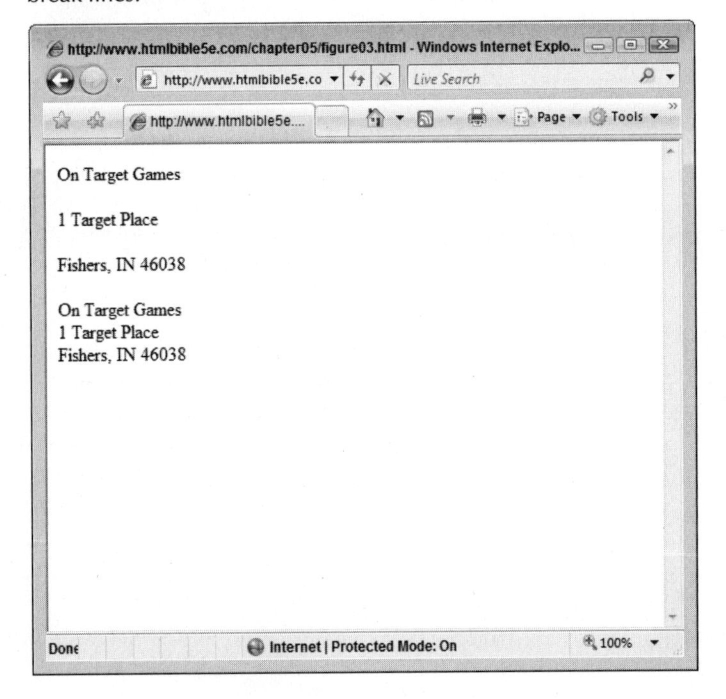

Note that the line break tag does not have a closing mate and requires the ending slash. As such, the line break tag *does not* qualify as a block tag and must be contained within block tags. Notice in the preceding code example that the second address is still contained within paragraph tags — the line break tag is used within the paragraph to break lines.

Divisions

Divisions are the big brother of paragraphs and are used to keep related objects (paragraphs, graphics, and so on) together. Divisions also allow the grouped objects to inherit most of the same formatting by applying the formatting to the division itself, which obviates the need to apply the formatting individually to each object contained within it.

Cross-Ref

Applying styles to divisions and affecting the divisions' contents is covered in Chapter 34. ■

Division tags (<div> and </div>) are one of the highest-level block tags available in HTML. It is very typical to see HTML document bodies coded with blocks of divisions, similar to the following:

```
<body>
  <div>
    ...HTML content...
  </div>
  <div>
    ...some other HTML content...
  </div>
  <div>
    ...still some other HTML content...
  </div>
</body>
```

Because divisions are high-level block tags, they should be used to contain other block tags such as paragraph tags. While rarely done, placing a division within another block tag is not unheard of.

Conceptually, it helps to think of divisions as chapters in a book, keeping the paragraphs together. Better yet, given the rich visual nature of Web pages, think of divisions as defining the areas of a magazine page — the left-most column of text, the ad in the upper-right corner of the page, the right-most column of text, the author's bio block, and so on. In fact, given a few well-designed divisions and the appropriate content, you can design a Web page to resemble almost any magazine layout.

For example, consider the following example, which defines four divisions to encapsulate different content on the page. The result of this code is shown in Figure 5-4.

```
<!DOCTYPE html PUBLIC "-//W3C//DTD XHTML 1.1//EN"
"http://www.w3.org/TR/xhtml11/DTD/xhtml11.dtd">
<html>

<head>
<meta http-equiv="content-type"
    content="text/html; charset=iso-8859-1"/>
<meta name="description" content="description"/>
<meta name="keywords" content="keywords"/>
<meta name="author"
    content="Template design by Arcsin -
 http://templates.arcsin.se"/>
<link rel="stylesheet" type="text/css" href="default.css"
    media="screen"/>
<title>The Oasis of Tranquility</title>
</head>

<body>

<div class="container">
```

```
<div class="top">
  <img src="img/OoTHeader.jpg" style="margin-top: 10px;" /> <!--
      <a href="index.html"><span>Bitter Sweet</span></a> -->
</div>

<div class="header"></div>

  <div class="main">

    <div class="item">
      <div class="date">
        <div></div>
        <span></span>
      </div>
      <div class="content">
        <h1>About The Oasis of Tranquility</h1>
        <div class="body">
        <p>The Oasis of Tranquility is a premier spa, with an
        environment designed to embrace you in an air of calming
        relaxation. When you walk through our doors, the
        outside world will slip away, as you allow our
        dedicated team of professionals to pamper you in an
        experience focused on personalized care. Browse our site
        for the full experience that can be your own Oasis.</p>
        </div>
      </div>
    </div>

  <div class="item">
    <div class="date">
      <div>APR</div>
      <span>21</span>
    </div>
    <div class="content">
      <h1>2 For 1 Manicure Special</h1>
      <div class="body">
      <p>Treat a friend to the experience of the Oasis. Use the
      coupon below to receive two manicures for the price of one
      through the month of May.</p>
      <div class="coupon">
        <p>Present this coupon for a free manicure with the
        purchase of a similar manicure. Good during the same visit
        only, one per customer, other limitations may apply.</p>
        <p class="barcode">241 Manicure, valid May 2009 <img
        src="img/barcode.jpg"
            width="126px" height="15px"></p>
      </div>
      </div>
    </div>
  </div>
```

```
    <div class="item">
      <div class="date">
        <div>APR</div>
        <span>10</span>
      </div>
      <div class="content">
        <h1>Visiting Hair Specialist</h1>
        <div class="body">
        <p>The Oasis is pleased to announce another visit from hair
        specialist Samual Hart.
        Make an appointment in the next two weeks for your
        personalized consultation on color, style, and product.</p>
        </div>
      </div>
    </div>

  </div> <!-- Main -->

  <div class="navigation">

    <h1>Salon Services</h1>
    <ul>
      <li><a href="index.html">Hair Care</a></li>
      <li><a href="index.html">Nail Care</a></li>
    </ul>
    <h1>Spa Services</h1>
    <ul>
      <li><a href="index.html">Skin Care</a></li>
      <li><a href="index.html">Massage</a></li>
    </ul>
    <h1>Relaxation Amenities</h1>
    <ul>
      <li><a href="index.html">Amenities</a></li>
    </ul>
    <h1>About the Oasis</h1>
    <ul>
      <li><a href="index.html">About the Oasis</a></li>
      <li><a href="index.html">About the Staff</a></li>
    </ul>
  </div>

  <div class="clearer"><span></span></div>

  <div class="footer">Copyright &copy; 2009 Oasis of Tranquility.
  All Rights Reserved.</div>

</div> <!-- Container -->

</body>

</html>
```

FIGURE 5-4

Many divisions can be created to hold various pieces of content on the same page.

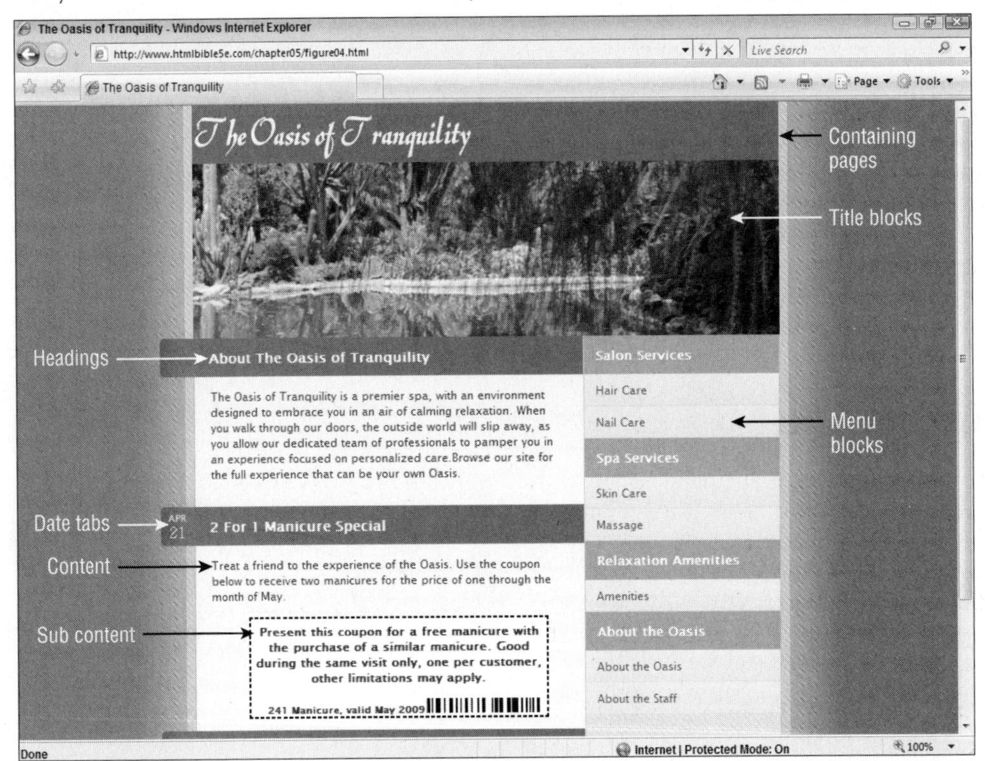

Rules

Rules are horizontal lines largely used to break sections of text into smaller chunks, or otherwise delimit the text in some way. For example, the headings in this book use rules under the heading text to set the heading off from the text to which it refers.

In HTML, rules are inserted into documents using the horizontal rule (`<hr />`) tag. Like many other empty tags that do not need to encapsulate anything, the `<hr />` tag is a solitary tag, having no closing mate, but therefore requiring the obligatory slash inside the tag.

An `<hr />` tag results in a gray, beveled line in most browsers, although the actual way the rule looks in the user agent is up to the agent itself. The rule results in a line break where the tag is placed, and the line itself stretches from margin to margin of the container (page, block, element, and so on) in which it is placed.

A default rule is shown in Figure 5-5.

FIGURE 5-5

A close-up of a horizontal rule rendered in Internet Explorer

---

The look of rules can be tailored to some extent using styles. For example, you can change the color using the `color` property, and the length of the line using the `width`. That being said, using styles to create and manipulate block element borders is generally a more flexible approach to custom rules.

Cross-Ref

More information on the available style properties can be found in Part III of this book. ■

Block Quotes

Occasionally, you will want to set blocks of text apart from the general text around it. One frequent example is the use of quotations, as shown in Figure 5-6.

FIGURE 5-6

Quotations or other text that needs to be set off from text around it can use blockquote tags

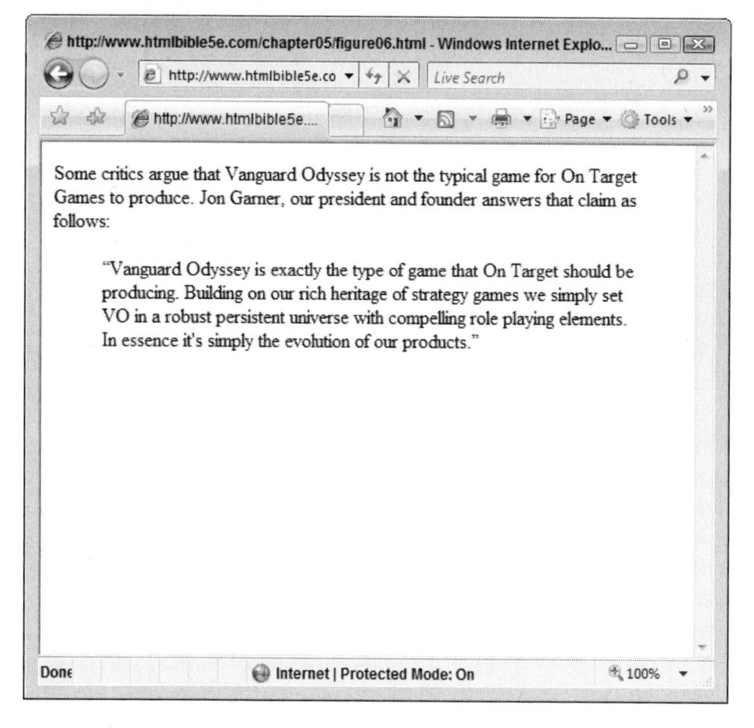

The blockquote tag (<blockquote>) indents the elements it encapsulates and inserts space above and below the blockquote section, although the latter depends on the rules of the individual user agent rendering the element.

Consistency with the HTML standards and other documents is the main reason to continue to use the <blockquote> tag for quotations, rather than styled paragraphs, but you might find using styles a better, more flexible solution for your purposes.

Note

Using the <blockquote> tag to simply indent text is discouraged in favor of using styles to accomplish such formatting. The use of <blockquote> should be limited to highlighting quoted text. ■

Preformatted Text

User agents do a great job of optimizing text. Extra spaces are reduced to a single space, and redundant formatting is reduced or removed. However, you may sometimes want to preserve particular formatting in your text — keeping extra spacing, and so on.

The preformatted tags (<pre> and </pre>) can be used to encapsulate text for which you want the formatting preserved. Such text is generally space-formatted, columnar text, but is not limited to that type of text.

Note that the preformatted tag also causes the encapsulated text to be rendered in a monospace font to ensure that the character spacing does not change. The following code demonstrates an example of how preformatted tags can be used, and Figure 5-7 shows the results in a browser:

```
<pre>
+----+---------------------+---------+
| id | dtime               | counter |
+----+---------------------+---------+
|  1 | 2005-09-13 04:18:02 |    1335 |
|  2 | 2005-09-13 04:18:02 |   85355 |
|  1 | 2005-09-13 04:23:02 |    1043 |
|  2 | 2005-09-13 04:23:02 |  127885 |
|  1 | 2005-09-13 04:45:59 |    1189 |
|  2 | 2005-09-13 04:45:59 |   29529 |
|  1 | 2005-09-13 04:50:59 |    1189 |
|  2 | 2005-09-13 04:50:59 |    9641 |
|  1 | 2005-09-13 04:55:59 |    1189 |
|  2 | 2005-09-13 04:55:59 |   23374 |
+----+---------------------+---------+
</pre>
```

FIGURE 5-7

Preformatted tags enable you to include sections of text that the browser will not reformat.

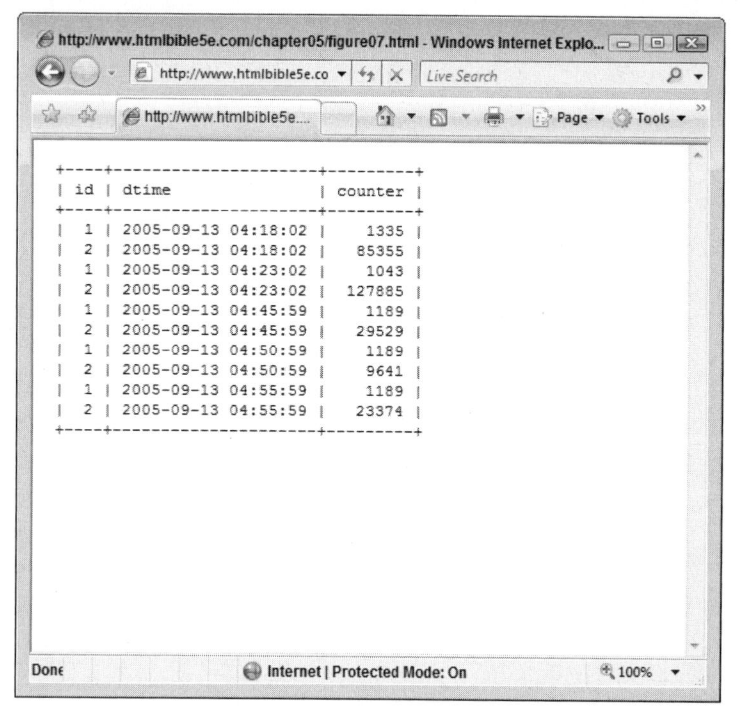

id	dtime	counter
1	2005-09-13 04:18:02	1335
2	2005-09-13 04:18:02	85355
1	2005-09-13 04:23:02	1043
2	2005-09-13 04:23:02	127885
1	2005-09-13 04:45:59	1189
2	2005-09-13 04:45:59	29529
1	2005-09-13 04:50:59	1189
2	2005-09-13 04:50:59	9641
1	2005-09-13 04:55:59	1189
2	2005-09-13 04:55:59	23374

Summary

At this point in the book you should have a good understanding of how to construct an HTML standards-compliant document and format paragraphs of text within it. The next few chapters delve into specific character and special object formatting to give you fine control over your documents, make them look their best, and keep them standards compliant.

The next chapter dives into character formatting, showing you how to achieve a finer grain of formatting control over your text. This part then continues to cover other HTML formatting controls including lists (Chapter 7), links to other documents (Chapter 8), tables (Chapter 9), and frames (Chapter 10). By the end of this part, you should have a good understanding of the HTML elements at your disposal and the appropriate parts of a document on which to use them.

CHAPTER 6

Character Formatting Essentials

IN THIS CHAPTER

Although the modern-day Web is a haven of multimedia, text is still vitally important. Only through text can some messages be succinctly communicated. Even then, diversity in text can help further clarify a message. For example, emphasizing one word with bold or italic font can change the entire tone and meaning of a sentence.

This chapter discusses the tags you can use to format elements inside of block elements (characters, words, or sentences inside of paragraphs).

Methods of Text Control

You can control the look and formatting of text in your documents using various means. It should come as no surprise that the more direct methods — `<font>` tags and the like — have been deprecated in favor of CSS controls in HTML 4.01 and XHTML. For historical context and completeness, the following sections cover the various means possible.

Tip

Although it is sometimes easier to drop a direct formatting tag into text, resist the urge and use styles instead. Your documents will be more flexible and more standards-compliant. ■

The <font> tag

The `<font>` tag enables you to directly affect the size and color of text. Intuitively, the `size` attribute is used to change the text's size; the `color` attribute is used to change the color. The size of the text is specified by a number, from 1 to 7, or by a signed number (also 1 to 7). In the latter case, the size change is relative to the size set by the <basefont> tag. The <basefont> tag has one attribute, size, which can be set to a number, 1 through 7.

Note

Default font type and size is left up to the user agent. No standard correlation exists between the size used in a <font> tag and the actual font size used by the user agent. As such, the default size of the font (1 to 7) can vary considerably between user agents. ■

For example, if you wanted larger text in a red color, you could use a tag similar to the following:

```
<font size="+3" color="red">this is larger, red text</font>
```

Note that using "+3" for the size increases the text within the tag by a factor of 3 from the base font size.

The <font> tag is one of the HTML tags that have been deprecated in favor of styles. If you need to change the size of some of the text within a block element, use a <span> tag and styles instead. (The <span> tag is covered later in this chapter.)

Emphasis and other text tags

You can use a handful of tags to emphasize portions of text. Although these tags have not been deprecated in HTML 4.01, it is strongly recommended that you make use of CSS instead, as CSS provides better control and flexibility, and the ability to cache formatting in style sheets for reuse.

Table 6-1 lists the emphasis tags and each one's use. A sample of their use is shown in Figure 6-1.

Because support for tags is somewhat haphazard, it is not standard across user agents — for example, you may not be able to tell the difference between text coded with <cite> or <em>.

CSS text control

CSS provides several different properties to control text. Table 6-2 lists some of the more popular properties.

As you can see, CSS offers a bit more control over your text, enabling you to specify actual fonts and font sizes. However, the advantage to using CSS properties over hard-coded tags is not found in the list of available properties, but in the flexibility in formatting and affecting later changes — culled from the concept of keeping structure (HTML) and presentation (CSS) separate.

For example, suppose you were creating documentation for a programming language and wanted to format all reserved words a particular way — perhaps in a slightly larger, red, bold font. With tags, the code would resemble the following:

```
<p>The <font size="+1" color="red"><b>date</b></font>
function can be used to ...
```

FIGURE 6-1

The different types of tags emphasizing text are rendered here.

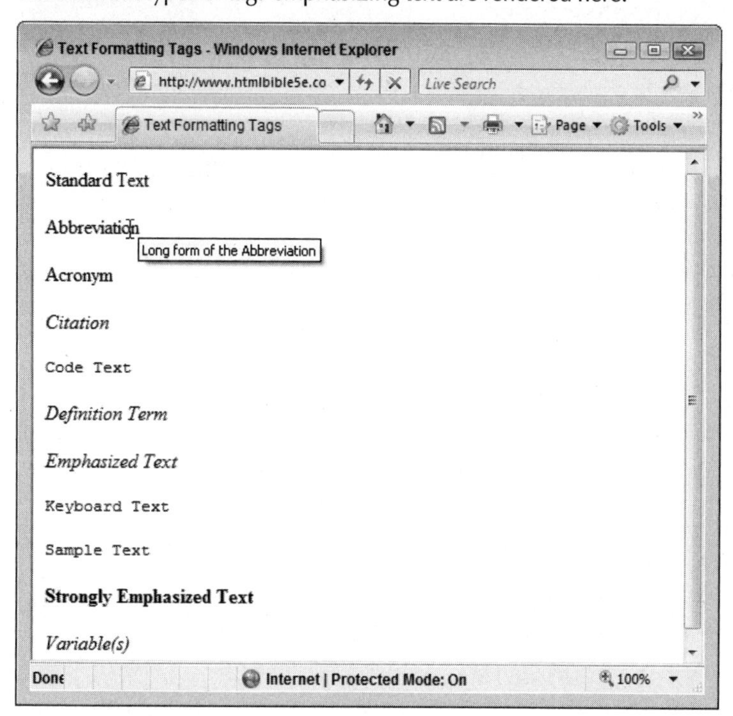

Later, you might decide that the red color is too much emphasis, and larger, bold text is enough. You must then change every <font> tag used around reserved words, as follows, removing the `color` attribute:

```
<p>The <font size="+1"><b>date</b></font>
function can be used to ...
```

Suppose, instead, that you used CSS, as shown in the following code:

```
<head>
  <style type="text/css">
    .reservedword { font: 14pt bold; color: red }
  </style>
</head>
<body>
<p>The <span class="reservedword">date</span> function can be
used to...
```

If you later decided to change the formatting of reserved words, you would have to make only one change to the style definition at the top of the document. That one change would result in changing all instances of the style within the document.

TABLE 6-1

Emphasis Tags

Tag	Use
<abbr>	Abbreviation
<acronym>	Acronym
<cite>	Citation
<code>	Code text
<dfn>	Definition term
<em>	Emphasized text
<kbd>	Keyboard text
<samp>	Sample text
<strong>	Strongly emphasized text
<var>	Variable(s)

TABLE 6-2

CSS Text Properties

Property	Values	Use
color	color value	Change the color of text.
font	font-style font-variant font-weight font-size line-height font-family	Shortcut property for setting font style, variant, weight, size, line height, and font family.
font-family	family name value	Set the font family (face).
font-size	font size value	Set the font size.
font-style	normal	italic	oblique	Set font to italic.
font-variant	normal	small-caps	Set small caps.
font-weight	normal	bold	bolder	lighter	Set font to bold.
text-decoration	none	underline	overline	line-through	blink	Set under/overlining.
text-transform	none	capitalize	uppercase	lowercase	Transform font capitalization.

Tip

If you used an external style sheet, that one change outlined in the preceding explanation could result in changing an unlimited number of documents that use the sheet. ■

Bold and Italic Text

Two well-known text emphasis tags that survive in HTML are bold and italic. As used in the following code example, their effect on text is shown in Figure 6-2:

```
<p>This is normal text.</p>
<p><b>This is bold text.</b></p>
<p><i>This is italic text.</i></p>
```

Note

Not every font has a bold and/or italic variant. When possible, the user agent will substitute a similar font when bold or italic is requested but not available. However, not all user agents are font-savvy. Your mileage with these tags may vary depending on the user agent being used, and the system on which it is being used. ■

FIGURE 6-2

Bold and italic tags at work

For the same reasons mentioned elsewhere, it is advisable to use CSS instead of hard-coded bold and italic tags.

Use of Emphasis Instead of Italics

There is some common wisdom among Web developers that the emphasis tag (<em>) should be used instead of the italic tag (<i>). The rationale behind this opinion is that the italic tag should be used to *emphasize* text, not necessarily to italicize it (which has the notable side effect of emphasizing the very text it italicizes).

Note

Although bold and italic tags have survived deprecation in HTML, their use is still discouraged in favor of CSS alternatives, for all the usual reasons highlighted throughout this chapter. ■

The one problem with specifying that text be italicized is that not all fonts have an italic variant. Some non-font-savvy user agents may choose to ignore the italic tag, rendering the text as normal, non-italicized, non-emphasized text. The emphasis tag, however, instructs the user agent to use its preferred method of emphasizing the coded text — italic, special symbols, a special font, bold characters, and so on. Regardless of the user agent, you can almost always rely upon text coded with the emphasis tag to appear differently than text not coded as such.

The bottom line: Use the emphasis tag when your goal is simply to have the coded text emphasized, regardless of how it is displayed by the user agent. Use the italic tag when you need the text to show up unconditionally as italic — if the user agent can render it as such.

Monospace (Typewriter) Fonts

Another text formatting tag that has thus far survived deprecation is the teletype tag (<tt>). This tag is named for the teletype terminals used with the first computers, which were capable of printing only in a monospaced font. This tag tells the user agent that certain text should be rendered in a monospaced font. Suggested uses for this tag include reserved words in documentation, code listings, and so on. The following code shows an example of the teletype tag in use:

```
<p>Consider using the <tt>date</tt> function instead.</p>
```

Tip

Again, the use of styles is preferred over individual inline tags. If you need text rendered in a monospace font, consider directly specifying the font parameters using styles instead of relying upon the <tt> tag. ■

Superscripts and Subscripts

There are two tags, <sup> and <sub>, for formatting text in superscript and subscript, respectively. The following code shows an example of each tag, the output of which is shown in Figure 6-3:

```
<p>This is normal text.</p>
<p>This is the 16<sup>th</sup> day of the month.</p>
<p>Water tanks are clearly marked as H<sub>2</sub>O.</p>
```

FIGURE 6-3

Examples of superscript and subscript

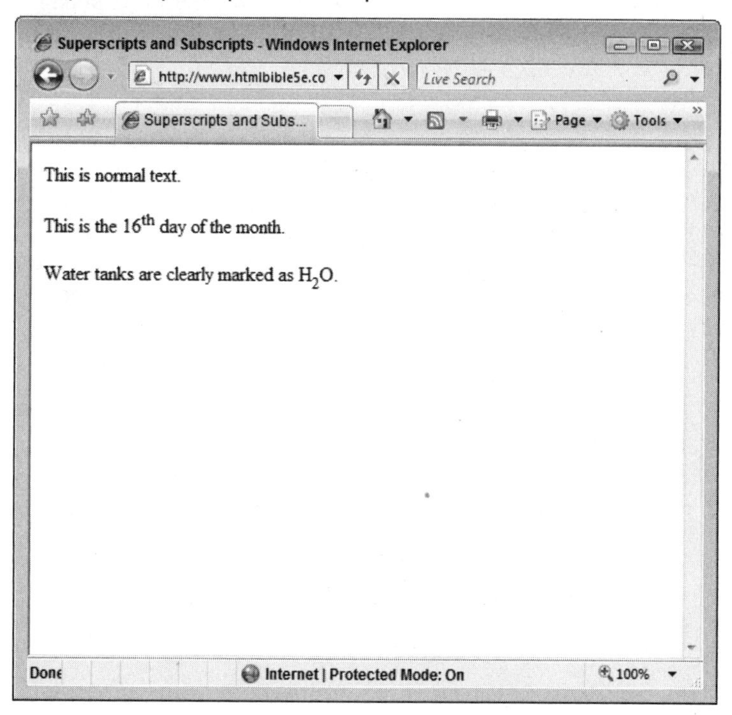

Abbreviations

You can use the abbreviation tag (<abbr>) to mark abbreviations, and, optionally, when using the title attribute, give readers the expansion of the abbreviation used. For example, you could use this tag with acronyms such as HTML:

```
<abbr title="Hypertext Markup Language">HTML</abbr>
```

Note that the expansion of the abbreviation is placed in the <abbr> tag's title attribute. Some user agents will display the value of the title attribute when the mouse/pointer is over the abbreviation, as previously shown in Figure 6-1. Other user agents may totally disregard the tag and its expansion title attribute.

The acronym tag (<acronym>) is very similar to the abbreviation tag but is used for acronyms. It, too, supports a title attribute for optionally supplying the expansion of the acronym.

Marking Editorial Insertions and Deletions

To further strengthen the bond between HTML documents and printed material, the insert (<ins>) and delete (<del>) tags have been added to HTML. Both tags are used for redlining documents — that is, creating a visually marked-up document showing changes made to the document.

For example, the following code has been marked up with text to be inserted (underlined) and deleted (strikethrough). The output of this code is shown in Figure 6-4.

```
<p>Peter <del>are</del><ins>is</ins> correct, the proposal from Acme
is lacking a few <del>minor </del>details.</p>
```

Note

The underline tag (<u>) has been deprecated in favor of the insert tag (<ins>), and the strikethrough tag (<strike>) has been deprecated in favor of the delete tag (<del>). ■

Grouping Inline Elements with the Span Tag

When using CSS for text formatting, you need a method to code text with the appropriate styles. If you are coding block elements, you can use the <div> tag to delimit the block, but with smaller chunks (inline elements) you should use <span>.

The <span> tag is used like any other inline tag (<b>, <i>, <tt>, and so on), surrounding the text/elements that it should affect. However, the <span> tag itself does not directly affect the text it encapsulates. You must use the style or class attribute to define what style(s) should be applied. For example, both of the following code paragraph samples would render the word red in a red-colored font:

```
<head>
  <style type="text/css">
    .redtext { color: red; }
  </style>
</head>
```

```
<body>
<!-- Paragraph 1, using direct style coding -->
<p>We should paint the document <span style="color: red">
red</span>.</p>
<!-- Paragraph 2, using a style class -->
<p>We should paint the document <span class="redtext">
red</span>.</p>
</body>
```

FIGURE 6-4

The ins and del tags can provide for suitable redlined documents.

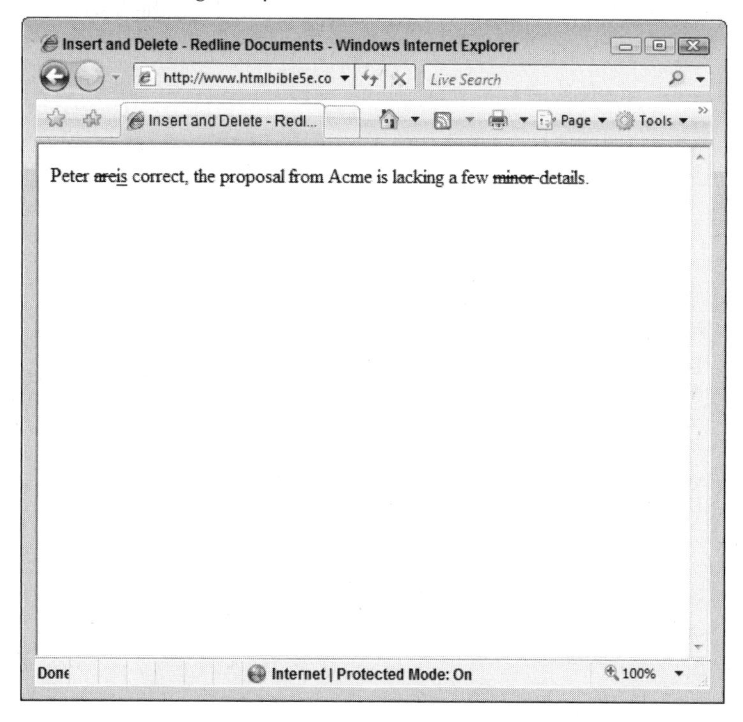

Of the two methods, using the `class` attribute is preferred over using the `style` attribute because `class` avoids directly (and individually) coding the text. Instead, it references a separate style definition that can be repurposed with other text.

Note

Throughout this chapter, I have advocated using styles in lieu of direct formatting using inline tags. The `<span>` tag is the vehicle you should use to accomplish that feat. For example, instead of coding individual instances of bold, italic text (`<b><em>`) throughout a document, create a style class using `font-weight` and `font-style` attributes and code each instance with a `<span>` tag that specifies that class. ■

Summary

This chapter covered the formatting of text using inline tags. You learned two distinct methods (direct tags and styles) and the various tags to supplement textual formatting. Keep in mind that you should use `<div>` or other block tags to format larger sections of a document.

The following chapters (7 through 11) introduce you to larger formatting elements such as lists, tables, frames, and forms, and explain how to link documents to one another. All of this information gives you more formatting options for the text and character formatting techniques you have already learned.

CHAPTER

Lists

IN THIS CHAPTER

HTML and its various derivatives were originally intended to reproduce academic and research text. For this reason, particular care was taken to ensure that specific elements, such as lists and tables, were implemented and robust enough to handle the tasks for which they serve.

In the case of lists, HTML defines three different types of lists: *ordered lists* (numbered), *unordered lists* (bulleted), and *definition lists* (term and definition pairs). This chapter covers all three types of lists and the various syntax and formatting possibilities of each.

Understanding Lists

All lists, whether ordered, unordered, or definition, share similar elements. Each HTML list has the following structure:

```
<list_tag>
  <item_tag>Item text</item_tag>
  <item_tag>Item text</item_tag>
  ...
</list_tag>
```

Note

Definition lists are slightly different in syntax because they use a term tag (<dt>) and a definition description tag (<dd>). See the "Definition Lists" section later in this chapter for more information. ■

For each list, you need the list opening tag, a corresponding closing tag, and individual item tags for each element actually in the list. Essentially, the entire list must be delimited by list open and close tags, with list items appearing between the two tags with open and close tags of their own. This structure will become abundantly clear throughout the chapter.

Each type of list has its own display format:

- An ordered list precedes its items with a number or letter.
- An unordered list precedes its items with a bullet (as in this list).
- A definition list has two pieces for each item: a term and a definition.

The ordered and unordered lists have many different display options available:

- Ordered lists can have their items preceded by the following:
  - Arabic numbers
  - Roman numerals (uppercase or lowercase)
  - Letters (uppercase or lowercase)
  - Numerous other language-specific numbers/letters
- Unordered lists can have their items preceded by the following:
  - Several styles of bullets (filled circle, open circle, square, and so on)
  - Images

More information on the individual list types is provided in the following sections.

Ordered (Numbered) Lists

Ordered lists have elements that are preceded by numbers or letters. They are meant to provide a sequence of ordered steps for an activity. For example, this book uses numbered lists when stepping you through a process. Such a list might resemble the following:

1. Press and hold the reset button until the power light blinks rapidly.
2. Release the reset button.
3. Wait until the power light returns to a steady state.

Ordered lists use the ordered list tag (`<ol>`) to delimit the entire list, and the list item tag (`<li>`) to delimit each individual list item.

In the preceding example, the list has three elements numbered with Arabic numbers. This is the default for ordered lists in HTML, as shown in the following code, whose output is shown in Figure 7-1:

```
<!DOCTYPE HTML PUBLIC "-//W3C//DTD HTML 4.01//EN"
   "http://www.w3.org/TR/html4/strict.dtd">
<html>
```

```
<head>
  <title>Example Ordered List</title>
</head>
<body>
<p>
<ol>
  <li> Press and hold the reset button until the power light blinks
       rapidly.</li>
  <li> Release the reset button.</li>
  <li> Wait until the power light returns to a steady state.</li>
</ol>
</p>
</body>
</html>
```

FIGURE 7-1

The default ordered list uses Arabic numbers for its items.

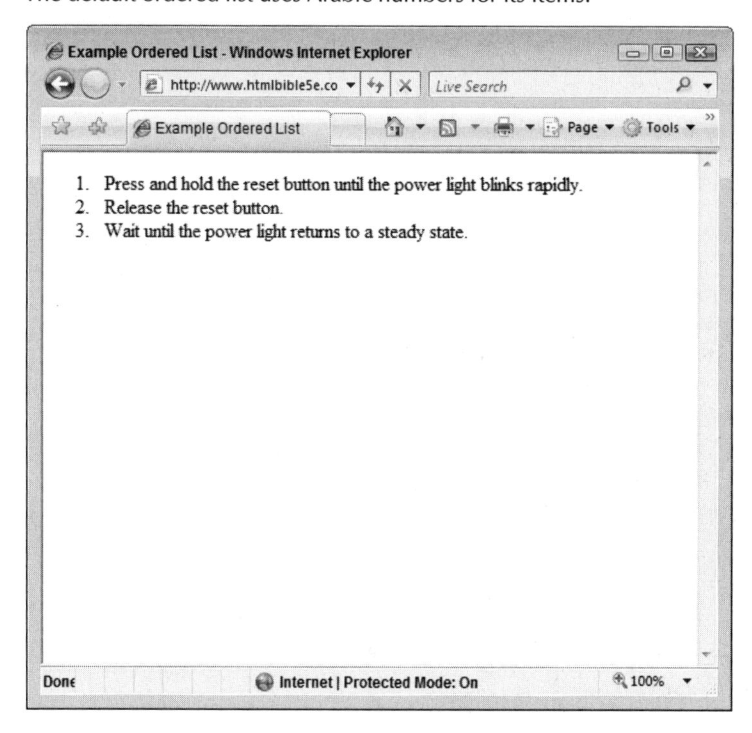

To specify a different type of identifier for each item, you use the `list-style-type` attribute and define a style for the list, as shown in the following code:

```
<!DOCTYPE HTML PUBLIC "-//W3C//DTD HTML 4.01//EN"
   "http://www.w3.org/TR/html4/strict.dtd">
<html>
```

```
<head>
  <title>Example Ordered List - Letters</title>
</head>
<body>
<p>
<ol style="list-style-type: upper-alpha">
  <li> Press and hold the reset button until the power light blinks
       rapidly.</li>
  <li> Release the reset button.</li>
  <li> Wait until the power light returns to a steady state.</li>
</ol>
</p>
</body>
</html>
```

Cross-Ref

Style properties for lists are covered in Chapter 31. ■

This code results in the list items being prefaced with uppercase letters, as shown in Figure 7-2.

FIGURE 7-2

The upper-alpha value of the list-style-type attribute causes the ordered list elements to be prefaced with uppercase letters.

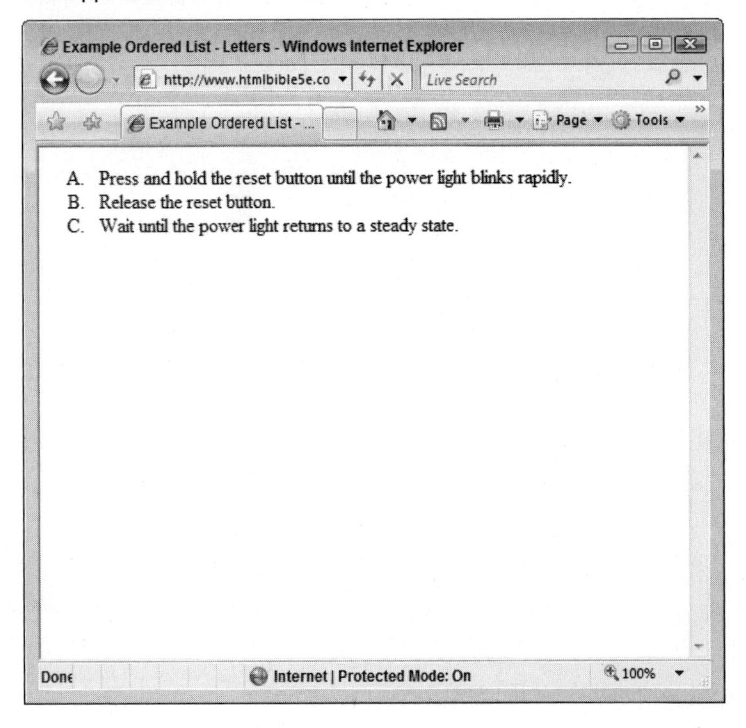

Note

Using letters or Roman numerals only makes sense for organizational lists (outlines, and so on), not for lists that outline a series of steps that must be followed in order. ■

The `list-style-type` property supports the following values in CSS2:

- `decimal`
- `decimal-leading-zero`
- `lower-roman`
- `upper-roman`
- `lower-greek`
- `lower-alpha`
- `lower-latin`
- `upper-alpha`
- `upper-latin`
- `Hebrew`
- `Armenian`
- `Georgian`
- `cjk-ideographic`
- `hiragana`
- `katakana`
- `hiragana-iroha`
- `katakana-iroha`
- `none`

Note

Some of the values for `list-style-type` are font-dependent, meaning they are supported on certain fonts only. If you are using a type such as `hiragana` with a Latin-based font, you will not achieve the results you intended. ■

The values for `list-style-type` are self-explanatory. The default type is typically decimal, but it can be defined by the individual user agent. Keep in mind that your document's font and language options must support the language character sets used by the `list-style-type`.

Ordered lists also support the `list-style-position` property. This property controls where the number or character preceding each item appears. The property has two possible values:

- `outside` — The number or character appears outside the left margin of the item text.
- `inside` — The number or character appears inside the left margin of the item text.

The default is outside, and the difference between the two options is shown in Figure 7-3.

Tip

The various list properties can all be defined within one property, `list-style`. The `list-style` property has the following syntax:

```
list-style: <list-style-type> <list-style-image>
   <list-style-position>
```

You can use this one property to specify one, two, or all three `list-style` properties in one declaration. For example, to define an ordered list with lowercase letters and inside positioning, you could use the following tag:

```
<ol style="list-style: lower-alpha inside;">
```

See Part III of this book for more information on styles. ■

FIGURE 7-3

The list-style-position property controls where the list item numbers/characters appear — outside or inside the list item margins.

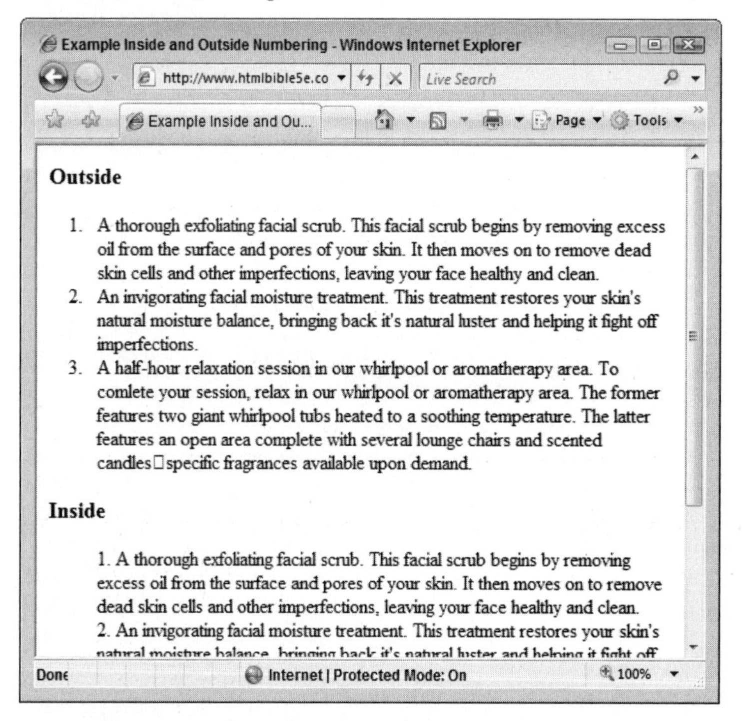

Changing the Start Value of Ordered Lists

Previous versions of HTML allowed the use of the `start` attribute in the `<ol>` tag to control what number or letter the list began with. For example, the following code starts a list with the decimal number 12:

```
<ol start="12" style="list-style-type: decimal;">
```

However, the `<ol>` tag's `start` attribute was deprecated and a replacement CSS equivalent has yet to be defined. Although you can use the `start` attribute, your document will no longer validate against *strict* HTML.

If you find yourself needing consistent yet flexible numbering, consider using the new CSS2 automatic counters and numbering feature. This feature uses the `content` property along with the new `counter-increment` and `counter-reset` properties to provide a fairly flexible automatic counter function.

The following style code defines a counter and causes any `<ol>` list to begin with an item number of 11:

```
<style type="text/css">
ol.eleven { counter-reset: list 10; }
li { list-style-type: none; }
li:before {
    content: counter(list,decimal) ". ";
    counter-increment: list; }
</style>
```

This code introduces quite a few CSS2 concepts: pseudo-elements, counters, and related properties and methods. However, it isn't as complex as it might first appear:

- The `ol` definition causes the counter (list) to be reset to 10 every time the `<ol>` tag is used — that is, at the beginning of every ordered list with a class of `eleven`.
- The `li` definition sets the list style type to `none` — the counter will display our number; if we left the `list-style-type` set to decimal, there would be an additional number with each item courtesy of the tag itself.
- The `li:before` definition does two things: It causes the counter to be displayed before the item (using the `before` pseudo-element and the `content` property) along with a period and a space. It increments the counter. Note that the counter increment happens first, before the display. That is why you need to reset the counter to one lower than your desired start.

Using the preceding styles along with the following list code in a document results in a list with items numbered 12–15:

```
<ol class="eleven">
   <li>Item 11</li>
   <li>Item 12</li>
   <li>Item 13</li>
   <li>Item 14</li>
</ol>
```

Counters are a relatively new feature of CSS2. Unfortunately, at the time of this writing, few user agents fully support counters. However, the other browsers are sure to follow suit at some point. Until then, you might consider using JavaScript or another client/server scripting method to generate dynamic numbers. You'll find more information on counters and the content property in Chapter 35.

Unordered (Bulleted) Lists

Unordered lists are similar to numbered lists except that they use bullets instead of numbers or letters before each list item. Bulleted lists are generally used when providing a list of nonsequential items. For example, consider the following list:

- Action
- Role Playing
- Puzzle
- Adventure

Unordered lists use the unordered list tag (<ul>) to delimit the entire list and the list item tag (<li>) to delimit each individual list item.

In the preceding example, the list has four elements, each preceded by a small, round, filled bullet. This is the default for unordered lists in HTML, as shown in the following code, whose output is shown in Figure 7-4:

```
<!DOCTYPE HTML PUBLIC "-//W3C//DTD HTML 4.01//EN"
   "http://www.w3.org/TR/html4/strict.dtd">
<html>
<head>
  <title>Example Unordered List</title>
</head>
<body>
<p>
<ul>
  <li>Action</li>
  <li>Role Playing</li>
  <li>Puzzle</li>
  <li>Adventure</li>
</ul>
</p>
</body>
</html>
```

Unordered lists also support the `list-style-type` property, but with slightly different values:

- `disc`
- `circle`
- `square`
- `none`

The default bullet type is `disc`, although the client browser can define the default differently. The different bullet types are shown in Figure 7-5.

As with ordered lists, you can define the `list-style-position` property, which in the case of unordered lists controls where the bullet appears — outside or inside the left margin of the item. For example, to move the bullet inside the item's margins, use a style with the <ul> tag, similar to the following:

```
<ul style="list-style-position: inside;">
```

Unordered lists support one other type of bullet for each item, an image. An image for use in unordered lists must fit the following criteria:

- Be accessible to the document via HTTP (be on the same Web server or accessible from another Web source)
- Be in a suitable format for the Web (JPEG, GIF, or PNG)
- Be sized appropriately for use as a bullet

FIGURE 7-4

Example of an unordered list

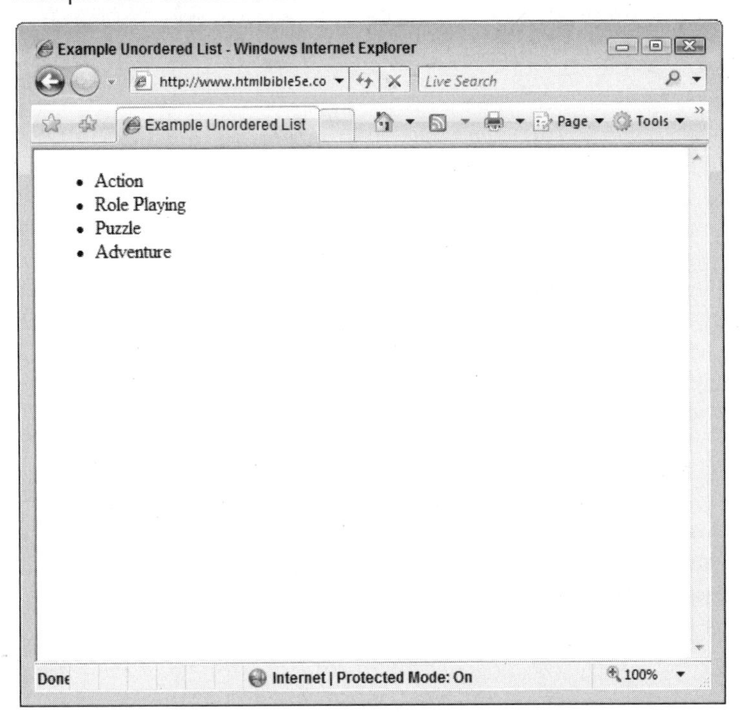

To specify an image for the list, use the `list-style-image` property. This property has the following syntax:

```
list-style-image: url(url_to_image);
```

This property can be used to add more dimension to standard bullets (for example, creating spheres to use instead of circles) or to use specialty bullets that match your content.

Of course, the graphics must be scaled to an appropriate "bullet" size and saved in a Web-friendly format. In the following example, two images were reduced to 10–20 pixels square and saved on the Web server as `sphere.jpg` and `sight.jpg`. The code uses the images as bullets, and the output is shown in Figure 7-6:

```
<!DOCTYPE HTML PUBLIC "-//W3C//DTD HTML 4.01//EN"
   "http://www.w3.org/TR/html4/strict.dtd">
<html>
<head>
  <title>Example Unordered List with Image Bullets</title>
</head>
<body>
<p><b>sphere</b></p>
```

```
<p>
<ul style="list-style-image: url(sphere.jpg);">
  <li>Action</li>
  <li>Role Playing</li>
  <li>Puzzle</li>
  <li>Adventure</li>
</ul>
</p>
<p><b>sight</b></p>
<p>
<ul style="list-style-image: url(sight.jpg);">
  <li>Action</li>
  <li>Role Playing</li>
  <li>Puzzle</li>
  <li>Adventure</li>
</ul>
</p>
</body>
</html>
```

FIGURE 7-5

Different bullet types for unordered lists

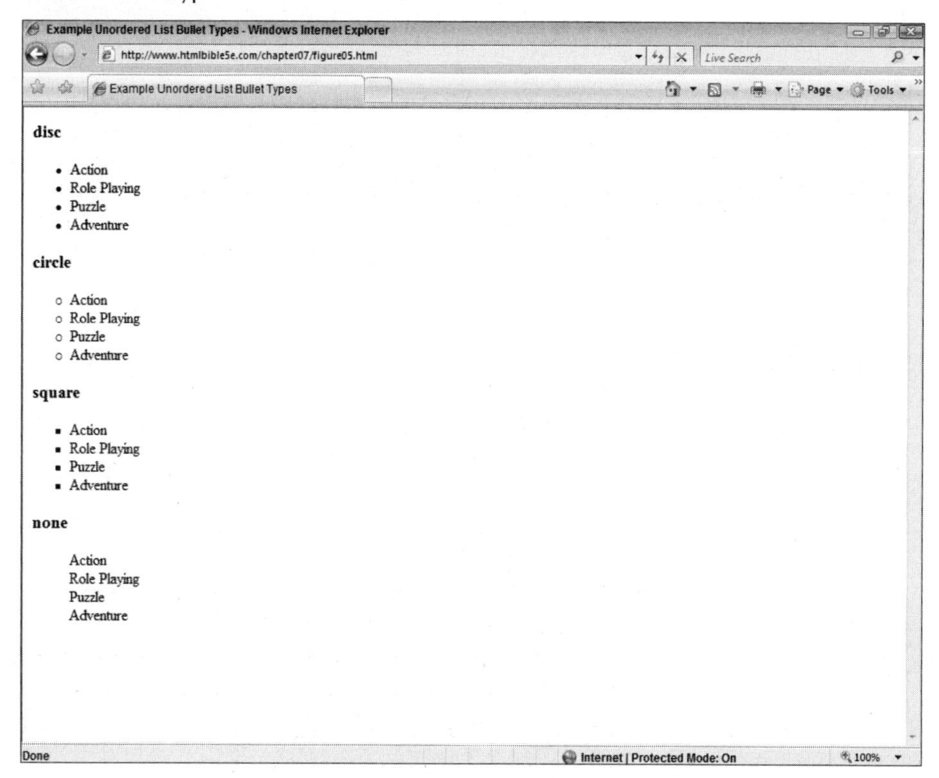

Note

A few references state that the closing item tags (</li>) are not necessary in lists. Although most browsers will render the list properly without them, your code will not validate against strict HTML unless you include them. ■

FIGURE 7-6

Using graphic images for bullets in unordered lists

Definition Lists

Definition lists are slightly more complex than the other two types of lists because they have two elements for each item: a term and a definition. However, there aren't many formatting options for definition lists, so their implementation tends to be simpler than that of the other two lists.

Consider this list of definitions:

E for Everyone. Games rated E contain content suitable for anyone age 6 or older. Games may contain minimal violence and language, typically in animated fashion.

T for Teen. Games rated T contain content suitable for anyone age 13 or older. Games rated T may contain violence, suggestive content, crude humor, blood, and use of strong language.

M for Mature. Games rated M contain content suitable for anyone age 17 or older. Games rated M may contain intense violence, blood, sexual content, and strong language.

FIGURE 7-7

Definition lists provide term and definition pairs for each list item.

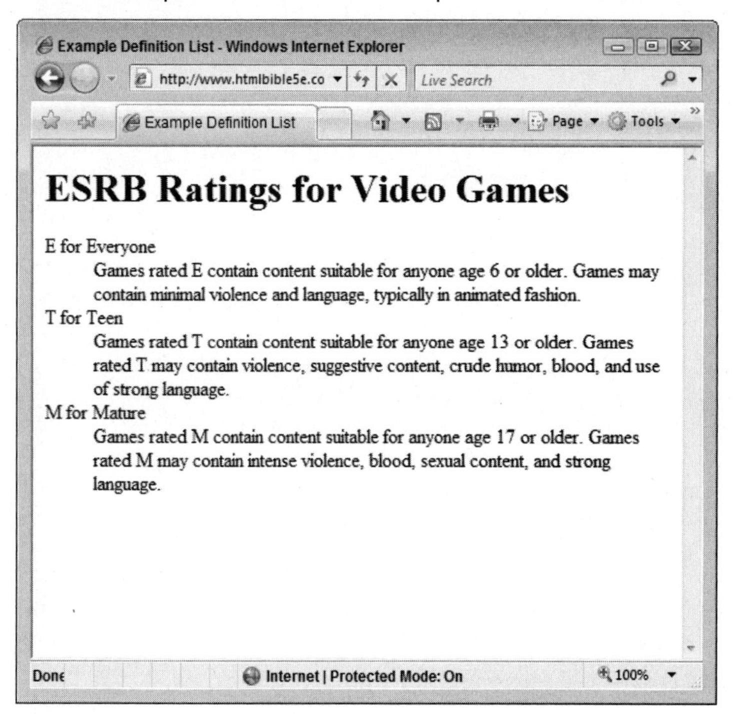

The definition items can be coded as list terms and their definitions as list definitions, as shown in the following code. The output of this code is shown in Figure 7-7.

```
<!DOCTYPE HTML PUBLIC "-//W3C//DTD HTML 4.01//EN"
   "http://www.w3.org/TR/html4/strict.dtd">
<html>
<head>
  <title>Example Definition List</title>
</head>
<body>
<h1>ESRB Ratings for Video Games</h1>
<p>
<dl>
  <dt>E for Everyone</dt>
  <dd>Games rated E contain content suitable for anyone age 6
      or older. Games may contain minimal violence and language,
      typically in animated fashion.</dd>
  <dt>T for Teen</dt>
  <dd>Games rated T contain content suitable for anyone age 13
      or older. Games rated T may contain violence, suggestive
```

```
        content, crude humor, blood, and use of strong
        language.</dd>
    <dt>M for Mature</dt>
    <dd>Games rated M contain content suitable for anyone age 17
        or older. Games rated M may contain intense violence,
        blood, sexual content, and strong language.</dd>
</dl>
</p>
</body>
</html>
```

Note

To add clarity to your definition lists, construct styles that set the definition term in a different font or textual style. For example, you might want the definition terms to be red, bold, and italic. The following style definition accomplishes this:

```
<style type="text/css">
  dt { color: red; font-style: italic;
    font-weight: bold }
</style> ■
```

Nested Lists

You can nest lists of the same or different types. For example, suppose you have a bulleted list and need a numbered list beneath one of the items, as shown:

- Send us a letter detailing the problem. Be sure to include the following:
  1. Your name
  2. Your order number
  3. Your contact information
  4. detailed description of the problem

In such a case, you would nest an ordered list inside an unordered one, as shown in the following code:

```
<!DOCTYPE HTML PUBLIC "-//W3C//DTD HTML 4.01//EN"
   "http://www.w3.org/TR/html4/strict.dtd">
<html>
<head>
  <title>Example Definition List</title>
</head>
<body>
<p>
<ul style="list-style-type: disc;">
  <li>Send us a letter detailing the problem. Be sure to
     include the following:</li>
  <ol style="list-style-type: decimal;"> <li>Your name.</li>
    <li>Your order number.</li>
```

```
        <li>Your contact information.</li>
        <li>A detailed description of the problem.</li>
      </ol>
    </ul>
    </p>
    </body>
    </html>
```

The code's output is shown in Figure 7-8.

FIGURE 7-8

You can nest different types of lists within one another.

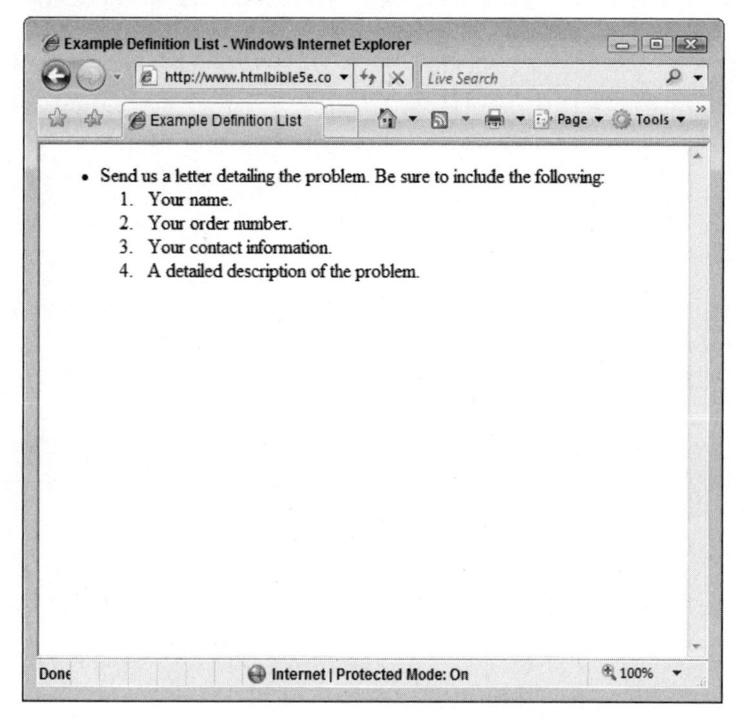

Note that the nested list does not span any open or close tags — it starts after the close tag of the parent's item and before any other tags in the parent list. It is also formatted (indented) to make it easier to identify in the code. Using this method, you can nest any list within any other list.

Summary

This chapter covered the ins and outs of the three different list types in HTML: numbered, bulleted, and definition. You learned how to define and format each type of list and how you can nest lists for more flexibility.

From here, you should work through the rest of the HTML formatting essential chapters (Chapters 8 through 12), covering links, tables, frames, forms, and more. This will help round out your knowledge of how to format document elements using HTML. Furthermore, reading the CSS basic chapters (Chapters 25 through 28) will give you the basics to apply to the specific CSS concepts in Chapters 29 through 38.

CHAPTER

8

Links

IN THIS CHAPTER

Links are what make the World Wide Web weblike. One document on the Web can link to several other documents, and those in turn link to other documents, and so forth. The resulting structure, if diagrammed, resembles a web. The comparison has spawned many "web" terms commonly used on the Internet; for example, electronic robots that scour the Web are known as *spiders*.

Besides linking to other documents, you can link to just about any content that can be delivered over the Internet — media files, e-mail addresses, FTP sites, and so on.

This chapter covers the ins and outs of linking to references inside and outside the current document and how to provide more information about your documents' relationships to others on the Web.

What's in a Link?

Web links have two basic components: the *link* and the *target, or destination*.

- The link is the tag in the main document (source) that refers to another document.
- The target, or destination, is the document (or particular location in the document) to which the link leads.

For example, suppose the Acme Games website reviews video games, and the site posts an extremely positive review of a game by On Target Games. Acme could put a link in the review on its site, leading to the game's product page on On Target's site. Such an arrangement would resemble the diagram shown in Figure 8-1.

FIGURE 8-1

The relationship of documents on the Web via links— the user clicks the link in the review document to reach the specified page on the On Target Games website.

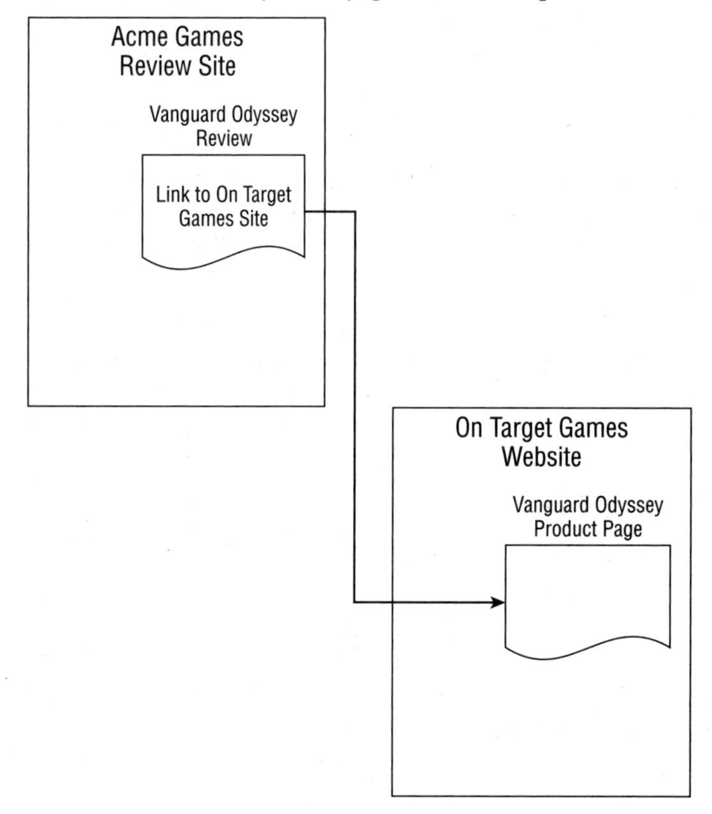

Links have two components: a descriptor and a reference to the target. The target is a document that can be delivered via the Internet. In the preceding example, the review might list the manufacturer's name as the descriptor, and the actual Web URL would be the reference. Both are specified in the anchor tag (`<a>`), as follows:

```
<a href= "url_of_target">descriptor</a>
```

The target reference is specified via the `href` attribute, and the descriptor appears between the start and end anchor tags. For example, a link to On Target Games would resemble the following, if the domain for On Target is `on-target-games.com`:

```
<a href="http://www.on-target-games.com">On Target Games' Website</a>
```

If you don't provide the name of a document in the link, the Web server (in this case, `on-target-games.com`) will send the defined top-level document (known as an *index document*). Typically, this document is named `index.html` or `home.html`. If such a document doesn't exist or one has not been defined for the server, the server will either display an index page or send a "not found" error to the client's user agent.

The text "On Target Games' Website" would be highlighted in the document to indicate it is a link. The default highlight for a link is a different color font and underlined — you will see how to change the highlight later in this chapter.

Note

As mentioned in the introduction to this chapter, you can link to other things besides HTTP documents. All you need is the URL of the item to which you wish to link and the protocol necessary to reach the item. For example, if you wanted to link to a document on an FTP site, you could use an anchor tag similar to the following:

```
<a href="ftp://ftp.on-target-games.com/demos/vanguarddemo.zip">
Vanguard Demo</a>
```
■

Note that the protocol is specified (`ftp:` instead of `http:`) and the server name is specified (`ftp.on-target-games.com`), as is the path and filename (`demos` and `vanguarddemo.zip`). A similar method can be used to link to an e-mail address (`href="mailto:someone@on-target-games.com"`). Clicking such a link will generally spawn the user's e-mail client, ready to send an e-mail to the address specified.

Note

The rest of this chapter concentrates on linking to HTML documents on the Web. However, all the concepts addressed here apply when linking to other content types. ■

Linking to a Web Page

The most popular link style on the Web is a link to another Web page or document. When activated, such a link causes the target page to load in the user agent. Control is then transferred to the target page — its scripts run, and so on.

To link to another page on the Internet, simply specify the target's URL in the anchor tag. Suppose you want to link to the products page of the On Target Games Website and the page is named `vanguard.html` and resides in the `products` directory on the Web server. The `href` parameter of the link would be as follows:

```
http://www.on-target-games.com/products/vanguard.html
```

Note that the URL contains the protocol, the server name, the directory name, and the filename. Figure 8-2 shows a breakdown of the various pieces of the URL.

FIGURE 8-2

The various pieces of a URL

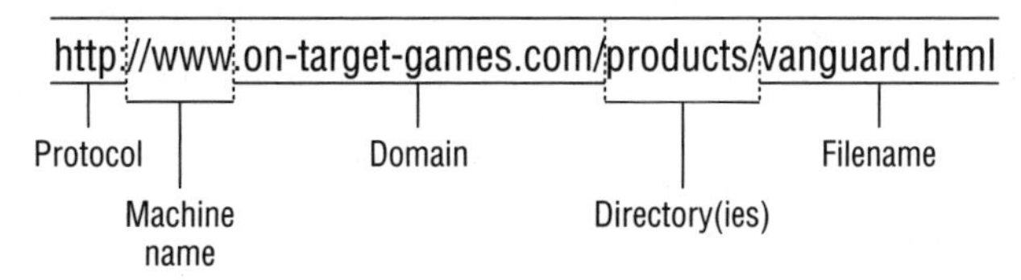

In the case of this URL, the various pieces are separated by various key characters:

- The protocol is first, and ends with a colon (`http:`).
- The server name is next, prefaced with a double slash (`//www.on-target-games.com`).
- The directory (or directories) comes next, separated with slashes (`/products/`).
- The page's filename is last, separated from the preceding directory by a slash (`/vanguard.html`).

Note

The server name is actually two pieces: the server's name and the domain on which it resides. In `www.on-target-games.com`, `www` is the server name and `on-target-games.com` is the domain. There is a common misconception that all Web server names need to begin with `www`. Although `www` is a standard name for a Web server, the name can be almost anything. For example, the U.S.-based Web server for the Internet Movie Database (`imdb.com`) is `us.imdb.com`. ■

Absolute versus Relative Links

There are two types of URL styles, and therefore two link types that you need to understand: *absolute links* and *relative links*. You have seen absolute links, where the URL used in the link provides the full path, including the protocol and full server address. These links are called *absolute* links because the URL itself is absolute — that is, it does not change no matter where the document in which it appears is kept.

The other type of link, a *relative* link, does not provide all of the details to the referenced page; hence, its address is treated as relative to the document where the link appears. Relative links are useful only for linking to other pages on the same website because any reference off of the same site requires the remote server's name.

Suppose you are the Webmaster of a company website on the Internet. You have several pages on the site, including the home page, a main products page, and hardware and software products pages. The home page is in the root directory of the server, while the product pages (all three) are in a products directory. The relative links back and forth between the pages are shown in Figures 8-3 and 8-4.

FIGURE 8-3

Relative links to subpages

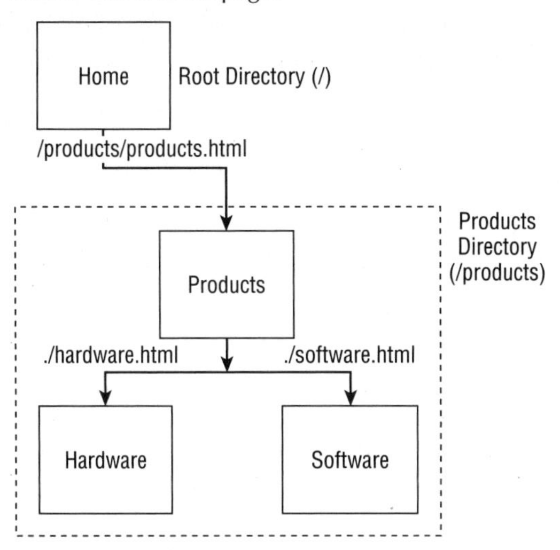

FIGURE 8-4

Relative links to parent pages

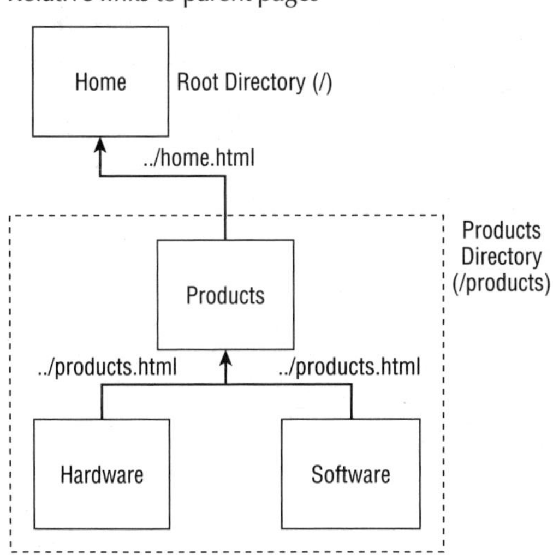

Note that you can use directory shortcuts to specify where the pages are:

- Starting a directory with a slash (/) references it in a subdirectory of the root directory.
- Starting a directory with a period and a slash (./) references it in a subdirectory of the current directory (the directory where the current page resides).
- Starting a directory with a double period and a slash (../) references it in a parent directory to the current directory.

Relative links are easier to maintain on sections of websites where the pages in that section never change in relationship to one another. For example, in the case of the site shown in Figures 8-3 and 8-4, if the products pages move as a whole unit to another place on the site, the relative links between the product pages won't change. If the links were coded as absolute (for example, `http://www.domain-name/products/hardware.html`), they would all have to change.

Link Targets

Normally, links open the page they refer to in the active user agent window, replacing the page currently displayed. However, you can control where the page opens using the `target` attribute in the anchor tag.

Note

The `target` attribute has been deprecated in strict HTML because it directs the destination of a link to be opened in a specific frame target. Because frames have been deprecated in the strict version of HTML 4.01, so has the `target` attribute. It appears here because most user agents still support the attribute and it can be useful. However, keep in mind that using this attribute means your documents will not validate against strict HTML. ■

The `target` attribute supports the values shown in Table 8-1.

TABLE 8-1

Target Attribute Values

Value	Description
`_blank`	Opens the linked document in a new window.
`_self`	Opens the linked document in the same frame as the link.
`_parent`	Opens the linked document in the parent frameset.
`_top`	Opens the linked document in the main window, replacing any and all frames present.
`name`	Opens the linked document in the window with the specified name.

Cross-Ref

Frames are covered in Chapter 10. ■

For example, to open a linked document in a new window, rather than replace the contents of the current window with the linked document, you would use a tag similar to the following:

```
<a href="http://www.oasisoftranquility.com" target="_blank">
Monthly Drawing (new window)</a>
```

Caution

The debate about whether you should *ever* open a new window is fierce. Most users are accustomed to all new windows being of the pop-up ad variety — and very unwelcome. However, from a user interface standpoint, new windows can be utilized very effectively if they are used like dialog boxes or new windows that an operating system spawns. In any case, you should form a habit of informing users when you are going to open a new window so you don't surprise them. ■

The last value listed for target, *name*, can also aid in the user interface experience, if used correctly. Certain methods of opening windows (such as the JavaScript `window.open` method) enable you to give a window a unique name. You can then use that name to push a linked document into that window. For example, the following code displays two links; the first opens a new, empty user agent window named `NEWS`, and the second pushes the content at `www.yahoo.com` into the window:

```
<!DOCTYPE HTML PUBLIC "-//W3C//DTD HTML 4.01//EN"
   "http://www.w3.org/TR/html4/strict.dtd">
<html>
<head>
<script type="text/javascript">
function NewsWindow(){
  var fin=window.open("","NEWS","width=400,height=400");
}
</script>
</head>
<body>
<p><a href="#" onclick="NewsWindow()">Open a Blank Window</a></p>
<p><a href="http://www.yahoo.com" target="NEWS">Fill Window with
Yahoo Content</a></p>
</body>
</html>
```

Cross-Ref

For more information on JavaScript, refer to Chapter 16. ■

Link Titles

You can also title a link using the `title` attribute in the anchor tag. This causes most current user agents to display the title text as a tooltip when the mouse hovers over it. For example, the following link will cause Internet Explorer to display "Read the review at On Target Games," as shown in Figure 8-5:

```
Read what others think of our game <a
href="http://www.on-target-games.com/reviews/vanguard.com"
title="Read the review at On Target Games">here</a>.
```

You can use this feature to give users more information about a link before they click it.

FIGURE 8-5

The title attribute causes a tooltip display when the mouse hovers over the link.

Keyboard Shortcuts and Tab Order

In the modern world of computers it is easy to make assumptions about users, their hardware, and capabilities. Several years ago, no one would have dreamt of delivering rich, multimedia content over the Web. Today, however, it is often assumed that everyone is using the latest user agent, on a high-end computer, across a broadband connection.

That isn't always the case. In fact, some users who visit your site may not even have a mouse to aid in browsing. The reason could be a physical handicap, a text-only agent, or just a fondness for using the keyboard. You can accommodate these users by adding additional methods to access links on your page.

Keyboard shortcuts

Each link can be assigned a shortcut key for easy keyboard-only access using the `accesskey` attribute with the anchor tag. The `accesskey` attribute takes one letter as its value: the letter that can be used to access the link. For example, the following link defines "R" as the access key:

```
<a href="http://www.on-target-games.com/reviews"
accesskey="R"><b>R</b>eviews</a>
```

Note that different user agents and different operating systems handle access keys differently. Some user agent and operating system combinations require special keys to be pressed with the defined access key. For example, Windows users on Internet Explorer must hold the Alt key down while they press the access key. Note also that different user agents handle the actual access of the link differently. Some user agents will activate the link as soon as the access key is pressed, while others only select the link, requiring another key to be pressed to actually activate it.

Tip

Keyboard shortcuts won't help your users if you don't give them a clue as to what the shortcut is. In the example earlier in this section, the defined shortcut key ("R") was used in the link text and highlighted using the bold font attribute. ■

Tab order

Defining a tab order for the links in your document will also help your users. As with most graphical operating systems, the Tab key can be used to move through interface elements, including links. Typically, the default tab order is the same as the order in which the links appear in the document. However, on occasion, you might wish to change the order using the `tabindex` attribute. The `tabindex` attribute takes an integer as its value, and that integer is used to define the tab sequence in the document. For example, the following code switches the tab order of the second and third links in a document:

```
<!DOCTYPE HTML PUBLIC "-//W3C//DTD HTML 4.01//EN"
   "http://www.w3.org/TR/html4/strict.dtd">
<html>
<head>
<title>Tab Ordered Document</title>
</head>
<body>
<p>This is the <a href="http://www.example.com"
   tabindex="1">first link</a>.</p>
<p>This is the <a href="http://www.example.com"
   tabindex="3">second link</a>.</p>
<p>This is the <a href="http://www.example.com"
   tabindex="2">third link</a>.</p>
</body>
</html>
```

Note

As with most interface elements in HTML, the user agent defines how `tabindex` is implemented and how tabbed elements are accessed. ■

Creating an Anchor

Anchor tags have another use; they can be a marker in the current document to provide a bookmark that can be directly linked to. For example, a large document might have several sections. You can place links at the top of the document (or in a special navigation frame) to each section, enabling the user to easily access each section.

To create an anchor in a document, use the anchor tag with the `name` attribute. For example, the following code creates an `introduction` anchor at the "Introduction" heading:

```
<h1><a name="introduction">Introduction</a></h1>
```

To link to the anchor you use a standard link, but add the anchor name to the end of the URL in the link. To identify the name as an anchor, separate it from the rest of the URL with a pound sign (#). For example, suppose the `introduction` anchor appears in the document `vanguard.html`. To link to the `introduction` anchor, you could use the following code:

```
<a href="vanguard.html#introduction">Introduction</a>
```

Note

Because the URL in the link tag can contain the server and document names as well as the anchor name, you can link to anchors in the same document or any accessible document. If you are linking to an anchor in the same document, you can use an abbreviated form of the URL that includes only the pound sign and the anchor name. ■

In addition to using the anchor tag for bookmarks, you can link to a block element's `id` attribute. For example, if the Introduction appears inside an `<h1>` tag, you can set the `<h1>` tag's `id` attribute to `introduction` and omit the anchor link altogether, as shown in the following example:

```
<h1 id="introduction">Introduction</h1>
```

Choosing Link Colors

Links should stand out from the rest of the content in your documents. They need to be easily recognizable by users. Each link has four different status modes:

- **Link** — The standard link in the document. It is neither active nor visited (see other modes).
- **Active** — The link's target is active in another window.
- **Visited** — The link's target has been previously visited (typically, this means the target can be found in the user agent's cache).
- **Hover** — The mouse pointer is over the link.

Each of these modes should be colored differently so that users can tell the status of each link on your page. The usual colors of each link status are as follows:

- **Link** — Blue, underlined text
- **Active** — Red, underlined text
- **Visited** — Purple, underlined text
- **Hover** — No change in the appearance of the link (remains blue, red, or purple)

Note

As with other presentation attributes in HTML, the user agent plays a significant role in setting link colors and text decorations. Most agents follow the color scheme outlined in this section, but some agents don't conform to this scheme. ■

To change the text color and other link attributes, you can modify the properties of each type of anchor tag. For example, the following style, when used in an HTML document, sets the default visited link text to bold and yellow:

```
a:visited { color: yellow; font-weight: bold; }
```

Tip

Setting the anchor tag properties without specifying a mode changes all of the link modes to the characteristics of the style. For example, the following style sets all links (link, active, visited) to red:

```
a { color: red; }
```
■

Why would you want to change the color of links in your document? One reason would be that the normal text in your document is the same color as the default link. For example, if your document's text is blue, you probably want to change the default color of existing links from blue to another color to enable users to easily recognize them.

Make a habit of defining all of the link attributes instead of haphazardly defining only one or two of the link status colors. The following styles define each type of link, ensuring that they appear how you want in the document:

```
a:link { color: #003366;
  font-family:verdana, palatino, arial, sans-serif;
  font-size:10pt;  text-decoration: underline; }
a:visited  {color: #D53D45;
  font-family:verdana, palatino, arial, sans-serif;
  font-size:10pt;  text-decoration: underline; }
a:active {color: #D53D00;
  font-family:verdana, palatino, arial, sans-serif;
  font-size:10pt;  font-weight: bold;
  text-decoration: underline; }
```

```
a:hover  {color: #D53D45;
  font-family:verdana, palatino, arial, sans-serif;
  font-size:10pt;  text-decoration: none; }
```

Note the redundancy in the styles — there are only subtle changes in each. You should strive to eliminate such redundancy whenever possible, relying instead upon the cascade effect of styles. You could effectively shorten each style by defining the anchor tag's attributes by itself, and defining only the attributes that are different for each variant:

```
a { color: #003366;
 font-family:verdana, palatino, arial, sans-serif;
 font-size:10pt; text-decoration: underline; }
a:visited {color: #D53D45; }
a:active {color: #D53D00; font-weight: bold; }
a:hover {color: #D53D45; text-decoration: none; }
```

Link Destination Details

You can add a host of other attributes to your anchor tags to describe the form of the destination being linked to, the relationship between the current document and the destination, and more.

Table 8-2 lists these descriptive attributes and their possible values.

TABLE 8-2

Link Destination Details

Attribute	Meaning	Value(s)
`charset`	The character encoding of the target	For example, `charset="ISO 8859-1"`
`hreflang`	The base language of the target	For example, `hreflang="en-US"`
`rel`	The relationship between the current document and the destination	`alternate stylesheet start next prev contents index glossary copyright chapter section subsection appendix help bookmark`
`rev`	The relationship between the destination and the current document	`alternate stylesheet start next prev contents index glossary copyright chapter section subsection appendix help bookmark`
`type`	The MIME type of the destination	Any valid MIME type

The following code snippet demonstrates how the relationship attributes (`rel`, `rev`) can be used:

```
<!DOCTYPE HTML PUBLIC "-//W3C//DTD HTML 4.01//EN"
   "http://www.w3.org/TR/html4/strict.dtd">
<html>
<head>
<title>Chapter 10</title>
</head>
<body>
<p><a href="contents.html" rev="chapter" rel="contents">Table of
Contents</a></p>
<p><a href="chapter9.html" rev="next" rel="prev">Chapter 9</a></p>
<p><a href="chapter11.html" rev="prev" rel="next">Chapter 11</a></p>
.......
```

Here, the anchor tags define the relationships between the chapters (next, previous) and the table of contents (chapter, contents).

The Link Tag

You can use the link tag (`<link>`) to provide additional information about a document's relationship to other documents, independently of whether the current document actually links to other documents or not. The link tag supports the same attributes as the anchor tag, but with a slightly different syntax:

- The link tag does not encapsulate any text.
- The link tag does not have an ending tag.

For example, the following code could be used in `chapter10.html` to define that document's relationship to `chapter9.html` and `chapter11.html`:

```
<link href="chapter9.html" rev="next" rel="prev" />
<link href="chapter11.html" rev="prev" rel="next" />
```

The link tag does not result in any visible text being rendered, but it can be used by user agents to provide additional navigation or other user-interface tools.

Another important use of the link tag is to provide alternate content for search engines. For example, the following link references a French version of the current document (`chapter10.html`):

```
<link lang="fr" rel="alternate"hreflang="fr"
      href="chapter10-fr.html" />
```

Other relationship attribute values (`start`, `contents`, and so on) can likewise be used to provide relevant information about document relationships to search engines.

Summary

This chapter covered links — what they are and how to use them to reference other content on the Web. You learned how to construct a link and what attributes are available to the anchor and link tags. You also learned how to define relationships between your document and other documents, and why this is important.

From here, you should progress through the next few chapters, continuing to familiarize yourself with the other various pieces of an HTML document, such as tables, frames, and forms (Chapters 9 through 11). This part of the book then covers colors and multimedia (Chapters 12 and 13), and special characters and internationalization (Chapters 14 and 15), and wraps up with the basics of coding in HTML.

CHAPTER

Tables

IN THIS CHAPTER

Parts of an HTML Table

Table Width and Alignment

Cell Spacing and Padding

Borders and Rules

Rows

Cells

Table Captions

Row Groups — Header, Body, and Footer

Background Colors

Spanning Columns and Rows

Grouping Columns

Formatting with Tables

Tables are a powerful HTML tool with many uses. Developed originally to help communicate tabular data (usually scientific or academic-based data), tables are now used for many purposes — from simply holding tabular data to the layout of entire pages. This chapter covers the basics of tables and then progresses into more complex uses of this versatile HTML structure.

Parts of an HTML Table

An HTML table is made up of the following parts:

- Rows
- Columns
- Header cells
- Body cells
- Caption
- Header row(s)
- Body row(s)
- Footer row(s)

Figure 9-1 shows an example of an HTML table, with the various parts labeled. The table is defined by the following code:

```
<!DOCTYPE HTML PUBLIC "-//W3C//DTD HTML 4.01//EN"
  "http://www.w3.org/TR/html4/strict.dtd">
<html>
<head>
```

```
  <title>An HTML Table</title>
</head>
<body>
<p>
  <table border="1">
    <caption>Table Caption</caption>
    <thead>
      <tr><td colspan="2">Table Header</td></tr>
    </thead>
    <tfoot>
      <tr><td colspan="2">Table Footer</td></tr>
    </tfoot>
    <tbody>
      <tr><th>Header Cell 1</th><th>Header Cell 2</th></tr>
      <tr><td>Body Cell 1</td><td>Body Cell 2</td></tr>
    </tbody>
  </table>
</p>
</body>
</html>
```

FIGURE 9-1

HTML table elements

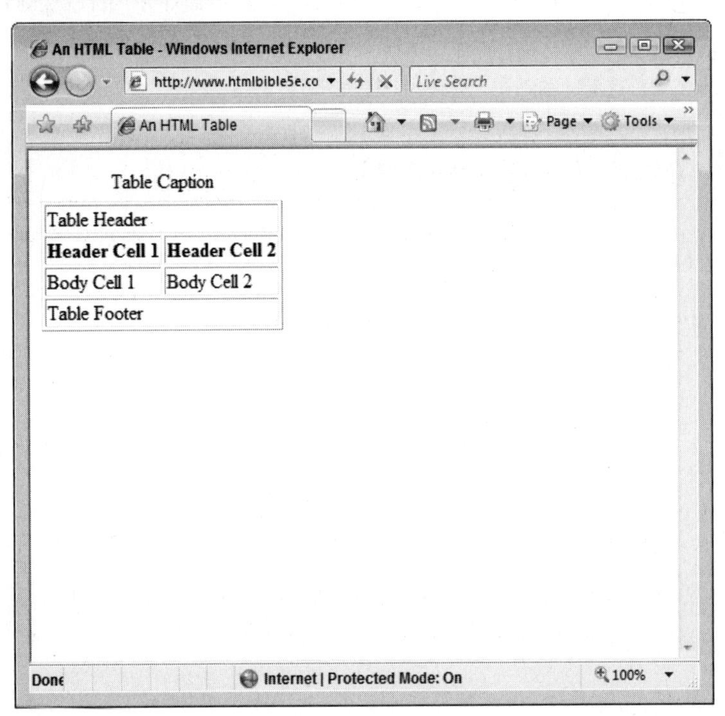

Many parts of the HTML table are optional — you need only to delimit the table (with <table> tags) and define rows (via <tr> tags) and columns (via <td> tags). For example, code for a table with these minimum requirements would resemble the following:

```
<!DOCTYPE HTML PUBLIC "-//W3C//DTD HTML 4.01//EN"
  "http://www.w3.org/TR/html4/strict.dtd">
<html>
<head>
  <title>A Minimal HTML Table</title>
</head>
<body>
<p>
  <table border="1">
    <tr>
      <td>Body Cell 1</td>
      <td>Body Cell 2</td>
    </tr>
  </table>
</p>
</body>
</html>
```

Tip

It is possible to nest tables within one another. In fact, using tables for layout (covered later in this chapter) depends on this capability. Tables must be nested within table cells (<td> tags). See the "Cells" section later in this chapter for more information on the <td> tag. ■

Table Width and Alignment

Typically, an HTML table expands to accommodate the contents of its cells. For example, consider the following code and the resulting tables shown in Figure 9-2:

```
<!DOCTYPE HTML PUBLIC "-//W3C//DTD HTML 4.01//EN"
  "http://www.w3.org/TR/html4/strict.dtd">
<html>
<head>
  <title>HTML Table Widths</title>
</head>
<body>
<p>
  Short Text Table<br />
  <table border="1">
      <tr><td>Short Text 1</td><td>Short Text 2</td></tr>
  </table>
</p>
<p>
  Longer Text Table<br />
```

```
    <table border="1">
        <tr><td>Longer Text 1</td><td>Longer Text 2</td></tr>
    </table>
</p>
<p>
    Mixed Text Table<br />
    <table border="1">
        <tr><td>Short Text</td><td>Even Longer Text</td></tr>
    </table>
</p>
</body>
</html>
```

FIGURE 9-2

HTML tables expand to accommodate their content.

Once a table expands to the limits of its container object — whether the browser window, another table, or a sized frame — the contents of the cells will wrap, as shown in Figure 9-3.

Sometimes you will want to manually size a table, either to fill a larger space or to constrain the table's size. Using the width attribute in the table tag (`<table>`), you can set a table's size by specifying the table width in absolute pixels or a percentage of the table's containing object.

FIGURE 9-3

Cell contents wrap if a table cannot expand any further.

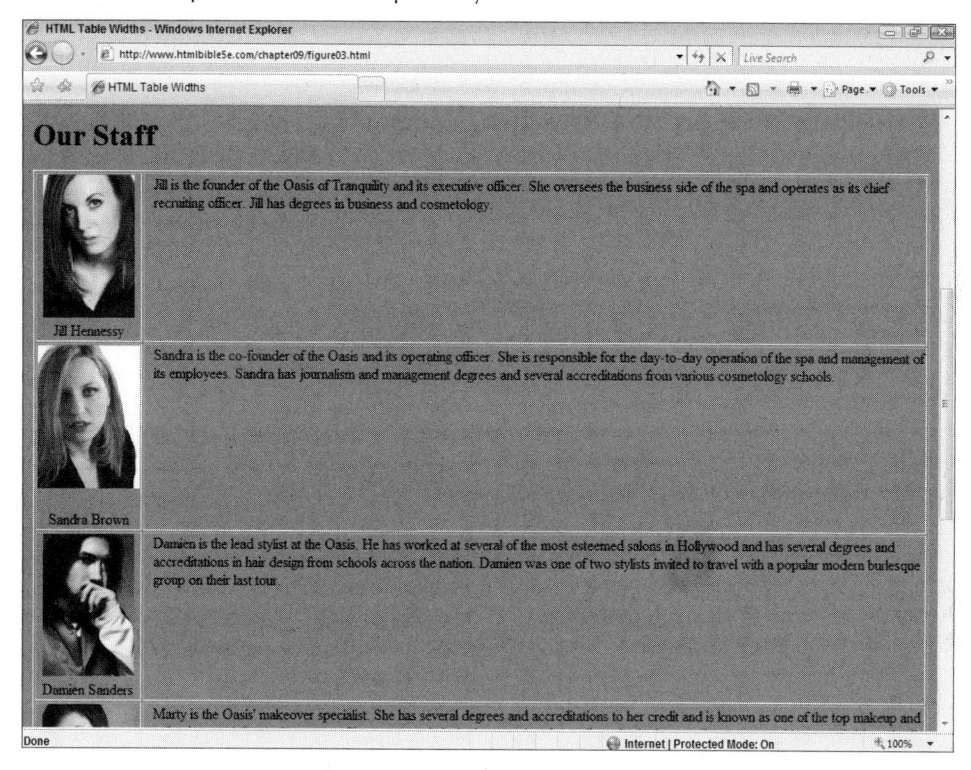

For example, if you specify 50%, as in the following code snippet, the table's width will be 50 percent of the containing object (which is the width of the browser), as shown in Figure 9-4:

```
<table border="1" width="50%">
```

Note

Besides specifying the width of the full table, you can also specify the width of each column within the table using width attributes in the table header (<th>) and table cell (<td>) tags. These techniques are covered in the "Cells" and "Grouping Columns" sections later in this chapter. ■

Using a percentage width enables the table to size itself dynamically to the size of its container. For example, if a table is set to 50%, the table will display as 50 percent of its container — paragraph tag, division, or other block object. Note that if the container is not the width of the user agent, then the scaled table width will not be proportional to the user agent window, but rather the container.

FIGURE 9-4

The width of this table is set to occupy 50 percent of the available width of its containing object — in this case, the user agent window.

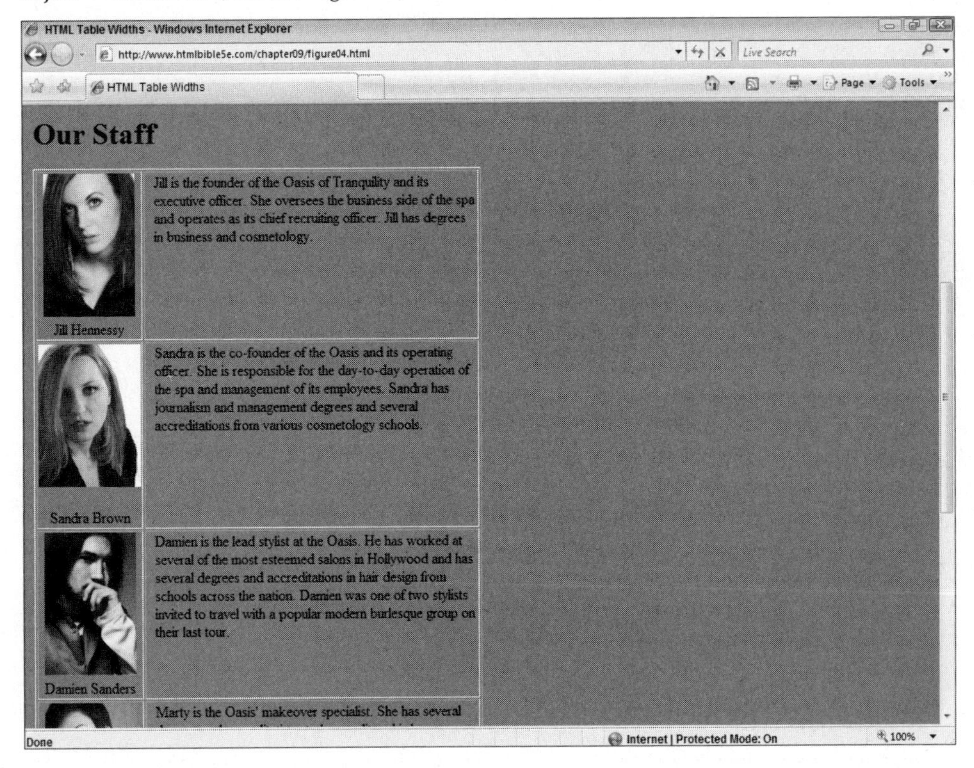

If you need to specify the exact width of a table, you should specify the width of the table in pixels instead. For example, if you need a table to be 400 pixels wide, you would specify the table with the following tag:

```
<table width="400px">
```

Keep in mind that if the specified table width exceeds the width of its container object, the width will be adjusted to the size of the container. An exception is containers that support horizontal scroll bars; if the container supports scroll bars, then the table will be sized as instructed and the container will spawn scroll bars to accommodate its full width, as shown in Figure 9-5.

Note

If the table's specified width exceeds the container's width and the container is not scroll bar–enabled, it is up to the browser to handle the table. Most browsers will resize the table to fit the width of its container. ■

FIGURE 9-5

Tables too wide for their environment can get some help from scroll bars.

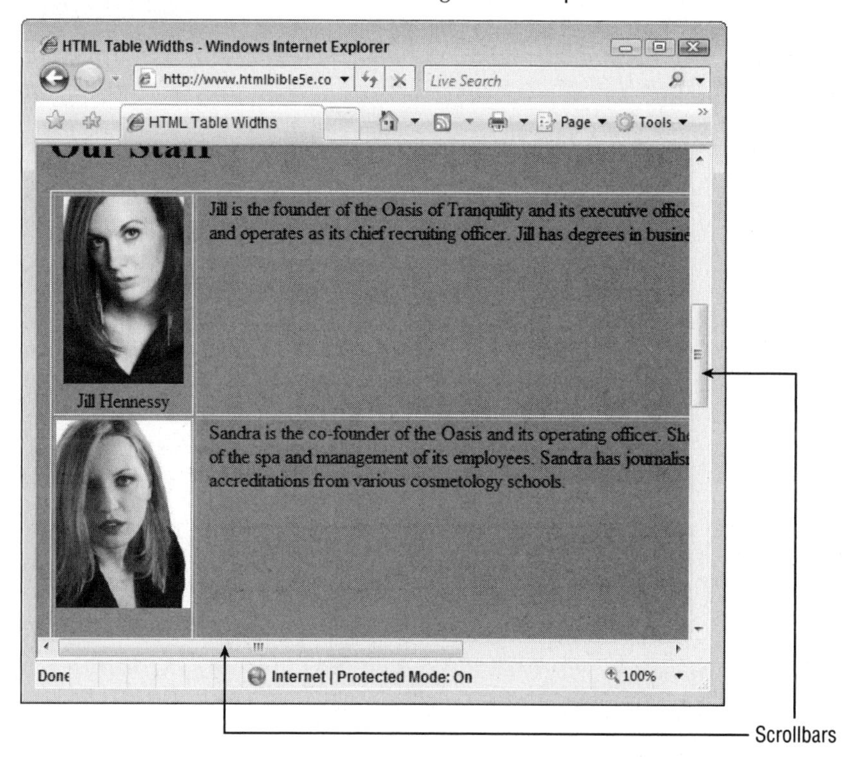

Cell Spacing and Padding

You can control two cell spacing options in your HTML tables: spacing and padding. Cell *spacing* is the space between cells. Cell *padding* is the space between the cell border and its contents. Figure 9-6 shows the relationship between the two and the cell data itself.

Cell spacing is controlled with the `cellspacing` attribute and can be specified in pixels or percentages. When specified by percentage, the browser uses half of the specified percentage for each side of the cell.

Cell padding is controlled with the `cellpadding` attribute. As with cell spacing, you can specify padding in pixels or a percentage.

Tip

Keep in mind that cell spacing and cell padding can have a drastic effect on the available size for cell content. Increasing both spacing and padding decreases the cell content size. ■

FIGURE 9-6

Cell padding and spacing

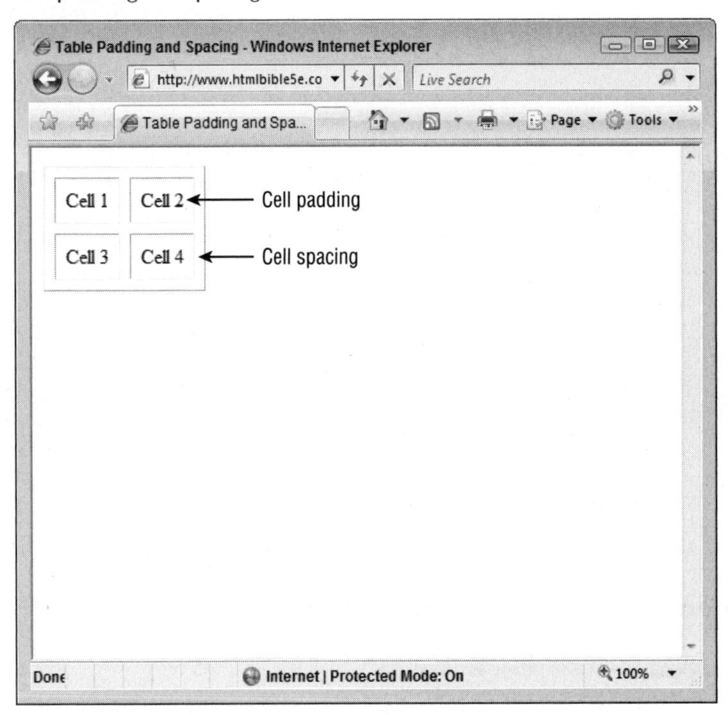

Borders and Rules

The border around HTML tables and in between cells can be configured in many ways. The following sections cover the various ways you can configure table borders and rules.

Table borders

You can use the `border` attribute of the table tag (`<table>`) to configure the outside border of the table. For example, consider the following code containing three tables (the resulting output is shown in Figure 9-7):

```
<!DOCTYPE HTML PUBLIC "-//W3C//DTD HTML 4.01//EN"
  "http://www.w3.org/TR/html4/strict.dtd">
<html>
<head>
  <title>Table Outside Borders</title>
</head>
<body>
<p>
```

```
    No Borders<br />
    <table border="0">
        <tr><td>Cell 1</td><td>Cell 2</td></tr>
        <tr><td>Cell 3</td><td>Cell 4</td></tr>
    </table>
  </p>
  <p>
    Border = 1<br />
    <table border="1">
        <tr><td>Cell 1</td><td>Cell 2</td></tr>
        <tr><td>Cell 3</td><td>Cell 4</td></tr>
    </table>
  </p>
  <p>
    Border = 5<br />
    <table border="5">
        <tr><td>Cell 1</td><td>Cell 2</td></tr>
        <tr><td>Cell 3</td><td>Cell 4</td></tr>
    </table>
  </p>
  </body>
  </html>
```

FIGURE 9-7

Examples of table border widths

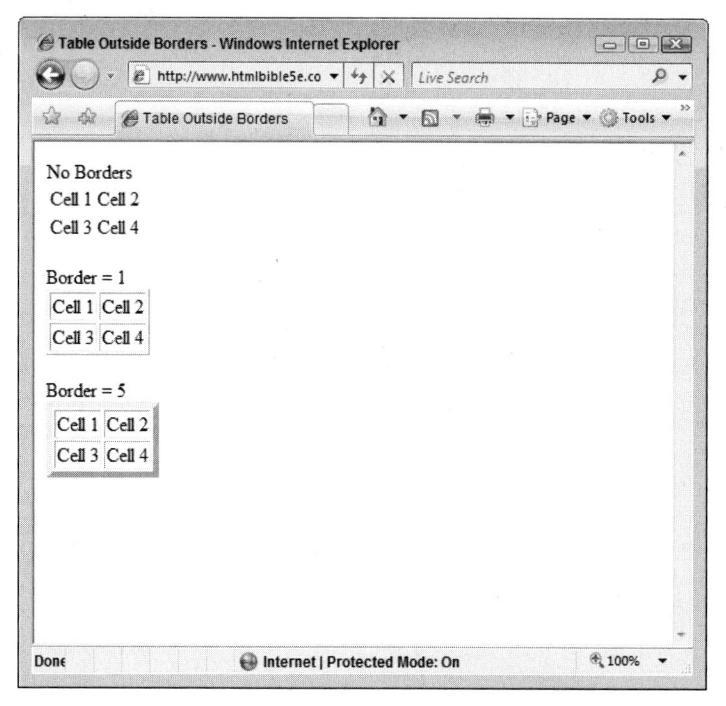

The `border` attribute's value specifies the width of the border in pixels. The default border width is 0, or no border.

Tip

Borders are an effective troubleshooting tool when dealing with table problems in HTML. If you are having trouble determining what is causing a problem in a table, try turning on the borders to better visualize the individual rows and columns. If you are using nested tables, turn on the borders of tables individually until you narrow down the scope of the problem. ■

To specify which outside borders are displayed, use the `frame` attribute with one of the values displayed in Table 9-1.

Note

Not all user agents follow the defaults for table borders (no borders, or box/border when a border width is specified). If you want a table to appear with particular formatting, take care to specify all appropriate options, or use CSS to style the table elements. (Table-based CSS properties are covered in Chapter 30.) ■

TABLE 9-1

frame Attribute Values

Value	Definition
`void`	Display no borders.
`above`	Display a border on the top of the table only.
`below`	Display a border on the bottom of the table only.
`hsides`	Display borders on the horizontal sides (top and bottom) only.
`lhs` or `rhs`	Display only the left side or the right side border only.
`vsides`	Display borders on the vertical sides (right and left) only.
`box` or `border`	Display borders on all sides of the table (the default when the border attribute is set without specifying frame).

Table rules

You can use the table tag's `rules` attribute to control what rules (borders between cells) are displayed in a table. Table 9-2 shows the `rules` attribute's possible values.

Note that the width of rules is governed by the table spacing attribute. For example, setting `cellspacing` to a value of `5px` results in rules five pixels wide.

TABLE 9-2

rules Attribute Values

Value	Definition
none	Display no rules.
groups	Display rules between row groups and column groups only.
rows	Display rules between rows only.
cols	Display rules between columns only.
all	Rules will appear between all rows and columns.

Rows

Table rows are the horizontal elements of the table grid and are delimited with table row tags (<tr>). For example, a table with five rows would use the following pseudocode:

```
<table>
  <tr> row 1 </tr>
  <tr> row 2 </tr>
  <tr> row 3 </tr>
  <tr> row 4 </tr>
  <tr> row 5 </tr>
</table>
```

The rows are divided into individual cells by embedded <td> or <th> tags (see the next section, "Cells," for more details).

Note

The table row ending tag (</tr>) is mandatory. ■

The table row tag supports the attributes shown in Table 9-3.

For an example of how baseline vertical alignment differs from bottom alignment, consider the two tables in Figure 9-8.

If you use the alignment attributes in a <tr> tag, that alignment will be applied to all cells in that row. To format cell alignment individually, specify the alignment attribute(s) in individual cell tags (<th> or <td>) or in <col> or <colgroup> tags.

Note

The bgcolor attribute, used to set the background color for the row, has been deprecated in HTML 4.01. Instead of using this attribute, I recommend using applicable styles to accomplish the same effect. ■

TABLE 9-3

Table Row Tag Attributes

Attribute	Definition
align	Set to right, left, center, justify, or char, this attribute controls the horizontal alignment of data in the row. Note that if you use char alignment, you should also specify the alignment character with the char attribute described below.
char	Specifies the alignment character to use with character (char) alignment.
charoff	Specifies the offset from the alignment character to align the data on. Can be specified in pixels or percentage.
valign	Set to top, middle, bottom, or baseline, this attribute controls the vertical alignment of data in the row. Baseline vertical alignment aligns the text baseline across the cells in the row.

FIGURE 9-8

Baseline alignment aligns the baseline of the text.

Bottom Alignment

Baseline Alignment

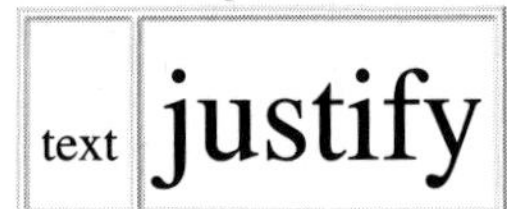

Cells

The individual cells of a table are the elements that actually hold data. In HTML, cell definitions also define the columns for the table. You delimit cells/columns with table data tags (<td>).

For example, consider the following code:

```
<table border="1" cellpadding="5">
  <tr>
    <td>Column 1</td><td>Column 2</td><td>Column 3</td>
  </tr>
  <tr>
    <td>Column 1</td><td>Column 2</td><td>Column 3</td>
```

```
    </tr>
  </table>
```

Tip

Formatting your tables with ample white space (line breaks and indents) will help you accurately format and understand your tables. There are just as many ways to format a table in HTML as there are Web programmers — find a style that suits your taste and use it consistently. ■

The preceding code defines a table with two rows and three columns, as evidenced by the three sets of <td> tags.

You can also use table header tags (<th>) to define columns that are headers for the columns. Expanding on the previous example, the following adds column headers:

```
<table border="1" cellpadding="5">
  <tr>
    <th>Header 1</th><th>Header 2</th><th>Header 3</th>
  </tr>
  <tr>
    <td>Column 1</td><td>Column 2</td><td>Column 3</td>
  </tr>
  <tr>
    <td>Column 1</td><td>Column 2</td><td>Column 3</td>
  </tr>
</table>
```

Table header tags make it easy to format column headings without having to resort to character formatting. For example, the preceding code results in most user agents rendering the table header cells in a bold font (the default for <th>). To accomplish the same formatting without header tags, you would need to include bold character formatting similar to the following:

```
<tr>
  <td><b>Header 1</b></td>
  <td><b>Header 2</b></td>
  <td><b>Header 3</b></td>
</tr>
```

Using CSS, your formatting options with <th> are practically limitless; simply define appropriate formatting or several formatting classes, as necessary.

Note

Most user agents will not properly render an empty cell (for example, <td></td>). When you find yourself needing an empty cell, get in the habit of placing a nonbreaking space entity ( ) in the cell (for example, <td> </td>) to ensure that the user agent renders your table correctly. Technically, this "fix" should not be necessary — setting the empty-cells style property to show should ensure that empty cells are rendered as such. ■

Although cells represent the smallest element in a table, surprisingly, they have the most attributes for their tags. Supported attributes include those shown in Table 9-4.

TABLE 9-4

Cell Attributes

Attribute	Definition
`abbr`	An abbreviated form of the cell's contents. User agents can use the abbreviation where appropriate (indicating a short form of the contents, displaying on a small device, and so on). As such, the value of the `abbr` attribute should be as short and concise as possible.
`align`	The horizontal alignment of the cell's contents — `left`, `center`, `right`, `justify`, or `char` (character).
`axis`	Used to define a conceptual category for the cell, which can be used to place the cell's contents into dimensional space. How the categories are used (if at all) is up to the individual user agent.
`char`	The character used to align the cell's content if the alignment is set to `char`.
`charoff`	The offset from the alignment character to use when aligning the cell content by character.
`colspan`	How many columns the cell should span (default = 1). See the section "Spanning Columns and Rows" for more information.
`headers`	A space-separated list of header cell `id` attributes that corresponds with the cells used as headers for the current cell. User agents use this information at their discretion — a verbal agent might read the contents of all header cells before the current cell's content.
`rowspan`	How many rows the cell should span (default = 1). See the section "Spanning Columns and Rows" for more information.
`scope`	The scope of the current cell's contents when used as a header — `row`, `col` (column), `rowgroup`, `colgroup` (column group). If set, the cell's contents are treated as a header for the corresponding element(s).
`valign`	The vertical alignment of the cell's contents — `top`, `middle`, `bottom`, or `baseline`.

Note

Previous versions of HTML also supported a `nowrap` attribute to control whether a cell's contents wrapped or not. In HTML 4.01, this attribute has been deprecated in favor of styles. See Chapters 30 and 32 for more information on styles pertaining to tables and table cells. ■

Table Captions

Table captions (`<caption>`) provide an easy method to add descriptive text to a table. For example, suppose you wanted to caption a table detailing the benefits of certain membership levels. The following code adds an appropriate caption to a table whose output is shown in Figure 9-9:

```
<!DOCTYPE HTML PUBLIC "-//W3C//DTD HTML 4.01//EN"
  "http://www.w3.org/TR/html4/strict.dtd">
<html>
<head>
<title>Table Captions</title>
</head>
<body>

  <table width="400" border="1">
    <caption>The Benefits of Membership</caption>
    <tr>
      <th>Service</th>
      <th>Silver</th>
      <th>Gold</th>
    </tr>
    <tr>
      <td>Valet Parking</td>
      <td> </td>
      <td align="center">X</td>
    </tr>
    <tr>
      <td>Manicure Guarantee</td>
      <td align="center">X</td>
      <td align="center">X</td>
    </tr>
    <tr>
      <td>Monthly Makeover</td>
      <td> </td>
      <td align="center">X</td>
    </tr>
    <tr>
      <td>Hair Maintenance</td>
      <td align="center">X</td>
      <td align="center">X</td>
    </tr>
    <tr>
      <td>Massage Discount</td>
      <td align="center">X</td>
      <td align="center">X</td>
    </tr>
    <tr>
      <td>Monthly 30min Massage Included</td>
      <td> </td>
      <td align="center">X</td>
    </tr>
    <tr>
      <td>Light Lunch During Stay</td>
      <td> </td>
      <td align="center">X</td>
    </tr>
```

```
        <tr>
          <td>Unlimited Tranquility Room Use</td>
          <td align="center">X</td>
          <td align="center">X</td>
        </tr>
        <tr>
          <td>Unlimited Whirlpool Use</td>
          <td> </td>
          <td align="center">X</td>
        </tr>
        <tr>
          <td>8 Hour Appointment Guarantee</td>
          <td> </td>
          <td align="center">X</td>
        </tr>
      </table>

    </body>
    </html>
```

FIGURE 9-9

The table caption, ''The Benefits of Membership,'' is placed above the table in this example.

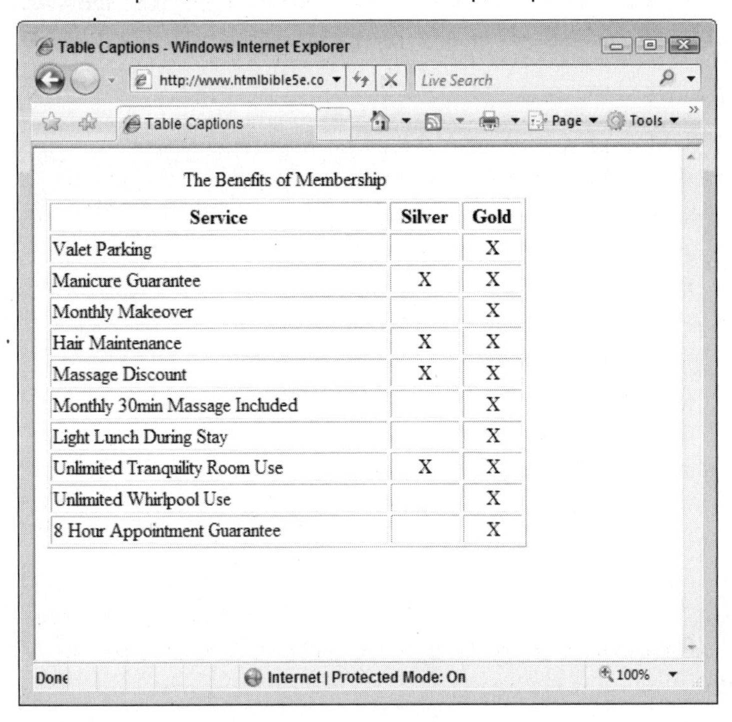

The Benefits of Membership

Service	Silver	Gold
Valet Parking		X
Manicure Guarantee	X	X
Monthly Makeover		X
Hair Maintenance	X	X
Massage Discount	X	X
Monthly 30min Massage Included		X
Light Lunch During Stay		X
Unlimited Tranquility Room Use	X	X
Unlimited Whirlpool Use		X
8 Hour Appointment Guarantee		X

Note that the caption tag must appear immediately after the table tag. Captions typically appear centered above the table to which they are attached, although different user agents may interpret the caption differently.

Cross-Ref

You can use styles to format the caption however you like. For more information on styles, see Part III of this book. ■

Row Groups — Header, Body, and Footer

Simple tables have only one section, the body, which consists of rows and columns. However, you might want to include additional information in your table by defining a table header and footer to complement the information in the body.

For example, the header could contain the header rows, the body could contain the data, and the footer could contain totals for each column. The advantage to breaking up the table into three sections is that some user agents will then allow users to scroll the body of the table separately from the header and footer.

Note

The HTML 4.01 specification dictates that you must use all three sections — header, body, and footer — if you use any one section. You cannot use only a header section and body section without a footer section, for example. If you don't intend to use one of the elements, you must still include tags for the section, even if the section is otherwise empty. ■

The table header is delimited by `<thead>` tags — otherwise, its content is exactly like any other table section, delimited by `<tr>`, `<td>`, and optionally `<th>` tags. For example, consider the following table header section:

```
<thead>
  <tr>
    <th>Name</th>
    <th>Hire Date</th>
    <th>Title</th>
  </tr>
</thead>
```

Other than being delimited by `<tbody>` tags, the table body is defined and formatted just like any other table element. The table footer is delimited by `<tfoot>` tags and is formatted like the other two sections.

Tip

Although it seems counterintuitive, you should place the `<tfoot>` section *before* the `<tbody>` section in your code. This enables the user agent to correctly anticipate the footer section and appropriately format the table body section. ■

All three section tags support `align` and `valign` attributes for controlling text alignment within the section for which it applies. (The `char` and `charoff` attributes are also supported for `align = "char"`.)

For an example of a table with all three sections, consider the following code and its output, shown in Figure 9-10:

```
<!DOCTYPE HTML PUBLIC "-//W3C//DTD HTML 4.01//EN"
  "http://www.w3.org/TR/html4/strict.dtd">
<html>
<head>
  <title>Loose Part Inventory</title>
</head>
<body>
<p>
<h3>Loose Part Inventory</h3>
<table border="1" cellpadding="10" cellspacing="2"
    rules="groups">
<thead align="center">
  <tr>
    <th>Controllers</th><th>Power Cords</th><th>Video Cords</th>
  </tr>
</thead>
<tfoot align="center">
  <tr>
    <td>Totals</td><td>51</td><td>13</td>
  </tr>
</tfoot>
<tbody align="center">
  <tr>
    <td>Nintendo</td><td>10</td><td>0</td>
  </tr>
  <tr>
    <td>Sony PS</td><td>12</td><td>4</td>
  </tr>
  <tr>
    <td>XBOX</td><td>9</td><td>2</td>
  </tr>
  <tr>
    <td>Misc</td><td>20</td><td>7</td>
  </tr>
</tbody>
</table>
</p>
</body>
</html>
```

Note how the three sections are set off by rules, but the table is otherwise devoid of rules. This is because of the `rules = "groups"` attribute in the table tag. Also note how alignment attributes are used in the section tags to center the text in the table.

FIGURE 9-10

The three table sections (header, body, footer) can be set off by custom rules.

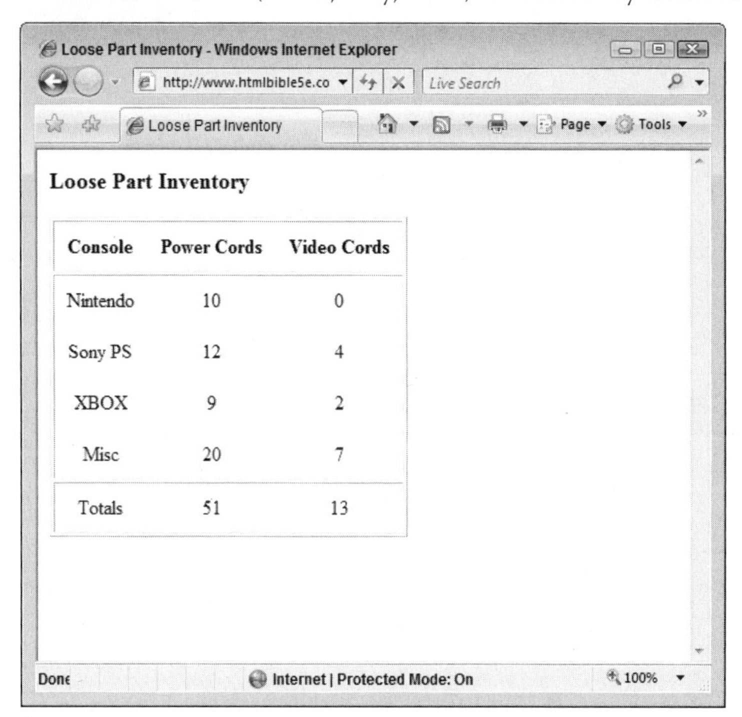

Background Colors

In previous versions of HTML, you could use the bgcolor attribute in the <table> and <tr>, <th>, and <td> tags to set a color background for the element. This attribute has been deprecated in HTML 4.01 in favor of using styles to set the background color of table elements.

That said, if you must use the deprecated method, you can set the background of a header row to green with code similar to the following:

```
<tr bgcolor="green">
  <th>Controllers</th><th>Power Cords</th><th>Video Cords</th>
</tr>
```

If you were to use CSS to accomplish the same effect, the code would resemble the following (output is shown in Figure 9-11):

```
<tr style="background-color: green;">
  <th>Controllers</th><th>Power Cords</th><th>Video Cords</th>
</tr>
```

FIGURE 9-11

Use the background-color CSS property to control table element backgrounds.

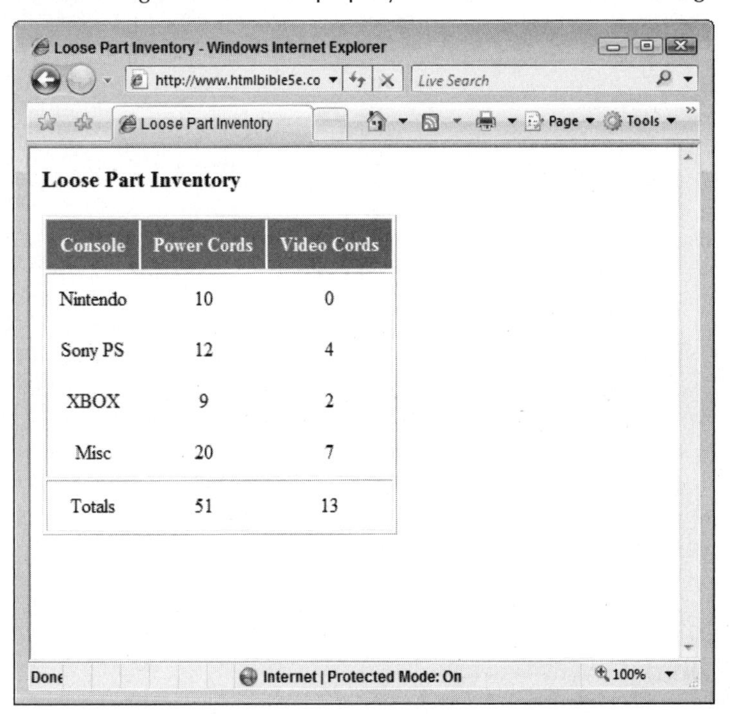

However, not all user agents adequately support background colors in tables. Older browsers are particularly finicky about correctly representing background colors. When in doubt, test.

Spanning Columns and Rows

It is possible to span data cells across multiple columns and rows using the `colspan` and `rowspan` attributes. Usually such spanning is used to provide column or row headings for groups of columns. For example, consider the following table code utilizing the `colspan` attribute and the resulting output shown in Figure 9-12:

```
<!DOCTYPE HTML PUBLIC "-//W3C//DTD HTML 4.01//EN"
  "http://www.w3.org/TR/html4/strict.dtd">
<html>
<head>
<title>Spanning Columns</title>
</head>
<body>

  <table width="400" border="1">
```

```
    <tr>
      <td> </td>
      <td colspan="2">Membership<br />Levels</td>
      <!-- Above cell spans the two membership columns /-->
    </tr>
  <tr>
    <th>Service</th>
    <th>Silver</th>
    <th>Gold</th>
  </tr>
  <tr>
    <td>Valet Parking</td>
    <td> </td>
    <td align="center">X</td>
  </tr>
  <tr>
    <td>Manicure Guarantee</td>
    <td align="center">X</td>
    <td align="center">X</td>
  </tr>
  <tr>
    <td>Monthly Makeover</td>
    <td> </td>
    <td align="center">X</td>
  </tr>
  <tr>
    <td>Hair Maintenance </td>
    <td align="center">X</td>
    <td align="center">X</td>
  </tr>
  <tr>
    <td>Massage Discount </td>
    <td align="center">X</td>
    <td align="center">X</td>
  </tr>
  <tr>
    <td>Monthly 30min Massage Included</td>
    <td> </td>
    <td align="center">X</td>
  </tr>
  <tr>
    <td>Light Lunch During Stay</td>
    <td> </td>
    <td align="center">X</td>
  </tr>
  <tr>
    <td>Unlimited Tranquility Room Use </td>
    <td align="center">X</td>
    <td align="center">X</td>
  </tr>
  <tr>
```

```
        <td>Unlimited Whirlpool Use </td>
        <td> </td>
        <td align="center">X</td>
      </tr>
      <tr>
        <td>8 Hour Appointment Guarantee</td>
        <td> </td>
        <td align="center">X</td>
      </tr>
    </table>

  </body>
  </html>
```

FIGURE 9-12

You can span cells across columns.

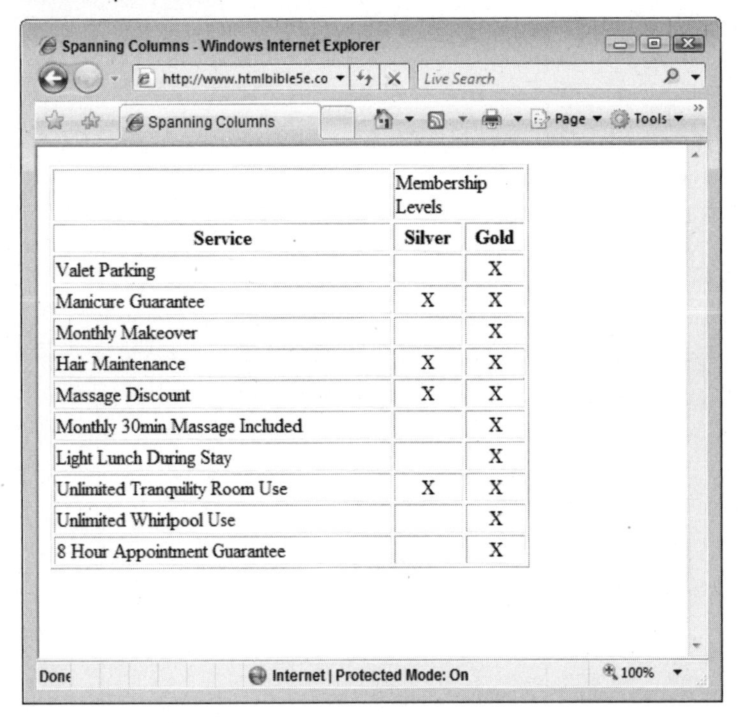

	Membership Levels	
Service	**Silver**	**Gold**
Valet Parking		X
Manicure Guarantee	X	X
Monthly Makeover		X
Hair Maintenance	X	X
Massage Discount	X	X
Monthly 30min Massage Included		X
Light Lunch During Stay		X
Unlimited Tranquility Room Use	X	X
Unlimited Whirlpool Use		X
8 Hour Appointment Guarantee		X

You can span cell rows using the `rowspan` attribute in a similar fashion, as shown in the following code and resulting output in Figure 9-13:

Note

Rows that include a previously spanned cell omit the declaration of their first cell. ■

FIGURE 9-13

Spanning rows with the rowspan attribute

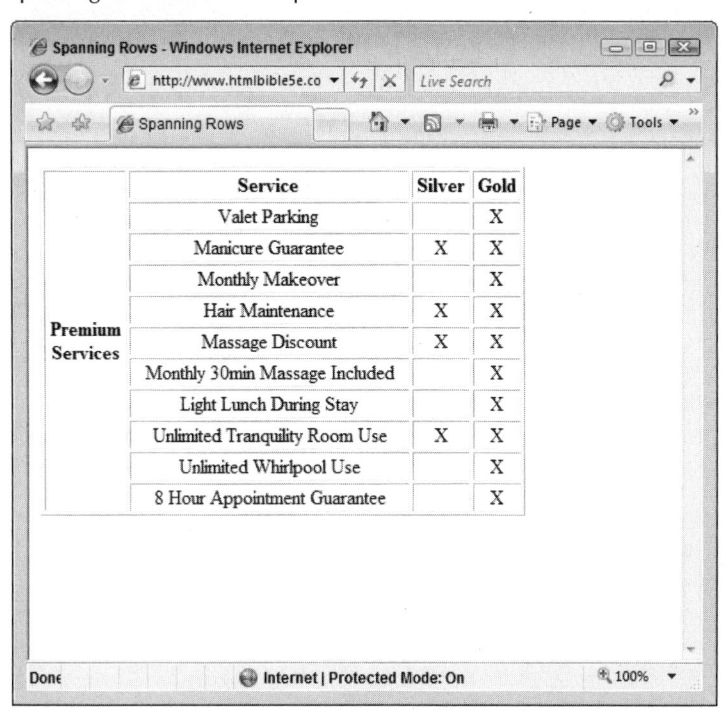

Premium Services	Service	Silver	Gold
	Valet Parking		X
	Manicure Guarantee	X	X
	Monthly Makeover		X
	Hair Maintenance	X	X
	Massage Discount	X	X
	Monthly 30min Massage Included		X
	Light Lunch During Stay		X
	Unlimited Tranquility Room Use	X	X
	Unlimited Whirlpool Use		X
	8 Hour Appointment Guarantee		X

```
<!DOCTYPE HTML PUBLIC "-//W3C//DTD HTML 4.01//EN"
  "http://www.w3.org/TR/html4/strict.dtd">
<html>
<head>
<title>Spanning Rows</title>
</head>
<body>

  <table width="400" border="1">
    <colgroup>
      <col></col>
      <col span="2" style="text-align: center;"></col>
    </colgroup>
    <tr>
      <th rowspan="11">Premium<br/>Services</th>
      <!-- Above cell spans 11 rows. Remaining rows omit
           their first cell declaration. /-->
      <th>Service</th>
      <th>Silver</th>
      <th>Gold</th>
    </tr>
```

```
    <tr>
      <td>Valet Parking</td>
      <td> </td>
      <td align="center">X</td>
    </tr>
    <tr>
      <td>Manicure Guarantee</td>
      <td align="center">X</td>
      <td align="center">X</td>
    </tr>
    <tr>
      <td>Monthly Makeover</td>
      <td> </td>
      <td align="center">X</td>
    </tr>
    <tr>
      <td>Hair Maintenance</td>
      <td align="center">X</td>
      <td align="center">X</td>
    </tr>
    <tr>
      <td>Massage Discount</td>
      <td align="center">X</td>
      <td align="center">X</td>
    </tr>
    <tr>
      <td>Monthly 30min Massage Included</td>
      <td> </td>
      <td align="center">X</td>
    </tr>
    <tr>
      <td>Light Lunch During Stay</td>
      <td> </td>
      <td align="center">X</td>
    </tr>
    <tr>
      <td>Unlimited Tranquility Room Use</td>
      <td align="center">X</td>
      <td align="center">X</td>
    </tr>
    <tr>
      <td>Unlimited Whirlpool Use</td>
      <td> </td>
      <td align="center">X</td>
    </tr>
    <tr>
      <td>8 Hour Appointment Guarantee</td>
      <td> </td>
      <td align="center">X</td>
    </tr>
  </table>
```

```
</body>
</html>
```

You can also span columns and rows within the same table by using appropriate `colspan` and `rowspan` attributes. However, such use is not recommended without a GUI HTML editor because the code becomes exponentially complex the more spans you make to a table.

Cross-Ref

For more information on GUI HTML editors, see Chapter 19. ■

Grouping Columns

HTML 4.01 added a few extra tags to make defining and formatting groups of columns easier. The tags `<colgroup>` and `<col>` are used together to define and optionally format column groups and individual columns, respectively.

The `colgroup` tag is used to define and optionally format groups of columns. The tag supports the same formatting attributes as the `<tr>` and `<td>/<th>` tags (`align`, `valign`, and so on). Any columns defined by the column group tag will inherit the formatting contained within the tag.

To define columns in a group, use the `span` attribute with the `<colgroup>` tag to indicate how many columns are in the group. For example, the following HTML table code places the first three columns in a group:

```
<table>
<colgroup span="3">
</colgroup>
...
```

Note that additional `<colgroup>` tags can be used to create additional column groups. You must use additional column groups if the columns you are grouping are not contiguous or do not start with the first column. For example, the following HTML table code creates three column groups:

- Columns 1 and 2, formatted with centered alignment
- Columns 3–5, formatted with decimal alignment
- Columns 6–10, formatted with right alignment and bold text

```
<table>
<colgroup span="2" align="center">
<!-- This group contains columns 1 & 2 /-->
</colgroup>
<colgroup span="3" align="char" char=".">
<!-- This group contains columns 3 - 5 /-->
</colgroup>
```

```
<colgroup span="5" align="right" style="font-weight: bold;" >
<!-- This group contains columns 6 - 10 /-->
</colgroup>
...
```

Note

Column groups that do not have explicit formatting attributes defined in their respective `<colgroup>` tags inherit the standard formatting of columns within the table. However, the group is still defined as a group and will respond accordingly to table attributes that affect groups (`rules = "groups"`, and so on). ■

What if you don't want all the columns within the group formatted identically? For example, in a group of three columns, suppose you wanted the center column (column number 2 in the group) to be formatted with bold text. That's where the `<col>` tag comes into play, defining individual columns within the group. To format a group using the preceding example (middle column bold), you could use code similar to the following:

```
<table>
<colgroup span="3">
<!-- This group contains columns 1 & 3 /-->
<col></col>
<col style="font-weight: bold;"></col>
<col></col>
</colgroup>
...
```

The `<col>` tag follows similar rules to that of the `colgroup` tag — namely, the following:

- Empty tags (those without explicit formatting) are simply placeholders and inherit the formatting of the parent `<colgroup>`.
- You must define columns in order, and in a contiguous group, using blank `<col>` tags where necessary.
- You can use the `span` attribute with a `<col>` tag if you want it to format more than one contiguous column.
- Missing `<col>` tags result in the corresponding columns inheriting the formatting from the parent `colgroup`.

Note that in standard HTML, the column tag has no closing tag. However, in XHMTL, the `<col>` tag must be closed by a corresponding `</col>` tag.

Tip

Column definitions via the `<colgroup>` or `<col>` tags do not eliminate or change the necessity of `td` tags (which actually form the columns). You must still take care in placing your `<td>` tags to ensure proper data positioning within columns. ■

Formatting with Tables

Formatting your documents with HTML tags enables you to create many useful designs for a variety of purposes. The HTML tag (and related tags) with humble beginnings that revolutionized document formatting with HTML is the table tag (`<table>`).

The table tag was originally designed to represent tabular data, numbers, and other data in columns. However, using a few tricks, such as embedding tables within one another, it is possible to achieve some pretty fantastic layouts. This section explains how to best utilize tables for page layout purposes.

Note

With the advent of CSS, there are many who proclaim that tables should no longer be used for any layout purposes, and that instead CSS should be used to style and position elements for the sake of layout. However, this is not necessarily the case. Despite the existence of CSS, HTML tables still make a perfectly acceptable layout mechanism, either on a micro level (such as a simple table of headers and values) or on a macro level (such as the layout basis for an entire page or document).

Arguments can be made for both technologies and the debate can get very heated (try searching for "html table layout versus CSS layout" at `www.google.com`). My advice is to use whichever technology makes sense to you — what you are most comfortable with, what presents your documents in the best light, or what appears to be the best tool for the job. ■

Rudimentary Formatting with Tables

It's not hard to see how tables can help with formatting elements. For example, consider the following code and the output shown in Figure 9-14:

```
<!DOCTYPE HTML PUBLIC "-//W3C//DTD HTML 4.01//EN"
  "http://www.w3.org/TR/html4/strict.dtd">
<html>
<head>
  <title>A Simple Form</title>
</head>
<body>
<form>
<p>Name: <input type="text" size="40"></p>
<p>Age: 
<input type="radio" name="20to30" value="20to30">
 20-30 
<input type="radio" name="31to40" value="31to40">
 31-40 
<input type="radio" name="41to50" value="41to50">
 41-50 
</p>
</form>
</body>
</html>
```

FIGURE 9-14

A rudimentary form using spaces for layout purposes

A simple table can help better align the elements in this form, as shown in the following code and Figure 9-15:

```
<!DOCTYPE HTML PUBLIC "-//W3C//DTD HTML 4.01//EN"
  "http://www.w3.org/TR/html4/strict.dtd">
<html>
<head>
  <title>Rudimentary Form Alignment</title>
</head>
<body>
<form>
<table width="50%" border="1">
<tr>
<td width="25%"><p>Name:</p></td>
<td><p><input type="text" size="40"></p></td>
</tr>
<tr>
<td><p>Age:</p></td>
<td><p>
<input type="radio" name="20to30" value="20to30">
 20-30 
<input type="radio" name="31to40" value="31to40">
 31-40 
```

```
<input type="radio" name="41to50" value="41to50">
 41-50 
</p></td>
</table>
</form>
</body>
</html>
```

FIGURE 9-15

Aligning the labels and fields in a form using a simple table

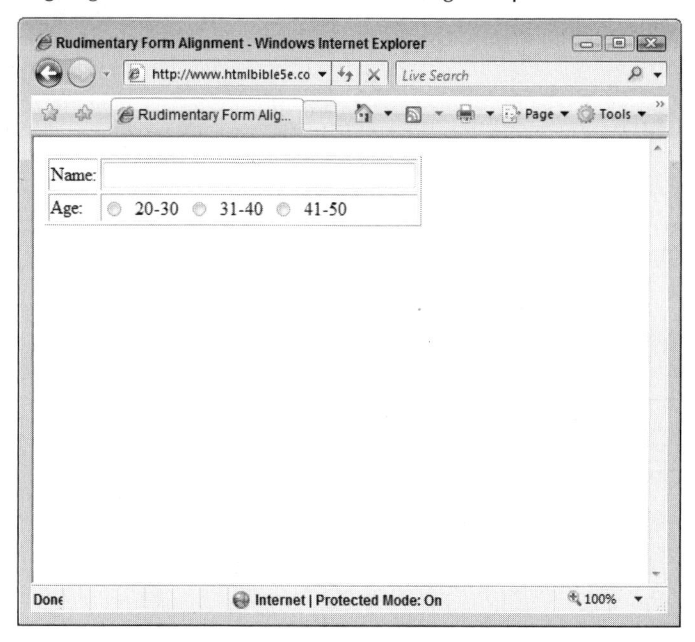

However, this serves only to align the labels and fields in two columns. This is better than no alignment, but if you add a nested table, you can add more order to the radio buttons, as shown in the following code and Figure 9-16:

```
<!DOCTYPE HTML PUBLIC "-//W3C//DTD HTML 4.01//EN"
  "http://www.w3.org/TR/html4/strict.dtd">
<html>
<head>
  <title>Formatting with Nested Tables</title>
</head>
<body>
<form>
<table width="50%" border="1">
<tr>
<td width="25%"><p>Name:</p></td>
<td><p><input type="text" size="40"></p></td>
```

```
</tr>
<tr>
<td><p>Age:</p></td>
<td>
<table width="100%" border="1">
<colgroup span="3" style="text-align:center;">
</colgroup>
<tr>
<td><p><input type="radio" name="20to30" value="20to30"></p></td>
<td><p><input type="radio" name="31to40" value="31to40"></p></td>
<td><p><input type="radio" name="41to50" value="41to50"></p></td>
</tr>
<tr>
<td><p>20-30</p></td>
<td><p>31-40</p></td>
<td><p>41-50</p></td>
</tr>
</table>
</td>
</table>
</form>
</body>
</html>
```

FIGURE 9-16

Nested tables allow for even more alignment and formatting control

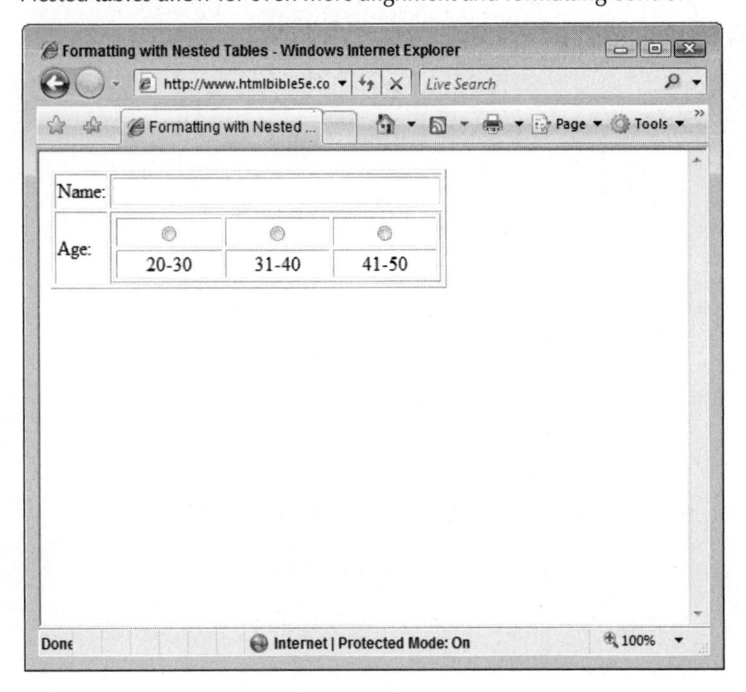

Note

Of course, in real life the tables in the examples would have even more formatting attributes and/or CSS to fine-tune the alignment, and the borders would be off or set to accent the formatting. ■

Even though these examples are fairly small in scope, it should be easy to see the power and flexibility tables can lend to alignment, formatting, and even page layout.

Real-world examples

You might be surprised by how many tables are hiding under the veneer of the Web pages you frequent. For example, take a look at Figure 9-17, which shows a corporate website.

FIGURE 9-17

A corporate website that doesn't visibly use tables

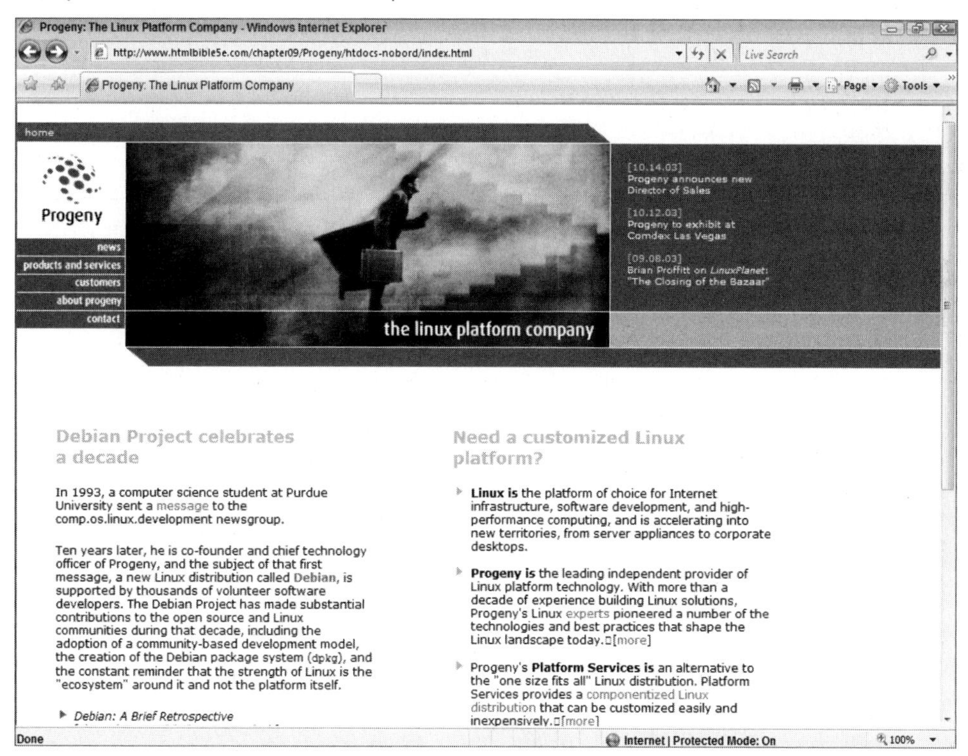

Figure 9-18 shows the same website with the table borders on. Note the multitude of nested tables used to achieve the layout.

FIGURE 9-18

A corporate website with the tables made visible

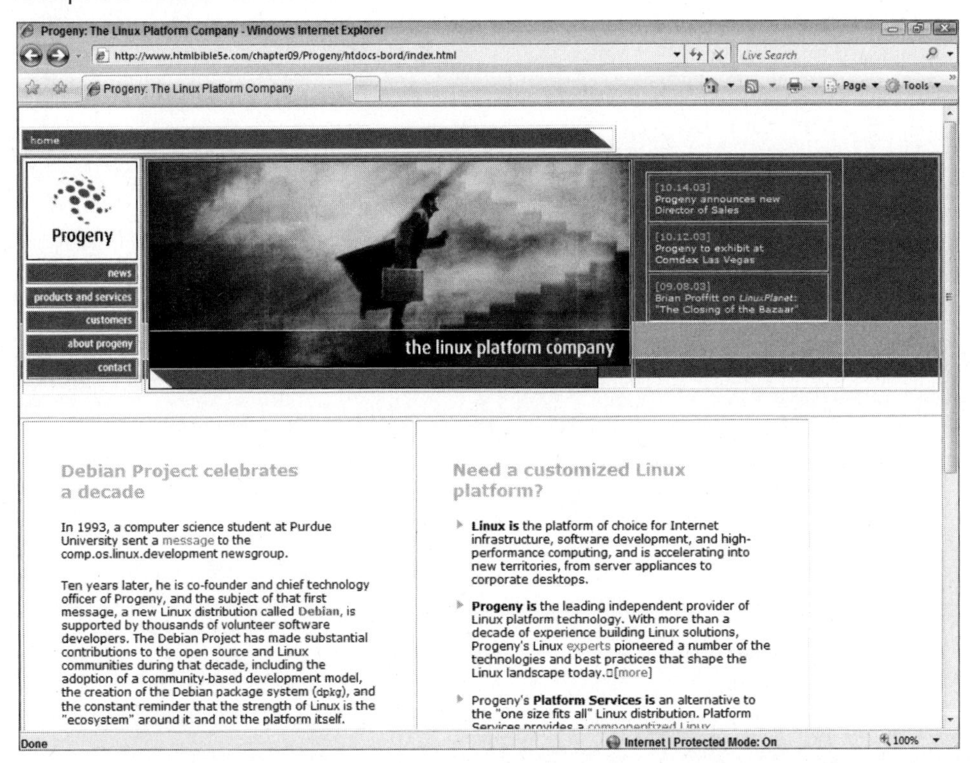

Figure 9-19 shows another popular layout format, a floating page and two columns of content. Again, note that the use of tables, visible in Figure 9-20, isn't readily apparent.

The rest of this chapter shows you how to achieve some of these effects.

Floating page

The floating page layout has become quite popular and is used in pages of all kinds, from corporate sites to personal Web logs. The effect simulates a piece of paper on a desktop and is fairly easy to create using a few nested tables, as shown in the following code, the output of which is shown in Figure 9-21:

```
<!DOCTYPE HTML PUBLIC "-//W3C//DTD HTML 4.01//EN"
  "http://www.w3.org/TR/html4/strict.dtd">
<html>
<head>
  <title>Floating Table Format</title>
  <style type="text/css">
    <!-- Sets "desktop" color (behind page) -->
```

```
    body {background-color: #B0C4DE;}
  </style>
</head>
<body>
<!-- /Body container -->
  <!-- (background = border, padding = border width
       margin = centered table) -->
<table border="0" cellpadding="4px" cellspacing="0"
    style="background-color: black;
    margin: 0 auto;">
 <tr>
  <td>
    <!-- Floating page -->
      <!-- (padding = page margin) -->
    <table border="0" cellpadding="5px" cellspacing="0"
      width="732px"
      style="background-color: #FFFFFF;">
     <tr valign="top">
       <td>
         <!-- Page content -->
         <p>Content goes here.</p>
         <!-- Page content -->
       </td>
     </tr>
    </table>
    <!-- /Floating page -->
  </td>
</tr>
</table>
<!-- /Body container -->
</body>
</html>
```

Tip

Note the comments in the code delimiting the individual tables and content areas. It is a best practice to follow standard code formatting (indentation, liberal white space, and so on) and add sufficient comments to easily keep track of all your tables, how they are formatted, and what they accomplish. ■

If you want more of a drop shadow effect, you can play with the borders of the floating page, setting two adjacent borders to a nonzero value, as shown in the following code:

```
<!-- Floating page -->
  <!-- (padding = page margin) -->
<table border="0" cellpadding="5px" cellspacing="0"
  width="732px" height="900px"
  style="background-color: #FFFFFF;
   border-right: 4px solid black;
   border-bottom: 4px solid black;">
```

FIGURE 9-19

Another popular layout: floating page and multiple columns of content

This code will visually increase the width of the right and bottom borders, giving the page a more realistic, three-dimensional drop shadow effect.

Tip

Keep in mind that you can combine various techniques within the same document. For example, you can put a two-column layout on a floating page by nesting a two-column table in the content area of the floating page table. Then, within one of the columns, you can evenly space out a handful of graphics by nesting another table in the column. The possibilities are endless. ■

Odd graphics and text combinations

You can also use tables to combine text and graphics in nonstandard layouts. For example, note the header in Figure 9-22. The header graphic is actually several pieces, as shown in Figure 9-23.

A table with no padding and no spacing is used to put the pieces back together into a complete image, while enabling text to flow to the right of the face portion.

FIGURE 9-20

The floating page and two-column layout with visible tables

Code for the completed header is shown here:

```
<!-- Heading container -->
<table border="0" cellpadding="0" cellspacing="0">
  <tr>
  <td valign="top">
    <img border="0" src="images/home_top.gif"
      width="240" height="118">
  </td>
  <td>
<!-- Nav and main graphic -->
<table border="0" cellpadding="0" cellspacing="0">
  <tr>
  <td width="100%">
  <!-- Nav bar -->
  <table border="0" cellpadding="0" cellspacing="0"
   width="100%">
    <tr>
    <td width="25%">
    <a href="archive/index.html" onfocus="this.blur()"
    onMouseOver="archive.src=`images/archive_punch_on.gif'"
```

```
    onMouseOut="archive.src=`images/archive_punch_off.gif'"
    >
    <img name="archive" border="0"
src="images/archive_punch_off.gif" width="132" height="38" />
</a>
   </td>
   <td width="25%">
   <a href="guest/index.html" onfocus="this.blur()"
   onMouseOver="guest.src=`images/g_punch_on.gif'"
   onMouseOut="guest.src=`images/g_punch_off.gif'" >
   <img name="guest" border="0"
    src="images/g_punch_off.gif" width="116" height="38" /></a>
   </td>
   <td width="25%">
   <a href="mailto:email@example.com"    onfocus="this.blur()"
   onMouseOver="email.src=`images/e_punch_on.gif'"
   onMouseOut="email.src=`images/e_punch_off.gif'" >
   <img name="email" border="0"
    src="images/e_punch_off.gif" width="113" height="38"/></a>
   </td>
   <td width="25%">
<a href="about/index.html" onfocus="this.blur()"
   onMouseOver="about.src=`images/a_punch_on.gif'"
   onMouseOut="about.src=`images/a_punch_off.gif'">
   <img name="about" border="0"
    src="images/a_punch_off.gif" width="131" height="38" /></a>
   </td>
   </tr>
 </table>
 <!-- /Nav bar -->
 </td>
 </tr>
   <tr>
   <td width="100%"><img border="0"
   src="images/home_flag.gif" height="80" />
   </td>
   </tr>
 </table>
 <!-- /Nav and main graphic -->
 </td>
 </tr>
 <tr>
   <td height="158" valign="top"><img border="0"
      src="images/home_left.gif" width="239"
      height="156" />
      <p>SECONDARY CONTENT HERE</p>
    </td>
    <td valign="top">
      <p>MAIN CONTENT HERE</p>
    </td>
  </tr>
</table>
<!-- /Heading container -->
```

FIGURE 9-21

A floating page can add a bit of simple design to your documents.

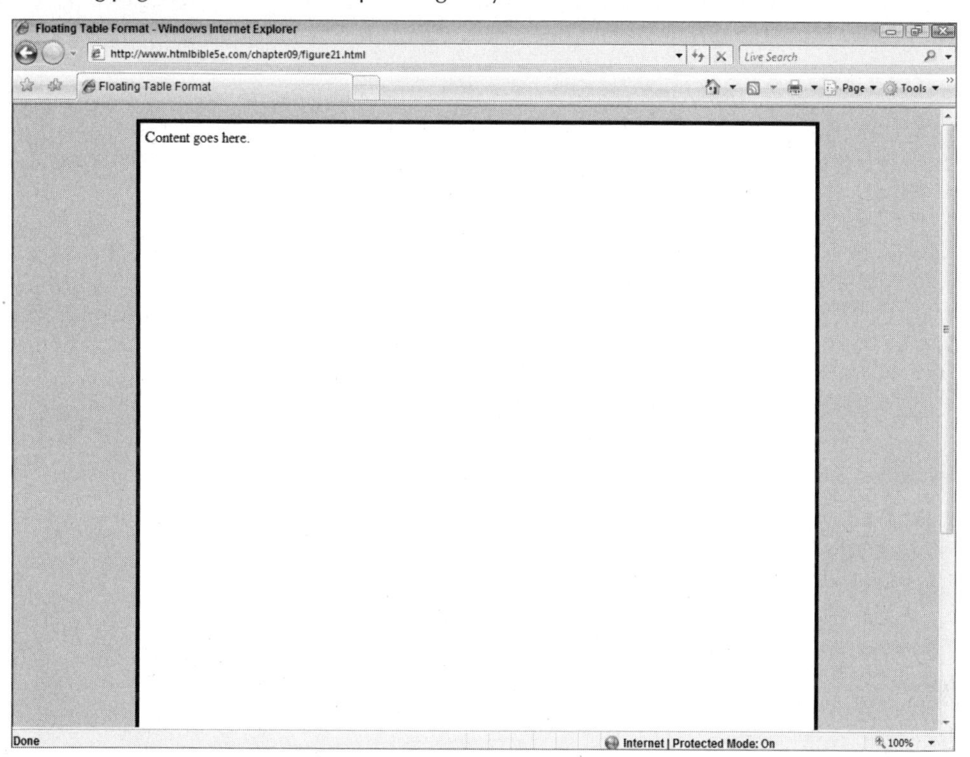

Note

The preceding listing has been formatted for legibility. However, when put into use on an actual Web page, all spaces and line breaks that aren't contained within tags themselves should be removed from between the `<td>` and `</td>` tags. For example, consider the following code from the listing:

```
   <td width="25%">
   <a href="guest/index.html" onfocus="this.blur()"
   onMouseOver="guest.src=`images/g_punch_on.gif'"
   onMouseOut="guest.src=`images/g_punch_off.gif'" >
   <img name="guest" border="0"
src="images/g_punch_off.gif" width="116" height="38"
/></a>
   </td> ■
```

This code should be changed to resemble the following, where the only spaces and line breaks are within the angle brackets of a tag (< and >):

```
<td width="25%"><a href="guest/index.html"
onfocus="this.blur()"
onMouseOver="guest.src=`images/g_punch_on.gif'"
```

```
onMouseOut="guest.src=`images/g_punch_off.gif'" ><img
name="guest" border="0" src="images/g_punch_off.gif"
width="116" height="38"></a></td>
```

Using this technique, you can wrap text and graphics around each other in a variety of ways. For example, if the graphic used in the preceding example descended on the right as well, you could use three columns — pieces of the graphic in the first and third, text in the middle.

Caution

It's important to watch for errant white space in and around your tags when formatting a page using tables. For example, one single space within a <td> pair can create a visible seam in between the graphics that make up your header. To avoid this problem, place the line breaks in your code within the tags, between attributes and such. ■

FIGURE 9-22

Presenting graphics and text in a nonstandard format

FIGURE 9-23

The various pieces of the header graphic

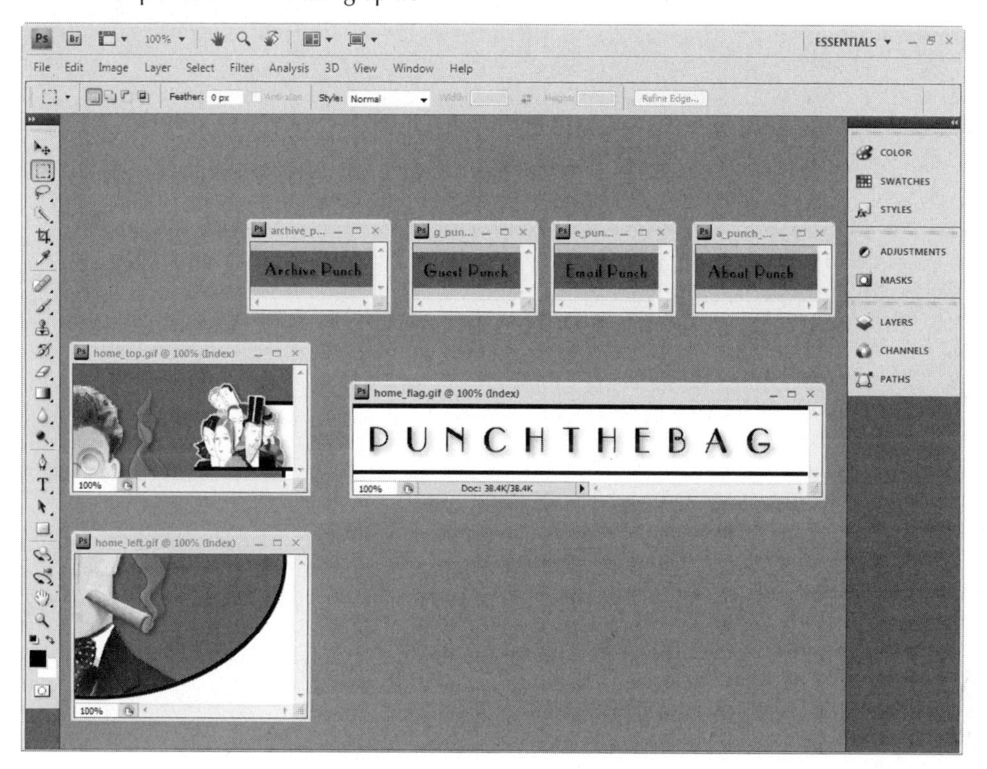

Navigational menus and blocks

The sample page header has its navigational elements in a row at the top of the page. You can construct similar, vertical layouts for your navigational elements using `rowspan` attributes in your tables. For example, consider the following code and the output shown in Figure 9-24:

```
<table border="1" width="100%">
  <tr>
    <td rowspan="4" >
      <p>Header graphic</p>
    </td>
    <td>
      <p>Nav_1</p>
    </td>
  </tr>
  <tr>
```

```
        <td>
          <p>Nav_2</p>
        </td>
      </tr>
      <tr>
        <td>
          <p>Nav_3</p>
        </td>
      </tr>
      <tr>
        <td>
          <p>Nav_4</p>
        </td>
      </tr>
    </table>
```

FIGURE 9-24

Using rowspan, you can create vertically stacked elements.

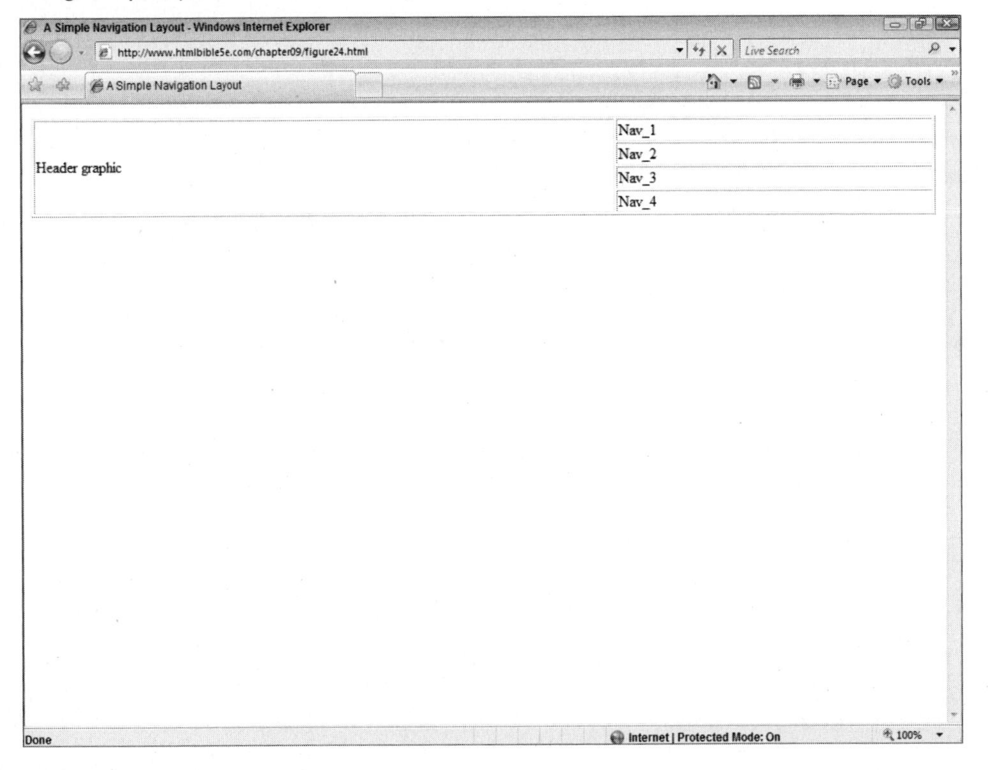

Note

As you have no doubt realized, there are multiple ways to accomplish many of the designs shown in this chapter. For example, you could just as easily nest a one-column table in a cell instead of using `rowspan`. ■

Multiple columns

As covered earlier in this chapter, you can use tables to position elements in columns. This technique can be used for a variety of layout purposes:

- Providing navigation bars to the right or the left of text
- Putting text into columns
- More precise positioning controls, putting text next to graphics, and so forth

Columnar formatting is simple to accomplish, as shown in the following code:

```
<table border="1" cellspacing="0" cellpadding="5px"
  width="100%">
  <colgroup>
    <col width="50%">
    <col width="50%">
  </colgroup>
  <tr>
    <td colspan="2">Header graphic or navigation can go here</td>
  </tr>
  <tr>
    <td>First column content...</td>
    <td>Second column content...</td>
  </tr>
</table>
```

The output of this code is shown in Figure 9-25.

Note

One caveat to creating columns with tables is that the content doesn't automatically wrap from one column to the next (as in a newspaper). You must split the text between the columns manually. ■

The columns do not have to be the same size or proportional to each other. You can define the columns in any size you need by using the appropriate formatting attributes. For example, to create a navigation column to the left that is 200 pixels wide and a text column to the right that is 400 pixels wide, you could use this column definition:

```
<colgroup>
  <col width="200px">
  <col width="400px">
</colgroup>
```

FIGURE 9-25

A simple two-column format

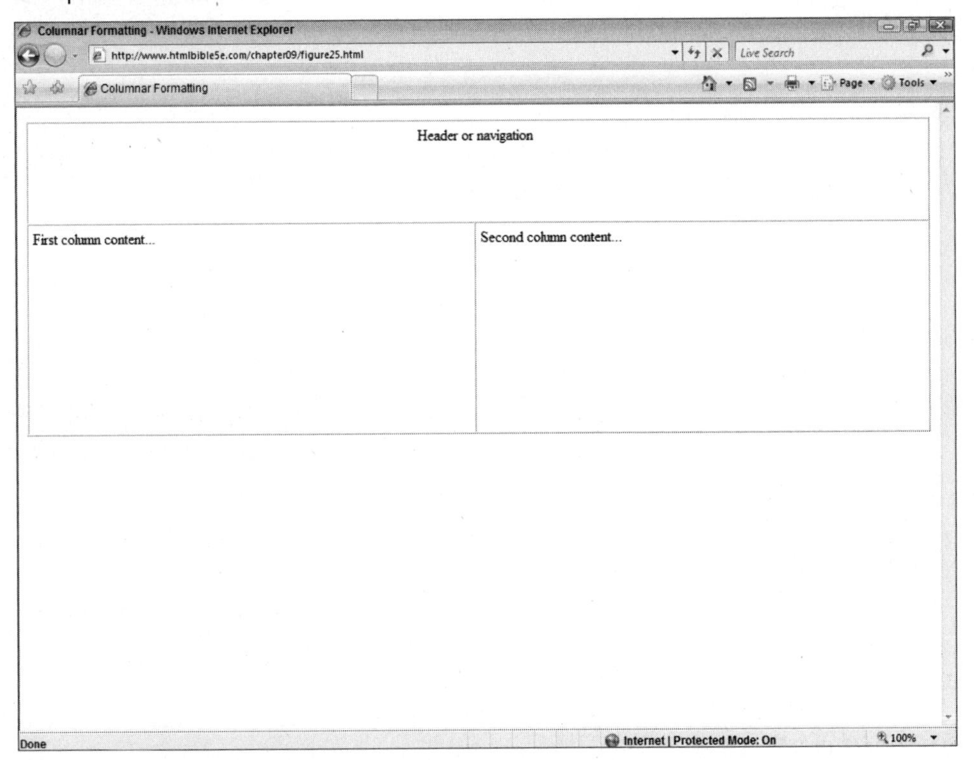

Summary

This chapter covered the basics of HTML tables. You learned how to define a table, what each table element is used for, and how to format table elements to achieve various desired effects.

This chapter also showed you the glamorous side of tables, how they can be used to provide complex formatting structures in HTML. As mentioned throughout this book, CSS provides a better mechanism for creating and controlling layout while maintaining the laudable goal of keeping presentation and content separate. That said, tables still provide a viable means to align, format, and lay out blocks of text.

From here you will learn about additional structured elements — namely, frames and forms (Chapters 10 and 11) and continue through the rest of the HTML element categories. Once you venture into Part III of this book, you will first learn about the basics of CSS (Chapters 25 through 28) before learning about tags for specific elements, such as in Chapter 30, which describes table- and text-specific CSS.

CHAPTER 10

Frames

Several years ago, almost every document on the Web contained frames. The frameset structure provided an easy way to create multiple, separate scrolling areas in a user agent window and a flexible mechanism to modify the content of frames.

However, frames have turned out to be more of a fad. You can have many of the benefits provided by using frames through the infinitely more flexible and powerful CSS formatting methods.

That said, frames still have their uses and have even spawned their own official Document Type Definitions (DTDs) to handle their special tags and needs. This chapter introduces the concept of frames and shows you how to add them to your documents.

IN THIS CHAPTER

Frames Overview

At their simplest level, frames provide multiple separately scrollable areas within one user window. Many non-Web applications use the technique of separate panes to provide organization and controls. For example, Figure 10-1 shows Windows Explorer using the left panes to display Favorite Links and Folders, and the right pane to display files within the selected folder.

As you have no doubt noticed, the different panes in applications such as Windows Explorer can be manipulated separately from other panes. The same is true for documents utilizing frames.

For example, Figures 10-2 and 10-3 show the same document but the window in Figure 10-3 has been scrolled to view the bottom of the text in the document. This has caused the navigation bar to scroll as well, in this case almost off the screen, where part of it can no longer be immediately accessed.

FIGURE 10-1

Applications such as Windows Explorer use multiple panes to display a variety of information and controls.

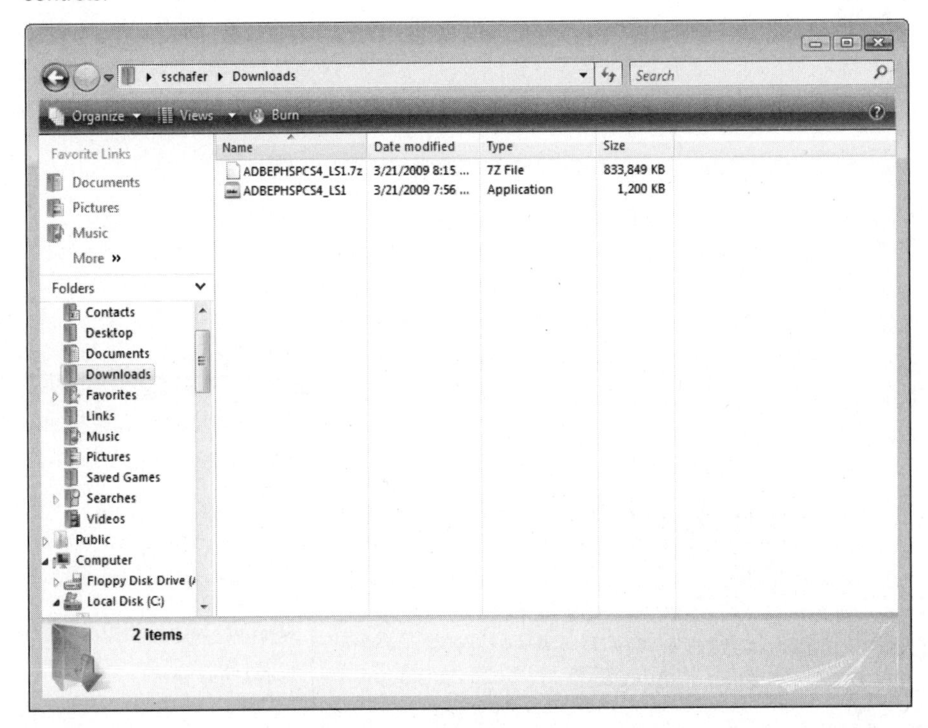

Now take a look at Figure 10-4. Each element — the top banner, the navigation bar, and the main content — has been placed in a separate frame. When the main content is scrolled, the banner and the navigation menu remain static within their own regions.

Framesets and Frame Documents

Frames are a bit complex to implement, as they require a separate document to define the frame layout as well as individual documents to actually occupy the frames. This section describes the pieces of the defining document, the frameset, and shows you how to create a frame-based layout.

Creating a frameset

A frameset is created like any other HTML document except that its content is limited to frame-related tags. The following skeletal code is an example of a frameset document:

```
<!DOCTYPE HTML PUBLIC "-//W3C//DTD HTML 4.01 Frameset//EN"
    "http://www.w3.org/TR/html4/frameset.dtd">
```

```
<html>
<head>
...
</head>
  <frameset attributes>
    <frame attributes></frame>
    <frame attributes></frame>
    ...
  </frameset>
</html>
```

FIGURE 10-2

A long document uses scroll bars to enable users to see the entire document.

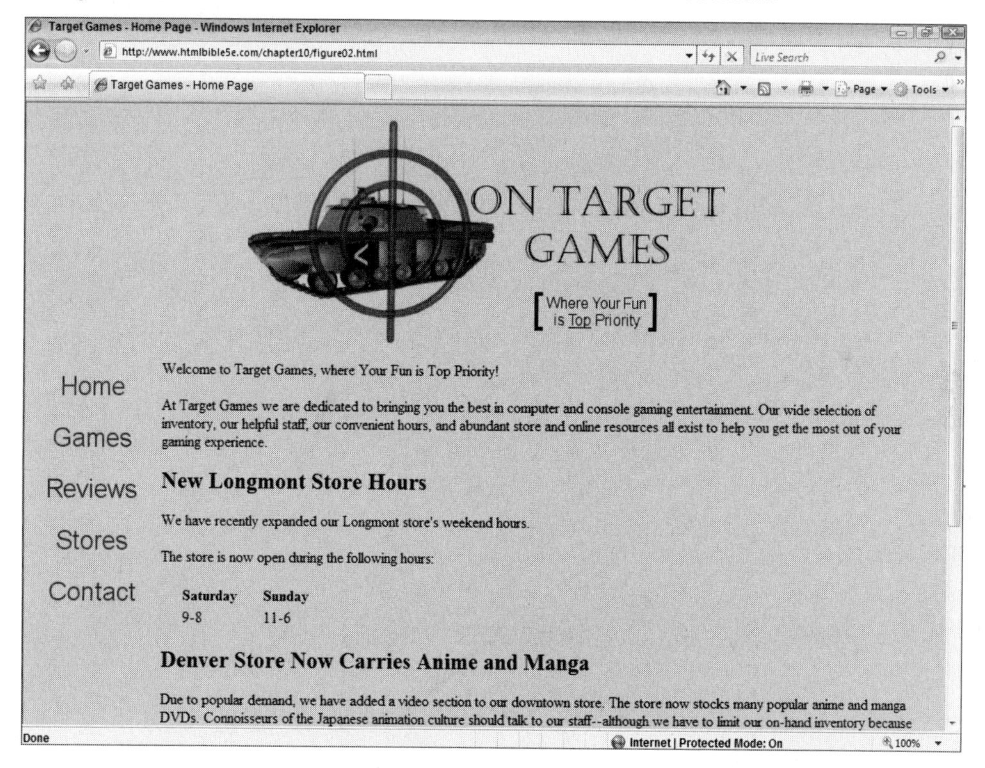

Note the following about this code:

- The document uses the frameset DTD. The frameset DTD is essentially the same as the transitional DTD except for the addition of the frame-specific tags (and replacement of the `<body>` tag, covered shortly).
- There is no `body` element. Instead, the `<frameset>` tag provides the next level container under `<html>`.

- The <frame> tags, nestled inside the <frameset> tag, define the content for the frames and various properties of the frame itself.
- Other than the <frameset> and <head> sections, there is no other content in the document.

FIGURE 10-3

When the document is scrolled, the entire view, including the navigation bar on the left and the banner graphic on top, is moved.

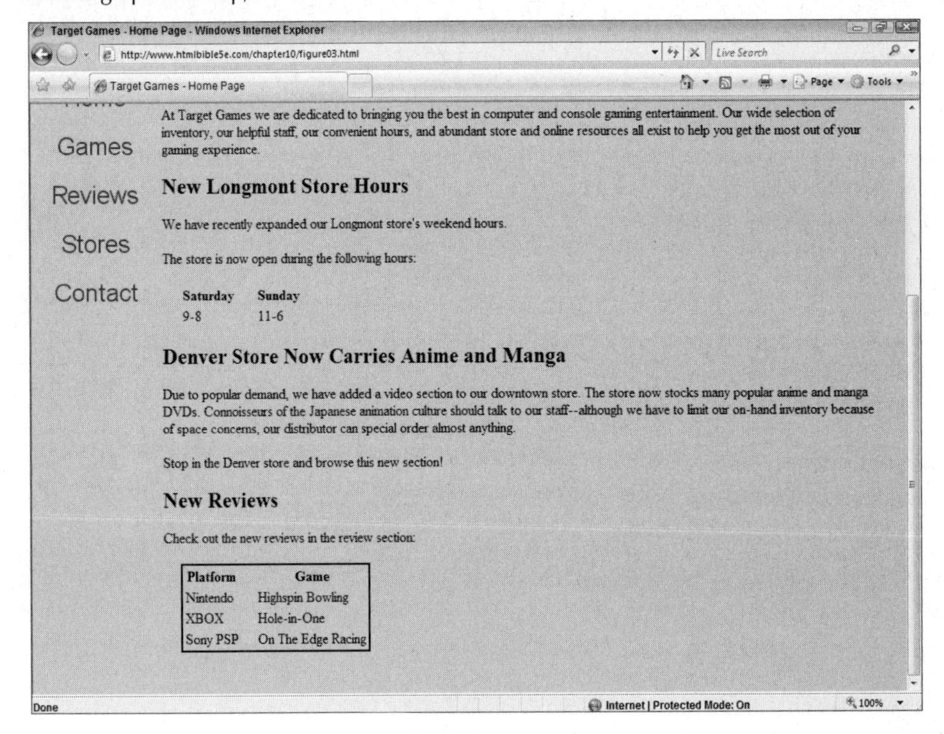

The basics of the frameset and frame tags are covered in the next two sections.

The frameset tag

The frameset tag (<frameset>) defines the layout of the frames in the document. It does so by specifying whether the frames should be laid out in columns or rows and what each column's width should be.

The frameset tag has the following format:

```
<frameset cols|rows = "column_or_row_size(s)">
```

The column or row sizes can be specified as percentages of the user agent window; pixels; or an asterisk (*), which enables the user agent to assign the size. In the last case, the user agent typically splits the remaining space across the columns or rows that specify * as their width. In any case, the resulting frameset will occupy the entire user agent window. The number of entries of the `cols` or `rows` attribute also defines how many frames will be used — each entry needs a corresponding `<frame>` tag within the `<frameset>` tag.

FIGURE 10-4

Frames enable one region to scroll while others remain static.

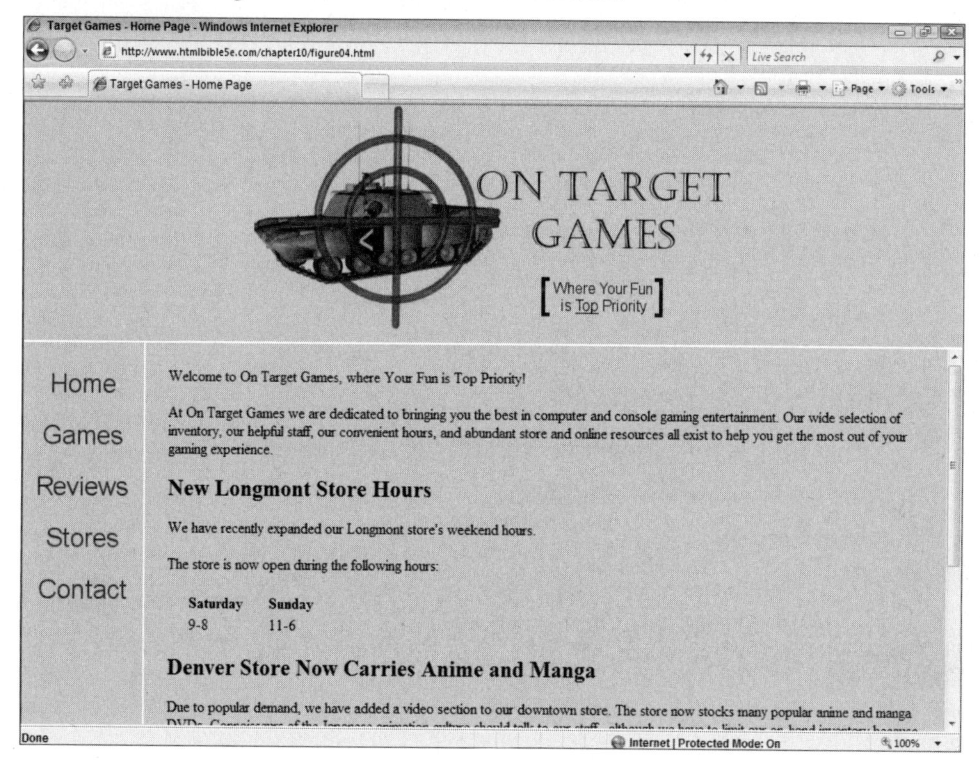

For example, consider these definitions:

```
<!-- Two columns, 25% of the window, the other
   75% of the window -->
<frameset cols = "25%, 75%">
<!-- Two columns, 25% of the window, the other
   75% of the window -->
<frameset cols = "25%, *">
<!-- Three rows, the first 50% of the window, the other
   two 25% of the window each -->
<frameset rows = "50%, *, *">
<!-- Two rows, the first 100 pixels high, the second is the
   size of the remaining window space -->
<frameset rows = "100px, 200px">
```

Note

In the last frameset example, the second row is defined at 200px. However, if the user agent's window is larger than 300 pixels high (the total of the rows defined), the second row will be expanded to fill the space. ■

The frame tag

While the frameset tag (`<frameset>`) is responsible for defining the layout of the entire page (in terms of number of frames and their size), the frame tag (`<frame>`) is responsible for defining properties of each frame.

The frame tag has the following minimal syntax:

```
<frame name="name_of_frame" src="url_of_content"></frame>
```

The `name` attribute gives the frame a unique name that can be referenced by URLs, scripts, and so on to control the frame's contents. The `src` attribute is used to specify the URL of the content the frame should display.

Using only these two attributes results in a frame with minimal margins, no borders, and automatic scroll bars. More information on controlling these frame attributes is covered in the next few sections.

Frame margins, borders, and scroll bars

The frame tag supports the additional attributes shown in Table 10-1.

TABLE 10-1

Frame Tag Attributes

Attribute	Value(s)	Definition
`frameborder`	`0 = no border` (default) `1 = border`	Indicates whether the frame has a border or not
`longdesc`	`url`	A document's URL to use as a long description for the frame (note that this is largely unsupported by user agents)
`marginheight`	`pixels`	Sets the top and bottom margins for the frame — the distance of the frame's content from its border
`marginwidth`	`pixels`	Sets the left and right margins for the frame — the distance of the frame's content from its border
`scrolling`	`yes no auto` (default)	Controls whether the frame displays scroll bars to help scroll the content displayed in the frame

As mentioned in Table 10-1, the `longdesc` attribute is not fully supported by most user agents. Use it if you need to specify a long description, but don't count on its functionality.

The margin attributes, marginheight and marginwidth, are self-explanatory, controlling the inside margin of the frame. They should be used to provide enough white space around the frame's content to help make the content clear.

Tip

When using images in a frame, consider setting the margins to zero so the graphic fills the frame entirely without superfluous white space. ■

The frameborder attribute controls whether or not the bounding border of the frame is visible. Figure 10-5 shows a frameset without borders, and Figure 10-6 shows the same frameset with borders.

Note

As of this writing, the latest crop of browsers (including the latest versions of Microsoft Internet Explorer and Firefox) display a white border for each frame, despite the frameborder setting. If frameborder is set to 1, the border appears as a 3-D, stylized bar, as shown in Figure 10-6. However, setting frameborder to 0 does not totally eradicate the border as expected. One, non-standards-compliant solution to remove the border entirely is to place the attribute border="0" in the frameset tag. ■

FIGURE 10-5

Without borders, the frame divisions are hard to distinguish, which may work well for a seamless page design.

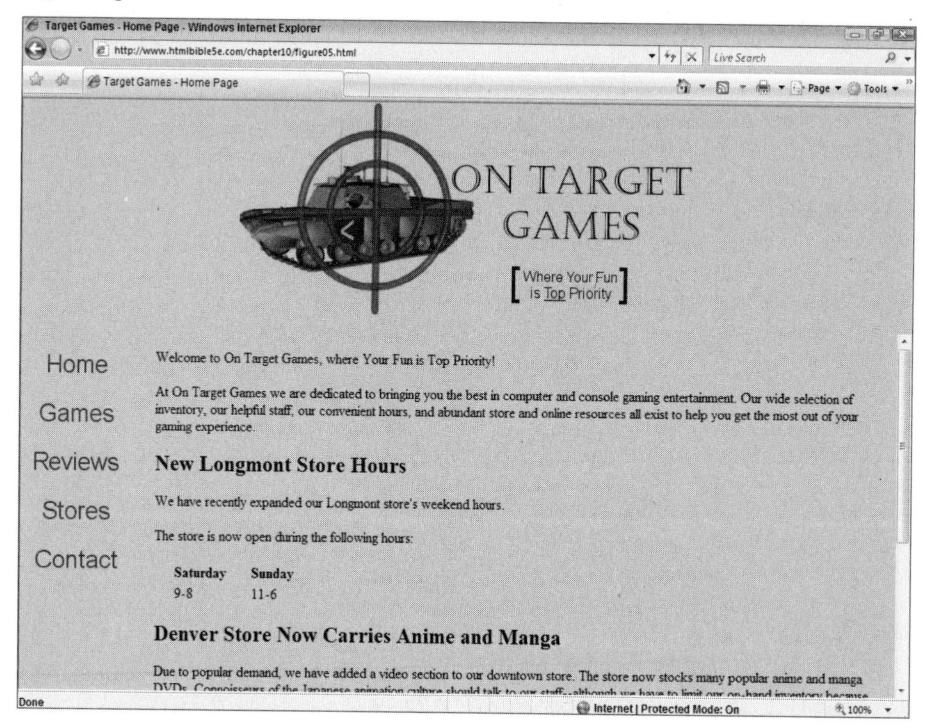

FIGURE 10-6

Frame borders can help users understand the layout of your document and where the edges of each frame are so they can better manipulate them.

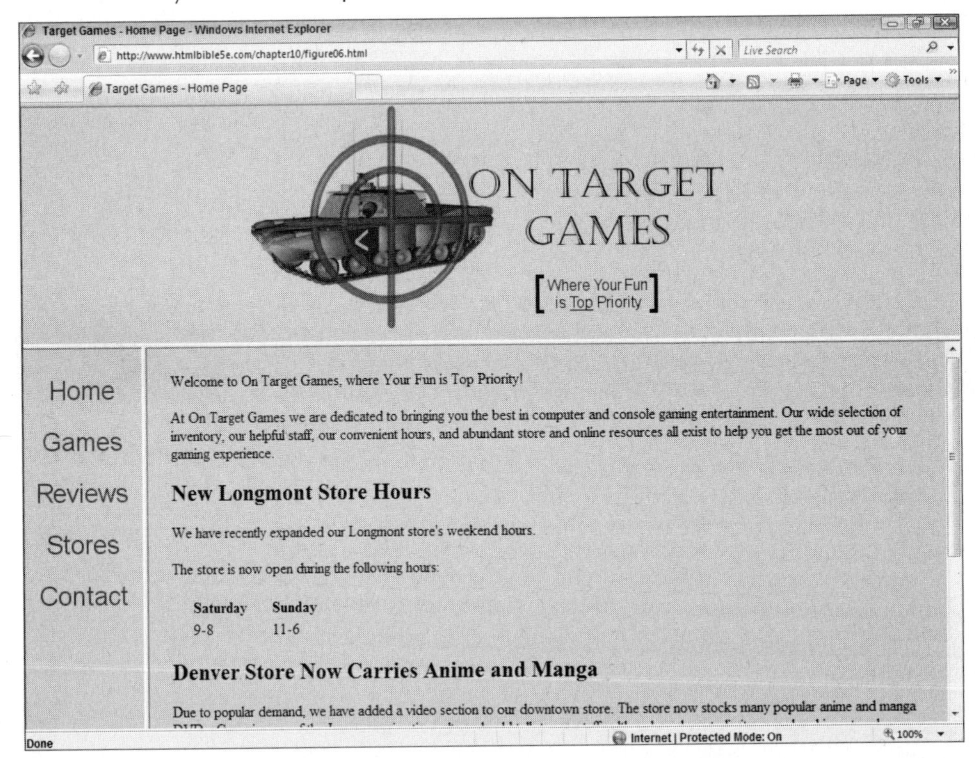

The `scrolling` attribute controls whether the frame will display scroll bars. The default setting, auto, allows the user agent to decide. If the frame contains too much content to be displayed, the user agent will add scroll bars; if the content fits within the frame, the user agent will not display scroll bars. Use the `scrolling` attribute accordingly — if you want scroll bars all the time, or don't want scroll bars regardless of how the frame's content displays.

Permitting or prohibiting user modifications

The frame tag also has a `noresize` attribute that, when set, will not allow a user to modify the frame's size. The default is to allow the user to resize the frame.

To resize a frame, you position the pointer over the frame division and drag the border. Figures 10-7 and 10-8 show the left frame being enlarged. As a consequence, the right frame shrinks to compensate.

FIGURE 10-7

To resize a frame, position the pointer over the frame border until a double-headed arrow cursor appears.

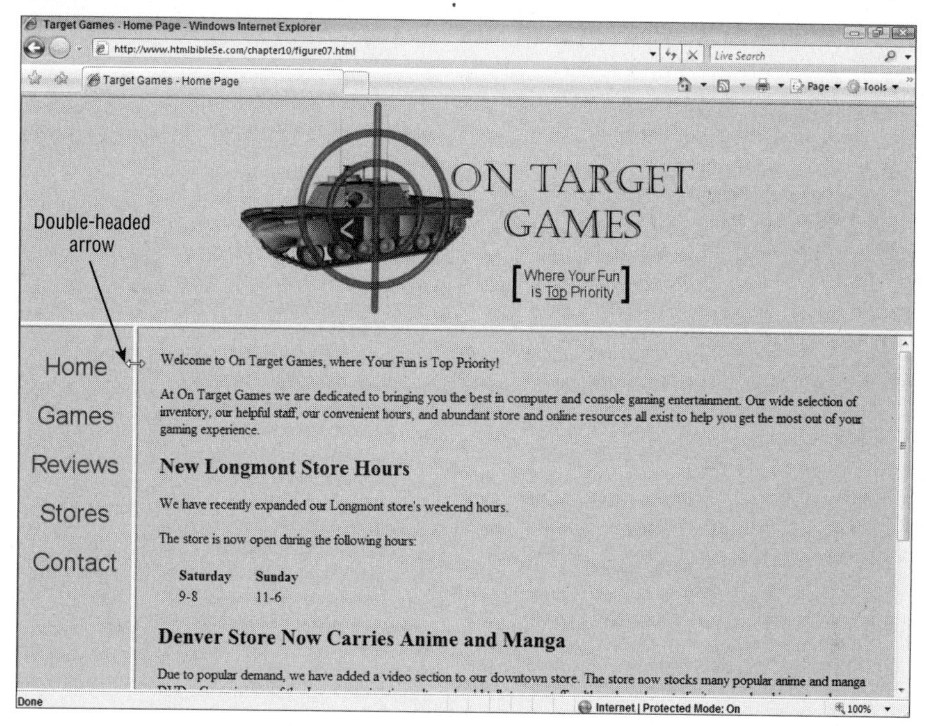

Targeting Links to Frames

To change a frame's content, you must be able to target a frame. To do so, you use the `name` attribute to uniquely identify your frames. You can then use those names in scripts and anchor tags to direct new content to the frame.

Scripting languages can use the document's frame collection to target a frame. For example, JavaScript can reference the content of a frame named `news` by changing the value of the following property:

```
parent.news.location.href
```

For example, to fill the news frame with the content of `www.yahoo.com`, a script could use the following statement:

```
parent.news.location.href = "http://www.yahoo.com";
```

FIGURE 10-8

Dragging the curser resizes the frames accordingly.

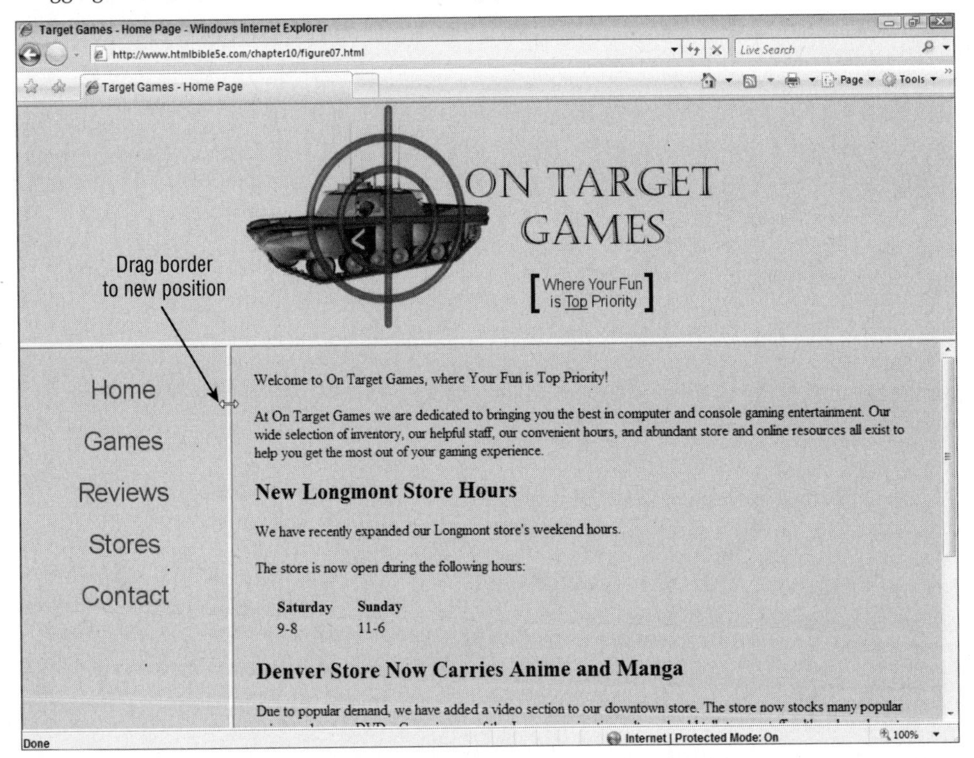

You can use similar methods and properties to otherwise manipulate the frame content and properties.

Cross-Ref

For more information on JavaScript and how it can be used to affect a document's properties, see Chapters 16 and 17. ■

When you use the frameset DTD, the anchor tag (<a>) supports the `target` attribute, which can be used to target a frame for content. The `target` attribute supports the values shown in Table 10-2.

Note

To understand the difference between the `target` attribute's `_parent` and `_top` values, you must understand nested frames, which are covered in the next section. ■

The easiest way to direct content to a frame is to use the frame's name in the `target` attribute of an anchor. This technique is often used to control one frame independently from another, especially where one frame has a navigation control and the other displays variable content. For example, the following code provides a handful of navigation links in the left (menu) frame, and the content is displayed in the right (content) frame. Each button in the menu frame is wrapped in an appropriate anchor that specifies the content frame as the destination for the URL to which it links:

```
<!DOCTYPE HTML PUBLIC "-//W3C//DTD HTML 4.01 Frameset//EN"
  "http://www.w3.org/TR/html4/frameset.dtd">
<html>
<head>
  <title>On Target Games - Menu</title>
  <style type="text/css">
    p { font: Arial;
        font-size: 24pt;
        color: blue; }
  </style>
</head>
<body style="background-color: #CBCC66;">
<table border="0" width="100%">
<colgroup>
<col style="text-align: center;"></col>
</colgroup>
<tr><td><a href="home.html" target="content"><p>Home</p></a></td></tr>
<tr><td><a href="games.html" target="content"><p>Games</p></a></td></tr>
<tr><td><a href="reviews.html" target="content"><p>Reviews</p></a></td></tr>
<tr><td><a href="stores.html" target="content"><p>Stores</p></a></td></tr>
<tr><td><a href="contact.html" target="content"><p>Contact</p></a></td></tr>
</table>
</body>
</html>
```

TABLE 10-2

Target Attribute Values

Value	Definition
frame_name	Displays the content in the frame specified by frame_name
_blank	Opens a new window to display the content
_parent	Displays the content in the parent frameset of the current frame
_self	Displays the content in the current frame
_top	Displays the content in the current window, without frames

Note that each anchor specifies a different document, and that the document specified should be loaded into the content frame via the target attribute. Figure 10-9 shows what this code looks like in a browser; notice the menu on the left edge of the window.

FIGURE 10-9

In this simple frame-based navigation scheme, when the user clicks a link in the menu (left) frame, the content changes in the content (right) frame.

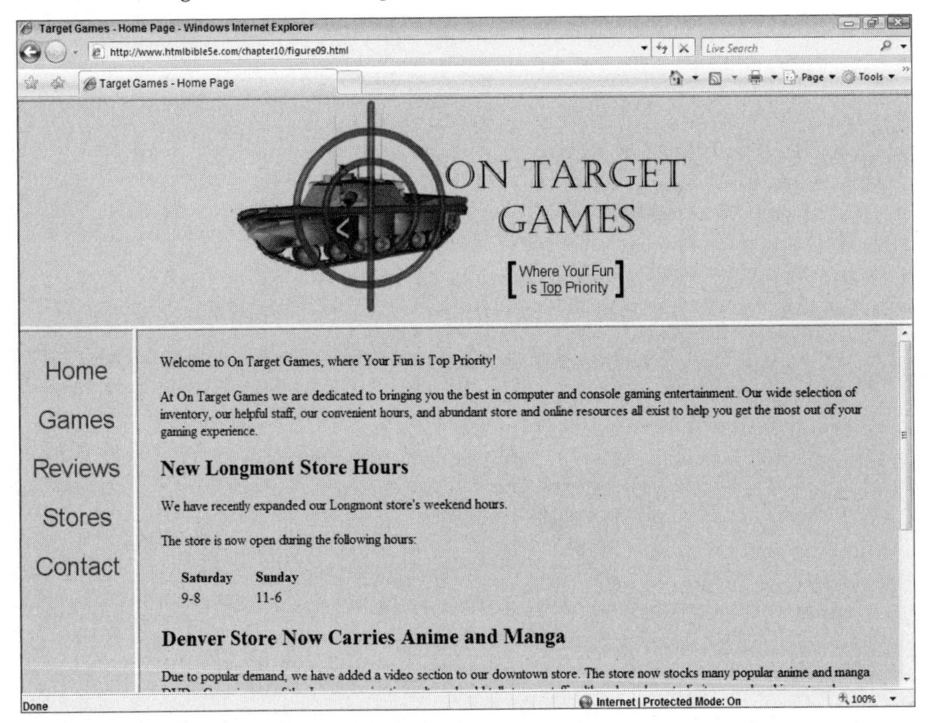

Nested Framesets

You have seen how to create rows and columns using framesets, but what if you want a little of both, as shown in the examples in this chapter (two rows, the second one having two columns)?

In such cases, you need to nest one frameset inside of another. For example, the following frameset code results in the layout shown in the document example used throughout this chapter (as in Figure 10-9, for example):

```
<!-- The master frameset, specifying two rows / -->
<frameset rows="250px,*">
  <!-- The first row, one column / -->
  <frame name="top" src="top.html" marginheight="0px"
         frameborder="0" scrolling="no"></frame>
<!-- The nested frameset, specifying two columns / -->
  <frameset cols="130px,*">
    <frame name="menu" src="menu.html" frameborder="0"
           scrolling="no"></frame>
```

```
        <frame name="content" src="maincontent.html"
               marginwidth="25px" marginheight="25px"
               frameborder="0" scrolling="auto"></frame>
    </frameset>
</frameset>
```

To achieve the layout, a column-based frameset is nested inside the second row of the row-based frameset. In essence, the second row of the top frameset becomes its own frameset. You could conceivably nest other framesets within this layout, but using more than two or three frames tends to clutter the document and confuse the user.

Note

The `_parent` and `_top` values of the anchor tag's `target` attribute were mentioned earlier in this chapter. Looking at the example in this section, you can see how those two values would each affect the target.

The `_parent` value causes the content to load within the frameset — that is, the immediate parent of the current frame. For example, using `_parent` in a link within the `content` frame would cause the specified content to load in the area defined for the column-based frameset.

The `_top` value causes the content to load within the top-most frameset. For example, using `_top` in a link within the `content` frame causes the specified content to load in the area defined for the row-based frameset, effectively taking up the entire user agent window. ■

Inline Frames

Inline frames were conceived as a method to enable smaller pieces of content to be incorporated in scrollable containers within a larger document. Although you can use regular framesets to create individually scrolling regions, the layout is somewhat hampered by the stringent row and column layout design inherent in framesets.

Figure 10-10 shows a sample inline frame placed in a document. Note that the frame is truly "inline" within the objects around it.

Note

Inline frames are not fully supported by all user agents. Inline frames are safe to use only if you are relatively certain that your entire audience will be using an `inline-frame`-compatible browser to view your documents. If this is not the case, you should stay away from inline frames, or code your documents to offer incompatible browsers an alternative.

If you do decide to use inline frames, keep in mind that, like other frame constructs, your documents will validate against frameset DTDs only. ■

Inline frames are accomplished with the `<iframe>` tag. This tag has the following minimal format:

```
<iframe src="url_of_content"></iframe>
```

FIGURE 10-10

Inline frames define separate scrollable regions truly inline within the document.

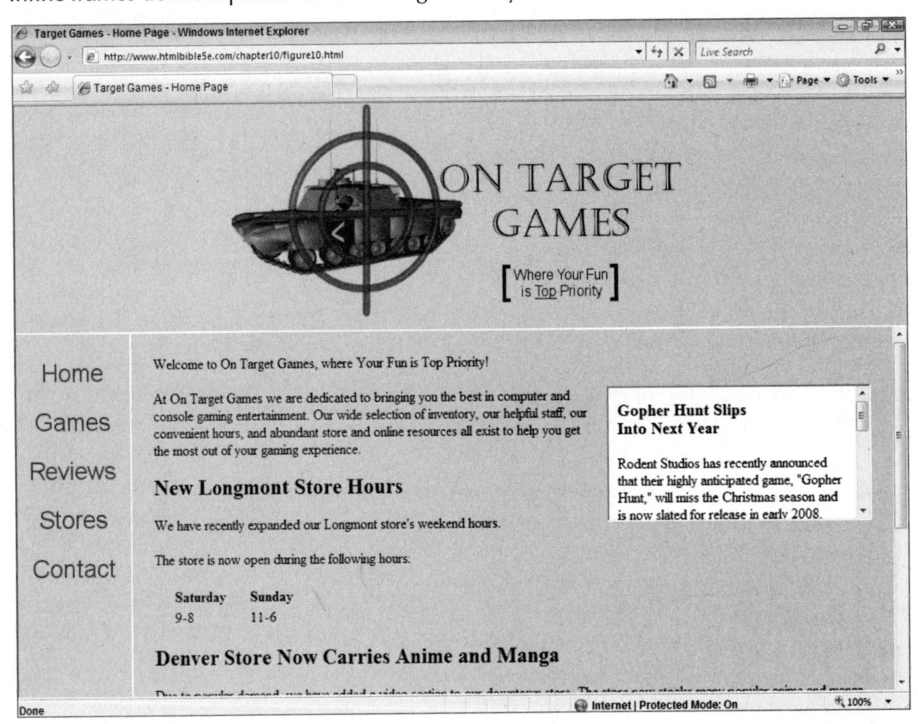

The inline frame tag has a handful of additional attributes, as shown in Table 10-3.

TABLE 10-3

Inline Frame Tag Attributes

Attribute	Value(s)	Definition
`align`	`Left right top middle bottom`	Alignment of the frame to surrounding text
`frameborder`	`0 = no border 1 = border` (default)	Indicates whether the frame has a visible border or not
`height`	`pixels %`	Height of the frame
`longdesc`	`url`	URL to a document containing the long description of the frame
`marginheight`	`pixels`	Size of the internal top and bottom margins of the frame

Attribute	Value(s)	Definition
marginwidth	pixels	Size of the internal left and right margins of the frame
name	name_ of_ frame	Name of the frame (for use in scripting and otherwise referencing the frame and its properties)
scrolling	Yes no auto	Indicates whether the frame has scroll bars or not
src	url	URL of the content to display in the frame
width	pixels %	The width of the frame

These attributes function exactly like their frame-based kin. It is recommended that you use as many attributes as possible to clearly specify how your inline frame layout will be rendered.

The following code snippet shows how the inline frame was inserted into the document displayed in Figure 10-10:

```
content.html
...
 <p>Welcome to On Target Games, where Your Fun is Top Priority!</p>
 <iframe src="newsflash.html" align="right"
  style="margin-left:10px;"></iframe>
 <p>At On Target Games we are dedicated to bringing you the best in
 computer and console gaming entertainment. Our wide selection of
 inventory, our helpful staff, our convenient hours, and abundant
 store and online resources all exist to help you get the most out of
 your gaming experience.</p>
 ...
```

```
newsflash.html
 <!DOCTYPE HTML PUBLIC "-//W3C//DTD HTML 4.01 Frameset//EN"
   "http://www.w3.org/TR/html4/frameset.dtd"><html>
 <head>
   <title>On Target Games - News Flash!</title>
 </head>
 <body > <!-- style="background-color: #CBCC66;" /-->
 <h3>Gopher Hunt Slips<br />Into Next Year</h3>
 <p>Rodent Studios has recently announced that their highly
anticipated game, "Gopher Hunt," will miss the Christmas season and
is now slated for release in early 2008. Gopher Hunt is the
semi-sequel to "Badger Brigade," Rodent Studios smash hit of last
year.</p>
 <p>Company president Samuel Perry could not be reached for comment,
but all release dates for the game have been removed from the
company website. As you may recall, "Badger Brigade" is one of the
few titles to which On Target Games awarded 5-stars to and the only
game to stay on the best seller list for a whopping 24 week.</p>
```

```
<p>We hope this slip isn't a sign of bigger problems at RS, but we
will keep you in the loop.</p>
</body>
</html>
```

Summary

This chapter introduced the concept of frames, including the inline frame construct. Using frames or inline frames, you can insert separately scrollable and formatted regions inside a larger document. As with most older HTML technologies, you should take care when choosing to use frames; in many instances, you're better off learning and using CSS instead.

The next chapter covers how to use HTML to collect data via forms. Following that, Chapters 12 and 13 round out our coverage of HTML with images, colors, and multimedia.

CHAPTER

11

Forms

HTML's somewhat humble beginnings were send only; that is, the user could receive data sent from a Web server, but the server could not receive data sent from the user. This was quickly identified as a deficiency of HTML. Because most user agents were being run in graphical environments that included rich user interfaces, creating a similar interface to allow users to submit data back to a server seemed a natural extension.

Today, HTML forms present a complex yet flexible framework to allow users basic controls over data. These controls can be used to provide input back to scripts or to submit data. This chapter delves into the particulars of HTML forms.

IN THIS CHAPTER

Understanding Forms

HTML forms simply place a handful of GUI controls on the user agent screen to allow the user to enter data. The controls can allow text input and selection of predefined options from a list, radio buttons or check boxes, or other standard GUI controls.

After the data is entered into the fields, a special control is used to pass the entered data on to a program that can do something useful with it. Such programs are typically referred to as *form handlers* because they "handle" the form data submitted to the server.

The following code shows a basic HTML form whose output is shown in Figure 11-1:

```
<!DOCTYPE HTML PUBLIC "-//W3C//DTD HTML 4.01//EN"
  "http://www.w3.org/TR/html4/strict.dtd">
<html>
<head>
```

```
  <title>A Simple Form</title>
</head>
<body>
<form name="sample" id="sample" action="formhandler.cgi"
method="post">
  <table cellspacing="20">
  <tr><td>
    <!-- Text boxes -->
    <table border="0">
    <tr>
    <td><p><label for="fname">First Name: </label></p></td>
    <td><p><input type="text" name="fname" id="fname"
        size="20" /></p></td>
    </tr><tr>
    <td><p><label for="lname">Last Name: </label></p></td>
    <td><p><input type="text" name="lname" id="lname"
        size="20" /></p></td>
    </tr>
    </table>
    <!-- Text area -->
    <p><label for="address">Address:</label><br />
      <textarea name="address" id="address"
        cols=20 rows=4 /></textarea>
    </p>
    <!-- Password -->
    <table border="0">
    <tr>
    <td><p><label for="password">Password:</label></p></td>
    <td><p><input type="password" name="password" id="password"
        size="20" /></p></td>
    </tr>
    </table>
    </td>
    <td>
    <!-- Select list -->
    <p><label for="products">What gaming consoles do you<br />
    own or are you interested in?</p>
    <select name="consoles[]" id="consoles" multiple="multiple"
      size="4" />
      <option id="PS3">Sony Playstation 3
      <option id="XBOX">XBOX 360
      <option id="NINTENDO">Nintendo Wii
      <option id="OTHER">Other
    </select>
    </p>

    <!-- Check boxes -->
    <fieldset>
      <legend>Contact me via: </legend>
      <p><input type="checkbox" name="email" id="email"
          Checked />
```

```
        <label for="email">Email</label><br />
      <input type="checkbox" name="postal" id="postal" />
        <label for="postal">Postal Mail</label></p>
    </fieldset>
    </td>
    </tr>
    <tr>
    <td>
    <!-- Radio buttons -->
    <fieldset>
    <legend>How many games do you buy in a year?</legend>
    <p><input type="radio" name="buy" value="onethree"
        id="onethree" checked="checked" />
      <label for="onethree">1-3</label><br />
    <input type="radio" name="buy" value="fiveten" id="fiveten" />
      <label for="fiveten">5-10</label><br />
    <input type="radio" name="buy" value="tenfifteen"
     id="tenfifteen" />
      <label for="tenfifteen">10-15</label></p>
    </fieldset>
    </td>
    <td>
    <!-- Submit and Reset buttons -->
    <p>
    <input type="submit" />   
    <input type="reset" />
    </p>

    <!-- Generic Button -->
    <p>
    <input type="button" name="Leave" value="Leave site!" />
    </p>
    <!-- Image -->
    <input type="image" name="sirveybutton"
     src="images/SirVeyButton.jpg" />
    <!-- Hidden field -->
    <input type="hidden" name="referredby" value="Google" />
  </td>
  </tr>
  </table>
</form>
</body>
</html>
```

The individual form fields are covered in the following sections.

Note

Many form tags do not have closing tags. However, XML and its variants require that all elements be closed. If you are coding for XML or one of its variants (such as XHTML), be sure to close your tags by including the closing slash (/) at the end of tags that lack a formal closing tag. ■

FIGURE 11-1

A simple HTML form

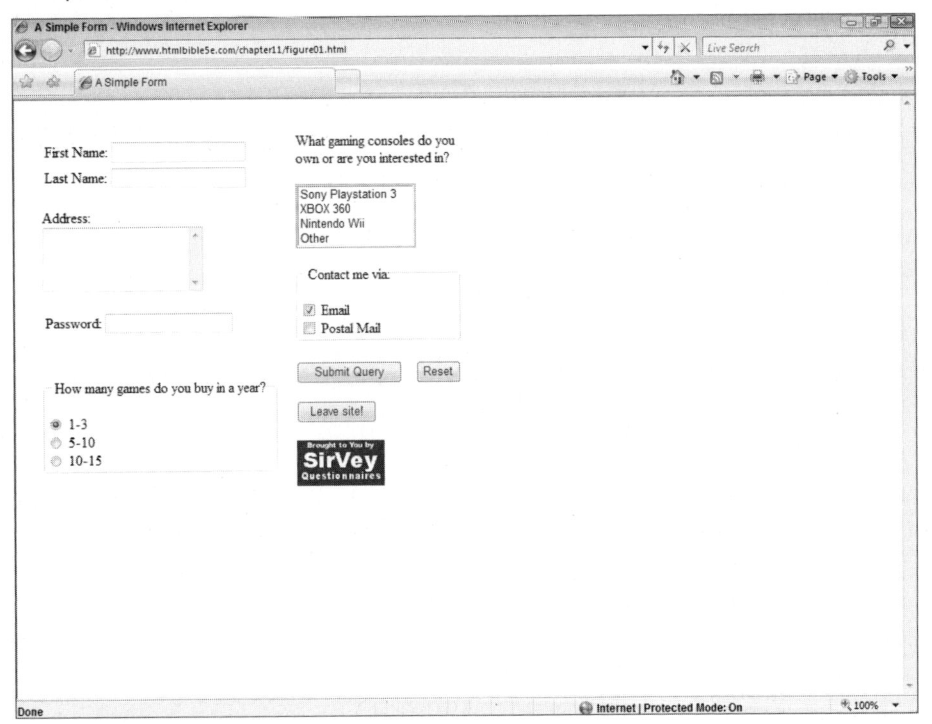

Inserting a Form

You insert a form into your document by placing form fields within `<form>` tags. The entire form or any of the tags can be formatted like any other element in your document, and can be placed within any element capable of holding other elements (paragraphs, tables, and so on).

The `<form>` tag has the following minimum format:

```
<form action="url_to_send_data" method="get/post">
```

The `action` attribute defines a URL where the data from the form should be sent to be handled. Although you can use just about any URL, the destination should be a script or other construct capable of correctly interpreting and doing something useful with the data.

Note

Form actions and form data handlers are covered in the section "Form Scripts and Script Services" later in this chapter. ■

The second attribute, `method`, controls how the data is sent to the handler. The two valid values are `GET` and `POST`. Each value corresponds to the HTTP protocol of the same name.

HTTP GET

The HTTP `GET` protocol attaches data to the actual URL text to pass the data to the destination specified in the `action` attribute. You have probably noticed URLs that resemble the following:

```
http://www.on-target-games.com/forms.cgi?id=45677&data=Taarna
```

The data appears after the question mark and is in name/value pairs. For example, the name `id` has the value of `45677`, and the name `data` has the value of `Taarna`.

Note

In most cases, the name corresponds to field names from the form and may relate to variables in the data handler. ■

Because the data is passed in the text of the URL, it is easy to implement — you can pass data by simply adding appropriate text to the URL used to call the data handler. However, `GET` is also inherently insecure. Never use `GET` to send confidential, unencrypted data to a handler because the data is clearly visible in most user agents and can be easily sniffed by hackers.

HTTP POST

The HTTP `POST` method passes data encoded in the HTTP data stream. As such, it is not typically visible to a user and is therefore a more secure method to pass data, but it can be harder to implement. Thankfully, HTML forms and most other Web technologies make passing data via `POST` a trivial task.

Additional <form> attributes

The `<form>` tag has many additional attributes, which are listed in Table 11-1.

Although you may not need these attributes in simple forms, these attributes can be very useful. The `accept`, `accept-charset`, and `enctype` attributes are invaluable for processing nontextual and international data. The `id` and `name` attributes should be used to uniquely identify a form in your document, especially if you use more than one form in the same document.

Note

Although you can set a field's `id` and `name` to the same value, it's important to understand the use of each. The `id` attribute is used primarily in client-side scripts (like JavaScript) to uniquely identify and manipulate a control. The `name` attribute is used to uniquely reference a field value when a form is passed to a form handler on the server side. ■

TABLE 11-1

<form> Tag Attributes

Attribute	Values
accept	A comma-separated list of content types that the handler's server will accept
accept-charset	A comma-separated list of character sets the form data may be in
enctype	The content type of the form data
id	A unique identifier for the form object (replaces the name attribute)
name	The name of the form (deprecated, use the id attribute instead)
target	Where to open the handler URL (deprecated)

Field Labels

The <label> tag defines textual labels for form fields. It has the following format:

```
<label for="id_of_related_tag">text_label</label>
```

For example, the following code defines a label for a text box:

```
<p><label for="FirstName">First Name: </label>
<input type="text" id="FirstName" value="" size="30"
maxlength="40" /></p>
```

The purpose of the <label> tag is related to accessibility. Most users can rely upon the layout of your forms to determine which labels go with what fields. However, if the user agent does not have a visual component, or if the user is visually impaired, the form's visual layout cannot be relied upon to match labels and fields. The <label> tag's for attribute ensures that the user agent can adequately match labels with fields.

Text Input Boxes

One of the most frequently used fields of HTML forms is the simple text field. This field allows for the input of smaller pieces of text — names, addresses, search terms, and so on.

The text input field tag has the following format:

```
<input type="text" id="id_of_field" value="initial_value"
   size="size_of_field" maxlength="max_characters_allowed" />
```

Although not all of the attributes previously listed are strictly required, they do represent the minimum attributes that you should always use with your text boxes. The following sample text box is designed to accept a name, appears 30 characters long, accepts a maximum of 40 characters, and has no initial value:

```
<p>Name: <input type="text" id="username" value=""
   size="30" maxlength="40" /></p>
```

The following code example defines a text box to accept an e-mail address. It appears 40 characters wide, accepts only 40 characters, and has an initial value of `info@oasisoftranquility.com`:

```
<p>Email: <input type="text" id="email"
value="info@oasisoftranquility.com" size="40"
maxlength="40" /></p>
```

Password Input Boxes

The password input box is similar to the text box but visually obscures data entered into the box by displaying asterisks instead of the actual data entered into the field. The following example displays a password field that accepts 20 characters:

```
<p>Password: <input type="password" id="password" value=""
size="20" maxlength="20" /></p>
```

The `password` field accepts the same attributes as the `text` field.

Caution

The `password` field only visibly obscures the data onscreen to help stop casual snoops from seeing what a user inputs into a field. It does not encode or in any way obscure the information at the data level. As such, be careful how you use this field. ■

Radio Buttons

Radio buttons are groups of small, round buttons that enable the user to choose one option in each group. The name "radio" button comes from how old-fashioned radios used to be tuned — you pushed one of many buttons to tune to a preset station. When one button was pushed, the rest were reset to the out, or off, position. Like those buttons, form radio buttons are mutually exclusive: Only one of the group can be set. When one is selected, the others in the group are deselected.

The radio button field has the following format:

```
<p><input type="radio" id="control_id" name="group_name" [checked="checked"]
value="value_if_selected" /> Descriptive Text for Button</p>
```

Note that the `value` attribute defines what value is returned to the handler if the button is selected. This attribute should be unique between buttons in the same group. However, the `name` attribute should be *the same* for all buttons in a group.

The following example code defines a group of radio buttons that enables users to select their gender:

```
<p>Gender:<br />
<input type="radio" id="gender_male" name="gender" value="male" /> Male
<input type="radio" id="gender_female" name="gender" value="female" />
   Female</p>
```

If you want a button selected by default, add the `checked` attribute to the appropriate button's tag. For example, to have "Male" checked by default, you would change the preceding code to the following:

```
<p>Gender:<br />
<input type="radio" id="gender_male" name="gender" value="male"
  checked="checked" /> Male
<input type="radio" id="gender_female" name="gender" value="female" />
  Female</p>
```

It is good form to always set a default button checked in a group of radio buttons.

Tip

XML and its variants do not allow attributes without values. HTML will allow the `checked` attribute to be used with or without a value. To ensure that your code remains as compliant as possible, specify a checked box with the checked attribute as `checked="checked"` instead of just `checked`. ■

Check Boxes

Check boxes are small, square boxes used to select non-mutually exclusive options. They are so named because when selected, they display a checkmark (or more commonly an X) in the box like the check boxes in paper lists.

The `checkbox` field has the following format:

```
<input type="checkbox" id="id_of_field" [checked="checked"]
  value="value_if_selected" />
```

As you can see, other than the mutually exclusive issue, check boxes are very similar in definition to radio buttons. The following example displays a check box that enables users to select whether they want to receive solicitation e-mails:

```
<p><input type="checkbox" id="spam_me" checked="checked" value="spamme" />
Add me to your email list</p>
```

Note that the `checked` attribute can be used to preselect check boxes in your forms. Also, just like radio buttons, the `value` attribute is used as the value of the check box if it is selected. If no value is given, selected check boxes are given the value of "on."

List Boxes

List boxes enable users to pick one or more textual items from a list. The list can be presented in its entirety, with each element visible, or as a pull-down list from which users can scroll to their choices.

List boxes are implemented using `<select>` and `<option>` tags, and optionally the `<optgroup>` tag.

The `<select>` tag provides the container for the list and has the following format:

```
<select id="id_of_field" size="items_to_show"   [multiple="multiple"] />
```

The `<option>` tag defines the items for the list. Each item is given its own `<option>` tag. This tag has the optional attributes shown in Table 11-2.

TABLE 11-2

<option> Tag Attributes

Attribute	Values
`label`	A shorter label for the item that the user agent can use
`selected`	Indicates that the item should be initially selected
`value`	The value that should be sent to the handler if the item is selected; if this attribute is omitted, the text of the item is sent instead.

The following is an example of a minimum set of `<option>` tags:

```
<option>Sunday</option>
<option>Monday</option>
<option>Tuesday</option>
<option>Wednesday</option>
<option>Thursday</option>
<option>Friday</option>
<option>Saturday</option>
```

Occasionally, you might want to group options of a list together for clarity. For this you use `<optgroup>` tags, which encapsulate items that should be in that group. For example, the following code defines two groups for the preceding list of options, weekend and weekday:

```
<optgroup label="Weekend">
  <option>Sunday</option>
  <option>Saturday</option>
</optgroup>
<optgroup label="Weekday"
```

```
    <option>Monday</option>
    <option>Tuesday</option>
    <option>Wednesday</option>
    <option>Thursday</option>
    <option>Friday</option>
  </optgroup>
```

Different user agents display option groups differently, but the default behavior is to display the option group labels above the options to which they apply, as shown in Figure 11-2.

FIGURE 11-2

Option groups are displayed in the list as nonselectable items.

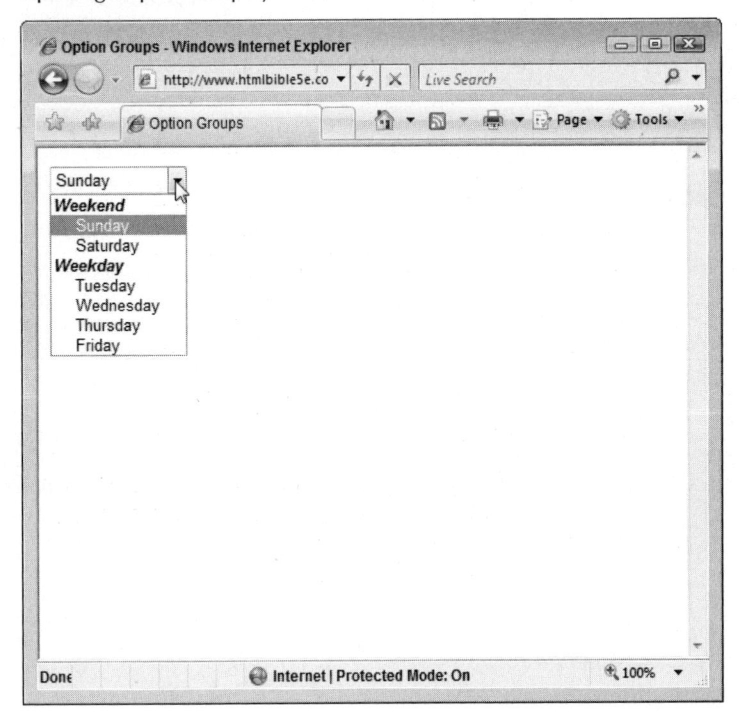

The code to combine all three tags to create a list would resemble the following:

```
<p>Select the days you are available:
<select id="AvailDays[]" name="AvailDays[]" size="5"
multiple="multiple">
   <optgroup label="Weekend">
     <option>Sunday</option>
     <option>Saturday</option>
  </optgroup>
  <optgroup label="Weekday"
```

```
    <option>Monday</option>
    <option>Tuesday</option>
    <option>Wednesday</option>
    <option>Thursday</option>
    <option>Friday</option>
  </optgroup>
</select>
</p>
```

Note

Notice the brackets ([ ]) after the select field's ID. These brackets are used because some languages that form handlers are written in require notification if a field will contain multiple items. In the preceding case, the `select` field has included the `multiple` attribute, so the field can indeed return multiple values. The brackets signal the form handler to expect this, whether multiple values are actually returned or not.

As of this writing, only handlers written in PHP are known to require this convention. However, the use of brackets will not harm handlers written in other languages, so it's a good habit to adopt. ■

Large Text Input

For large pieces of text, you can use the <textarea> tag. This tag can accept textual input of up to 1,024 characters and uses a multiline text box for input.

The <textarea> tag has the following format:

```
<textarea id="id_of_field" name="name_of_field" cols="number_of_columns"
rows="number_of_rows"></textarea>
```

Note that the <textarea> tag is one of the few form tags that requires both an open tag and a close tag. If you want the field to have default content, the content should be placed between the tags. For example, the following code results in the initial form shown in Figure 11-3:

```
<textarea cols="50" rows="6">
John Doe
123 Main Street
Anywhere, USA
</textarea>
```

Tip

Whatever is placed between the <textarea> tags appears verbatim in the text box when the form is first displayed. Therefore, it is important to carefully watch the formatting of your HTML code. For example, if you want the field to be initially blank, you cannot place the open and close tags on separate lines in the code:

```
<textarea>
</textarea>
```

This would result in the field containing a newline character — it would not be blank. ■

FIGURE 11-3

You can set a default value for the <textarea> tag by placing content between the open and close tags.

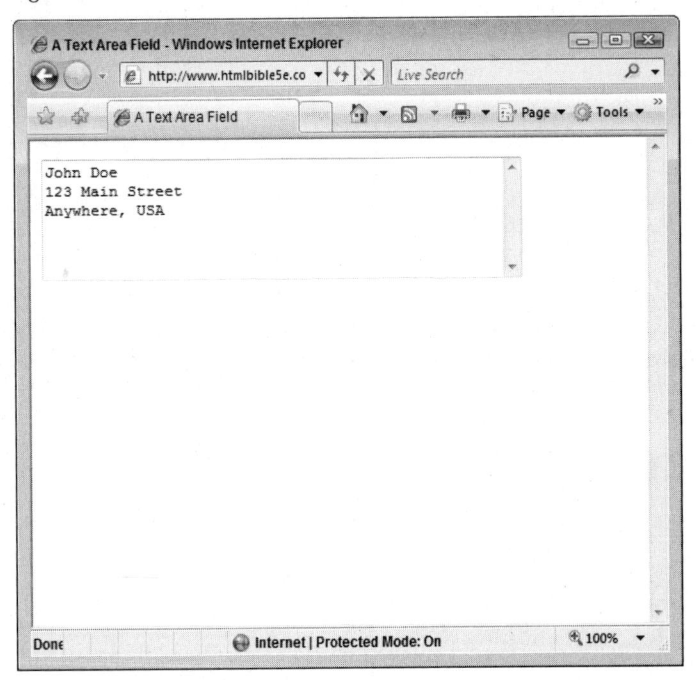

Note that the text entered into the `textarea` field wraps within the width of the box, but the text is sent verbatim to the handler. If the user enters line breaks, then those breaks are also sent to the handler. However, the wrapped text (without hard line breaks) is sent without breaks of any kind.

Note

Previous versions of HTML supported a `wrap` attribute for the `<textarea>` tag. This attribute could be used to control how text wrapped in the text box as well as how it was sent to the handler. Unfortunately, user agent support for this attribute was inconsistent — you could not rely on a browser to follow the intent of the attribute. As such, the attribute has been deprecated and should not be used. ■

Hidden Fields

Hidden fields are used to add data to your form without displaying it to the user. The hidden field has the following format:

```
<input type="hidden" id="id_of_field" name="name_of_field"
value="value_of_field" />
```

Hidden fields are used mostly for tracking data, and other than not being visibly displayed, are like any other field. For example, in a multipage form, a userid field can be hidden in the form to ensure that subsequent forms, when submitted, are tied to the same user data.

Keep in mind that hidden fields do not display on the user agent but are still visible in the document's code. As such, hidden fields should never be used for sensitive data.

Buttons

Occasionally, you might need additional, custom buttons on your form. For those cases, you can use the `button` field, which has the following format:

```
<input type="button" id="id_of_field" name="name_of_field"
value="text_for_button" />
```

This tag results in a standard graphical button being displayed on the form. The following code example results in the button shown in Figure 11-4:

```
<input type="button" id="BuyNow" name="buy_button" value="Buy Now!" />
```

FIGURE 11-4

You can use the button field to add custom buttons to your form.

Buttons by themselves, however, are fairly useless on a form. To have the button actually do something, you must link it to a script via onclick or other event attributes. For example, the following code results in a button that, when clicked, runs the script "buynow":

```
<input type="button" id="BuyNow" name="buy_button" value="Buy Now!"
onClick="buynow();" />
```

Cross-Ref

For more information on onclick and other form field event handlers, see the section "Using Events with Forms" later in this chapter. You can also refer to Chapters 16 and 17. ■

Images

Images provide a graphical means to convey a message. Using the image type of the <input> tag, you can add images to your form, images that can be used along with other form elements to gather data. The image field has the following format:

```
<input type="image" id="id_of_field" name="name_of_field"
src="url_to_image_file" />
```

The image type of the <input> tag also serves as a submit button, giving you the option of easily providing a graphical button. Simply put, if you include an image type <input> tag in your form and click the resulting image, it will behave like a Submit button (and likely submit the form).

Note

Submit buttons are covered later in this chapter. ■

However, like the button field, image fields by themselves do not provide any actual form controls. To use the image for input purposes beyond submitting the form, it must be linked to a script. The following example causes the image buynow.jpg to be displayed on a form. When the image is clicked, the script buynow is run.

```
<input type="image" id="BuyNow" name="BuyNow_graphic" src="buynow.jpg"
onclick="buynow()" />
```

File Fields

File fields enable users to browse for a local file and send it as an attachment to the form data. The file field has the following format:

```
<input type="file" id="id_of_field" name="name_of_field"
size="display_size_of_field" />
```

The `file` field results in a text box with a button that enables users to browse for a file using their platform's file browser. Alternately, users can simply type the path and name of the file in the text box. Figure 11-5 shows an example of a file field in Internet Explorer.

FIGURE 11-5

The file field enables users to send a local file.

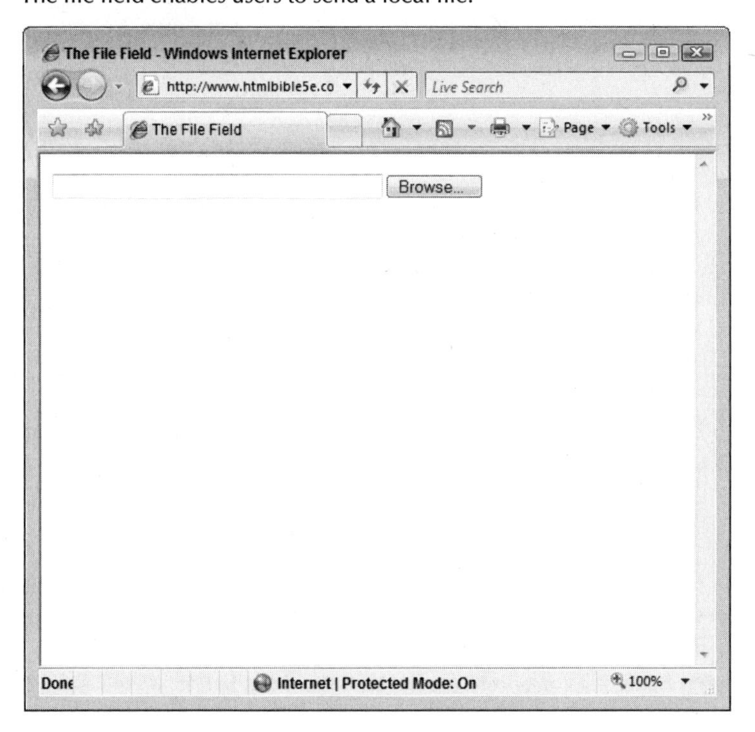

However, in order to use this control in your forms you must do the following:

- Specify your form as multipart, which allows the file to be attached to the rest of the data.
- Use the `POST`, not the `GET`, method of form delivery.

This means your `<form>` tag should resemble the following:

```
<form action="formhandler.cgi" method="post"
enctype="form/multipart">
```

The form handler you send your form's data to must also be multipart-aware to be able to handle the data sent to it.

Submit and Reset Buttons

Submit and Reset buttons provide control mechanisms for users to submit the data entered to a handler and reset the form to its default state. These buttons have the following format:

Submit button

```
<input type="submit" id="id_of_field" name="name_of_field"
[value="text_for_button"] />
```

Reset button

```
<input type="reset" id="id_of_field" name="name_of_field"
[value="text_for_button"] />
```

The `value` attribute for both tags is optional — if this attribute is omitted, the buttons will display default text (usually `Submit` and `Reset`, but ultimately determined by the user agent). Note that some user agents use fairly inappropriate text, such as "Submit Query." It is a good idea to include the `value` attribute and appropriate text of your own.

The Submit button, when clicked, causes the form to be submitted to the handler specified in the `<form>` tag's `action` attribute. Alternately, you can use the `onclick` attribute to call a script to preprocess the form data before it is passed on to the handler.

The Reset button, when clicked, causes the form to be reloaded and its fields reset to their default values. You can also use the `onclick` attribute to change the button's behavior, calling a script instead of reloading the form.

Tip

Use of `onclick` to change the Reset button's behavior is not recommended. Using `onclick` to cause the Submit button to run a script for preprocessing is an expected process, but the Reset button should always reset the form. If you need a button to perform some other function, use a custom button that is appropriately labeled. ■

Tab Order and Keyboard Shortcuts

Two additional attributes, `tabindex` and `accesskey`, should be used with your form fields to increase their accessibility.

The `tabindex` attribute defines what order the fields are selected in when the user presses the Tab key. This attribute takes a numeric argument that specifies the field's order on the form.

The `accesskey` attribute defines a key the user can press to directly access the field. This attribute takes a single letter as an argument — that letter becomes the key the user can press to directly access the field.

Note

Keys specified in `accesskey` attributes usually require an additional key to be pressed simultaneously with the chosen key. For example, user agents running on Windows require the Alt key to be pressed along with the letter specified by `accesskey`. Other platforms require similar key combinations, which typically follow the GUI interface conventions of the platform. ■

The following example defines a text box that can be accessed by pressing Alt+F on Windows platforms, and is third in the tab order:

```
<p><label for="FirstName"><u>F</u>irst Name: </label>
<input type="text" id="FirstName" name="FirstName" value="" tabindex="3"
accesskey="F" size="30" maxlength="40" /></p>
```

Notice the visual cue given to users, clueing them in to the available shortcut key, via underlining the F in the field's label. Although it is not always possible to provide such cues, doing so will greatly improve the usability of your forms.

Preventing Changes

There are two ways to display information in common form fields but not allow users to change the data: by setting the field to read-only or disabled.

You can add the `readonly` attribute to text fields to prevent users from being able to edit the data contained therein.

The `disabled` attribute effectively disables a control (usually graying out the control, consistent with the user agent's platform method of showing disabled controls) so the user cannot use it.

The following code shows examples of both a read-only and a disabled control. The output of this code is shown in Figure 11-6:

```
<!DOCTYPE HTML PUBLIC "-//W3C//DTD HTML 4.01//EN"
  "http://www.w3.org/TR/html4/strict.dtd">
<html>
<head>
  <title>Read Only and Disabled Fields</title>
</head>
<body>
  <form name="sample" id="sample" action="formhandler.cgi"
     method="post">
  <table cellspacing="10" width="600">
  <tr><td width="25%">
  <p>Customer Code (readonly):</p>
  </td><td>
  <input type="text" size="12" value="X234GG"
```

```
      readonly="readonly" />
    </td></tr>
    </table>
    <table>
    <tr><td>
    <p>Zip Code (disabled):</p>
    </td><td>
    <input type="text" size="10" value=""
      disabled="disabled" />
    </td></tr>
    </table>
</form>
</body>
</html>
```

FIGURE 11-6

Disabled and read-only fields can be used to show data without the data being editable.

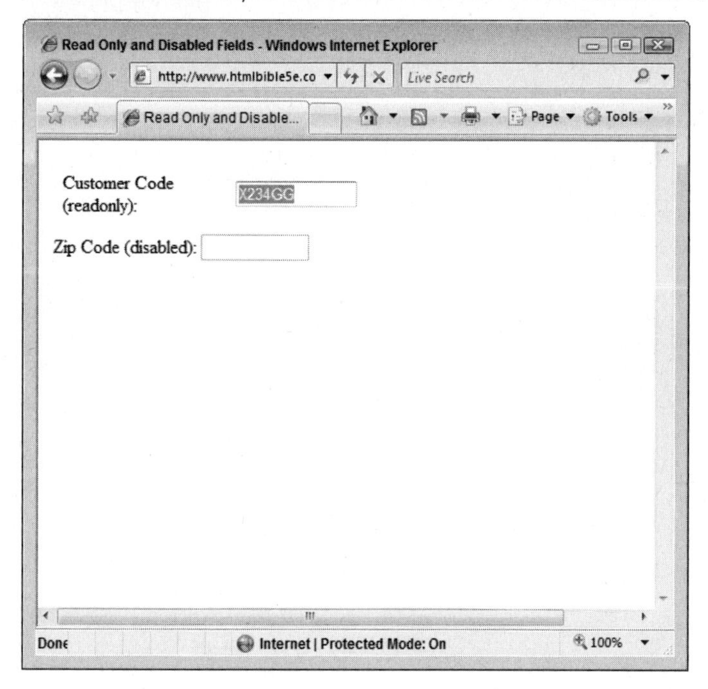

Although the two attributes make the fields look similar when displayed, the `readonly` field can be selected, but not edited. The `disabled` field cannot be selected at all.

Tip

Disabling a control that is not applicable in certain instances is common practice. For example, international addresses do not have a U.S. zip code. When users indicate that they have an international address, you might decide to disable the zip code field so they do not enter data in it.

You can use client-side scripts to dynamically disable controls. Use the `onblur` or `onchange` actions to call a script from fields that could change the enabled status of other fields — those scripts check the data entered and enable or disable other fields by changing the value of that field's `disabled` attribute. For more information on `onclick` and other form field actions, see the section "Using Events with Forms" later in this chapter, and Chapter 16. ■

Fieldsets and Legends

Sometimes it is advantageous to visually group certain controls on your form. This is a standard practice for graphical user agents, as shown in Figure 11-7, where the dialog controls are separated into distinct sections: Home page, Browsing history, Search, Tabs, and Appearance.

FIGURE 11-7

Grouping controls enables users to better understand a form's organization.

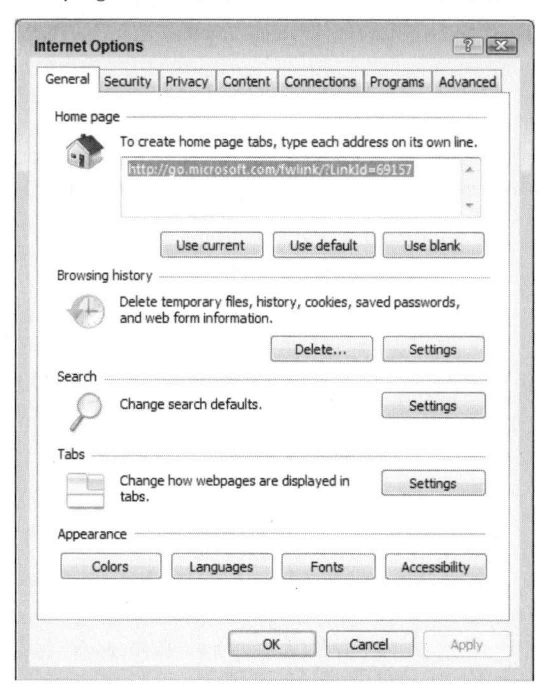

The <fieldset> tag is used as a container for form elements, and results in a thin border being displayed around the elements it surrounds. For example, the following code results in the output shown in Figure 11-8:

```
<fieldset>
<p>Gender: <br />
<input type="radio" id="gender" value="male" /> Male <br>
<input type="radio" id="gender" value="female" /> Female</p>
</fieldset>
```

FIGURE 11-8

The <fieldset> tag can help add organization to your forms.

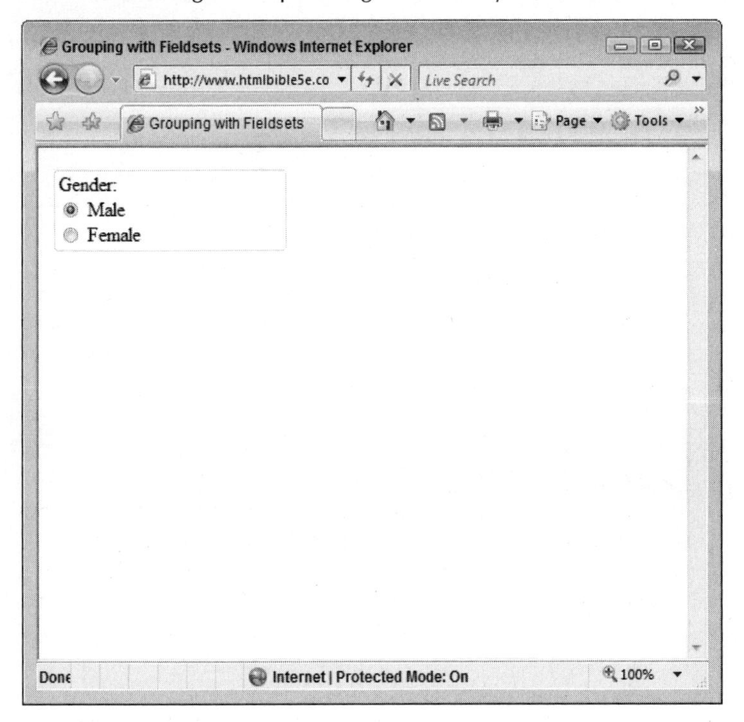

The <legend> tag allows the surrounding fieldset box to be captioned. The following code adds a caption to the previous example, the output of which is shown in Figure 11-9:

```
<fieldset>
<p><legend> Gender </legend></p>
<input type="radio" name="gender" value="male"/ > Male <br />
<input type="radio" name="gender" value="female" /> Female</p>
</fieldset>
```

FIGURE 11-9

The <legend> tag can add captions to your fieldsets.

Using Events with Forms

Another important enhancement to HTML 4 is the addition of events. Events are user or user agent actions that can be captured and acted upon by HTML code. The action is captured via special event attributes added to key tags in your HTML code. These attributes specify the event to watch for and the script to run if the event is encountered.

For example, the `onclick` event can be used to run a script if an element is clicked. This event is particularly handy for `button` fields in a form, which otherwise perform no action when clicked. For example, the following HTML code specifies that the JavaScript function `addCoupon` should be run when the `coupon` button is clicked:

```
<input type="button" id="coupon" name="coupon" value="Add Coupon"
    onClick="addCoupon()" />
```

The `addCoupon` script is defined elsewhere — in the document or external script file — and can do any number of things when called. Typically, events and scripts are used to manipulate form data — for example, add shipping costs, validate information entered, dynamically change the form depending on information entered, and more.

Note

Event attributes can be added to any HTML entity. However, they are most useful in conjunction with forms or other dynamic elements. For more information on scripting, see Chapter 16. For more information on dynamic HTML, see Chapter 17. ■

A full list of available event attributes is shown in Table 11-3.

TABLE 11-3

Event Attributes

Event	Trigger
onAbort	An element's loading is interrupted.
onBlur	An element loses focus.
onChange	An element's content is changed.
onClick	An element is clicked.
onDblclick	An element is double-clicked.
onError	An error occurs while loading an element or document.
onFocus	An element receives focus.
onKeydown	A key is pressed.
onKeypress	A key is pressed or held down.
onKeyup	A key is released.
onLoad	An element or document finishes loading.
onMousedown	A mouse button is pressed.
onMousemove	The mouse pointer is moved.
onMouseout	The mouse pointer is moved away from an element.
onMouseover	The mouse pointer is moved over an element.
onMouseup	A mouse button is released.
onReset	The Reset button is clicked.
onResize	A window or frame is resized.
onSelect	Text in an element is selected.
onSubmit	The Submit button is clicked.
onunload	The current document is exited or closed.

The following code shows a sample use of the `onClick` event. When the user clicks the Evaluate button, a script takes the equation in the `equation` field, evaluates it, and places the value in the `results` field. A sample run of the process is shown in Figure 11-10.

```
<!DOCTYPE HTML PUBLIC "-//W3C//DTD HTML 4.01//EN"
  "http://www.w3.org/TR/html4/strict.dtd">
<html>
<head>
  <title>A Simple Calculator</title>
  <script type="text/JavaScript">
    function eval_eq() {
      // Get the value of the equation field
      var x=document.getElementById("equation").value;
      // Evaluate it (eval) and put the results in
      //   the results field
     document.getElementById("results").value=eval(x);
    }
  </script>
</head>
<body>
<form name="sample" id="sample" action="formhandler.cgi"
      method="post">
<p>Type an equation into the field below and click the
Evaluate button to evaluate it. Click Reset to clear
the form and start over.<br />
<table border="0" cellpadding="10px">
<tr style="padding-bottom: 10px;">
<td><label for="equation">Type your equation here: </label></td>
<td><input type="text" id="equation" size="40" value="" /></td>
</tr>
<tr>
<td><label for="results">Your results: </label></td>
<td><input type="text" id="results" size="40" value=""
     disabled="disabled" /></td>
</tr>
<tr>
<td><input type="button" id="evaluate" value="Evaluate"
     onClick="eval_eq();" /></td>
<td><input type="Reset" id="Reset" /></td>
</tr>
</table>
</p>
</form>
</body>
</html>
```

Don't worry if this isn't clear to you at this point. Adding scripting to the HTML mix is a fairly advanced concept. It is introduced here for completeness, but more information on scripting can be found in Chapters 16 and 17.

Tip

If you plan to do a lot of scripting in your HTML documents, you will be best served by picking up a dedicated JavaScript book. Although you may learn the basics here, more advanced script usage is outside the scope of this book. ■

FIGURE 11-10

The onClick event enables the button object to perform tasks on other form elements via JavaScript.

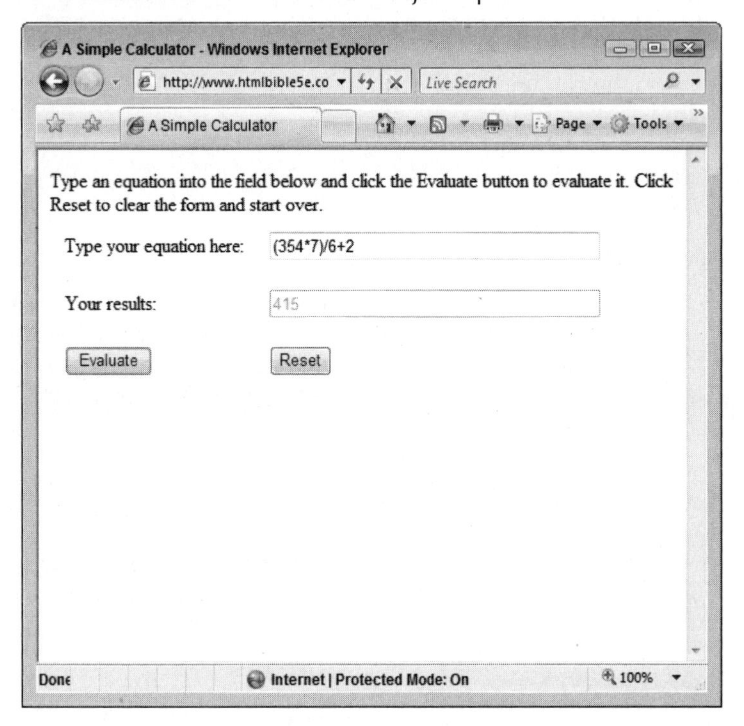

Form Scripts and Script Services

As previously mentioned in the section "Understanding Forms," form data is typically passed to a data handler, a script or program that does something useful with the data.

Form handlers typically do one or more of the following actions with the form data:

- Manipulate or verify the data
- E-mail the data
- Store the data in a file or database
- Process the data and return some result

There are many ways to construct a form handler, but the usual method is by using a server-side programming language to create a script that does what you need to the data. Common form handlers are created in Perl, Python, PHP, or another server-side programming language.

Security is an important issue you should consider when creating form handlers. One of the earliest, most popular form handlers, `formmail.cgi`, was found to have a vulnerability that allowed anyone to send data to the script and have it e-mail the data to whomever the sender wanted. This functionality was an instant hit with e-mail spammers who still use unsecured formmail scripts to send anonymous spam.

Because form-handling scripts can be so diverse (performing different functions, written in different languages), it is hard to give tangible examples here. Use a server-side language you are comfortable with to create a form handler that does exactly what you want.

If you want a generic form handler to simply store or e-mail the data, you can choose from a few routes.

Download a handler

Several sites on the Internet offer generic form handlers. One of my favorites is the CGI Resource Index, http://cgi.resourceindex.com/. This site has several dozen scripts that you can download and use for your form handling. Keep in mind that most scripts require a processing language such as Perl or PHP — ensure your server has such prerequisites before downloading scripts.

Use a script service

Also available are several services that enable you to process your form data through their server and scripts. You may need such a service if you cannot run scripts on your server or you want a generic, no-hassle solution.

A partial list of script services is available at the CGI Resource Index, http://cgi.resourceindex.com/. From the main page, select Remotely Hosted and browse for a service that meets your needs.

Summary

This chapter showed you the particulars of HTML forms. It demonstrated how to include them in your documents and what each form tag can accomplish, and the methods and handlers you might employ to get the most of the data your forms supply.

The next few chapters cover colors, images, and multimedia, and then delve into HTML niche formatting and encoding topics. Chapters 16 and 17 provide basic and then advanced coverage of JavaScript, which can be used for tasks such as automating your forms and documents.

CHAPTER 12

Colors and Images

The Web is not a black-and-white place. In fact, it never has been — the Web and HTML language was born with 16 named colors and blossomed quickly into more than 200 other supported colors. So, although it had its share of growing spurts, unlike most of the other information mediums, the Web didn't have to grow out of a colorless beginning.

This chapter shows how to use colors with fonts, borders, backgrounds, and more. It also covers the image tag, which can be used to insert graphical images into your documents.

IN THIS CHAPTER

Web Color Basics

When the Web was first conceived, most computers were not capable of displaying the multitude of colors possible today. Most computers in that era supported a maximum of 16 colors (via Enhanced Graphics Adapter, or EGA), or a few years later, 256 colors (via Video Graphics Array, or VGA).

To create an initial, standard color palette, the W3C created a color palette of 16 named colors: aqua, black, blue, fuchsia, gray, green, lime, maroon, navy, olive, purple, red, silver, teal, white, and yellow. These color names are still the only color names that will properly validate against HTML 4.

To accommodate colors in elements, several `color` and `bgcolor` attributes were added to the element tags that support color. For example, the following two tags would produce a red background in a document, and text in a white font, respectively:

```
<body bgcolor="red">
<font color="white">
```

Note

It bears mentioning at this point that most of the `color` and `bgcolor` attributes have been deprecated in favor of using styles. As such, you should not use them — they are presented here for completeness and historical context. ■

Other Means to Specify Colors

Besides using assigned names to specify colors, there are several other ways to choose specific colors in your documents, mostly by specifying an exact mix of red, green, and blue that make up the target color.

You can code the mix of colors to create the color you want to use in two main ways: by denoting a hexadecimal number containing the color values to mix, or by using an `rgb()`function, also containing the color values to mix but in decimal format. Either way allows for color values between 0 (no color) and 255 (full color).

The hexadecimal format typically looks as follows:

```
#RRGGBB;
```

The format begins with a pound sign (#), has two hexadecimal digits for each color value, and ends with a semicolon (;). For the values, the smaller the number, the less the presence of the color in the mix. To create purple, for example (which is equal parts red and blue), you could use code similar to the following:

```
#FF00FF;
```

Lighter shades of purple can be accomplished by lowering the values. Conversely, you can create deeper purple shades by increasing the values.

The second function/decimal value method resembles the following:

```
rgb(rrr,ggg,bbb);
```

In this case, the function begins with `rgb` and encapsulates the color values in parentheses in a comma-separated list. This method also ends with a semicolon. In terms of the preceding example, you would use the following code with `rgb` to define purple:

```
rgb(255,0,255);
```

The Evolution of Color on the Web

Within a few years of the Web's creation, it was clear that more colors, not fewer, were in its future. To answer the call for a standard palette with more colors, the W3C created a so-called "Web-safe" palette of 216 colors, shown in Table 12-1.

TABLE 12-1

The Web-Safe Palette

000000	#000033	#000066	#000099	#0000CC	#0000FF
003300	#003333	#003366	#003399	#0033CC	#0033FF
006600	#006633	#006666	#006699	#0066CC	#0066FF
009900	#009933	#009966	#009999	#0099CC	#0099FF
00CC00	#00CC33	#00CC66	#00CC99	#00CCCC	#00CCFF
00FF00	#00FF33	#00FF66	#00FF99	#00FFCC	#00FFFF
330000	#330033	#330066	#330099	#3300CC	#3300FF
333300	#333333	#333366	#333399	#3333CC	#3333FF
336600	#336633	#336666	#336699	#3366CC	#3366FF
339900	#339933	#339966	#339999	#3399CC	#3399FF
33CC00	#33CC33	#33CC66	#33CC99	#33CCCC	#33CCFF
33FF00	#33FF33	#33FF66	#33FF99	#33FFCC	#33FFFF
660000	#660033	#660066	#660099	#6600CC	#6600FF
663300	#663333	#663366	#663399	#6633CC	#6633FF
666600	#666633	#666666	#666699	#6666CC	#6666FF
669900	#669933	#669966	#669999	#6699CC	#6699FF
66CC00	#66CC33	#66CC66	#66CC99	#66CCCC	#66CCFF
66FF00	#66FF33	#66FF66	#66FF99	#66FFCC	#66FFFF
990000	#990033	#990066	#990099	#9900CC	#9900FF
993300	#993333	#993366	#993399	#9933CC	#9933FF
996600	#996633	#996666	#996699	#9966CC	#9966FF
999900	#999933	#999966	#999999	#9999CC	#9999FF

continued

TABLE 12-1 *(continued)*

99CC00	#99CC33	#99CC66	#99CC99	#99CCCC	#99CCFF
99FF00	#99FF33	#99FF66	#99FF99	#99FFCC	#99FFFF
CC0000	#CC0033	#CC0066	#CC0099	#CC00CC	CC00FF
CC3300	#CC3333	#CC3366	#CC3399	#CC33CC	#CC33FF
CC6600	#CC6633	#CC6666	#CC6699	#CC66CC	#CC66FF
CC9900	#CC9933	#CC9966	#CC9999	#CC99CC	#CC99FF
CCCC00	#CCCC33	#CCCC66	#CCCC99	#CCCCCC	#CCCCFF
CCFF00	#CCFF33	#CCFF66	#CCFF99	#CCFFCC	#CCFFFF
FF0000	#FF0033	#FF0066	#FF0099	#FF00CC	#FF00FF
FF3300	#FF3333	#FF3366	#FF3399	#FF33CC	#FF33FF
FF6600	#FF6633	#FF6666	#FF6699	#FF66CC	#FF66FF
FF9900	#FF9933	#FF9966	#FF9999	#FF99CC	#FF99FF
FFCC00	#FFCC33	#FFCC66	#FFCC99	#FFCCCC	#FFCCFF
FFFF00	#FFFF33	#FFFF66	#FFFF99	#FFFFCC	#FFFFFF

This palette was chosen because it represented the 216 colors that were common between the PC and MAC platforms — each having its own set of 40 or so reserved colors different from the other platform.

In today's computing environments, most user agents on most platforms are capable of producing or approximating several million colors. However, you should still be aware of your audience and their ability to see a particular color before designing your page to use that color prominently.

In addition to the original 16 named colors, a palette of 150 additional named colors should be recognized by most browsers. Keep in mind, however, that using the names of the colors in this palette will cause your documents not to validate against the HTML 4 standard. If you need your document to validate, stick with the names in the 16-color palette or use the hex codes shown next to the names in Table 12-2.

Tip

Most image-editing programs include a hexadecimal value field in their color picker or palette dialog. Using that feature you can easily sample colors from graphics, obtain their hexadecimal value, and include that value in your styles and other color codes within your HTML documents. ■

TABLE 12-2

Extended Named Color Palette

Name	Hex Value	Name	Hex Value
AliceBlue	#F0F8FF	DarkMagenta	#8B008B
AntiqueWhite	#FAEBD7	DarkOliveGreen	#556B2F
Aqua	#00FFFF	DarkOrange	#FF8 C00
Aquamarine	#7FFFD4	DarkOrchid	#9932CC
Azure	#F0FFFF	DarkRed	#8B0000
Beige	#F5F5DC	DarkSalmon	#E9967A
Bisque	#FFE4 C4	DarkSeaGreen	#8FBC8F
Black	#000000	DarkSlateBlue	#483D8B
BlanchedAlmond	#FFEBCD	DarkSlateGray	#2F4F4F
Blue	#0000FF	DarkSlateGrey	#2F4F4F
BlueViolet	#8A2BE2	DarkTurquoise	#00CED1
Brown	#A52A2A	DarkViolet	#9400D3
BurlyWood	#DEB887	DeepPink	#FF1493
CadetBlue	#5F9EA0	DeepSkyBlue	#00BFFF
Chartreuse	#7FFF00	DimGray	#696969
Chocolate	#D2691E	DimGrey	#696969
Coral	#FF7F50	DodgerBlue	#1E90FF
CornflowerBlue	#6495ED	FireBrick	#B22222
Cornsilk	#FFF8DC	FloralWhite	#FFFAF0
Crimson	#DC143C	ForestGreen	#228B22
Cyan	#00FFFF	Fuchsia	#FF00FF
DarkBlue	#00008B	Gainsboro	#DCDCDC
DarkCyan	#008B8B	GhostWhite	#F8F8FF
DarkGoldenRod	#B8860B	Gold	#FFD700
DarkGray	#A9A9A9	GoldenRod	#DAA520
DarkGrey	#A9A9A9	Gray	#808080
DarkGreen	#006400	Grey	#808080
DarkKhaki	#BDB76B	Green	#008000

continued

TABLE 12-2 *(continued)*

Name	Hex Value	Name	Hex Value
GreenYellow	#ADFF2F	Maroon	#800000
HoneyDew	#F0FFF0	MediumAquaMarine	#66CDAA
HotPink	#FF69B4	MediumBlue	#0000CD
IndianRed	#CD5C5C	MediumOrchid	#BA55D3
Indigo	#4B0082	MediumPurple	#9370D8
Ivory	#FFFFF0	MediumSeaGreen	#3CB371
Khaki	#F0E68C	MediumSlateBlue	#7B68EE
Lavender	#E6E6FA	MediumSpringGreen	#00FA9A
LavenderBlush	#FFF0F5	MediumTurquoise	#48D1CC
LawnGreen	#7CFC00	MediumVioletRed	#C71585
LemonChiffon	#FFFACD	MidnightBlue	#191970
LightBlue	#ADD8E6	MintCream	#F5FFFA
LightCoral	#F08080	MistyRose	#FFE4E1
LightCyan	#E0FFFF	Moccasin	#FFE4B5
LightGoldenRodYellow	#FAFAD2	NavajoWhite	#FFDEAD
LightGray	#D3D3D3	Navy	#000080
LightGrey	#D3D3D3	OldLace	#FDF5E6
LightGreen	#90EE90	Olive	#808000
LightPink	#FFB6C1	OliveDrab	#6B8E23
LightSalmon	#FFA07A	Orange	#FFA500
LightSeaGreen	#20B2AA	OrangeRed	#FF4500
LightSkyBlue	#87CEFA	Orchid	#DA70D6
LightSlateGray	#778899	PaleGoldenRod	#EEE8AA
LightSlateGrey	#778899	PaleGreen	#98FB98
LightSteelBlue	#B0C4DE	PaleTurquoise	#AFEEEE
LightYellow	#FFFFE0	PaleVioletRed	#D87093
Lime	#00FF00	PapayaWhip	#FFEFD5
LimeGreen	#32CD32	PeachPuff	#FFDAB9
Linen	#FAF0E6	Peru	#CD853F
Magenta	#FF00FF	Pink	#FFC0CB

Name	Hex Value	Name	Hex Value
Plum	#DDA0DD	SlateGrey	#708090
PowderBlue	#B0E0E6	Snow	#FFFAFA
Purple	#800080	SpringGreen	#00FF7F
Red	#FF0000	SteelBlue	#4682B4
RosyBrown	#BC8F8F	Tan	#D2B48C
RoyalBlue	#4169E1	Teal	#008080
SaddleBrown	#8B4513	Thistle	#D8BFD8
Salmon	#FA8072	Tomato	#FF6347
SandyBrown	#F4A460	Turquoise	#40E0D0
SeaGreen	#2E8B57	Violet	#EE82EE
SeaShell	#FFF5EE	Wheat	#F5DEB3
Sienna	#A0522D	White	#FFFFFF
Silver	#C0C0C0	WhiteSmoke	#F5F5F5
SkyBlue	#87CEEB	Yellow	#FFFF00
SlateBlue	#6A5ACD	YellowGreen	#9ACD32
SlateGray	#6A5ACD		

Using Proper Means to Specify Colors

As previously mentioned, the old HTML tag attributes of `color` and `bgcolor` have been deprecated. If you use them, your documents will not validate against the HTML 4 standard, and you run the risk that modern user agents will not interpret the attributes correctly.

Instead, you should use styles.

Many different color style properties can be applied to almost any element in HTML. Of course, not all elements support color changes, but you might be surprised to learn how many do.

The most common style properties to change an element's color are `color` and `background-color`. These two properties do what you would expect: change the foreground color of an element and change the background color of an element, respectively.

As an example, the following tag would cause the text within the paragraph to be rendered in yellow:

```
<p style="color: yellow;">
```

FIGURE 12-1

Changing an element's color or background affects the element and possibly its children, but not its parent.

The following tag would cause the entire document to have a green background:

```
<body style="background-color: green;">
```

Many other properties also have color components — that is, arguments that can be used to affect the color of elements to which the property is applied. These include the following:

- `background`
- `border`
- `border-color`
- `border-top, right, bottom, left`
- `border-top, right, bottom, left-color`
- `outline`
- `outline-color`
- `text-shadow`

Each of these properties affects the elements to which it is applied in a slightly different manner. Using the `color` attribute of the `text-shadow` property, for example, affects only the color of the text shadow, not the element itself, despite how the `color` attribute might work elsewhere.

Cross-Ref

More information on using styles to influence backgrounds and colors can be found in Chapter 33. ■

Also, keep in mind that using a color property on one element nested within another will change only the color of the nested element, and perhaps elements nested within it (its children). For example, the table shown in Figure 12-1 has the following style added to its opening tag:

```
style="background-color: yellow;"
```

As you can see, the background of the table has been changed. However, the document background remains unaffected.

Image Formats for the Web

Most user agents support, to some degree, three graphics file formats: GIF, JPEG, and PNG. The GIF and JPEG formats have been supported for quite some time (since the origin of the Web), whereas PNG is relatively new. This section covers the basics of these image formats.

Image compression

All three of these graphics file formats use some form of compression to store your image. Why is compression important? Uncompressed images can be large — consider Table 12-3, which compares image dimensions, number of colors, and file size for some sample, uncompressed images.

TABLE 12-3

Uncompressed Image File Size Comparison by Dimensions and Number of Colors

Dimensions (in Inches)	Colors	File Size
1 × 1	2	9K
1 × 1	256	9K
1 × 1	16.7 million	18K
2 × 2	2	16K
2 × 2	256	24K
2 × 2	16.7 million	63K
3 × 3	2	16K
3 × 3	256	49K
3 × 3	16.7 million	139K

As you can see, with file sizes like this, you would have to limit yourself to mighty tiny images, or two-color, black-and-white images. Or, you could compress the files.

Note

With the predominance of broadband in the workplace and in homes worldwide, keeping documents and images small has become an afterthought for designers, not a primary concern. However, the number of graphics on a page has also increased, in some cases exponentially. The net result is the same: bulky, graphical Web documents that can make browsing the Web a tedious prospect.

When designing pages, you should also consider the new wave of user agents — deployed on handheld devices such as cell phones. These devices do not possess speedy processors and blazing fast connections. If you don't keep your pages slim, or offer specialized content for such devices, you risk alienating this relatively new, but growing, audience.

Although it might seem "old school," consider using text instead of graphics wherever possible. ■

Compression options

When you implement file compression, you either have to throw away some information about the image or find a way to store the existing information about the image in a more intelligent manner. GIF files throw away some color information. JPEG files throw away some information about the image itself. PNG files store the information using a more intelligent algorithm.

GIF

GIF was the earliest format in use in inline images on the Web. Version 1 browsers could open GIF images inline, but required that JPEG images be opened out-of-line. GIF uses a compression scheme — called *LZW compression* — that predates CompuServe, even though you might see it called CompuServe GIF. CompuServe implemented LZW compression thinking it was in the public sphere and then found out it was proprietary. A lot of lawyers sorted it out.

How does GIF work? Simply put, GIF indexes images to an 8-bit palette. The system palette is 256 colors. Before you can save your file in GIF format, the utility you are using simply makes its best guess at mapping all your colors to one of the 256 colors in an 8-bit palette.

Is a reduction in color depth a problem? That depends. GIF uses dithering to achieve colors between two colors on the palette. Even with dithering, however, GIF images of a sunset have stripes of color where a smooth gradation would be more natural. GIF images also tend to have more cartoonish colors because flesh tones aren't part of the palette. A GIF image of a drawing of something like a checkerboard, however, will look just fine.

One distinct advantage the GIF format offers is transparency. This feature enables part of the feature to appear transparent when rendered, revealing the elements below the figure through the transparent areas of the figure. As a result, the figure can be more seamlessly incorporated into the page's design because there is no obvious rectangular area encapsulating the figure.

Note
Transparency in images is covered in the section, "Using transparency" later in this chapter. ■

JPEG

JPEG takes a different approach than that of the GIF format. JPEG stands for the *Joint Photographic Experts Group*, the name of the group that created the standard. With JPEG, you get to keep all your colors, but you don't get to keep all the data about the image. What kinds of images lend themselves to being compressed with JPEG? Most any image that doesn't require absolute detail works well in a JPEG format. Keep in mind that the loss is typically very minor and unnoticeable to all but those trained in photography or graphic arts. Of course, there are some images for which you should avoid using JPEG, including text, schematic drawings, and any line art.

Note
Most graphics packages give the user the option of choosing the level of compression when saving an image in JPEG format. A good rule of thumb is that the more compression selected, the more detail that is lost in the final image. Therefore, try to save your JPEG images with a compression level of 30 percent or lower, unless absolutely necessary. ■

Every user agent, version 3 and later, can handle inline JPEGs. JPEGs are also ideal for showing gradient-filled graphics (when the color changes gradually from one color to another). The same graphic would suffer enormously under the GIF format because the color depth wouldn't support all the in-between colors.

PNG

The *Portable Network Graphics*, or *PNG* format, was developed exclusively for the Web and is in the public domain. The PNG format takes advantage of a clever way to store information about the image so you don't lose as much color or image quality. As a lossless format, images in PNG format tend to be larger than those in the JPEG format.

The adoption of PNG graphics got off to a rocky start because of slow adoption by user agents and incomplete support for its features, such as levels of transparency. However, the latest crop of desktop browsers fully support the PNG standard and all its advantages. Keep in mind that mobile browsers, kiosks, and older browsers still lack adequate PNG support, if they have it at all.

The PNG format supports a variety of transparency options, but does not have any animation features.

Note
Fireworks, a graphics editing package from Adobe, uses the PNG format for its natively saved files. Fireworks embeds unique metadata in the saved PNG file to keep track of objects and features used in the image, such as tweening. However, the raw image saved by Fireworks should not be used in your Web documents. Use the export feature of Fireworks to save a Web-suitable file with the advanced metadata stripped out. ■

Creating Graphics

If you need to create top-notch graphics, the tool of choice among professionals is Adobe Photoshop, available for the Mac and the PC. Freeware and shareware software programs also are available that perform subsets of the functions performed by Photoshop. Photoshop LE, the "lite" version of Photoshop, ships with many scanners. Photoshop Elements — primarily used for photo editing — ships with many digital cameras.

Essential functions

What should your graphics package be able to do? For existing images, such as photographs, you want to sharpen, blur, and perform some special effects on the image (for example, posterize, swirl, and mosaic). For images you create on the screen, you want to create your own custom palette (so you can send as few colors as you need). You also need some basic artist tools, such as a paintbrush, a pencil, a spray can, and a magnifying glass to enlarge parts of the image to see it better.

Keep in mind that it takes a bit of skill and training to be able to use such features effectively. If your needs or skill level are meager, consider a lower-end, cheaper, less complicated package to begin with. However, be sure to pick a package that supports any graphic images you wish to edit, and one that is able to export to the major Web formats — GIF, JPEG, and PNG.

Tip
If you aren't ready to commit to a $500 software package to get all these great functions, you can work with a number of small, free software packages and services that perform many of the tasks previously listed. On the Web, you can find sites that turn your TIF file into a GIF, or make your GIF an interlaced GIF. The trade-off is the time. Finding, learning, and using a variety of small packages to solve all your imaging needs obviously takes longer than learning one package and using it on your desktop. ■

Capturing Images from Other Sites

As you build your documents you may be tempted to borrow images from other sites. The temptation is common; the Web is rich with content that seems "just perfect for your use."

However, this is not a good practice. In general, unless you clearly own the image in question, you cannot use it for *any* purpose. Using an image from another source requires express (usually written) permission from the image's owner. Moreover, keep in mind that the owner of the image and the owner of the Web page on which it appears may be two different individuals. When it comes down to a suit in copyright court, you would bear the burden of proving you had clear rights to use the image, and to use it in the way you did in your documents.

Instead, create your own images or buy suitably licensed images from one of the stock photography houses, including the following:

- Fotolia (`www.fotolia.com`)
- Getty Images (`www.gettyimages.com`)
- iStockphoto (`www.istockphoto.com/index.php`)

Progressive JPEGs and interlaced GIFs

There was a time on the Web when you had to wait for an image to finish loading before you knew what it was. Today, you can save your files using the progressive JPEG format or the interlaced GIF format and watch the image come into focus as it loads.

The advantage to this approach is that a visitor to your site knows roughly what an image is before the entire image has downloaded. If download times are long because of a poor Internet connection, for example, the site visitor can actually take a link off the page before the image has finished loading without missing anything.

Finally, these two image formats are good because the visitor participates in the download time. Watching the images become clearer as the page downloads gives visitors to the site a sense of reward for waiting.

Note

Specifying the size of the image in the image tag can also speed up the display of your Web pages, as it enables the user agent to reserve space for the image and keep rendering, instead of waiting for the entire image to load before progressing. See the "Sizing an image" section later in this chapter for more information. ■

The sense of "coming into focus" that these types of images provide is the result of the way the images are stored. Progressive JPEGs and interlaced GIFs download only every eighth line at first, then every fourth line, then every second line, and then, finally, the odd-numbered lines. As a result, the image goes from blurry to focused.

You create a progressive JPEG or an interlaced GIF by saving it into this format. In Adobe Photoshop, when you save a file as a GIF, you can choose whether you want the file to be normal or interlaced (see Figure 12-2). Freeware packages that convert your regular JPEGs and GIFs into progressive JPEGs and interlaced GIFs are also available.

FIGURE 12-2

Adobe Photoshop enables you to choose whether you want your GIF to be interlaced or not.

Using transparency

Two of the Web-supported graphics formats, GIF and PNG, support transparency, which enables parts of images to be completely transparent. Typically, transparency is used to soften the edges of images, creating an illusion that the image is not rectangular. For example, Figure 12-3 shows an image with a standard opaque background and the same figure with a transparent background. The image with transparency allows the page background to show through.

Using transparency can open up a document's design, making it more airy and less "blocky." It gives the document a more professional appearance, looking more like a published document than a Web page of the 1980s.

Different graphics editing programs handle transparency differently. Some assign transparency to the background layer; some allow you to pick one color that should be transparent; some programs allow multiple colors to be transparent. Check the Help file for your editor to determine how to accomplish transparency.

FIGURE 12-3

Transparency can soften an image, creating the appearance that the image is not rectangular.

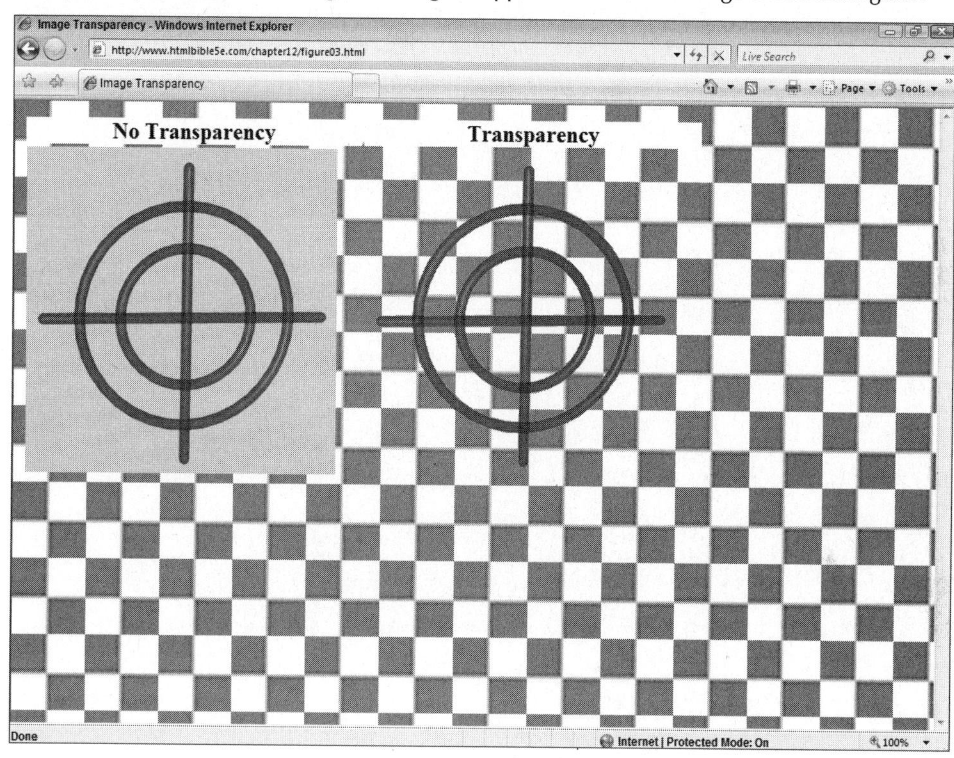

Animated images

The GIF format also supports rudimentary animation by showing different frames of an image one after another. The effect is similar to drawing individual frames of animation on different pages of a sketchbook and rapidly flipping the pages. Animated GIF images are not supported by all user agents and should be used sparingly due to their size — the image must store all the frames of the animation, increasing the size of the image with each new frame.

Some image editors, such as Adobe Fireworks, shown in Figure 12-4, include tools to help create animated GIF images.

FIGURE 12-4

Programs such as Fireworks can help you create animated GIFs, in this case the animation of a spinning CD-ROM.

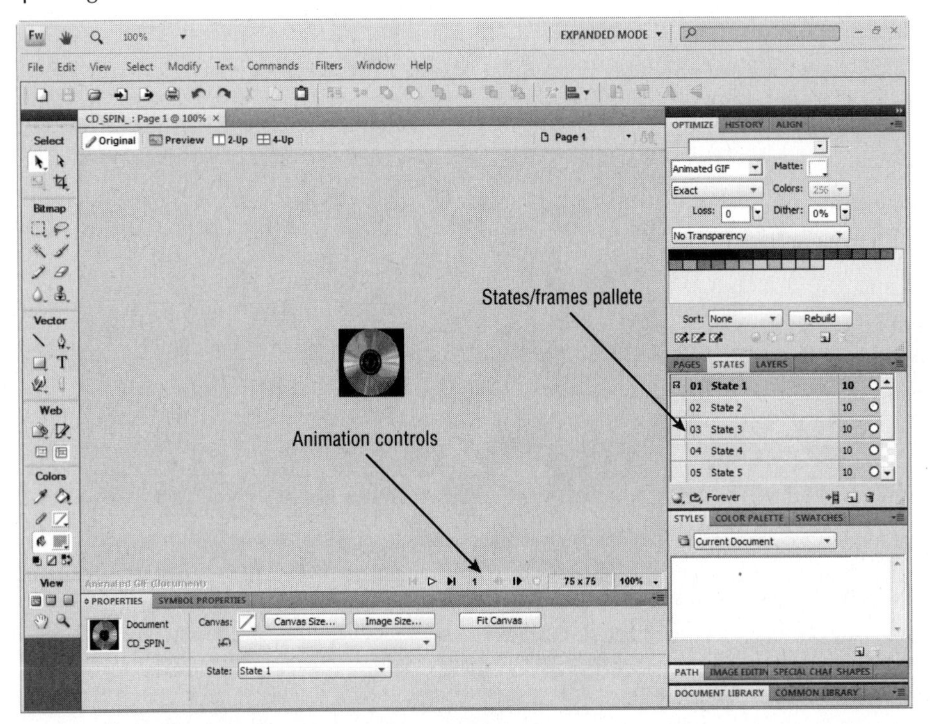

Inserting an Image

Images are inserted into HTML documents using the image tag (`<img>`). This tag, at a minimum, takes two attributes, `alt` and `src`.

The `alt` attribute specifies text that should be displayed in lieu of the image in nongraphical browsers (see the section "Specifying Text to Display for Nongraphical Browsers" later in this chapter). The `src` attribute tells the user agent what image file should be displayed. For example, if you wanted to include the graphic `gunsight.jpg` in your document, you could use code similar to the following:

```
<img alt="A gunsight" src="gunsight.jpg" />
```

The `<img>` tag has no closing tag. As such, you should include the slash at the end of the tag itself.

Cross-Ref

For more information about absolute and relative URLs, see Chapter 8. ■

The `src` attribute's value can be any valid URL of an image on the Web — local or remote. Just as with the anchor tag, you can use absolute or relative URLs to specify the location of the image to display. The reasons for using either URL are the same as the reasons for using absolute or relative URLs in anchor tags.

Note

The src attribute of an image tag can also be a server-side program that produces a graphic. For example, some chart-producing PHP libraries work by calling the PHP script directly from an image tag, similar to:

```
<img alt="A pie chart" src="piechart.php" />
```

This allows dynamic means to produce graphics without first having to store the dynamic graphic on the server. Note that the graphic producing script or program must supply the full header and graphic for the user agent to properly render the graphic. ■

Image Alignment

Most user agents will attempt to display the image exactly where the `<img>` tag is inserted in the document. For example, consider the following HTML code and the resulting display shown in Figure 12-5:

```
<!DOCTYPE HTML PUBLIC "-//W3C//DTD HTML 4.01//EN"
   "http://www.w3.org/TR/html4/strict.dtd">
<html>
<head>
   <title>Default Image Placement</title>
</head>
<body >
<p><img src="images/smsight.gif" height="100px" width="100px"
alt="OTG Logo" />Rodent Studios has recently announced that their
highly anticipated game, "Gopher Hunt," will miss the Christmas
season and is now slated for release in early 2008. Gopher Hunt is
the semi-sequel to "Badger Brigade," Rodent Studios smash hit of
last year.<img src="images/smsight.gif" height="100px" width="100px"
alt="OTG Logo" /></p>
<p>Company president Samuel Perry could not be reached for comment,
but all release dates for the game have been removed from the
company website. As you may recall, "Badger Brigade" is one of the
few titles to which On Target Games awarded 5-stars to and the only
game to stay on the best seller list for a whopping 24 week.</p>
<p>We hope this slip isn't a sign of bigger problem at RS, but will
keep you in the loop.</p>
</body>
</html>
```

If the user agent cannot fit the image on the current line, it will wrap it to the next line and follow the paragraph's alignment and formatting.

Note how the default formatting (at least for Internet Explorer) of the image is to be aligned with the baseline of neighboring text. This isn't always ideal. Sometimes you will want to specify the image's alignment as it relates to the text and other objects around it. Image alignment can be controlled by using the `align` attribute with the `<img>` tag. The `align` attribute can be set to the values shown in Table 12-4.

Figure 12-6 shows an example of each of these alignment options.

FIGURE 12-5

The browser displays the image at the beginning and the end of the paragraph where the image tags are located.

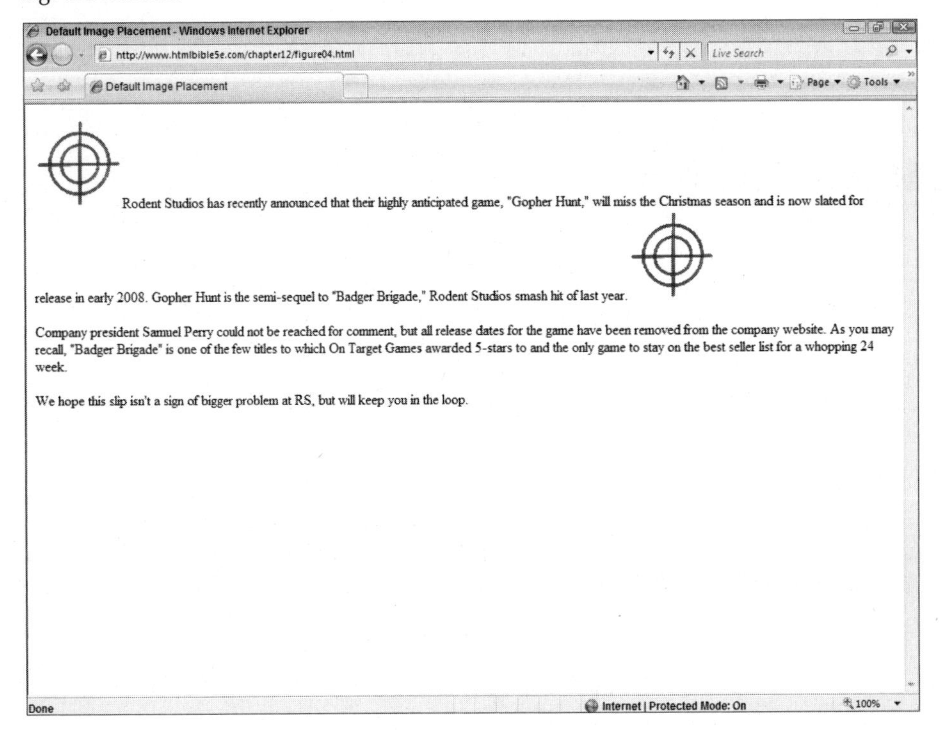

Note

Most user agents render items in the order in which they appear in the document. If you are using left-aligned images, they should appear *before* the text that they should be positioned to the left of. ■

However, the `align` attribute has been deprecated in favor of using styles for image alignment. The following CSS properties can be used to help align images:

- `text-align` — Used in surrounding text, this property aligns the text around an image (versus aligning the image itself). See Chapter 8 for more information on using the `text-align` property.
- `float` — Floats the image to the right or left of the user agent. The `float` property allows text and other objects to wrap next to the image.
- `vertical-align` — Aligns the image vertically with neighboring text or objects.

TABLE 12-4

Align Attribute Values

Value	Definition
`top`	Align with the top of nearby text or object
`bottom`	Align with the bottom of nearby text or object
`middle`	Align with the middle of nearby text or object
`left`	Align to the left of nearby text or object
`right`	Align to the right of nearby text or object

FIGURE 12-6

The various alignment options for images

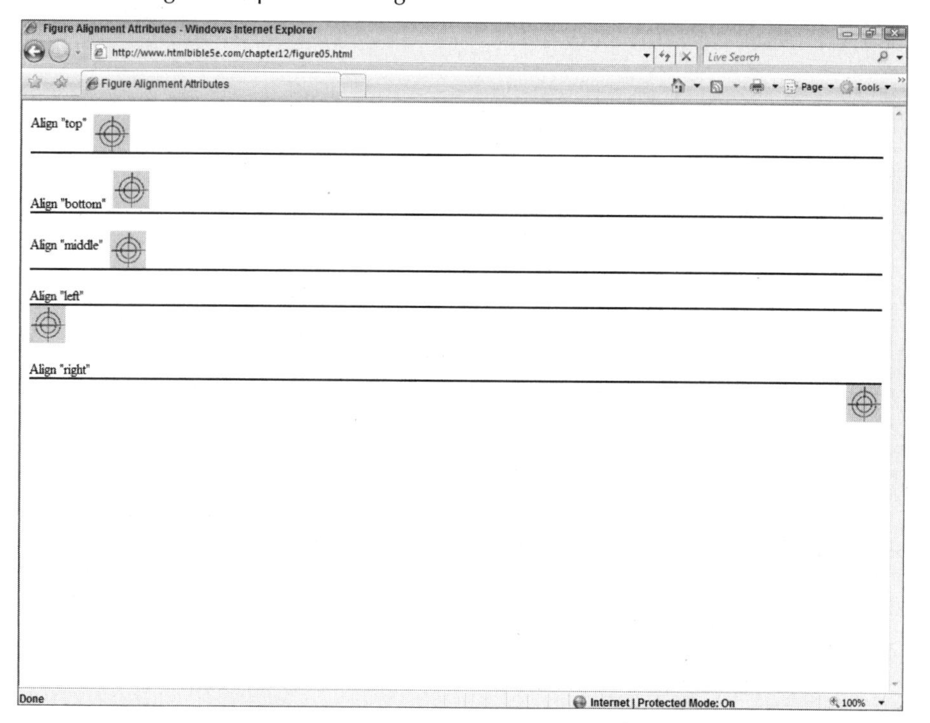

Note that with the `align left` and `align right` attributes, the image is placed after the first line of its containing block, unless the image is placed first in the block. This is evident by the position of the bottom border of the paragraph tag relative to the image. However, this is not consistent behavior across browsers and shouldn't be relied upon. Also, some user agents need to process the image alignment prior to the text around it. If you are using CSS to position your images, it is usually best to position them before neighboring text in your HTML document.

Specifying Text to Display for Nongraphical Browsers

As mentioned repeatedly in this book, it is important not to get caught up in the graphical nature of the Web, and forget that not all user agents support graphics to the extent that the Web designer would like. You should use the image tag's `alt` attribute to specify text that should be displayed when the image cannot. For example, consider the following text and the display shown in Figure 12-7:

```
<p><img src="images/smsight.gif" height="100px" width="100px"
alt="OTG Logo" style="float: right;"/>Rodent Studios has recently
announced that their highly anticipated game, "Gopher Hunt," will
miss the Christmas season and is now slated for release in early
2008. Gopher Hunt is the semi-sequel to "Badger Brigade," Rodent
Studios smash hit of last year.</p>
```

FIGURE 12-7

The alt attribute specifies text to use (in this case, ''TG Logo'') when the image cannot be displayed.

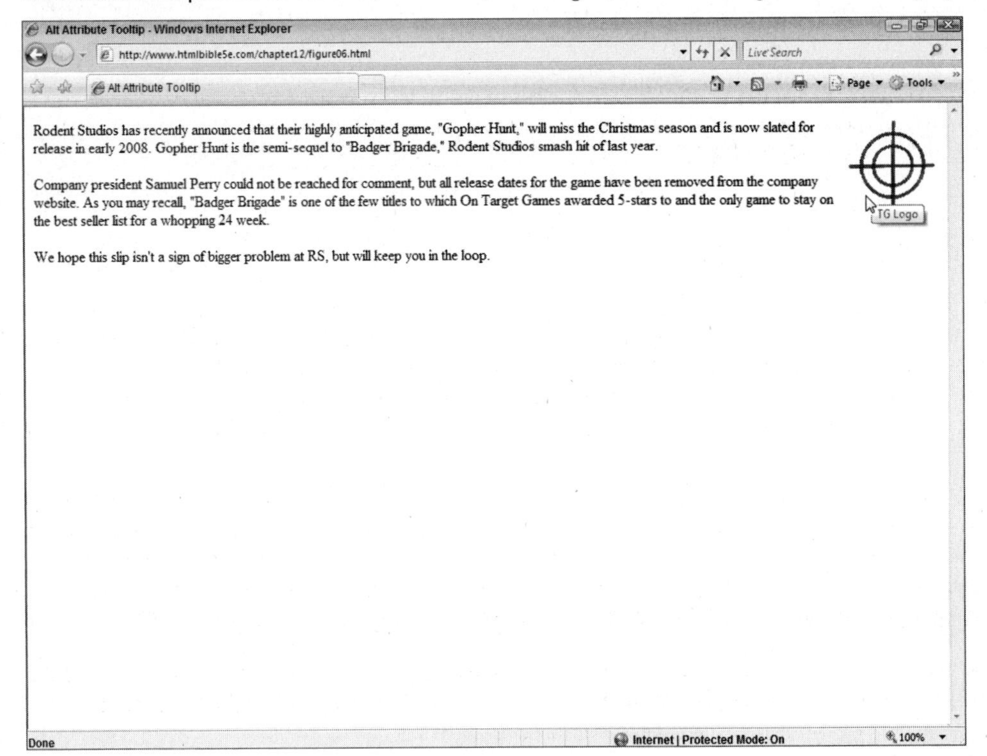

Some user agents display the alt attribute text when the user mouses over the image. This enables you to use the alt attribute to include additional information about an image. If you have a lot of information to convey, consider using the longdesc (long description) attribute, as well. The longdesc attribute specifies a URL to a document that is to be used as the long description for the figure. Remember that it is up to the user agent to decide how to enable access to the long description, if at all.

Sizing an Image

You can specify the size of an image by using the height and width attributes of the image tag. These attributes accept pixel and percentage values, enabling you to specify the exact size of an image or a size relative to the current size of the image's containing object.

Tip

Get in the habit of always using the width and height attributes with your <img> tags. These attributes enable the user agent to reserve the correct amount of space for the image while it continues to render the rest of the document. Without these attributes, the user agent must wait for the image to be loaded before continuing to load the rest of the document. ■

For example, suppose you have a large, high-resolution image but want to display a smaller version. Using the pixel values of the sizing attributes, you can specify a custom size of the larger image. Consider the following code and the resulting display in Figure 12-8:

```
<!-- Full image is 200px square -->
<p>Full Size Image<img alt="Full size image"
  src="images/mdsight.gif" width="200px" height="200px" /></p>
<p>Half Size Image<img alt="Half-size image"
  src="images/mdsight.gif" width="100px" height="100px" /></p>
```

Note

It is important to use both the correct height and width when specifying image dimensions in an <img> tag. If you change the proportions of the figure (by specifying a wrong width or height), you will end up with a funhouse mirror effect — the image will be stretched or shrunk in one dimension. While this can be used for effect, it is usually accidental. In addition, although pixel values are the default, it is good practice to always be specific in your measurements — that is, always include the px when you specify pixel values. ■

You might think that using percentage values in the width and height attributes would be an easier way to scale an image to a percentage of its size. Unfortunately, using percentage values isn't quite that intuitive — the result is an image that is the specified percentage of the available space. For example, for an image in an unconstrained paragraph (user agent screen width), using a width of 50 percent would be scaled to 50 percent of the screen's width.

You can specify only one of the dimensions and have the user agent automatically figure out the other. However, the user agent must then wait for the entire image to load before rendering the rest of the page, so it is best to specify both dimensions.

FIGURE 12-8

Using height and width values, you can display an image at any size other than its normal size, although it is better to use a properly sized image.

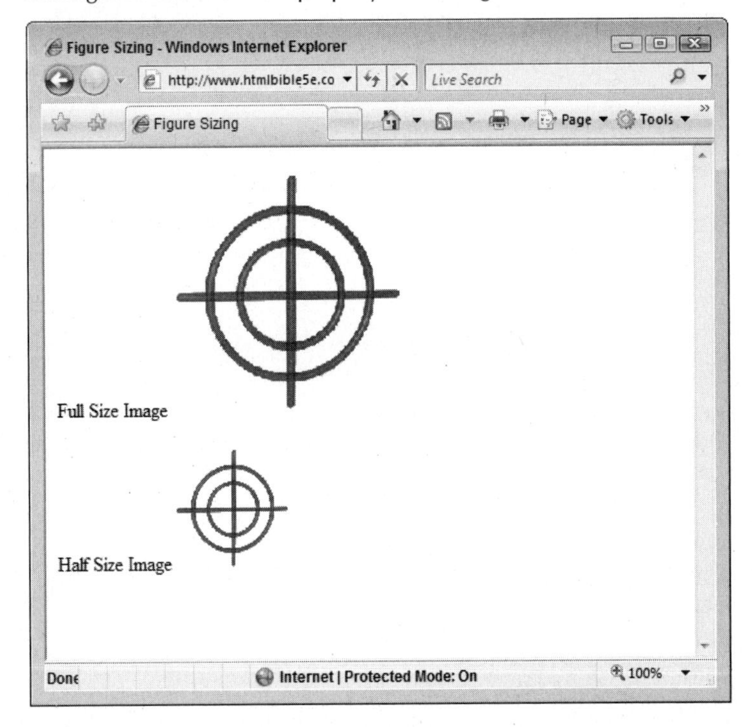

Image size attributes should not be used as a substitute for an appropriately sized graphic. If you need a different sized image, create the appropriate size in an image editor and use the new image instead. Although you can use the width and height attributes to display an image smaller than it actually is, the user agent must still download the entire image and then scale the image accordingly.

Image Borders

You can use CSS styles to create borders around images. Previous versions of HTML supported a `border` attribute for the `<img>` tag, which worked similarly to the table tag's `border` attribute. However, this attribute has been deprecated for use with the image tag. Instead, use styles. CSS supports quite a few border properties, including the following:

- All-inclusive (color, style, width) attribute setting properties:
  - `border`
  - `border-top`
  - `border-right`

    - border-bottom
    - border-left
- Color-setting properties:
    - border-color
    - border-top-color
    - border-right-color
    - border-bottom-color
    - border-left-color
- Style-setting (type of line used for border) properties:
    - border-style
    - border-top-style
    - border-right-style
    - border-bottom-style
    - border-left-style
- Width-setting properties:
    - border-width
    - border-top-width
    - border-right-width
    - border-bottom-width
    - border-left-width

Cross-Ref

More information on CSS borders can be found in Chapter 32. ■

For example, to define a 4-pixel-wide border around an entire image, you can use the following code:

```
<img alt="A gunsight" src="sight.jpg"
style="border: 4px solid black;" width="50px" height="50px" />
```

To define a border on just the left and right sides of an image, you would use the following:

```
<img alt="A gunsight" src="sight.jpg"
style="border-left: 4px solid black;
border-right: 4px solid black;"
width="50px" height="50px" />
```

To simplify defining a different border on one side of an image, use the `border` property first to define a border on all sides and then the appropriate `border-`*side* property for the side that is the exception, overriding the previous setting for that side. For example, to create a border on all sides of an image except the right, you could specify `border-top`, `border-bottom`, `border-left`, and `border-right` properties individually. Or, you could use just `border` and `border-right`:

```
<img alt="A gunsight" src="sight.jpg"
style="border: 4px solid black;
border-right: none;" width="50px" height="50px" />
```

Note

An image placed inside an anchor tag will display with a border that is the color of the appropriate link status. (See Chapter 8 for more information on links.) The border is designed to highlight the image as a link, but can have undesired effects on the design of your pages. If you wish to remove the border, use styles to specify no border for the image tag (that is, `border: none`). ■

Image Maps

Image maps provide a way to map certain areas of an image to actions. For example, a company might want to provide a map of the United States on its website that enables customers to click a state to find a local office or store.

There are two types of image maps, *client-side* and *server-side*. Client-side image maps rely on the user agent to process the image, the area where the user clicks, and the expected action. Server-side image maps rely on the user agent only to tell the server where the user clicked; all processing is done by an agent on the Web server.

Between the two methods, client-side image maps are generally preferred, as they enable the user agent to offer immediate feedback to the user (like being over a clickable area) and they are supported by most user agents. Server-side agents can bog down a server if the map draws consistent traffic, hides many details necessary to provide immediate feedback to the user, and might not be compatible with some user agents.

Tip

If you want an image to be clickable and take the user to one particular destination, you don't have to use an image map. Instead, embed the image tag (`<img>`)in an appropriate anchor tag (`<a>`) similar to the following:

```
<a href="catpage.html"><img alt="Link to home page"
  src="sight.jpg" /></a> ■
```

Specifying an image map

A client-side image map is generally specified within the contents of a `map` tag and linked to an appropriate `img` tag with the `<img>` tag's `usemap` attribute. For example, to specify a map for an image, `shapes.jpg`, you could use this code:

```
<img alt="Pick a Shape" src="shapes.jpg"
  usemap="#map1" />
<map name="map1">
........
</map>
```

Inside the `<map>` tags you specify the various clickable regions of the image, as covered in the next section.

Specifying clickable regions

To specify an image map, a list of polygonal regions must be defined on an image and referenced in the HTML document. Three different types of polygons are supported: rectangle, circle, and free-form polygon.

- `rect` — Defines a rectangular area by specifying the coordinates of the upper-left and lower-right corners of the rectangle.
- `circle` — Defines a circular area by specifying the coordinates of the center of the circle and the circle's radius.
- `poly` — Defines a free-form polygon area by specifying the coordinates of each point of the polygon.

Note that all coordinates of the image map are relative to the top-left corner of the image (effectively 0, 0) and are measured in pixels. For example, consider the image shown in Figure 12-9, depicting a polygon (star), circle, and rectangle. Figure 12-10 shows the same image but with callouts — the numbered callouts indicate the coordinates necessary to map each shape.

FIGURE 12-9

An image ready to be used as an image map

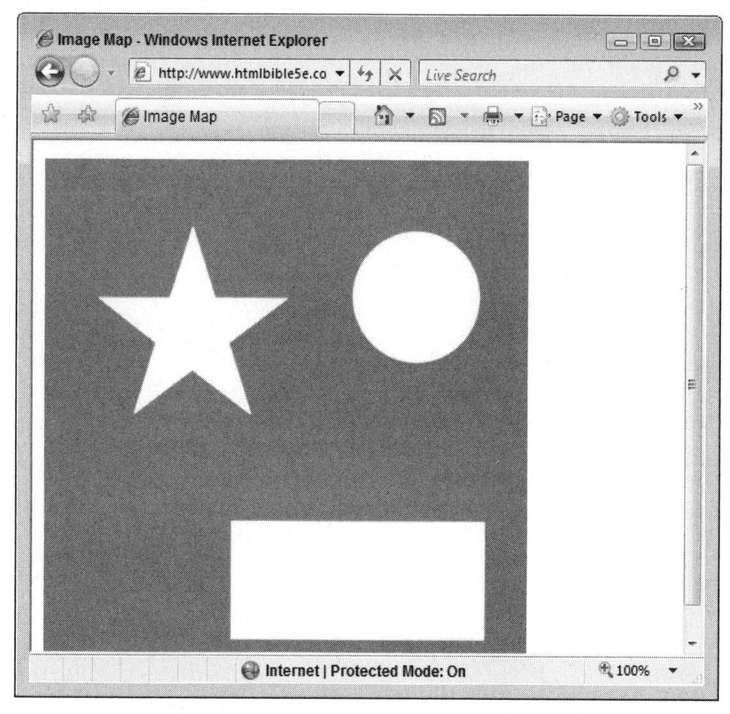

FIGURE 12-10

The points for which coordinates need to be entered for each shape

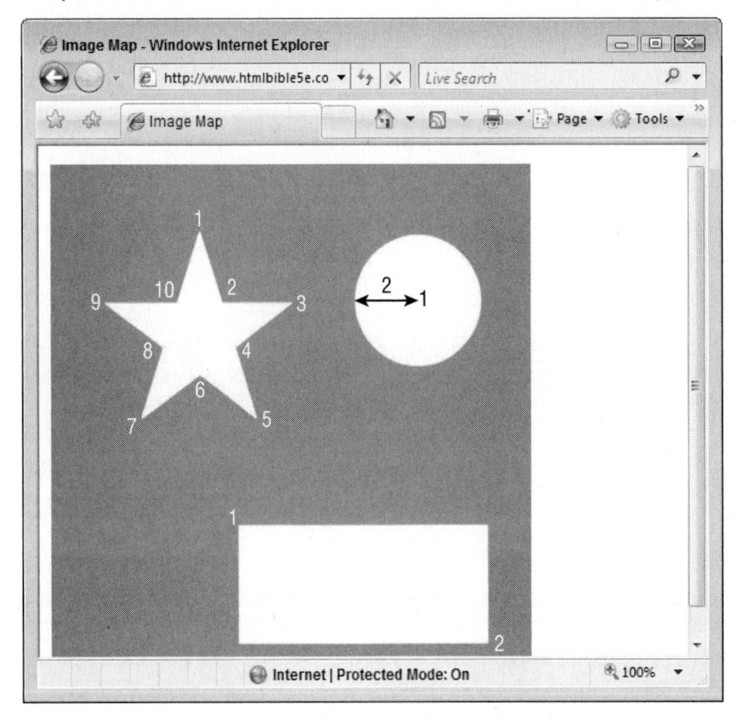

The regions that will be used for image mapping are the white areas. The coordinates that are necessary for each area are as follows:

- Polygon: 123, 54, 142, 110, 201, 111, 154, 147, 171, 203, 123, 169, 75, 204, 91, 147, 45, 110, 104, 109
- Circle: 307, 109, 53
- Rectangle: 156, 289, 364, 384

Tip

Several tools are available to help create image map coordinates. Use your favorite search engine to find a dedicated piece of software to map regions, or check your graphics program to see if it can create regions for you. ■

In a pinch, you might be able to use your graphics program's status bar. Most graphics programs display the current position of the mouse cursor in their status bar — simply point at the area of the graphic for which you need coordinates and then transpose the numbers in the status bar into your HTML code.

Specifying regions using anchor tags

You can specify regions using anchor tags with `shape` and `coords` attributes. For example, to specify the three regions previously outlined, you could use the following:

```
<map name="map1">
<a href="polygon.html" shape="poly" coords="123,54,142,
110,201,111,154,147,171,203,123,169,75,204,91,147,45,110,
104,109">Polygon Link</a>
<a href="circle.html" shape="circle" coords="307,109,53">
Circle Link</a>
<a href="rectangle.html" shape="rect" coords="156,289,364,384">
Rectangle Link</a>
</map>
```

Note that the link text helps the user determine where the clickable area links to. The user agent will typically provide a tooltip or other visual clue using the text.

Specifying regions using area tags

You can also define regions with the area (`<area>`)tags instead of anchors:

```
<map name="map1">
<area href="polygon.html"
  shape="poly" coords="123,54,142,110,201,
  111,154,147,171,203,123,169,75,204,91,147,45,110,104,109"
  alt="Polygon Link" />
<area href="circle.html"
  shape="circle" coords="307,109,53"
  alt="Circle Link" />
<area href="rectangle.html"
  shape="rect" coords="156,289,364,384"
  alt="Rectangle Link" />
</map>
```

In the case of the `<area>` tag, using the `alt` attribute helps the user determine what the clickable area leads to, usually via a tooltip when the user mouses over the area.

Putting it all together

Code for a document with a working image map (as outlined in this section) would resemble the following:

```
<!DOCTYPE HTML PUBLIC "-//W3C//DTD HTML 4.01//EN"
   "http://www.w3.org/TR/html4/strict.dtd">
<html>
<head>
  <title>Pick a Shape</title>
</head>
```

```
<body>
<img alt="Pick a Shape" src="shape.jpg" usemap="#map1" />
<map name="map1">
<area href="polygon.html"
  shape="poly" coords="123,54,142,110,201,
  111,154,147,171,203,123,169,75,204,91,147,45,110,104,109"
  alt="Polygon Link" />
<area href="circle.html"
  shape="circle" coords="307,109,53"
  alt="Circle Link" />
<area href="rectangle.html"
  shape="rect" coords="156,289,364,384"
  alt="Rectangle Link" />
</map>
</body>
</html>
```

Note

Image maps can be used for more complex purposes, such as the clickable U.S. map mentioned earlier in this chapter, or to enable users to obtain more information, such as clicking various buildings on a map, or individual parts of a complex diagram of a machine. ■

Summary

This chapter explained the basics of image formats. You learned the benefits and drawbacks of each supported image type, as well as how to include and format them in an HTML document, bringing the basics of multimedia to your documents.

The next chapter builds on the multimedia concept by showing you how to bring full animation, movies, Flash animations, and other pieces of multimedia to the table. This part of the book wraps up with a few HTML tidbits (special characters in Chapter 14, and internationalization in Chapter 15), and then covers scripting (Chapters 16 and 17).

CHAPTER

13

Multimedia

In the early days of the Web, the word multimedia caused quite a bit of excitement. Hearing digital sounds over a previously text-only protocol was captivating. Today, the word "multimedia" simultaneously brings users excitement and dismay. The difference in the emotion encountered is driven by how much control the user has over coming in contact with the media — live or on-demand broadcast of TV shows is generally a good thing, whereas a multitude of Flash banners that bring your user agent to a standstill is a bad thing.

But that still begs the question, "What is multimedia?"

Wikipedia (www.wikipedia.org) defines multimedia as "media that uses multiple forms of information content and information proc... such as text, audio, graphics, animation, video, inter... tertain the (user) audience." So, for th... her-wise considered text. This inclu... audio, video, and combinations thereo... eb today qualifies as having multim...

I've gone through this exercise fo...

- To help define what this c...
- To illustrate that multimed... daunting prospect, but a ve... e

The following sections cover the var... specific and general means to incorp...

Animated Images

Animated images are a simple type of multimedia that incorporates visual animation but has no audible component. Animated images are built and displayed by frames — individual images that vary slightly, which, when played back in rapid succession, produce simulated motion. Think of the process like the flip books you might have created when you were younger, drawing images on the pages and flipping them rapidly to produce an animated effect.

Figure 13-1 shows an example of an animated image: six frames of a spinning CD animation.

FIGURE 13-1

An animation of a spinning CD, animated over six frames.

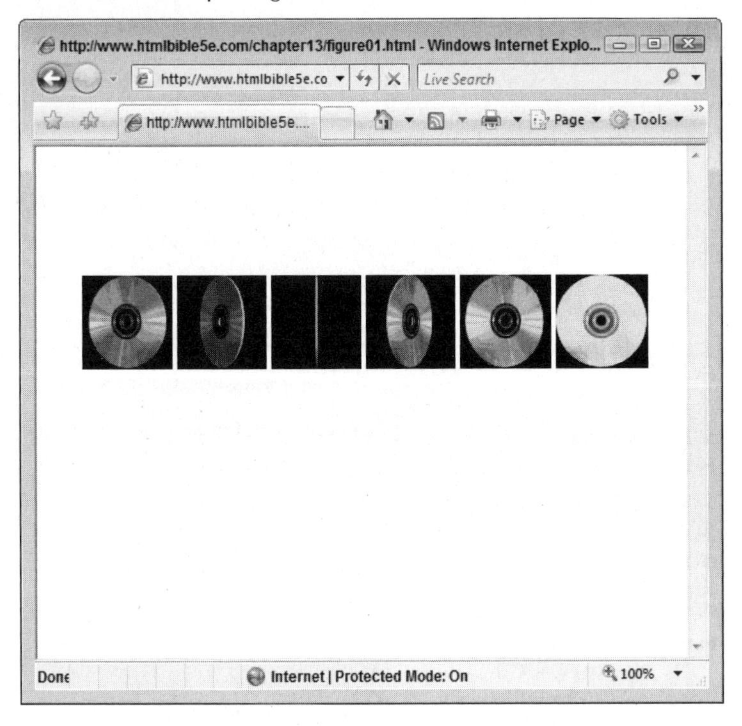

Cross-Ref

Non-animated images and the image tag (`<img>`) are covered in Chapter 12. ■

One downside to animated images is their size. Each frame in the animation increases the size of the image file incrementally. For example, if you have a 75 KB image and animate its contents across ten frames, you would create a 750 KB file (75×10 = 750). With animations, it is easy to get carried away and produce even more frames, which can increase the file to a cumbersome size.

Animated images need to be stored in a Web-friendly format that supports animation. Today, only the GIF format fits this bill. You also need an image editing program capable of creating animated GIF files. Several high-end image editors are capable of creating animated images, and provide tools that aid in the image's creation.

As an example, Adobe Fireworks enables you to build an animation frame by frame (using the Edit ➤ Insert ➤ Frame menu option) and save the result in the animated GIF format. Figure 13-2 shows the spinning CD animation in Adobe Fireworks; notice the animation controls to move from frame to frame, and the frame palette showing the state of each frame and enabling easy access to each one.

FIGURE 13-2

Adobe Fireworks makes building animated images relatively easy.

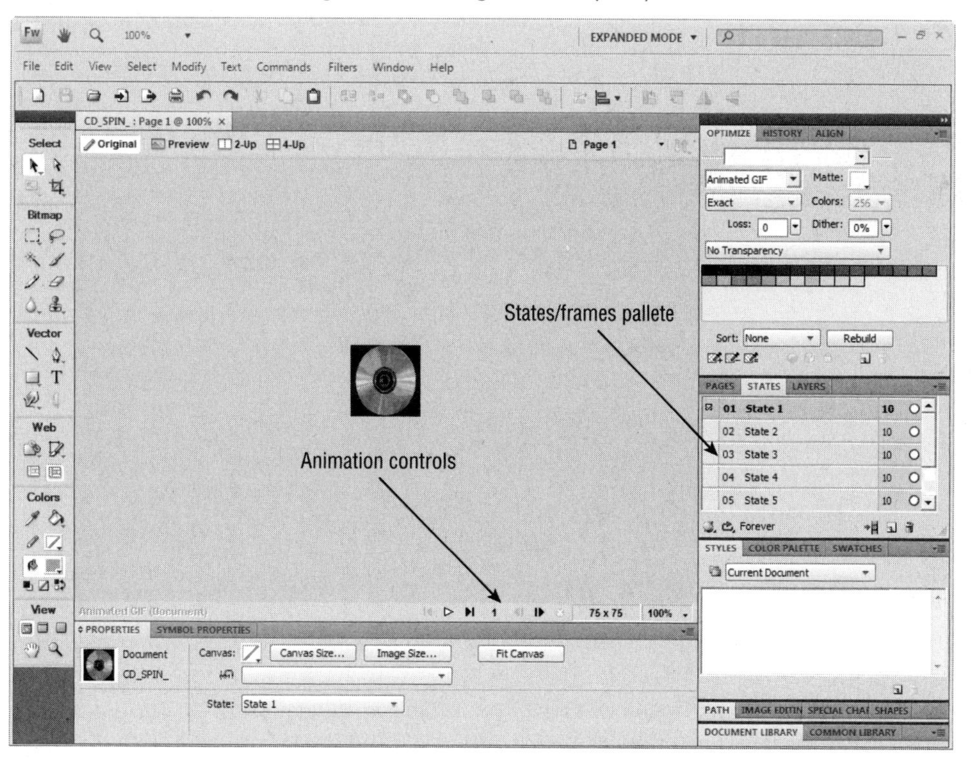

Tip

If you don't want to spend the money for an image editor that includes creating animations, consider using a cheaper image editor to build the frames, and a cheap or even free utility to assemble the frames into an animated GIF file. Search utility sites such as Tucows (`www.tucows.com`) or Winfiles (`www.winfiles.com`) for suitable utilities.

You add an animated image to your documents in the same way you add any other image, using the image tag (`<img>`). Image tag specifics are covered in detail in Chapter 12, but the tag's basic syntax is shown here:

```
<img src="url_to_image" alt="alternative_text"
width="width_of_image" height="height_of_image" />
```

Using the spinning CD image as an example, which is 75 pixels square, you could use the following tag:

```
<img src="cdspin.gif" alt="a spinning cd"
width="75px" height="75px" />
```

You can then use other tags and styles to place the image, control the flow of other objects around it, add ornamentation, and more.

Animation and Video Formats, Plug-ins, and Players

The standard user agents do not natively support animation outside of animated images or video. Instead, they rely on add-on programs, typically known as *plug-ins*, to bring the content to the user. The content is embedded in Web documents via tags with URLs pointing to the actual media, just like other objects and content. However, when the page is decoded and rendered by the user agent, an appropriate plug-in is required to play, view, or otherwise do something useful with the content. The process resembles the diagram shown in Figure 13-3.

The process generally proceeds like this:

1. The user agent encounters an `<object>` tag.
2. The user agent tries to determine the type of media encased in the tag via the MIME type — either specified in the `type` attribute or inferred from the media file's extension (`.avi`, `.mpg`, and so on). If the MIME type cannot be determined, then the user agent won't know what to do with the media and cannot play/display it.
3. Once the MIME type has been determined, the user agent compares the type against the players it already knows about. If an appropriate player plug-in is found, it is loaded to play/display the media.
4. If an appropriate player isn't already available, the `<object>` tag is again examined, this time for an appropriate player to acquire for playback of the media. If a URL is supplied,

then the user is prompted to download the player. If the user responds in the affirmative, the player is downloaded and used to play/display the media.

5. If for any reason this process fails — invalid or missing MIME types, user refused to download player, and so on — the user agent will generally display a placeholder (as it does for missing or broken graphic links) and will not play the media.

For example, if you haven't installed the Flash plug-in and you load a page with Flash content, you can install the Flash plug-in quickly by following the prompts. However, not every plug-in works as well as Flash.

FIGURE 13-3

The process a user agent goes through when unknown content is encountered.

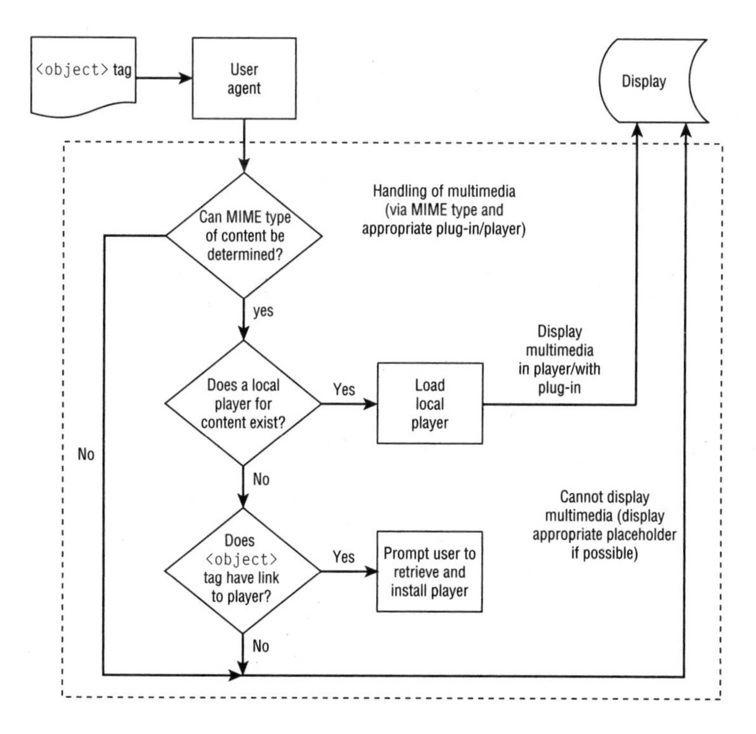

Tip

More information on inserting objects into your document can be found in the HTML standards at: `www.w3.org/TR/html401/struct/objects.html`. ■

Popular formats and players (plug-ins)

Four animation and video players dominate the Web space today. Windows Media Player's capabilities have also been enhanced over the years to enable it to play a lot of content that would otherwise have taken a dedicated player. The following sections detail the four dominant multimedia programs used for the Web.

Flash

Flash, which has become arguably the most prevalent multimedia format, began life as a plug-in for something called FuturePlayer. FuturePlayer was purchased by Macromedia, which made significant refinements to the original product. Macromedia had already enjoyed reasonable success with its own Shockwave format, which was quite similar to Flash files but was generated by Macromedia Director. Macromedia did a good job of commingling the two formats, and eventually Shockwave pretty much disappeared in favor of Flash. Today's Flash can display MP3-based video and sound along with vector graphics, and can harness data sources from relational databases and XML.

In fact, Flash has become a serious application platform in its own right, enabling developers to display changing data in real time.

RealOne

RealOne is a media player that reads video and audio files. Real, Inc., the developer of RealOne, was one of the first companies to introduce the concept of streaming audio to desktops. Streaming media (audio and video) is sent in real time through special servers. If you're doing professional-level streaming media, you'll want to check whether your host provider (if you're using one) offers access to a Real Audio server. If you're planning on developing for RealOne, you can find comprehensive software development kits (SDKs) and tutorials at `www.realnetworks.com/support/index.html`.

QuickTime

QuickTime has distinguished itself by consistently raising the bar on video quality. QuickTime has long been a staple in the Apple world, but its quality is so good it has made inroads into the Wintel world too.

YouTube

More of a platform than format or player, YouTube has become the most popular way to embed video in documents. Using Flash, YouTube provides a stable and known platform for displaying and controlling video. Using YouTube to embed video is covered later in this chapter.

Windows Media Player

Windows Media Player has a huge installed base because it is included as part of the Windows operating system. Its functionality is virtually identical to RealOne, offering video and music playing capabilities. To properly display Windows Media Player files, you should use the ASX markup language, which is an XML-based proprietary language developed by Microsoft.

When a user clicks an ASX link, the browser spawns an instance of the Windows Media Player. Consider the following link:

```
<a href="http://webserver/path/yourfile.asx">Link to Streaming Content</a>
```

This links to the following file and opens up a Media Player:

```
<asx version = "3.0">
<title> ASX Demo</title>
  <entry>
   <title>Gopher Hunt Theme Song</title>
   <author>Rodent Studios</author>
    <copyright>(c)2009 Rodent studios</copyright>
    <ref href="mms://windowsmediaserver/path/mysong.asf" />
  </entry>
</asx>
```

For the specifics of what the various elements mean in an ASX file, go to http://msdn2.microsoft.com/en-us/library/ms910265.aspx.

Embedding Media via the Object Tag

The best way to embed multimedia in your documents is via the object tag (<object>). This tag embeds a link to media in your document and specifies what a user agent needs in order to play the media (plug-in/player).

An example of an object tag follows; it is configured to embed a Flash file named myFlashMovie.swf:

```
<object
 classid="clsid:D27CDB6E-AE6D-11cf-96B8-444553540000"
 codebase=
"http://download.macromedia.com/pub/shockwave/cabs/flash/swflash.cab#
 version=9,0,45,0"
 width="550" height="400" id="myMovieName">
   <param name=movie value="myFlashMovie.swf" />
   <param name=quality value=high />
   <param name=bgcolor value=#FFFFFF />
 </object>
```

The object tag includes a wealth of information for the user agent and plug-in alike. The classid and codebase attributes specify information about which plug-in is necessary to play the content — the codebase attribute includes the player/plug-in necessary to play the content, including the specific (or usually minimum) version of the plug-in.

Where do you get the appropriate information for the classsid and codebase attributes? Usually from the vendor's website. For example, the following page from Adobe's TechNote site outlines all the attributes for the <object> and <embed> tags (although the version code is a bit dated): www.adobe.com/go/tn_12701.

Note

Embedding media in your document via <object> or <embed> tags causes the media to display within your document alongside other HTML objects. The other method of including media is simply linking to it via a standard anchor. For example, to link to a media file — causing it to display exclusively in the user agent window — you could use a tag similar to this:

```
<a href="myFlashFile.swf">A Flash File</a>
```

When the user clicks the link, the Flash file (myFlashFile.swf) will load in the user agent window and play according to the player's defaults. This technique can be used for most media formats that can be played by the players typically installed on an end user's machine (wav, mpg, avi, aiff, and so on).

However, this method relies upon the user agent finding a suitable player based solely on the extension (wav, mpg, avi, aiff, and so on) of the media file. To help the user agent, consider adding a type attribute that directly specifies the media type, similar to the following:

```
<a href="myFlashFile.swf"
type="application/x-shockwave-flash">
A Flash File</a> ■
```

Table 13-1 shows the other attributes that you can use with the object tag. The specific attributes used depend on your specific needs and the plug-in being used.

For extra functionality and customization of the user agent's handling of the media, you can embed parameter tags (<param>) within the object tag. The parameter tags have the following format:

```
<param name="name_of_parameter" value="value_of_parameter" />
```

These tags are used to set the value of parameters that the plug-in/player understands. For example, the Flash Player supports a parameter named loop, which controls whether the movie will play only once or multiple times. To set the Flash animation to loop, you would include the following parameter tag:

```
<param name="loop" value="true" />
```

TABLE 13-1

Attributes of the Object Element

Attribute Name	HTML Standard and Description
archive (optional)	(HTML 4.01) A space-separated list of URIs for archives of classes and resources to be preloaded. Using this attribute can significantly improve the loading speed of an object.
classid (optional)	(HTML 4.01) Specifies the location of the object's implementation by URI. Depending on the type of object involved, it can be used with, or as an alternative to, the data attribute.
codebase (optional)	(HTML 4.01) Indicates the base URI for the path to the object file. The default is the same base URI as the document.
codetype (recommended)	(HTML 4.01) Specifies the content type of data expected. If this is omitted, the default is the same as the type attribute.
data (optional)	(HTML 4.01) Specifies the location of the object's data. If given as a relative URI, it is relative to the code-based URI.
height (optional)	(HTML 4.01) Specifies the initial height in pixels or percentages of the element.
hspace (optional)	(HTML 4.01) Defines the number of pixels on the horizontal sides of the element.
id (optional)	(HTML 4.01) (CSS enabled) Formats the contents of the tag according to the style ID. Note: IDs must be unique within a document.
name (optional)	(HTML 4.01) The name attribute assigns the control name to the element.
standby (optional)	(HTML 4.01) This specifies a message that is shown to a user while the object is loading.
style (optional)	(HTML 4.01) (CSS enabled) Formats the contents of the element according to the listed style.
type (recommended)	(HTML 4.01) Indicates the content type at the link target. Specify the type as a MIME-type. This attribute is case insensitive.
vspace (optional)	(HTML 4.01) Defines the number of pixels on the vertical sides of the element.
width (optional)	(HTML 4.01) Specifies the initial width in pixels or a percentage of the element.

When the <object> Tag Is Not Supported

A handful of user agents do not support the relatively new `<object>` tag. These user agents typically *do* support an older embedded media tag, embed (`<embed>`). This deprecated tag has the following syntax when embedding a Flash file named `myFlashMovie.swf`:

```
<embed src="myFlashMovie.swf"
  quality="high" bgcolor="#FFFFFF" width="550" height="400"
  name="myMovieName" align="" type="application/x-shockwave-flash"
  pluginspage="http://www.macromedia.com/go/getflashplayer">
</embed>
```

The embed tag contains similar information to that in the `<object>` tag and its `<param>` tags, but in attribute format — that is, the options are embedded as attributes within the `<embed>` tag, not as children tags. As with the `<object>` tag, `<embed>` supports a variety of attributes and values, depending on the desired use and player/plug-in being utilized. The preceding example uses the attributes listed in the accompanying table.

Attribute	Definition
`src`	URL to the media file
`quality` (optional)	Quality setting at which the movie should be played (not supported by all plug-ins)
`bgcolor` (optional, not supported with all players/plug-ins)	Background color that should be used for the media
`width` (optional, but should be included)	Width of the media file
`height` (optional, but should be included)	Height of the media file
`name`	Name used to identify the particular embed tag
`type`	MIME type of the media file
`pluginspage`	URL to a page to download the appropriate player/plug-in

Because the `<embed>` tag has been deprecated, direct use of this tag will cause your documents not to validate. However, you can use the following technique to include both an `<object>` tag and an `<embed>` tag to support a wider range of user agents. Simply encase the `<embed>` tag within the `<object>` tag as shown:

```
<object
 classid="clsid:D27CDB6E-AE6D-11cf-96B8-444553540000"
 codebase=
"http://download.macromedia.com/pub/shockwave/cabs/flash/
 swflash.cab#version=9,0,45,0"
 width="550" height="400" id="myMovieName">
```

```
    <param name=movie value="myFlashMovie.swf" />
    <param name=quality value=high />
    <param name=bgcolor value=#FFFFFF />
    <embed src="myFlashMovie.swf"
      quality="high" bgcolor="#FFFFFF" width="550" height="400"
      name="myMovieName" align=""
      type="application/x-shockwave-flash"
      pluginspage="http://www.macromedia.com/go/getflashplayer">
    </embed>
  </object>
```

This method effectively hides the <embed> tag from validation programs — they do not check the children tags embedded within the <object> tag. Older user agents still find and use the <embed> tag, whereas modern user agents will use the <object> tag instead, ignoring the <embed> tag.

Embedding a Windows Media Player Using <object>

Earlier in this chapter, I discussed using ASX for delivering media via Windows Media Player. That method spans an instance of the player to play the media. Using the <object> tag, you can also embed the player in your Web pages.

Caution

To work, this method relies on your entire target audience running Windows, as it utilizes Windows ActiveX controls to integrate with Windows Media Player. No Windows, no ActiveX controls, no interface into Windows Media Player. In addition, if a user agent doesn't fully support ActiveX, it won't be able to take full advantage of the features described in this section. In other words, if your audience isn't running Internet Explorer, you can't bank on the full feature set of the embedded Media Player video.

It's generally more useful to port your media into a Flash-friendly format and wrap it with one of many Flash projector scripts, if necessary, to give it appropriate playback controls. ■

The <object> tag format should be familiar by this point. The following is a sample of a tag supporting an embedded Windows Media Player instance:

```
<object id="video" width="320" height="240"
   classid="CLSID:6BF52A52-394A-11d3-B153-00C04F79FAA6"
   codebase="http://activex.microsoft.com/activex/controls/
```

```
mplayer/en/nsmp2inf.cab#Version=6,4,5,715"
  standby="Loading Microsoft Windows Media Player components..."
  type="application/x-oleobject">
  <param name="URL" value="GamePLaySample.avi" />
  <param name="SendPlayStateChangeEvents" value="True" />
  <param name="AutoStart" value="True" />
  <param name="uiMode" value="mini" />
  <param name="Volume" value="20" />
  <param name="CurrentPosition" value="0" />
  <param name="PlayCount" value="1" />
  <embed type="application/x-mplayer2"
    pluginspage=
    "http://www.microsoft.com/Windows/Downloads/Contents/MediaPlayer/"
    width="320" height="240"
    src="GamePlaySample.avi"
    autostart="True"
    showcontrols="True" showstatusbar="False"
    showdisplay="False" autorewind="True">
  </embed>
</object>
```

Note that the codebase line is broken into two lines in this listing because of the limitations of the printed page. In your code, it should be on one line.

The codebase and classid shown in the preceding listing are specific to Windows Media Player 6, a stable player that is a common denominator in older user agents. Additional pairs of parameters for other versions and other useful information can be found on the following reference site: www.jakeludington.com/project_studio/20051015_embedding_windows_media_player_wma.html.

The Windows Media Player object takes a wide variety of parameters, some of which appear in the preceding listing, but most are shown in Table 13-2.

Note

Many additional parameters and control settings are available for Windows Media Player, but not all of them are necessarily suitable for delivering media over the Web. Visit Microsoft's Windows Media Developer Center site for more information about Windows Media Player settings and controls: http://msdn2.microsoft.com/en-us/windowsmedia/default.aspx. ■

Figure 13-4 shows examples of each of the four user interface settings. Note that the user interface, if enabled, occupies a certain amount of the object's area. This amount is determined largely by the skin being used by Windows Media Player on the user's machine. However, if you intend to enable the interface to any degree, you should compensate by adjusting the object's height to avoid compacting the media.

TABLE 13-2

Parameters for a Windows Media Player Object

Parameter	Value Type	Use/Effect
`AutoStart`	True/False	Controls whether the media will begin playing automatically upon loading
`BaseURL`	URL	Specifies the base URL to be used for any scripting commands embedded in the media
`CaptioningID`	HTML element ID	The ID of the element supplying alternate captioning for the media, if any
`CurrentMarker`	Numeric	Specifies the marker number where the media should begin playing. Specifying 0 starts the media from the beginning.
`CurrentPosition`	Numeric (seconds)	Specifies the timecode (in seconds) where the media should begin playing. Specifying 0 starts the media from the beginning.
`EnableContextMenu`	True/False	Controls whether the right-click context menu will be available to the user to aid in controlling playback, etc.
`Enabled`	True/False	Controls whether the Windows Media Player controls are enabled at all
`FullScreen`	True/False	Controls whether playback occurs in full-screen mode
`Mute`	True/False	Controls whether the volume is muted on initial playback
`Playcount`	Numeric	Specifies how many times the media will play. The minimum value for this parameter is 1.
`Rate`	Numeric	The relative rate of speed at which the media will play. The value specified is multiplied by 1, so specifying .5 will result in half-speed, while specifying 2 results in double-speed.
`StretchToFit`	True/False	Specifies whether the media should be stretched to fit the player window, if/when the player window is larger than the media size
`UIMode`	invisible, none, mini, full	Specifies the type and size of the player controls to display with the player. See Figure 13-4 for an example of each.

continued

TABLE 13-2 *(continued)*

Parameter	Value Type	Use/Effect
URL	URL	The location of the media file to play
Volume	Numeric (percentage)	The initial setting of the player's volume. The default value is the last setting used by the local user. Values specified with this parameter are treated as a percentage from 0 (no volume) to 100 (full volume).

FIGURE 13-4

The various UIMode settings control how much of the Windows Media Player interface is displayed for the user to control playback of the media.

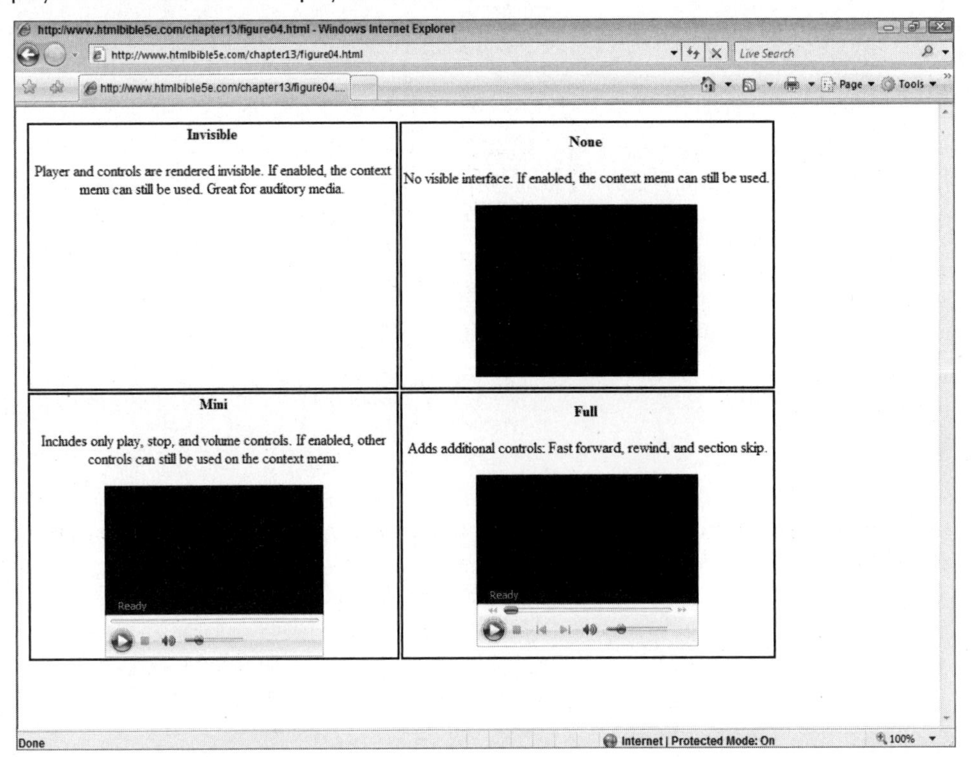

Embedding YouTube Videos

One popular and easy way to add movies to your documents is to use YouTube as the medium. Adding a YouTube video to your documents is very easy thanks to YouTube's embed display, which accompanies all videos on their site. A sample video with the embed code is shown in Figure 13-5.

FIGURE 13-5

Every video on YouTube has accompanying code to embed the video in a document.

Note

Keep in mind that YouTube videos require the Flash plug-in, so your audience needs to have the plug-in installed to see the video. ■

The embed code resembles the following:

```
<object width="425" height="344">
<param name="movie"
    value="http://www.youtube.com/v/XT6XPHXK4e4&hl=en&fs=1">
</param>
<param name="allowFullScreen" value="true">
</param>
<param name="allowscriptaccess" value="always"></param>
<embed src="http://www.youtube.com/v/XT6XPHXK4e4&hl=en&fs=1"
type="application/x-shockwave-flash" allowscriptaccess="always"
allowfullscreen="true" width="425" height="344"></embed>
</object>
```

Note

If you use the YouTube embed code in your documents, you should be aware that the documents will no longer validate against HTML 4. That's because the code needs to work on most browsers and as such employs loose HTML 4 code. ■

To embed a YouTube video, follow these steps:

1. Locate the video on YouTube and navigate to its page.
2. Select the code in the embed field and copy it to the clipboard.
3. Paste the code into your document where you want the video to appear.

You can customize the look of the video by clicking the gear next to the embed field and choosing from a handful of options, like border color and size of the video, before copying the embed code to your document.

You can also add parameters to the URL contained in the `<param>` and `<embed>` tags to cause the video to autoplay when the page is loaded or to start at a particular place in the video.

To cause the video to autoplay, add `&autoplay=1` to the end of the URL. For example,

```
www.youtube.com/v/XT6XPHXK4e4&hl=en&fs=1
```

becomes

```
www.youtube.com/v/XT6XPHXK4e4&hl=en&fs=1&autoplay=1
```

Tip

The number used with the autoplay parameter also controls how many times the video will play. For example, using 2 (instead of 1) will cause the video to play two times without user intervention. ■

To cause the video to start at a designated place, use the `&start` parameter, with the number of seconds into the video as an argument. For example, to start the video 10 seconds into it, add `&start=10` to the end of the URL.

Adding Sound to Web Pages

There are two deprecated ways to add sound files to Web pages. Generally speaking, you shouldn't use these methods, but if you need to add a MIDI or WAV file to your page and can't embed either into a player supported by `<object>`, you might find it necessary to use one.

The first method is using the background sound tag (`<bgsound>`). This tag has the following format:

```
<bgsound src="url_to_sound_file" loop="times_to_play" />
```

This tag causes the specified sound file to be delivered to the user agent and played the number of times specified by the `loop` attribute.

The other method is to use the `<embed>` tag as previously described in this chapter.

Note

Remember that the media file delivered to the user agent must be supported on that platform; that is, the target platform must have a player or plug-in to play the file. Also, using the `<bgsource>` tag doesn't give you the chance to specify a player that the user agent can retrieve, if necessary. ■

Creating Multimedia Files

Creating multimedia files takes dedicated applications geared to create the appropriate file for the format you want to use. For example, creating Flash files requires the Adobe Flash application. QuickTime file production requires a suitable video encoder for MPEG or other QuickTime formats. RealOne is one of the few formats that requires a bit more work and dedicated servers to deliver the media files.

Unfortunately, most of the creation programs are fairly expensive. There are less capable video creation tools on the market, most of which are sold to translate and edit video from personal camcorders and the like. While these programs can create video that can be used on the Web, the file sizes are usually too large to be practical. If you want to develop directly for the Web, look for a professional program such as Adobe Premier to do your video editing and creation.

Note

Many files output their content in Flash format and/or can be used to create original Flash content. If you already have a 3D or animation program, check its export options for Flash format. In addition, search the utility sites for Flash-capable creation tools; more are cropping up every day. ■

A Final Word About Multimedia

Keep in mind that most multimedia is not natively supported by user agents — specific plug-ins or operating system players are required to play a multimedia file delivered over the Web. When a user's system has the correct player installed, the embedded or otherwise delivered multimedia can be played rather seamlessly. However, if users don't have the right player software installed, you are asking them to go through one more step to view your content — a step they might not want to take.

Although the `<object>` tag can be used to deliver almost any content *and* a link to an appropriate player, consider sticking to the most popular players — Flash, QuickTime, RealOne, and Windows Media Player — and porting your content to formats supported by those players.

The best route today, in this author's opinion, is to encapsulate your multimedia content in Flash files whenever possible. Most user agents will already have the Flash Player installed and can instantly play your content.

Also, avoid using anchor tags to link to the media file(s). Use the `<object>` and `<embed>` tags to embed the media in a properly validated HTML document.

Last, remember that the best kind of multimedia to use on your site might be no multimedia at all, which saves the user the aggravation of encountering unwanted multimedia, downloading unwanted plug-ins, and so on.

Summary

This chapter showed how easy it is to embed multimedia into your Web documents, and what concerns you need to be aware of in doing so. You saw how using the `<object>` tag is easy and flexible and that with it you can deliver just about any content. You also learned about other tags that have been deprecated but can still be used in a pinch.

The next two chapters wrap up the HTML coverage with special characters and internationalization. The final two chapters in this section (Chapter 16 and 17) cover scripting.

CHAPTER 14

Special Characters

IN THIS CHAPTER

As its roots are firmly grounded in plain text, HTML needs to be able to display a wide range of characters — many that cannot be typed on a regular keyboard. Language is rich with extended and accented characters, and there are many reserved characters in HTML.

The HTML specification defines many entities — specific codes — to insert special characters. This chapter introduces you to the concept of entities and lists the various entities available for use.

Note

The W3C website is a good source of information about entities. The HTML entities are listed at `www.w3.org/TR/html4/sgml/entities.html`. ■

Understanding Character Encodings

Character encoding at its simplest is the method that maps binary data to its proper character equivalents. For example, in a standard American English document character, 65 is matched to a capital A.

Most English fonts follow the American Standard Code for Information Interchange (ASCII) coding. So when Web designers insert a capital A, they can be assured that users will see the appropriate "A" in their user agent.

There are, of course, plenty of caveats to that statement. The document must be encoded as English, the specified font must also be encoded as English, the font must be an alphanumeric font capable of producing the letter, and the user agent must not interfere with either encoding.

Note

Document encoding is typically passed to the user agent in the `Content-Type` **HTTP header, such as the following:**

```
Content-Type: text/html; charset=EN-US
```

However, some user agents don't correctly handle encoding in the HTTP header. If you need to explicitly declare a document's encoding, you should use an appropriate meta tag in your document, similar to the following:

```
<meta http-equiv="Content-Type" content="text/html; charset=EN-US">
```
■

What happens when any of the necessary pieces are different or changed from what they were intended to be? For example, what if your document is viewed in Japan, where the requisite user agent font is in Japanese instead of English? In those cases, using the proper document encoding helps ensure that the right characters are represented.

Most fonts have international characters encoded in them as well as their native language character set. When a non-native encoding is specified, the user agent tries to use the appropriate characters in the appropriate font. If appropriate characters cannot be found in the current font, then alternative fonts can be used.

However, none of this can be accomplished if the document does not declare its encoding. Without knowing the document encoding, the user agent simply uses the character that corresponds to the character position arriving in the data stream. For example, a capital A is translated to whatever character is in the 65th place in the font table the user agent is using.

Cross-Ref

More information on character encoding and internationalizing documents can be found in Chapter 15. ■

Special Characters

Several characters have special meaning in HTML. For example, the less than symbol (<) signals the beginning of a tag. As such, you cannot use that character in normal text. Instead, you must encode the character using a means that user agents understand. Such codes are referred to as *entities*. When the user agent renders a document and encounters an entity, the entity is rendered as the correct character.

Entities in HTML begin with an ampersand (&), end with a semicolon (;), and contain a numeric code or mnemonic phrase in between.

Numerically coded entities can use decimal or hexadecimal numbers. Either must be preceded by a pound sign (#). Hexadecimal numbers also need to be preceded by an x. For example, a nonbreaking space is character number 160. The following entity in decimal references this character:

```
 
```

The following entity in hexadecimal also references character 160:

```
 
```

Mnemonic entities use a few characters to specify the entity — the characters usually are an abbreviation or mnemonic representation of the character they represent. For example, the following entity represents a nonbreaking space:

```
 
```

Other essential entities are listed in Table 14-1.

TABLE 14-1

Essential Entities

Decimal Entity	Mnemonic Entity	Character
"	"	Double quote mark
&	&	Ampersand
<	<	Less than symbol
>	>	Greater than symbol
		Nonbreaking space

Additional special-use characters are covered in the following sections.

Note

Specifying special characters via their mnemonic codes is the only way to ensure that the correct character is used by the user agent. Using the decimal or hexadecimal equivalent only instructs the user agent to use the corresponding character at that place in the current font map — it doesn't guarantee that the character is the one you intended. However, the user agent will use the character mapped to the mnemonic, despite its position in the font map.

All that said, remember that entity use is not a substitution for correctly internationalizing your documents. Refer to Chapter 15 for more information. ■

En and Em Spaces and Dashes

The en space and dash characters got their name from their relative size; they are as wide as a capital N. Likewise, em characters are as wide as a capital M.

These characters have specific uses in the English language:

- *En spaces* are used when you need a larger space than a normal space provides. For example, en spaces can be used between street numbers and street names for clarity (e.g., 123 Main Street).

- *Em spaces* are used to separate elements such as dates and headlines, figure numbers and captions, and so on (e.g., Figure 02 A simple prompt).
- *En dashes* are used instead of hyphens in constructs such as phone numbers, element numbering, and so on.
- *Em dashes* are used grammatically when you need to divide thoughts in a sentence (e.g., "The excuse was nonsense — at least that's how it seemed to me.").

Table 14-2 lists the entities for en and em elements.

TABLE 14-2

En and Em Entities

Decimal Entity	Mnemonic Entity	Character
		En space
		Em space
–	–	En dash
—	—	Em dash

Copyright and Trademark Symbols

Copyright and trademark symbols are special symbols that indicate a legal relationship between individuals (or companies) and text.

The copyright symbol (©) is used to indicate that someone has asserted certain rights on written material — text included with the symbol usually indicates which rights. For example, many written works include the following phrase as a copyright: "Copyright © 2009. All rights reserved."

The trademark and registered marks (™ and ®) are used to indicate that a particular word or phrase is trademarked — that is, marked (trademarked) or registered for unique use by an individual or company. For example, "Windows" is a registered trademark of Microsoft, and "For Dummies" is a registered trademark of Wiley Publishing.

Note

Trademark and registered trademark symbols are typically superscripted after the word or phrase to which they apply. As such, you should generally use each within superscript (<sup>) tags. ■

Table 14-3 lists the entities for copyright, trademark, and registered trademark symbols.

Note that some fonts include the trademark symbol. However, because the symbol is actually two characters, it is included as an exception, not a rule. As such, you shouldn't rely on an entity to display the symbol, but use specific small and superscript font coding such as the following:

```
<small><sup>TM</sup></small>
```

TABLE 14-3

Copyright, Trademark, and Registered Entities

Decimal Entity	Mnemonic Entity	Character
©	©	Copyright symbol
™	™	Trademark symbol
®	®	Registered trademark symbol

Note

Use of styles is preferred over the use of the <small> tag. ■

Currency Symbols

There are many currency symbols, including the U.S. dollar ($), the English pound (£), the European euro (€), and the Japanese yen (¥). There is also the general currency symbol (¤). Table 14-4 lists many of the most common currency symbols.

TABLE 14-4

Currency Entities

Decimal Entity	Mnemonic Entity	Character
¢	¢	The cent symbol (¢)
£	£	English pound
¤	¤	General currency
¥	¥	Japanese yen
€	€	European euro

Note that the dollar symbol ($) is typically ASCII character 24 (in U.S. fonts) and can be accessed directly from the keyboard.

"Real" Quotation Marks

Real quotation marks, used in publishing, do not exist on a standard keyboard. The quote marks available on the keyboard (" and ') are straight quotes; that is, they are small, superscripted, vertical lines.

Quote marks used in publishing typically resemble the numbers 6 and 9 — that is, dots with a serif leading off of them. For example, the following sentence is set off with real quote marks:

"This sentence is a real quote."

Table 14-5 lists the entities for real quotes.

TABLE 14-5

Quote Mark and Apostrophe Entities

Decimal Entity	Mnemonic Entity	Character
`‘`	`‘`	Left/Opening single quote
`’`	`’`	Right/Closing single quote and apostrophe
`“`	`“`	Left/Opening double quote
`”`	`”`	Right/Closing double quote

Arrows

A variety of arrow symbols are available as entities. Table 14-6 lists these entities.

TABLE 14-6

Arrow Entities

Decimal Entity	Mnemonic Entity	Character
`←`	`←`	Left arrow
`↑`	`↑`	Up arrow
`→`	`→`	Right arrow
`↓`	`↓`	Down arrow
`↔`	`↔`	Left right arrow
`↵`	`↵`	Down arrow with corner leftwards
`⇐`	`⇐`	Leftwards double arrow
`⇑`	`⇑`	Upwards double arrow
`⇒`	`⇒`	Rightwards double arrow
`⇓`	`⇓`	Downwards double arrow
`⇔`	`⇔`	Left right double arrow

Accented Characters

Many accented character entities are available in the HTML standard. These characters can be used in words such as résumé. Table 14-7 lists the accented character entities.

TABLE 14-7

Accented Character Entities

Decimal Entity	Mnemonic Entity	Character
À	À	Latin capital letter A with grave
Á	Á	Latin capital letter A with acute
Â	Â	Latin capital letter A with circumflex
Ã	Ã	Latin capital letter A with tilde
Ä	Ä	Latin capital letter A with diaeresis
Å	Å	Latin capital letter A with ring above
Æ	Æ	Latin capital letter AE
Ç	Ç	Latin capital letter C with cedilla
È	È	Latin capital letter E with grave
É	É	Latin capital letter E with acute
Ê	Ê	Latin capital letter E with circumflex
Ë	Ë	Latin capital letter E with diaeresis
Ì	Ì	Latin capital letter I with grave
Í	Í	Latin capital letter I with acute
Î	Î	Latin capital letter I with circumflex
Ï	Ï	Latin capital letter I with diaeresis
Ð	Ð	Latin capital letter ETH
Ñ	Ñ	Latin capital letter N with tilde
Ò	Ò	Latin capital letter O with grave
Ó	Ó	Latin capital letter O with acute
Ô	Ô	Latin capital letter O with circumflex
Õ	Õ	Latin capital letter O with tilde
Ö	Ö	Latin capital letter O with diaeresis
Ø	Ø	Latin capital letter O with stroke

continued

TABLE 14-7 *(continued)*

Decimal Entity	Mnemonic Entity	Character
Ù	Ù	Latin capital letter U with grave
Ú	Ú	Latin capital letter U with acute
Û	Û	Latin capital letter U with circumflex
Ü	Ü	Latin capital letter U with diaeresis
Ý	Ý	Latin capital letter Y with acute
Þ	Þ	Latin capital letter THORN
ß	ß	Latin small letter sharp s = ess-zed
à	à	Latin small letter a with grave
á	á	Latin small letter a with acute
â	â	Latin small letter a with circumflex
ã	ã	Latin small letter a with tilde
ä	ä	Latin small letter a with diaeresis
å	å	Latin small letter a with ring above
æ	æ	Latin small letter ae
ç	ç	Latin small letter c with cedilla
è	è	Latin small letter e with grave
é	é	Latin small letter e with acute
ê	ê	Latin small letter e with circumflex
ë	ë	Latin small letter e with diaeresis
ì	ì	Latin small letter i with grave
í	í	Latin small letter i with acute
î	î	Latin small letter i with circumflex
ï	ï	Latin small letter i with diaeresis
ð	ð	Latin small letter eth
ñ	ñ	Latin small letter n with tilde
ò	ò	Latin small letter o with grave
ó	ó	Latin small letter o with acute
ô	ô	Latin small letter o with circumflex
õ	õ	Latin small letter o with tilde
ö	ö	Latin small letter o with diaeresis

Decimal Entity	Mnemonic Entity	Character
ø	ø	Latin small letter o with stroke
ù	ù	Latin small letter u with grave
ú	ú	Latin small letter u with acute
û	û	Latin small letter u with circumflex
ü	ü	Latin small letter u with diaeresis
ý	ý	Latin small letter y with acute
þ	þ	Latin small letter thorn
ÿ	ÿ	Latin small letter y with diaeresis

Greek and Mathematical Characters

Table 14-8 lists various Greek symbol entities available in HTML.

TABLE 14-8

Greek Symbol Entities

Decimal Entity	Mnemonic Entity	Character
Α	Α	Greek capital letter alpha
Β	Β	Greek capital letter beta
Γ	Γ	Greek capital letter gamma
Δ	Δ	Greek capital letter delta
Ε	Ε	Greek capital letter epsilon
Ζ	Ζ	Greek capital letter zeta
Η	Η	Greek capital letter eta
Θ	Θ	Greek capital letter theta
Ι	Ι	Greek capital letter iota
Κ	Κ	Greek capital letter kappa
Λ	Λ	Greek capital letter lambda
Μ	Μ	Greek capital letter mu

continued

TABLE 14-8 *(continued)*

Decimal Entity	Mnemonic Entity	Character
Ν	Ν	Greek capital letter nu
Ξ	Ξ	Greek capital letter xi
Ο	Ο	Greek capital letter omicron
Π	Π	Greek capital letter pi
Ρ	Ρ	Greek capital letter rho
Σ	Σ	Greek capital letter sigma
Τ	Τ	Greek capital letter tau
Υ	Υ	Greek capital letter upsilon
Φ	Φ	Greek capital letter phi
Χ	Χ	Greek capital letter chi
Ψ	Ψ	Greek capital letter psi
Ω	Ω	Greek capital letter omega
α	α	Greek small letter alpha
β	β	Greek small letter beta
γ	γ	Greek small letter gamma
δ	δ	Greek small letter delta
ε	ε	Greek small letter epsilon
ζ	ζ	Greek small letter zeta
η	η	Greek small letter eta
θ	θ	Greek small letter theta
ι	ι	Greek small letter iota
κ	κ	Greek small letter kappa
λ	λ	Greek small letter lambda
μ	μ	Greek small letter mu
ν	ν	Greek small letter nu
ξ	ξ	Greek small letter xi
ο	ο	Greek small letter omicron
π	π	Greek small letter pi
ρ	ρ	Greek small letter rho

Decimal Entity	Mnemonic Entity	Character
`ς`	`ς`	Greek small letter final sigma
`σ`	`σ`	Greek small letter sigma
`τ`	`τ`	Greek small letter tau
`υ`	`υ`	Greek small letter upsilon
`φ`	`φ`	Greek small letter phi
`χ`	`χ`	Greek small letter chi
`ψ`	`ψ`	Greek small letter psi
`ω`	`ω`	Greek small letter omega
`ϑ`	`ϑ`	Greek small letter theta symbol
`ϒ`	`ϒ`	Greek upsilon with hook symbol
`ϖ`	`ϖ`	Greek pi symbol

Table 14-9 lists a variety of mathematical symbols.

TABLE 14-9

Mathematical Symbol Entities

Decimal Entity	Mnemonic Entity	Character/Symbol
`×`	`×`	Multiplication sign
`÷`	`&division;`	Division sign
`∀`	`∀`	For all
`∂`	`∂`	Partial differential
`∃`	`∃`	There exists
`∅`	`∅`	Empty set = null set = diameter
`∇`	`∇`	Nabla = backward difference
`∈`	`∈`	Element of
`∉`	`∉`	Not an element of
`∋`	`∋`	Contains as member
`∏`	`∏`	n-ary product = product sign
`∑`	`∑`	n-ary summation

continued

TABLE 14-9 *(continued)*

Decimal Entity	Mnemonic Entity	Character/Symbol
−	−	Minus sign
∗	∗	Asterisk operator
√	√	Square root = radical sign
∝	∝	Proportional to
∞	∞	Infinity
∠	∠	Angle
∧	∧	Logical and = wedge
∨	∨	Logical or = vee
∩	∩	Intersection = cap
∪	∪	Union = cup
∫	∫	Integral
∴	∴	Therefore
∼	∼	Tilde operator = varies with = similar to
≅	≅	Approximately equal to
≈	≈	Almost equal to = asymptotic to
≠	≠	Not equal to
≡	≡	Identical to
≤	≤	Less than or equal to
≥	≥	Greater than or equal to
⊂	⊂	Subset of
⊃	⊃	Superset of
⊄	⊄	Not a subset of
⊆	⊆	Subset of or equal to
⊇	⊇	Superset of or equal to
⊕	⊕	Circled plus = direct sum
⊗	⊗	Circled times = vector product
⊥	⊥	Up tack = orthogonal to = perpendicular
⋅	⋅	Dot operator
⌈	⌈	Left ceiling
⌉	⌉	Right ceiling

Decimal Entity	Mnemonic Entity	Character/Symbol
⌊	⌊	Left floor
⌋	⌋	Right floor
〈	⟨	Left-pointing angle bracket
〉	⟩	Right-pointing angle bracket

Other Useful Entities

Table 14-10 lists other miscellaneous entities.

TABLE 14-10

Miscellaneous Entities

Decimal Entity	Mnemonic Entity	Character/Symbol
¡	¡	Inverted exclamation mark
¦	¦	Broken bar = broken vertical bar
§	§	Section sign
¨	¨	Diaeresis = spacing diaeresis
ª	ª	Feminine ordinal indicator
«	«	Left-pointing double angle quotation mark = left pointing guillemet
¬	¬	Not sign
		Soft hyphen = discretionary hyphen
¯	¯	Macron = spacing macron = overline = APL overbar
°	°	Degree sign
±	±	Plus-minus sign = plus-or-minus sign
²	²	Superscript two = superscript digit two = squared
³	³	Superscript three = superscript digit three = cubed
´	´	Acute accent = spacing acute
µ	µ	Micro sign

continued

TABLE 14-10 *(continued)*

Decimal Entity	Mnemonic Entity	Character/Symbol
¶	¶	Pilcrow sign = paragraph sign
·	·	Middle dot = Georgian comma = Greek middle dot
¸	¸	Cedilla = spacing cedilla
¹	¹	Superscript one = superscript digit one
º	°	Masculine ordinal indicator
»	»	Right-pointing double angle quotation mark = right-pointing guillemet
¼	¼	Vulgar fraction one-quarter = fraction one-quarter
½	½	Vulgar fraction one-half = fraction one-half
¾	¾	Vulgar fraction three-quarters = fraction three-quarters
¿	¿	Inverted question mark = turned question mark
Œ	Œ	Latin capital ligature OE
œ	œ	Latin small ligature oe
Š	Š	Latin capital letter S with caron
š	š	Latin small letter s with caron
Ÿ	Ÿ	Latin capital letter Y with diaeresis
ˆ	°	Modifier letter circumflex accent
˜	˜	Small tilde
		Thin space
‌	‌	Zero width non-joiner
‍	‍	Zero width joiner
‎	‎	Left-to-right mark
‏	‏	Right-to-left mark
‚	‚	Single low-9 quotation mark
„	„	Double low-9 quotation mark
†	†	Dagger

Decimal Entity	Mnemonic Entity	Character/Symbol
`‡`	`‡`	Double dagger
`‰`	`‰`	Per mille sign
`‹`	`‹`	Single left-pointing angle quotation mark
`›`	`›`	Single right-pointing angle quotation mark

Summary

Although most of your Web documents will contain standard characters, there are times when you need accented or special characters as well. Taking character and language encoding into account, you can also fall back on HTML entities to insert these special characters.

The next, and final, HTML chapter in this section covers internationalization (Chapter 15). The next two chapters (16 and 17) cover JavaScript and DHTML, bringing scripting to your now robust knowledge of HTML. Part II covers tools and utilities, and Part III provides in-depth coverage of CSS.

CHAPTER

15

Internationalization and Localization

IN THIS CHAPTER

Even though this book is written in English, chances are good it will be translated into other languages. From a website perspective, if your site is only in English, you may eliminate a huge portion of your potential world audience. This chapter takes a look at some options for improving your documents' access to the world's population.

Note

The terms Internationalization and Localization are often used interchangeably. To Internationalize an online document refers to making it more suitable to a global audience, while Localizing an online document refers to making the document suitable for one particular locale. In this chapter we deal with the latter. ■

Internationalization and Localization

Only a small percentage of the world's population uses English as a first language. If you anticipate a wide range of international visitors to your site, then you should consider localizing your site.

Localization is the process of creating different sites for each language you intend to support. By creating documents in Japanese, Chinese, German, French, and Spanish, for example, you vastly increase the size of your potential audience.

The actual implementation of localization can be very straightforward: create different URL "branches" for your site, one branch for each language. For example, if you need to support English, German, and Japanese, your home page URLs might resemble the following:

```
http://www.on-target-games.com/en/index.htm
http://www.on-target-games.com/de/index.htm
http://www.on-target-games.com/jp/index.htm
```

On your Web server, each URL branch would be linked to document directories that store the appropriate language version. Other sites that link to your site can simply use the proper URL — that is, include "en," "de," or "jp" in the URL pointing to a document on your site — depending on the audience's preferred language. In addition, each version of your home page should include a prominent navigational link at the top of the document to the other language versions of the document, as shown in Figure 15-1.

FIGURE 15-1

Localized sites should include navigational aids for users to reach the other versions of a document.

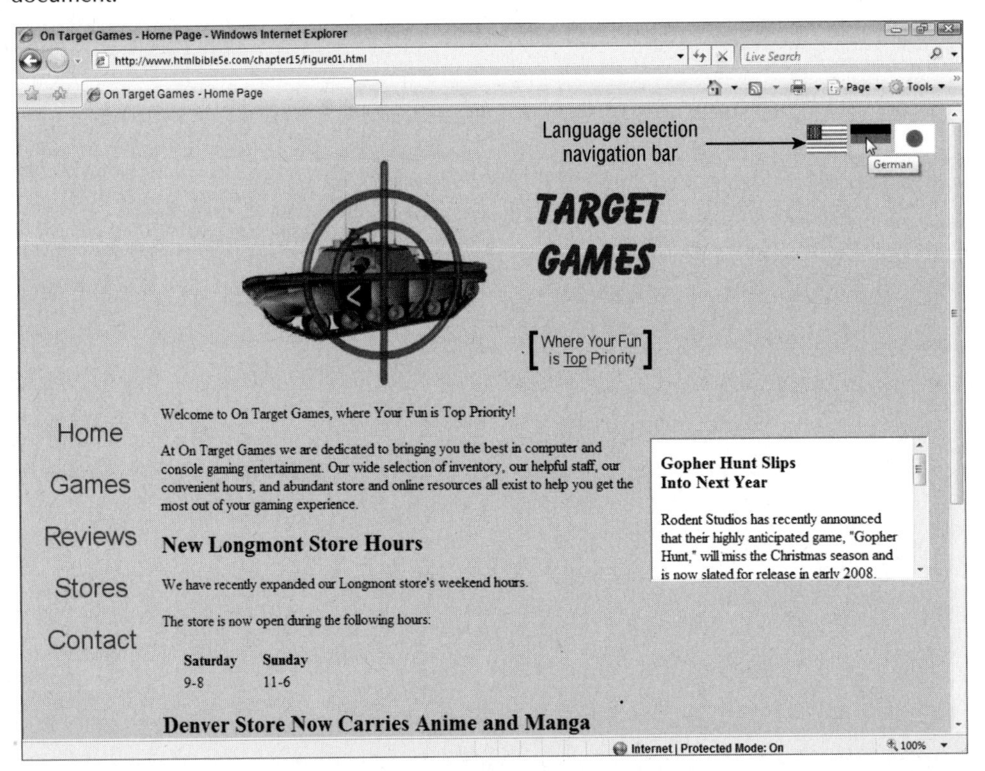

However, maintaining such an implementation can quickly become overwhelming. When a document changes on the site, the change must be translated and incorporated into each of the mirrored sites as well. This exponential increase in labor is why many sites avoid localization.

Translating Your Web Site

There's much more to localization than simply creating branches on your Web server. To be truly global you need to create documents in the native language of your audience — that means translating your text into those languages. Of course, simply changing the words from one language to another won't always accomplish your goals. Simple, colloquial phrases in English won't always carry the same meaning when translated to other languages.

Tip

You can download free localization software from The RWS Group at: `www.translate.com/technology/tools/index.html`. ■

For this reason, you should try to use native speakers of any language to which you are translating. This can be an expensive proposition, and may not be an option if you run a small site that is only marginally profitable. But if you have already made the decision to localize, it's important to do it right.

You can also use translation services that specialize in such endeavors. Use Google or another search engine to point you to "translation services" and see which options may be right for you. Another, often overlooked, resource is International sales partners — companies that want to sell your products or services in their area of the world. If your company or business has ties to other locales, see if you can take advantage of those resources for your localization needs.

If you have only a small amount of text to translate, you can try using an online translator like Yahoo's Babel Fish (`http://babelfish.yahoo.com/`). Babel Fish enables you to translate blocks of text or entire pages between several different languages. Babel Fish's main purpose is to aid in translating pages and text *from* other languages — a snippet of Japanese to English for an English-speaking person — but in a pinch it can be used to translate from English as well.

Understanding Unicode

Unicode is a standard developed by the Unicode Consortium for processing the world's alphabets in a consistent way. Unicode consists of a number of tables, each containing numerical references to alphanumeric characters. Every character in nearly every written language in the world is represented in Unicode, as shown in Table 15-1.

The Unicode tables are also known as *code pages*. Each code page serves a specific set of languages and has a table of numeric references for each character. Each row in Table 15-1 represents a code page, and each code page consists of several rows of numeric references for the characters in the corresponding language.

Basic Latin (U + 0000–U + 007F)

All nations in America, most European nations, most African nations, as well as Australia and New Zealand use the Latin encoding. In Unicode, the Latin encoding is broken down into different parts, with the most basic called Basic Latin. Only a few languages can be written entirely with a Basic Latin encoding. You generally need to incorporate additional Latin encodings because Basic Latin consists of only characters between 0 and 7F (hexadecimal).

Tip

All of these Latin encodings are automatically included as part of the UTF-8 encoding. In fact, Unicode-based UTF-8 includes most of the world's written languages. ■

TABLE 15-1

Alphabets Represented in Unicode

Start Code	End Code	Block Name
\u0000	\u007F	Basic Latin
\u0080	\u00FF	Latin-1 Supplement
\u0100	\u017F	Latin Extended-A
\u0180	\u024F	Latin Extended-B
\u0250	\u02AF	IPA Extensions
\u02B0	\u02FF	Spacing Modifier Letters
\u0300	\u036F	Combining Diacritical Marks
\u0370	\u03FF	Greek and Coptic
\u0400	\u04FF	Cyrillic
\u0530	\u058F	Armenian
\u0590	\u05FF	Hebrew
\u0600	\u06FF	Arabic
\u0700	\u074F	Syriac
\u0750	\u077F	Arabic Supplement
\u0780	\u07BF	Thaana
\u07C0	\u07FF	N'Ko
\u0900	\u097F	Devanagari
\u0980	\u09FF	Bengali
\u0A00	\u0A7F	Gurmukhi
\u0A80	\u0AFF	Gujarati
\u0B00	\u0B7F	Oriya
\u0B80	\u0BFF	Tamil
\u0C00	\u0C7F	Telugu

Start Code	End Code	Block Name
\u0C80	\u0CFF	Kannada
\u0D00	\u0D7F	Malayalam
\u0D80	\u0DFF	Sinhala
\u0E00	\u0E7F	Thai
\u0E80	\u0EFF	Lao
\u0F00	\u0FFF	Tibetan
\u1000	\u109F	Myanmar
\u10A0	\u10FF	Georgian
\u1100	\u11FF	Hangul Jamo
\u1200	\u137F	Ethiopic
\u1380	\u139F	Ethiopic Supplement
\u13A0	\u13FF	Cherokee
\u1400	\u167F	Unified Canadian Aboriginal Syllabics
\u1680	\u169F	Ogham
\u16A0	\u16FF	Runic
\u1700	\u171F	Tagalog
\u1720	\u173F	Hanunoo
\u1740	\u175F	Buhid
\u1760	\u177F	Tagbanwa
\u1780	\u17FF	Khmer
\u1800	\u18AF	Mongolian
\u1900	\u194F	Limbu
\u1950	\u197F	Tai Le
\u1980	\u19DF	New Tai Lue
\u19E0	\u19FF	Khmer Symbols
\u1A00	\u1A1F	Buginese
\u1B00	\u1B7F	Balinese
\u1D00	\u1D7f	Phonetic Extensions
\u1D80	\u1DBF	Phonetic Extensions Supplement
\u1DC0	\U1DFF	Combining Diacritical Marks Supplement

continued

TABLE 15-1 *(continued)*

Start Code	End Code	Block Name
\u1E00	\u1EFF	Latin Extended Additional
\u1F00	\u1FFF	Greek Extended
\u2000	\u206F	General Punctuation
\u2070	\u209F	Superscripts and Subscripts
\u20A0	\u20CF	Currency Symbols
\u20D0	\u20FF	Combining Diacritical Marks for Symbols
\u2100	\u214F	Letterlike Symbols
\u2150	\u218F	Number Forms
\u2190	\u21FF	Arrows
\u2200	\u22FF	Mathematical Operators
\u2300	\u23FF	Miscellaneous Technical
\u2400	\u243F	Control Pictures
\u2440	\u245F	Optical Character Recognition
\u2460	\u24FF	Enclosed Alphanumerics
\u2500	\u257F	Box Drawing
\u2580	\u259F	Block Elements
\u25A0	\u25FF	Geometric Shapes
\u2600	\u26FF	Miscellaneous Symbols
\u2700	\u27BF	Dingbats
\u27C0	\u27EF	Miscellaneous Mathematical Symbols-A
\u27F0	\u27FF	Supplemental Arrows-A
\u2800	\u28FF	Braille Patterns
\u2900	\u297F	Supplemental Arrows-B
\u2980	\u29FF	Miscellaneous Mathematical Symbols-B
\u2A00	\u2AFF	Supplemental Mathematical Operators
\u2B00	\u2BFF	Miscellaneous Symbols and Arrows
\u2C00	\u2C5F	Glagolitic
\u2C60	\u2C7F	Latin Extended-C
\u2C80	\u2CFF	Coptic
\u2D00	\u2D2F	Georgian Supplement

Start Code	End Code	Block Name
\u2D30	\u2D7F	Tifinagh
\u2D80	\u2DDF	Ethiopic Extended
\u2E00	\u2E7F	Supplemental Punctuation
\u2E80	\u2EFF	CJK Radicals Supplement
\u2F00	\u2FDF	KangXi Radicals
\u2FF0	\u2FFF	Ideographic Description Characters
\u3000	\u303F	CJK Symbols and Punctuation
\u3040	\u309F	Hiragana
\u30A0	\u30FF	Katakana
\u3100	\u312F	Bopomofo
\u3130	\u318F	Hangul Compatibility Jamo
\u3190	\u319F	Kanbun
\u31A0	\u31BF	Extended Bopomofo
\u31C0	\u31EF	CJK Strokes
\u31F0	\u31FF	Katakana Phonetic Extensions
\u3200	\u32FF	Enclosed CJK Letters and Months
\u3300	\u33FF	CJK Compatibility
\u3400	\u4DBF	CJK Unified Ideographs Extension A
\u4DC0	\u4DFF	Yijing Hexagram Symbols
\u4E00	\u9FBB	CJK Unified Ideographs
\uA000	\uA48F	Yi Syllables
\uA490	\uA4CF	Yi Radicals
\uA700	\uA71F	Modifier Tone Letters
\uA720	\uA7FF	Latin Extended-D
\uA800	\uA82F	Syloti Nagri
\uA840	\uA87F	Phags-pa
\uAC00	\uD7A3	Hangul Syllables
\uD800	\uDB7F	High Surrogates
\uDB80	\uDBFF	Private Use High Surrogates
\uDC00	\uDFFF	Low Surrogates

continued

TABLE 15-1 *(continued)*

Start Code	End Code	Block Name
\uE000	\uF8FF	Private Use Area
\uF900	\uFAFF	CJK Compatibility Ideographs
\uFB00	\uFB4F	Alphabetic Presentation Forms
\uFB50	\uFDFF	Arabic Presentation Forms-A
\uFE00	\uFE0F	Variation Selectors
\uFE10	\uFE1F	Vertical Forms
\uFE20	\uFE2F	Combining Half Marks
\uFE30	\uFE4F	CJK Compatibility Forms
\uFE50	\uFE6F	Small Form Variants
\uFE70	\uFEFF	Arabic Presentation Forms-B
\uFF00	\uFFEF	Halfwidth and Fullwidth Forms
\uFFF0	\uFFFF	Specials

ISO-8859-1

If you are working on websites for Western audiences, you will most likely use ISO-8859-1, which, although not officially a subset of UTF-8, does map to the Latin Basic and Latin Extended A Unicode sets.

The most familiar encoding to Western HTML developers, ISO-8859-1, is a subset of Unicode and can be used safely because most modern user agents support Unicode. Although ISO-8859-1 is not part of the Unicode standard, the two bodies governing both standards have worked together to standardize the models.

Note

The entire set of ISO-8859-1 numeric references can be found at `www.w3 .org/MarkUp/html3/latin1.html`. ■

Table 15-2 shows the entities you are likely to encounter as an HTML developer. If your encoding is UTF-8, then you can use the decimal references, but for compatibility with older user agents you should use HTML entities, because many older user agents don't support Unicode.

Latin-1 Supplement (U + 00 C0 - U + 00FF)

The Latin-1 Supplement also contains values from ISO-8859-1. The characters in this Unicode block are used for the following languages:

- Danish
- Dutch

- Faroese
- Finnish
- Flemish
- German
- Icelandic
- Irish
- Italian
- Norwegian
- Portuguese
- Spanish
- Swedish

It extends the Basic Latin encoding with a miscellaneous set of punctuation and mathematical signs.

TABLE 15-2

ISO-8859-1 HTML Entities

Description	Decimal-Based Code Value	HTML Entity	How Character Appears on Web Page
Quotation mark	"	"	"
Ampersand	&	&	&
Less-than sign	<	<	<
Greater-than sign	>	>	>
Nonbreaking space			
Inverted exclamation	¡	¡	¡
Cent sign	¢	¢	¢
Pound sterling	£	£	£
General currency sign	¤	¤	¤
Yen sign	¥	¥	¥
Broken vertical bar	¦	¦	|
Section sign	§	§	§
Umlaut (diaeresis)	¨	¨ &dia;	¨
Copyright	©	©	©

continued

TABLE 15-2 *(continued)*

Description	Decimal-Based Code Value	HTML Entity	How Character Appears on Web Page
Feminine ordinal	ª	ª	ª
Left angle quote, guillemotleft	«	«	«
Not sign	¬	¬	¬
Soft hyphen			-
Registered trademark	®	®	®
Macron accent	¯	¯	¯
Degree sign	°	°	°
Plus or minus	±	±	±
Superscript two	²	²	^{2}
Superscript three	³	³	^{3}
Acute accent	´	´	´
Micro sign	µ	µ	µ
Paragraph sign	¶	¶	¶
Middle dot	·	·	·
Cedilla	¸	¸	¸
Superscript one	¹	¹	^{1}
Masculine ordinal	º	°	°
Right angle quote, guillemotright	»	»	»
Fraction one-fourth	¼	¼	¼
Fraction one-half	½	½	½
Fraction three-fourths	¾	¾	¾
Inverted question mark	¿	¿	¿
Capital A, grave accent	À	À	À
Capital A, acute accent	Á	Á	Á
Capital A, circumflex accent	Â	Â	Â
Capital A, tilde	Ã	Ã	Ã
Capital A, diaeresis or umlaut mark	Ä	Ä	Ä
Capital A, ring	Å	Å	Å
Capital AE diphthong (ligature)	Æ	Æ	Æ

Description	Decimal-Based Code Value	HTML Entity	How Character Appears on Web Page
Capital C, cedilla	Ç	Ç	Ç
Capital E, grave accent	È	È	È
Capital E, acute accent	É	É	É
Capital E, circumflex accent	Ê	Ê	Ê
Capital E, diaeresis or umlaut mark	Ë	Ë	Ë
Capital I, grave accent	Ì	Ì	Ì
Capital I, acute accent	Í	Í	Í
Capital I, circumflex accent	Î	Î	Î
Capital I, diaeresis or umlaut mark	Ï	Ï	Ï
Capital Eth, Icelandic	Ð	Ð	Ð
Capital N, tilde	Ñ	Ñ	Ñ
Capital O, grave accent	Ò	Ò	Ò
Capital O, acute accent	Ó	Ó	Ó
Capital O, circumflex accent	Ô	Ô	Ô
Capital O, tilde	Õ	Õ	Õ
Capital O, diaeresis or umlaut mark	Ö	Ö	Ö
Multiplication sign	×	×	×
Capital O, slash	Ø	Ø	Ø
Capital U, grave accent	Ù	Ù	Ù
Capital U, acute accent	Ú	Ú	Ú
Capital U, circumflex accent	Û	Û	Û
Capital U, diaeresis or umlaut mark	Ü	Ü	Ü
Capital Y, acute accent	Ý	Ý	Ý
Capital THORN, Icelandic	Þ	Þ	Þ
Small sharp s, German (sz ligature)	ß	ß	ß
Small a, grave accent	à	à	à
Small a, acute accent	á	á	á
Small a, circumflex accent	â	â	â
Small a, tilde	ã	ã	ã

continued

TABLE 15-2 *(continued)*

Description	Decimal-Based Code Value	HTML Entity	How Character Appears on Web Page
Small a, diaeresis or umlaut mark	ä	ä	ä
Small a, ring	å	å	å
Small ae diphthong (ligature)	æ	æ	æ
Small c, cedilla	ç	ç	ç
Small e, grave accent	è	è	è
Small e, acute accent	é	é	é
Small e, circumflex accent	ê	ê	ê
Small e, diaeresis or umlaut mark	ë	ë ë	ë
Small i, grave accent	ì	ì	ì
Small i, acute accent	í	í	í
Small i, circumflex accent	î	î	î
Small i, diaeresis or umlaut mark	ï	ï	ï
Small eth, Icelandic	ð	ð	ð
Small n, tilde	ñ	ñ	ñ
Small o, grave accent	ò	ò	ò
Small o, acute accent	ó	ó	ó
Small o, circumflex accent	ô	ô	ô
Small o, tilde	õ	õ	õ
Small o, diaeresis or umlaut mark	ö	ö	ö
Division sign	÷	÷	÷
Small o, slash	ø	ø	ø
Small u, grave accent	ù	ù	ù
Small u, acute accent	ú	ú	ú
Small u, circumflex accent	û	û	û
Small u, diaeresis or umlaut mark	ü	ü	ü
Small y, acute accent	ý	ý	ý
Small thorn, Icelandic	þ	þ	þ
Small y, diaeresis or umlaut mark	ÿ	ÿ	ÿ
Trademark symbol	™	™	™

Latin Extended-A (U + 0100 - U + 017F)

Once you extend coding past Latin-1 Supplement in Unicode, you begin to veer away from ISO-8859-1 as well. There are specific ISO encodings for different Latin languages. You can find the names of these encodings at `www.alanwood.net/unicode/latin_extended_a.html`.

Alternately, you can simply guarantee the incorporation of these encodings by using UTF-8. The characters in this Unicode block are used in the following languages (among others):

- Afrikaans
- Basque
- Breton
- Catalan
- Croatian
- Czech
- Esperanto
- Estonian
- French
- Frisian
- Greenlandic
- Hungarian
- Latin
- Latvian
- Lithuanian
- Maltese
- Polish
- Provencal
- Rhaeto-Romanic
- Romanian
- Romany
- Sami
- Slovak
- Slovenian
- Sorbian
- Turkish
- Welsh

Latin Extended-B and Latin Extended Additional

The characters in this block are used to write additional languages and to extend Latin encodings. These characters include seldom used characters such as the bilabial click. By the time you reach this territory of encoding, you should definitely be using UTF-8.

Tip

It might seem that encoding your documents in UTF-8 is the best bet. However, mixing encodings is a bad idea and you should consider using a specific codepage for each region — ISO-8859-1 for a largely Western language audience, for example. ■

Summary

This chapter introduced you to the concept of localization of your site. It also covered the basics of Unicode and the different code pages you are likely to encounter when coding your documents for an international audience.

The next two chapters, 16 and 17, cover JavaScript and dynamic HTML.

CHAPTER

16

Scripts

IN THIS CHAPTER

Standard HTML was designed to provide static, text-only documents. No innate intelligence is built into plain HTML, but it is desired, especially in more complex documents or documents designed to be interactive. Enter scripts — svelte programming languages designed to accomplish simple tasks while adhering to the basic premise of the Web, easily deployable content that can play nicely with plain-text HTML.

This chapter covers scripting basics and then provides the details of how to use client-side scripting in your documents.

Client-Side versus Server-Side Scripting

There are two basic varieties of scripting, *client-side* and *server-side*. As their names imply, the main difference is where the scripts are actually executed.

Client-side scripting

Client-side scripts are run by the client software — that is, the user agent. As such, they impose no additional load on the server, but the client must support the scripting language being used.

JavaScript is the most popular client-side scripting language, but JScript and VBScript are also widely used. Client-side scripts are typically embedded in HTML documents and deployed to the client. Client users can usually easily view these scripts.

For security reasons, client-side scripts generally cannot read or write to the server or client file system.

Server-side scripting

Server-side scripts are run by the Web server. Typically, these scripts are referred to as CGI scripts, CGI being an abbreviation for Common Gateway Interface, the first interface for server-side Web scripting. Server-side scripts impose more of a load on the server, but generally don't influence the client — even output to the client is optional. The client may have no idea that the server is running a script.

Perl, Python, PHP, Java, ASP, and ASP.NET are all examples of server-side scripting languages. The script typically resides only on the server, but is called by code in the HTML document.

Although server-side scripts cannot read or write to the client's file system, they usually have some access to the server's file system. Therefore, it is important that the system administrator take appropriate measures to secure server-side scripts and limit their access.

Note

Unless you are a system administrator on the Web server you use to deploy your content, your ability to use server-side scripts is probably limited. Your Internet service provider (ISP) or system administrator has policies that allow or disallow server-side scripting in various languages and performing various tasks.

If you intend to use server-side scripts, you should check with your ISP or system administrator to determine what resources are available to you. ■

This chapter deals only with client-side scripting.

Setting the Default Scripting Language

To embed a client-side script in your document, you use the script (`<script>`) tag. This tag has the following, minimal format:

```
<script type="script_type">
```

The value of `script_type` depends on the scripting language you are using. The following are generally used script types:

- `text/ecmascript`
- `text/javascript`
- `text/jscript`
- `text/vbscript`
- `text/vbs`
- `text/xml`

For example, if you are using JavaScript, your script tag would resemble the following:

```
<script type="text/javascript">
```

Note

The W3C recommends that you specify the default script type you are using in an appropriate `META` tag in your document. Such a tag resembles the following:

```
<META http-equiv="content_script_type"
content="text/javascript">
```

This does not obviate the need for the `type` attribute in each `script` tag. You must still specify each `script` tag's type for your documents to validate against HTML 4.01. ■

If your script is encoded in a character set other than the one used for the rest of the document, you should also use the `charset` attribute to specify the script's encoding. This attribute has the same format as the `charset` attribute for other tags:

```
charset="character_encoding_type"
```

Including a Script

To include a script in your document, place the script's code within `<script>` tags. For example, consider the following script:

```
<script type="text/javascript">
  function NewWindow(url){
    var fin=window.open(url,"","width=800,height=600,
    scrollbars=yes,resizable=yes");
}
</script>
```

You can include as much scripting code between the tags as needed, providing that the script is syntactically sound. Scripts can be included within a document's head or body sections, and you can include as many script sections as you like. Note, however, that nested `script` tags are not valid HTML.

Generally, you will want to place your scripts in the head section of your document so the scripts are available as the rest of the page loads. You may occasionally want to embed a script in a particular location in the document — in those cases, place an appropriate `script` block in the body of the document. For example, you may want a script in close proximity to a paragraph it affects. In that case, you would place it in-line, as shown in the following example:

```
<h2>Spa Services</h2>
<p>The Oasis of Tranquility offers a full menu of services to
renew the real you that lies within. Begin in one of our two
relaxation centers, then enjoy an invigorating body and facial care,
deep soothing massage therapies, and a host of other indulgent
treatments that pamper you on the outside, and revive you from
within. In addition to our many spa services, take a refreshing dip
in the swimming pool, melt in one of our whirlpool spas, or
rejuvenate in the sauna.</p>
```

```
<script type="text/javascript">
   ... script contents go here ...
</script>
<h2>Give the Gift of Tranquility</h2>
<p>All services at the Oasis of Tranquility can be experienced
individually, or selected a la carte to create you own personalized
day of pampering.  Gift certificates are excellent for surprising
your loved ones with an hour or a day of pampering and
rejuvenation.</p>
```

Calling an External Script

If you have some scripts that you want to use in multiple documents, consider placing them in an external file. You can then use the `script` tag's `src` attribute to specify that the script content can be found in that file. For example, suppose you want to include the following script in multiple documents:

```
function NewWindow(url){
  var fin=window.open(url,"","width=800,height=600,
  scrollbars=yes,resizable=yes");
}
```

You can place the script in a text file on the server and specify the file's URL in the appropriate `script` tag's `src` attribute. Suppose the preceding file were stored in the file `scripts.js` on the server. Your script tag would then resemble the following:

```
<script type="text/javascript" src="scripts.js"></script>
```

Note that even though the script element's body is empty, it still requires the closing `</script>` tag.

One major advantage to external script files is that if you need to edit the script, you can edit it in one place — the external file — and the change is effected in all the documents that include it.

Triggering Scripts with Events

Most HTML tags can include event attributes that can be used to trigger scripts. Table 16-1 lists these attributes and their use for triggering scripts.

Cross-Ref

See Appendix A for a comprehensive list of what tags support event attributes. ■

Note

Many of the event attribute triggers are dependent on the element(s) to which they apply being "in focus" at the time of the trigger. ■

TABLE 16-1

Event Attributes

Attribute	Trigger Use
`onclick`	When item enclosed in the tag is clicked
`ondblclick`	When item enclosed in the tag is double-clicked
`onmousedown`	When mouse button is pressed while mouse pointer is over the item enclosed in the tag
`onmouseup`	When mouse button is released while mouse pointer is over item enclosed in the tag
`onmouseover`	When mouse pointer is placed over the item enclosed in the tag
`onmousemove`	When mouse is moved within the item enclosed in the tag
`onmouseout`	When mouse is moved outside of the item enclosed in the tag
`onblur`	When item enclosed in the tag has focus removed
`onfocus`	When item enclosed in the tag receives focus
`onload`	When the document finishes loading (valid only in the `<body>` tag)
`onunload`	When the document is unloaded — when the user navigates to another document (valid only in the `<body>` tag). This event is often used to create pop-ups when a user leaves a site.
`onsubmit`	When a form has its Submit button pressed (valid only in `<form>` tags)
`onreset`	When a form has its Reset button pressed (valid only in `<form>` tags)
`onkeypress`	When a key is pressed while the mouse pointer is over the item enclosed in the tag
`onkeydown`	When a key is pressed down while the mouse pointer is over the item enclosed in the tag
`onkeyup`	When a key is released while the mouse pointer is over the item enclosed in the tag

Event triggers have a variety of uses, including the following:

- **Form data verification** — Using the `onchange` and `onselect` attributes, you can verify each field as it is changed or selected. Using `onsubmit` and `onreset`, you can verify or reset an entire form when the appropriate button is clicked.
- **Image animation** — Using the `onmouseover` and `onmouseout` attributes, you can animate an image when the mouse pointer passes over it.
- **Mouse navigation** — Using the `onclick` and `ondblclick` attributes, you can trigger user agent navigation when a user clicks or double-clicks an element.

For example, you can create images to use as buttons on your page. Figure 16-1 shows two images for use on a button. The image on the left is used for general display, while the image on the right is used when the mouse is over the button.

FIGURE 16-1

Two images for use as a button

Tip

Users appreciate visible feedback from active elements on your page. As such, it is important to always provide visible changes to navigation elements. Links should have a visibly different style when moused over, as should navigation buttons. ■

Combining `onmouseover`, `onmouseout`, and `onclick` events, you can easily create a button that reacts when the mouse is over it and navigates to a new page when clicked. Consider the following document, which uses a few JavaScript scripts and events to create a navigation button:

```
<!DOCTYPE HTML PUBLIC "-//W3C//DTD HTML 4.01//EN"
  "http://www.w3.org/TR/html4/strict.dtd">
<html>
<head>
<META http-equiv="Content-Script-Type"
     content="text/javascript">
```

```
<title>Event Buttons</title>
<script type="text/javascript">
  // Get the specified object by ID
  //  (browser specific method used)
  function getObj(id) {
    if (document.getElementById) {
      this.obj = document.getElementById(id);
}     else if (document.all) {
      this.obj = document.all[id];
}     else if (document.layers) {
      this.obj = document.layers[id];
}
}
   // Activate the specified button
   function activate(bname) {
     imageid = bname + "button";
     iname = bname + "On.jpg";
     x = new getObj(imageid);
     x.obj.src = iname;
}
   // Deactivate the specified button
   function deactivate(bname) {
     imageid = bname + "button";
     iname = bname + "Off.jpg";
     x = new getObj(imageid);
     x.obj.src = iname;
}

</script>
</head>
<body>
<p>
<img alt="Home page" id="homebutton"
  src="HomeOff.jpg"
  onmouseover="activate('home')"
  onmouseout="deactivate('home')"
  onclick="document.location='home.html"'
/>
</p>
</body>
</html>
```

When the document loads, the button is displayed in its inactive (off) state, as shown in Figure 16-2. When the mouse is placed over the button, the `onmouseover` event launches the JavaScript `activate` function, which changes the image's `src` attribute, causing the button to be displayed as active (on), as shown in Figure 16-3.

When the mouse leaves the button, the `onmouseout` event launches the `deactivate` function, returning the button display to its inactive display state by changing the `src` attribute back to the original image. When the button is clicked, the `onclick` event changes the `location` property of the user agent, effectively navigating to a new page (in this case `home.html`).

Note that the JavaScript code for the `onclick` attribute is contained directly in the value of the attribute — because the code is short, placing it in-line within the attribute is more economical than creating a separate function.

FIGURE 16-2

The button is initially displayed in its inactive (off) state.

Tip

You can place several lines of code within the value section of the event attributes. Just ensure that you end each line (where appropriate) with a semicolon. ■

This example only scratches the surface of what JavaScript can do within an HTML document. Similar methods can be used to manipulate form objects and other elements within your documents.

Cross-Ref

Additional methods and examples are covered in Chapter 17. ■

FIGURE 16-3

The button is changed to active (on) when the mouse is over it.

Hiding Scripts from Older Browsers

Not all user agents support JavaScript. Many of the older user agents are not JavaScript-enabled, and some of the latest user agents may have JavaScript disabled by their users.

Note

Most modern browsers will ignore scripts of types they do not recognize. ■

If you are concerned about older browsers not recognizing your scripts, you should *hide* your scripts so that older browsers will ignore them (instead of trying to render them).

To hide your scripts, simply place them within a special set of comment tags. The only difference between normal comment tags and script-hiding tags is that the closing tag contains two slashes (//). Those two slashes enable browsers that support scripting to find the script.

For example, the following structure will effectively hide the scripts within the <script> tag:

```
<script type="text/javascript">
  <!-- hide scripts from older browsers
  --- Script content ---
  // -->
</script>
```

Summary

This chapter introduced how to add basic intelligence and dynamic content to your site via client-side scripting. You learned how to embed scripts in your documents and how to utilize external script files. The chapter also covered the use of event attributes to trigger scripts from user actions.

The next chapter covers Dynamic HTML, which enables you to influence a document's content using scripting, and shows how to put the basic knowledge of scripting you learned here to maximum use.

Dynamic HTML

Dynamic HTML (DHTML) is a combination of HTML, CSS, and JavaScript, used to create dynamic Web page effects. These can be animations, dynamic menus, text effects such as drop shadows, text that appears when a user rolls over an item, and other similar effects.

This chapter introduces DHTML by reviewing some JavaScript basics and providing a look at the Document Object Model (DOM), which enables you to access HTML elements so you can change their properties and/or content. Examples of common DHTML techniques are provided.

IN THIS CHAPTER

Note

In a very strict, technical sense, DHTML is thought of as containing code that is targeted toward level 4 browser architecture with a lot of proprietary code. For example, such a script would be written for a particular platform, use proprietary hooks and code existing only on that platform, and would be incompatible with other platforms.

However, Document Object Model (DOM) scripting has emerged to enable scripts that follow cross-browser–compatible standards, and hence are more compatible with more platforms.

That said, DHTML is still the predominant term used for the dynamic combination of HTML, CSS, and JavaScript, and as such is used here. ■

The Need for DHTML

DHTML, when used correctly, can significantly enhance the user experience. DHTML was originally best known for its flashy effects. These still exist, but their importance is questionable, and when used improperly they can be annoying for your users. Fancy text animations and bouncing balls might be fun to write, but they're not so much fun for the user. This chapter focuses on the more practical aspects of DHTML, most of which are related to navigation. After all, your website should be all about the user experience.

Tip

Whenever you create an enhancement to your website, you should always ask, "Does this improve the user experience? Can they navigate my site more easily? Read my Web page more easily?" If the answer to any of these questions is no, rethink the enhancement. ■

How DHTML Works

DHTML can work either by applying certain CSS properties or by using JavaScript to directly manipulate HTML elements. When using JavaScript, DHTML takes advantage of a browser's object model, which is a tree of objects based on the element set of HTML and the property set of CSS. When you code against that object model, you can change an element's properties, which are associated with an element's attributes. An element's attributes, in fact, are referred to as *properties* in a JavaScript environment. How these properties are referred to, and what actions (methods) you can take on them, is determined by the DOM.

Actually, several DOMs are available for your scripting needs. However, only two are pertinent for typical websites — the pure object DOM created by the World Wide Web Consortium (W3C) and the JavaScript DOM consisting of JavaScript methods mapped to document objects. The following sections cover both of these models.

The Document Object Model

Most Web developers are familiar with the concept of DHTML and the underlying DOMs developed by Netscape and Microsoft for their respective browsers. However, a unifying DOM developed by the W3C is even more powerful, because of its compatibility, and is much more popular with more professional developers. The W3C DOM has several advantages over the DHTML DOMs — using its node structure, it is possible to easily navigate and change documents despite the user agent employed to display them. This chapter covers the basics of the W3C DOM and explains how to use JavaScript to manipulate it.

Note

The W3C DOM is much more complex than shown within this chapter. Several additional methods and properties are at your disposal to use in manipulating documents, many more than we have room to address in this chapter. Further reading and information on the standard can be found on the W3C site at `www.w3.org/TR/2000/WD-DOM-Level-1-20000929/Overview.html`. **■**

The history of the DOM

The DOM was developed by the W3C to allow programming languages access to the underlying structure of a Web document. Using the DOM, a program can access any element in the document, determining and changing attributes and even removing, adding, or rearranging elements at will.

It's important to note that the DOM is a type of application program interface (API), allowing any programming language access to the structure of a Web document. The main advantage of using the DOM is the capability to manipulate a document without another trip to the document's server. As such, the DOM is typically accessed and used by client-side technologies, such as JavaScript.

The first DOM specification (Level 0) was developed at the same time as JavaScript and early browsers. It is supported by Netscape 2 onward.

Two intermediate DOMs were supported by Netscape 4 onward and Microsoft Internet Explorer (IE) versions 4 and 5 onward. These DOMs were proprietary to the two sides of the browser coin — Netscape and Microsoft IE. The former used a collection of elements referenced through a `document.layers` object, whereas the latter used a `document.all` object. To be truly cross-browser compatible, a script should endeavor to cover both of these DOMs instead of only one or the other.

The latest, well-supported DOM specification (Level 2) is supported by Mozilla and Microsoft Internet Explorer version 5 onward. Both browser developers participated in the creation of this level of the DOM. However, Microsoft chose to continue to support its `document.all` model as well, while Netscape discontinued its `document.layers` model.

Keep in mind that because the DOM was originally intended to allow programs to navigate and change XML, not HTML, documents, it contains many features a Web developer dealing only with HTML may never need.

Understanding the DOM

The basis of the DOM is to recognize each element of the document as a node connected to other nodes in the document and to the document root itself. The best way to understand the structure is to look at an example. The following code shows a document that renders as shown in Figure 17-1, and whose DOM is illustrated in Figure 17-2:

```
<!DOCTYPE HTML PUBLIC "-//W3C//DTD HTML 4.01//EN"
   "http://www.w3.org/TR/html4/strict.dtd">
<html>
<head>
<title>Sample DOM Document</title>
<style type="text/css">
  div.div1 { background-color: #999999; }
```

```
  div.div2 { background-color: #BBBBBB; }
  table, table * { border: thin solid black; }
  table { border-collapse: collapse; }
  td { padding: 5px; }
</style>
<script type="text/JavaScript">
</script>
</head>
<body>
<div class="div1">
  <h1>Heading 1</h1>
  <table>
    <tr><td>Cell 1</td><td>Cell 2</td></tr>
    <tr><td>Cell 3</td><td>Cell 4</td></tr>
  </table>
  <p>Lorem ipsum dolor sit amet, consectetuer adipiscing
  elit, sed diam <b>nonummy nibh euismod</b> tincidunt ut laoreet
  dolore magna aliquam erat volutpat. Ut wisi enim ad minim
  veniam, quis nostrud exerci tation ullamcorper suscipit
  lobortis nisl ut aliquip ex ea commodo consequat.</p>
</div>
<div class="div2">
  <h1>Heading 2</h1>
  <p>Lorem ipsum dolor sit amet, consectetuer adipiscing
  elit, sed diam nonummy nibh euismod tincidunt ut laoreet
  dolore magna aliquam erat volutpat. Ut wisi enim ad minim
  veniam, quis nostrud exerci tation ullamcorper suscipit
  lobortis nisl ut aliquip ex ea commodo consequat.</p>
  <ol id="sortme">An ordered list
    <li>Gamma</li>
    <li>Alpha</li>
    <li>Beta</li>
  </ol>
</div>
</body>
</html>
```

As you can see, each node is joined to its neighbors using a familiar parent/child/sibling relationship. For example, the first div node is a child of the body node, and the div node in turn has three children: an h1 node, a P node, and an ol node. Those three children (h1, p, and ol) have a sibling relationship to one another.

Plain text and usually the content of nodes such as paragraphs (p) are referenced as textual nodes and are broken down, as necessary, to incorporate additional nodes. This can be seen in the first p node, which contains a bold (b) element. The children of the P node include the first bit of text up to the bold element, the bold element, and the text after the bold element. The bold element (b) in turn contains a text child, which contains the bolded text.

The relationships between nodes can be explored and traversed using the DOM JavaScript bindings, as described in the next section.

FIGURE 17-1

A sample document

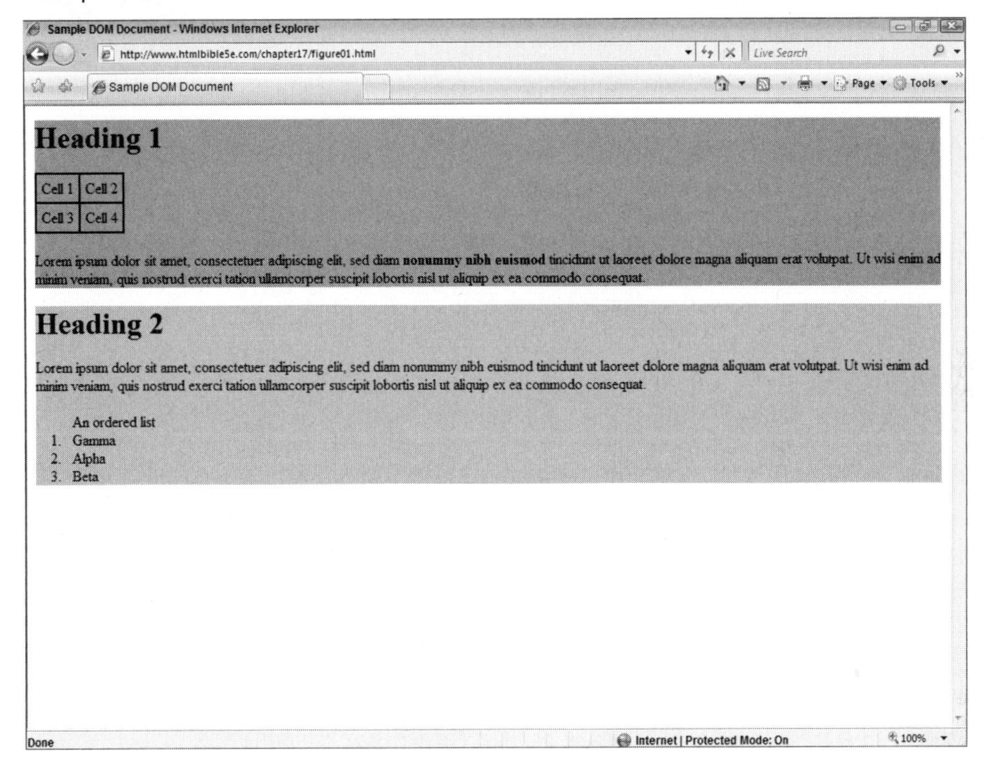

DOM node properties and methods

The W3C DOM includes several JavaScript bindings that can be used to navigate a document's DOM. A subset of those bindings, used in JavaScript as properties and methods, is listed in Tables 17-1 and 17-2. The first table describes JavaScript's properties.

Note

A full list of DOM Level 1 JavaScript bindings can be found on the W3C's Document Object Model Level 1 pages, at `www.w3.org/TR/2000/WD-DOM-Level-1-20000929/ecma-script-language-binding.html`. ■

Note

A full list of DOM Level 2 JavaScript bindings can be found on the W3C's Document Object Model Level 2 pages, at `www.w3.org/TR/2000/REC-DOM-Level-2-Core-20001113/ecma-script-binding.html`. ■

FIGURE 17-2

Diagram of the sample document's DOM

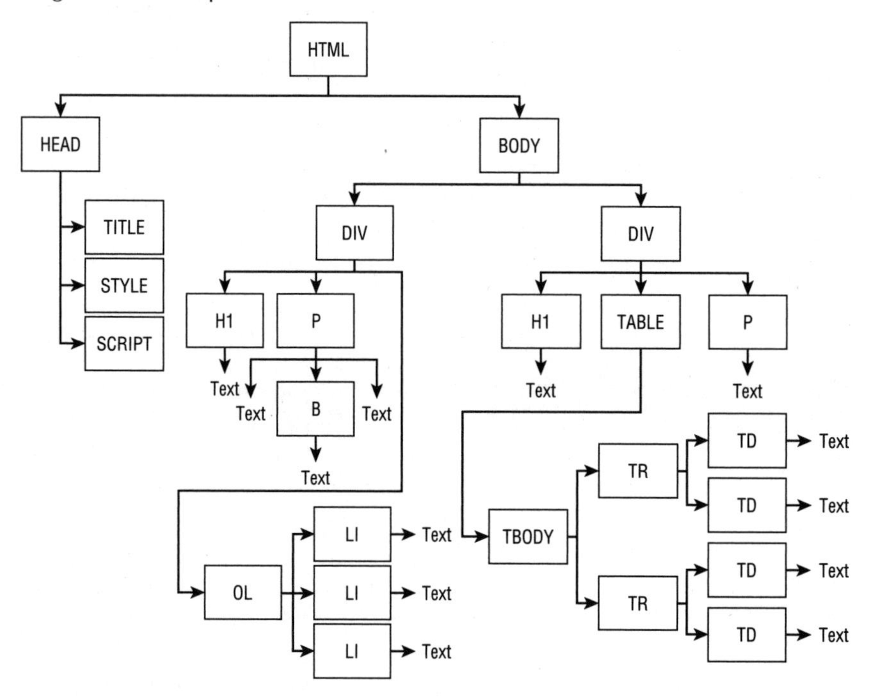

TABLE 17-1

JavaScript DOM Property Bindings

Property	Description
`attributes`	This read-only property returns a `NamedNodeMap` containing the specified node's attributes.
`childNodes`	This read-only property returns a node list containing all the children of the specified node.
`firstChild`	This read-only property returns the first child node of the specified node.
`lastChild`	This read-only property returns the last child node of the specified node.
`nextSibling`	This read-only property returns the next sibling of the specified node.
`nodeName`	This read-only property returns a string containing the name of the node, which is typically the name of the element (`p`, `div`, `table`, and so on).
`nodeType`	This read-only property returns a number corresponding to the node type (1 = element, 2 = text).

Property	Description
`nodeValue`	This property returns a string containing the contents of the node and is only valid for text nodes.
`ownerDocument`	This read-only property returns the root document node object of the specified node.
`parentNode`	This read-only property returns the parent node of the specified node.
`previousSibling`	This read-only property returns the previous sibling of the specified node. If there is no node, then the property returns `null`.

TABLE 17-2

JavaScript DOM Method Bindings

Method	Description
`appendChild(newChild)`	Given a node, this method inserts the `newChild` node at the end of the children and returns a node.
`cloneNode(deep)`	This method clones the node object. The parameter `deep` — (a Boolean) — specifies whether the clone should include the source object's attributes and children. The return value is the cloned node(s).
`createElement(element)`	This method creates an HTML `element` of the specified type.
`createTextNode("text")`	This method creates a new text node using the specified text.
`getAttribute(attrib)`	This method returns the value of the specified `attribute`.
`getElementById(id)`	This method returns a reference to the element having the `id` specified.
`getElementByTagName(element)`	This method returns the number of a specified `element` found in the document.
`hasChildNodes()`	This method returns `true` if the node object has children nodes, `false` if the node object has no children nodes.
`insertBefore(newChild, refChild)`	Given two nodes, this method inserts the `newChild` node before the specified `refChild` node and returns a node object.
`removeChild(oldChild)`	Given a node, this method removes the `oldChild` node from the DOM and returns a node object containing the node removed.

continued

TABLE 17-2 *(continued)*

Method	Description
replaceChild(newChild, oldChild)	Given two nodes, this method replaces the oldChild node with the newChild node and returns a node object. Note that if the newChild is already in the DOM, it is removed from its current location to replace the oldChild.
setAttribute(attribute, value)	This method sets the specified attribute to the specified value.

Traversing and changing a document's nodes

Using the bindings from the preceding section, it is possible to write JavaScript to navigate through a document using nodes and change node attributes. Remember that nodes typically correspond to HTML elements, so changing nodes changes the document's HTML.

The following code includes a recursive JavaScript function, findNode(), that looks at each node and child node in a document, searching for the node that is an ol element with an id of sortme. The comments in the code outline how the function operates:

```
<!DOCTYPE HTML PUBLIC "-//W3C//DTD HTML 4.01//EN"
   "http://www.w3.org/TR/html4/strict.dtd">
<html>
<head>
<title>DOM Find Node</title>
<style type="text/css">
  div.div1 { background-color: #999999; }
  div.div2 { background-color: #BBBBBB; }
  table, table * { border: thin solid black; }
  table { border-collapse: collapse; }
  td { padding: 5px; }
</style>
<script type="text/JavaScript">
// Starting at node "startnode," transverse the document
//   looking for an element named "nodename" with an id
//   of "nodeid"
//////////////////////////////////////////////////////
function findNode(startnode,nodename,nodeid) {
  var foundNode = false;
  // Check if our starting node is what we are looking for
  if ( startnode.nodeName == nodename &&
       startnode.id == nodeid ) {
    foundNode = startnode;
  // If startnode is not what we are searching for
}   else {
    look_thru_children:
    // If current startnode has children
```

```
    if ( startnode.hasChildNodes() ) {
      var children = startnode.childNodes;
      // Look through each child and its children
      //   (by recursing through this function)
      for (var i = 0; i < children.length; i++) {
        foundNode = findNode(children[i],nodename,nodeid);
         // If we find what we are looking for, stop recursion
         if (foundNode) { break look_thru_children;}
}
}
}
  // Return the node
  return foundNode;
}
///////////////////////////////////////////////////
// Kick off the search (runs from <body> onload)
function dofind() {
  alert("Click OK to find 'sortme' node");
  var node = findNode(document,"OL","sortme");
  alert("Found node: " + node.nodeName);
}
</script>
</head>
<body onload="dofind()">
<div class="div1">
  <h1>Heading 1</h1>
  <table>
    <tr><td>Cell 1</td><td>Cell 2</td></tr>
    <tr><td>Cell 3</td><td>Cell 4</td></tr>
  </table>
  <p>Lorem ipsum dolor sit amet, consectetuer adipiscing
  elit, sed diam <b>nonummy nibh euismod</b> tincidunt ut laoreet
  dolore magna aliquam erat volutpat. Ut wisi enim ad minim
  veniam, quis nostrud exerci tation ullamcorper suscipit
  lobortis nisl ut aliquip ex ea commodo consequat.</p>
</div>
<div class="div2">
  <h1>Heading 2</h1>
  <p>Lorem ipsum dolor sit amet, consectetuer adipiscing
  elit, sed diam nonummy nibh euismod tincidunt ut laoreet
  dolore magna aliquam erat volutpat. Ut wisi enim ad minim
  veniam, quis nostrud exerci tation ullamcorper suscipit
  lobortis nisl ut aliquip ex ea commodo consequat.</p>
  <ol id="sortme">An ordered list
    <li>Gamma</li>
    <li>Alpha</li>
    <li>Beta</li>
  </ol>
</div>
</body>
</html>
```

The script opens an alert window displaying the found node's name.

Tip

The DOM provides another, easier mechanism to find an element with a particular `id` — namely, the `getElementById()` method of the document object. In fact, the entire search function in the preceding script can be replaced with one line:

```
node = document.getElementById("sortme");
```

The previous method of traversing the DOM was used only to illustrate how you can manually navigate and search the DOM, if necessary. ■

Just as you can navigate downward through the document using the `childNodes` method, you can also navigate across the DOM with `previousSibling` or `nextSibling` (selecting adjacent siblings of a particular node) or up the DOM using `parentNode`.

You can also use the JavaScript bindings to change a node's value. For example, suppose you have a paragraph element with an ID of `"edit"` similar to this:

```
<p id="edit"> ... </p>
```

You can change the text within the element using the following JavaScript code:

```
// Find the element, assign it to "node"
var node = document.getElementById("edit");
  // Make sure the node is text (nodeType = 3)
  if (node.firstChild.nodeType == 3) {
    // Change the text to "Changed text"
    node.firstChild.nodeValue = "Changed text";
}
```

You can also copy one element's text to another, using code similar to the following:

```
node2.nodeValue = node1.nodeValue;
```

Ultimately, you can copy an entire node to another, using code similar to this:

```
// Copy a node and all of its properties to another
node2 = node1;
```

The JavaScript DOM

The standardized form of JavaScript is called ECMAScript. This is a relevant fact because, usually, if you confine your scripting to the conventions of the W3C's Level 1 DOM and ECMAScript, you'll be pretty successful at achieving cross-browser scripting compatibility.

Note

You can find the specification for ECMAScript at `www.ecma-international.org/publications/standards/Ecma-262.htm`. ■

The W3C's Level 1 Core DOM is basically a set of properties and methods that can be accessed from a given element. For example, one of the most ubiquitous (and dastardly, in many people's opinion) methods is the `window.open()`method, which makes it possible for JavaScript to open a new browser window in which advertising pop-ups appear the majority of the time. The `open()`method acts on the `window` object, which, although not an element (the DOM isn't restricted to elements), is still an object that can be manipulated by script.

JavaScript has a host of built-in objects that can be used to access the user agent and the document it contains. This section introduces the various objects and how JavaScript can use them. Figure 17-3 shows the ECMAScript (JavaScript) Core DOM, consisting of the various objects, properties, and methods to access document objects. The sections that follow provide more detail on the DOM's elements.

Note

Use of the JavaScript DOM is a stark contrast to using the W3C DOMs. The former has a host of built-in objects that allow you to directly access objects in a document, whereas the latter utilizes a set of standard methods for accessing and manipulating elements as nodes. Generally, use of the JavaScript DOM is easier and more straightforward, but it does require more advanced knowledge of a document's layout and contents, whereas the W3C DOM tools can act upon more abstract documents. ■

Tip

For quick-and-dirty scripts, stick with the JavaScript DOM. For more robust and variable scripting, consider the W3C DOM. ■

The window object

The `window` object is the top-level object for an XHTML document. It includes properties and methods to manipulate the user agent window. The `window` object is also the top-level object for most other objects.

Using the `window` object, not only can you work with the current user agent window, you can also open and work with new windows. The following code will open a new window displaying a specific document:

```
NewWin = window.open("example.htm","newWindow",
  "width=400,height=400,scrollbars=no,resizable=no");
```

The `open` method takes three arguments: the URL of the document to open in the window, the name of the new window, and options for the window. For example, the preceding code opens a window named `newWindow` containing the document `example.htm` and will be 400 pixels square, be non-resizable, and have no scroll bars.

FIGURE 17-3

The Core DOM used by ECMAScript (JavaScript)

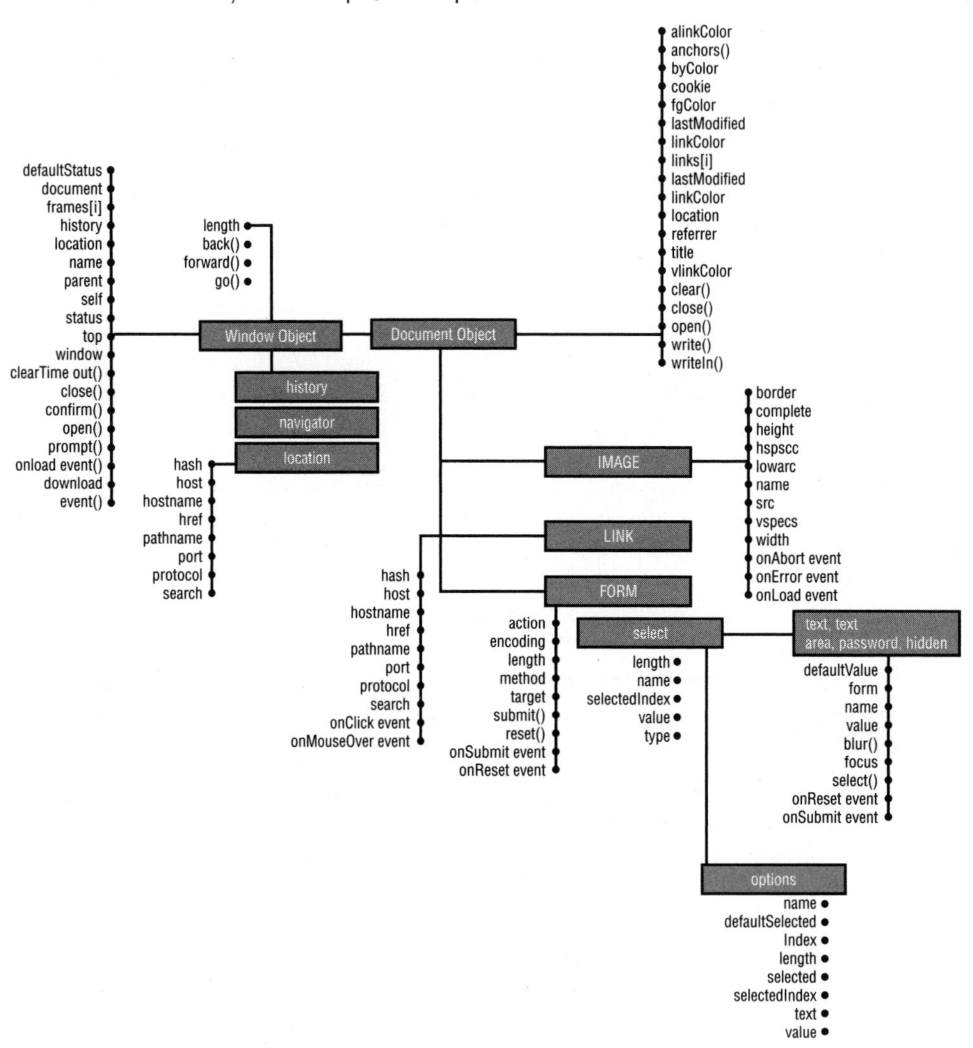

The options supported by the `open` method include the following:

- `toolbar = yes|no` — Controls whether the new window will have a toolbar
- `location = yes|no` — Controls whether the new window will have an address bar
- `status = yes|no` — Controls whether the new window will have a status bar
- `menubar = yes|no` — Controls whether the new window will have a menu bar
- `resizeable = yes|no` — Controls whether the user can resize the new window

- `scrollbars = yes|no` — Controls whether the new window will have scrollbars
- `width = pixels` — Controls the width of the new window
- `height = pixels` — Controls the height of the new window

Note

Not all user agents support all options. ■

The `window` object can also be used to size and move a user agent window. One interesting DHTML effect is to shake the current window. The following function can be used to cause the user agent window to visibly shudder:

```
function shudder() {
  // Move the document window up and down 5 times
  for (var i=1; i<= 5; i++) {
    window.moveBy(8,8);
    window.moveBy(-8,-8);
}
}
```

You can use other methods to scroll a window (`scroll`, `scrollBy`, `scrollTo`) and to resize a window (`resizeBy`, `resizeTo`).

The document object

You can use the JavaScript `document` object to access and manipulate the current document in the user agent window. Many of the collection objects (`form`, `image`, and so on) are children of the `document` object.

The `document` object supports a `write` and `writeln` method, both of which can be used to write content to the current document. For example, the following code results in the current date being displayed (in mm/dd/yyyy format) wherever the code is inserted in the document:

```
<script type="text/JavaScript">
  today = new Date();
  document.write((today.getMonth()+1) + "/" + today.getDate() +
    "/" + today.getFullYear());
</script>
```

The `open` and `close` methods can be used to open and then close a document for writing. Building on the examples in the earlier section "The window object," the following code can be used to spawn a new document window and write the current date to the new window:

```
<script type="text/JavaScript">
  today = new Date();
  newWin = window.open("","","width=400,height=400,
     scrollbars=no,resizable=no");
```

```
    newDoc = newWin.document.open();
    newDoc.write((today.getMonth()+1) + "/" + today.getDate() +
      "/" + today.getFullYear());
    newDoc.close();
  </script>
```

The form object

You can use the `form` object to access form elements in a document. The `form` object supports `length` and `elements` properties — the former property returns how many elements (fields) are in the form; the latter contains an array of form element objects, one per field. You can also access the form elements by their `name` attribute. For example, the following code will set the value of the `addlength` field to the length of the address field using the form name and element names to address the various values:

```
...
<head>
<script type="text/JavaScript">
  function dolength() {
    document.form1.addlength.value =
      document.form1.address.value.length;
}
</script>
</head>
<body>
<p>
<form name="form1" action="handler.cgi" method="post">
Length: <input type="text" name="addlength" size="5" /><br />
Address: <input type="text" name="address" size="30"
          onkeyup="dolength();" />
</form>
</p>
...
```

The `form` object can be used for a variety of form automation techniques.

The location object

The `location` object can be used to manipulate the URL information about the current document in the user agent. Various properties of the `location` object are used to store individual pieces of the document's URL (protocol, hostname, port, and so on). For example, you could use the following code to piece the URL back together:

```
with (document.location) {
  var url = protocol + "//";
  url += hostname;
  if (port) { url += ":" + port;}
  url += pathname;
```

```
    if (hash) { url += hash;}
  }
```

The preceding example is shown only to illustrate how the various pieces relate to one another; the `location.href` property contains the full URL.

One popular method of using the `location` object is to cause the user agent to load a new page. To do so, your script simply has to set the `document.location` object to the desired URL. For example, the following code will cause the user agent to load the Yahoo.com home page:

```
document.location = "http://www.yahoo.com";
```

The history object

The `history` object is tied to the history function of the user agent. Using the `history` object, your script can navigate up and down the history list. For example, the following code acts as though the user used the browser's back feature, causing the user agent to load the previous document in the history list:

```
history.back();
```

Other properties and methods of the `history` object allow more control over the history list. For example, the `history.length` property can be used to determine the number of entries in the history list.

The self object

You can use the `self` object to refer to an element making the function call. This object is typically used when calling JavaScript functions, allowing the function to operate on the object initiating the call. For example, the following code passes a reference to the button to the `dosomething()` function:

```
<input type="button" value="Click Me" id="button"
onclick="dosomething(self);" />
```

The function can then use that reference to operate on the object that initiated the call:

```
function dosomething(el) {
... // do something with the element referenced by el ...
}
```

For example, the following function can be used to change the color of an element when called with a reference to that element:

```
function changecolorRed(el) {
  el.style.color = "red";
}
```

That function can then be added to an event of any element, as in the following `onclick` event example:

```
<p onclick="changecolorRed(this);">When clicked,
   the text will change to red.</p>
```

Using Event Handlers

Notice the `onclick` attribute in the following code fragment:

```
<div onClick="this.style.fontSize='60px';
this.style.color='red'">
```

This tells the browser that when the user clicks the `div` element something should happen. In this case, that something is that the following two attributes of the style element will change:

- `style.fontSize` tells the browser to change the font size to 60 pixels.
- `style.color` tells the browser to change the color to red.

The two statements are JavaScript code, making use of the JavaScript hook into the document's CSS. The `onClick` attribute is actually an event handler. An event is something that happens, as you probably already know. A party, for example, is an event. When a human triggers the `onparty` event, sometimes that human falls down drunk. When a human triggers an `onClick` event in a browser, more benign things take place, such as text color changes, menu changes, and so on.

Besides placing spurious code in the element, you can also place a function call as a function call to the `onClick` event. For example, if you have a function named "ChangeDiv" defined in a `<script>` section earlier in your document, you could use the following `onClick`:

```
<div onClick="ChangeDiv(this);">
```

All the code to change the `div` element could then be placed in the function and used by multiple elements.

Note

The "this" used in the previous examples is shorthand for referring to the element in which the code was placed, or in this case, the `div`. ■

Table 17-3 shows the common event handlers associated with JavaScript.

When one of these events takes place and the appropriate handler is included in one or more elements, the corresponding code is executed.

Note

Many browsers have their own, custom event handlers, but if you stick with those found in Table 17-3, you'll find cross-compatibility issues much easier to solve. ■

TABLE 17-3

JavaScript Event Handlers

Event Handler	Usage
onAbort	Occurs when a user stops an image from loading.
onBlur	Occurs when a user's mouse loses focus on an object. Focus is when the cursor is active on an object, such as a form input field. When a cursor is clicked within the field, it has focus, and when the mouse is taken out of the field, it loses focus, causing an onBlur event.
onChange	Occurs when a change takes place in the state of an object — for example, when a form field loses focus after a user changes some text within the field.
onClick	Occurs when a user clicks an object.
onError	Occurs when an error occurs in the JavaScript.
onFocus	Occurs when a user's mouse enters a field with a mouse click.
onLoad	Occurs when an object, such as a page (as represented by the body element), is loaded into the browser.
onMouseOut	Occurs when a mouse no longer hovers over an object.
onMouseOver	Occurs when a mouse begins to hover over an object.
onSelect	Occurs when a user selects text.
onSubmit	Occurs when a form is submitted.
onUnload	Occurs when an object is unloaded.

Accessing an Element by Its ID

One of the surest methods to access a document's elements is to use the getElementById() function. This function is supported by any DOM Level 1-compliant user agent, so it can be relied upon to access elements that have a properly assigned ID attribute.

The getElementById() function's syntax is straightforward:

```
element = document.getElementById("elementID");
```

For example, the following code would assign a reference to the address field to the element variable:

```
element = document.getElementById("address");
...
<input type="text" size="30" id="address">
```

Once assigned, the `element` variable can be used to access the referenced field's properties and methods:

```
addresslength = element.length;
```

Tip

Before using `getElementById()`, you should test the user agent to ensure that the function is available. The following `if` statement will generally ensure that the user agent supports the appropriate DOM level and thus `getElementById()`:

```
if (document.all || document.getElementById) {
  ...getElementById should be available, use it here...
} ■
```

Cross-Browser Compatibility Issues

The most important caveat to exploring DHTML is that there are a ton of compatibility issues. The newest iterations of Firefox/Mozilla/Netscape and Internet Explorer have actually begun to come closer together, but developers working with DHTML during the height of the browser wars quickly learned that developing cross-browser DHTML was a very difficult proposition. As a result, most large professional sites eschew complex DHTML in favor of simpler cross-browser routines to improve navigation and other facets of the user experience, rather than excessive visual effects.

Browser detection: querying for identification

You can detect what kind of a browser a user is using by running a browser-detection script. This kind of script, along with some more finely tuned type of object detection, described in the next section, is sometimes referred to as *browser sniffing*. At its simplest, a typical browser-detection script looks like this:

```
<script language="JavaScript">
<!--
var bName =navigator.appName;
var bVer = parseFloat(navigator.appVersion);
if (bName == "Netscape")
  var browser = "Netscape Navigator"
else
  var browser = bName;
document.write("You are currently using ", browser, " ",
bVer, ".");
// -->
</script>
```

However, this method is inexact at best. Many browsers report erroneous data in their ID strings, and knowing a browser's name and version doesn't guarantee that it supports particular features. A better method is to test for each key feature you use — or objects that exist to support that feature — as described in the next section.

Browser detection: object detection

Object detection is a more precise way of browser sniffing. It examines a browser's support for various aspects of the object model. This avoids the potential for successfully checking a browser version but not confirming that the browser actually supports a specific object property or method. For this reason, object detection is the preferred method for browser sniffing and is considered a best practice. In addition, unless you have the object model of all the different browsers memorized, it's difficult to know which browser supports which object. It's easier to just check and see if a browser supports a specific object's properties or methods.

The principles used in object detection are quite similar to those used in browser detection. You make use of JavaScript `if` statements to check a browser's support for a named object's properties or methods. If the browser does support the object, you execute some given code. For example, using regular expressions can be very handy in JavaScript, but not if your users' browsers don't support them. So you create a simple detection script to see if they do:

```
if (window.RegExp) {
  // execute some regular expressions
} else {
  // provide an alternative to regular expressions
}
```

DHTML Examples

This section offers a few practical examples of DHTML. The scripts you'll see here are necessarily simple to get you started. You'll find a ton of resources on the Internet for additional help, including a vast array of freely available scripts you can customize for your own use. We'll take a look at a few of the most popular DHTML routines.

Form Automation: Check boxes

Dynamic HTML is very useful when used with `form` elements. By using events to tie specific elements to JavaScript functions, you can perform a wide array of automated tasks.

One popular automation technique is to add a special check box that enables you to check all of the check boxes in a series at the same time, rather than having to check each one individually. Take the document shown in Figure 17-4, for example.

FIGURE 17-4

A series of check boxes might benefit from an "(un)check all" check box.

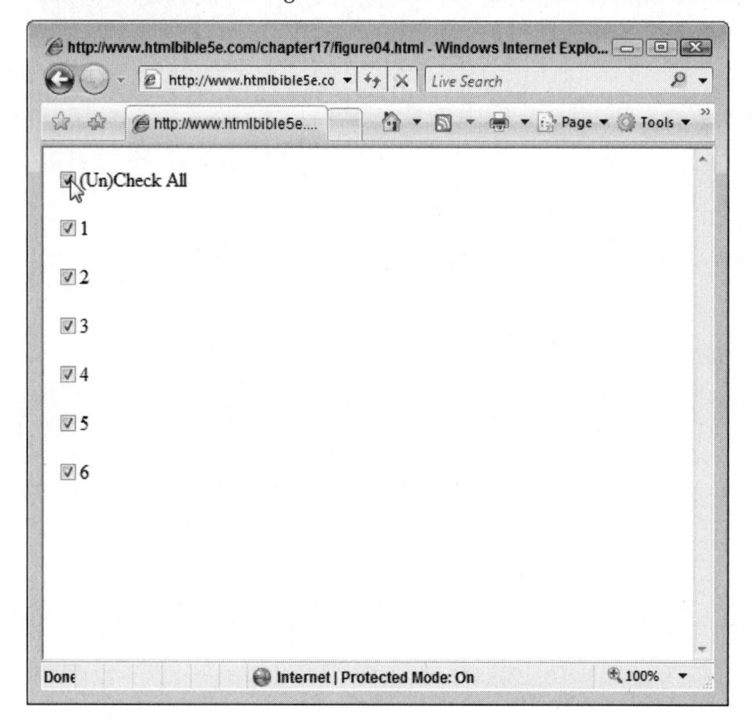

When the (Un)Check All box is checked, all the check boxes will become checked. Likewise, when the (Un)Check All box is unchecked, all the check boxes will be unchecked.

This technique is accomplished using the code and document snippet shown here:

```
<html>
<head>

<script type="text/JavaScript">
function checkall() {
  var chk = form1.checks[0].checked;
  for (i = 1; i < document.form1.checks.length; i++) {
    form1.checks[i].checked = chk;
  }
}
</script>

</head>
<body>
<form name="form1" action="formhandler.cgi" method="POST">
<p><input id="allboxes" type="checkbox" name="checks"
```

```
        onClick="checkall();" />(Un)Check All</p>
<p><input type="checkbox" name="checks" />1</p>
<p><input type="checkbox" name="checks" />2</p>
<p><input type="checkbox" name="checks" />3</p>
<p><input type="checkbox" name="checks" />4</p>
<p><input type="checkbox" name="checks" />5</p>
<p><input type="checkbox" name="checks" />6</p>
</form>
</body>
</html>
```

In this case, the trigger is the `onClick` event tied to the (Un)Check All check box. When the box is clicked, it changes state — to and from being checked — and the JavaScript function `checkall()`is called. This function iterates through the check boxes in the form and sets them to the same state as the triggering check box. Hence, if the box is checked, then all the check boxes will be checked. If the box is unchecked, then all the boxes will likewise be unchecked.

Note

It is important to assign a unique name to the `form` element and its children (in this case check boxes). It enables the JavaScript code to identify and act upon that form and its elements. ■

You can use similar techniques with other form elements. For example, you could use an `onChange` event with a select box. When a new selection is made, the form could morph to suit the new selection.

Rollovers

Creating rollovers using JavaScript can be as simple or as tedious as you wish it to be. Best practice would suggest you should create rollovers, like any other JavaScript-based functionality, in a way that creates the fewest problems for the most users.

Cross-Ref

You can also create rollover effects using the CSS anchor pseudo-class `:hover`. Samples of this technique are covered in Chapter 35. ■

You can take advantage of the narrowing gap in differences among browsers by relying on the event models of the main browsers. For example, the following bit of code creates a rollover of sorts that displays a JavaScript alert box when a user mouses over a portion of text:

```
To use this rollover, <span style="color:red; cursor:hand;"
onMouseOver="alert('AMAZING!!!')"> mouse over these
words</span>.
```

The result of this simple bit of code is shown in Figure 17-5.

Mozilla and IE allow all elements to use event handlers such as `onmouseover`. But because it's an attribute, browsers that don't support event handlers in all their elements will ignore the call to the JavaScript because they simply ignore the attribute itself. Keep this concept in mind when you're working with DHTML. In other words, try to limit the damage. The beauty of CSS is that if you use it right, browsers that don't support CSS will simply ignore your styling. The same is true for the use of event handlers in HTML.

FIGURE 17-5

When a user mouses over a portion of text, an alert box is displayed.

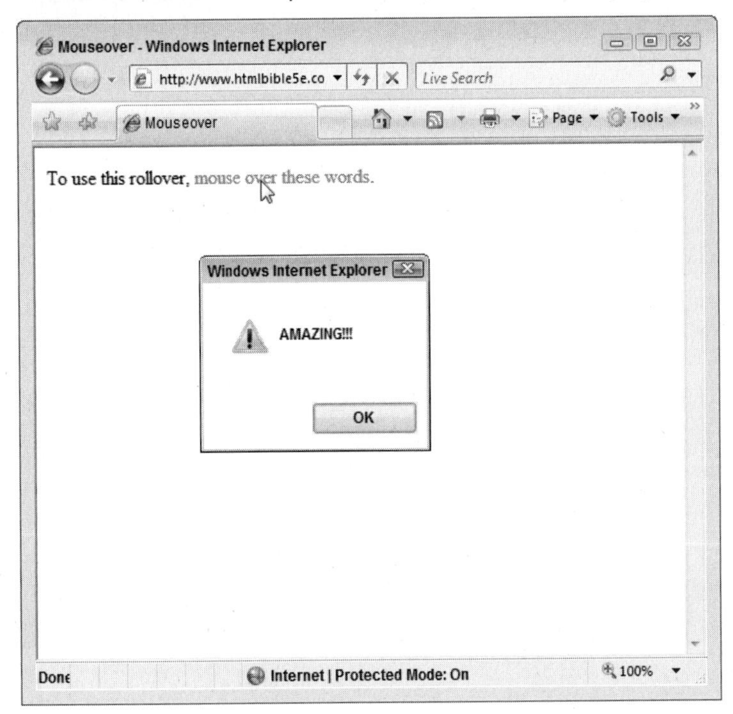

Collapsible menus

Collapsible menus have become a staple in Web development, and you can generally avoid the hassle of creating your own from scratch by simply searching the Internet for something that is close to what you want; then make any adaptations necessary to reflect your own site's needs. Collapsible menus generally come in two styles:

- **Vertical menus that expand and collapse on the left side of a Web page and within a reasonably small space** — When a user clicks his or her mouse on an item, a group of one or more sub-items is displayed and, generally, remains displayed until the user clicks the main item again, which then collapses the tree.
- **Horizontal menus that live at the top of a page** — When a user rolls his or her mouse over an item, a group of one or more sub-items is displayed and, generally, disappears when the mouse loses focus on the item.

How they work

Most collapsible menus rely on either the CSS `display` property or the CSS `visibility` property. The JavaScript used to manage these menus turns the display/visibility on or off depending on where a user's mouse is, or turns the display on or off to collapse or expand a menu. The difference between the `visibility` property and the `display` property is that when you hide an element's visibility, the element still takes up visible space in the browser document. When you turn the `display` property off by giving it a `none` value (`display = "none"`), the space where the affected element lives collapses.

The following code shows an example of a pull-down menu, using JavaScript event triggers and a hidden table. Figure 17-6 shows the menu in action.

```
<html>
<head>
<style type="text/css">

table.topmenu { background-color: black; }

table.topmenu td  { background-color: lightblue;
                    width: 200px;  }

table.menu { background-color: black; }

table.menu td { color: black; }

</style>

<script type="text/JavaScript">

function showmenu(menu) {
  obj = document.getElementById(menu);
  obj.style.visibility = "visible";
}
function hidemenu(menu) {
  obj = document.getElementById(menu);
  obj.style.visibility = "hidden";
}

</script>
</head>
<body>
<table class="topmenu" border="0">
<tr>
  <td onMouseOver="showmenu('products');"
      onMouseOut="hidemenu('products');">Products<br />
    <table id="products" class="menu" border="0"
      style="visibility: hidden; position: absolute;">
    <tr><td>Hardware</td></tr>
    <tr><td>Software</td></tr>
    </tr>
```

```
      </table>
    </td>
    <td onMouseOver="showmenu('services');"
        onMouseOut="hidemenu('services');">Products<br />
      <table id="services" class="menu" border="0"
        style="visibility: hidden;
         position: absolute;">
      <tr><td>Documentation</td></tr>
      <tr><td>Translations</td></tr>
      </tr>
      </table>
    </td>
    <td onMouseOver="showmenu('company');"
        onMouseOut="hidemenu('company');">Products<br />
      <table id="company" class="menu" border="0"
        style="visibility: hidden; position: absolute;">
      <tr><td>About</td></tr>
      <tr><td>Contact</td></tr>
      </tr>
      </table>
    </td>
  </tr>
  </table>
  </body>
  </html>
```

FIGURE 17-6

DHTML menus can be as simple or complex as your code will allow.

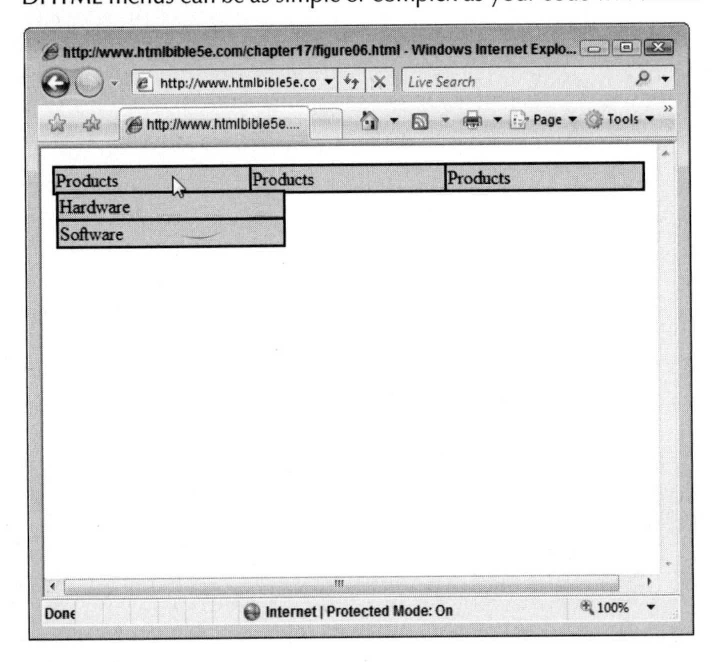

The mechanics of this menu are fairly straightforward. A series of table cells is filled with the top menu item ("Products," etc.) and contains a hidden table of sub-elements (`visibility="hidden"` in the elements' `style` attribute. The `onMouseover` event is used to call the `showmenu()` JavaScript function when the user mouses over a top menu. The JavaScript function changes the embedded table's visibility to "visible," revealing the table of sub-elements. When the mouse leaves the top menu item, the `onMouseOut` event triggers the `hidemenu()` function, which changes the embedded table's visibility back to hidden, hiding the submenu.

Tip

As previously mentioned, you often don't need to write your own menu from scratch because so many developers have made them freely available. Instead, you can download someone else's menu and change the CSS and some of the other specifics, such as the location to which the links refer. ■

Summary

This chapter covered DHTML, or how you can use JavaScript along with HTML and CSS to create dynamic documents. You learned how to reference elements within the document and how to use JavaScript to interact with them.

Note that this book's primary focus is HTML and CSS, and although JavaScript and DHTML remain in the requisite coverage along with those two topics, it cannot be given the depth necessary to make one highly proficient in the subject. If JavaScript interests you, refer to a book, such as the JavaScript Bible (Wiley, 2009), that is more specific to the topic.

CHAPTER

18

The Future of HTML: HTML5

HTML has come a long way since its inception back in 1991. If you examine the specification by release version numbers alone — 2, 3.2, 4.0, and 4.01 — you might be tempted to disregard the evolutionary changes brought forth with each version. However, now that we stand on the edge of the release of HTML5, the jump in technology and intended use of the language becomes very apparent.

This chapter presents an overview of HTML5.

IN THIS CHAPTER

Note

This chapter was written based on a draft specification of HTML5. Currently, this version is still several years away from release and general adoption. As such, documentation within this chapter may not exactly match the final release of HTML5. To keep tabs on the latest happenings with HTML5, visit the official W3C site: `http://dev.w3.org/html5/spec/Overview.html`. ■

More Publishing and Layout Features

The most interesting new aspects of HTML5 are two-fold:

- Elements created for publishing purposes, not just markup
- Elements created to provide easier avenues for nontextual elements (like multimedia)

Some examples of new elements created for publishing purposes are the new `section` elements — `header`, `hgroup`, `nav`, `section`, `article`, `aside`, and `footer`. These elements are designed to free Web authors from overusing `div` elements to delimit document elements. For example, Figure 18-1 shows a suggested page layout created using the new section elements in place of `div` elements.

FIGURE 18-1

This use of the new page division tags bears a distinct resemblance to the layout of most documents on the Web.

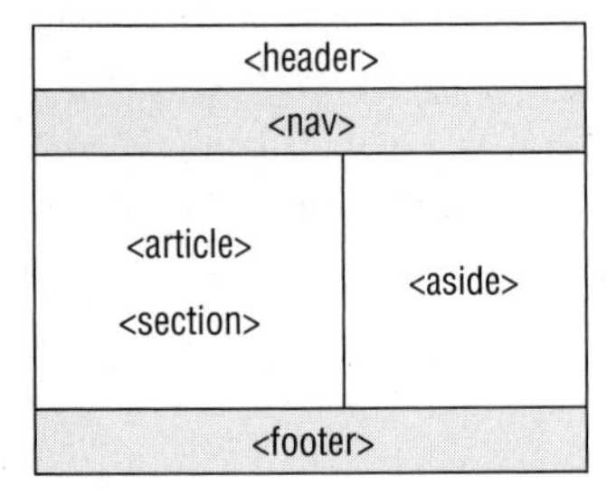

A snippet of documents using the older `<div>` tags and newer specific section tags (e.g., `<header>`) illustrates the difference between the markups. The first listing shows the traditional, `div`-heavy method of markup, which can be hard to read and navigate. The second listing shows the same general markup but uses the new document sectioning elements:

```
<!-- Standard div layering -->
<div id="header"> ...  </div>
<div id="nav"> ... </div>
<div id="section">
    <div id="article"> ...  </div>
    <div id="article"> ...  </div>
    ...
</div>
<div id="aside"> ...  </div>
<div id="footer"> ...  </div>

<!-- New section element  layering -->
<header> ...  </header>
<nav> ... </nav>
<section>
    <article> ...  </article>
    <article> ...  </article>
    ...
</section>
<aside> ...  </aside>
<footer> ...  </footer>
```

Note

The `section` elements were created to help create documents like the one shown in Figure 18-1. As you might have guessed, blogs and news sites played a large part in this evolution. ■

Accessible Multimedia

Another big change coming with HTML5 is access to native multimedia — sound, video, and vector drawing. Although HTML5 will rely on the platform to supply the output means for the multimedia, the intent is to provide more native, and less plug-in-reliant, multimedia.

Note

Due to the large user base of certain plug-ins, such as Flash, the new multimedia features of HTML cannot hope to actually replace plug-ins. However, the new features enable other methods of creating simple multimedia options. ■

One powerful feature that has already made headlines is the canvas-drawing feature. Using a new element (`canvas`), the Web author can delimit an area within the document for drawing and use new JavaScript methods to draw within the canvas. The following code produces the canvas drawing shown in Figure 18-2:

```
<!DOCTYPE html>
<html lang="en">
  <head>
    <meta charset="utf-8">
    <title>Using the Canvas</title>
    <style type="text/css">
      canvas { border: thin solid black; }
    </style>

    <script type="text/javascript">
window.addEventListener('load', function () {

  // Get the canvas element.
  var elem = document.getElementById('myCanvas');
  if (!elem || !elem.getContext) {
    return;
  }

  // Get the canvas 2d context.
  var context = elem.getContext('2d');
  if (!context) {
    return;
  }

  // Draw a blue rectangle.
  context.fillStyle = '#00f';
  context.fillRect(0, 0, 150, 100);
  context.fillStyle = "rgba(255, 0, 0, .5)";

  // Draw a red circle with transparency
  context.beginPath();
  context.arc(200, 200, 150, 0, Math.PI*2, true);
  context.closePath();
  context.fill();
}, false);
    </script>

  </head>
  <body>
```

```
        <p><canvas id="myCanvas" width="200" height="150">Your
         browser does not have support for Canvas.</canvas></p>

      </body>
    </html>
```

Tip

For more information on the canvas features, see the tutorial at `https://developer.mozilla.org/en/Canvas_tutorial`. ■

The `canvas` element provides a mechanism for those user agents that don't support this feature. If the agent doesn't support the canvas feature, it will display fallback content that says "Your browser does not have support for Canvas" (or whatever markup appears between the canvas tags). Note in Figure 18-2 how the canvas clips any element drawn outside of its border — the circle in this case.

FIGURE 18-2

The new canvas feature provides drawing mechanisms to HTML documents.

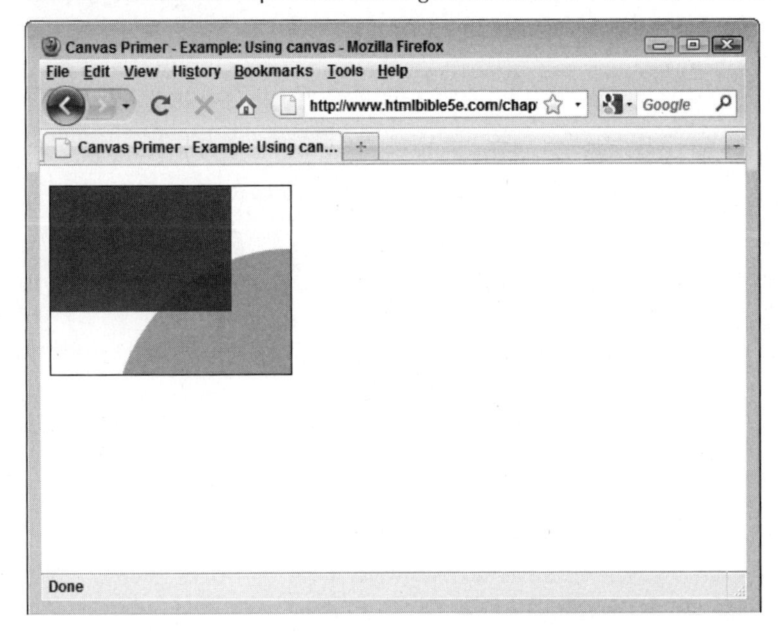

The `canvas` element also has a border applied. Because it is an HTML block element, it can have all the usual block element properties applied to it — positioning, decorative, and so on.

Changes: Elements and Attributes

There have been many changes to the elements and attributes that make up HTML5. The following sections provide an overview of the more noticeable changes.

Note

Throughout this book we have continually suggested XHTML formatting standards and techniques. Both will come in handy with the advent of HTML5, which has deep roots in XHTML. ■

New elements

Several new elements have been added to extend the capabilities of HTML5's markup, as shown in the following table.

Element(s)	Use
`section`	Represents a generic section of a document
`article`	Represents an independent piece of the document whole
`aside`	Represents a piece of content slightly related to the document whole
`hgroup`	Represents the header of a section
`header`	Represents a group of introductory or navigational aids
`footer`	Represents the footer of a section of the document
`nav`	Represents a section of the document intended for navigation
`dialog`	Used with `dt` and `dd` elements to mark up a conversation
`figure`	Used to provide a caption to embedded content
`video`, `audio`	Used to provide multimedia content
`embed`	Used to provide plug-in content
`mark`	Used to designate marked content
`progress`	Used to provide a status or progress bar
`meter`	Used to represent a measurement
`time`	Represents a date or time
`ruby`, `rt`, and `rp`	Used to provide an interface into Ruby applications
`canvas`	Used to contain rendered text or shapes
`command`	Used to reference a user-accessible command
`details`	Used to reference additional controls available to the user
`datalist`	Used to help build combo-boxes
`output`	Represents output generated by another source

New attributes by element

Several existing elements have been given additional attributes to help extend HTML5's capabilities, as shown on the following table.

Element(s)	Attribute(s)
a, area	media, ping, target
area	hreflang, rel
base	target
li	value
ol	start
meta	charset
input	autofocus (except type of hidden)
input, textarea	placeholder
input, output, select, textarea, button, and fieldset	form
input	required (except type of hidden, image, or button), autocomplete, min, max, multiple, pattern, and step
fieldset	disabled
form	novalidate
input, button	formaction, formenctype, formmethod, formnovalidate, and formtarget
menu	type, label
style	scoped
script	async
html1	manifest
link	sizes
ol	reversed
iframe	seamless, sandbox

New input types (form input element)

The input element's type attribute supports several new values to aid in the input of additional values:

tel
search
url
email
datetime
date

```
month
week
time
datetime-local
number
range
color
```

These new input types provide HTML form support of new data formats without requiring additional scripting.

New global attributes

The new specification also adds more global attributes, shown in the following table, that can be applied to most elements, giving the author better control over specifying or exempting element-level features.

Attribute	Use
`contenteditable`	Marks an editable area of the document
`contextmenu`	Points to an optional context menu
`data-`	Author-defined attributes
`draggable`	Marks content as draggable (via mouse)
`hidden`	Remove element
`item`, `itemprop`, `subject`	Provides Microdata elements
`role`, `aria-`	Used to provide assistive technology
`spellcheck`	Indicates that the content can be spell-checked

Deprecated elements

The following elements have been deprecated either in favor of other elements or because of their frequent misuse or consistent confusion surrounding their use:

```
basefont
big
center
font
s
strike
tt
u
frame
frameset
noframes
```

acronym (use abbr instead)
applet (use object instead)
isindex
dir (use ul instead)

Deprecated attributes

The following attributes have been deprecated with HTML5 in favor of more consistent usage (such as the use of styles to produce the same effect).

Attribute	Deprecated from (Element)
rev, charset	link, a
shape, coords	a
longdesc	img, iframe
target	link
nohref	area
profile	head
version	html
Name	img (use id instead)
scheme	meta
archive, classid, codebase, codetype, declare, standby	object
valuetype, type	param
axis, abbr	td, th
Scope	td

In addition, many presentation attributes have been deprecated in favor of styles, as shown in the following table.

Attribute	Deprecated from (Element)
align	caption, iframe, img, input, object, legend, table, hr, div, h1, h2, h3, h4, h5, h6, p, col, colgroup, tbody, td, tfoot, th, thead, tr
alink, link, text, vlink	body
background	body
bgcolor	table, tr, td, th, body

Attribute	Deprecated from (Element)
border	table, object
cellpadding, cellspacing	table
char, charoff	col, colgroup, tbody, td, tfoot, th, thead, tr
clear	br
compact	dl, menu, ol, ul
frame	table
frameborder	iframe
height	td, th
hspace, vspace	img, object
marginheight, marginwidth	iframe
noshade	hr
nowrap	td, th
rules	table
scrolling	iframe
size	hr
type	li, ol, ul
valign	col, colgroup, tbody, td, tfoot, th, thead, tr
width	hr, table, td, th, col, colgroup, pre

Summary

As you can see from the information in this chapter, HTML continues to march forward toward mainstream publishing mechanisms. The rift between content (HTML) and presentation (CSS) is also becoming more pronounced, forcing Web developers to use the right tool for the right purpose. Although HTML5 is still quite a ways off, its feature set will provide some welcome changes.

Part II

HTML Tools and Variants

IN THIS PART

CHAPTER 19

Web Development Software

IN THIS CHAPTER

As you have seen throughout this book, Web development is an area rich in features. The Web has come a long way from its early beginnings as a text-only medium. As online documents get more complex, the tools to create them become more powerful. Although you can still create large, feature-rich sites with a simple text editor, using more complex and powerful tools can make the task much easier. This chapter introduces several popular tools that can help you create the best online documents possible.

Note

This chapter provides several recommendations for tools you should consider for online document development. However, the recommendations are just that, recommendations. Only you can decide what tools will work best for you. Luckily, most of the tools covered in this chapter have demo versions you can download and try out for a limited time. Be sure to visit the websites referenced for each tool to get more information and perhaps even download a trial version. ■

Text-Oriented Editors

Text-oriented editors have been around since the dawn of the cathode-ray tube (CRT), the technology used in most computer display screens. However, today's editors can be quite powerful and feature-rich, doing much more than simply enabling you to create text documents. This section covers the latest in text-oriented editing.

Simple text editors

Simple text editors — such as Windows Notepad or vi on UNIX/Linux — provide an invaluable service. They enable you, without intervening features, to easily edit text-based documents. As such, they are a logical addition to your Web development toolkit.

However, although you could create an entire site with one of these simple tools, there are better tools for actual creation.

Smart text editors

Smart text editors are editors that understand what you are editing and attempt to help in various ways. For example, Linux users should look into vim or Emacs and enable syntax highlighting when editing documents with embedded code (HTML, CSS, JavaScript, and so on). Figure 19-1 shows an example of a large PHP file in vim.

FIGURE 19-1

Syntax highlighting can help you avoid simple errors.

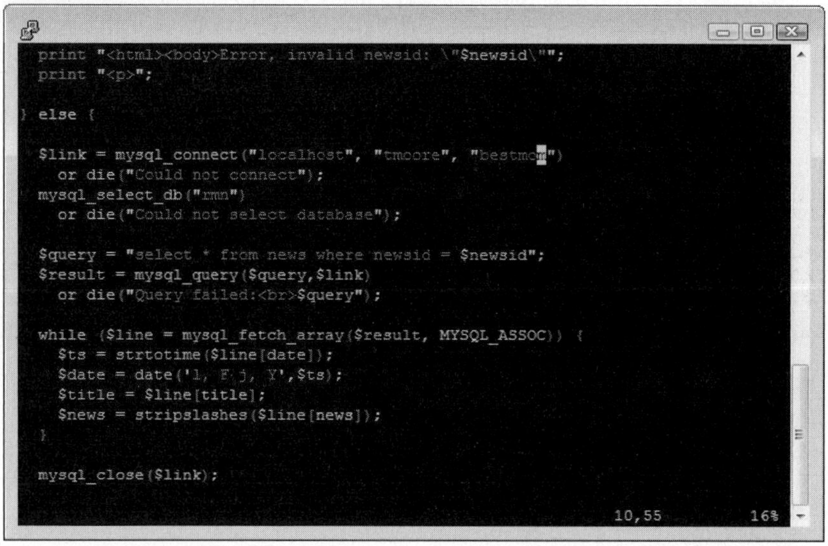

```
  print "<html><body>Error, invalid newsid: \"$newsid\"";
  print "<p>";

} else {

  $link = mysql_connect("localhost", "tmoore", "bestmo")
    or die("Could not connect");
  mysql_select_db("rmn")
    or die("Could not select database");

  $query = "select * from news where newsid = $newsid";
  $result = mysql_query($query,$link)
    or die("Query failed:<br>$query");

  while ($line = mysql_fetch_array($result, MYSQL_ASSOC)) {
    $ts = strtotime($line[date]);
    $date = date('l, F j, Y',$ts);
    $title = $line[title];
    $news = stripslashes($line[news]);
  }

  mysql_close($link);
                                                    10,55          16%
```

Although it may be hard to tell in the black-and-white figure, various elements have been colorized to show where they begin or end. Using methods like this, the editor keeps you abreast of what elements have been opened and which have been closed. For example, the editor may highlight quoted text in green. If most of the document turns green, it is likely that you forgot to close a quote somewhere. These editors also offer features such as auto-indenting, which can help you keep your documents structured.

Windows users have a few options for smart editors, as well. My favorite is TextPad, which uses document class templates to understand the syntax of almost any coded document.

TextPad is loaded with standard editor features. You can find TextPad on the Internet at `www.textpad.com`.

HTML-specific editors

A few non-WYSIWYG editors understand HTML and provide specific features to help you code. However, HomeSite (now owned by Adobe) has always stood out from the crowd.

HomeSite provides the next level of functionality for HTML editing with special tools for entering tags and their parameters, codes for entities, macros for repeating steps, and more. Although the program is a bit dated (no support for HTML version 4.01), it is still a great choice for a full-featured HTML text editor.

Figure 19-2 shows the HomeSite main interface, and Figure 19-3 shows a tab of the dialog for creating a `<table>` tag.

FIGURE 19-2

HomeSite includes several features to make HTML editing a breeze.

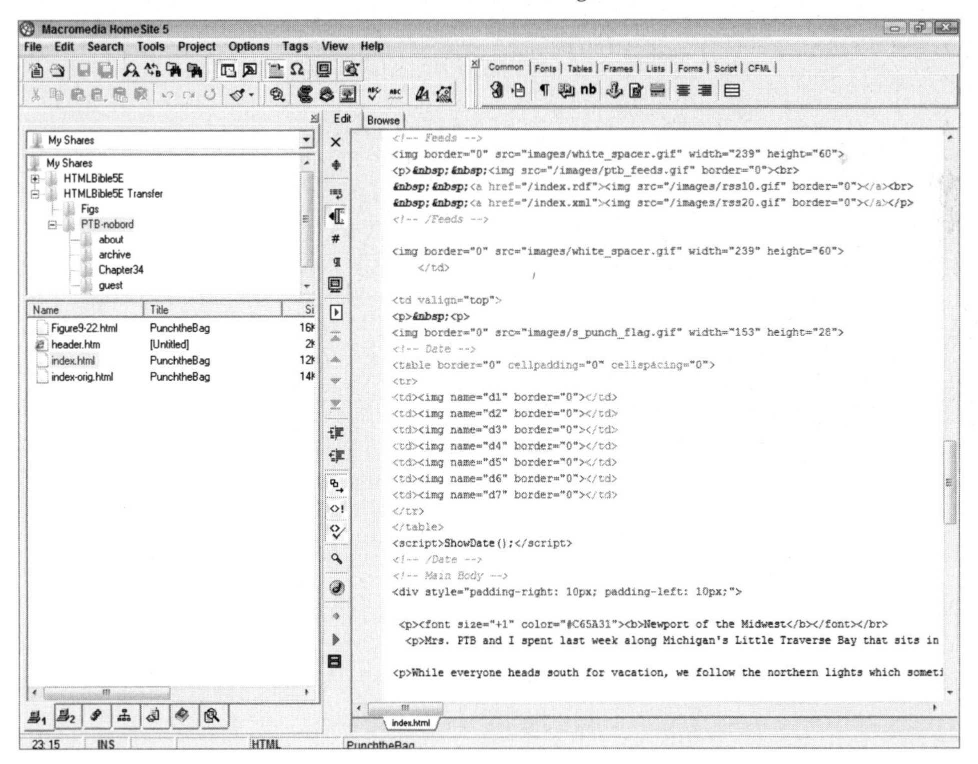

TopStyle Lite, which installs with HomeSite, provides an interface for editing and managing your external style sheets.

Visit Adobe's website for more information on HomeSite (www.adobe.com/products/homesite/).

FIGURE 19-3

HomeSite includes comprehensive mechanisms for building more complex tags such as tables.

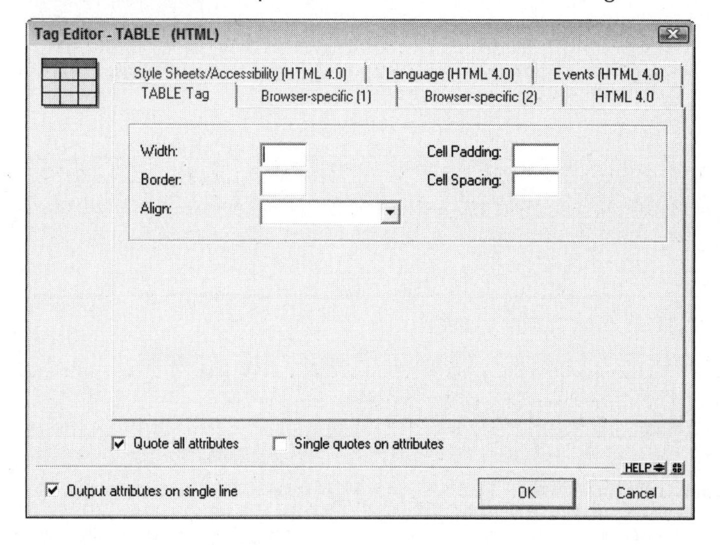

Note

In 2005, Adobe Systems, Inc., acquired Macromedia lock, stock, and barrel. Most former Macromedia products are still available on the market, but under the Adobe brand name. ■

WYSIWYG HTML Editors

Just as *what you see is what you get* (WYSIWYG) editors revolutionized word processing, WYSIWYG HTML editors have revolutionized Web publishing. Using such tools, designers can design their pages visually and let the tools create the underlying HTML code. This section highlights the three most popular visual tools available for WYSIWYG editing.

NetObjects Fusion

NetObjects Fusion is another site-level design tool that offers WYSIWYG editing. The advantages of using NetObjects Fusion include easy management of entire sites, pixel-accurate designs, and a plethora of features that make publishing on the Web a breeze. Such features include the following:

- Advanced scripting support
- Automatic e-commerce catalog building

- Enhanced photo gallery support
- Hooks for including external pages and code
- Incremental publishing capability
- Flexible meta tag management
- Powerful, full-site management tools

Note

NetObjects Fusion should not be confused with Macromedia's ColdFusion product. The former is owned by Website Pros and is a WYSIWYG Web editor. The latter is owned by Macromedia and is a database integration tool for the Web. ■

Figure 19-4 shows the page design view for NetObjects, and Figure 19-5 shows the site layout view. In the latter, you can easily create, delete, and move pages around your site — NetObjects Fusion will automatically adjust all links, navigation bars, and other references between the pages.

FIGURE 19-4

NetObjects Fusion provides a good framework for designing pages visually.

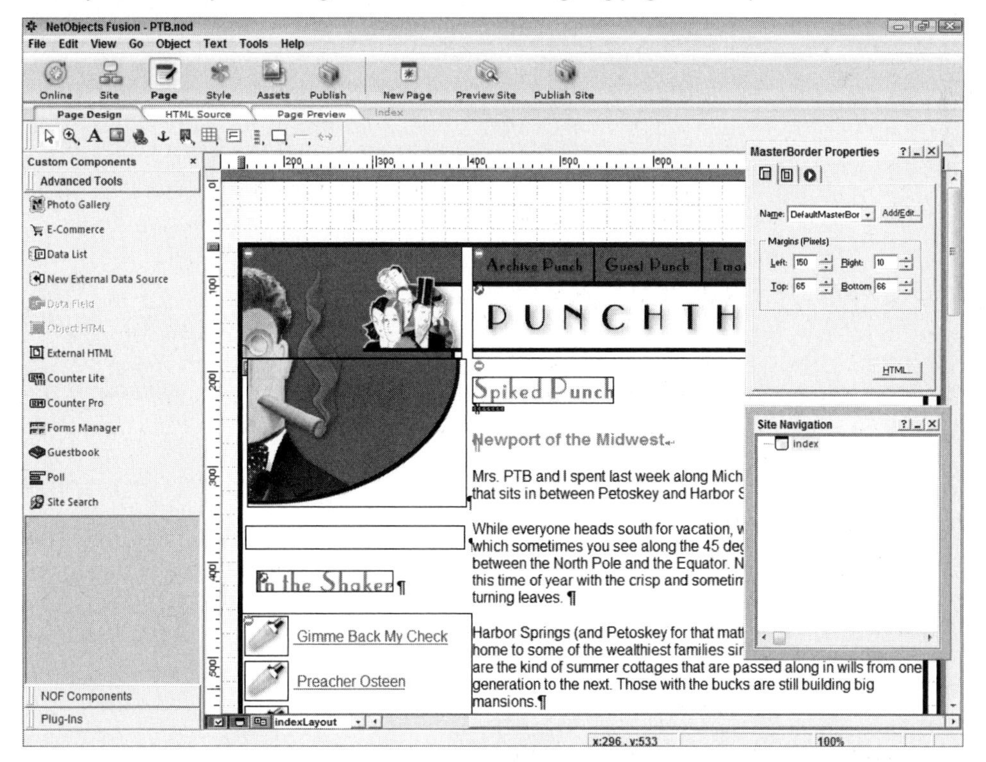

In addition to the visual tools, NetObjects Fusion provides many ways to customize the actual code behind your documents as well. You can learn more about NetObjects Fusion on the Web at `www.netobjects.com`.

FIGURE 19-5

At the site level, NetObjects Fusion gives you complete control over your site's organization; behind the scenes, it adjusts links between pages automatically.

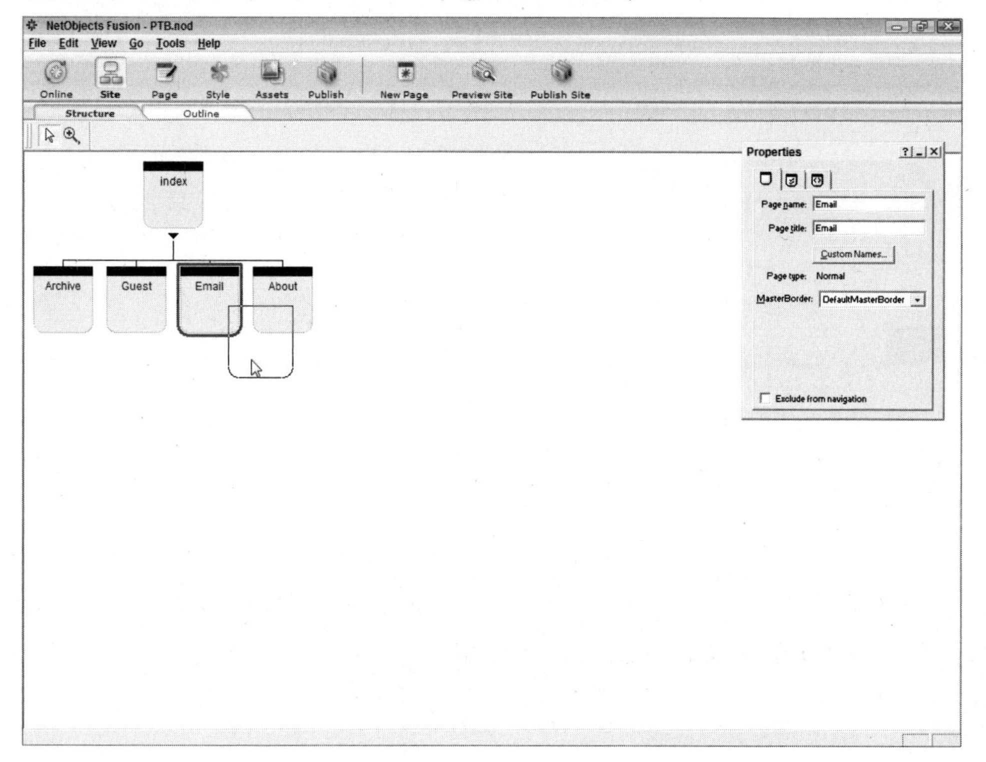

Dreamweaver

The king of all Web document editing programs is currently Adobe Dreamweaver. Combining the best visual and nonvisual editing tools with several development features, Dreamweaver is the most feature-rich program covered here.

Dreamweaver provides as much or as little automation during creation of new documents as you would like. You can create the entire site in text mode, editing HTML code directly. Alternatively, you can use the WYSIWYG design editor to create your documents visually. Figure 19-6 shows Dreamweaver's main editing window, displaying both the code and visual design windows. Figure 19-7 shows the Check Browser Compatibility feature, which enables you to test your code against the compatibility of specific browsers.

The feature-rich nature of Dreamweaver does come at a price — it is easily the most complicated program covered in this chapter. The learning curve for Dreamweaver can be quite steep, even to create simple sites. However, once you get used to Dreamweaver, it is easy to appreciate its powerful features.

You can learn more about Dreamweaver at `www.adobe.com/products/dreamweaver/`.

FIGURE 19-6

Dreamweaver's main editing window can show the code view, the design (visual) view, or both.

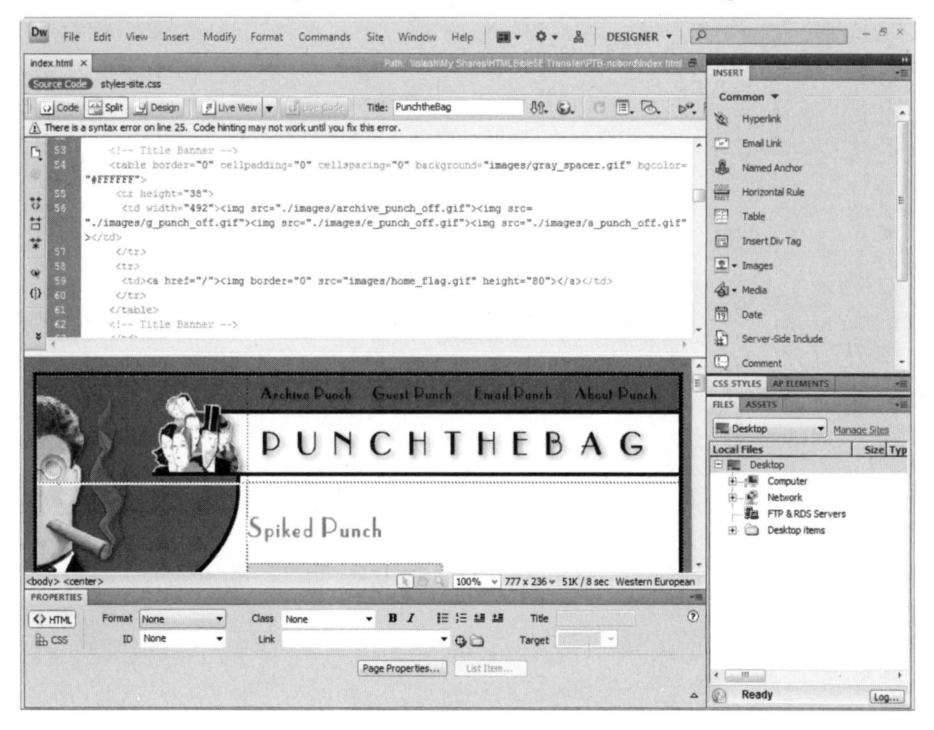

Firefox Add-ons

Firefox is a favorite browser for Web developers for one reason: add-ons. Using Firefox's robust application programming interface, developers can create simple widgets or extensive programs to add to the Firefox interface.

Several add-ons, Firebug in particular, enable you to view and edit your documents in unique ways. Firebug, for example, enables you to inspect individual elements to see their styles, where the styles are applied from (given the cascade), and even edit the HTML and styles on the current *live* document to help tweak your formatting. Figure 19-8 shows Firebug in action.

Find more information on Firefox, Firebug, and other Firefox add-ons at `www.mozilla.org`.

FIGURE 19-7

The Check Browser Compatibility feature checks your code against the compatibility of specific browsers.

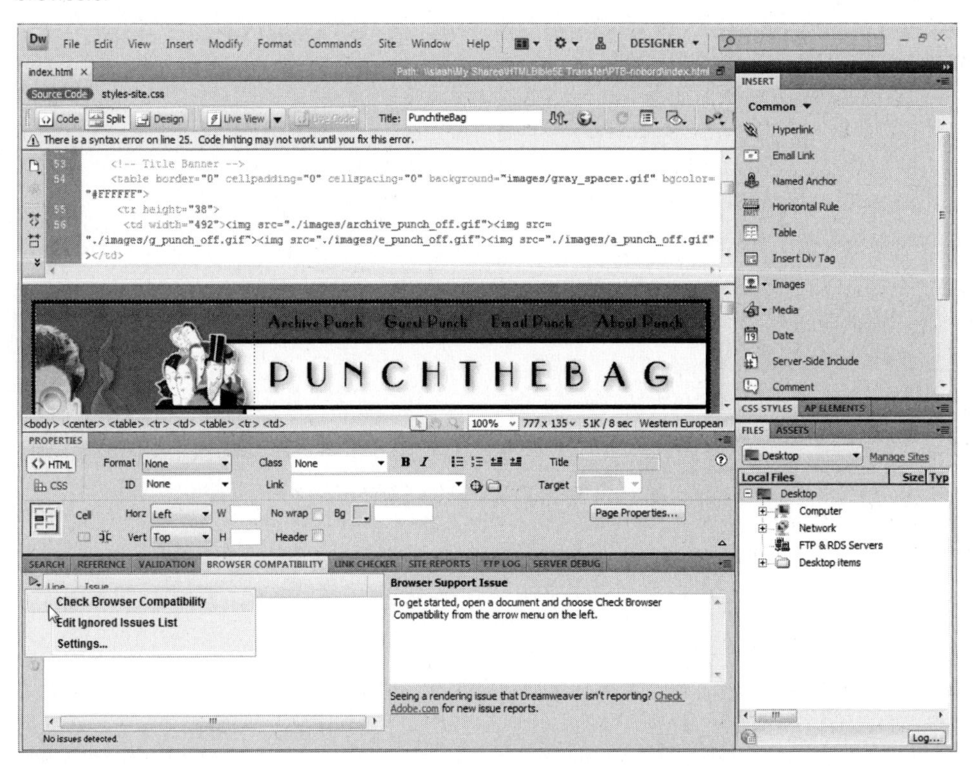

FIGURE 19-8

When inspecting an element, Firebug displays all the information on styles affecting the element (their source and settings), and allows you to tweak the styles on the live document.

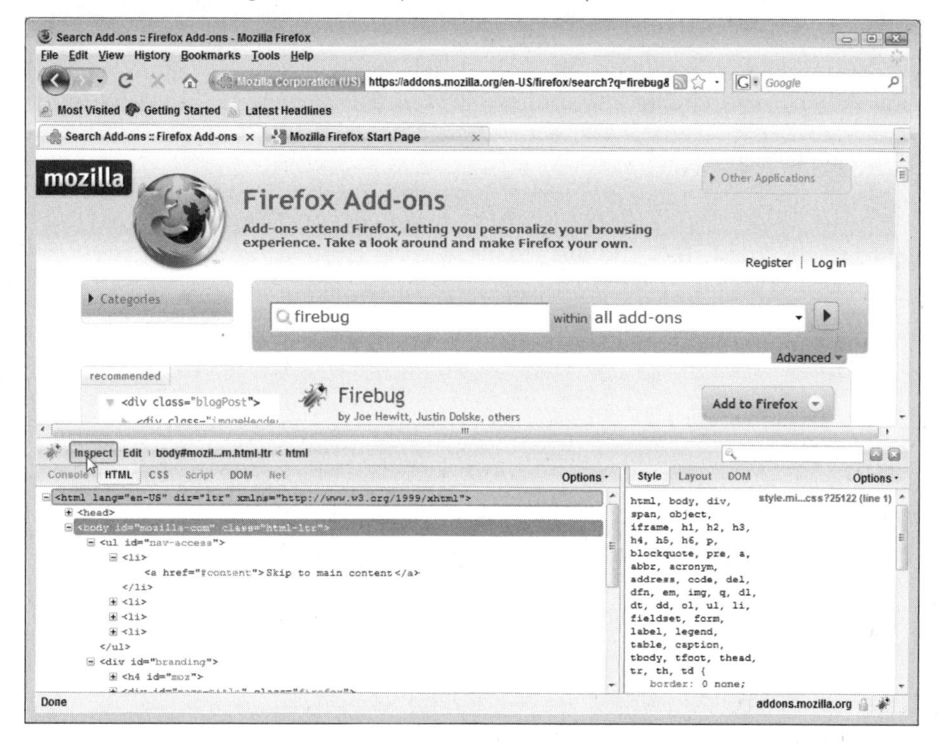

Other Tools

Tools to create HTML are only half of the equation when creating online documents. You must also have tools available to do graphics editing and supply any multimedia content you use. This section covers a handful of additional tools necessary to create rich, online content.

Graphics editors

Years ago, text-only Web pages were the norm. However, today's Web is a visual feast, and your documents must incorporate as much imagery as possible in order to be noticed.

Almost every operating system comes with at least one graphics editor, but the capabilities of the included editors are quite limited, and you shouldn't rely on them for much. The same goes for graphics programs bundled with many scanners, printers, and other graphics peripherals.

Ideally, you should consider using both a vector-based and a raster-based editing program. Vector-based editors use shapes and lines to create images, whereas raster-based editors use individual dots (pixels) to create images. Vector-based images are traditionally more exact and clear, but raster-based images allow for more visually striking effects. The best results can be obtained using both — use the vector tools to create solid imagery, and the raster tools for special effects and finishing work.

Note
Only raster-based images (specifically JPEG, GIF, and PNG images) are supported by common user agents. ■

Vector-based editing tools include the following:

- Adobe Illustrator
  `www.adobe.com/products/illustrator/main.html`
- Adobe Freehand
  `www.adobe.com/products/freehand`

Raster-based editing tools include the following:

- Paint Shop Pro Photo X2
  `http://store.corel.com/webapp/wcs/stores/servlet/ProductDisplay?partNumber=OL_PR12`
- Adobe Photoshop
  `www.adobe.com/products/photoshop`
- Adobe Fireworks
  `www.adobe.com/products/fireworks`
- The GIMP
  `www.gimp.org`

Note
Paint Shop Pro Photo X2 actually supports both raster and vector editing. ■

Note that these tools can be quite expensive — the latest version of Photoshop is several hundred dollars. Of course, Photoshop is without equal for raster editing; no other tool provides as much power and extensibility. Paint Shop Pro Photo X2 is quite capable at around $100, and The GIMP provides suitable editing without a price tag (it's open source).

Adobe Flash

Adobe Flash is the staple for most multimedia on the Web. Flash provides an animation platform with plenty of power via ActionScript, a flexible scripting language, and can be used for simple buttons or full-blown product demos.

Although the interface is a bit idiosyncratic, Flash is an indispensable tool for online animation. Figure 19-9 shows a Flash document in development.

The main draw of Flash is two-fold:

- It has become a standard on the Web that users expect.
- Flash can provide even complex animations in a small package (small file size).

Flash is another tool you should consider adding to your collection. You can learn more about Flash at `www.adobe.com/products/flash`.

FIGURE 19-9

Flash can be used for simple or complex animations.

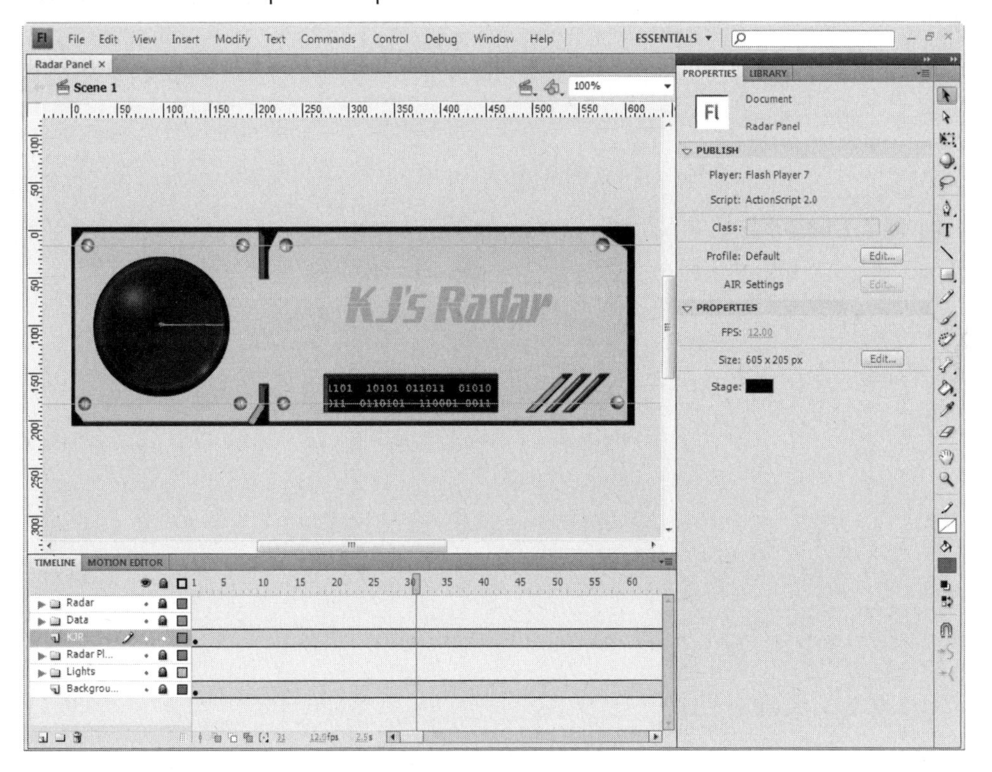

Summary

This chapter introduced you to a handful of HTML, CSS, and graphics editing tools you can use to make the creation of Web documents easier. Of course, there are many more Web-oriented tools on the market; the ones presented here only scratch the surface. When evaluating tools for your own use, keep in mind that there is a balance between cost and effectiveness. The tools included on the free disc from your ISP may be very affordable, but implementing them may wind up costing more than a tool you have to buy. The sweet spot lies somewhere in between, in capable but budget-minded tools. Many software manufacturers provide evaluation copies of their software that you can download and try before you purchase.

The next several chapters (20 through 24) continue the coverage of tools and utilities you can employ to develop and deploy your documents.

CHAPTER

20

Publishing Your Site

IN THIS CHAPTER

Now that you have documents to deploy on the Web, how do you actually move the files to the Web server? If you don't have an automated publishing tool (as covered in Chapter 19), you will probably use File Transfer Protocol (FTP). This chapter provides an introduction to FTP and explains how you can use it to deploy your files to a server.

Introducing FTP

File Transfer Protocol was created to easily move files between computers on the Internet. Dating back to the very early days of the Internet, FTP hasn't evolved much during the years it has been in service. FTP encapsulates several functions to transfer files, view files on both sides of the connection, and more.

FTP servers use the same protocol as the rest of the Internet: TCP/IP. TCP/IP is a packet-switching protocol that enables computers all over the world to communicate with one another via the Internet. The protocol uses well-defined ports — data doorways reserved for particular applications — to segregate the types of information traveling over the network. FTP uses TCP/IP ports 20 and 21. These ports are unique to the FTP service, allowing a computer to run a Web server (port 80), an FTP server (ports 20 and 21), as well as other services at the same time.

The FTP server sits patiently waiting for a client to request a connection on port 21. The client opens a port greater than port 1024 and requests a connection from the server. After the connection is authenticated — that is, a user logs in — the client can initiate commands to transfer files, and so on. When data is transferred between the client and the server, the server initiates the connection using port 20 — the client uses one port higher than the port used for commands. Figure 20-1 shows a graphical representation of the connection and port arrangement.

FIGURE 20-1

A typical FTP connection

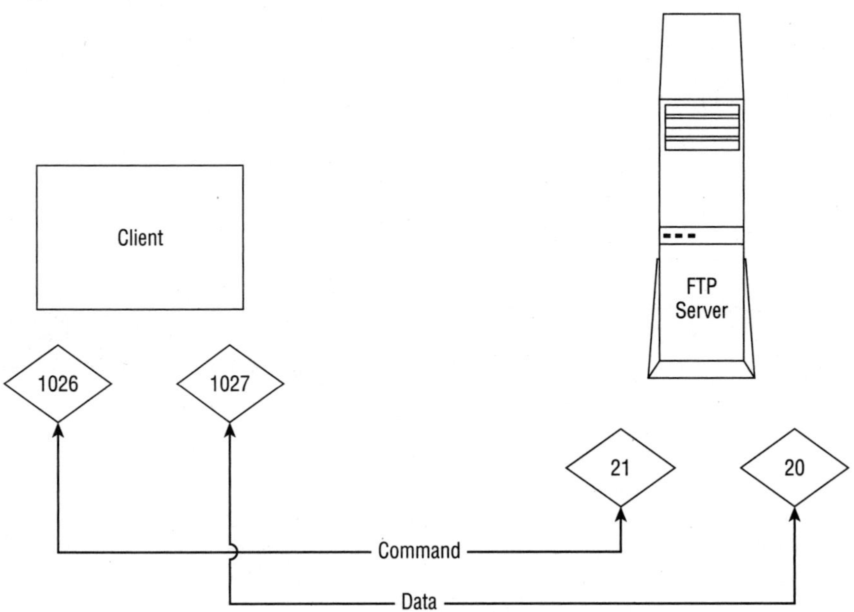

One problem with the traditional FTP process is that the server must initiate the data connection. This requires that the server be able to access the requisite port on the client to initiate the connection. If the client is using a firewall, the firewall might prevent the server from accessing the correct port. Because the client port isn't consistent, configuring the firewall to allow access is problematic.

To solve this problem, a new mode of FTP was created. Passive mode (typically referred to as *PASV*) allows the client to initiate both connections.

Note

If you are behind a firewall, you should always try to use passive mode. ■

FTP Clients

The first FTP clients were text-only applications, meaning the connection is initiated and data is transferred using textual commands. The latest FTP clients employ the same graphical interface as most modern operating systems, using standard file manager-like interfaces to accomplish FTP operations.

Note

Graphical FTP clients use the same methods and commands to communicate with the FTP server, but typically hide the communication from the user. The term "client" comes from the fact that the software — "application" by any other name — is connecting to a "server." As such, the application inherits the client moniker because of its role in the connection relationship. ■

The following code example shows a typical dialogue using a textual FTP client. The client initiates a connection, and the user logs in, gets a directory listing on the server, and then transfers a file. For clarity, the commands entered by the user are in boldface:

```
$ ftp ftp.example.com
Connected to ftp.example.com.
220 ftp.example.com FTP server ready.
Name: sschafer
331 Password required for sschafer.
Password: ******
230 User sschafer logged in.
Remote system type is UNIX.
Using binary mode to transfer files.
ftp> cd www
250 CWD command successful.
ftp> ls
200 PORT command successful.
150 Opening ASCII mode data connection for file list.
drwxr-xr-x  2 sschafer sschafer  4096 Jun 20 16:45 Products
drwxr-xr-x  2 sschafer sschafer  4096 Jun 16 18:41 About
drwxr-xr-x  2 sschafer sschafer  4096 Jun 6 15:16 Images
-rwxr-xr-x  1 sschafer sschafer  1571 Jun 12 17:58 index.html
drwxr-xr-x  2 sschafer sschafer  4096 Jun 15 04:16 Scripts
226-Transfer complete.
226 Quotas off
ftp> put index.html
local: index.html remote: index.html
200 PORT command successful.
150 Opening BINARY mode data connection for index.html.
226 Transfer complete.
2095 bytes sent in 0.3 secs (3.6 kB/s)
ftp> close
221 Goodbye.
ftp> quit
$
```

Figure 20-2 shows a graphical FTP application accessing the same site. The application shows the file listing of the remote server. To transfer a file, the user simply drags the file into or out of the application window to a local window or a destination pane within the same FTP application. Notice the underlying FTP commands and output in the lower-right corner of the application. Some graphical FTP client applications allow you to take manual control, entering various commands as required.

FIGURE 20-2

Graphical FTP clients use graphical user interface methods to transfer files.

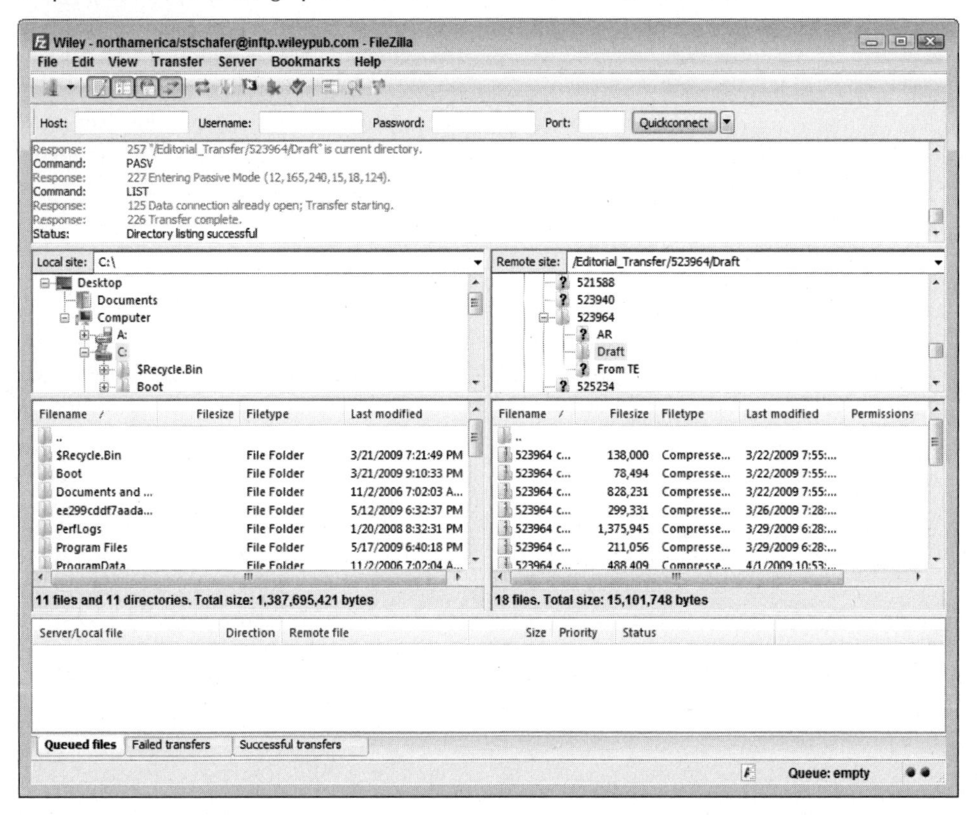

Table 20-1 shows a list of common FTP commands.

TABLE 20-1

Common FTP Commands

Command	Syntax	Use
`ascii`	`ascii` or `asc`	Switch to ASCII mode for file transfers.
`binary`	`binary` or `bin`	Switch to binary mode for file transfers.
`cd`	`cd` ***`directory_name`***	Change the remote directory.
`close`	`close`	Close the current connection to the server (log off).
`get`	`get` ***`filename`***	Download a file from the server.

Command	Syntax	Use
`lcd`	`lcd` ***`directory_name`***	Change the directory on the local machine.
`ls`	`ls` ***`[file_spec]`***	List files on the server (in the current directory).
`mget`	`mget` ***`file_spec`***	Download multiple files from the server.
`mkdir`	`mkdir` ***`directory_name`***	Create a new directory on the server.
`mput`	`mput` ***`file_spec`***	Upload multiple files to the server.
`user`	`user` ***`username`***	Initiate login as username (prompt for password).
`pasv`	`pasv`	Enter passive mode.
`put`	`put` ***`filename`***	Upload a file to the server.
`quit`	`quit`	Exit the client.
`rmdir`	`rmdir` ***`directory_name`***	Remove a directory on the server.
`open`	`open` ***`server_address`***	Open a new connection to the server.

Notable FTP Clients

Most operating systems include a textual FTP client, aptly named FTP. To use the client, type **ftp** at a command prompt. For example, on Windows XP, you would click the Start button, choose Run, type **command**, and press Enter. When the system prompt appears, type **ftp** and press Enter. Once the FTP program loads, an `ftp>` prompt appears. Other operating systems utilize different means to access their command prompt, but the concept is similar.

However, not all textual clients use the same commands or have the same options. Most clients support a help command: Type **help** followed by the name of the command for which you need help. Unfortunately, the standard help output simply tells you what the command does, not the syntax or options.

Tip

There are many ways to place files on the Web server. The easiest, of course, is to create and edit the files directly on the server. If you are using a development application, you can use its features to upload your content (typically such programs use FTP to transfer files). ■

Quite a few graphical FTP clients are available, from $100 commercial solutions to open-source and shareware solutions. The following list is a subset of available clients:

- Cross-platform clients:
  - **FileZilla** — This FTP client provides a host of valuable features in an open-source, cross-platform (and free) package. FileZilla is available for Windows, Linux, Mac OS X, and BSD platforms and supports a wide range of languages. Visit the FileZilla project page at `http://filezilla-project.org` for more information.

    - **FireFTP** — This FTP client is courtesy of a free add-on for Firefox. It provides the basic functionality to copy files to and from FTP sites as well as some nifty features like file compression. More on FireFTP can be found at `http://fireftp.mozdev.org/`.
- Windows clients:
    - **FTP Voyager** — This client enables you to transfer files between servers, resume aborted downloads, and more. It also has a scheduler that can automatically transfer files at set times.
    - **CoffeeCup FTP client** — This freeware client contains the usual options for graphical clients.
    - **CuteFTP** — This popular client contains a number of features to make FTP transfers easier. It provides a download queue, macro recording, and a scheduler to automate file transfers.
    - **WS-FTP** — This FTP client has the typical features found in other commercial solutions.
- Linux clients:
    - **Desktop-specific clients** — Both K Desktop Environment (KDE) and Gnome include graphical clients specific to the desktop environment.
    - **Additional open-source solutions** — Many graphical FTP clients are available for Linux. Each distribution contains several from which you can choose. Even more are available from various online sources.

Tip

Your Web browser can be used as a graphical client. Simply specify the FTP protocol (`ftp:`) and the server address, as in the following example:

```
ftp://ftp.example.com
```

If the server requires authentication, you will be prompted for your login information.

Principles of Web Server File Organization

Files on a Web server typically follow a tiered organization, placing subordinate pages in subdirectories. Furthermore, supplemental files — scripts, images, and so on — are typically placed in separate directories. Keeping the same hierarchical structure on both your computer and the server is an advisable tactic. Figure 20-3 shows the organizational structure of a typical website.

Note

There really isn't anything *typical* on the Web. As such, you should use a file and directory structure that suits your needs. The examples in this chapter are just that, examples. The important thing is that you use *some* logical organizational structure in your files and directories, and be consistent. ■

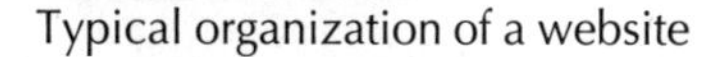

FIGURE 20-3

Typical organization of a website

Root of site
Main/home page/document

Images
All images for the site

Scripts
External scripts

Products
Documents for the Products section

About
Documents for the About section

Contact
Documents for the Contact section

If your site is small enough, it can be contained in one single directory. A site with many files, however, should be organized within several directories. Use your FTP client's features to create subdirectories, and transfer your files into the directories accordingly.

Summary

Although you can host HTML documents on a local machine, their true potential is realized when you publish your documents on a public server, where the rest of the world can view and interact with them. This chapter taught you the basics of FTP — the File Transfer Protocol of the Internet — which is used to transfer most of the world's HTML documents from local machines to public servers. You learned the basics of using an FTP application or client to connect and transfer files. You also learned that most Web development applications have built-in FTP services to help you get your content online.

The rest of this part covers variants of the version of HTML covered in Part I, including XML (Chapter 21) and XHTML Basic (Chapter 22).

CHAPTER

21

An Introduction To XML

Extensible Markup Language (XML) is a popular scheme for representing data. Although created as a more portable version of Standard Generalized Markup Language (SGML), XML lives mostly on the application side of the computer world. XML is used to store preferences and data from applications, provide a unified data structure for transferring data, encapsulate syndicated feeds from websites, and more. XML standards are being adopted by other data formats such as HTML (creating XHTML).

This chapter presents a primer on XML, including its format, methods, and tools.

IN THIS CHAPTER

Note

Full coverage of XML can occupy an entire book on its own, and is therefore outside the scope of this one. In the case of the Web, XML is a bystander technology, useful to know but not entirely critical for publishing on the Web. However, because XHTML is XML-compliant, coverage is mandatory. If you desire more information about XML, you can pick up a book dedicated to the subject, such as *WROX Beginning XML*, Third Edition, *WROX XSLT 2.0 Programmer's Reference*, Third Edition, or Wiley's *XML Weekend Crash Course* or *XML Programming Bible*. ■

XML Basics

XML was created to bring the advantages of the SGML standard to smaller platforms such as Web browsers. XML retains the flexibility of its older sibling but has been redesigned for the Web, enabling it to be easily transmitted via the Internet's architecture and displayed with less overhead.

The XML design strategy attempted to address the following points:

- Form should follow function. In other words, the language should be flexible enough to encapsulate many types of data. Instead of shoehorning multiple forms of data into one structure, the structure should be able to change to adequately fit the data.
- Documents should be easily understood by their content alone. The markup should be constructed in such a way that there is no doubt about the content it frames. XML documents are often referred to as *self-describing* because of this attribute.
- Format should be separated from presentation. The markup language should represent the difference in pieces of data only, and should make no attempt to describe how the data will be presented. For example, elements should be marked with tags such as `<emphasis>` instead of `<b>` (bold), leaving the presentation of the data (which should be emphasized, but not necessarily bold) to the platform using the data.
- The language should be simple and easily parsed, with intrinsic error checking.

These attributes are evident in the goals stated in the W3C's Recommendation for XML 1.0 (found at `www.w3.org/TR/1998/REC-xml-19980210`):

- XML shall be straightforwardly usable over the Internet.
- XML shall support a wide variety of applications.
- XML shall be compatible with SGML.
- It shall be easy to write programs that process XML documents.
- The number of optional features in XML is to be kept to the absolute minimum, ideally zero.
- XML documents should be human-legible and reasonably clear.
- The XML design should be prepared quickly.
- The design of XML shall be formal and concise.
- XML documents shall be easy to create.
- Terseness in XML markup is of minimal importance.

As is, XML is ill suited for the World Wide Web. Because XML document elements can be author defined, user agents cannot possibly interpret and display all XML documents in the way the author intended. However, standardized XML structures are excellent for storing application data. For example, consider the following applications of XML:

- The popular RSS syndication format defines particular element tags in XML format to encapsulate syndicated news and blog feeds. This enables many applications to easily disseminate the information contained within the feed.
- Several online statistic sites (computer game stats, and so on) store their information in XML because it can be easily parsed by a variety of applications.
- Many applications store their preferences in XML-formatted files. This format proves to be easily parsed, changed, and rewritten, as necessary.

- Many word-processing and other document-based applications (e.g., spreadsheets) store their documents in XML format.
- Many business-to-business applications use XML to share and transfer data between each other.

Note that while XML provides an ideal data structure for some applications, it should be used only for smaller, sequential collections of data. Data collections that require random access or have thousands of records would benefit from an actual database format, rather than XML.

Note

XHTML was designed to bring HTML into XML compliance (each element being properly closed, and so on), not the other way around (to add extensibility to HTML). In short, XHTML adheres to XML standards but is not itself an extensible markup language. ■

XML Syntax

XML and XHTML follow many of the guidelines already set forth for HTML but are slightly more stringent:

- Element and attribute names are case sensitive.
- All elements must be properly closed.
- Elements must be properly nested, not overlapping.
- All attributes must have values.
- All attribute values must be quoted.

Note

This book espouses the formatting syntax of XHTML, which is more exacting than straight HTML. As such, you already know many of the conventions for XML. ■

Within documents, the structure is similar to that of HTML, where element tags are used to encapsulate content that may itself contain tag-delimited content.

The following sections outline the particular syntax of the various XML elements.

XML Declaration and DOCTYPE

Each XML document must begin with an XML declaration similar to the following:

```
<?xml version="1.0" encoding="UTF-8"?>
```

The declaration is `<?xml?>`, with `version` and `encoding` attributes. The `version` attribute specifies the version of XML the document uses, and the `encoding` attribute specifies the character encoding used within the document's content.

As with other markup languages, XML supports Document Type Definitions (DTDs), which specify the rules used for the elements within documents using the DTD. Applications can then use the DTD to check the document's syntax. An XML document's DTD declaration resembles that of an XHTML document, specifying a SYSTEM or PUBLIC definition. For example, the following DTD is used for OpenOffice documents:

```
<!DOCTYPE office:document-content PUBLIC
   "-//OpenOffice.org//DTD OfficeDocument 1.0//EN" "office.dtd">
```

The following is an example of an XHTML document's DTD:

```
<!DOCTYPE html PUBLIC "-//W3C//DTD XHTML 1.0 Strict//EN"
   "http://www.w3.org/TR/xhtml1/DTD/xhtml1-strict.dtd">
```

Elements

XML elements resemble HTML elements. However, because XML is extensible, elements are generally not of the HTML variety. For example, consider the following snippet from an RSS feed, presented in XML format:

```
<?xml version="1.0" encoding="UTF-8"?>
<?xml-stylesheet href="/externalflash/NASA_Detail/NASA_Detail.xsl"
   type="text/xsl"?>
<rss version="2.0">
  <channel>
    <title>NASA Breaking News</title>
    <link>http://www.nasa.gov/audience/formedia/features/index.html</link>
    <description>A RSS news feed containing the latest NASA news
      articles and press releases.</description>
    <language>en-us</language>

    <item>
      <title>Atlantis Set for Return to Kennedy Space Center</title>
      <link>./HQ_M07077_Atlantis_ferry_flight.html</link>
      <description>The shuttle's ferry flight aboard a modified 747
         is expected to occur this weekend.</description>
      <pubDate>Fri, 29 Jun 2007 00:00:00 EDT</pubDate>
    </item>
    <item>
      <title>ISS Status Report: SS07-32</title>
      <link>./HQ_SS0732_station_status.html</link>
      <description>Operations and research occupied the crew this
         week.</description>
      <pubDate>Fri, 29 Jun 2007 00:00:00 EDT</pubDate>
    </item>
    <item>
      <title>Satellite Captures First View of 'Night-Shining'
         Clouds</title>
      <link>./HQ_07145_AIM_First_Light.html</link>
      <description>A NASA satellite has captured the first occurrence
         this summer of mysterious iridescent polar clouds that form 50
```

```
        miles above Earth's surface.</description>
      <pubDate>Thu, 28 Jun 2007 00:00:00 EDT</pubDate>
    </item>
    <item>
      <title>NASA Mars Rover Ready for Descent Into Crater</title>
      <link>./HQ_07145_Rover_Victoria_Crater.html</link>
      <description>NASA's Mars rover Opportunity is scheduled to begin a
         descent down a rock-paved slope into the Red Planet's massive
         Victoria Crater.</description>
      <pubDate>Thu, 28 Jun 2007 00:00:00 EDT</pubDate>
    </item>
</channel>
</rss>
```

In this case, the following elements are used:

- `channel` — The container for the channel, that is, the feed itself. The `channel` container has the following subcontainers:
  - `title` — The title of the channel or feed
  - `link` — The link to the feed on the Web
  - `description` — The description of the feed
  - `language` — The language of the feed's content
- `item` — The feed encapsulates each news item within an `item` element, which has the following sub-elements:
  - `title` — The title of the item
  - `link` — A link to the item on the Web
  - `description` — A short description of the item
  - `pubDate` — The publication date of the item

Note that several elements have multiple contexts. For example, the `channel` and `item` elements both provide context for `title` elements — the placement of each `title` element (usually its parent) determines to what element the `title` refers.

Attributes

XML elements support attributes much like XHTML. Again, the difference is that the attributes can be defined in accordance with the document's purpose. Consider the following code snippet:

```
<employee sex="female">
  <lastName>Moore</lastName>
  <firstName>Terri</firstName>
  <hireDate>2003-02-20</hireDate>
</employee>
<employee sex="male">
  <lastName>Robinson</lastName>
  <firstName>Branden</firstName>
  <hireDate>2000-04-30</hireDate>
</employee>
```

In this example, the sex of the employee is coded as an attribute of the `employee` element.

In most cases, the use of attributes instead of elements is arbitrary. For example, the preceding example could have been coded with sex as a child element instead of as an attribute, as in the following:

```
<employee>
  <sex>female</sex>
  <lastName>Moore</lastName>
  <firstName>Terri</firstName>
  <hireDate>2003-02-20</hireDate>
</employee>
<employee>
  <sex>male</sex>
  <lastName>Robinson</lastName>
  <firstName>Branden</firstName>
  <hireDate>2000-04-30</hireDate>
</employee>
```

The mitigating factor in deciding how to code data is whether the content is ever to be used as data, instead of just a modifier. If an application will use the content as data, it's best to code it within an element where it is more easily parsed as such.

Comments

XML supports the same comment tag as HTML:

```
<!-- comment_text /-->
```

You can embed comments anywhere inside an XML document as long as the standard XML conventions and corresponding DTD rules are not violated by doing so.

Non-parsed data

On occasion, you will need to define content that should not be parsed (interpreted by the application reading the data). Such data is defined as character data, or CDATA. Nonparsed data is formatted within a CDATA element, which has the following syntax:

```
<!CDATA [non_parsed_data]]>
```

Generally, CDATA elements are used to improve the legibility of documents by placing reserved characters within a CDATA element instead of using cryptic entities. For example, both of the following paragraph elements result in identical data, but the first is more legible because the CDATA elements are used instead of entities:

```
The table element should be used instead of the pre element
whenever possible.
```

```
The <!CDATA [table]]> element should be used instead of the
<!CDATA
[pre]]> element whenever possible.
```

Entities

XML also allows for user-defined entities. Entities are content mapped to mnemonics — the mnemonics can then be used as shorthand for the content within the rest of the document. Entities are defined using the following syntax:

```
<!ENTITY entity_name "entity_value">
```

Entities are defined within a document's DTD. For example, the following document prologue defines `"Acme, Inc."` as the entity `customer`:

```
<?xml version="1.0"?>
<!DOCTYPE report SYSTEM "/xml/dtds/reports.dtd" [
  <!ENTITY customer "Acme, Inc.">
]>
```

Elsewhere in the document the entity (referenced by `&entityname;`) can be used to insert the customer name:

```
<report>
  <title>TPS Report</title>
  <date>2005-01-25</date>
  <summary>The latest run of the regression test have yielded
  perfect results. The engagement for &customer; can now be
  completed and the final code delivered.</summary>
...
```

Entities can also be declared as external resources. Such external resources are generally larger than a few words or a phrase, such as complete documents. A system entity, used for declaring external resources, is defined using the following syntax:

```
<!ENTITY entity_name SYSTEM "URL">
```

For example, the following code defines a `chapter01` entity that references a local document named `chapter01.xml`:

```
<!ENTITY chapter01 SYSTEM "chapter01.xml">
```

The `chapter01` entity can then be used to insert the contents of `chapter01.xml` in the current document.

Namespaces

The concept of namespaces is relatively new to XML. Namespaces enable you to group elements together by their purpose using a unique name. Such groupings can serve a variety of purposes, but are commonly used to distinguish elements from one another.

For example, an element named `table` can refer to a data construct or a physical object, such as a dining room table:

```
<!-- Data construct in one document-->
<table>
  <tr><th>Date</th><th>Customer</th><th>Amount</th></tr>
  <tr><td>2005-01-25</td><td>Acme, Inc</td><td>125.61</td></tr>
...
</table>

<!-- Home furnishing definition in another document /-->
<table>
  <type>Dining</type>
  <width>4</width>
  <length>8</width>
  <color>Cherry</color>
</table>
```

If both elements are used in the same document there will be a conflict because the two refer to two completely different things. This is a perfect place to specify namespaces. Namespace designations are added as prefixes to element names. For example, you could use a furniture namespace to identify the table elements that refer to furnishings:

```
<furniture:table>
  <type>Dining</type>
  <width>4</width>
  <length>8</width>
  <color>Cherry</color>
</furniture:table>
```

The prefix should be uniquely tied to a namespace using a namespace declaration with an appropriate `xmlns` attribute. The namespace declaration has the following form:

```
<prefix:tag xmlns:tag="url">
```

For example, using our furniture prefix with the table tag, we would have something similar to the following:

```
<furniture:table xmlns:table="http://www.w3.org/XML/">
```

Note that the URL in the declaration serves only as a unique identifier — it is not perceived by the XML parser as an actual Uniform Resource Identifier (URI) of any type and might not even exist. It does, however, need to be unique within its sphere of influence.

Stylesheets

XML also offers support for stylesheets. Stylesheets are linked to XML documents using the `xml-stylesheet` tag, which has the following syntax:

```
<?xml-stylesheet type="mime_type" href="url_to_stylesheet"?>
```

For example, to link a stylesheet to an XML document, you could use a tag similar to the following:

```
<?xml-stylesheet type="text/css" href="mystyles.xsl"?>
```

Working with Document Type Definitions

As previously mentioned, an XML document that follows the syntax rules of XML is called a well-formed document. You can also have, or not have, a *valid* document. A document is valid if it validates against a DTD. Just as with HTML, an XML DTD is a document containing a list of rules that define the structure of the XML document. For example, a DTD can dictate whether all contact elements contain a phone element, as in the following code:

```
<contact>
   <name>Jill Hennessy</name>
   <address>111 East Main St.</address>
   <phone>1-303-555-4444</phone>
</contact>
```

The preceding code fragment is well formed as it stands. However, you may wish to define rules that more clearly delineate the purpose of each element and the position of each element within the framework or document as a whole. You might also want to define how many times each element can (or should) appear in the document.

A DTD can exist either outside the XML document that validates against it or within that same document. If the DTD exists outside of the document, you must declare it within the XML document so the XML parser knows you're referring to an *external* DTD, similar to the following:

```
<!DOCTYPE root SYSTEM "filename">
```

For example, for our contact XML document, an external `DOCTYPE` declaration might look like this (the `DOCTYPE` declaration is in bold):

```
<?xml version="1.0"?>
<!DOCTYPE contact SYSTEM "contact.dtd">
<contact>
   <name>Jill Hennessy</name>
   <address>111 East Main St.</address>
   <phone>1-303-555-4444</phone>
</contact>
```

The definitions would then be placed in a separate file, `contact.dtd`, accessible by the document.

You can also place the DOCTYPE rules within the XML document itself, as in the following example:

```
<?xml version="1.0"?>
<!DOCTYPE contact [
 <!ELEMENT contact (name, address, phone)>
  <!ELEMENT name        (#PCDATA)>
  <!ELEMENT address     (#PCDATA)>
  <!ELEMENT phone       (#PCDATA)>
]>
<contact>
   <name>Jill Hennessy</name>
   <address>111 East Main St.</address>
   <phone>1-303-555-4444</phone>
</contact>
```

Although DTDs are not XML documents, DTD and XML structure alike is defined using the following core components of XML:

- Elements
- Attributes
- Entities
- PCDATA
- CDATA

Each of these is described in the sections that follow.

Using elements in DTDs

Elements are the main data-containing components of XML. They are used to structure a document. You've seen them in HTML, and the core principles are the same as that of HTML. Elements can contain data or be empty. If they are empty they normally include an attribute, but it isn't a requirement. The HTML `br` and `img` elements are good examples of empty elements, as they don't encapsulate any data.

XML elements are declared with an element declaration using the following syntax:

```
<!ELEMENT name datatype>
```

The first part of the declaration (`!ELEMENT`) says that you are defining an element. The next part (`name`) is where you declare the name of your element. The last part (*`datatype`*) declares the type of data that an element can contain. An element can contain the following types of data when defined by DTDs:

- `EMPTY` data, which means there is no data within the element
- `PCDATA`, or parsed character data
- One or more child elements

Using element declaration syntax for empty elements

Empty elements are declared by using the keyword EMPTY:

```
<!ELEMENT name EMPTY>
```

For example, to declare an empty rug element, you would write the following:

```
<!ELEMENT rug EMPTY>
```

This element would appear as follows in an XML document:

```
<rug />
```

Using element declaration syntax for elements with PCDATA

Elements that do not contain any child elements and contain only character data are declared with the keyword #PCDATA inside parentheses, like this:

```
<!ELEMENT name (#PCDATA)>
```

A typical example of such an element follows:

```
<!ELEMENT note (#PCDATA)>
```

An XML parser might then encounter an actual note element that looks like this:

```
<note>The saunas will be closed for maintenance all of next
week. Please be sure to let your clients know.</note>
```

As you can see, the note element contains only text (PCDATA), and no child elements.

Using element declaration syntax for elements with child elements

Elements can contain sequences of one or more children, and are defined with the name of the children elements inside parentheses:

```
<!ELEMENT name (child_name)>
```

If you have more than one child element, separate each element with a comma:

```
<!ELEMENT name (child_name_1, child_name_2)>
```

An example, using the code you saw earlier for the contact document, might look like this:

```
<!ELEMENT contact (name, address, phone)>
```

Declaring the number of occurrences for elements

You can also declare how often an element can appear within another element by using an *occurrence operator* in your element declaration. The plus sign (+) indicates that an element *must* occur one or more times within an element. Therefore, if you create the following declaration, the phone element must appear at least once within the contact element:

```
<!ELEMENT contact (phone+)>
```

You can declare that a group of elements must appear at least one or more times:

```
<!ELEMENT contact (name, address, phone)+>
```

To declare that an element can appear zero or more times (in other words, it's an optional element), use an asterisk instead of a plus sign, as in the following:

```
<!ELEMENT contact (phone*)>
```

If you want to limit an element to zero or one occurrence (meaning it can't appear more than once), use a question mark (?) operator instead:

```
<!ELEMENT contact (phone?)>
```

The following XML would not be valid when the declaration uses a ? operator for the phone element:

```
<contact>
   <phone>303-555-4444</phone>
   <phone>303-555-4447</phone>
</contact>
```

You can also use a pipe operator (|) to indicate that one element *or* another element can be contained within an element:

```
<!ELEMENT contact (name,address,phone,(email | fax))>
```

In the preceding declaration, the sequence of name, address, and phone elements must all appear in the order shown, followed by either the email or fax elements. This means the following XML is valid:

```
<contact>
   <name>Jill Hennessy</name>
   <address>111 East Main St.</address>
   <phone>1-303-555-4444</phone>
   <email>jill@oasisoftranquility.com</email>
</contact>
```

However, the following XML would not be valid if validating against the same DTD:

```
<contact>
   <name>Jill Hennessy</name>
   <address>111 East Main St.</address>
   <phone>1-303-555-4444</phone>
   <email>jill@oasisoftranquility.com</email>
   <fax>303-555-4447</fax>
</contact>
```

Using attributes in DTDs

Attributes define the properties of an element. For example, in HTML, the img element has an src property, or attribute, that describes where an image can be found.

To define attributes for elements, you use an ATTLIST declaration. The ATTLIST declaration has the following format:

```
<!ATTLIST  element_name  attribute_name
  attribute_type  default_value>
```

The element_name and attribute_name parameters are what you would expect — the element to which the attribute applies and the name of the actual attribute. The attribute_type and default_value parameters are more complex, as they must handle several different values.

Table 21-1 shows the various values possible for the attribute_type parameter.

TABLE 21-1

Attribute Types

Value	Definition
CDATA	Character data
(value|value|...)	Enumerated data
ID	Unique ID
IDREF	ID of another element
IDREFS	List of IDs of other elements
NMTOKEN	An XML name
ENTITY	An entity
ENTITIES	A list of entities
NOTATION	Name of a notation
xml:	A predefined value

Table 21-2 shows the list of acceptable values for the default_value of the attribute.

For example, the following DTD declaration defines a phonenumber element with a default type attribute of home:

```
<!ELEMENT phonenumber  (#PCDATA)>
  <!ATTLIST phonenumber   type  CDATA "home">
```

TABLE 21-2

Default Value Settings

Value	Definition
value	The attribute has a default value of value.
#REQUIRED	The attribute is always required in the element.
#IMPLIED	The attribute does not need to be included in the element.
#FIXED value	The attribute has a default value of value and that value is fixed — it cannot be changed by the author.

To limit the values of the type attribute to home, work, cell, or fax — with a default of home — you could change the declaration as follows:

```
<!ATTLIST phonenumber type (home|work|cell|fax)>
```

Using entities in DTDs

You saw how to create entities in XML in the "Entities" section of this chapter. As a reminder, you use an ENTITY declaration of the following syntax:

```
<!ENTITY entity_name "entity_value">
```

Entities are defined within a document's DTD. For example, the following document prologue defines "Acme, Inc." as the entity customer:

```
<?xml version="1.0"?>
<!DOCTYPE report SYSTEM "/xml/dtds/reports.dtd" [
  <!ENTITY customer "Acme, Inc.">
]>
```

Elsewhere in the document the entity (referenced by &customer;) can be used to insert the customer name.

Using PCDATA and CDATA in DTDs

PCDATA is parsed character data, which means that all character data is parsed as XML; any starting or closing tags are recognized, and entities are expanded. Elements contain PCDATA.

CDATA is data that is not parsed by the processor. This means that tags are not recognized, and entities are not expanded. Attributes do not contain PCDATA; they contain CDATA.

Introducing XML Schemas

However important, DTDs can be somewhat limiting. Consider, for example, the following XML document:

```
<datatypes>
  <Boolean>true</Boolean>
  <integer>1</integer>
  <double>563.34</double>
  <date>06-01-2007</date>
</datatypes>
```

As far as DTD rules might be concerned, every element contains character data. The value for the `integer` element is not actually an integer, and the `date` isn't a date. This is because DTDs don't have mathematical, Boolean, or date types of data.

The W3C introduced another rules development methodology called *XML Schema* to handle richer data typing and more granular sets of rules that allow for much greater specificity than DTDs. In addition to the types of rules DTDs manage, schemas manage the data types allowed in an element, such as Booleans and integers.

The use of datatyping is especially important because it facilitates working with traditional databases and application program interfaces (APIs) based on Java, C++, and other languages, such as JavaScript.

Working with Schemas

Now that you're familiar with DTDs, it should be fairly easy to see how their concepts can extend to a greater range of datatypes. XML Schema uses XML syntax to develop rule sets, so it is a bit more intuitive than the DTD syntax shown earlier in the chapter.

Recall that an example earlier created a simple XML document for contacts derived from `contact.dtd`. The following listing shows the same principles at work in a schema. Pay particular attention to the `xs:sequence` `xs:element` children (in bold) that live in the `xs:complexType` element:

```
<?xml version="1.0"?>
<xs:schema xmlns:xs="http://www.w3.org/2001/XMLSchema"
targetNamespace="http://www.tumeric.net/schemas"
xmlns="http://www.tumeric.net/schemas"
elementFormDefault="qualified">
<xs:element name="contact">
    <xs:complexType>
      <xs:sequence>
        <xs:element name="name" type="xs:string"/>
        <xs:element name="address" type="xs:string"/>
        <xs:element name="city" type="xs:string"/>
```

```
          <xs:element name="state" type="xs:string"/>
          <xs:element name="postalcode" type="xs:string"/>
          <xs:element name="age" type="xs:integer" />
        </xs:sequence>
      </xs:complexType>
  </xs:element>
  </xs:schema>
```

Note

The `contact` element is a complex type of element because it contains other elements. If an element isn't defined to contain child elements, it's a *simple* type of element. ■

In a DTD, the sequence of elements that should appear in the document is defined by placing a comma-delimited list of the elements in an element definition. In XML Schema, a sequence is defined by creating a sequence of elements in a specific order within an `xs:sequence` element. This is part of the larger definition of the XML document's root element, which is the `contact` element. Note the use of the `type` attribute in the `xs:element` elements, which defines the datatype of each element.

Numerous datatypes are available for XML elements using schema. If you're familiar with the Java programming language, it might help you to know that most of the XML Schema datatypes are similar to Java datatypes. If you're not familiar with Java, there are four basic datatypes:

- Numerical (such as integer and double)
- Date
- String
- Booleans

Tip

You can find out the specifics of various datatypes available in XML Schema at `www.w3.org/TR/xmlschema-2`. ■

You can also place your schema in an external document and reference it from within your XML document. To reference an external schema in an XML document, use the following syntax:

```
<?xml version="1.0"?>
<contact xmlns="http://www.tumeric.net/schemas"
xmlns:xsi="http://www.w3.org/2001/XMLSchema-instance"
xsi:schemaLocation=
"http://www.on-target-games.com/schemas/contact.xsd" >
   <name>Johhny Rude</name>
   <address>111 East Onion Ave.</address>
   <city>Big City</city>
   <state>CA</state>
   <postalcode>96777</postalcode>
   <phone>1-323-456-4444</phone>
```

```
    <fax>test</fax>
    <email>rude@rude.com</email>
</contact>
```

The schema is referenced through the namespace for the document. The specific syntax for the namespace declaration looks like this:

```
xmlns="http://www.tumeric.net/schemas"
xmlns:xsi="http://www.w3.org/2001/XMLSchema-instance"
xsi:schemaLocation="
http://www.on-target-games.com/schemas/contact.xsd"
```

The other two lines of code are additional namespaces, which serve as identifiers. They tell a parser that elements associated with them are unique and may have specially developed definitions. The important part of the namespace is the Uniform Resource Identifier (URI), which is what gives a namespace its unique identity. When elements live within a specific namespace governed by a schema, they must adhere to the rules of that schema.

The first namespace in the preceding code fragment refers to a namespace established in the schema that uniquely binds the schema to a specified resource, in this case a website. You don't have to refer to a website, and the reference is not actually a physical pointer. Instead, the URI is simply an easy way to establish identity because a website should be unique. While it isn't guaranteed to be unique, because anyone can hijack your website address name and use it for their own schema, using a website address has become fairly standard practice. Instead of a website name, you could use a long mash of characters, as in the following example:

```
xmlns="hk45kskds-scld456ksaldkttsslae697hg"
```

The second namespace refers to the W3C's schema location so that XML processors will validate the XML document against the schema. This is necessary because you then need to call the resource you're using — in this case, a schema that can be found on the path named in the `xsi:SchemaLocation` attribute. When the processor finds the schema, it attempts to validate the XML document as the document loads. If the XML document doesn't conform to the rules you set forth in the schema definition, an error will result (assuming your parser can work with XML Schema).

Using XML

Actual use of an XML document requires that the document be transformed into a usable format. There are many means and formats to translate XML — the limits are governed only by your imagination and the tools at hand.

Viewing XML documents doesn't require special tools. Many of the modern user agents assemble various functionality to view XML documents and even add capabilities such as tag highlighting and the ability to collapse portions of the document, as shown in Figure 21-1, where Internet Explorer is displaying an RSS document.

FIGURE 21-1

Internet Explorer is able to render XML documents in a fairly robust manner.

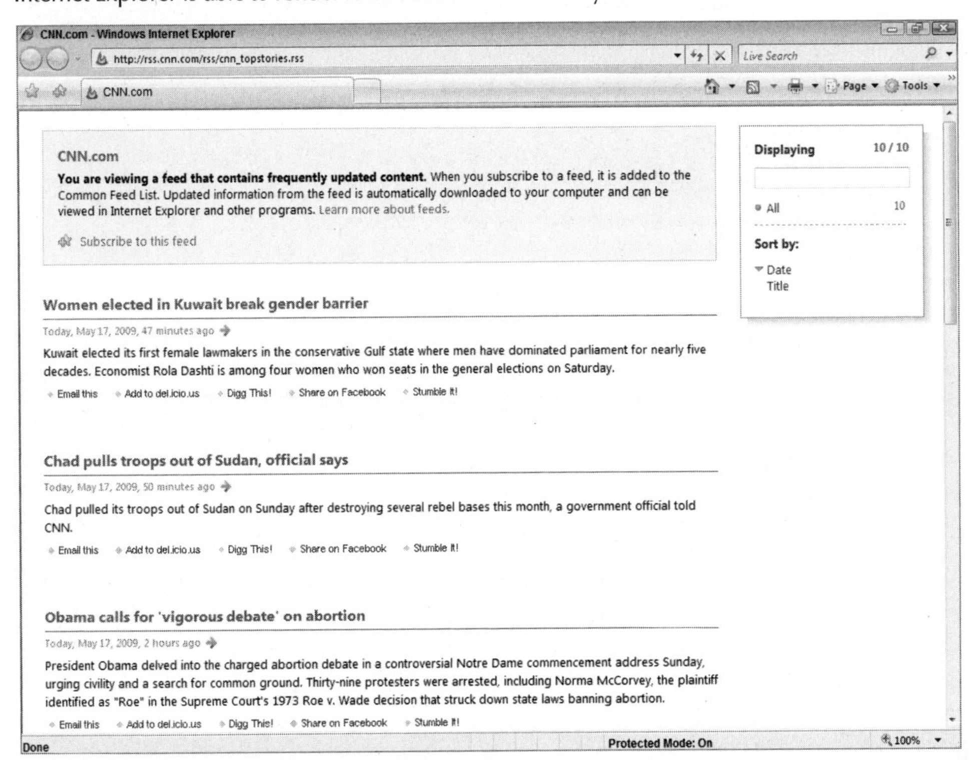

Extensible Stylesheet Language Transformations

Extensible Stylesheet Language Transformations (XSLT) change XML documents into formatted documents and can rearrange document contents to generate new document elements. XSLT takes two items as its input: the XML document (sometimes referred to as the *source tree*) and a stylesheet to determine the transformation. The output document (sometimes referred to as the *result tree*) is in the desired format, ready for output to the desired device.

Many tools are available to help you manage XML documents and perform XSLT, including many open-source solutions (search for "XSLT" on `www.sourceforge.org`).

XML editing

You have many options for editing XML files. Because XML is a text-only format, you can use any text editor (Emacs, vi, Notepad, and so on) to create and edit XML documents. However, dedicated XML editors make the editing job easier by adding syntax highlighting, syntax checking, validation, auto-code completion, and more. Following are some XML text editing options:

- Many open-source XML editors are available (search "XML editor" on `http://sourceforge.org`).
- Lennart Staflin has developed a major mode for Emacs called PSGML (`www.lysator.liu.se/projects/about_psgml.html`).
- XMetal — formerly owned by Corel, now owned by Blast Radius — is a well-known, capable (albeit commercial and expensive) XML editor (`www.xmetal.com`).
- XMLSpy, by Altova, is another capable XML editor in the same price range as XMetal, although the personal edition is free (`www.altova.com`).
- <oXygen/>, by SyncRO Soft Ltd., is a lower-cost, multiplatform XML editor and XSLT debugger (`www.oxygenxml.com`).

XML parsing

Many XML parsing applications are available, including many open-source applications (search for "XML parsing" on `http://sourceforge.org`). In addition, there are XML parsing modules for most programming languages:

- James Clark's XML parser, expat, is well known as the standard for XML parsing (`http://expat.sourceforge.net` and `www.jclark.com/xml/expat.html`).
- Many XML modules are available for Perl via CPAN (`www.cpan.org`).
- Several XML tools are available for Python, including the many found on the Python website (`http://pyxml.sourceforge.net/topics`).
- PHP has a handful of XML functions built in as extensions to support expat (`www.php.net/manual/en/ref.xml.php`).
- The PHP Extension and Application Repository has several additional extensions for XML maintenance and manipulation (`http://pear.php.net`).

Summary

This chapter covered the basics of XML, a fairly robust and extensible markup language that can be used to represent a wide range of data. You learned how similar XML and HTML were in structure, but also how different XML can be to suit its purposes. You learned how an XML document is defined, its elements declared, and how the language can be extended.

The rest of this part of the book covers XHTML Basic, as well as how to clean up and validate your documents, and presents a handful of HTML tips and tricks. The next part of the book covers CSS, the other half of the Web document equation.

CHAPTER 22

Creating Mobile Documents

IN THIS CHAPTER

As I've repeatedly pointed out, the Web and its technologies have grown up. Starting as a simple, text-only medium, the Web is now capable of delivering almost any kind of media. The underlying technologies, HTML and HTTP, have also evolved to better support this growth.

One inevitable side-effect of a popular delivery technology is its rapid adoption by other media devices. Today, it isn't just Web browsers on PCs that access Web content and use Web-related technologies — devices such as mobile phones, mall kiosks, and even ATMs utilize the technology. However, many of these devices have limited resources and cannot make full use of HTML or display the same rich content that a dedicated PC browser can. As a result, if you intend to deliver content via one of these resource-constrained devices, you must limit the scope of your code appropriately.

This chapter covers XHTML Basic, a specification designed for smaller devices. It also covers some ancillary technologies that help deploy content to these devices.

Tip

Before taking the time to create content for mobile devices, ask yourself these questions:

- **Does my audience need my content on their mobile devices?**
- **Does my content lend itself to mobile devices?**
- **Can I spend the time and other resources to keep both my mobile and traditional content up-to-date and in sync?**

If you answer even one of these questions with a "no," then creating and maintaining mobile content is not appropriate for you. ■

Understanding the Evolution of the Mobile Web

If you choose to develop Web content for mobile devices, it is important for you to understand the evolution of those devices and their relationship to the Web. This history is important because the mobile landscape is very different from that of the normal Web. The capabilities of mobile devices tend to be quite limited, and in many cases devices are quite different from one another — from the markup language they understand to their individual capabilities and their connectivity to the Internet (or lack thereof).

The following sections provide a short introduction to these topics.

The first, dark years of mobility

Web-enabled mobile devices have been around for many years. In the late 1990s, several cellular phones were launched with Web features. In the U.S., the technology was backed by a popular phone manufacturer (Nokia) and a mobile connectivity company (Openwave). The two companies created a protocol for mobile data connectivity called Wireless Access Protocol, or WAP. They also created a new minimalistic markup language, Wireless Markup Language (WML). WAP protocol used special gateways for mobile devices to connect to and receive their content, and WML language was very different from normal Web markup specifications like HTML. However, mobile devices were able to receive Web-like content.

Around the same time, the Japanese mobile communications company NTT DoCoMo launched its i-Mode service in Japan, bringing Web-like content to mobile devices. NTT DoCoMo created another HTML variant, Compact HTML, to support its content.

Note

Throughout this section, I use the phrase "Web-like content" because the early mobile content was not delivered via Web standard markup (HTML) or the standard Internet gateways. The content was coded in WML or Compact HTML, and as such could not be as rich. In addition, because it was delivered via proprietary gateways, it was prone to being filtered, and most of the content was created and delivered by the service provider — it was unusual to be able to reach a site of the user's choice. Therefore, the content was only "Web-like." ■

As mobile connectivity became more popular, and even expected, new devices appeared with even more capable user agents. However, more players in the market meant more proprietary solutions. Consumers found that what worked on one phone would not work on another, and the expectation of being able to browse the actual Web was an unrealized one. Thankfully, these consumer issues did not go unnoticed for long.

The Open Mobile Alliance and other standards

Several companies realized the shortcomings of mobile connectivity and the divergence of technologies taking place, and formed the Open Mobile Alliance. This alliance sought to help create better, more globally adopted standards and generally improve the mobile connectivity experience. Several new, exceedingly capable user agents began appearing on devices, while proprietary gateways began disappearing.

Around the same time as the formation of the Alliance, the W3C put together a mobile markup specification designed to bring more order to the mobility market. The new standard, known as *XHTML Basic*, was developed as a minimal set of XHTML tags for mobile user agent support. The Open Mobile Alliance embraced the standard and expanded it to create the XHTML Mobile Profile standard, designed to be adopted by future mobile user agents to enable a more capable and rich browsing experience.

As with everything else in the mobile environment, the new standards were met with spotty acceptance and adoption. Most mobile user agent vendors chose to support XHMTL Basic, but not the expanded Mobile Profile specification. A few vendors with more capable browsers (who were members in the Open Mobile Alliance) chose to support the expanded specification, enabling their users to enjoy a more rich experience while still being backward compatible with XHTML Basic.

However, as you can probably guess, most content developers chose to develop for XHMTL Basic, ensuring that the widest possible audience could use their content.

Note

Older devices (i.e., those two years or older as of this writing) support only WML or one of the older WAP variants. Even user agents that render almost perfect XHTML display their results on smaller screens, have less memory to utilize, and so on. Keep these points in mind as you develop your content — especially if owners of older devices are part of your target audience. ■

The bottom line

The bottom line of this retelling of mobile Web history is this: Although standards have evolved and browser manufacturers are adopting them, you can never be completely certain what browsing capabilities your audience will possess.

Coding to XHTML Basic is a fairly safe bet, but when possible it is best to test several devices in your target audience for compliance with your code.

Note

In the last few years, Web technology on mobile devices has leaped ahead in capabilities. A few user agents, running on select handheld devices, can interpret and display standard HTML content. In rare cases, the

user agents can even support more advanced technologies like Flash. However, when developing for handheld devices, never assume that such capabilities will be available to your entire audience; endeavor to create content for the most basic of devices. ■

XHTML Basic 1.1

XHTML Basic was developed as a subset of XHTML and is defined using a method known as XHTML Modularization. XHTML Modularization is a methodology for creating a markup language by first defining smaller components and then defining how those components fit together to create the entire language.

Note

The current XHTML Basic 1.1 specification can be found at `www.w3.org/TR/xhtml-basic/`. ■

The XHTML Basic 1.1 doctype

As with any other Web document, XHTML Basic documents must start with a proper doctype. In the case of XHTML Basic 1.1, the document header should be as follows:

```
<?xml version="1.0" encoding="UTF-8" ?>
<!DOCTYPE html PUBLIC "-//W3C//DTD XHTML Basic 1.1//EN"
    "http://www.w3.org/TR/xhtml-basic/xhtml-basic11.dtd">
```

Also, to ensure that your documents' file type is interpreted correctly from their name alone, they should be saved with a `.xhtml` extension, not `.htm` or `.html`.

XHTML Basic 1.1 elements

Because XHTML Basic was patterned after XHTML, you will find most of the elements familiar in structure, scope, and usage. Table 22-1 lists the modules created for XHMTL Basic, and the elements present in each.

TABLE 22-1

XHTML Basic 1.1 Modules and Related Elements

Module	Elements
Structure Module	body, head, html, title
Text Module	abbr, acronym, address, blockquote, br, cite, code, dfn, div, em, h1, h2, h3, h4, h5, h6, kbd, p, pre, q, samp, span, strong, var
Hypertext Module	a
List Module	dl, dt, dd, ol, ul, li

Module	Elements
Basic Tables Module	caption, table, td, th, tr
Image Module	img
Object Module	object, param
Presentation Module	b, big, hr, i, small, sub, sup, tt
Meta Information Module	meta
Link Module	link
Base Module	base
Intrinsic Events Module	event attributes
Scripting Module	script, noscript
Stylesheet Module	style element
Style Attribute Module (Deprecated)	style attribute
Target Module	target attribute

Unless otherwise indicated in Table 22-1, the items in the Elements column are tag elements — `<br />`, `<h5>`, `<ol>`, and so forth. Attributes are properly noted.

It is interesting to note that XHTML Basic retains all of the text formatting elements (including a few deprecated in HTML 4.01), but deprecates the `style` attribute, disallowing style definitions within tag elements.

Note

Most mobile devices are not JavaScript enabled, so you should not use JavaScript in any of your documents meant for mobile users. Instead, consider the use of server scripting technologies — PHP, Perl, Python, and so on — to do data processing on the back end to present dynamic, but compliant, XHTML Basic documents. ■

Special considerations

Although the XHTML Basic specification allows for many HTML constructs, a handful of considerations should be taken into account when using XHTML Basic.

Tip

For some excellent guidelines on mobile development, check out the "Mobile Web Best Practices" document by the W3C, found at `www.w3.org/TR/mobile-bp/`. ■

Screen size

It has often been mentioned that mobile devices have limited screen real estate. However, to fully appreciate the lack of display space on some devices, you should navigate to your favorite website and size your PC's browser window to fewer than 200 pixels. Figure 22-1 shows a similarly sized browser window trying to display the Yahoo! main page.

FIGURE 22-1

Most Web pages look entirely different when viewed through a tiny viewport.

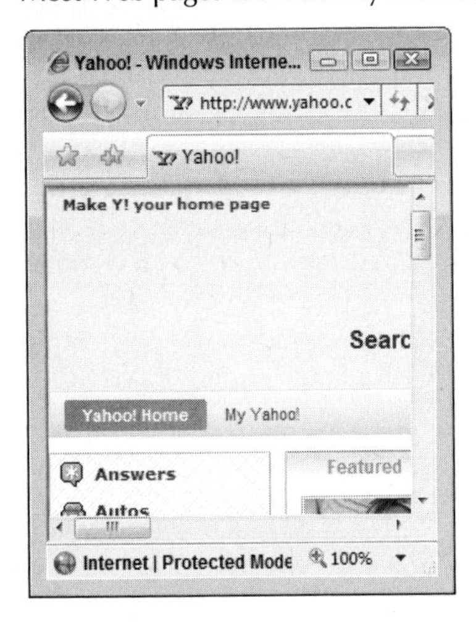

Balancing content for bandwidth and cost

It is easy to get carried away with content when developing for the Web and to assume that most of your audience has a fast computer connected to the Internet via a fast broadband connection. However, that is not the case with most mobile devices. In fact, some users pay a premium to have their device connected to the Internet.

When developing for mobile devices, keep a healthy balance between your content and what users might end up paying for it. This means self-censoring your content and not adding any fluff or out-of-context material. It also means keeping your content lean and mean, coding the bare minimum content, and realizing that mobile content will not be glitzy and flashy at this point in time.

Input restrictions

It is tempting to solicit various pieces of input from mobile users — location data for looking up local services, names for registering in databases, and so forth. However, keep in mind that most mobile devices lack a real keyboard, making a chore out of entering even the most trivial of data. Therefore, it becomes important to limit the amount of data entry required, relying more on alternative data entry schemes, such as select lists, option buttons, links, and so forth.

Easy URLs

Although it is advisable to put your mobile documents in a separate directory on your Web server, you want to keep that directory (and full URL) as easy to "type" as possible. For example, consider these guidelines:

- Keep your directory names short.
- Do not place content further than one level down from the root of the server.
- Avoid any special characters in the URL.
- Use abbreviations instead of long words in the URL (for example, `dev` instead of `developer`).
- Consider creating shorter URLs, decoded by the server.

Another alternative is to place your mobile content in a specific location and have the Web server redirect user agents to that location based upon their capabilities. Most user agents advertise their capabilities — whether they can accept HTML, XHTML MP, WML, and so on — when they request a document. Web servers can read this information and act accordingly. For example, the rewrite module for the Apache server can use the following code to detect a user agent that accepts XHTML Mobile Profile and WML content and deliver an `index.xhtml` document instead of the default `index.html` document:

```
# Test for acceptance of xhtml+xml (MP) and WML
RewriteCond %{HTTP_ACCEPT} application/xhtml+xml
RewriteCond %{HTTP_ACCEPT} text/vnd\.wap\.wml
# If user agent accepts both, it's MP enabled-give
# it the xhtml file instead
RewriteRule index.html$ index.xhtml [L]
```

Note

Full coverage of the Apache rewrite module and how to use it to redirect mobile user agents is outside the scope of this book. You can find more information on Apache's `mod_rewrite` module at `http://httpd.apache.org/docs/2.2/misc/rewriteguide.html`. An excellent primer on how to use several server-based methods of redirection can be found at `www.oreillynet.com/pub/a/wireless/2004/02/20/mobile_browsing.html`. ■

There are also several online scripting services to help you parse the agent trying to access your documents:

- Handset Detection provides a service that your documents can call to determine exactly which handset is accessing them. Visit `http://handsetdetection.com/pages/home` for more information.
- Studio Hyperset is a handful of scripts that can be run on or with your documents to determine the features of the accessing agent. Visit `http://studiohyperset.wordpress.com/2006/11/12/mobile-redirect-update/` for more information.

Small images

For practicality's sake, your images have to be small in terms of dimension, but you should ensure that they are as small as possible in terms of file size too. Run every image through a palette optimizer and consider using black-and-white images wherever possible.

Descriptive alt attributes and link text

When developing mobile content, it is also important to ensure that all images have short but highly descriptive `alt` tags. This ensures that devices that have images disabled or are on a slow network (slow to load images) can display *something* to alert the user of the actual content. In addition, provide descriptive text for all links to ensure that users know where each will take them.

Reliable navigation schemes

When display and usability are limited, reliable navigation schemes become much more significant. Logical access keys and logically structured tab order are two easy methods to improve usability. Placing frequently used navigation toward the top of the page where it can be easily found is another way to improve navigation.

Limit complex display structures

Tables were grudgingly included in XHTML Basic 1.1 by the W3C. Their inclusion was to help ensure that tabular data could be represented in mobile documents. However, tables *should not* be used to format entire documents, as discussed in Chapter 34. Stick to textual data in your tables to help keep mobile users happy.

Mobile Web Development Tools

Many development tools are available to aid your Web document efforts. Almost every phone manufacturer has a tool or two available to help developers create content for delivery on their devices. Table 22-2 lists a handful of the more prolific developer sites.

Each of these sites offers several resources, which are available only after you sign up for the respective developer program.

Tip

Several of the toolsets available from the mobile vendors contain full IDEs and debugging tools that can help you write compliant XHTML mobile code for a variety of devices. ■

TABLE 22-2

Popular Sites for Mobile Content Development Tools

Company	URL
Ericsson Mobility World Developer Program	`www.ericsson.com/mobilityworld`
ForumNokia	`http://forum.nokia.com/`
MOTODEV, the Motorola Developer Network	`http://developer.motorola.com/`

Summary

This chapter covered mobile HTML, from how Web mobility started to how it evolved through the components of XHTML Basic. You learned how easy it can be to create pages to be displayed on a variety of mobile devices, but also how difficult it can be to create content for resource-constrained devices. The next chapter covers how to clean and validate your code. Then you will learn a few HTML tips and tricks.

CHAPTER

Tidying and Validating Your Documents

Most of your documents will endure multiple rounds of editing before and after they are published. It is important to keep your code as tidy as possible so that you can easily read and change them in the future. Also, after creating your documents, it is important to test them to ensure that visitors to your site will not encounter any unforeseen problems. This chapter covers the basics of testing your code, including what tools are at your disposal.

IN THIS CHAPTER

Tidying Your HTML Code

One important step while developing HTML documents is to keep the code *tidy*. Tidy code is code that is kept orderly with logical line breaks and intelligent indentation. Although this may not seem like a crucial issue, it takes only small snippets of code to see the difference, as illustrated in Listings 23-1 and 23-2.

LISTING 23-1

Untidy code

```
<table border="1" rules="all">
<tr><td><img src="./images/JillHennessy.jpg" width="100px"
height="150px" alt="Jill" /><br />Jill Hennessy</td><td>Jill is
the founder of the Oasis of Tranquility and its executive
officer. She oversees the business side of the spa and operates
as its chief recruiting officer. Jill has degrees in business
and cosmetology.</td></tr><tr><td><img
src="./images/SandraBrown.jpg" width="100px" height="150px"
alt="Sandra" /><br />Sandra Brown</td><td>Sandra is the
co-founder of the Oasis and its operating officer. She is
```

continued

LISTING 23-1 *(continued)*

```
responsible for the day-to-day operation of the spa and
management of its employees. Sandra has journalism and
management degrees and several accreditations from various
cosmetology schools.</td></tr><tr><td><img
src="./images/DamienSanders.jpg" width="100px" height="150px"
alt="Damien" /><br />Damien Sanders</td><td>Damien is the lead
stylist at the Oasis. He has worked at several of the most
esteemed salons in Hollywood and has several degrees and
accreditations in hair design from schools across the nation.
Damien was one of two stylists invited to travel with a popular
modern burlesque group on their last tour.</td></tr><tr><td><img
src="./images/MartyTowers.jpg" width="100px" height="150px"
alt="Marty" /><br />Marty Towers</td><td>Marty is the Oasis
makeover specialist. She has several degrees and accreditations
to her credit and is known as one of the top makeup and nail
color specialists in the country. She was recently invited on a
nationally syndicated talk show to discuss women's image and
skin and nail techniques.</td></tr><tr><td><img
src="./images/TaliaOwens.jpg" width="100px" height="150px"
alt="Talia" /><br />Talia Owens</td><td>Talia is the lead
masseuse for the Oasis. She has over 2000 hours of instruction
in various massage techniques--from deep tissue to
neuromuscular--and holds certifications in each. Talia is also
an accredited acupuncturist and aromatherapy
specialist.</td></tr><tr><td><img src="./images/ThomasBaker.jpg"
width="100px" height="150px" alt="Thomas" /><br />Thomas
Baker</td><td>Thomas rounds out the massage team here at the
Oasis. He has over 1500 hours of instruction in several massage techniques
and is accredited in several. Thomas also holds a degree
in sports therapy and rehabilitation.</td></tr>
</table>
```

LISTING 23-2

Tidy code

```
<table border="1" rules="all">
<tr>
  <td><img src="./images/JillHennessy.jpg" width="100px"
         height="150px" alt="Jill" />
  <br />Jill Hennessy</td>
  <td>Jill is the founder of the Oasis of Tranquility and its
executive officer. She oversees the business side of the spa and
operates as its chief recruiting officer. Jill has degrees in
business and cosmetology.</td>
</tr>
```

```
<tr>
  <td><img src="./images/SandraBrown.jpg" width="100px"
         height="150px" alt="Sandra" />
  <br />Sandra Brown</td>
  <td>Sandra is the co-founder of the Oasis and its operating
officer. She is responsible for the day-to-day operation of the
spa and management of its employees. Sandra has journalism and
management degrees and several accreditations from various
cosmetology schools.</td>
</tr>
<tr>
  <td><img src="./images/DamienSanders.jpg" width="100px"
         height="150px" alt="Damien" />
  <br />Damien Sanders</td>
  <td>Damien is the lead stylist at the Oasis. He has worked at
several of the most esteemed salons in Hollywood and has several
degrees and accreditations in hair design from schools across
the nation. Damien was one of two stylists invited to travel
with a popular modern burlesque group on their last tour.</td>
</tr>
<tr>
  <td><img src="./images/MartyTowers.jpg" width="100px"
         height="150px" alt="Marty" />
  <br />Marty Towers</td>
  <td>Marty is the Oasis makeover specialist. She has several
degrees and accreditations to her credit and is known as one of
the top makeup and nail color specialists in the country. She
was recently invited on a nationally syndicated talk show to
discuss women's image and skin and nail techniques.</td>
</tr>
<tr>
  <td><img src="./images/TaliaOwens.jpg" width="100px"
         height="150px" alt="Talia" />
  <br />Talia Owens</td>
  <td>Talia is the lead masseuse for the Oasis. She has over
2000 hours of instruction in various massage techniques--from
deep tissue to neuromuscular--and holds certifications in each.
Talia is also an accredited acupuncturist and aromatherapy
specialist.</td>
</tr>
<tr>
  <td><img src="./images/ThomasBaker.jpg" width="100px"
         height="150px" alt="Thomas" />
  <br />Thomas Baker</td>
  <td>Thomas rounds out the massage team here at the Oasis. He
has over 1500 hours of instruction in several massage techniques
and is accredited in several. Thomas also holds a degree in
sports therapy and rehabilitation.</td>
</tr>
</table>
```

As you can see, with the table elements isolated by line breaks and indentations, the table is easier to read and troubleshoot. Although tables are some of the more complex and problematic elements, many HTML elements can become exponentially harder to read and troubleshoot without liberal formatting.

The act of tidying your code is simply adding the additional spacing, indentation, and other formatting to your HTML code in order to make it readable. Ideally, you would add this formatting as you write your code, but should you need to do so after the fact, there are a few ways, and one powerful tool, to help add the formatting later.

Note

When writing tidy code it is important to be careful of where you insert blank lines and spaces. Although important for readability, both of these entities can change the format of your final document, usually for the worse. As a general rule, always insert white space between closing and opening tags. For example, when adding space to table cells, place your white space between the ending tag of one cell (`</td>`) and the beginning tag of the next cell (`<td>`). Any white space in this area will simply be ignored by a user agent, and as such will not change the formatting of your document.

Consistency is also important while formatting your documents so you know exactly where to expect elements and when. ■

HTML Tidy

The HTML Tidy tool was created several years ago by Dave Raggett and maintained for several years by Dave and various entities at the W3C. HTML Tidy was originally created for two reasons:

- To clean up HTML code, adding liberal white space and indentation to help increase the readability of the code (also making it easier to troubleshoot)
- To check the HTML for basic errors — missing tags, inappropriate attributes, and so on

Today, the program has been taken over by a group of "enthusiastic volunteers" at Source Forge, where it is now actively maintained.

Note

The HTML Tidy home page is now at `http://tidy.sourceforge.net`. ■

Getting HTML Tidy

HTML Tidy exists mostly as an executable available for Linux/UNIX platforms and is downloadable from the HTML Tidy home page. Additional HTML Tidy projects have included the following:

- Java version of Tidy
- Perl XS version of Tidy
- Python wrapper for TidyLib
- HTMLTrim, a highly customizable X(HTML)/XML pretty-printer and fixer for Windows

- Jase, a simple editor with TidyLib integration
- mod_tidy for Apache 2

There are also ad hoc versions compiled for Windows, OS/2, and MAC OS (classic and OS X).

Running HTML Tidy

Running HTML Tidy is straightforward; you simply run the executable with an HTML file as an argument. For example, the following command line could be used to run our earlier non-tidy table example (refer to Listing 23-1) through Tidy:

```
tidy tableexample.html
```

Tidy, in return, provides a tidied example of the file, along with a few hints for our document, as shown in Listing 23-3.

LISTING 23-3

Tidy output

```
line 8 column 1 - Warning: <table> lacks "summary" attribute
Info: Doctype given is "-//W3C//DTD HTML 4.01//EN"
Info: Document content looks like HTML 4.01 Strict
1 warning, 0 errors were found!
<!DOCTYPE HTML PUBLIC "-//W3C//DTD HTML 4.01//EN"
"http://www.w3.org/TR/html4/strict.dtd">
<html>
<head>
<meta name="generator" content=
"HTML Tidy for Linux/x86 (vers 12 April 2005), see www.w3.org">
<title>Using Tidy</title>
</head>
<body>
<table border="1" rules="all">
<tr>
<td><img src="./images/JillHennessy.jpg" width="100" height="150"
alt="Jill" /><br>
Jill Hennessy</td>
<td>Jill is the founder of the Oasis of Tranquility and its
executive officer. She oversees the business side of the spa and
operates as its chief recruiting officer. Jill has degrees in
business and cosmetology.</td>
</tr>
<tr>
<td><img src="./images/SandraBrown.jpg" width="100" height="150"
alt="Sandra" /><br>
Sandra Brown</td>
<td>Sandra is the co-founder of the Oasis and its operating
officer. She is responsible for the day-to-day operation of the spa
```

continued

LISTING 23-3 *(continued)*

```
and management of its employees. Sandra has journalism and
management degrees and several accreditations from various
cosmetology schools.</td>
</tr>
<tr>
<td><img src="./images/DamienSanders.jpg" width="100" height="150"
alt="Damien" /><br>
Damien Sanders</td>
<td>Damien is the lead stylist at the Oasis. He has worked at
several of the most esteemed salons in Hollywood and has several
degrees and accreditations in hair design from schools across the
nation. Damien was one of two stylists invited to travel with a
popular modern burlesque group on their last tour.</td>
</tr>
<tr>
<td><img src="./images/MartyTowers.jpg" width="100" height="150"
alt="Marty" /><br>
Marty Towers</td>
<td>Marty is the Oasis makeover specialist. She has several
degrees and accreditations to her credit and is known as one of the
top makeup and nail color specialists in the country. She was
recently invited on a nationally syndicated talk show to discuss
women's image and skin and nail techniques.</td>
</tr>
<tr>
<td><img src="./images/TaliaOwens.jpg" width="100" height="150"
alt="Talia" /><br>
Talia Owens</td>
<td>Talia is the lead masseuse for the Oasis. She has over 2000
hours of instruction in various massage techniques--from deep
tissue to neuromuscular--and holds certifications in each. Talia
is also an accredited acupuncturist and aromatherapy
specialist.</td>
</tr>
<tr>
<td><img src="./images/ThomasBaker.jpg" width="100" height="150"
alt="Thomas" /><br>
Thomas Baker</td>
<td>Thomas rounds out the massage team here at the Oasis. He has
over 1500 hours of instruction in several massage techniques and is
accredited in several. Thomas also holds a degree in sports therapy
and rehabilitation.</td>
</tr>
</table>
</body>
</html>
```

Note the various lines at the beginning of the output: The table summary attribute should be used to describe the table structure. It is very helpful for people using nonvisual browsers. The scope and headers attributes for table cells are useful for specifying which headers apply to each table cell, enabling nonvisual browsers to provide a meaningful context for each cell.

For further advice on how to make your pages accessible, see www.w3.org/WAI/GL. You may also want to try www.cast.org/bobby, which is a free Web-based service that checks URLs for accessibility.

To learn more about HTML Tidy, see http://tidy.sourceforge.net. Please send bug reports to html-tidy@w3.org. HTML and CSS specifications are available from www.w3.org.

Lobby your company to join W3C — see www.w3.org/Consortium.

As you can see from Listing 23-3 and the suggestion of the <table> tag's summary attribute, Tidy is a bit aggressive in its diagnostics of documents. Thankfully, with several dozen options at your disposal, you can tailor Tiny's behavior to your liking.

To get a list of Tidy's options, either read the documentation or run Tidy with the help parameter:

```
tiny -h
```

Note

As with validation tools (covered in the next section), it is important to include a valid DOCTYPE in all the documents being run through Tidy. ■

Validating Your Code

Validating your document code is a very good idea. It helps double-check your document for simple errors — typos, unclosed tags, and so on — and verifies that your code meets expected standards.

Specifying the correct document type declaration

There are many ways to validate your documents, but they all rely on your documents containing a correct document type declaration that references a specific document type definition (DTD). For example, if you want to base your documents on Strict HTML 4.01, you would include the following document type declaration at the top of your document:

```
<!DOCTYPE HTML PUBLIC "-//W3C//DTD HTML 4.01//EN"
  "http://www.w3.org/TR/html4/strict.dtd">
```

The DOCTYPE declaration informs any user agent reading the document on what standard the document is based. The information is primarily used by validation clients in validating the code within the document, but it might also be used by a display agent to determine what features it must support.

Tip

You can find a list of valid DTDs at `www.w3.org/QA/2002/04/valid-dtd-list.html`. ■

Validation tools

You can use several tools to validate your documents. Tools at your disposal include the following:

- The online W3C HTML validation tool, found at `http://validator.w3.org/`
- The online Web Design Group (WDG) validation tool, found at `http://htmlhelp.com/tools/validator/`
- Validation utilities built into Web development tools such as Adobe's Dreamweaver, shown in Figure 23-1
- Any of the various separate applications that can be run locally. A comprehensive list is maintained on the WDG site at `www.htmlhelp.com/links/validators.htm`

FIGURE 23-1

Adobe's Dreamweaver includes a comprehensive code validation feature.

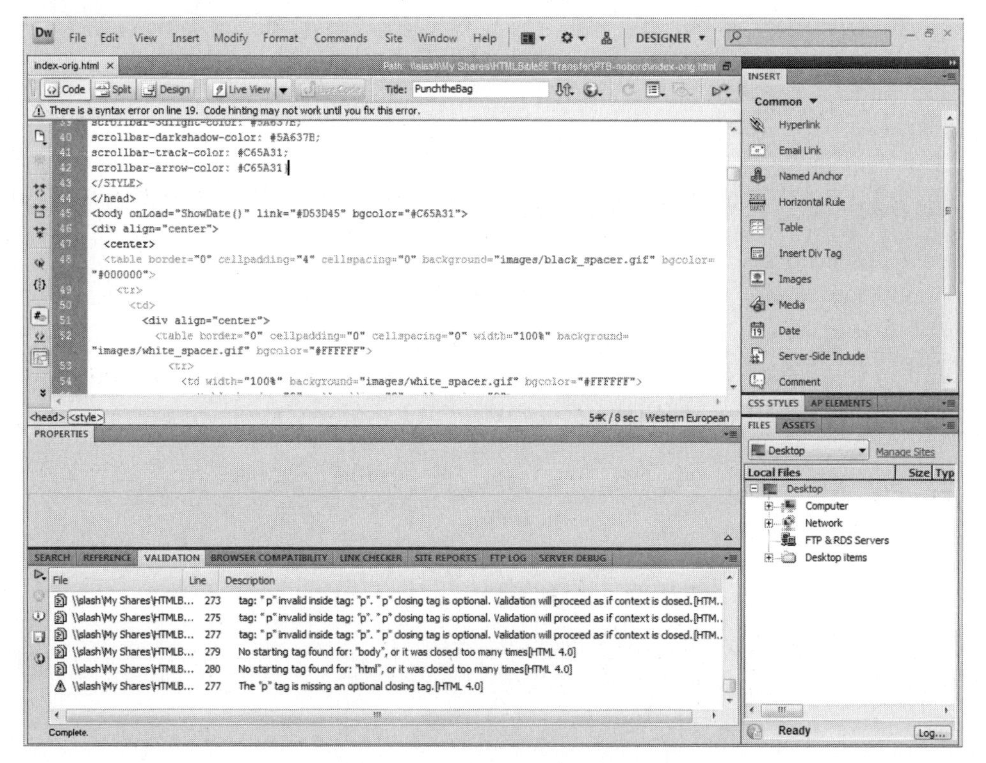

Understanding validation output

Consider the following HTML document:

```
<!DOCTYPE HTML PUBLIC "-//W3C//DTD HTML 4.01//EN"
  "http://www.w3.org/TR/html4/strict.dtd">
<html>
<head>
  <title>Validation Test</title>
</head>
<body>
  <form action="" method="POST">
    <input name="text" type="text" />
    <br>
    <input name="submit" type="submit" />
  </form>
</body>
</html>
```

When this code is passed through the W3C Markup Validation Service, the following first error is returned:

```
Line 9, column 30: document type does not allow element
"INPUT" here; missing one of "P", "H1", "H2", "H3", "H4",
"H5", "H6", "PRE", "DIV", "ADDRESS" start-tag
  <input name="text" type="text">
```

Although the document looks to be conforming HTML, the validation service thinks otherwise. But what exactly does the error mean?

In short, it means that the `input` element must be contained within a block element other than the `form` tag. Typically, the paragraph tag (`<p>`) is used, but you can also use `<div>`, a heading, `<pre>`, and so on.

Note

The W3C also has an online CSS validation tool, accessible at `http://validator.w3.org/`. Similar to the HTML validation tool, this tool will ensure that your CSS is free from typos and that all the attributes are paired with their matching styles. ■

Adding a paragraph container solves the problem and makes the document valid:

```
...
  <form action="" method="POST">
    <p>
    <input name="text" type="text" />
    <br>
    <input name="submit" type="submit" />
    </p>
  </form>
...
```

Tip

When working on making a document validate, always handle the errors in order. The example in this section actually results in four separate errors, each relating to the missing block elements. Adding the preceding elements solves all four problems. ■

Additional Testing and Validation

Besides using prefab Tidy and validation services, you can run other quick tests on your code to ensure that it runs well in the real world.

Testing with a variety of user agents

Despite being built on standards, no two user agents support HTML and CSS to the same degree. Some user agents don't implement certain features, while others implement them differently.

Note

Contrary to popular belief, Microsoft's Internet Explorer is no worse than other user agents regarding supporting standards. Even though Microsoft has created many proprietary technologies for its user agent, it does only a fair job of supporting the actual standards. ■

When coding your documents, it is important to understand your expected audience and what user agents they may be using. Although Microsoft Internet Explorer has market share on its side, many people use other user agents, such as Firefox, Opera, Konqueror, Safari, and so forth. As such, it is doubtful that everyone will be able to view your documents the way you originally intended, especially if you use some of the more esoteric features and technologies.

Make sure you test your pages on all target platforms to ensure that no show-stopping errors exist on any of the platforms. At a bare minimum, you should test on a current Microsoft (Internet Explorer) browser and a Firefox/Mozilla browser because most user agents incorporate one of these two technology bases.

Also, don't forget the non-computer user agents used by cell phones, PDAs, and other mobile devices. If your site will appeal to mobile device users, at least obtain the Software Development Kit (SDK) or emulator for each likely platform and preview your documents accordingly.

Testing for a variety of displays

Many Web designers make the mistake of designing their documents for specific screen resolutions. When the document is displayed at a smaller resolution, the page elements tend to jam together or break across unexpected lines.

Your documents should be suitable for many resolutions. Although most users will be running at resolutions of at least 800 × 600 pixels, you may have the occasional user running lower resolutions.

Always test your documents at various resolutions and color depths to look for any shortcomings.

Summary

This chapter taught you the importance of keeping your code tidy and consistent, and how to validate it using tools and a lot of testing. The next chapter wraps up the HTML coverage by providing a handful of tips and tricks you can employ in your documents. The next part of this book covers CSS in topical chapters.

HTML Tips and Tricks

IN THIS CHAPTER

Throughout this book, you have read about the ins and outs of the various HTML tags and entities. This chapter covers a few tips and tricks you can use to supplement your HTML knowledge to achieve real-world results.

Preloading Images

One of the things that can really slow down the display of Web pages is an abundance of images, each of which can contain the equivalent of 17,000 to 20,000 characters.

A trick that was developed to help overcome the delays experienced while image-rich documents load is *image preloading*. Through the use of JavaScript, image files are loaded into image objects. The net result is that the graphics are not displayed but are loaded into the browser's cache for later use. When it is time for the browser to actually display the image(s), they are taken from the local cache instead of having to make the trip across the Internet.

The script embedded in the following document is an example of an image preload script:

```
<!DOCTYPE HTML PUBLIC "-//W3C//DTD HTML 4.01//EN"
  "http://www.w3.org/TR/html4/strict.dtd">
<html>
<head>
  <title>Preloading Images</title>
  <script type="text/JavaScript">
  // Assign path of images to be preloaded to
  //   array, one image per index
```

```
        var imagenames = [];
        imagenames[0]  = "images/header.gif";
        imagenames[1]  = "images/logo.jpg";
        imagenames[2]  = "images/picture1.gif";
        imagenames[3]  = "images/picture2.gif";
        imagenames[4]  = "images/picture3.gif";
        imagenames[5]  = "images/rule.gif";
        imagenames[6]  = "images/button01.gif";
        imagenames[7]  = "images/button02.gif";
        imagenames[8]  = "images/button03.gif";
        imagenames[9]  = "images/footer.gif";
        imagenames[10] = "images/gradient.gif";
        imagenames[11] = "images/sphere.gif";
        // Create new image object for each image
        //   and then assign a path to the src, preloading
        //   the actual image
        function preload(imagenames) {
                var images = [];
                for (var i=0; i < imagenames.length; i++) {
                        images[i] = new Image();
                        images[i].src = imagenames[i];
                }
        }
        // Run script, preloading images, before document loads
        //   (alternately, place call in an onLoad in body tag to
        //   preload images after document loads
        preload(imagenames);
        </script>
      </head>
      <body>
        <p>Document body goes here.</p>
      </body>
      </html>
```

The script builds an array of image paths and then iterates through them, creating an image object and assigning an `src` property to cause the image to actually be preloaded. The script can be run via two different means: by a function call in the `head section`, which causes the script to run before the document loads, or by an `onLoad` handler in the `<body>` tag, which causes the script to run after the document loads.

Note

Image preloaders aren't useful for individual documents; they are most useful for sites of multiple documents that reuse the same images repeatedly (buttons, rules, backgrounds, and so on). When seeding the loader, don't forget to include images from all documents your audience may see. ■

The former, before the document loads, is handy when the document itself contains many images — running the preloader first can speed the display of the initial document. The latter, after the document loads, is a better choice when subsequent documents contain the majority of images. This enables the initial document to load more quickly because it doesn't have to wait for the script to run — the document is displayed for the user to peruse while the script runs in the background.

Controlling Text Breaks in Table Cells

Text in table cells is a fickle beast, especially when filled with long numbers. True text will typically allow for sane breaks, even in a narrow column. However, not much can be done with numeric data or other data that cannot be arbitrarily broken when a column changes size.

For example, consider the following number:

```
1,234,567,890.34
```

How would you break such a number in a column that supports only a four-character width? It's a tough decision, but probably one you would prefer to make yourself, rather than leave it up to HTML and CSS.

Tip

When deciding where to break numbers, keep in mind that the best places to break are around punctuation (e.g., commas or periods) or currency symbols. Doing so will preserve the readability of your numbers as much as possible. ■

You have two essential tools to use when controlling line breaks: the *nonbreaking space* and the *zero-width space.*

The nonbreaking space is best known by its HTML entity code . This resulting character looks and acts like a space but it doesn't allow the browser to break the line at this space. Although it is commonly used to space-fill elements, the nonbreaking space does have its textual uses. For example, you typically would not want the following line broken at the embedded spaces:

```
12344 Mediterranean Circle
```

To prevent the line from breaking, you would replace the spaces with nonbreaking space entities, similar to the following:

```
12344 Mediterranean Circle
```

Unlike the nonbreaking space, the zero-width space is not visible but allows the browser to break at the character. The zero-width space can be inserted by using its HTML entity code, ``.

Returning to our earlier example number, you can choose where you would like it to be divided if it must break (the original number is on the first line, the doctored number on the second):

```
1,234,567,890.34
1,&#8203;234,&#8203;567,&#8203;890.&#8203;34
```

Now, if the number needs to be broken, it will be broken after a comma or after the decimal point.

Stretching Title Bars

In Chapter 41 you will see how to use CSS to create elaborate expandable buttons. However, you can achieve similar results in HTML. This section demonstrates how to create an expandable header bar like that shown in Figure 24-1.

FIGURE 24-1

Using background graphic layering in a table, you can create expandable title bars.

This technique is very simple but employs a method that isn't thought of very often — the use of background images.

The goal is to create a bar that can be stretched to accommodate any page width, design implementation, or text length. At first blush, you might be tempted to simply place the bar as a graphic, increasing its width via a custom value for the image's `width` property. However, doing so will alter the image's aspect ratio and distort it accordingly.

The better choice is to use a sectioned image consisting of the bar's end caps and a slice of its midsection. Figure 24-2 shows a basic title bar created and sliced in a basic graphic editing program. The bar is sliced into four pieces: the two end caps, a slice of midsection, and the remainder of the midsection.

FIGURE 24-2

A title bar can be easily created and sliced into desired pieces with most graphic editing programs.

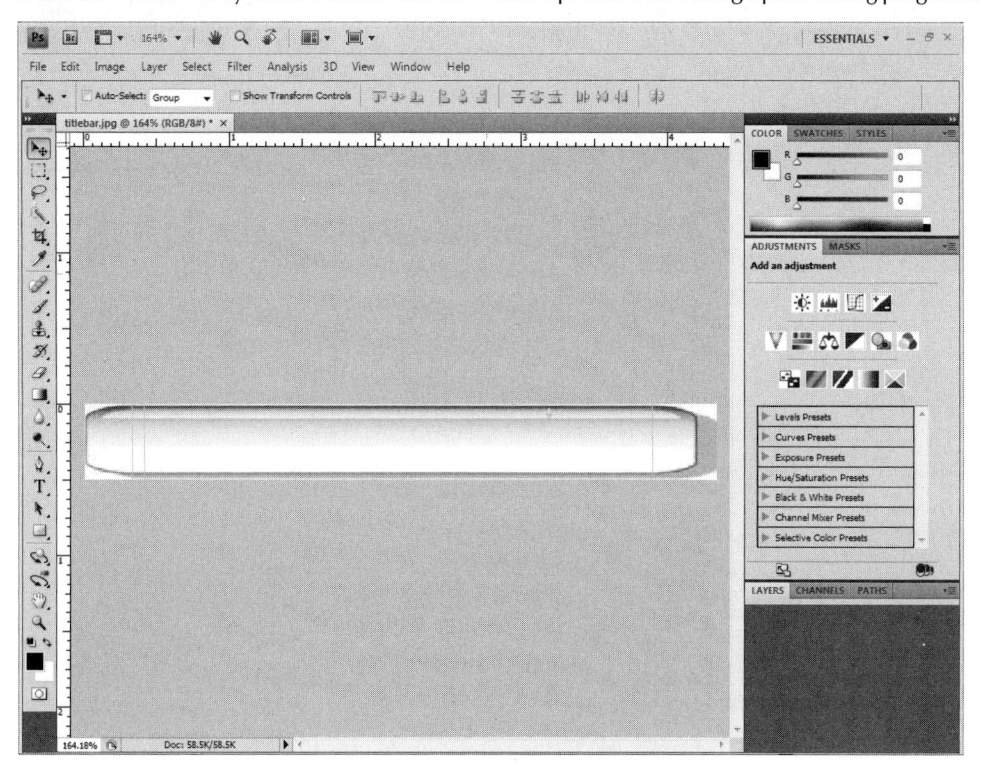

Note

The large section of the midsection is an unnecessary piece; you only need the small center slice. ■

Once you have the three pieces, you place them in a three-celled table, putting the end caps in the first and last cells and using the slice as the background for the middle cell. Use of the `background-repeat` property causes the slice to repeat through the width of the cell without any distortion. The text for the bar becomes the content of the middle cell. The following document shows how the bar is constructed:

```
<!DOCTYPE HTML PUBLIC "-//W3C//DTD HTML 4.01//EN"
  "http://www.w3.org/TR/html4/strict.dtd">
<html>
<body>
<table width="50%"  border="0" align="center"
         cellpadding="0" cellspacing="0">
  <tr>
```

```
    <td width="2%"><img src="BarLeft.jpg" width="43"
           height="50"></td>
    <td width="96%" style="background-image:
           url('BarSliver.jpg');
           background-repeat: repeat-x;">
      <strong>Title Text for Bar</strong></td>
    <td width="2%"><img src="BarRight.jpg" width="53"
           height="50"></td>
  </tr>
</table>
</body>
</html>
```

Figure 24-3 shows how the method achieves the desired effect.

FIGURE 24-3

The top image shows how the bottom image is achieved.

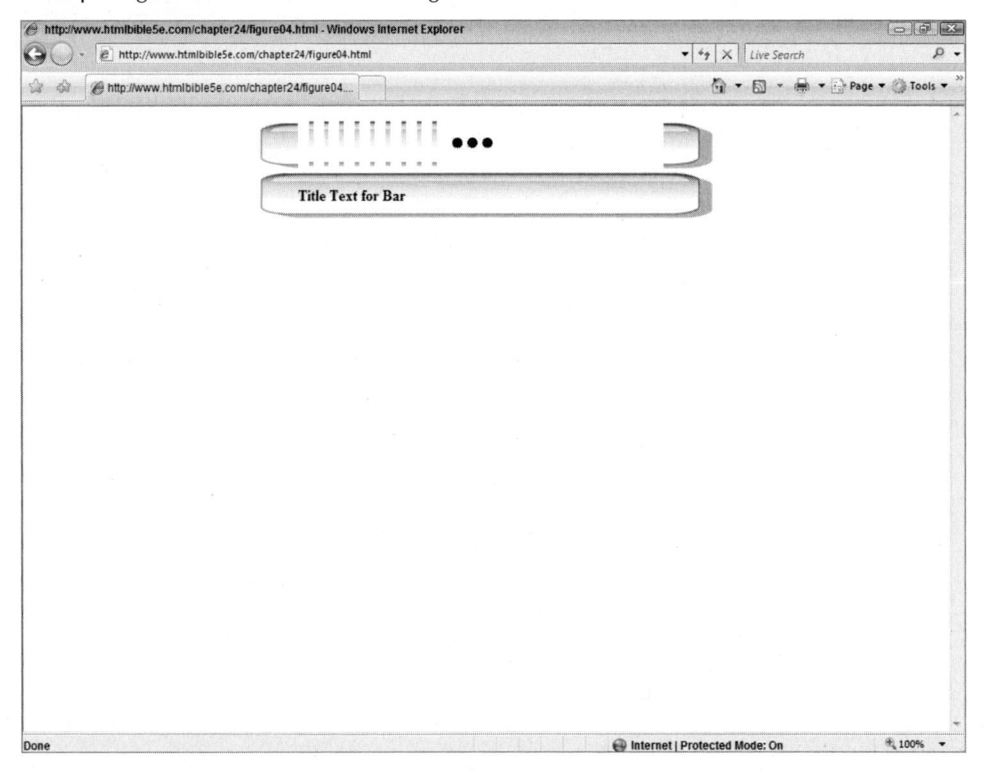

The bar can easily be extended by increasing the width of the middle cell — the slice will be tiled to fill the extra space. If the table is set to dynamically expand, then the bar will also expand dynamically with its table.

Simulating Newspaper Columns

Although CSS advocates are known to proclaim that table formatting is dead, you can still achieve many impressive layouts with tables. One in particular, newspaper columns, is often used.

Newspaper columns are narrow, parallel, vertical columns of text. This layout incorporates an optional heading that straddles the top of the columns just like a newspaper headline.

The key is to use the colspan attribute with the first table cell, causing it to span multiple columns. The text columns follow on the next row, occupying one table column each. For example, the following code sets up a table for two newspaper columns with a heading above them, as shown in Figure 24-4:

```
<!DOCTYPE HTML PUBLIC "-//W3C//DTD HTML 4.01//EN"
  "http://www.w3.org/TR/html4/strict.dtd">
<html>
<head>
  <title>Newspaper Columns</title>
  <style type="text/css">
    #newspaper { height: 100px;
                 width: 700px; }
    #headline { font-size: xx-large;
                text-align: center; }
    #column { height: 400px; }
  </style>
</head>
<body>
<table id="newspaper" border="1" cellpadding="10px">
  <tr>
    <td id="headline" colspan="2">Headline</td>
  </tr>
  <tr>
    <td id="column" valign="top" width="50%"><p>Lorem ipsum
dolor sit amet, consectetur adipisicing elit, sed do eiusmod
tempor incididunt ut labore et dolore magna aliqua. Ut enim ad
minim veniam, quis nostrud exercitation ullamco laboris nisi ut
aliquip ex ea commodo consequat. Duis aute irure dolor in
reprehenderit in voluptate velit esse cillum dolore eu fugiat
nulla pariatur. Excepteur sint occaecat cupidatat non proident,
sunt in culpa qui officia deserunt mollit anim id est
laborum.</p><p>Lorem ipsum dolor sit amet, consectetur
adipisicing elit, sed do eiusmod tempor incididunt ut labore et
dolore magna aliqua. Ut enim ad minim veniam, quis nostrud
exercitation ullamco laboris nisi ut aliquip ex ea commodo
consequat. Duis aute irure dolor in reprehenderit in voluptate
velit esse cillum dolore eu fugiat nulla pariatur. Excepteur
sint occaecat cupidatat non proident, sunt in culpa qui officia
deserunt mollit anim id est laborum.</p</td>
    <td id="column" valign="top" width="50%"><p>Lorem ipsum
```

```
dolor sit amet, consectetur adipisicing elit, sed do eiusmod
tempor incididunt ut labore et dolore magna aliqua. Ut enim ad
minim veniam, quis nostrud exercitation ullamco laboris nisi ut
aliquip ex ea commodo consequat. Duis aute irure dolor in
reprehenderit in voluptate velit esse cillum dolore eu fugiat
nulla pariatur. Excepteur sint occaecat cupidatat non proident,
sunt in culpa qui officia deserunt mollit anim id est
laborum.</p><p>Lorem ipsum dolor sit amet, consectetur
adipisicing elit, sed do eiusmod tempor incididunt ut labore et
dolore magna aliqua. Ut enim ad minim veniam, quis nostrud
exercitation ullamco laboris nisi ut aliquip ex ea commodo
consequat. Duis aute irure dolor in reprehenderit in voluptate
velit esse cillum dolore eu fugiat nulla pariatur. Excepteur
sint occaecat cupidatat non proident, sunt in culpa qui officia
deserunt mollit anim id est laborum.</p></td>
  </tr>
</table>
</body>
</html>
```

FIGURE 24-4

A two-column newspaper layout

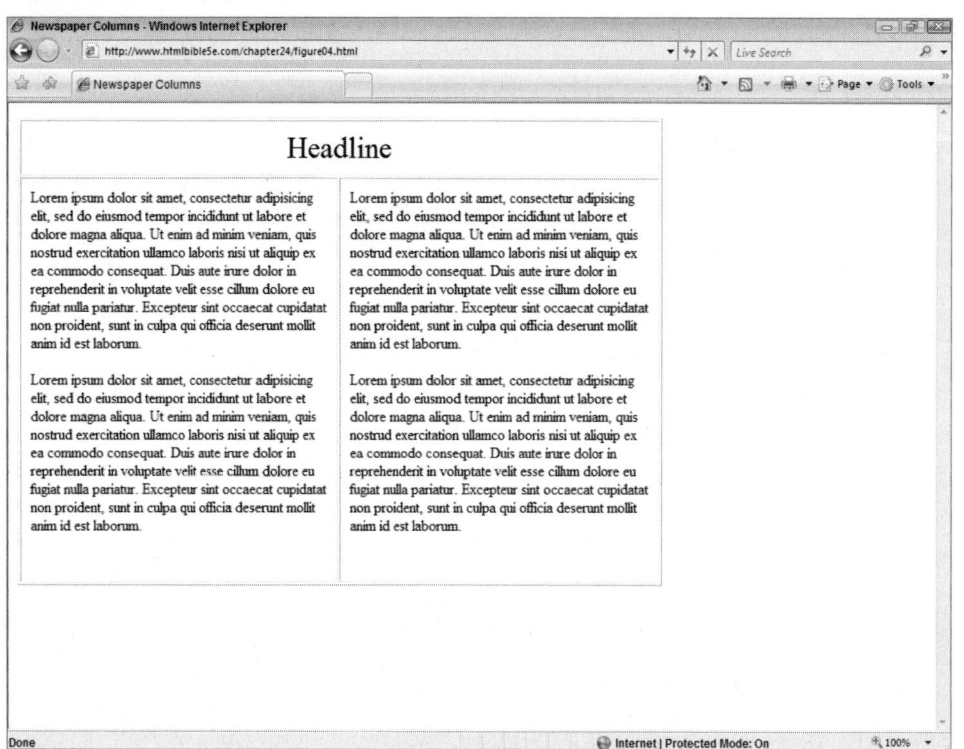

For a production layout you will probably want to set the table's `border` attribute to 0.

The keys to a good design are to either fix the table width or set it to 100 percent, and ensure that the columns occupy only their share of the table width (text oddities can cause column widths to shift) by explicitly setting their width, as well. Setting the column height isn't always necessary, but sometimes you will want to fix column lengths with a `height` property or set a minimum length with a `min-height` property.

Tip

You can use the `<td>` tag's `colspan` and `rowspan` attributes to make some very creative table designs. ■

Including Image Size for Fast Display

The importance of always specifying an image's dimensions was brought up in Chapter 12, but it bears repeating here. When a browser loads an image to display, it needs one of two things in order to ascertain the size of the image:

- The completion of the image load
- The availability of `width` and `height` properties in the `<img>` tag

Either option will result in a page displaying the image with its correct size. However, the first option causes a delay before the image displays correctly, which can lead to a few unwelcome side effects for the end user. One possible side effect is that the user agent will stop loading all content until the image is loaded, sized, and can be displayed properly. Another possible side effect is that the user agent will reserve a portion of the document for the image, and reformat the document to fit the final size after the image's size is known.

If the size is known, the user agent will reserve the proper amount of space for the image and continue to load the rest of the document. When the image is fully loaded it is dropped into the reserved area with no ill effects for the end user.

Protecting E-mail Addresses

Placing an e-mail address on a Web page is a dangerous prospect nowadays. If the document on which the address appears generates even a medium amount of traffic, it is a given that a robot or other harvester will pick up the e-mail address and add it to dozens of spam lists.

These bots and harvesters collect the e-mail address by simply accessing the document and examining the document's source. For example, to insert a link to e-mail Jill at The Oasis of Tranquility, the following code can be inserted into a document:

```
<a href="mailto:jill@oasisoftranquility.com">Email Jill</a>
```

Although this is displayed as simply "Email Jill" on a user agent's screen, the harvester is able to look at the code to find `mailto:jill@oasisoftranquility.com`. The `mailto` protocol confirms that an e-mail address is within the anchor tag.

The key to protecting your e-mail address is to avoid adding it to documents in an unencoded format. Instead, obfuscate it using one of several methods, including the following:

- Break it into pieces that are reassembled by a script, which can't be easily discerned by the harvesters.
- Encode it using a method that can preserve its functionality.

Tip

One low-security method for obscuring an e-mail address is to replace the at sign (@) with its entity equivalent, @. This method relies on the assumption that most harvesters search documents for the literal "@" in their quest for e-mail addresses. By removing the literal at sign, you impede the harvester's ability to recognize e-mail addresses. Using the equivalent entity ensures that compliant browsers will still render the at sign properly. Unfortunately, most harvesters are now aware of this trick and recognize the entity as well as the literal at sign. ■

The first method is fairly straightforward and uses a script similar to the following:

```
<script type="text/JavaScript">
  document.write('<a href="');
  t1 = "mai";
  t2 = "lto";
  t3 = ":";
  t4 = "jill";
  t5 = "&#64;";
  t6 = "oasi";
  t7 = "softra";
  t8 = "nquil";
  t9 = "ity";
  t10 = ".";
  t11 = "com";
  text = t1+t2+t3+t4+t5+t6+t7+t8+t9+t10+t11;
  document.write(text);
  document.write('">Mail Jill</a>');
</script>
```

The preceding script breaks the e-mail portion into small chunks, assigns each chunk to a variable, concatenates the chunks into one variable, and then outputs the entire anchor tag. The key to this method is that the pieces of the e-mail address never appear together in the file. For additional security, you could scramble the order of the chunks — for example, placing number 6 before number 3, and so on.

The other method, encoding the address, is a little more complicated. It requires that you first run a program to encode the address and then use those results in your document. The encoding can be done in a variety of ways, one of which is shown in the following listing, an HTML document with form entry and JavaScript for the encoding:

```
<html>
<head>
  <title>Email Encoder</title>
  <script type="text/JavaScript">
    function encode (email) {
      var encoded = "";
      for (i = 0; i < email.length; i++) {
        encoded += "&#" + email.charCodeAt(i) + ";";
      };
      return (encoded);
    };
  </script>
</head>
<body>
<form action="" name="encoder"
  onsubmit="encoded.value = encode(email.value);
  return false;">
<table border="0" cellpadding="3px">
  <tr>
    <td>Enter your<br/>email address:</td>
    <td><input type="text" name="email" size="30" /></td>
    <td><input type="submit" value="Encode" /></td>
  </tr>
  <tr>
    <td>Encoded email:</td>
    <td colspan="2"><input type="text" name="encoded"
        size="60" /></td>
  </tr>
</table>
</form>
</body>
</html>
```

This document displays a form in which you can enter your e-mail address. When you click the `Encode` button, the e-mail address you entered is converted, character by character, into entity equivalents and placed in the `Encoded email` field where you can copy it to the clipboard for use in your documents. Note that you can encode the e-mail address only or, optionally, the `mailto:` protocol string or even the entire anchor tag. Just be sure to replace the same amount of text in your document as you encoded.

Note

Although the encoded method might seem to be the most secure method of protecting e-mail, it has a fatal flaw. Any bot that can decode entities — which, at their root, are ASCII codes — can read the encoded address very easily. ■

Automating Forms

A traditional use of JavaScript is the automation of forms. Using JavaScript, you can easily manipulate the status of form controls, validate form content, and more.

Manipulating form objects

One popular use of JavaScript and forms is to provide a special check box to check or uncheck the rest of the check boxes in the group. A bare-bones document with such a purpose resembles the following code, whose output is shown in Figure 24-5:

```
<?xml version="1.0" encoding="utf-8"?>
<!DOCTYPE html PUBLIC "-//W3C//DTD XHTML 1.1//EN"
   "http://www.w3.org/TR/xhtml11/DTD/xhtml11.dtd">
<html>
<head>
<script type="text/JavaScript">

function checkall() {

  // Get the state of the first checkbox (0)
  var chk = document.form1.checks[0].checked;

  // Set the rest of the checkbox group to that value
  for (i = 1; i < document.form1.checks.length; i++) {
    document.form1.checks[i].checked = chk;
  }

}

</script>
</head>
<body>

<form name="form1">
<p><input id="allboxes" type="checkbox" name="checks"
      onClick="checkall();">(Un)Check All</p>
<p><input type="checkbox" name="checks">First check box</p>
<p><input type="checkbox" name="checks">Second check box</p>
<p><input type="checkbox" name="checks">Third check box</p>
<p><input type="checkbox" name="checks">Fourth check box</p>
<p><input type="checkbox" name="checks">Fifth check box</p>
<p><input type="checkbox" name="checks">Sixth check box</p>
</form>

</body>
</html>
```

FIGURE 24-5

JavaScript can help automate forms, making them easier to access, like the (Un)Check All check box shown here.

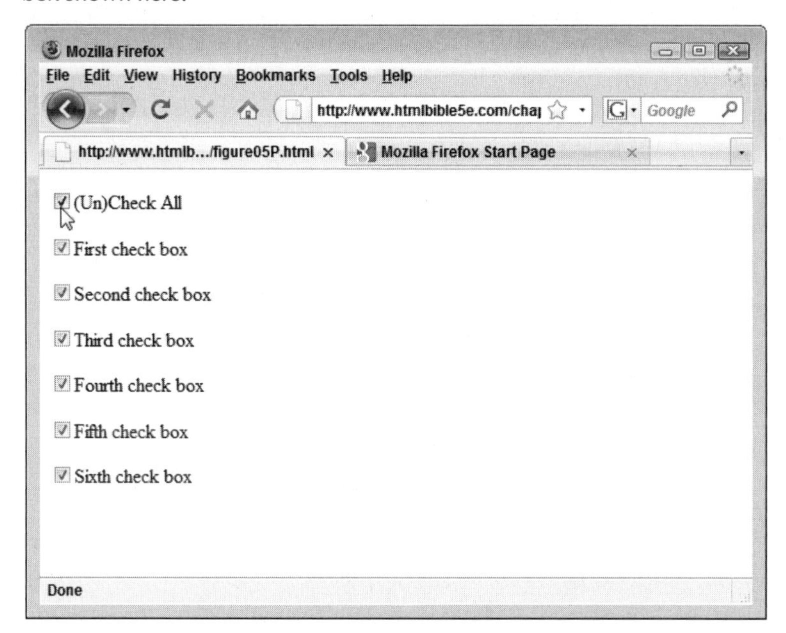

The automation works thanks to a few, basic HTML and JavaScript constructs:

1. The group of check boxes, including the special check box, have the same `name` attribute, creating a collection of check boxes that can be accessed by a single JavaScript object.
2. The first check box, appropriately labeled "(Un)Check All," includes an `onClick` event handler that calls the JavaScript function `checkall()`when it is clicked (and changes states).
3. The `checkall()`JavaScript function reads the state of the special check box and iterates through the remaining check boxes setting their state to match the special check box's state. This causes the rest of the check boxes to be checked when the special check box is checked, and unchecked when the special check box is unchecked.

In this case the JavaScript function is hard-coded to work on the `checks` collection of check boxes, accessed via the JavaScript object `document.form1.checks`.

Such routines can be quite complex, identifying and modifying elements in the whole document, and even across forms. For example, the following JavaScript function will cause every check box with similar value attributes to be checked when one of its kin, anywhere in the document, is checked:

```
// Called from a checkbox's "onClick" event,
//   check all boxes with the same value attribute
function checkboxes(field) {

  // Get settings of the checkbox that called us
      checked = field.checked;
      value = field.value;

  // Retrieve all <input> elements into the MyElements array
      myBody = document.getElementsByTagName("body")[0];
      myElements = myBody.getElementsByTagName("input");

      // Iterate through the retrieved <input> elements,
      //   looking for checkboxes
      for( var x = 0; x < myElements.length; x++ ) {
             if (myElements[x].getAttribute('type') == "checkbox") {

     // If this checkbox (myElements[x]) has the same value
     //   as the checkbox that called us, set this box to
     //   the caller's value
     if (myElements[x].value == value) {
       myElements[x].checked = checked;
     }

             } // if myElements

      } // for x

} // End function
```

All that's left is to ensure that related check boxes have the same value and to place the following code in each check box tag so that when it is clicked it executes the function:

```
onClick = "checkboxes(this);"
```

Note

The preceding example relies upon the `value` attribute in check boxes. However, by modifying the code you can easily match other attributes to trigger the mass checking. ■

Validating form input

Another popular use of JavaScript is to validate form contents before submission to the server-side handler. Using Dynamic HTML, JavaScript can easily pick up form field values, evaluate them, and make decisions based on the values.

For example, the following code checks whether the field x, in the form named form1, is empty:

```
if (document.form1.x.value == "")
```

Similar JavaScript code can determine the length of content in a field, compare two dates in two fields, test for a valid e-mail address, and more. How does this code execute? Each decision-based piece of code could be tied to an `onChange` event in each field on the form, but that forces you to build several functions, one for each field. It's simpler to tie the decision-based code together in one function and call it when the form is submitted. At that point the code can check the whole form to determine whether it should be submitted or rejected.

To tie a function to a form's submission action, you use the `onSubmit` event handler in the `<form>` tag, similar to the following:

```
<form action="handler.cgi" method="POST" onSubmit="return validation()">
```

The `onSubmit` handler causes the JavaScript function `validation()` to execute when the form's `submit` button is pressed (or any other action results in the form being submitted). The return value of the function determines whether the form is actually submitted — a return value of `true` allows the form to be submitted, whereas a return value of `false` prevents the form from being submitted.

The JavaScript function is constructed like the following pseudocode:

```
function validate() {

  test condition1
  if test fails:
    display message
    return false

  test condition1
  if test fails:
    display message
    return false

  test condition1
  if test fails:
    display message
    return false

  test condition1
  if test fails:
    display message
    return false

  ...

  return true
```

Note that in each case that the function returns `false`, the function's execution stops and the form is not submitted. However, the function also displays a message to users indicating the error encountered, giving them the chance to correct the error. This method of validating forms is serial — that is, each field is validated in order, and a single failure stops the validation. In such a case the user must deal with each error before validation can progress to the next test.

The following code shows a validation function that checks a handful of fields in a form. The comments in the code are self-explanatory as to what is checked and how:

```
function validate() {

  // Check to see if the "y" field's value exceeds 80
  if (parseFloat(document.form1.y.value) >= 80) {
    alert("The value of Y cannot exceed 80.
           Please enter an appropriate value.");
    document.form1.field.focus();
    return false;
  }

  // Check to see if the "x" field is blank
  if (document.form1.x.value == "") {
    alert("X is a required field.");
    document.form1.field.focus();
    return false;
  }

  // Check to see if the "ending_date field" is greater
  //   than the "starting_date field" (end after beginning)
  // Only check if we have both values
  if(document.form1.ending_date.value!="" &&
     document.form1.starting_date.value!="" )
  {
    // Split the dates by their dashes
    var from_date = document.form1.starting_date.value.split("-");
    var to_date = document.form1.ending_date.value.split("-");

    // Re-assemble dates in sortable method
    str_from_date = from_date[2]+from_date[0]+from_date[1];
    str_to_date = to_date[2]+to_date[0]+to_date[1];

    // Check date order
    if(str_from_date > str_to_date){
      alert("Ending Date should be greater then starting Date.");
      document.form1.ending_date.focus();
      return false;
    }
  }


  // Test for a valid email address in email field
  // Use a regular expression to match against the field's contents
  var regx = new
      RegExp(/^\w+([\.-]?\w+)*@\w+([\.-]?\w+)*(\.\w{2,3})+$/);
```

```
    if (!regx.test(document.form1.email.value)) {
      alert("The email address is invalid.
             Please enter a valid address.");
      return false;
    }

    return true;

} // End validate function
```

Note
The preceding example uses simple field and form names. In an actual environment you would use more descriptive names that match your usage. In addition, the preceding examples use some fairly complex methods such as regular expression matching. If you intend to do a lot of form work with JavaScript, you are encouraged to pick up a comprehensive JavaScript book, like Wiley's JavaScript Bible, 7th Edition. ■

Modifying the User Agent Environment

Not only can JavaScript modify CSS settings and HTML, it can also modify the user agent. For example, you can move and resize the user agent's window, manipulate its scroll bars, and more. To demonstrate this, we will create JavaScript to scroll the current document vertically, in both directions (up and down).

The concept

The concept for this exercise is simple — provide a control that when moused over will scroll the current document. When the end of the document is reached, the scrolling will scroll upward to the top of the document where it will again scroll downward. When the mouse is moved off of the control, the scrolling will stop.

Note
Although this example has limited usage — thanks to the scroll wheel on most mice — it is a good example of using a controlling element to orchestrate several events. ■

For this example we will use a `<div>` with a fixed position as the control.

The implementation

The code for this exercise appears in the next two listings. Listing 24-1 contains the JavaScript for the document (in an external file); Listing 24-2 contains the HTML document itself, which is shown in Figure 24-6.

LISTING 24-1

JavaScript to control the scroll bar

```
//////////////////////////////////////////////////
// Retrieve and return the current offsets
//   for both scrollbars (x = horizontal,
//   y = vertical)
//////////////////////////////////////////////////
function getScrollXY() {
  // Set offsets to zero
  var scrOfX = 0, scrOfY = 0;

  // Determine browser mode and set
  //  offsets to current scroll position
  if (typeof(window.pageYOffset) == 'number') {
    //Netscape compliant
    scrOfY = window.pageYOffset;
    scrOfX = window.pageXOffset;

  } else if(document.body &&
          (document.body.scrollLeft ||
           document.body.scrollTop)) {
    //DOM compliant
    scrOfY = document.body.scrollTop;
    scrOfX = document.body.scrollLeft;

  } else if(document.documentElement &&
          (document.documentElement.scrollLeft ||
           document.documentElement.scrollTop)) {
    //IE6 standards compliant mode
    scrOfY = document.documentElement.scrollTop;
    scrOfX = document.documentElement.scrollLeft;
  }

  // Return array with offsets
  return [ scrOfX, scrOfY ];
} // Function getScrollXY


//////////////////////////////////////////////////
// Change the direction (dir) of the scroll and
//   the background image of the scroller (to match
//   direction)
//////////////////////////////////////////////////
function chdirscroll () {
  dir = dir * -1;
  obj = document.getElementById("scroller");
  if (dir == 1) {
    obj.style.backgroundImage = "url(images/dn_arrow.gif)";
  } else {
```

```
      obj.style.backgroundImage = "url(images/up_arrow.gif)";
    }
  }


  /////////////////////////////////////////////////
  // Scroll the document in the y direction (vertical) by the
  //   currently set amount (increment * direction)
  /////////////////////////////////////////////////
  function doscroll() {

    // Initialize values
    var y = -1;
    var yy = 0;

    // Get current scroll position
    xy = getScrollXY();
    y = xy[1];

    // Scroll the document
    scrollBy(0,inc*dir);

    // Check new position, if it is the same as the old
    //   position, the scrollbar did not move -- it is
    //   at the top or bottom of the document
    xy = getScrollXY();
    yy = xy[1];
    // If scrollbar is at the top or bottom, reverse the
    //   direction and bounce, if bounce option set. If,
    //   bounce is not set, stop the scrollbar's movement
    if (y == yy) {
      if (bounce == 1) {
        chdirscroll();
      } else {
        clearInterval(scrollIt);
      }
    }
  } // End function doscroll()


  /////////////////////////////////////////////////
  // Begin scrolling according to previously set speedmod
  /////////////////////////////////////////////////
  function setscroll () {
    inc = speedmod * 20;  // Set the increment to move, in
                          //   multiples of 20 (by speedmod)
    // Start scrollbar movement (by inc) every 25 milliseconds
    scrollIt = setInterval("doscroll(inc);",25);
  }
  /////////////////////////////////////////////////
```

continued

LISTING 24-1 *(continued)*

```
// Stop the scrolling
//////////////////////////////////////////////////
function stopscroll () {
  clearInterval(scrollIt);
}

//////////////////////////////////////////////////
// Initialize the scroll values and settings
//////////////////////////////////////////////////
function initscroll () {
  // Init the scroll variables
  dir = 1;       // The direction to move (positive = down)
  bounce = 1;    // Whether to bounce (bounce = 1) or not (bounce = 0)
  speedmod = 1; // The speed modifier (higher = faster)
  // Assign the down arrow to the scroller
  obj = document.getElementById("scroller");
  obj.style.backgroundImage = "url(images/dn_arrow.gif)";
}
```

LISTING 24-2

The document with a scrollbar control

```
<!DOCTYPE html PUBLIC "-//W3C//DTD HTML 4.01//EN"
   "http://www.w3.org/TR/html4/strict.dtd">

<html>
<head>

  <script type="text/JavaScript" src="scroll.js"></script>

  <style type="text/css">

    #scroller {
      width: 20px;
      height: 20px;
      background-color: none;
      background-repeat: no-repeat;
      background-position: center center;
      border: 1px solid black;
      position: fixed;
      top: 0px;
      left: 0px;
      }

    #content {
      margin-left: 30px;
    }
```

```
  </style>

</head>

<body onLoad="initscroll();">

<div id="scroller" onMouseOver="setscroll();" onMouseOut="stopscroll();"
     onClick="chdirscroll();"> </div>

<div id="content">
      <p>Lorem ipsum dolor sit amet, consectetur adipisicing elit, sed
do eiusmod tempor incididunt ut labore et dolore magna aliqua. Ut enim
ad minim veniam, quis nostrud exercitation ullamco laboris nisi ut
aliquip ex ea commodo consequat. Duis aute irure dolor in reprehenderit
in voluptate velit esse cillum dolore eu fugiat nulla pariatur.
Excepteur sint occaecat cupidatat non proident, sunt in culpa qui officia
deserunt mollit anim id est laborum.</p>

      ...

      <p>Lorem ipsum dolor sit amet, consectetur adipisicing elit, sed
do eiusmod tempor incididunt ut labore et dolore magna aliqua. Ut enim
ad minim veniam, quis nostrud exercitation ullamco laboris nisi ut
aliquip ex ea commodo consequat. Duis aute irure dolor in reprehenderit
in voluptate velit esse cillum dolore eu fugiat nulla pariatur. Excepteur sint
occaecat cupidatat non proident, sunt in culpa qui officia deserunt mollit
anim id est laborum.</p>

</div>  <!-- /Content -->

</body>
</html>
```

The desired implementation is straightforward:

- An `onLoad` event trigger is attached to the `<body>` tag so that the scrolling options are set (globally) in preparation for scrolling when the document is first loaded.
- A fixed `<div>`, positioned at the upper-left corner of the user agent window, is used to control the scrolling.
- Two event triggers, `onMouseOver` and `onMouseOut`, are attached to the controlling `<div>` and are used to start and stop the scrolling. When the mouse is placed over the `<div>`, the scrolling starts. When the mouse is moved off of the `<div>`, the scrolling stops.
- A third event trigger, `onClick`, is used to change the direction of the scroll. When the controlling `<div>` is clicked, the scrolling changes direction.
- By default, the scrolling "bounces" — that is, when it reaches the bottom of the document it begins traveling upward to the top of the document where it bounces back down.

FIGURE 24-6

The scroll control division appears and stays in the upper-left corner of the window.

The document layout is accomplished with two divisions. The "scroller" `<div>` is a small square with an arrow pointing in the direction the document will scroll. It is used for turning on and off the scroll. The `<div>` position is set to fixed so it will stay where it was placed when the document scrolls.

A second `<div>` is used to contain the actual content of the document. Note how the "content" `<div>` has a larger left margin specified so as to not conflict with the scroll `<div>`. For this example, the document simply contains several paragraphs of the Lorem Ipsum placeholder text to provide a simple document long enough to scroll.

The JavaScript functions

The scrolling control is accomplished by six JavaScript functions:

- `initscroll()`: Called by the `<body>` tag's `onLoad` event, this function sets the initial values, preparing for the scrolling action — the initial direction (`dir`) of the scroll (1 = down, -1 = up), whether the scroll should bounce (1 = yes, 0 = no), and the speed modification (speedmod, faster values = faster movement). The settings in this function should be used to tailor your scrolling actions.

- `getScrollXY()`: This function is called to retrieve the current position of the scroll bars. It performs basic browser detection to determine how to retrieve the horizontal (x) and vertical (y) coordinates of the scroll bars. The coordinates are returned in an array, with x being index 0, and y being index 1.
- `setscroll()`: This function begins the scrolling action by setting the requisite variables and setting an Interval timer to move the scroll bar by the specified increment (`speedmod` * 20) every 25 milliseconds.
- `doscroll()`: This function moves the scroll bar every so often as defined by the Interval timer. Every 25 milliseconds the function is called by the timer and the scroll bar moves via the `scrollBy()`JavaScript function. The function then uses the `getScrollXY()`function to check whether the before position (y) is the same as the after position (yy). If the two values are the same, then the scroll bar didn't move and must be at the beginning or the end of the document. If that's the case, then the function `chdirscroll()`is called to reverse the scroll bar's direction (providing `bounce` is set to 1).
- `chdirscroll()`: This function reverses the direction of the scroll bar's movement by changing the value of `dir` to 1 (move down) or −1 (move up). The actual movement is handled by the `doscroll()`function.
- `stopscroll()`: This function is used to remove the Interval timer, effectively stopping the scroll. It is tied to the control `<div>`'s `onMouseOut` event and can also be called by other events or functions that require the scroll bar's movement to stop.

Tip

To perform other operations on the user agent's environment, use Google to search for applicable JavaScript functions. For example, to see how to move the user agent window, search for JavaScript move window. ■

Summary

This chapter presented a handful of HTML tips and tricks you can employ in your documents, including those related to presenting content, as well as a few on optimizing or speeding up your document's delivery. This is the last chapter in the HTML section (Parts I and II). The next part starts the coverage of CSS.

Part III

Controlling Presentation with CSS

IN THIS PART

CHAPTER

25

CSS Basics

IN THIS CHAPTER

The Web was founded on HTML and plain-text documents. Over the last few years the Web has become a household and industrial mainstay, maturing into a viable publishing platform thanks in no small part to Cascading Style Sheets (CSS).

CSS enables Web authors and programmers to finely tune elements for publishing both online and across several different types of media, including print format. This chapter serves as the introduction to CSS. Subsequent chapters in this section will show you how to use styles with specific elements.

The Purpose of Styles

Styles are an electronic publishing invention for dynamically coding text and other document elements with formatting. For example, a style called "Heading" would be attached to every heading in the document. The style definition would contain information about how headings should be formatted. In this book, for example, headings (such as "The Purpose of Styles," above) use a larger, bold font.

Note

Anyone who has spent an appreciable amount of time in and around a word-processing program has no doubt encountered styles. The concept of styles used by word processors does not differ appreciably from that of CSS and the Web — if you understand the former, you should have a good grasp on usage of the latter. ■

The advantage of styles is that you can change a definition once and that change affects every element using that style. Coding each element individually, by contrast, would require that each element be recoded individually whenever you wanted them all to change. Thus, styles provide an easy means to update document formatting and maintain consistency across multiple documents.

Coding individual elements is best done while the document is being created. This means that the document formatting is usually done by the author — not always the best choice. Instead, the elements can be tagged with appropriate styles (such as `heading`) while the document is created, and the final formatting can be left up to another individual who defines the styles.

Styles can be grouped into purpose-driven style sheets. *Style sheets* are like blueprints, holding groups of styles relating to a common purpose. Style sheets enable multiple styles to be attached to a document all at once and for all the style formatting in a document to be changed at once. Therefore, documents can be quickly formatted for different purposes — one style sheet can be used for documents meant for online consumption, another style sheet can be used (on the same documents) for brochures, and so on.

Styles and HTML

For a tangible example that uses HTML, consider the following code:

```
<p><b><u>Rabbit Run Racing</u></b></p>
<p>Rabbit Run Racing is similar to many of the "cart" racing games
on the market. You pick a character from one of six available and
race around a small track, picking up power ups and trying to beat
your opponent(s) to the finish line. Rabbit Run Racing supports 1-4
players.</p>
<p><b><u>Driving Range III</u></b></p>
<p>Driving Range III is one of the first games to take advantage of
the momentum joystick, using its pendulum-weighted motion to
simulate a golf driving iron. Unfortunately, the game is too simple
to hold much replay value--you drive balls on three different
ranges, two with a handful of trick-shot areas. Driving Range III is
a single-player only game, though you can compare high-scores with
your buddies.</p>
<p><b><u>Run, Gun, Gore</u></b></p>
<p>Capitalizing on the revitalized run and gun genre, RGG bring
plenty of everything in its title to the table. The graphics are
surprisingly crisp and the levels are designed well for
deathmatch-style play. Although there are surprisingly few levels in
the current release (10), soon to be released add on packs promise
more theme-driven levels. RGG is a single-player game, but supports
up to 100 players when linked across the NGame network.</p>
```

Note

For the purpose of this example, ignore the fact that most of the text formatting tags (underline, center, and so on) have been deprecated. ■

All three heading elements are coded bold and underlined. Now suppose that you wanted the heading elements to be larger and italicized. Each heading would have to be individually recoded, similar to the following:

```
<p><font size="+2"><i>Rabbit Run Racing</i></font></p>
```

Although using a decent text editor with global search and replace makes this change pretty easy, consider managing an entire site, with several — if not tens or hundreds of — documents, each with numerous headings. Each document makes the change exponentially harder.

Now, let's look at how styles would change the example. With styles, the example could be coded similarly to the following:

```
<p class="heading">Rabbit Run Racing</p>
<p>Rabbit Run Racing is similar to many of the "cart" racing games
on the market. You pick a character from one of six available and
race around a small track, picking up power ups and trying to beat
your opponent(s) to the finish line. Rabbit Run Racing supports 1-4
players.</p>
<p class="heading">Driving Range III</p>
<p>Driving Range III is one of the first games to take advantage of
the momentum joystick, using its pendulum-weighted motion to
simulate a golf driving iron. Unfortunately, the game is too simple
to hold much replay value--you drive balls on three different
ranges, two with a handful of trick-shot areas. Driving Range III is
a single-player only game, though you can compare high-scores with
your buddies.</p>
<p class="heading">Run, Gun, Gore</u></b></p>
<p>Capitalizing on the revitalized run and gun genre, RGG bring
plenty of everything in its title to the table. The graphics are
surprisingly crisp and the levels are designed well for
deathmatch-style play. Although there are surprisingly few levels in
the current release (10), soon to be released add on packs promise
more theme-driven levels. RGG is a single-player game, but supports
up to 100 players when linked across the NGame network.</p>
>
```

Cross-Ref

There are several methods for applying styles to document elements. Chapter 26 covers ways to define and use styles. ■

The style is defined in the head section of the document, similar to the following:

```
<head>
  <style type="text/css">
    p.heading { font-weight: bold; text-decoration: underline; }
  </style>
</head>
```

This definition defines a heading class that formats text appearing in a paragraph with a heading as bold and underlined.

Cross-Ref

Style definitions and selectors are covered in Chapter 26. Style property values and units are covered in Chapter 27. Individual CSS properties are covered in appropriate chapters later in this part of the book. ■

To change all the headings in the document to a larger, italic font, the *one* definition can be recoded:

```
<head>
  <style type="text/css">
    p.heading { font-size: larger; font-style: italic; }
  </style>
</head>
```

CSS Levels 1, 2, and 3

There are three levels of CSS — two levels are actual specifications, whereas the third level is in recommendation status. The main differences between the three levels are as follows:

- CSS1 defines basic style functionality, with limited font and limited positioning support.
- CSS2 adds aural properties, paged media, and better font and positioning support. Many other properties have also been refined.
- CSS3 will add presentation-style properties, enabling you to effectively build presentations from Web documents (similar to Microsoft PowerPoint presentations).

You don't have to specify the level of CSS you are using, but you should be aware of what user agents will be accessing your site. Most modern browsers support CSS, but the level of support varies dramatically between user agents. It's always best to test your implementation on target user agents before widely deploying your documents.

Note

When using styles, keep in mind that not all style properties are well supported by all user agents. This book attempts to point out major inconsistencies and differences in the most popular user agents, but the playing field is always changing. ■

Defining Styles

Styles can be defined in several different ways and attached to a document. The most popular method for defining styles is to add a style block to the head of a document:

```
<head>
  <style type="text/css">
    ...Style definitions...
  </style>
</head>
```

If you use this method, all style definitions are placed within a style element, delimited by `<style>` tags. This tag has the following syntax:

```
<style type="MIME_type" media="destination_media">
```

In most cases, the MIME type is "text/css," as used throughout this chapter. The `media` attribute is typically not used unless the destination media is nontextual. The media attribute supports the following values:

- `all`
- `aural`
- `braille`
- `embossed`
- `handheld`
- `print`
- `projection`
- `screen`
- `tty`
- `tv`

Note

Multiple style definitions, each defining a style for a different medium and encased in its own `<style>` tags, can appear in the same document. This powerful feature enables you to easily define document styles for a variety of uses and deployment. ■

Alternately, the style sheet can be contained in a separate document and linked to documents using the link (`<link>`) tag:

```
<head>
  <link rel="stylesheet" type="text/css" href="mystyles.css" />
</head>
```

The style sheet document, `mystyles.css`, contains the necessary styles:

```
...
p.heading { font-size: larger; font-style: italic; }
...
```

This way, when the style definitions in the external style sheet change, *all* documents that link to the external sheet reflect the change. This provides an easy way to modify the format of many documents — whether to affect new formatting for visual reasons, or for another specific purpose.

Attaching external style sheets via the link tag should be your preferred method of applying styles to a document, as it provides the most scalable use of styles — you can change only one external style sheet to affect many documents.

Tip

You can add comments to your style section or style sheet by delimiting the comment with /* and */. For example, the following is a style comment:

```
/*  Define a heading style with a border */
```

■

Cascading Styles

So where does the "cascading" in Cascading Style Sheets come from? It comes from the fact that styles can stack, or override, each other. For example, suppose that an internal corporate website's appearance varies according to the department that owns the various documents. All the documents need to follow the corporate look and feel, but the Human Resources department might use people-shaped bullets or apply other small changes unique to that department. The HR department doesn't need a separate, complete style sheet for its documents — it needs only a sheet containing the differences from the corporate sheet. For example, consider the following two style sheet fragments:

```
/*  corporate.css */
body {
  font-family:verdana, palatino,  georgia,  arial, sans-serif;
  font-size:10pt;
}
p {
  font-family:verdana, palatino,  georgia,  arial, sans-serif;
  font-size:10pt;
}
p.quote {
  font-family:verdana, palatino,  georgia,  arial, sans-serif;
  font-size:10pt;
  border: solid thin black;
  background: #5A637B;
  padding: .75em;
}
h1, h2, h3 {
  margin: 0px;
  padding: 0px;
}
ul {
  list-style-image: url("images/corporate-bullet.png")
}
...
/* humanresources.css */
ul {
  list-style-image: url("images/people-bullet.png")
}
```

The humanresources.css sheet contains only the style definitions that differ from the corporate.css sheet; in this case, only a definition for ul elements (using the different bullet). The two sheets are linked to the HR documents using the following <link> tags:

```
<head>
  <link rel="stylesheet" type="text/css" href="corporate.css" />
  <link rel="stylesheet" type="text/css" href="humanresources.css" />
</head>
```

Note

When a user agent encounters multiple styles that could be applied to the same element, it uses CSS rules of precedence, covered at the end of this section. ■

Likewise, other departments would have their own style sheets and their documents would link to the corporate and individual department sheets. As another example, members of the Engineering department might use their own style sheet and declare it in the head of their documents:

```
<head>
  <link rel="stylesheet" type="text/css" href="corporate.css" />
  <link rel="stylesheet" type="text/css" href="engineering.css" />
</head>
```

Furthermore, individual HTML elements can contain styles themselves:

```
<ul style="list-style-image: url("images/small-bullet.png");" >
```

Note

Styles embedded in elements take precedence over all previously declared styles. ■

CSS refers to the location of declarations as follows:

- **Author origin** — The author of a document includes styles in a style section or linked sheets (via <link>).
- **User origin** — The user (viewer of document) specifies a local style sheet.
- **User Agent origin** — The user agent specifies a default style sheet (when no other exists).

Tip

Styles that are critical to the document's presentation should be coded as important by placing the text `!important` at the end of the declaration. For example, the following style is marked as important:

```
.highlighted { color: blue  !important; }
```

Such styles are treated differently from normal styles when the style to use is determined from the cascade — styles coded as important override the next level of precedence when being evaluated. ■

The CSS standard uses the following rules to determine which style to use when multiple styles exist for an element:

1. Find all style declarations from all origins that apply to the element.
2. For normal declarations, author style sheets override user style sheets, which override the default style sheet. For `!important` style declarations, user style sheets override author style sheets, which override the default style sheet.
3. More specific declarations take precedence over less specific declarations.
4. Styles specified last have precedence over otherwise equal styles.

Summary

This chapter covered the basics of CSS — how styles are attached to a document, how they are best used, the different levels of CSS, and how the "cascade" in Cascading Style Sheets works. You learned the various ways to embed and define styles, and more about the separation between content and formatting that CSS can provide. The next chapter delves into the ins and outs of style definitions. Subsequent chapters in this part of the book will show you how styles are best used with various elements.

CHAPTER

26

Style Definitions

IN THIS CHAPTER

By this point in the book, you should recognize the power and versatility that styles can bring to your documents. You have seen how styles can make format changes easier and how they adhere to the content versus formatting separation. Now it's time to learn how to create styles — the syntax and methods used to define styles for your documents.

The Style Definition Format

CSS style definitions all follow the same basic format. A definition starts with a selector expression used to match elements within the documents(s), and is followed by one or more style properties and value sets. Roughly, this format approximates the following structure:

```
selector {
  property: value(s);
  property: value(s);
  ...
}
```

The `selector` is an expression that can be used to match specific elements within HTML documents. Its simplest form is an element's name, such as `h1`, which would match all `h1` elements. At its most complex, the selector expression can be used to match individual sub-elements of particular elements or to specify text to include before or after matched elements.

Cross-Ref

Selectors are covered in depth within the next section of this chapter. Acceptable property values are covered in Chapter 27. Individual CSS properties are covered in topical chapters, Chapter 29 through Chapter 37. ■

The property component of a style rule specifies which properties of the element the definition will affect. For example, to change the color of an element you would use the color property. Note that some properties affect only one aspect of an element, whereas others combine several properties into one declaration. For example, the border property can be used to define the width, style, and color of an element's border — and each of the properties (width, style, color) has its own property declarations as well (border-width, border-style, and border-color).

The values(s)component of a style rule contains one or more values that should be assigned to the properties. For example, to specify an element's color as red, you would use red as the value for the color property.

Now, let's look at all these elements of a style declaration in a real example. The following style definition can be used to change all the first-level headings (h1 elements) in a document to red text:

```
h1 {
  color: red;
}
```

The actual formatting of the style declarations can vary, but must follow these rules:

- The selector or selector expression must be first.
- Braces ({ and }) must follow the selector and enclose the style property-value pairs.
- Each style property-value pair must end with a semicolon (;).

It is also suggested, but not absolutely necessary, that style definitions be formatted with liberal white space — spaces between elements of the definition, line breaks between property-value pairs, sub-elements indented, and so on. Feel free to add as many spaces, line breaks, and tabs as you like, as the amount of white space does not matter. What is important is that the definitions are legible.

For example, both of the following definitions produce identical results, but they are formatted quite differently:

```
h1 { color: red; border: thin dotted black; font-family: helvetica,
sans-serif; text-align: right;}

h1 {
  color: red;
  border: thin dotted black;
  font-family: helvetica, sans-serif;
  text-align: right;
}
```

Understanding Selectors

Selectors are patterns that enable a user agent to identify what elements should get what styles. For example, the following style says, in effect, "If it is a paragraph element (p), then give it this style":

```
p { text-indent: 2em;}
```

The rest of this section shows you how to construct selectors of different types to best match styles to the elements within your documents.

Matching elements by type

The easiest selector to understand is the plain element selector, as in the following example:

```
h1 { color: red;}
```

Using the actual element type (h1) as the selector causes all objects within h1 elements to be formatted with the property-value section of the definition (color: red). You can also specify multiple selectors by listing them all in the selector area, separated by commas. For example, the following definition will affect all levels of heading elements (1 through 6) in the document:

```
h1, h2, h3, 4h, h5, h6 { color: red;}
```

Matching using the universal selector

The universal selector, designated by an asterisk (*), can be used to match any element in the document. As an extreme example, you can use the universal selector to match *every* tag in a document:

```
* { color: red;}
```

Using this rule, every tag will have the color:red property-value applied to it. You would rarely want a definition to apply to all elements of a document, of course, although you can also use the universal selector to match other elements than the selector specifically defines. The following selector matches any ol element that is a descendant of a td element, which is a descendant of a tr element (an ordered list in a cell in a row of a table):

```
tr td ol  { color: red;}
```

Cross-Ref

More information on child/descendant selectors can be found in the section "Matching child, descendant, and adjacent sibling elements" later in this chapter. ■

This selector rule is very strict, requiring all three elements. If you also wanted to include descendant ol elements of th elements or ol elements occurring within p elements, you would need to specify additional selectors, or use the universal selector to match all elements that might occur between tr and ol, as in the following example:

```
tr * ol  { color: red;}
```

You can use the universal selector within any of the selector forms discussed in this chapter.

Matching elements by class

You can use selectors to match element classes. Suppose you had two areas in your document with different backgrounds, one light and one dark. You would want to use dark-colored text within the light background area and light-colored text within the dark background area. You could use light_bg and dark_bg classes in your style selector and applicable elements to ensure that the appropriate text colors were applied within the areas.

To specify a class to match with a selector, you append a period and the class name to the selector. For example, the following style will match any paragraph element with a class of dark_bg:

```
p.dark_bg  { color: white;}
```

Suppose the following paragraph were in the area of the document with the dark background:

```
<p class="dark_bg">Based on the preview we were given at Rodent Studios, Gopher Hunt promises to be a great game.</p>
```

The specification of the dark_bg class with the paragraph tag will match the defined style, causing the paragraph's text to be rendered in white.

The universal selector can be used to match multiple elements with a given class. For example, this style definition will apply to *all* elements that specify the dark_bg class:

```
*.dark_bg  { color: white;}
```

You can omit the universal selector, specifying only the class itself (beginning with a period):

```
.dark_bg  { color: white;}
```

Tip

One little-known and infrequently used trick is to give HTML elements more than one class. For example, we can give our sample paragraph both the dark_bg and bold_text classes:

```
<p class="dark_bg bold_text"> ...
```

Using this method, the tag can be influenced by two different styles: one influencing the dark_bg class and one influencing the bold_text class.

You can give HTML elements as many classes as you like, but if two class-based styles conflict, the last one listed will be used. ■

Matching elements by identifier

You can also use selectors to match element identifiers — the `id` attribute of element(s). To match identifiers, use the pound sign (#) as a prefix for the selector, followed by the `id`. For example, the following style will match any tag that has an `id` of `comment`:

```
#comment { background-color: green;}
```

Matching elements by specific attributes

You can use a selector to match any attribute in elements, not just `class` and `id`. To do so, you specify the attribute and the value(s) you want to match at the end of the selector, offset in square brackets. This form of the selector has the following format:

```
element[attribute="value"] { property: value(s);}
```

For example, if you want to match any `table` element with a `border` attribute set to `3`, you can use this selector:

```
table[border="3"]
```

You can also match elements that contain the attribute, no matter what the value of the attribute, by omitting the equal sign and attribute value. To match any `table` element that contains a `border` attribute (of any value), you can use this selector:

```
table[border]
```

Tip

You can combine two or more selector formats for even more specificity. For example, the following selector will match `table` elements with a `class` value of `datalist`, and a `border` value of 3:

```
table.datalist[border="3"] ■
```

Multiple attributes within the same selector can also be specified. Each attribute is specified in its own bracketed expression. For example, if you wanted to match `table` elements with a `border` value of `3` and a `width` value of `100%`, you would use the following selector:

```
table[border="3"][width="100%"]
```

In addition, you can match single values that are contained within a space- or hyphen-separated list value. To match a value in a space-separated list, use tilde equal (~=) instead of the usual equal sign (=). To match a value in a hyphen-separated list, you use bar equal (|=) instead of the usual equal sign. For example, the following selector would match any attribute that has "us" in a space-separated value of the `language` attribute:

```
[language~="us"]
```

Matching child, descendant, and adjacent sibling elements

The most powerful selector methods match elements by their relationships to other elements within a document. For example, you can specify a selector style that matches italic elements only when appearing within a heading, or list items only within ordered (not unordered) lists.

Understanding document hierarchy

The elements in an HTML document are related to each other in a hierarchical manner. The hierarchy follows the same nomenclature as family trees — ancestors, parents, children, descendants, and siblings — with the `<html>` tag as the root of the document tree. For example, consider the following, fairly simplistic document code. Figure 26-1 shows a document and its hierarchy.

```
<html>
<body>
<div class="div1">
  <h1>Heading 1</h1>
  <table>
    <tr><td>Cell 1</td><td>Cell 2</td></tr>
    <tr><td>Cell 3</td><td>Cell 4</td></tr>
  </table>
  <p>Lorem ipsum dolor sit amet, consectetuer adipiscing
  elit, sed diam nonummy nibh euismod tincidunt ut laoreet
  dolore magna aliquam erat volutpat. Ut wisi enim ad minim
  veniam, quis nostrud exerci tation ullamcorper suscipit
  lobortis nisl ut aliquip ex ea commodo consequat.</p>
</div>
<div class="div2">
  <h1>Heading 2</h1>
  <p>Lorem ipsum dolor sit amet, consectetuer adipiscing
  elit, sed diam nonummy nibh euismod tincidunt ut laoreet
  dolore magna aliquam erat volutpat. Ut wisi enim ad minim
  veniam, quis nostrud exerci tation ullamcorper suscipit
  lobortis nisl ut aliquip ex ea commodo consequat.</p>
  <ol>An ordered list
    <li>First element,</li>
    <li>Second element</li>
    <li>Third element</li>
  </ol>
</div>
</body>
</html>
```

Ancestors and descendants

Ancestors and descendants are elements that are linked by lineage, no matter the distance between them. For example, in Figure 26-1, the list elements under `div2` are descendants of the `body` element, and the `body` element is their ancestor, even though multiple elements separate the two.

Parents and children

Parents and children are elements that are directly connected in lineage. For example, in Figure 26-1 the table rows (`tr`) under `div1` are children of the `table` element, which is their parent.

FIGURE 26-1

Diagram of a document's hierarchy

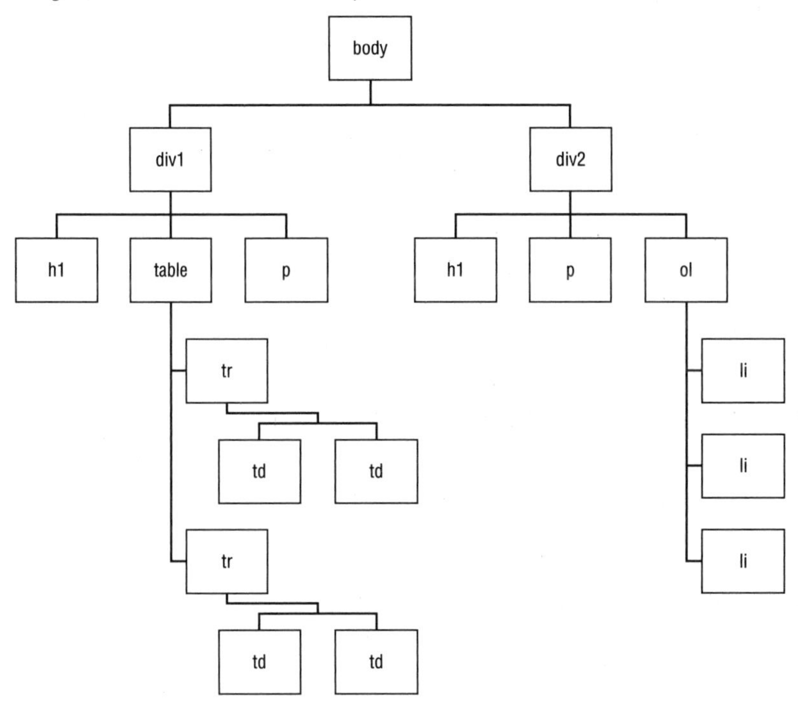

Siblings

Siblings are children that share the same, direct parent. In Figure 26-1, the list elements (li) under `div2` are siblings of each other. The header (`h1`), paragraph (`p`), and table (`table`) elements are also siblings because they share the same, direct parent (`div1`).

Selecting by hierarchy

Several selector mechanisms are available that enable you to match elements by their hierarchy in the document.

To specify ancestor and descendant relationships, list all involved elements, separated by spaces. For example, the following selector matches the `li` elements in Figure 26-1 (`li` elements within a `div` that has a class of `div2`):

```
div.div2 li
```

To specify parent and child relationships, list all involved elements, separated by a right angle bracket (>). For example, the following selector matches the table element in Figure 26-1 (a table element that is a direct descendant of a div element that has a class of divl):

```
div.divl > table
```

To specify sibling relationships, list all involved elements, separated by plus signs (+). For example, the following selector matches the p element under divl in Figure 26-1 (a p element that has a sibling relationship with a table element):

```
table + p
```

Of course, you can mix and match the hierarchy selector mechanisms for even more specificity. For example, the following selector will match only table and p sibling elements that are also children of the div with a class value of divl:

```
div.divl > table + p
```

Understanding Style Inheritance

Style inheritance is an important concept when working with CSS. The term *inheritance* reflects the fact that an element acquires the properties of its ancestors. In CSS, all *foreground* properties are inherited by descendant elements. For example, the following definition would result in all elements being rendered in green because every element in the document descends from the body tag:

```
body { color: green;}
```

Note that this inheritance rule is valid only for foreground properties. Background properties (background color, image, and so on) are not automatically inherited by descendant elements.

You can override inheritance by defining a style for an element with a different value for the otherwise inherited property. For example, the following definitions result in all elements being rendered with a green foreground, *except* for paragraphs with a nogreen class, which are rendered with a red foreground:

```
body { color: green;}
p.nogreen { color: red;}
```

Attributes that are not in conflict are cumulatively inherited by descendant elements. For example, the following rules result in paragraphs with an emphasis class being rendered in green, bold text:

```
body { color: green;}
p.emphasis { font-weight: bold;}
```

Using Pseudo-Classes

You have at your disposal a handful of pseudo-classes to match attributes of elements in your document. Pseudo-classes are identifiers that are understood by user agents, and they apply to elements of certain types without the elements having to be explicitly styled. Such classes are typically dynamic in nature; as such, they are tracked by means other than the static `class` attribute.

For example, there are pseudo-classes used to modify visited and unvisited anchors in the document. Using the pseudo-classes, you don't have to specify classes in individual anchor tags — the user agent determines which anchors are in which class (visited or not) and applies the style(s) appropriately in real time as the user browses.

The following sections discuss the available pseudo-classes.

Anchor styles

A handful of pseudo-classes can be used with anchor tags (`<a>`). The anchor pseudo-classes are listed in Table 26-1.

TABLE 26-1

Pseudo-Classes for Anchor Tags

Pseudo-Class	Matches
`:link`	Unvisited links
`:visited`	Visited links
`:active`	Active links
`:hover`	The link over which the browser pointer is hovering
`:focus`	The link that currently has the user interface focus

For example, the following definition will cause all unvisited links in the document to be rendered in blue, all visited links in red, and when hovered over, in green:

```
:link  { color: blue;}
:visited { color: red;}
:hover {color: green;}
```

Note

All pseudo-class definitions begin with a colon (:) and the pseudo-class name. ■

The order of the definitions is important; because the link membership in the classes is dynamic, `:hover` must be the last definition. If the order of `:visited` and `:hover` were reversed, then visited links would not turn green when hovered over because the `:visited` color attribute would override the `:hover` color attribute. Ordering is also important when using the `:focus` pseudo-class — it should be placed last in the definitions.

Pseudo-class selectors can also be combined with other selector methods. For example, if you wanted all nonvisited `a` elements with a class attribute of `boldme` to be rendered in a bold font, you could use the following code:

```
/* Add explicit "boldme" class to non-visited pseudo class */
:link.boldme { font-weight: bold;}
...
<!-- The following link is important! -->
<a href="http://something.example.com/important.html"
  class="important">An important message</a>
```

The :first-child pseudo-class

The `:first-child` pseudo-class is used to assign style definitions to the first child element of a specific element. You can use this pseudo-class to add more space or otherwise change the formatting of a first child element. For example, if you need to indent the first paragraph inside specific `div` elements (having an `indent` class), you could use the following definition:

```
div.indent > p:first-child { text-indent: 25px;}
```

This code results in only the first paragraph (p) element of all `div` elements having a class of `indent` being indented by 25px (pixels).

The :lang pseudo-class

The `:lang` pseudo-class is used to change elements according to the language being used for the document. For example, the French language uses angle brackets (< and >) to offset quotes, whereas the English language uses quote marks (" and "). If you need to address this difference in a document (seen by both French and English native readers), you could use a definition similar to the following:

```
/* Two levels of quotes for two languages */
.quote:lang(en) { quotes: "" "" ""' ""';}
.quote:lang(fr) { quotes: "{\ll}" "{\gg}" "<" ">";}
/* Add quotes (before and after) to quote class */
.quote:before { content: open-quote;}
.quote:after  { content: close-quote;}
```

This code would cause any element having a class of `quote` to be placed in appropriate quote characters, depending on the current language setting of the document or user agent.

Note

The pseudo-elements `:before` and `:after` are used in the preceding example to automatically place quote characters around elements. These two pseudo-classes are covered in the next section. ■

Pseudo-Elements

Pseudo-elements are another virtual construct to help apply styles dynamically to elements within a document. For example, the `:first-line` pseudo-element applies a style to the first line of an element dynamically — that is, as the first changes size (longer or shorter), the user agent adjusts the style coverage accordingly.

First line

The `:first-line` pseudo-element specifies a different set of property values for the first line of elements. This is illustrated in the following document listing and in Figure 26-2, which shows two browser windows of different widths, highlighting how the underlining of the first sentence is dynamic thanks to the pseudo-element first-line style:

```
<!DOCTYPE HTML PUBLIC "-//W3C//DTD HTML 4.01//EN"
  "http://www.w3.org/TR/html4/strict.dtd">
<html>
<head>
  <title>First-line formatting</title>
  <style type="text/css">
    p:first-line { text-decoration: underline;}
    p.noline:first-line { text-decoration: none;}
  </style>
</head>
<body>
<h1>The Oasis of Tranquility</h1>
<p class="noline">The Founding and Mission of The Oasis</p>
<p>Founded in 2001, The Oasis of Tranquility strives to be a
different, pleasurable experience for those seeking to get away from
their daily routine. Staffed by individuals each with specific
specialties, The Oasis provides the luxuries of many day spas, but at
salon prices. The main mission of The Oasis is that personal luxury
doesn't have to be expensive.</p>
</body>
</html>
```

Note

The preceding code example manages element formatting by exception. Most paragraphs in the document should have their first line underlined. A universal selector is used to select all paragraph tags. A different style, using a class selector (`noline`), is defined to select elements that have a class of `noline`. Using this method, you only need to add class attributes to the exceptions (the minority), rather than the rule (the majority). ■

The `:first-line` pseudo-element can affect only a finite range of properties. Only properties in the following groups can be applied using `:first-line` — font properties, color properties, background properties, `word-spacing`, `letter-spacing`, `text-decoration`, `vertical-align`, `text-transform`, `line-height`, `text-shadow`, and `clear`.

FIGURE 26-2

You can use the first-line pseudo-element to dynamically apply properties to a paragraph's first line — when the first line's length changes, so does application of the properties.

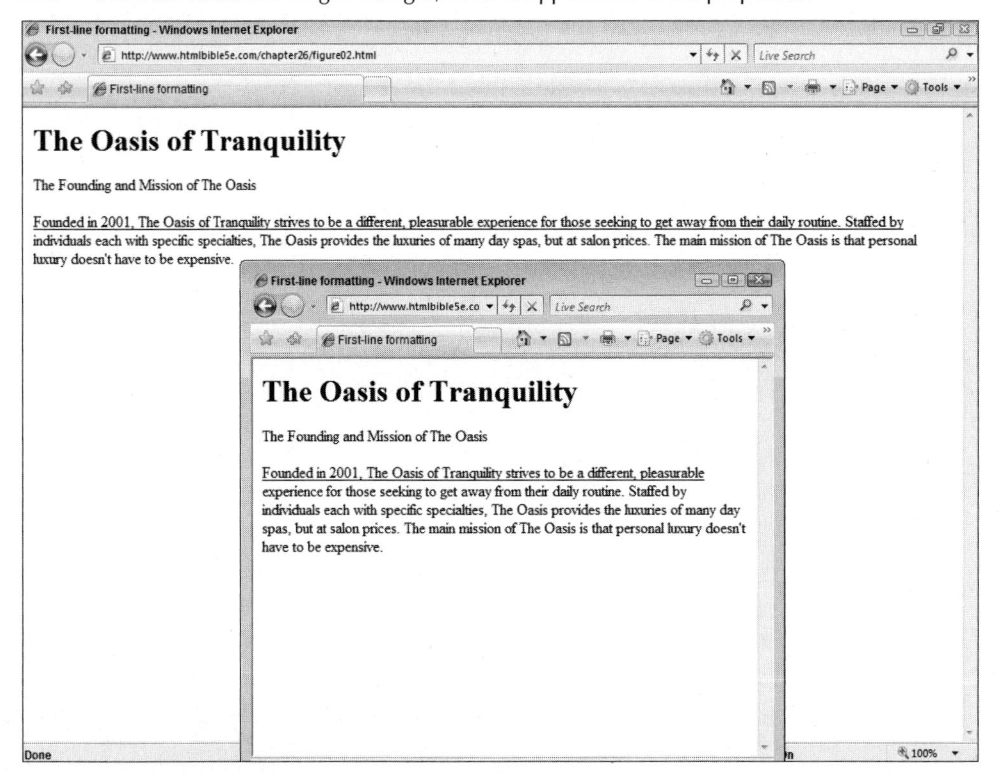

First letter

The `:first-letter` pseudo-element is used to affect the properties of an element's first letter. This selector can be used to achieve typographic effects such as drop caps, as illustrated in the following code and Figure 26-3:

```
<!DOCTYPE HTML PUBLIC "-//W3C//DTD HTML 4.01//EN"
  "http://www.w3.org/TR/html4/strict.dtd">
<html>
<head>
  <title>Drop cap formatting</title>
  <style type="text/css">
    p.dropcap:first-letter { font-size: 3em;
       font-weight: bold; float: left;
       border: solid 1px black; padding: .1em;
       margin: .2em .2em 0 0;}
  </style>
</head>
```

```
<body>
<h1>The Oasis of Tranquility</h1>
<p>The Founding and Mission of The Oasis</p>
<p class="dropcap"> Founded in 2001, The Oasis of Tranquility
strives to be a different, pleasurable experience for those seeking
to get away from their daily routine. Staffed by individuals each
with specific specialties, The Oasis provides the luxuries of many
day spas, but at salon prices. The main mission of The Oasis is that
personal luxury doesn't have to be expensive.</p>
</body>
</html>
```

FIGURE 26-3

The first-letter pseudo-element can be used for effects such as drop caps on user agents that support it.

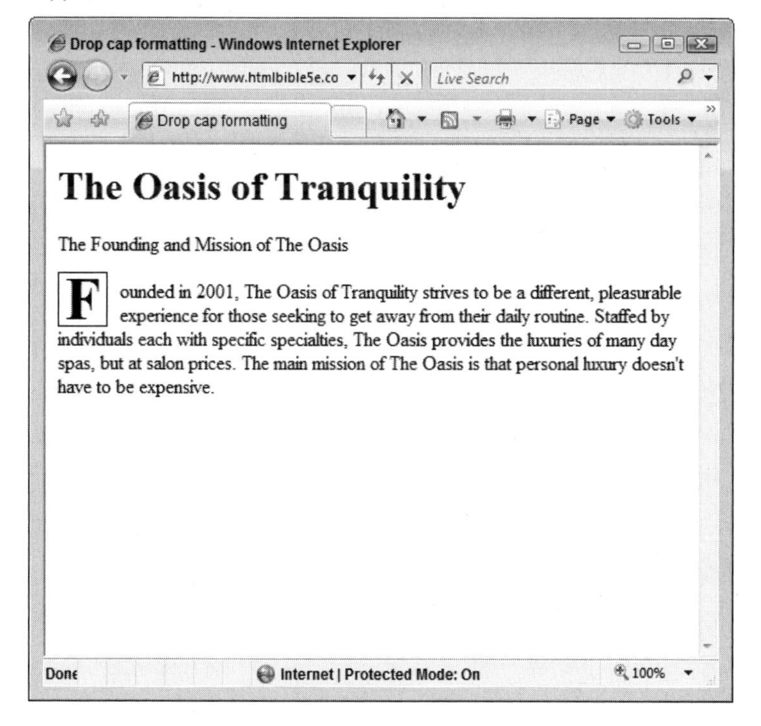

Before and after

You can use the `:before` and `:after` pseudo-elements to add additional text to specific elements. These pseudo-elements were used in the section "The :lang pseudo-class," to add quote marks to the beginning and ending of elements with a `quote` class:

```
.quote:before { content: '"';}
.quote:after  { content: '"';}
```

Notice the use of the `content` property. This property assigns the actual value to content-generating elements such as `:before` and `:after`. In this case, quote marks are assigned as the content to add before and after elements with a `quote` class. The following code and Figure 26-4 illustrate how a user agent that supports these classes generates content from the `:before` and `:after` pseudo-elements:

```
<!DOCTYPE HTML PUBLIC "-//W3C//DTD HTML 4.01//EN"
  "http://www.w3.org/TR/html4/strict.dtd">
<html>
<head>
  <title>Auto-quote marks</title>
  <style type="text/css">
  .quote:before { content: '"';}
  .quote:after  { content: '"';}
  </style>
</head>
<body>
<p class="quote">I set out to create a spa different from any other.
I was tired of seeing the average, every-day consumer pay top dollar
for a personal luxury service that wasn't even as good as a salon
service. I decided that with the right people and minimized overhead
I could create a day spa like experience for much less.</p>
</body>
</html>
```

Generated content breaks the division of content and presentation. However, adding presentation content is sometimes necessary to enhance the overall appeal of a document. Besides adding elements such as quote marks, you can also create counters for custom numbered lists, and other more powerful features.

Note

Some user agents have poor support for pseudo-elements. ■

Shorthand Expressions

CSS supports many properties for control over elements. Many of the properties overlap or affect only slightly different areas of an element. For example, consider the following properties, all of which apply to element borders:

- `border`
- `border-collapse`
- `border-spacing`
- `border-top`
- `border-right`
- `border-bottom`
- `border-left`
- `border-color`
- `border-top-color`

- border-right-color
- border-bottom-color
- border-left-color
- border-style
- border-top-style
- border-right-style
- border-bottom-style
- border-left-style
- border-width
- border-top-width
- border-right-width
- border-bottom-width
- border-left-width

FIGURE 26-4

The :before and :after pseudo-elements can be used to add characters such as quote marks to text.

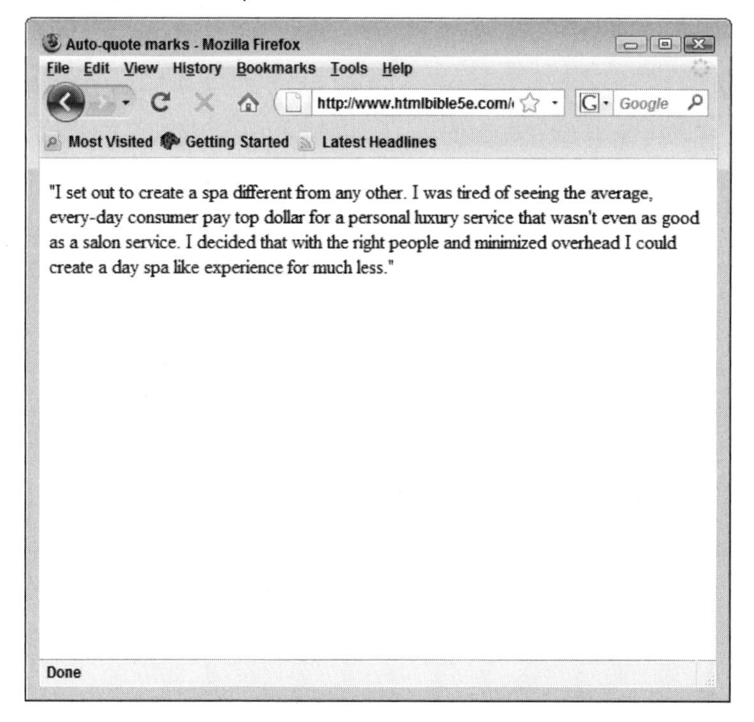

Several of these properties can be used to set multiple properties within the same definition. For example, to set an element's four-sided border you can use code similar to the following:

```
p.bordered {
  border-top-width: 1px;
  border-top-style: solid;
```

```
    border-top-color: black;
    border-right-width: 2px;
    border-right-style: dashed;
    border-right-color: red;
    border-bottom-width: 1px;
    border-bottom-style: solid;
    border-bottom-color: black;
    border-left-width: 2px;
    border-left-style: dashed;
    border-left-color: red;
}
```

Alternately, you could use the shorthand property border-*side* to shorten this definition considerably:

```
p.bordered {
  border-top: 1px solid black;
  border-right: 2px dashed red;
  border-bottom: 1px solid black;
  border-left: 2px dashed red;
}
```

This definition could be further simplified by use of the `border` property, which sets all sides of an element to the same values:

```
p.bordered {
  border: 1px solid black;
  border-right: 2px dashed red;
  border-left: 2px dashed red;
}
```

The preceding code shortens the definition by first setting all sides to the same values and then setting the exceptions (right and left borders).

Tip

As with all things code, avoid being overly ingenious when defining your styles. Otherwise, you will dramatically decrease your code's legibility. ■

Summary

This chapter explained the basics of defining styles — from the format and use of the various selector methods to the format of property declarations and setting their values. You also learned about special pseudo-classes and pseudo-elements that can make your definitions more dynamic. The next series of chapters in this book delve into specific style use for text, borders, tables, and more.

CHAPTER

CSS Values and Units

IN THIS CHAPTER

General Property Value Rules

Property Value Metrics

CSS is a rich language offering property-based control over many aspects of your HTML documents. Because the many aspects of the document differ from one another, several different types of metrics must be available — scales of units, such as inches, picas, and such — to be able to adequately apply values to their properties. This chapter covers the various types of metrics available in CSS and some reasoning regarding where and why to use each.

Cross-Ref

This chapter summarizes the syntax of values in CSS definitions and the various metric values available in CSS. For specific uses of each metric with each property, see the specific coverage of the individual properties in Chapters 29 through 35. ■

General Property Value Rules

A style definition's property/value section is contained within the braces of the definition. For example, in the following definition, `border-width: 3pt` is the property/value clause:

```
p.bordered  { border-width: 3pt; }
```

In this clause, the property (`border-width`) and value (`3pt`) are separated by a colon and the clause is terminated by a semicolon.

Tip

Technically speaking, the last (or only) property/value clause in a style definition does not need a closing semicolon. However, it is generally good practice to include a semicolon at the end of every property/value clause. ■

The property half of the clause is fairly straightforward; it is a CSS property keyword. The property/value-separating colon comes next, terminating the property half of the clause.

The value half of the clause is a bit more complex, and a myriad of values and units can be used. However, the general structure of this half is uniform, and contains the following elements, in the following order:

1. An optional unary sign (+/-)
2. A keyword, number, function (`url`, `rgb`, and so on), or textual string
3. An optional abbreviation signifying the metric value of the value (`%`, `cm`, `pt`, and so on)

There can be no white space between the items listed; they must be one contiguous string of characters. Also note that the "optional" component of the metric abbreviation is driven by the value, not by the style coder's whim. For example, the percentage metric identifier is always necessary when you want a value specified as a percentage. Omitting the metric would create ambiguity, and most user agents would just treat the value as if it were pixels, which would not create the result you desired. However, properties such as `font-size-adjust` can have only numeric values — as such, no metric abbreviation is necessary.

Tip

Although there can be no white space in the value of a property, there can be white space around the value. You can use this space (after the colon and before the semicolon) to format your definitions for legibility. ■

An illustrated example of the value half of a property/value clause is shown in Figure 27-1.

FIGURE 27-1

Illustrated example of a CSS property's value clause

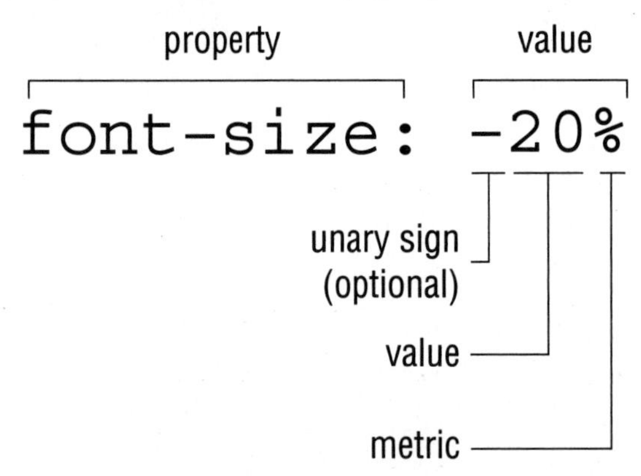

Some properties support more than one value in a property/value statement. For example, the shortcut property `border` can specify an element's border width, style, and color all in one definition. Such a definition would resemble the following:

```
p.bordered  { border: thin solid black; }
```

To specify multiple values within one property/value statement, simply separate each value from the others using white space — one or more spaces, a line break, and so on. The list of values should still begin after the colon and should still end with a semicolon, just like single-valued statements.

Property Value Metrics

Throughout this chapter you have seen how to apply values to properties using CSS. Now let's look at the values themselves. Property values can be expressed in several different metrics according to the individual property and the desired result.

CSS supports the following metrics for property values:

- Keywords such as `thin`, `thick`, `transparent`, `ridge`, and so forth
- Real-world measures
  - inches (in)
  - centimeters (cm)
  - millimeters (mm)
  - points (pt) — The points used by CSS2 are equal to $\frac{1}{72}$ of an inch
  - picas (pc) — 1 pica is equal to 12 points
- Screen measures in pixels (px)
- Relational to font size (font size [em] or x-height size [ex])
- Percentages (%)
- Color codes (keywords, `#rrggbb`, or `rgb(r,g,b)`)
- Angles — Used with aural style sheets
  - degrees (deg)
  - grads (grad)
  - radians (rad)
- Time values (seconds [s] and milliseconds [ms]) — Used with aural style sheets
- Frequencies (hertz [Hz] and kilohertz [kHz]) — Used with aural style sheets
- Textual strings
- URLs — Links to other resources on the Web (via the `url()` function)

Which metric is used depends on the value you are setting and your desired effect. For example, it doesn't make sense to use real-world measures (inches, centimeters, and so on) unless the user agent is calibrated to use such measures or your document is meant to be printed.

The following sections cover the various unit values.

Note

As with other elements in CSS (property names, reserved names, keywords, and so on), metric abbreviations are case sensitive. Be sure to use them as shown in this chapter, mostly lowercase (`pt` for points, and so on). ■

Keyword values

Many keywords have distinct meaning when used as CSS property values. For example, you can define a border property as follows:

```
border: thin solid black;
```

In this case, `thin`, `solid`, and `black` are all keywords applied to one property. The last keyword (`black`) is a specific keyword — a color keyword — that is used in a variety of places in Web coding, including HTML attribute values. The other two keywords, `thin` and `solid`, are used only with border-related properties.

That brings up an important point with keyword values: Most of them are valid only when used with specific properties. For example, the value `solid` is meaningless when used with the `font` property.

Cross-Ref

The various keywords available in CSS, along with the respective properties to which they can apply, are covered within Chapters 29 through 35. The keywords are covered in Appendix C. ■

One specific keyword, `inherit`, can be applied to almost any CSS property. This keyword implies that the property to which it applies should inherit the values of its parent. Of course, omitting a definition for the specific property would generally have the same effect due to the inheritance rules of CSS. However, there are times when intervening style rules might affect an object's inheritance, in which case you will need to explicitly specify that an object should inherit properties.

As an example, the following definition explicitly specifies that paragraph tags with a class of `highlight` should inherit their parent element's border properties but have their text rendered in a bold font:

```
p.highlight  { border: inherit;
               font-weight: bold; }
```

Real-world measures

CSS property values can be specified in the following real-world measures:

- Inches (in)
- Centimeters (cm)
- Millimeters (mm)
- Points (pt)
- Picas (pc)

These metrics can be used with almost any property that defines the length, width, or depth of an element. To use these metrics, you would use an appropriate numeric value with the suffix corresponding to the metric you are using. For example, to specify that an element with a class of `tall` should have a height of 2 inches, you can use the following definition:

```
.tall  { height: 2in; }
```

Note

Points and picas are traditionally font-related measures. As such, they are typically used with font-related CSS properties. However, because they both have absolute measures — a point is equal to $\frac{1}{72}$ of an inch and a pica is equal to 12 points — you can use these metrics with any property that can take a length, width, or depth measure. ■

The border properties are good examples of where real-world metrics are often used. In the following example, the style definition specifies that all `td` elements should have a 2-point top and left border and a 4-point bottom and right border:

```
td  {  border-top:    2pt;
       border-left:   2pt;
       border-bottom: 4pt;
       border-right:  4pt;  }
```

These values can be translated by several means, resulting in a proper border displayed on the user agent's screen. Typically, the user agent uses the same rules it uses for fonts, resulting in the points of a border width being the same scale as the points of a display font. This method helps keep everything in scale if the user agent employs a zoom function or other screen-scaling function — if the screen is magnified, then the fonts *and* border grow larger. Still, if you want a border in a particular size no matter the scaling on the user agent, specify your measures in screen metrics (pixels).

Specifying metrics in real-world measures is especially important in documents that are meant to be printed or that have some other real-world metric connection.

Screen measures

Any property that expresses a length, width, or depth value can be expressed in pixels. Pixels are the dots that make up a computer screen — one pixel equals one dot on screen. Pixels are expressed as a metric in style definitions by suffixing a value with `px`. For example, the following style definition specifies that the top border of all `td` elements should be 2 pixels wide:

```
td  { border-top: 2px; }
```

Pixel metrics are often used to ensure that a user agent's screen renders a document to an exact size. Because the pixel metric is not relative and directly influences the screen, it can be a powerful tool. However, it can have undesired side effects if the user agent screen is an odd size or it employs any type of display scaling mechanism. In the latter case, your specified pixel metric elements may not scale appropriately.

Note

Many user agents assume that a property's value is given in pixels if no other metric is specified. This means that the following two definitions will typically produce the same results:

```
p.px_specified       {  border: 2px;  }
p.px_notspecified    {  border: 2;  }
```

This is not always the case, however, and should not be relied upon; some user agents may ignore your styles if they do not include proper metric identifiers. Always specify the proper metrics for your property values to ensure that they are rendered properly on screen. ■

Relational measures

Three metrics can be used to specify that a value should be set in relation to another value. For example, the following definition sets all table widths to half (50 percent) of their parent element's width:

```
table  { width: 50%; }
```

The other two metric specifications — `em` and `ex` — refer to font sizes. The `em` metric refers to the height of the current font, whereas the `ex` metric refers to the height of the letter *x* in the current font (generally half the font's height). These two metrics specify their values as related to the current element's `font-height` property value. However, if either metric is used to specify an element's `font-height` property, the value specified is related to the parent's `font-height` property. The percentage metric (%) always relates to the parent's properties.

That last statement, "always relates to the parent's properties," is an important one. Many people assume that a table whose width is set to 50 percent will span half the user agent screen because the parent element of the table in question spans the entire screen width. But what happens when that isn't the case, when the parent element is not 100 percent as wide as the user agent?

Consider the following example and Figure 27-2, which shows how a table with a width specified as 50 percent can be a smaller fraction (25 percent) as wide as the user agent if its parent element is set to a smaller percentage width (50 percent):

```
<!DOCTYPE HTML PUBLIC "-//W3C//DTD HTML 4.01//EN"
  "http://www.w3.org/TR/html4/strict.dtd">
<html>
<head>
<title>Specifying Widths of Parent Elements</title>
<style type="text/css">
  body    { border: thin solid black;
            padding: 5px; }
  div     { width: 50%;
            border: thin dotted black;
            margin: 5px;
            padding: 5px; }
  table   { width: 50%; }
</style>
</head>
<body>
<div>
  <table border="1">
    <tr><td>Table Row 1</td></tr>
    <tr><td>Table Row 2</td></tr>
  </table>
</div>
</body>
</html>
```

The elements in the preceding example were given borders and extra padding to make the borders more evident. Using the borders, it is easy to see how the `body` element stretches to 100 percent of the user agent window's width, the `div` element occupies 50 percent of the `body` element's width (and hence 50 percent of the window), and the `table` element occupies only 25 percent of the window (50 percent of the `div`). In short, the `table` element is only 25 percent of the window because its `width` property is relative to its parent element's `width` property, not the user agent's window width.

The em and percent metrics can be quite powerful, specifying a value that changes as the element sizes around it change. The em and percent metrics are best used when you need a relational, not absolute, value.

FIGURE 27-2

The percentage metric always relates to the element's parent properties.

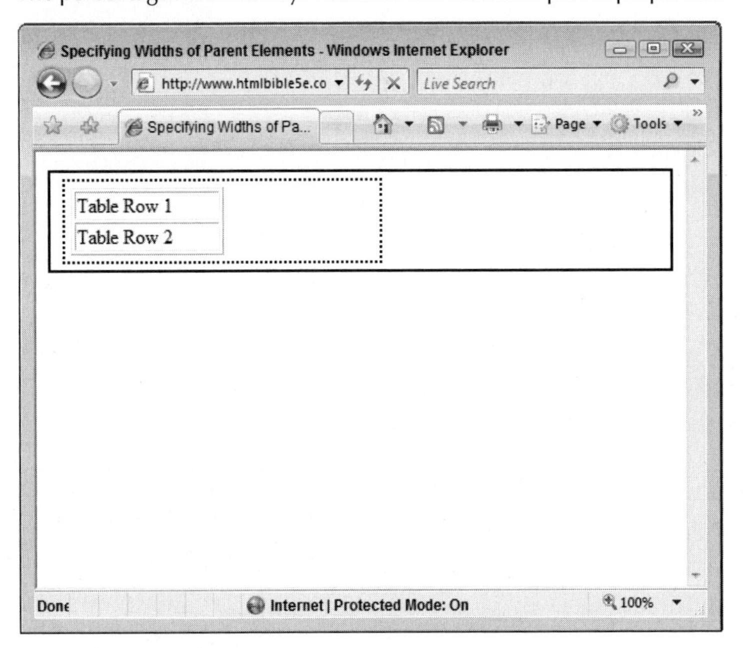

Color and URL functions

Two functions provide `color` and `url` values to properties.

The `rgb()` function (red, green, blue) takes three arguments to provide a color to a property via the mix of the values given. The arguments are values of the colors red, green, and blue to be mixed together to create the color desired. The values themselves are decimal numbers between 0 and 255 or percentage values between 0 and 100. In either case, 0 signifies no amount of the color specified, and the highest number (255 or 100 percent) is the most mix of the color specified. For example, consider the following:

```
border-color: rgb(0,0,0);          /* black (absence of color) */
border-color: rgb(255,255,255);    /* white (full mix of all colors) */
border-color: rgb(100%,0%,100%);   /* purple (red and blue mix) */
border-color: rgb(100%,0%,0%);     /* red (100% red only) */
border-color: rgb(255,125,0);      /* orange (red and green mix) */
```

The `rgb()` function can only be used where a color value can be provided, such as for a `color`, `background-color`, or `border-color` property. Keep in mind that the HTML-style, hexadecimal shorthand method of specifying color values is also available in CSS. This method has the following syntax:

```
#rrggbb
```

The letters signify hexadecimal digits for the colors red (rr), green (gg), and blue (bb). Using the two digits you can specify values between 0 and 255, as in the rgb() function. For example, the following is an example of the value orange, mixing a value of 255 red with 125 green:

```
border-color: #FF7D00;
```

The url() function is used to specify a URL — the Web or Internet address of a resource — to a property. The syntax of this function is very simple; the URL is encased between the parentheses in optional quote marks. For example, the following code specifies a background image for a table found in the images directory of the current site:

```
background-image:  url("images/star-background.jpg");
```

Keep in mind that the URL specified does not have to be a local path. You can specify a resource located on another server as long as it is accessible to the user agent. For example, this code specifies a similar image but one located on a remote server:

```
background-image:
url("http://www.on-target.com/images/star-background.jpg");
```

The URL can be encapsulated by single or double quotes. Although technically the quotes are optional, it's always a good idea to include them to help the parsing of your URL string. Note that, in any case, parentheses, commas, white space characters, single quotes, and double quotes must be escaped if they appear in the URL. To escape a character, simply prefix it with a backslash. For example, \ would adequately escape a comma.

Aural metrics

Several metrics are used with aural style properties, such as azimuth and pitch. These properties control the position and properties of sounds generated via aural style sheets. Metrics that can be used with such properties include the following:

- Angles — Used with positioning properties
  - degrees (deg)
  - grads (grad)
  - radians (rad)
- Time values (seconds [s] and milliseconds [ms]) — Used with sound properties
- Frequencies (hertz [Hz] and kilohertz [kHz]) — Used with sound properties

Each metric is used by specifying a decimal number and suffixing it with the appropriate suffix for the metric. For example, to specify an azimuth of 120 degrees, you can use the following property/value statement:

```
azimuth: 120deg;
```

Tip

For a good overview of aural style sheets, including a breakdown of browser support, visit `http://lab.dotjay.co.uk/tests/css/aural-speech/`. ■

Summary

There are almost as many metrics in CSS as there are properties. This has to do with the rich nature of the technology and its ability to influence many aspects of a document, because each characteristic of a document can use certain metrics, and the properties of these metrics are related to the characteristic where they're used. This may seem confusing at first, but the next few chapters help connect distinct metrics with distinct properties. In no time you will settle into your favorite metrics, and their use will become habit.

The next chapter covers the very important topics of cascade and inheritance, or how CSS styles and properties affect one another. From there, the other CSS chapters are broken into CSS topic areas — fonts, text, tables, and so on.

CHAPTER 28

CSS Inheritance and Cascade

IN THIS CHAPTER

Inheritance

Cascade

Specificity

The words "inheritance" and "cascade" are bandied about a lot in regard to CSS. They are often used interchangeably. However, they each have a unique style-related meaning. This chapter clarifies these terms and their meanings in CSS.

Inheritance

The word "inheritance" is defined by *Webster's Dictionary* as "a) the act of inheriting property; b) the reception of genetic qualities by transmission from parent to offspring; c) the acquisition of a possession, condition, or trait from past generations." This definition is accurate for the behavior of HTML elements controlled by CSS — child elements inherit the properties of their parents.

For example, consider the following document, whose output is shown in Figure 28-1:

```
<!DOCTYPE HTML PUBLIC "-//W3C//DTD HTML 4.01//EN"
   "http://www.w3.org/TR/html4/strict.dtd">
<html>
<head>
  <title>Inheritance Example</title>
  <style type="text/css">
    table { background-color: red; }
  </style>
</head>
<body>
<table border="1">
  <tr>
```

```
      <th>Column One</th>
      <th>Column Two</th>
    </tr>
    <tr>
      <td>Cell One</td>
      <td>Cell Two</td>
    </tr>
  </table>
  </body>
  </html>
```

FIGURE 28-1

The table rows and cells inherit the table's background-color property.

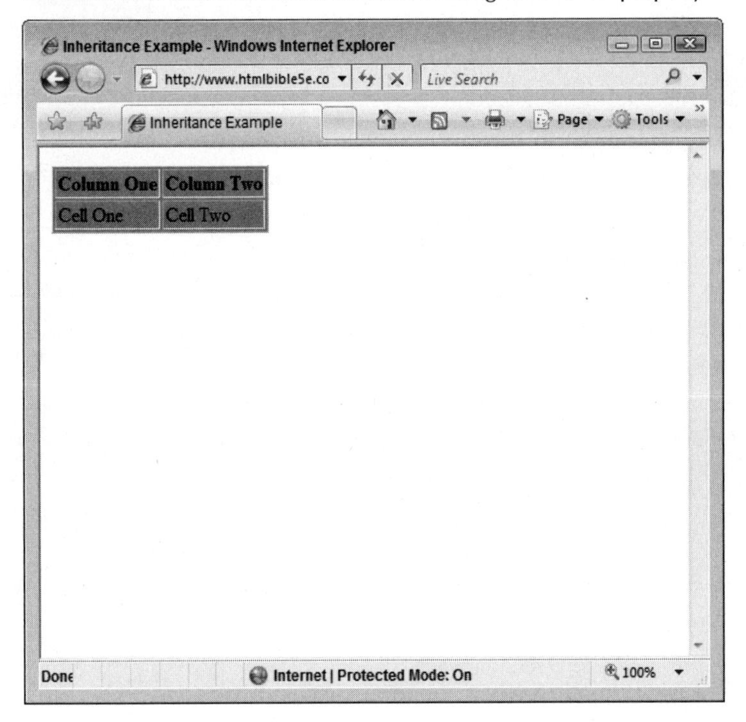

The table's `background-color` definition applies to all table elements (`table`), all table row elements (`tr`), and all table cell elements (`th` and `td`) in the document.

The rows and cells are also colored red because they are child elements of the table and inherit the table's background color property. The main body of the document, the parent of the table, does not inherit the background color because it is a parent of the table, not a child.

Inheritance can be more complex. For example, consider the following style definitions:

```
p           { border: thin solid black; }
p.redbottom { border-bottom: thin dotted red; }
```

The first definition will cause all paragraph elements (`p`) in the document to have solid black borders on all sides. The second definition will cause paragraph elements with a class of `red-bottom` to have solid black borders on three sides (top, right, and left) and a dotted red border on the bottom, as shown in Figure 28-2.

FIGURE 28-2

The second paragraph has its bottom border specified by a specific class-based style but inherits its other borders from a generic paragraph style.

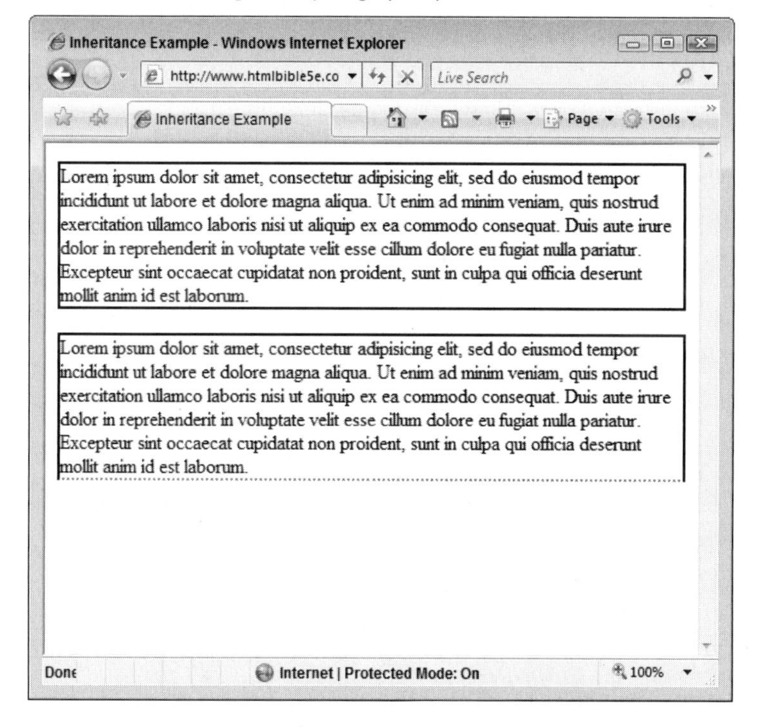

However, the second definition doesn't include property values for borders on any side other than the bottom. Where then do these other property values come from? They are inherited from the generic paragraph element definition.

Cascade

The term "cascade" has an entirely different meaning than "inheritance." The means by which styles come together to relate to a document is the cascade. Styles can be applied to a document from many different sources. These sources include the following:

- **Author styles** — Styles that the document author includes, whether embedded directly in the head of the document, linked in as a separate style sheet (using the `link` tag, or the

CSS `@import` rule), or inline in individual elements. These styles represent the way the author intends the document to look.

- **User styles** — Styles that the end user specifies should be used for the document. These styles are selected by the end user from local style sheets and can be used to modify a document's default look. The styles can be changed in Microsoft Internet Explorer, for example, within the Accessibility section of Internet Options, as shown in Figure 28-3.
- **User agent styles** — Styles that a user agent uses by default when no other styles are specified for a particular element or document. These styles are usually very simple in nature — black text on a white background, slightly larger fonts for headings, and so on.

FIGURE 28-3

Internet Explorer users can assign default styles that override the user agent's default styles.

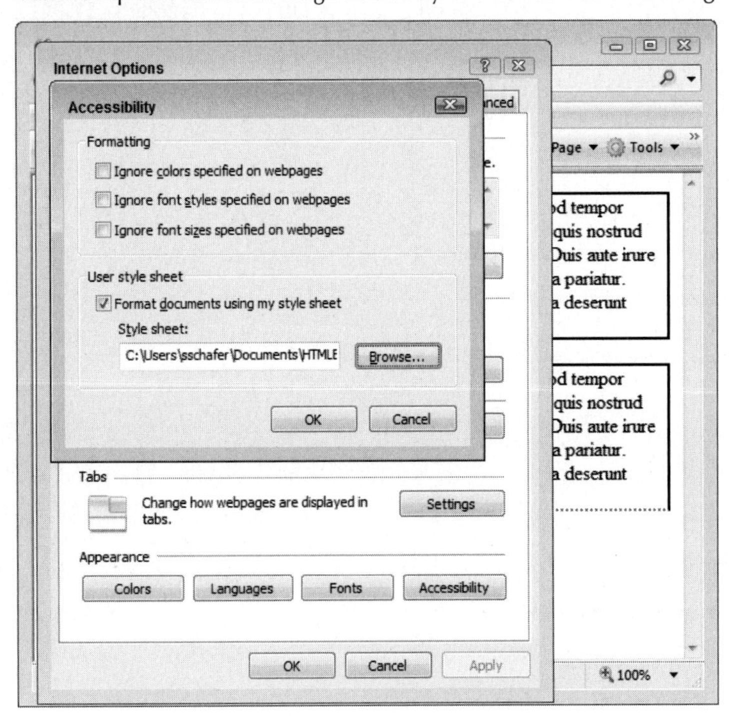

Each style from each source is assigned a weight. When styles conflict between the three sources, their assigned weight is used to determine which style should apply. By default, author styles have priority over user styles, which have priority over user agent styles.

An exception can be forced by use of the `!important` rule. The author or user can tag a style with this rule, which adds extra weight to that style's priority. To mark a style as important, place the `!important` keyword after the declaration, as shown in the following example:

```
p { font-weight: bold !important; }
```

In general, important styles trump non-important styles. However, in the case of two conflicting `important` styles, the order of precedence (author, user) is reversed — user important styles trump author important styles. This gives both the user and the user agent the ability to specify their preferences (or requirements) for display — the user agent might have hardware-specific requirements and the user might have accessibility needs.

Note

When considering style precedence, you must also consider the order in which style sheets are loaded if you attach more than one sheet to a document or import one sheet inside another. In the following example, styles in the `hr-dept.css` style sheet will trump styles in the `corporate.css` style sheet because the `hr-dept.css` sheet is loaded last:

```
<link rel=stylesheet type="text/css"
      href="corporate.css" title="corporate styles">
<link rel=stylesheet type="text/css"
      href="hr-dept.css" title="hr dept styles">
```

Care should be taken to observe inheritance between the sheets. Any individual element's properties specified in the `corporate.css` sheet that are not specified in the `hr-dept.css` sheet will be inherited and applied to the document. ■

The actual means to determine the cascade sorting order is specified by the World Wide Web Consortium (W3C) as follows:

1. Take all definitions that apply to the element and property in question.
2. Sort the definitions by weight and origin: Author styles override user styles, which override user agent styles. For `!important` definitions, user styles override author styles. All `!important` definitions override normal definitions. Any imported definitions are considered to have the same origin as the style sheet that imported them.
3. Sort the definitions by specificity of selector: The more specific selectors override the more general ones.
4. Sort by the order in which the definitions were specified: If two definitions have the same weight, origin, and specificity, the last one specified prevails. Rules in imported style sheets are considered before any rules in the style sheet itself.

The styles are applied according to the order resolved by this process.

Specificity

There is one other aspect to CSS conflict resolution: specificity. To understand how specificity is used, consider the following style definitions:

```
div p  { color:  red; }
p      { color:  blue; }
```

Given the discussion thus far in the chapter, you would expect that the font in every paragraph element, including those in `div` elements, would be rendered in blue. However, that's not the case. Paragraph elements contained within div elements would have their text rendered in red. The first definition is more specific — it specifies paragraph elements that are children of div elements. Therefore, it carries more weight than the more generic definition.

As with cascade precedence, the W3C has a specification for calculating a definition's specificity value based on the selector:

1. Count the number of ID attributes in the selector and assign that number to A.
2. Count the number of other attributes and pseudo-classes in the selector and assign that number to B.
3. Count the number of element names and pseudo-elements in the selector and assign that number to C.
4. Concatenate the values to make one number, ABC. That number is the definition's specificity.

Note that pseudo-elements are not given specificity and are ignored in the preceding calculation.

For example, consider the following selectors and their resultant specificity values:

```
*                  A=0 B=0 C=0 -> specificity =   0
p                  A=0 B=0 C=1 -> specificity =   1
div p              A=0 B=0 C=2 -> specificity =   2
ul ol+li           A=0 B=0 C=3 -> specificity =   3
h1 + *[REL=up]     A=0 B=1 C=1 -> specificity =  11
ul ol li.red       A=0 B=1 C=3 -> specificity =  13
li.red.level       A=0 B=2 C=1 -> specificity =  21
#columnhead        A=1 B=0 C=0 -> specificity = 100
```

Note that the selector #columnhead, which refers to an element with a specific ID attribute, is given a high specificity, whereas the wildcard selector (*) is given a low specificity, as you would expect.

Summary

CSS can be a complex beast if documents have several style sheets or otherwise create competing and conflicting styles. However, definite rules are in place to handle competing sheets and individual competing styles — rules that effectively address the needs of a document's author, the user of a document, and the user agent displaying the document. Understanding the style sheet cascade, style inheritance, and specificity eliminates any doubt as to how your documents will be displayed.

CHAPTER 29

Font Properties

IN THIS CHAPTER

As previously mentioned throughout this book, the Web began as a vehicle for displaying very plain documents. The documents in question were of the research variety, needing only basic font handling, tables for data display, and the inclusion of graphics.

However, the Web has come a long way from that simple beginning. As more entities embraced the medium, the technology became more robust and able to handle more desktop publishing–like capabilities. Today's Web technologies can produce documents almost as rich in content and presentation as those produced by modern, dedicated publishing programs.

The most important characteristics are typography and layout. This chapter covers typography — namely, fonts — and how CSS handles them.

Understanding Fonts

Fonts are stylized collections of letters and symbols, known as *glyphs*. Fonts can be used to convey information — for example, specialized fonts can provide special characters or symbols. Although fonts can be quite different from one another, they share the same basic characteristics, as shown in Figure 29-1.

FIGURE 29-1

Font characteristics

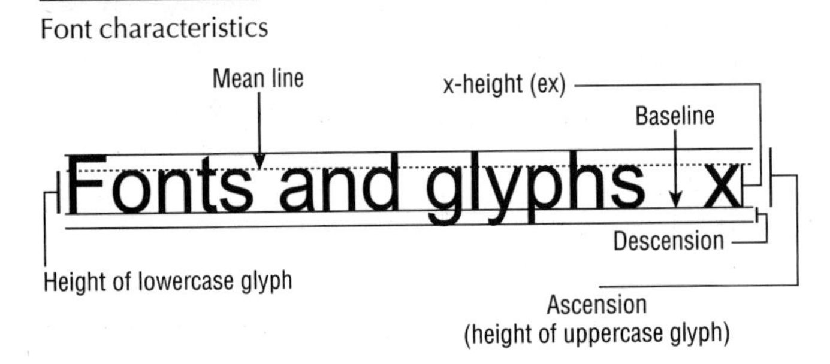

These elements are defined as follows:

- **Baseline** — The line on which glyphs of the font sit
- **Ascension** — The highest point reached by most capital glyphs in the font. Note that technically the ascension is the point at which the highest glyph reaches, as some fonts have special, ornate characters that reach higher than other, normal characters.
- **Descension** — The lowest position that some glyphs, such as *p*, *g*, or *q*, reach
- **Mean line** — The highest point that lowercase glyphs reach
- **x-height** — The height of the letter *x* in the font. Note that this is usually the same as the mean line, but occasionally the two heights are different. In addition, this value exists for all fonts, whether they contain an *x* or not.

Fonts are spaced vertically according to a system similar to ruled paper. Vertical font measurements, such as line spacing or leading, are typically measured between the baselines of text, at least as far as CSS is concerned. The spacing between individual glyphs is letter-spacing, and can vary between fonts and be adjusted within a font.

CSS offers many properties to control the fonts in your documents.

Font Types

CSS supports five different font family types (see Figure 29-2). These general types can be used to apprise a user agent of the type of font face it should use. The five families are as follows:

- **Serif** — Serif fonts have ornamentation on each glyph. Typically, serif fonts are used in body text. The finishing strokes, flared or tapering ends, or serifed endings, make the lines of characters flow and tend to be easier on the eyes.
- **Sans-serif** — These fonts are fairly plain, having little or no ornamentation on their glyphs. Sans-serif fonts are typically used for headings or other large areas of emphasis.
- **Cursive** — Cursive fonts are quite ornate, approximating cursive writing. Such fonts should be used only in extreme cases where the emphasis is on ornamentation, rather than legibility.

- **Fantasy** — Fantasy fonts, much like cursive fonts, emphasize ornamentation over legibility. Fantasy fonts come in many styles but still retain the basic shape of letters. Like cursive fonts, fantasy fonts are generally used for logos and other ornamentation purposes where legibility is secondary to a particular look or design.
- **Monospace** — Monospace fonts come in serif and sans-serif varieties but all share the same attribute: All characters in the font have the same width. The effect is much like characters on a text-based terminal or typewriter. Such fonts are generally used in code listings and other listings approximating terminal output.

FIGURE 29-2

The five CSS-supported font types

Serif
Sans-serif
Cursive
Fantasy
Monospace

The `font-family` property defines the font or fonts that should be used in the document or specific element to which the property is attached. The property has the following format:

```
font-family: [[ <family-name> | <generic-family> ][,
  <family-name> | <generic-family>]*] ;
```

Essentially, the property defines one or more font families that should be used, via an actual font name or a generic name. For example, to select a sans-serif font, you might use a definition similar to the following:

```
font-family: Verdana, Arial, Helvetica, Sans-Serif;
```

Tip

If the font family names contain any spaces they should be enclosed in quotes. ■

Note that this definition uses three specific family names (Verdana, Arial, Helvetica) and a generic family name (Sans-Serif) for versatility. The definition instructs the user agent that the sans-serif font Verdana should be used. If it is unavailable, the Arial font (popular on Windows-based platforms) should be used. If neither of those fonts is available, the Helvetica font should be used (popular on Macintosh-based platforms and other PostScript-based systems).

If none of the previously specified fonts are available, the user agent should use its default sans-serif font.

Tip

The preceding font-family definition is a good, universal sans-serif font specification that can be used for any platform. Likewise, the following definition can be used for a universal serif font specification:

```
font-family:  Palatino, "Times New Roman", "Times Roman", Serif; ■
```

The `font-family` definition doesn't control the font variant (bold, italic, and so on), size, letter spacing, and so forth. It does specify the font that should be used as the basis for fonts in the element where the `font-family` definition is placed. Individual font variant tags and elements (`<b>`, `<i>`, and so on) determine the variant of the font used when those variant elements are encountered by the browser. If the base font cannot be used for the variant, then the browser substitutes another font in the current font's stead.

Style definitions to set up a document in traditional serif font body text and bold sans-serif font headings would resemble the following:

```
body { font-family:  Palatino, "Times New Roman", "Times Roman", Serif; }
h1, h2, h3, h4, h5, h6 {
  font-family: Verdana, Arial, Helvetica, Sans-Serif;
  font-weight: bold; }
```

Font Sizing

Two properties can be used to control font sizing: `font-size` and `font-size-adjust`. Both properties can adjust a font absolutely or relative to the current font size. Possible value metrics are shown in Table 29-1.

The `font-size` property is used to set the actual size of the current font. For example, you could set an absolute font size of 12pt with the following property:

```
font-size: 12pt;
```

Likewise, you can adjust the font size relative to the current font size. For example, to set the font size to double its current size, you could use a property similar to this:

```
font-size: 200%;
```

TABLE 29-1

Font Size Value Metrics

Metric	Description
Absolute size keywords	Keywords corresponding to user agent absolute font sizes. These keywords include `xx-small`, `x-small`, `small`, `medium`, `large`, `x-large`, and `xx-large`.
Relative size keywords	Keywords corresponding to user agent relative font sizes. These keywords include `larger` and `smaller`.
Absolute size	An absolute value corresponding to a font size. Negative values are not supported, but supported values include point sizes (e.g., `12pt`) and, optionally (although not as exact), other size values such as pixels (e.g., `10px`).
Percentage size	A percentage corresponding to a percentage of the current font. These values can be expressed in actual percentages (e.g., `150%`) or other relative metrics such as ems (e.g., `1.5em`).

The `font-size-adjust` property adjusts the aspect of the current font. The aspect of a font is the ratio between its size and x-height values. Tweaking this aspect can improve the legibility of some fonts at smaller sizes, but usually the aspect should not be changed.

Font Styling

Four properties can be used to affect font styling: `font-style`, `font-variant`, `font-weight`, and `font-stretch`. The syntax of each is shown in the following listing:

```
font-style: normal | italic | oblique;
font-variant: normal | small-caps;
font-weight: normal | bold | bolder | lighter | 100 | 200 |
  300 | 400 | 500 | 600 | 700 | 800 | 900;
font-stretch: normal | wider | narrower | ultra-condensed |
  extra-condensed | condensed | semi-condensed | semi-expanded |
  expanded | extra-expanded | ultra-expanded;
```

The `font-style` property controls the italic style of the text, whereas the `font-weight` property controls the bold style of the text. The other two properties control other display attributes of the font; `font-variant` controls whether the font is displayed in small caps, and `font-stretch` does exactly what its name suggests — stretches the font by adjusting its letter spacing.

The various values for the `font-weight` property can be broken down as follows:

- `100-900` — The font's darkness, where `100` is the lightest and `900` the darkest. Various numbers correspond to other values, as described in the following bulleted points.
- `lighter` — Specifies the next lightest setting for a font unless the font weight is already near the weight value corresponding to `100`, in which case it stays at `100`.

- `normal` — The normal darkness for the current font; it corresponds to weight 400.
- `bold` — The darkness corresponding to the font's bold variety; it corresponds to weight 700.
- `bolder` — Specifies the next darkest setting for a font unless the font weight is already near the weight value corresponding to 900, in which case it stays at 900.

The `font-style` and `font-weight` properties can be used to control a font's bold and italic properties without coding document text directly with italic (`i`) and bold (`b`) elements. For example, you might define a bold variety of a style using definitions similar to the following:

```
p { font-family:  Palatino, "Times New Roman", "Times Roman", Serif; }
p.bold { font-weight: bold; }
```

The `bold` class of the paragraph element inherits the base font from its parent, the paragraph element. The `font-weight` property in the `bold` class of the paragraph element simply makes such styled elements render as a bold variety of the base font.

Line Spacing

The `line-height` property controls the line height of text. The line height is the distance between the baseline of two vertically stacked lines of text. This value is also known as *leading*.

Note

Refer to Figure 29-1 for an illustration of the baseline of a font. ■

The `line-height` property has the following syntax:

```
line-height: normal | <number> | <length> | <percentage>
```

This property sets the size of the surrounding box of the element for which it is applied, affecting the vertical distance between text lines. The normal value sets the line height to the default size for the current font. Specifying a number (for example, 2) causes the current line height to be multiplied by the number specified. Absolute lengths (for example, `1.2em`) cause the line height to be set to that absolute value. A percentage value is handled like a number value; the percentage is applied to the current font's value. Note that this property does not change the size of the font, only the distance between the lines of text.

For example, the following two definitions both set a class up to double-space text:

```
p.doublespace { line-height: 2; }
p.doublespace { line-height: 200%; }
```

Embedding Fonts in a Document

Two technologies exist to enable you to embed fonts in your documents, though support for either is almost non-existent. Embedding fonts enables your readers to download the specific font to their local machine so your documents use the *exact* font you designate.

Unfortunately, as with most progressive Web technologies, the market is split into distinct factions:

- OpenType is a standard developed by Microsoft and Adobe Systems. OpenType fonts, thanks to the creators of the standard, share similar traits with PostScript and TrueType fonts used in other publishing applications. Currently, only Internet Explorer supports OpenType.
- TrueDoc is a standard developed by BitStream, a popular font manufacturer. Currently, only Netscape-based browsers natively support TrueDoc fonts, but BitStream does make an ActiveX control for support on Internet Explorer.

Note

Even when a font is available for low cost or without cost, that doesn't mean you can reuse it, especially in a commercial application. When acquiring fonts for use on the Web, make sure that you have the appropriate rights for the use you intend. ■

To embed OpenType fonts in your document, you use an `@font-face` definition in the style section of your document. The `@font-face` definition has the following syntax:

```
@font-face { font-definition }
```

The `font-definition` contains information about the font, including stylistic information and the path to the font file. This information is contained in typical `property: value` form, similar to the following:

```
@font-face {
  font-family: Dax;
  font-weight: bold;
  src: url('http://www.example.com/fontdir/Dax.pfr');
}
```

To embed TrueDoc fonts in your document, you use the link tag (`<link>`) in a format similar to the following:

```
<link rel="fontdef" src="http://www.example.com/fontdir/Amelia.pfr" />
```

To use TrueDoc fonts in Internet Explorer you also have to include the TrueDoc ActiveX control using code like the following:

```
<script language="JavaScript" src="http://www.truedoc.com/activex/tdserver.js">
</script>
```

Tip

Several fonts are available for use from the TrueDoc website: `www.truedoc.com`. ■

Embedding fonts is not recommended for several reasons:

- The two standards make supporting embedded fonts difficult.
- Embedded fonts increase the download time of your document and increase the overall load on the user agent.

- Embedded fonts decrease the flexibility of your documents, limiting how user agents can adjust the display of text.

Instead of using embedded fonts, I recommend that you stick to CSS definitions for specifying font attributes. If you know your audience and their platform and you need your document to look *exactly* as you intend, investigate embedded fonts.

Summary

This chapter is the first of the topical coverage chapters in this CSS part. In this chapter, you learned about fonts — how to present them, control them, and even embed them, if you so choose. The following several chapters continue to present CSS subject matter in concrete, related chunks.

CHAPTER

30

Text Formatting

IN THIS CHAPTER

The Web was initially text-based, and text is still a major part of online content today. CSS offers many styles for text formatting, from simple justification to autogenerated text. Although CSS includes options for page layout without tables, it also includes styles for formatting HTML tables. This chapter covers the basics of text and table formatting with CSS.

Aligning Text

Multiple properties in CSS control the formatting of text. Several properties enable you to align text horizontally and vertically — aligning with other pieces of text or other elements around them.

Controlling horizontal alignment

You can use the `text-align` property to align blocks of text in four basic ways: left, right, center, or full. The following code and the output displayed in Figure 30-1 show the effect of the justification settings:

```
<!DOCTYPE HTML PUBLIC "-//W3C//DTD HTML 4.01//EN"
  "http://www.w3.org/TR/html4/strict.dtd">
<html>
<head>
  <title>Text Justification</title>
  <style type="text/css">
    p.left { text-align: left;}
    p.right { text-align: right;}
    p.center { text-align: center;}
    p.full { text-align: justify;}
  </style>
</head>
<body>
```

```
<div style="margin: 50px">
<h3>Left Justified (default)</h3>
<p class="left">The Oasis boasts three saunas, two whirlpools, and
a full-size swimming pool for the use of our clients. Each of these
facilities has a small usage fee, but many services include the use
of one or more of these facilities--be sure to ask your service
consultant about our many combination packages.</p>
<h3>Right Justified</h3>
<p class="right">The Oasis boasts three saunas, two whirlpools, and
a full-size swimming pool for the use of our clients. Each of these
facilities has a small usage fee, but many services include the use
of one or more of these facilities--be sure to ask your service
consultant about our many combination packages.</p>
<h3>Center Justified</h3>
<p class="center">The Oasis boasts three saunas, two whirlpools, and
a full-size swimming pool for the use of our clients. Each of these
facilities has a small usage fee, but many services include the use
of one or more of these facilities--be sure to ask your service
consultant about our many combination packages.</p>
<h3>Fully Justified</h3>
<p class="full">The Oasis boasts three saunas, two whirlpools, and
a full-size swimming pool for the use of our clients. Each of these
facilities has a small usage fee, but many services include the use
of one or more of these facilities--be sure to ask your service
consultant about our many combination packages.</p>
</div>
</body>
</html>
```

Note that the default justification is left; that is, the lines in the block of text are aligned against the left margin, and the lines wrap where convenient on the right, leaving a jagged right margin.

In addition to the four standard alignment options, you can also use `text-align` to align columnar data in tables to a specific character. For example, the following code results in the data in the Balance column being aligned on the decimal place:

```
<!DOCTYPE HTML PUBLIC "-//W3C//DTD HTML 4.01//EN"
  "http://www.w3.org/TR/html4/strict.dtd">
<html>
<head>
  <title>Table Column Justification</title>
  <style type="text/css">
    td.dec { text-align: ".";}
  </style>
</head>
<body>
  <table border="1">
  <tr>
    <th>Customer</th>
    <th>Balance</th>
  </tr>
```

```
    <tr>
      <td>Wendy Weatherbee</td>
      <td class="dec">$50.95</td>
    </tr>
    <tr>
      <td>Katy Keene</td>
      <td class="dec">$284.99</td>
    </tr>
    <tr>
      <td>Elizabeth Cooper</td>
      <td class="dec">$90.99</td>
    </tr>
    <tr>
      <td>Ronnie Lodge</td>
      <td class="dec">$525.99</td>
    </tr>
    <tr>
      <td>Nancy Woods</td>
      <td class="dec">$410.99</td>
    </tr>
    </table>
  </body>
  </html>
```

FIGURE 30-1

The four types of text justification

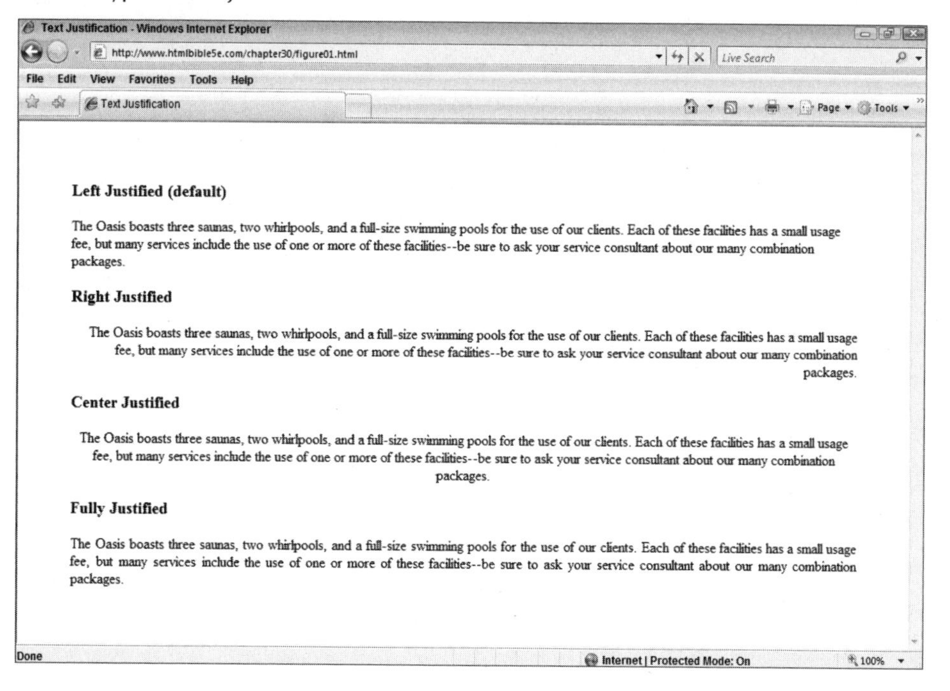

Note

Columnar alignment using the `text-align` property is not well supported in current user agents. You should test your target agents to ensure compliance before using `text-align` this way. ■

Controlling vertical alignment

In addition to aligning text horizontally, CSS also enables you to align text vertically via the `vertical-align` property. The `vertical-align` property supports the following values:

- `baseline` — This is the default vertical alignment; text uses its baseline to align to other objects around it.
- `sub` — This value causes the text to descend to the level appropriate for subscripted text based on its parent's font size and line height. (This value has no effect on the size of the text, only its position.)
- `super` — This value causes the text to ascend to the level appropriate for superscripted text based on its parent's font size and line height. (This value has no effect on the size of the text, only its position.)
- `top` — This value causes the top of the element's bounding box to be aligned with the top of the element's parent bounding box.
- `text-top` — This value causes the top of the element's bounding box to be aligned with the top of the element's parent text.
- `middle` — This value causes the text to be aligned using the middle of the text and the midline of objects around it.
- `bottom` — This value causes the bottom of the element's bounding box to be aligned with the bottom of the element's parent bounding box.
- `text-bottom` — This value causes the bottom of the element's bounding box to be aligned with the bottom of the element's parent text.
- `length` — This value causes the element to ascend (positive value) or descend (negative value) by the value specified.
- `percentage` — This value causes the element to ascend (positive value) or descend (negative value) by the percentage specified. The percentage is applied to the element's line height.

The following code and the output displayed in Figure 30-2 show the effect of each value:

```
<!DOCTYPE HTML PUBLIC "-//W3C//DTD HTML 4.01//EN"
  "http://www.w3.org/TR/html4/strict.dtd">
<html>
<head>
  <title>Vertical Text Alignment</title>
  <style type="text/css">
    .baseline { vertical-align: baseline;}
```

```
    .sub { vertical-align: sub;}
    .super { vertical-align: super;}
    .top { vertical-align: top;}
    .text-top { vertical-align: text-top;}
    .middle { vertical-align: middle;}
    .bottom { vertical-align: bottom;}
    .text-bottom { vertical-align: text-bottom;}
    .length { vertical-align: .5em;}
    .percentage { vertical-align: -50%;}
     /* All elements get a border */
     body * { border: 1px solid black;}
     /* Parent (paragraph) font larger for visibility
     p { font=size: 150%;}
     /* Reduce the spans' font by 50% */
     p * { font-size: 50%;}
  </style>
</head>
<body>
  <p>Baseline: Parent
    <span class="baseline">aligned text</span> text</p>
  <p>Sub: Parent
    <span class="sub">aligned text</span> text</p>
  <p>Super: Parent
    <span class="super">aligned text</span> text</p>
  <p>Top: Parent
    <span class="top">aligned text</span> text</p>
  <p>Text-top: Parent
    <span class="text-top">aligned text</span> text</p>
  <p>Middle: Parent
    <span class="middle">aligned text</span> text</p>
  <p>Bottom: Parent
    <span class="bottom">aligned text</span> text</p>
  <p>Text-bottom: Parent
    <span class="text-bottom">aligned text</span> text</p>
  <p>Length: Parent
    <span class="length">aligned text</span> text</p>
  <p>Percentage: Parent
    <span class="percentage">aligned text</span> text</p>
</body>
</html>
```

Of course, text isn't the only element that can be affected by the `vertical-align` property. Figure 30-3 shows an image next to text. The image has the `vertical-align` property set to middle. Note how the midpoint of the image is aligned to the text beside it.

FIGURE 30-2

The effect of various vertical-align settings. (Borders were added to the text to help contrast the alignment.)

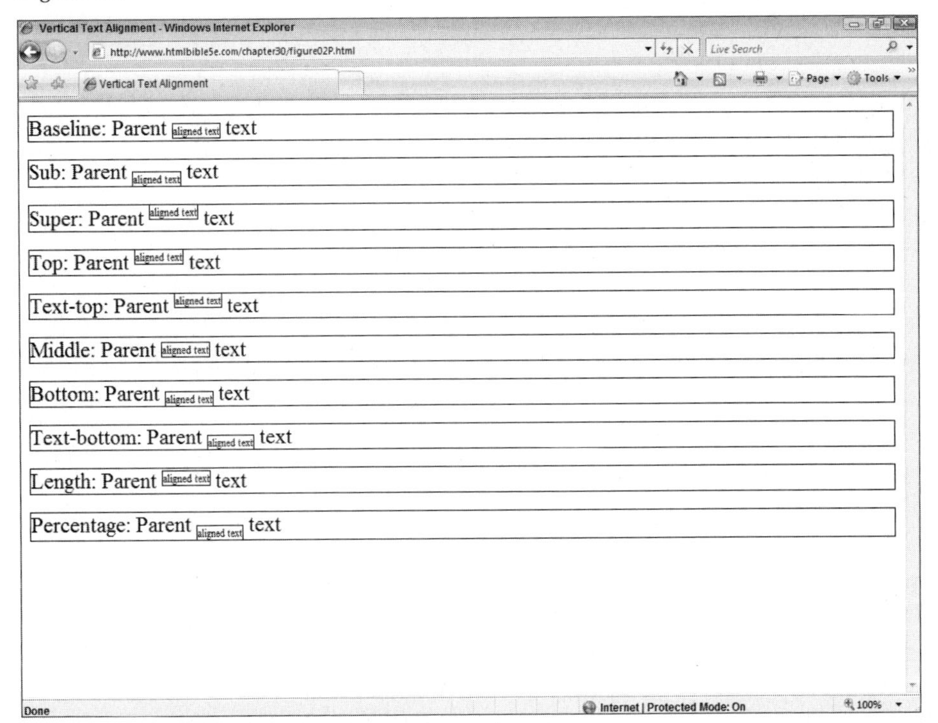

Indenting Text

You can use the `text-indent` property to indent the first line of an element. For example, to indent the first line of a paragraph of text by 25 pixels, you could use code similar to the following:

```
<p style="text-indent: 25px;">The Oasis boasts three saunas, two
whirlpools, and a full-size swimming pool for the use of our clients.
Each of these facilities has a small usage fee, but many services
include the use of one or more of these facilities--be sure to ask
your service consultant about our many combination packages.</p>
```

Note that the `text-indent` property indents only the first line of the element. If you want to indent the entire element, use the appropriate `margin` properties instead.

Cross-Ref

See Chapter 32 for more information about the `margin` properties. ■

FIGURE 30-3

The vertical-align property can be used to vertically align most elements.

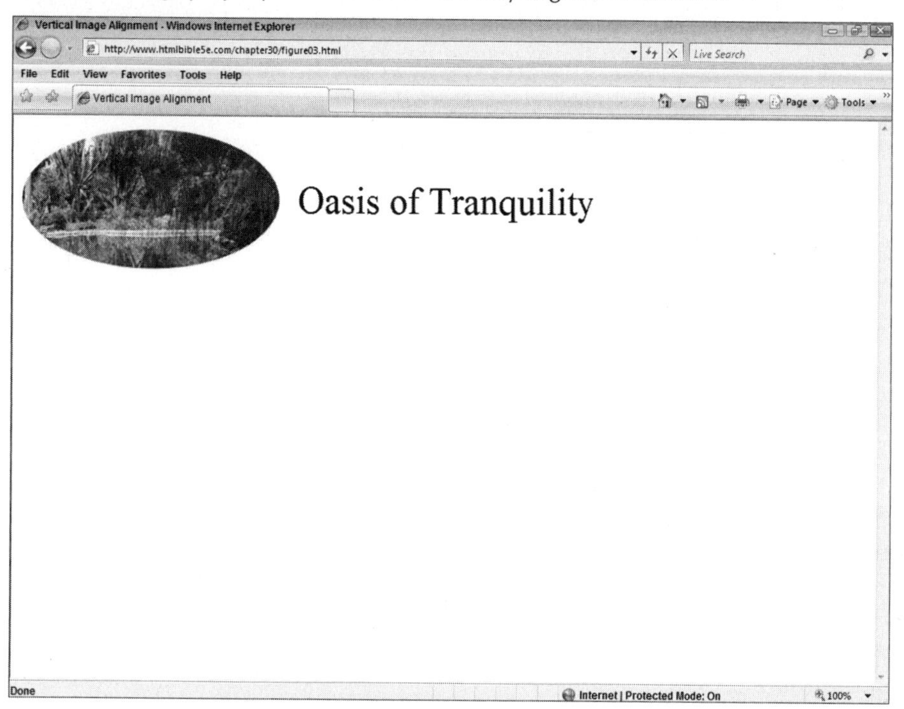

You can specify the indent as a specific value (`1in`, `25px`, and so on), or as a percentage of the containing element's width. When specifying the indent as a percentage, the width of the containing element(s) will play a prominent role in the actual size of the indentation. Therefore, when you want a uniform indent, use a specific value.

Controlling White Space Within Text

White space is typically not a concern in HTML documents. However, at times you'll want better control over how white space is interpreted and how certain elements line up to their siblings.

Clearing floating objects

The `float` property can cause elements to ignore the normal flow of the document and "float" against a particular margin. For example, consider the following code, whose resulting output is shown in Figure 30-4:

```
<!DOCTYPE HTML PUBLIC "-//W3C//DTD HTML 4.01//EN"
  "http://www.w3.org/TR/html4/strict.dtd">
<html>
```

```
<head>
  <title>Floating Image</title>
</head>
<body>
  <p><b>Floating Image</b><br>
  <img src="sphere.png" style="float: right;" />
  The Oasis boasts three saunas, two whirlpools, and a full-size
swimming pool for the use of our clients. Each of these facilities
has a small usage fee, but many services include the use of one or
more of these facilities--be sure to ask your service consultant
about our many combination packages.</p>
  <p><b>Non-Floating Image</b><br>
  <img src="sphere.png" />
  The Oasis boasts three saunas, two whirlpools, and a full-size
swimming pool for the use of our clients. Each of these facilities
has a small usage fee, but many services include the use of one or
more of these facilities--be sure to ask your service consultant
about our many combination packages.</p>
</body>
</html>
```

FIGURE 30-4

Floating images can add a dynamic feel to your document.

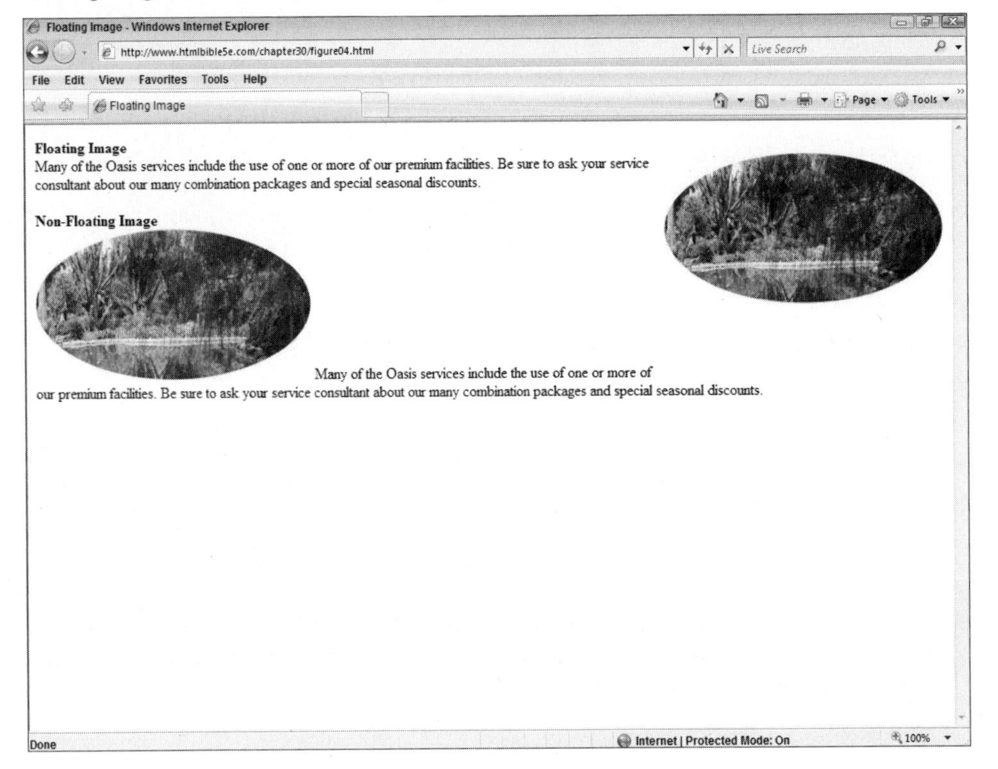

Although floating images can add an attractive, dynamic air to your documents, their placement is not always predictable. As such, it's helpful to be able to indicate that specific elements should not allow floating elements next to them. One good example of when you would want to disallow floating elements is next to headings. Consider the document shown in Figure 30-5.

FIGURE 30-5

Floating images can sometimes get in the way of positioning other elements, such as headings.

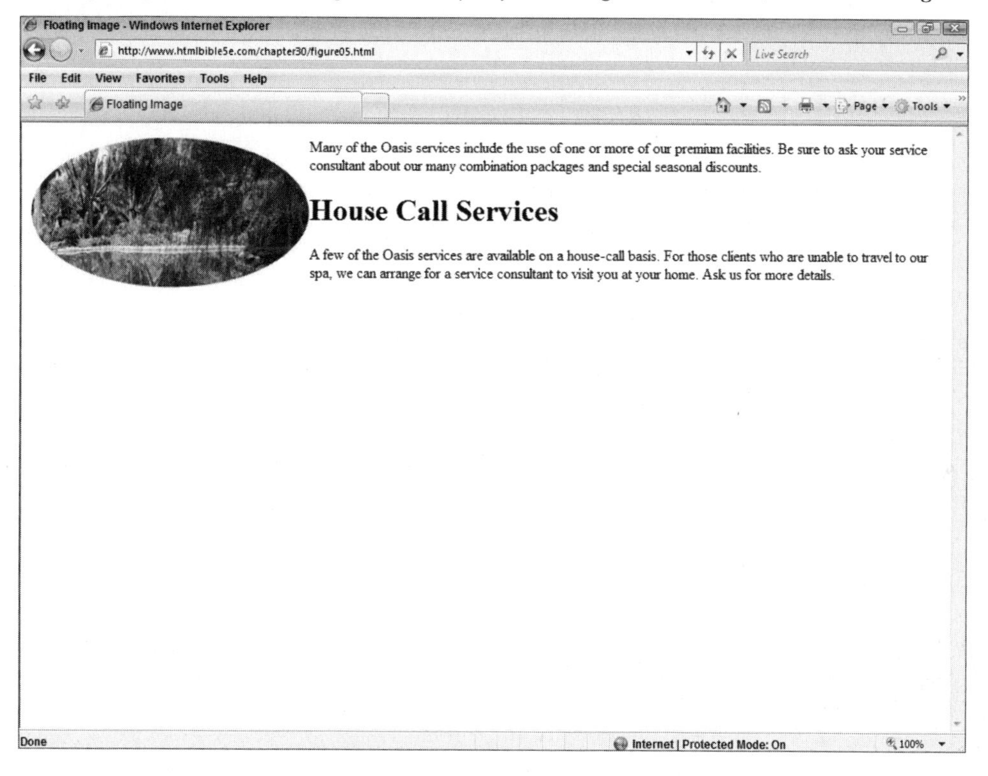

Using the `clear` property, you can ensure that one side or both sides of an element remain free of floating elements. You can specify `left`, `right`, `both`, or `none` (the default) for values of the `clear` property. Note that the `clear` property doesn't affect the floating element. Instead, it forces the element containing the `clear` property to avoid the floating element(s) by placing itself after the floating element(s).

For example, adding the following style to the document shown in Figure 30-5 ensures that both sides of all heading levels are clear of floating elements. This results in the display shown in Figure 30-6, with the heading being placed after the floating figure.

```
h1,h2,h3,h4,h5,h6 { clear: both;}
```

FIGURE 30-6

Use the clear property to force an element to start past the floating element's bounding box (and before any additional floating elements begin).

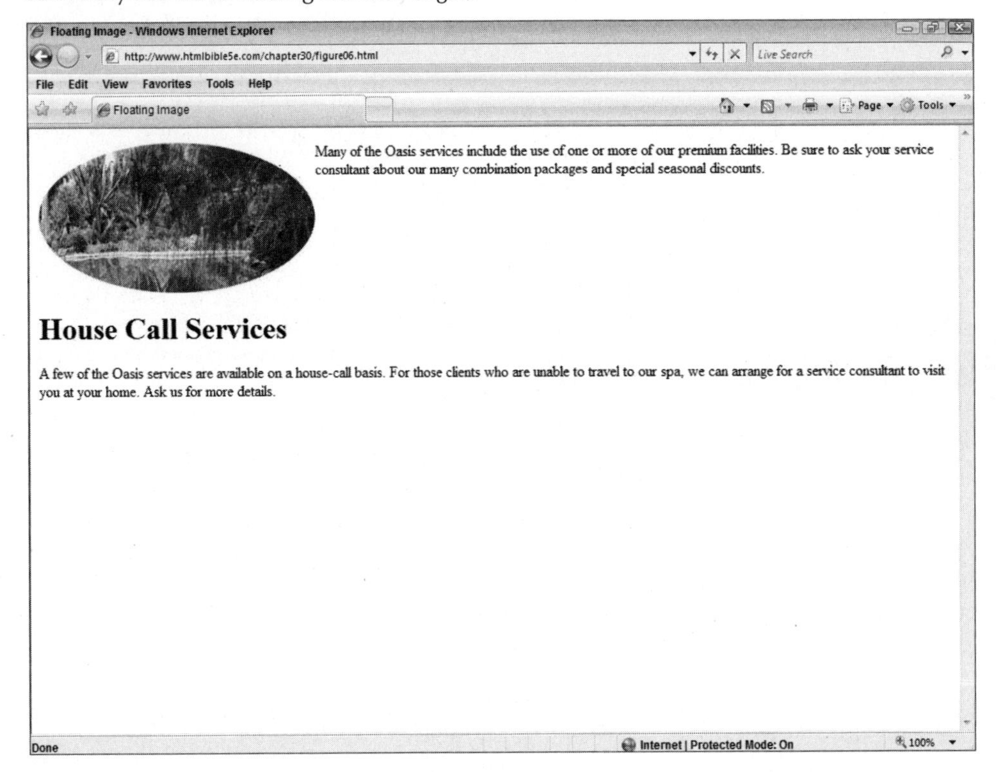

The white-space property

User agents typically ignore extraneous white space in documents. However, at times you want the white space to be interpreted literally, without having to use a <pre> tag to do so. Enter the `white-space` property.

The `white-space` property can be set to the following values:

- `normal`
- `pre`
- `nowrap`

The default setting is `normal` — that is, ignore extraneous white space.

If the property is set to `pre`, text will be rendered as though it were enclosed in a <pre> tag. Using `pre` does not affect the font or other formatting of the element; it just causes white space to be rendered verbatim. For example, the following text will be spaced exactly as shown in the following code:

```
<p style="white-space:  pre;">This         paragraph's   words
 are irregularly          spaced,       but will be rendered     as
     such
by       the                user             agent.</p>
```

Setting the `white-space` property to `nowrap` causes the element not to wrap at the right margin of the user agent. Instead, it continues to the right until the next explicit line break. User agents should add horizontal scroll bars to enable users to fully view the content.

Note

Text contained in a `pre` element is displayed using a monospace font. If you preserve white space by using the `white-space` property with a value of `pre`, your document will generally be rendered in a proportional font. ■

Controlling Letter and Word Spacing

The `letter-spacing` and `word-spacing` properties can be used to control the letter and word spacing in an element, respectively. Both elements take an explicit or relative value to adjust the spacing — positive values add more space, negative values remove space. For example, consider the following code, whose output is shown in Figure 30-7:

```
<!DOCTYPE HTML PUBLIC "-//W3C//DTD HTML 4.01//EN"
  "http://www.w3.org/TR/html4/strict.dtd">
<html>
<head>
  <title>Letter Spacing</title>
  <style type="text/css">
    .normal { letter-spacing: normal; }
    .tight  { letter-spacing: -.2em; }
    .loose  { letter-spacing: .2em; }
  </style>
</head>
<body>
  <h3>Normal</h3>
  <p class="normal"> The Oasis boasts three saunas, two whirlpools,
and a full-size swimming pool for the use of our clients. Each of
these facilities has a small usage fee, but many services include
the use of one or more of these facilities--be sure to ask your
service consultant about our many combination packages.</p>
  <h3>Tight</h3>
  <p class="tight"> The Oasis boasts three saunas, two whirlpools,
and a full-size swimming pool for the use of our clients. Each of
these facilities has a small usage fee, but many services include
```

```
the use of one or more of these facilities--be sure to ask your
service consultant about our many combination packages.</p>
   <h3>Loose</h3>
   <p class="loose"> The Oasis boasts three saunas, two whirlpools,
and a full-size swimming pool for the use of our clients. Each of
these facilities has a small usage fee, but many services include
the use of one or more of these facilities--be sure to ask your
service consultant about our many combination packages.</p>
 </body>
 </html>
```

FIGURE 30-7

The letter-spacing property does exactly what its name indicates; it adjusts the spacing between letters.

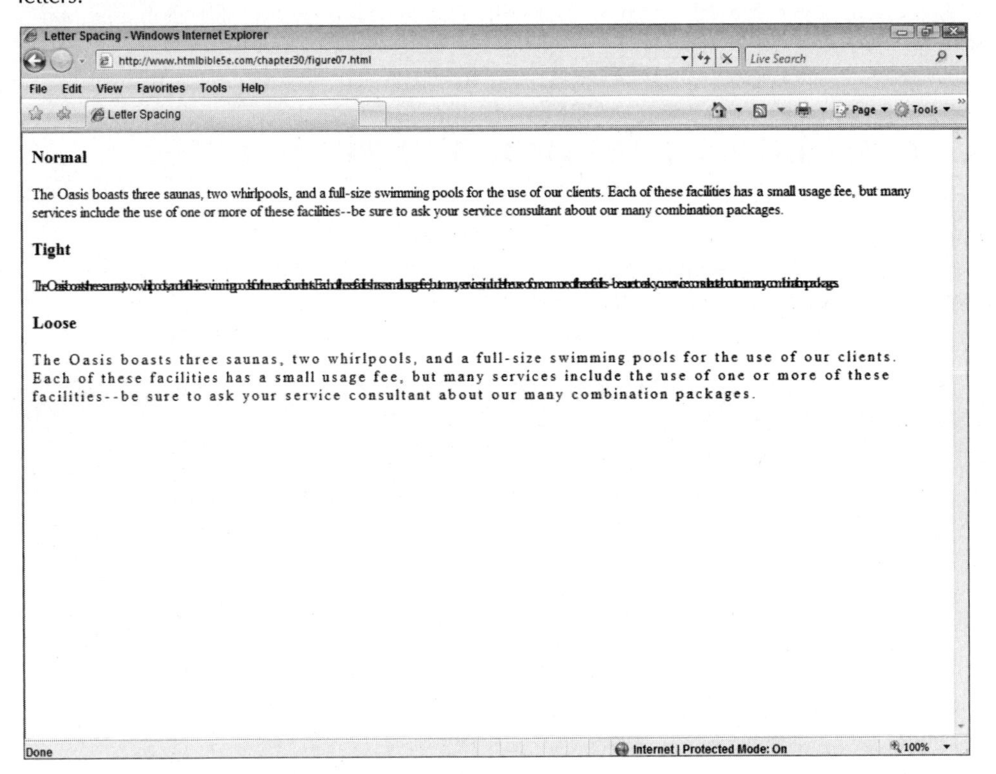

Note that the user agent can govern the minimum amount of letter spacing allowed. Setting the letter spacing to too small a value can have unpredictable results.

The word-spacing property behaves exactly like the letter-spacing property, except that it controls the spacing between words instead of letters. Like letter-spacing, using a positive value with word-spacing results in more space between words, and using a negative value results in less space.

Specifying Capitalization

You can also use styles to control the capitalization, or case, of text. The text-transform property can be set to four different values, as shown in the following code and Figure 30-8:

```
<!DOCTYPE HTML PUBLIC "-//W3C//DTD HTML 4.01//EN"
  "http://www.w3.org/TR/html4/strict.dtd">
<html>
<head>
  <title>Letter Spacing</title>
  <style type="text/css">
    .normal { text-transform: none;}
    .initcaps { text-transform: capitalize;}
    .upper { text-transform: uppercase;}
    .lower { text-transform: lowercase;}
  </style>
</head>
<body>
  <h3>Normal</h3>
  <p class="normal"> Many of the OASIS services include the use of
one or more of our premium facilities. Be sure to ask your service
consultant about our many combination packages and special seasonal
discounts.</p>
  <h3>Initial Caps</h3>
  <p class="initcaps"> Many of the OASIS services include the use of
one or more of our premium facilities. Be sure to ask your service
consultant about our many combination packages and special seasonal
discounts.</p>
  <h3>Uppercase</h3>
  <p class="upper"> Many of the OASIS services include the use of
one or more of our premium facilities. Be sure to ask your service
consultant about our many combination packages and special seasonal
discounts.</p>
  <h3>Lowercase</h3>
  <p class="lower"> Many of the OASIS services include the use of
one or more of our premium facilities. Be sure to ask your service
consultant about our many combination packages and special seasonal
discounts.</p>
</body>
</html>
```

FIGURE 30-8

The text-transform property enables you to influence the capitalization of elements.

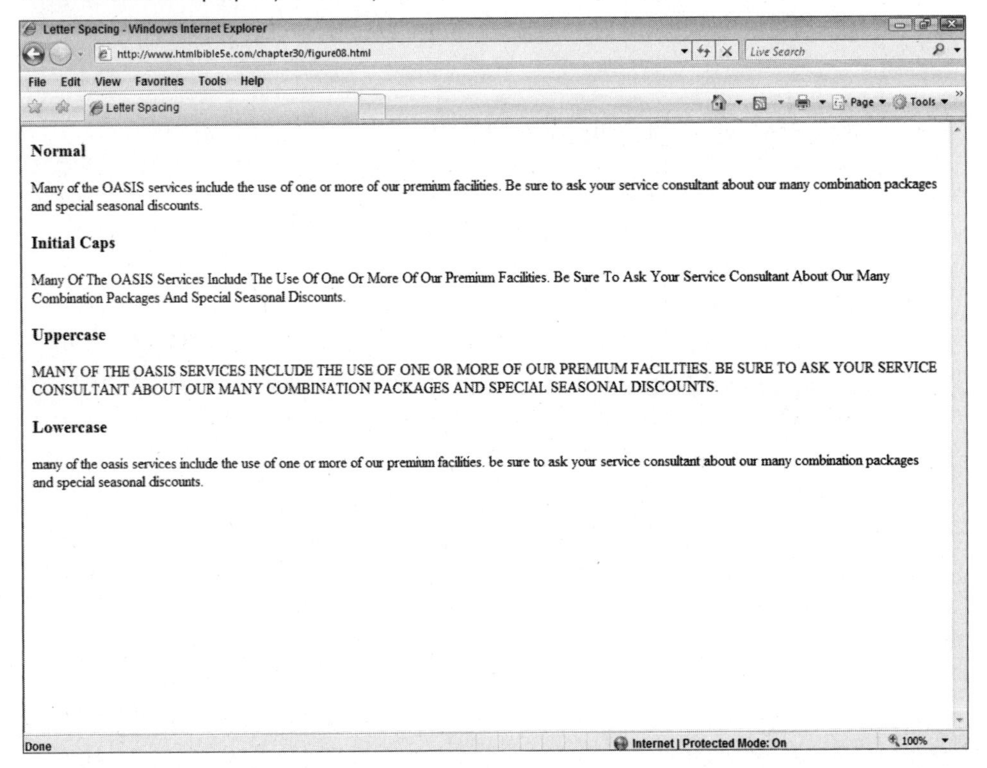

There are some rules as to what `text-transform` will and won't affect. For example, the `capitalize` value ensures that each word starts with a capital letter, but it doesn't change the case of the rest of the word. Likewise, setting the property to `normal` will not change the case of the element (for example, "OASIS" remains in all caps).

Using Text Decorations

You can add several different effects to text through CSS. Most are accomplished via the `text-decoration` and `text-shadow` properties.

The text-decoration property enables you to add the following attributes to text:

- underline
- overline (line above text)
- line-through
- blink

As with most properties, the values are straightforward:

```
<p style="text-decoration: none;">No Decoration</p>
<p style="text-decoration: underline;">Underlined</p>
<p style="text-decoration: overline;">Overlined</p>
<p style="text-decoration: line-through;">Line Through</p>
<p style="text-decoration: blink;">Blink</p>
```

The text-shadow property is a bit more complex but can add stunning drop shadow effects to text. The text-shadow property has the following format:

```
text-shadow: "[color] horizontal-distance
vertical-distance [blur]"
```

The property takes two values to offset the shadow: one horizontal, the other vertical. Positive values set the shadow down and to the right. Negative values set the shadow up and to the left. Using combinations of negative and positive settings, you can move the shadow to any location relative to the text it affects.

The optional color value sets the color of the shadow. The blur value specifies the blur radius — or the width of the effect — for the shadow. The exact algorithm for computing the blur radius is not specified by the CSS specification, so your experience may vary with this value.

The text-shadow property enables multiple shadow definitions for multiple shadows. Simply separate the definitions with commas.

The following code creates a drop shadow on all h1 headings. The shadow is set to display above and to the right of the text in a gray color:

```
h1 { text-shadow: #666666 2em -2em;}
```

The following definition provides the same shadow as the previous example but adds another, lighter gray shadow directly below the text:

```
h1 { text-shadow: #666666 2em -2em, #AAAAAA 0em 2em;}
```

Unfortunately, not many user agents support text-shadow. If you want such an effect, you might be better off creating it with a graphic instead of text.

Autogenerated Text

CSS has a few mechanisms for autogenerating text. Although this doesn't fit in well with the presentation-only function of CSS, it can be useful to have some constructs to automatically generate text for your documents. There are properties and elements to automatically supply quotation marks, provide arbitrary text before or after an element, or autogenerate a counter.

Cross-Ref

Although these properties bear mention here, they are covered in depth with the other pseudo-elements and generated content in Chapter 35. ■

Using CSS Table Properties

Because the `<table>` tag attributes, such as `border`, `rules`, `cellpadding`, and `cellspacing`, have not been deprecated, you might be tempted to use them instead of CSS properties when defining your tables. You should resist that temptation.

Using styles for tables provides the same advantages as using styles for any other element — consistency, flexibility, and the ability to easily change the format later.

For example, consider the following table tag:

```
<table border="1" width="200px" cellpadding="3px"
    cellspacing="5px">
```

Now suppose you had four tables using this same beginning tag in your document, and you had four other documents just like it. What if you decided to decrease the width of the table and increase the padding within the tables? You would have to edit each table manually, potentially 16 individual tables between four documents.

If the table formatting were contained in styles at the top of the documents, you would have to make only four changes, one change in each document. Better yet, if the formatting were contained in a separate, external style sheet, you would have to make only one change.

Note

The CSS `border` properties are used to control table borders, and the `padding` and `margin` properties are used to affect the spacing of cells and the padding of their contents. ■

Controlling Table Attributes

You can use CSS properties to control the formatting of tables, but note that some of the property names do not match up with the tag attributes. For example, there are no `cellspacing` or cellpadding CSS properties. The border-spacing and padding CSS properties fill those roles, respectively.

Table 30-1 shows how CSS properties match table tag attributes.

Each of the various properties is covered in the following sections.

TABLE 30-1

CSS Properties for Table Attributes

Purpose	Table Attribute	CSS Property(ies)
Borders	border	border properties
Spacing inside cell	cellpadding	padding properties
Spacing between cells	cellspacing	border-spacing property
Width of table	width	width and table-layout properties
Table framing	frame	border properties
Alignment	align, valign	text-align, vertical-align properties

Table borders

You can use the border properties to control the border of a table and its sub-elements, just like any other element. For example, the following definition causes all tables and their elements to have single, solid, 1-point borders around them (as shown in Figure 30-9):

```
table, table * { border: 1pt solid black;}
```

The preceding example specifies all tables and all table descendants (table, table *) to ensure that each cell, as well as the entire table, has a border. If you wanted only the cells or only the table to have borders, you could use the following definitions:

```
/* Only table cells have borders */
table * { border: 1pt solid black;}
 or
/* Only table body has borders */
table { border: 1pt solid black;}
```

The results of these two definitions are shown in Figure 30-10.

FIGURE 30-9

A table using CSS properties to define its borders

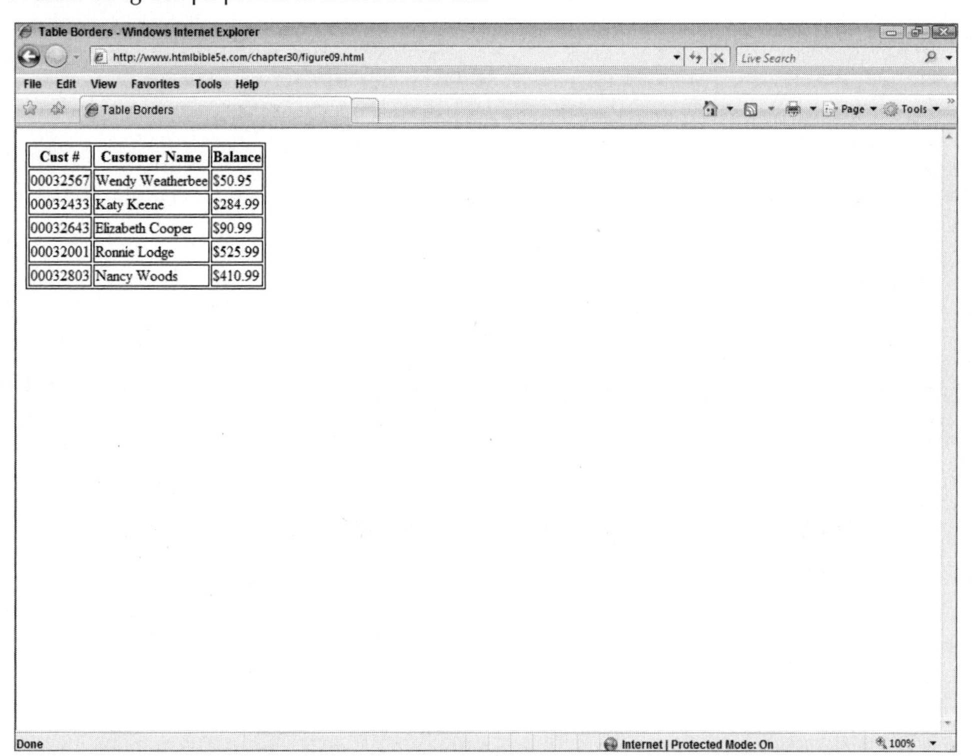

You can also combine border styles. For example, the following definitions create a table with borders similar to using the `table` element's `border` attribute. The result of this definition is shown in Figure 30-11.

```
table { border: outset 5pt;}
td, th { border: inset 5pt;}
```

Table border spacing

To increase the space around table borders, use the `border-spacing` and `padding` CSS properties. The `border-spacing` property adjusts the space between table cells much like the

<table> tag's `cellspacing` attribute. The `padding` property adjusts the space between a table cell's contents and the cell's border.

FIGURE 30-10

Tables using selective bordering

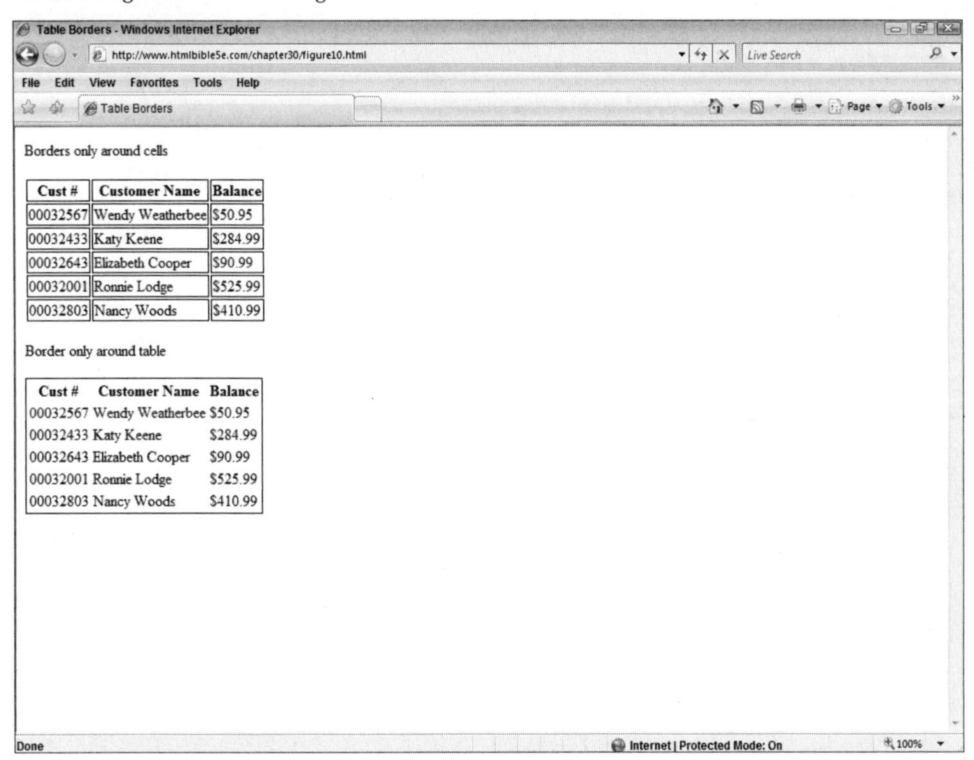

The `border-spacing` property has the following format:

```
border-spacing: horizontal_spacing  vertical_spacing;
```

Note that you can choose to include only one value, in which case the spacing is applied to both the horizontal and vertical border spacing.

For example, Figure 30-12 shows the same table shown in Figure 30-11, but with the following `border-spacing` definition:

```
Table { border-spacing: 5px 15px;}
```

Note

The `border-spacing` property works only with tables that have their `border-collapse` property set to `separate`. Also, some user agents, such as Internet Explorer, disregard the `border-spacing` property. ■

FIGURE 30-11

You can combine border styles to create custom table formats.

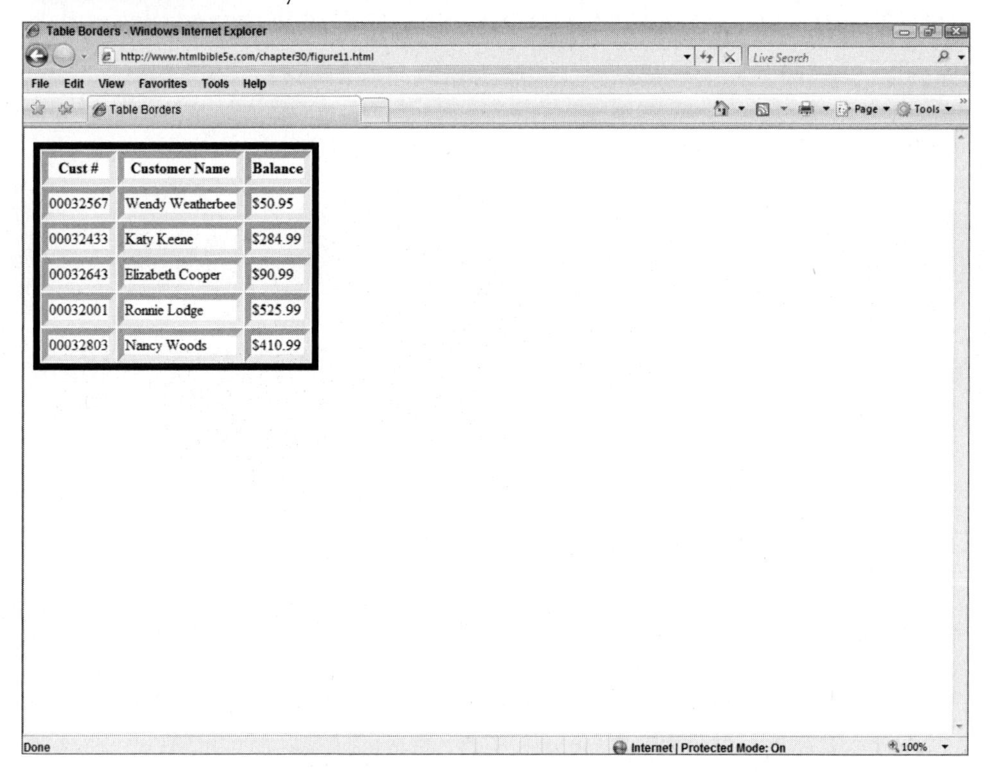

Collapsing borders

Sometimes you will want to remove the spacing between borders in a table, creating gridlines instead of distinct individual borders. To do so, use the `border-collapse` property. This property takes either the value of `separate` (default) or `collapse`. If you specify `collapse`, the cells merge their borders with neighboring cells (or the table) into one line. Whichever cell has the most visually distinctive border determines the collapsed border's look.

For example, consider the two tables in Figure 30-13, shown with their table definitions directly above them.

Notice how the borders between the table headers (th) and normal cells inherited the inset border, while the rest of the borders remained solid. This is because the border around the table headers was more visually distinctive and won the conflict between the borders styles being collapsed.

FIGURE 30-12

Different horizontal and vertical border-spacing can help distinguish data in columns or rows.

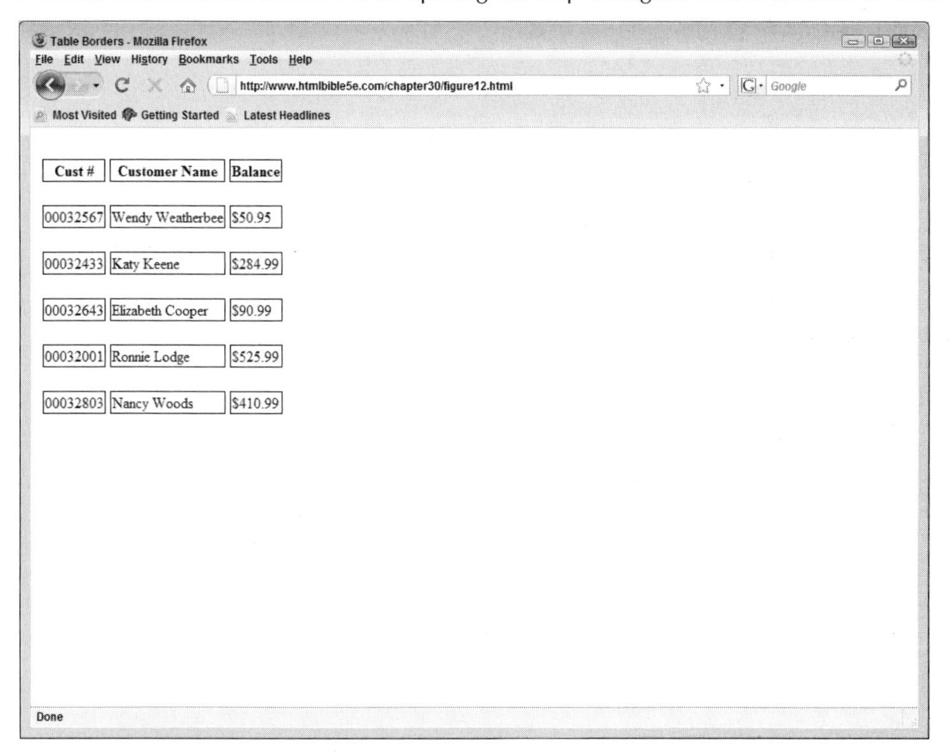

Borders on empty cells

Typically, the user agent does not render empty cells, but you can use the empty-cells CSS property to control whether the agent should or should not show empty cells. The empty-cells property takes one of two values: show or hide (default).

Figure 30-14 shows the following table with various settings of the empty-cells property:

```
<table>
  <tr><th>Heading</th><th>Heading</th><th>Heading</th></tr>
```

```
    <tr><td>X</td><td></td><td>X</td></tr>
    <tr><td></td><td>X</td><td></td></tr>
    <tr><td>X</td><td>X</td><td>X</td></tr>
</table>
```

FIGURE 30-13

Collapsing table borders turns individual borders into gridlines between cells.

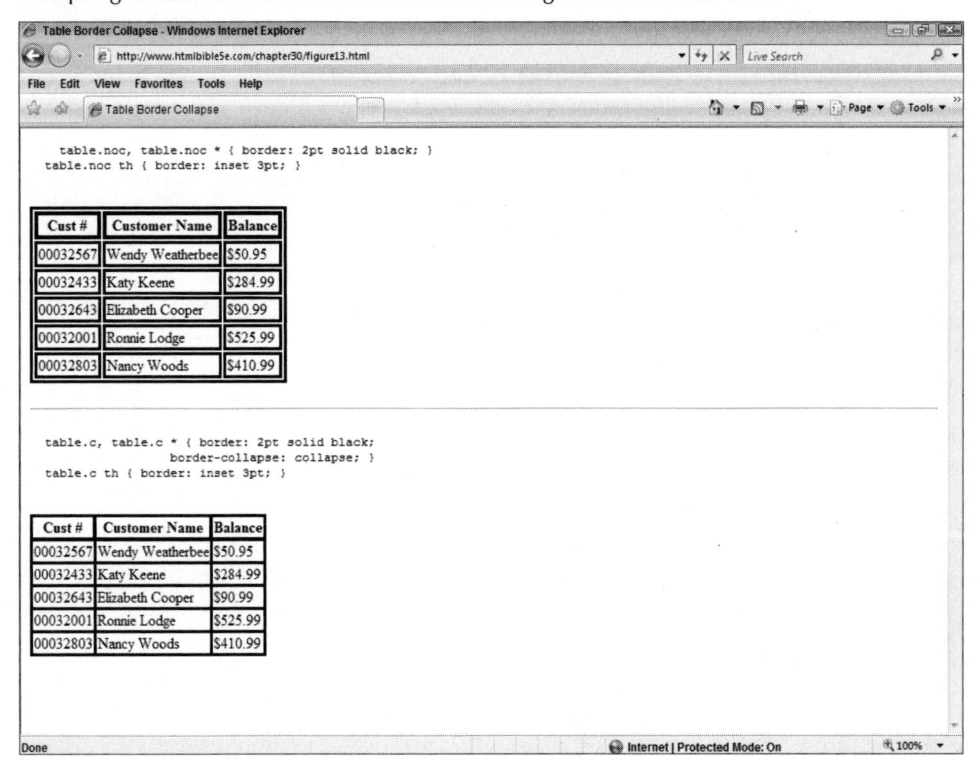

Note

Some user agents, such as Internet Explorer, disregard the `empty-cells` property. In such cases, the only recourse is to place a nonbreaking space (` `) or other non-printable character in each empty cell, making the cell not empty but containing no visible contents. ■

FIGURE 30-14

The empty-cells property controls whether the user agent displays empty cells or not.

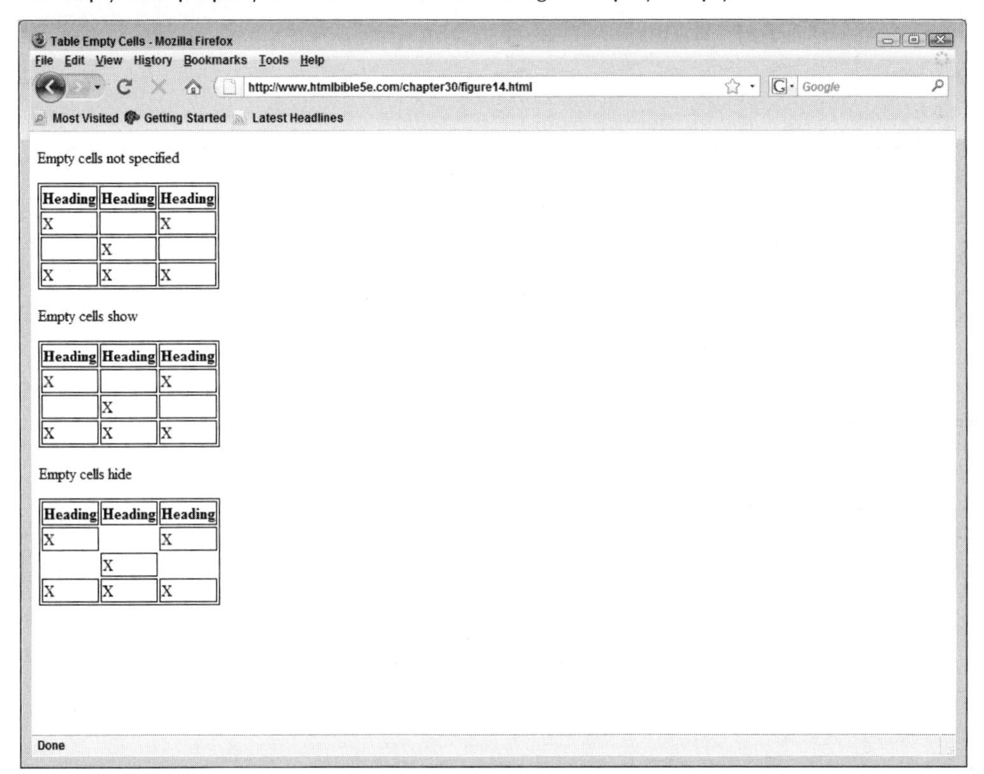

Table Layout

The `table-layout` property determines how a user agent sizes a table. This property takes one of two values: `auto` or `fixed`. If this property is set to `auto`, the user agent automatically determines the table's width primarily from the contents of the table's cells. If this property is set to `fixed`, the user agent determines the table's width primarily from the width values defined in the other properties and attributes affecting the table.

Aligning and Positioning Captions

CSS can also help control the positioning of table caption elements. The positioning of the caption is controlled by the `caption-side` property. This property has the following format:

```
caption-side: top | bottom | left | right;
```

The property's value determines where the caption is positioned in relationship to the table. To align the caption in its position, you can use typical text alignment properties such as `text-align` and `vertical-align`.

For example, the following code places the table's caption to the right of the table, centered vertically and horizontally, as shown in Figure 30-15:

```
<!DOCTYPE HTML PUBLIC "-//W3C//DTD HTML 4.01//EN"
  "http://www.w3.org/TR/html4/strict.dtd">
<html>
<head>
  <title>Table Caption Positioning</title>
  <style type="text/css">
    table { margin-right: 200px;}
    table, table * { border: 1pt solid black;
                     caption-side: right;}
    caption { margin-left: 10px;
              vertical-align: middle;
              text-align: center;}
  </style>
</head>
<body>
  <table>
  <tr>
    <th>Cust #</th>
    <th>Customer Name</th>
    <th>Balance</th>
  </tr>
  <tr>
    <td>00032567</td>
    <td>Wendy Weatherbee</td>
    <td>$50.95</td>
  </tr>
  <tr>
    <td>00032433</td>
    <td>Katy Keene</td>
    <td>$284.99</td>
  </tr>
  <tr>
    <td>00032643</td>
    <td>Elizabeth Cooper</td>
    <td>$90.99</td>
```

```
    </tr>
    <tr>
      <td>00032001</td>
      <td>Ronnie Lodge</td>
      <td>$525.99</td>
    </tr>
    <tr>
      <td>00032803</td>
      <td>Nancy Woods</td>
      <td>$410.99</td>
    </tr>
    <caption>Daily Balance for<br/>07/20/07</caption>
    </table>
  </body>
</html>
```

FIGURE 30-15

Using CSS you can position the caption of a table, in this case to the bottom of the table.

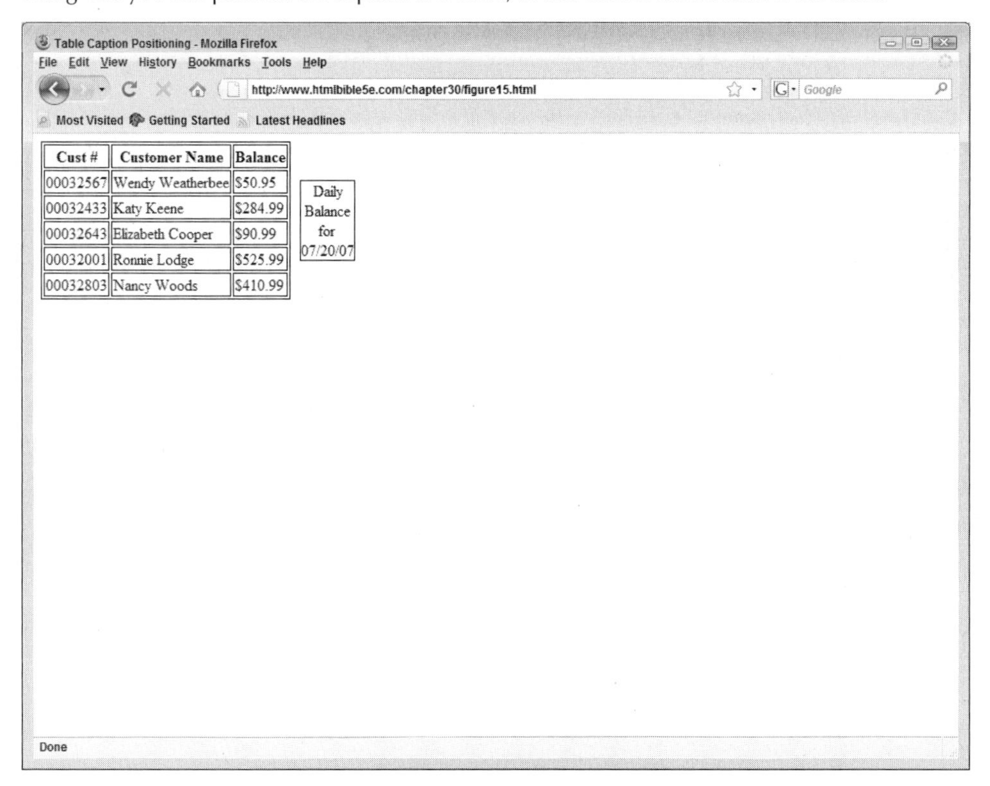

Note

This property does not currently work in Internet Explorer. ■

Note that the table's caption is positioned inside the table's margin. By increasing the table's margin, you allow more text per line of the caption. You can also explicitly set the width of the caption using the `width` property, which increases the table's margins accordingly.

Summary

This chapter covered CSS properties used to format tables and text. You learned how to affect basic text formatting such as aligning and indenting, as well as how to control spacing of various textual entities. You also learned how to use CSS to effectively format HTML tables, bringing even more versatility to an already powerful formatting tool.

The rest of the chapters in this part of the book continue to cover CSS in a topical manner: lists (Chapter 31), box elements (Chapter 32), and so on. The latter sections of this part cover topics such as page layout (Chapter 34) and using CSS to define a document for printing (Chapter 37).

CHAPTER 31

CSS Lists

Lists are one of the most versatile textual constructs in HTML. Many HTML authors rely on them to render text in a variety of ways — not just text in list form. Several CSS properties modify lists and you can take full advantage of those properties. You can change the list type or the position of the elements, and specify images to use instead of bullets. This chapter covers the CSS list-related properties.

IN THIS CHAPTER

Tip

HTML lists have been pressed into service for a variety of formatting and use functions online. The Max Design site (`http://css.maxdesign.com.au/index.htm`) contains many examples of lists serving other purposes. ■

An Overview of Lists

There are two types of lists in standard HTML: ordered and unordered. Ordered lists have each of their elements numbered and are generally used for steps that must follow a specific order. Unordered lists are typically a list of related items that do not need to be in a particular order (commonly formatted as bulleted lists).

Cross-Ref

HTML formatting of lists is covered in Chapter 7. ■

Ordered lists are enclosed in the ordered list tag, `<ol>`. Unordered lists are enclosed in the unordered list tag, `<ul>`. A list item tag (`<li>`) encapsulates each item in either list. The following code shows short examples of each type of list, and Figure 31-1 shows the output of this code:

```
<ol>An ordered list
  <li>Step 1</li>
  <li>Step 2</li>
```

```
  <li>Step 3</li>
</ol>
<ul>An unordered list
  <li>Item 1</li>
  <li>Item 2</li>
  <li>Item 3</li>
</ul>
```

FIGURE 31-1

The two types of lists, ordered (numbered) and unordered (bulleted)

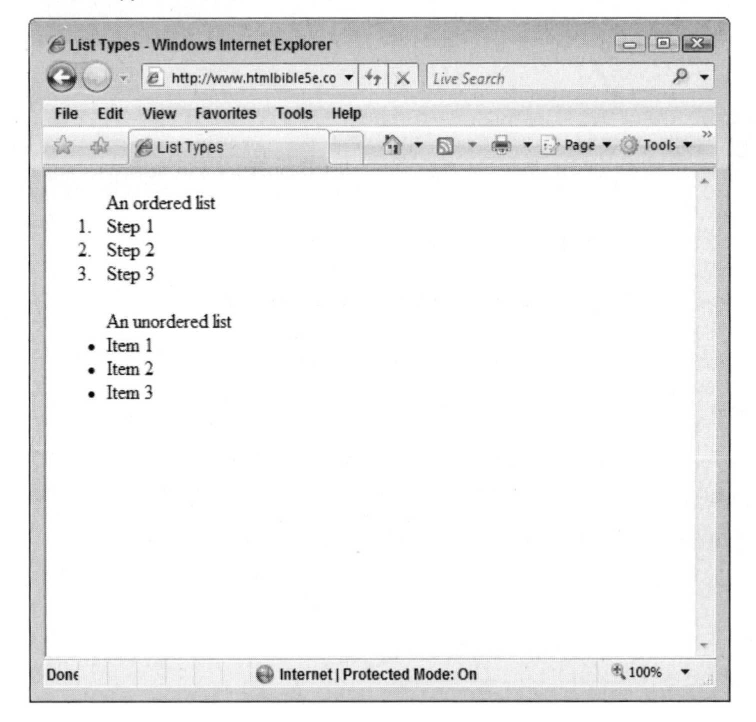

CSS Lists — Any Element Will Do

An important distinction of CSS lists is that you don't need to use the standard list element tag (`<li>`) for list items. CSS uses the `list-item` value of the `display` property, which, in effect, makes any inline element a list item. The `li` element is a list item by default.

Tip

There is a list style shortcut property that you can use to set list properties with a single property assignment. Use the `list-style` property to define the other list properties — style type, style position, and style image — as follows:

```
list-style: <list-style-type> <list-style-position>
<list-style-image>
```
■

For example, to create a new class that you can use to create a list item from almost any element, you can use the following definition:

```
.item { display: list-item;}
```

Thereafter, you can use that class to define elements as list items:

```
<p class="item">This is now a list item</p>
```

As you read through the rest of this section, keep in mind that list properties can apply to any element defined as a `list-item`.

Note

Any elements preceding list items, such as bullets or numbers, are known as *markers*. ■

List Style Type

The `list-style-type` property sets the type of the list and, therefore, what marker is used by default with each item within the list — bullet, number, Roman numeral, and so on.

The `list-style-type` property can have the following values:

- `disc`
- `circle`
- `square`
- `decimal`
- `decimal-leading-zero`
- `lower-roman`
- `upper-roman`
- `lower-greek`
- `lower-alpha`
- `lower-latin`
- `upper-alpha`
- `upper-latin`

- `hebrew`
- `armenian`
- `georgian`
- `cjk-ideographic`
- `hiragana`
- `katakana`
- `hiragana-iroha`
- `katakana-iroha`
- `none`

The values are all fairly mnemonic to the markers they generate; setting the style provides a list with the appropriate item marker. For example, consider this code and the output shown in Figure 31-2:

```
<ol style="list-style-type:lower-roman;">
  A Roman Numeral List
  <li>Step 1</li>
  <li>Step 2</li>
  <li>Step 3</li>
</ol>
```

FIGURE 31-2

Roman numeral list markers

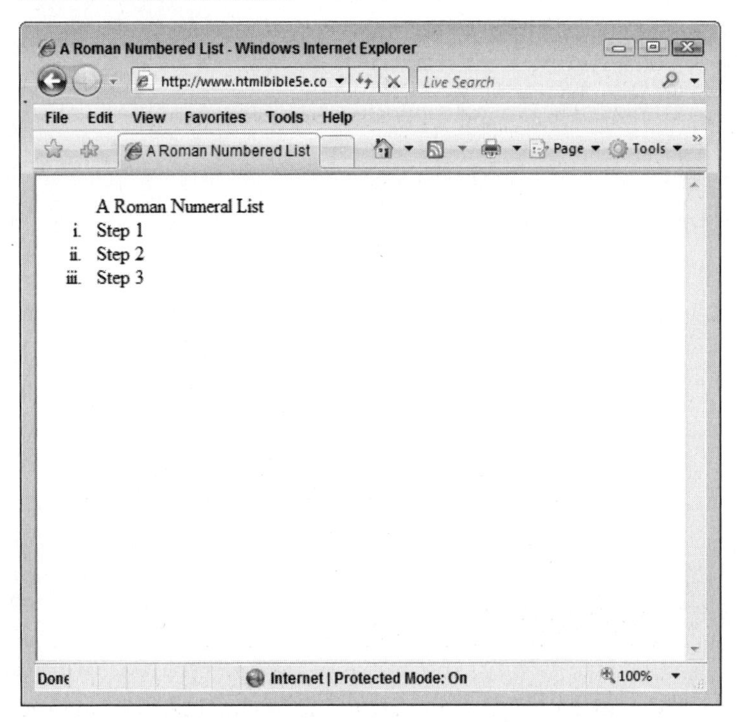

You can use the none value to suppress markers for individual items. However, this does not change the sequential generation of markers; the markers for that item in the sequence are just not displayed. For example, consider the following revised code and the output shown in Figure 31-3:

```
<ol style="list-style-type:lower-roman;">
  A Roman Numeral List
  <li>Step 1</li>
  <li style="list-style-type:none;">Step 2</li>
  <li>Step 3</li>
</ol>
```

FIGURE 31-3

Using the none value for list markers

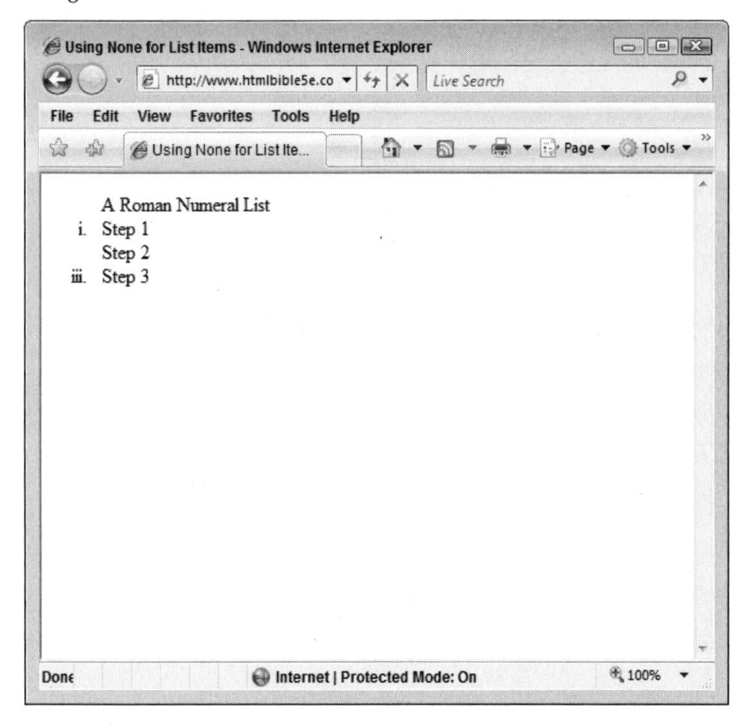

Note that the third item still has a marker of iii, despite suppressing the marker on the second item. Changing marker types in the middle of the list has a similar effect — the marker type may change, but its output will still reflect its proper sequence within the list.

Positioning of Markers

You can use the list-style-position property to change the position of the marker in relation to the list item(s). The valid values for this property are inside or outside. The outside value provides the more typical list style, whereby the marker is offset from the list item and the item's text is indented. The `inside` value sets the list to a more compact style, whereby the marker is indented with the first line of the item. Figure 31-4 shows an example of both positioning types.

FIGURE 31-4

Markers can be positioned either outside or inside the list element's margin.

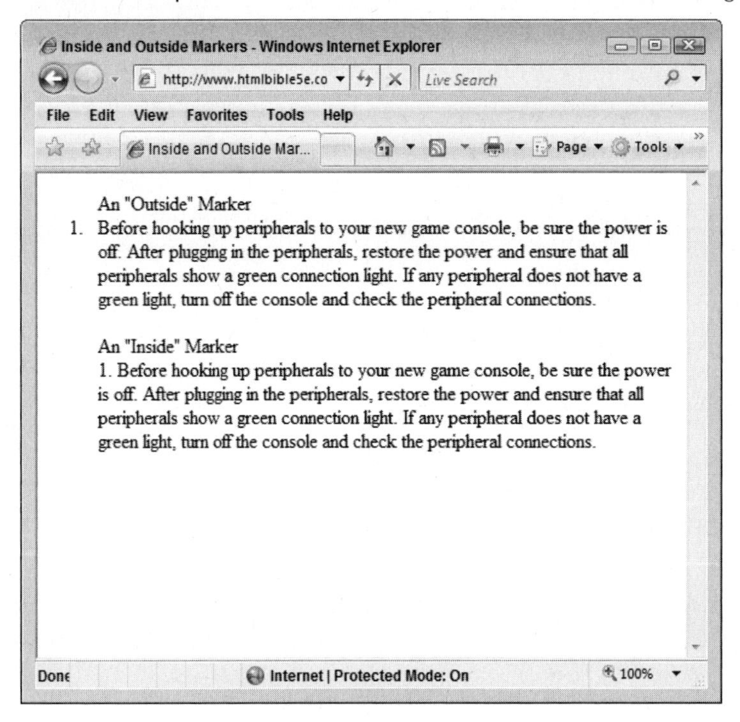

Of course, additional positioning and formatting styles can further change the position of the list item, but the position of the marker relative to the paragraph will be governed by the `list-style-position` property setting.

Using Images as List Markers

Using the `list-style-image` property, you can also specify an image to use as a marker. When this property's value is set, an image is used instead of the marker specified by the `list-style-type` property, even if the `list-style-property` value is set subsequently to the `list-style-image` value. The image to be used is specified via the `url` function. For example, the following code references `sight_bullet.jpg` and `burst_bullet.jpg` as images to use in the list, where both images reside in the `images` directory on the server:

```
<ol>
  <li style="list-style-image: url('images/sight_bullet.jpg')">
  Look for the gunsight icon which shows games we have our sights
  on!</li>
  <li style="list-style-image: url('images/burst_bullet.jpg')">
  Look for the burst icon which shows games we feel are bursting
  onto the scene.</li>
</ol>
```

The output is shown in Figure 31-5.

FIGURE 31-5

You can use images as list markers, such as the sight and burst shown here.

Note that you can use any URL-accessible image with the `list-style-image`. However, it is important to use images sized appropriately for your list.

Summary

This chapter demonstrated how you can use CSS to format HTML lists — formatting list elements and choosing or providing markers. Using the information in this chapter, you should be able to format a list to suit your particular needs. In the next few chapters, you'll learn how to use CSS to manipulate an element's box model, use colors for various design purposes, and use some of the more flexible, but esoteric CSS elements.

CHAPTER

32

Padding, Margins, and Borders

IN THIS CHAPTER

All elements in an HTML document can be formatted in a variety of ways using CSS. Previous chapters in this part of the book covered the CSS basics — how to write a style definition and how to apply it to various elements within your documents. This chapter begins coverage of the concentric areas that surround elements — also known as the *box model*.

The next chapter continues this discussion, covering colors and background images.

The CSS Box Formatting Model

Although not overtly obvious, all elements in an HTML document are contained within a box. That box has several properties — margins, padding, and borders — that can be configured to help distinguish the enclosed element from nearby elements.

Take a look at Figure 32-1, which shows a document that isn't overtly boxy.

The same document is shown in Figure 32-2, but a thin border has been added to every element courtesy of the following style:

```
* { border: thin solid black; }
```

Note how all the elements in the document pick up the border in a rectangular box shape. The border becomes much thicker at the intersection of two or more elements.

FIGURE 32-1

This Web document does not appear overly boxy in appearance.

All elements have a margin, padding, and border property. These properties control the space around the element's contents and other elements around it. These properties stack around an element in concentric box containers, as shown in Figure 32-3.

The element's content (text, image, and so on) are immediately surrounded by padding. The padding defines the distance between the element's contents and its border.

The element's border (if any) is typically drawn right inside the edge of the element's padding.

Note

Some user agents place the border on the outside of the edge of an element's padding. ■

The element's margin surrounds the element's border, or the space the border would occupy if no border is defined. The margin defines the distance between the element's padding and neighboring elements.

The next few sections cover each of these properties in more detail.

FIGURE 32-2

Every element in the document is in a box container, as shown when every element's border is enabled.

FIGURE 32-3

The box model comprises padding, a border, and a margin.

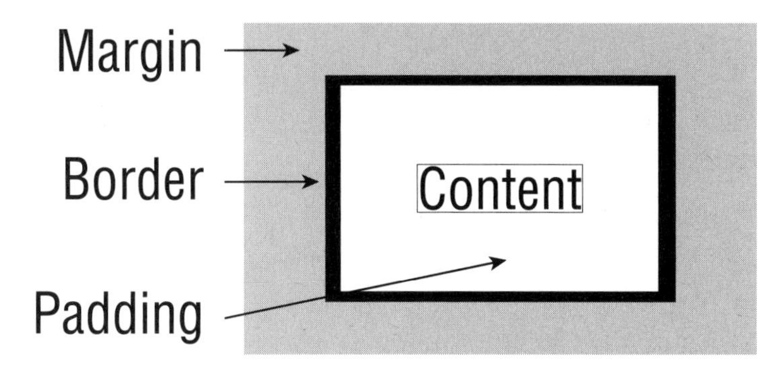

Element Padding

An element's padding defines the space between the element's contents and the space its border would occupy. This padding space can be increased, decreased, or set to an absolute value using the following CSS properties:

- `padding-top`
- `padding-right`
- `padding-left`
- `padding-bottom`
- `padding`

The first four properties are predictable in their behavior. For example, `padding-top` will change the padding on the top of the element, `padding-right` will change the padding on the right side of the element, and so forth. The fifth property, `padding`, is a shortcut for all sides; its effect is determined by the number of values provided, as explained in Table 32-1.

TABLE 32-1

Padding Values

Number of Values Provided	Effect of the Values
One	All sides are set to the value provided.
Two	The top and bottom are set to the first value provided; the left and right are set to the second value provided.
Three	The top is set to the first value provided, the left and right are set to the second value provided, and the bottom is set to the third value provided.
Four	The top is set to the first value provided, the right is set to the second value provided, the bottom is set to the third value provided, and the left is set to the fourth value provided. (In this case, the values are applied in a clockwise order around the element, starting with the top.)

For example, the following style will set the top and bottom padding value to 5 pixels and the right and left padding to 10 pixels:

```
padding:  5px 10px;
```

Note

Although changing an element's padding value will change its distance from neighboring elements, you should use an object's margin property to control that distance.

However, an element's background color typically extends to the edge of the element's padding. Therefore, increasing an element's padding can extend the background away from an element. This is one reason to use padding instead of margins to increase space around an element. For more information on backgrounds, see Chapter 33. ■

As with all CSS properties, you can specify an absolute value (as in the preceding example) or a relative value. When specifying a relative value, the value is applied to the size of the element's content (such as font size, and so on), not the default value of the padding. For example, the following code would define padding as two times the element's font size:

```
padding:  200%;
```

Element Borders

Borders are among the most versatile CSS properties. As you saw in Figure 32-2, every element in an XHTML document can have a border. However, that figure showed only one type of border — a single, thin, black line displayed around the entire element. Each side of an element can have a different size and style of border, all controlled by CSS properties corresponding to width (thickness), style (solid, dashed, dotted, and so on), and color of the border. The following sections detail how each of the respective CSS properties can be used to affect borders.

Border width

The width of an element's border can be specified using the border width properties, which include the following:

- `border-top-width`
- `border-right-width`
- `border-bottom-width`
- `border-left-width`
- `border-width`

As with other properties that have an effect on multiple sides of an element, there are border width properties for each side, and the `border-width` shortcut property can be used for all sides.

Note

The `border-width` shortcut property accepts one to four values. The way the values are mapped to the individual sides depends on the number of values specified. The rules for this behavior are the same as those used for the `padding` property. Revisit the "Element Padding" section earlier in this chapter for the specific rules. ■

As with other properties, the width can be specified in absolutes or relative units. For example, the first style in the following code sets all of an element's borders to two pixels wide. The second style sets all of an element's borders to 50 percent of the element's content size (generally font size):

```
p.two-pixel   { border-width: 2px;}
p.fifty-percent { border-width: 50%;}
```

You can also use keywords such as `thin`, `medium`, or `thick` to roughly indicate a border's width. The actual width used and what keywords are supported is up to the user agent. If you want exact control over a border's width, you should specify it using absolute values.

Border style

There are ten different types of predefined border styles. These types are shown in Figure 32-4, generated by the following code:

```
<!DOCTYPE HTML PUBLIC "-//W3C//DTD HTML 4.01//EN"
  "http://www.w3.org/TR/html4/strict.dtd">
<html>
<head>
  <title>Border Types</title>
  <style type="text/css">
    p { font-size: 12pt; border-width: 6pt;
        text-align: center; padding: 20px;
        margin: 10px; font-weight: bold;}
  </style>
</head>
<body>
<p>
<table width="100%" cellspacing="20px">
<tr><td width="50%">
  <p style="border-style:none ;">None & Hidden</p>
  <p style="border-style:dotted ;">Dotted</p>
  <p style="border-style:dashed ;">Dashed</p>
  <p style="border-style:solid ;">Solid</p>
  <p style="border-style:double ;">Double</p>
</td><td>
<p> </p>
<p style="border-style:groove;">Groove</p>
<p style="border-style:ridge ;">Ridge</p>
<p style="border-style:inset;">Inset</p>
<p style="border-style:outset;">Outset</p>
</td></tr>
</table>
</p>
</body>
</html>
```

Note
The border type `hidden` is identical to the border type `none`, except that the border type `hidden` is treated like a border for border conflict resolution. Border conflicts happen when adjacent elements share a common border (when there is no margin spacing between the elements). In most cases, the most eye-catching border is used. However, if either conflicting element has the conflicting border set to `hidden`, the border between the elements is unconditionally hidden. ■

As with other properties of this type, there are several different border style properties:

- `border-top-style`
- `border-right-style`

- `border-bottom-style`
- `border-left-style`
- `border-style`

FIGURE 32-4

The various border styles available via CSS

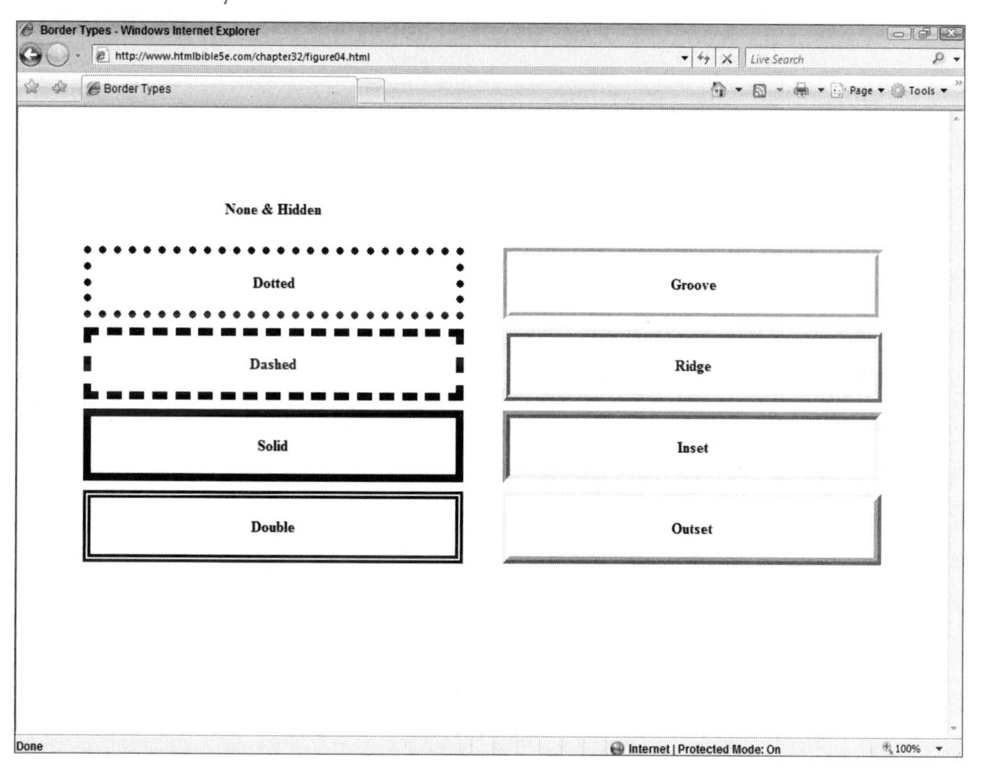

The first four properties affect the side for which they are named. The last, `border-style`, acts as a shortcut for all sides, following the same rules as other shortcuts covered in this chapter. Refer to the "Element Padding" section for more information.

Border color

The border color properties enable you to set the color of the element's visible border. As with the other properties in this chapter, there are border color properties for each side of an element (`border-top-color`, `border-right-color`, and so on) as well as a shortcut property (`border-color`) that can affect all sides.

You can choose from three different methods to specify colors in the border color properties:

- **Color keywords** — `Black`, `white`, `maroon`, and so on. Note that the exact color (mix of red, green, and blue) is left up to the browser and its default colors. (See Appendix A for a list of common color keywords.)
- **Color hexadecimal values** — Values specified in the form #`rrggbb`, where `rrggbb` is two digits (in hexadecimal notation) for each of the colors red, green, and blue. For example, #`FF0000` specifies red (255 red, 0 green, 0 blue) and #`550055` specifies purple (equal parts of red and blue, but no green).
- **Color decimal or percentage values** — Values specified using the `rgb()` function. This function takes three values, one each for red, green, and blue. The value can be an integer between 0 and 255, or a percentage designated with an ending percent sign. For example, the following specifies the color purple (equal parts red and blue, but no green) in integer form and then again in percentages:

```
rgb(100, 0, 100)
rgb(50%, 0%, 50%)
```

Tip

Most graphic editing programs supply color values in multiple formats, including percentage RGB values and perhaps even HTML-style hexadecimal format. ■

Border property shortcuts

You can use the `border` property as a shortcut when specifying an element's border properties. The `border` property has the following syntax:

```
border:  < border-width>  <border-style>  <border-color>;
```

For example, the following two styles set the same border for different paragraph styles:

```
p.one { border-width: thin;
        border-style: solid;
        border-color: black;}
p.two { border: thin solid black;}
```

Like the other properties, the border shortcut also has side-specific variants:

```
border-top
border-right
border-bottom
border-left
```

Each of these properties follows the same syntax as the `border` property, specifying the following properties within its definition:

```
<border-width>  <border-style>  <border-color>
```

Tip

Keep in mind that you can use CSS inheritance to your advantage when specifying an element's border. For example, suppose you want all but the top border to be thick and black, and you want the top border to be thin and red. Instead of specifying each side individually, you can use the `border` property to define all borders to be thick and black, and then use the `border-top` property to define the top border as an exception, similar to the following:

```
p.bordered  {  border:       thick solid black;
               border-top:   thin solid red;}
```
■

Border spacing

Two additional border properties are worth mentioning here, both of which are primarily used with tables:

- `border-spacing` — This property controls how the user agent renders the space between cells in tables.
- `border-collapse` — This property selects the collapsed method of table borders.

Cross-Ref

These properties are covered in more depth, along with other table properties, in Chapter 30. ■

Element Margins

Margins are the space between an element's border and neighboring elements. Margins are an important property to consider and adjust as necessary within your documents. Most elements have suitable default margins, but sometimes you will find it necessary to increase or decrease an element's margin(s) to suit your unique needs.

For example, consider the image and text shown in Figure 32-5, rendered using the following code:

```
<img src="square.png" style="float: left;"><p>Text next
 to an image using default margins</p>
```

Notice how the "T" in "Text" is almost touching the image next to it. In this case, additional margin space would be welcome.

As with other properties in this chapter, margin properties exist for each individual side (`margin-top`, `margin-left`, and so on) as well as a shortcut property to set all sides at once (`margin`). As with the other shortcut properties described herein, the `margin` property accepts one to four values, and the number of values specified determines how the property is applied to an element. See the "Element Padding" section earlier in this chapter for more information.

For example, you can increase the margins of the image in Figure 32-5 using a style similar to the following:

```
margin-right:  5px;
```

FIGURE 32-5

The default borders can sometimes cause elements to render too close to each other.

This would set the right border of the image (the edge next to the text) to five pixels. Likewise, you can change all four margins using a shortcut such as the following:

```
margin:  2px  4px  10px  4px;
```

Note

The `margin` property is used as a shortcut for all sides, following the same rules as other shortcuts covered in this chapter. See the "Element Padding" section for more information. ■

Just as with the other properties in this chapter, the margin properties have variants that affect each individual side of an element:

```
margin-top
margin-right
margin-bottom
margin-left
```

There are no guidelines for which margins you should adjust on what elements. However, it's usually best to modify the fewest margins possible or to be consistent with which margins you do change. This will help to ensure that your elements look the way you intend and are maintainable with the least amount of effort.

Dynamic Outlines

Outlines are an additional layer that exists around an element, enabling the user agent to highlight that element, if necessary. The highlight is generally used to indicate that a form element has focus. Note that outlines do not occupy any space whether active or not; the element occupies the same amount of space whether its outline is visible or not.

Figure 32-6 shows an example of a dynamic outline around the Phone label.

FIGURE 32-6

Dynamic outlines can be used to highlight objects that have focus or other importance.

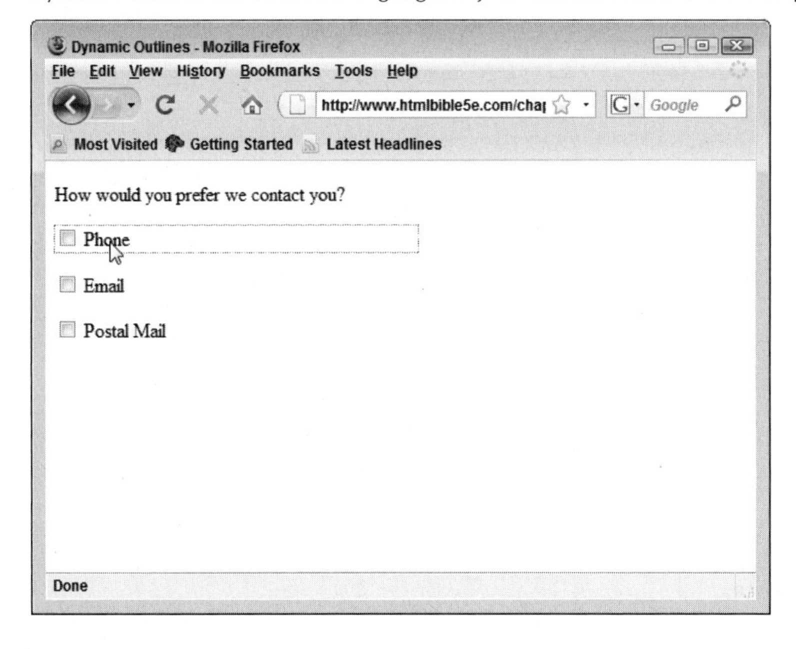

Note

Using CSS you can modify the look of outlines. However, unlike other properties of elements covered in this chapter, all sides of an outline must be the same. The CSS properties governing outlines include `outline-color`, `outline-style`, `outline-width`, and the shorthand property `outline`. These properties operate much like the other properties in this chapter, allowing the same values and having the same effects. The format of the `outline` shortcut property is as follows:

```
outline: <outline-color> <outline-style> <outline-width>;
```

■

To use the outline properties dynamically, use the :focus and :active pseudo-elements. These two pseudo-elements specify when an element's outline should be visible — when it has focus or when it is active. For example, the following definitions specify a thick, green border when form elements have focus, and a thin, blue border when they are active:

```
form *:focus { outline-width: thick; outline-color: green;}
form *:active { outline-width: thin; outline-color: blue;}
```

Be aware that, as of this writing, user agent support for outlines is very inconsistent, if support exists at all. If you intend to use outlines in your documents, you should test your code extensively on all platforms you expect your audience to use.

Summary

This chapter covered the box model concept of CSS, the pieces making up the model for each element, and the CSS properties that can be used to influence each. The box model is important because it is part of every element in your document. As you have seen in this chapter, using CSS to modify an element's box can have drastic effects on the element and the document's formatting. The next chapter covers colors and backgrounds.

Colors and Backgrounds

The previous chapter covered the box formatting model of CSS. You learned how you can manipulate an element's concentric boxes to better format your HTML documents. This chapter continues the discussion, covering element foreground and background colors, and the use of images for element backgrounds.

IN THIS CHAPTER

Element Colors

Most elements in an HTML document have two color properties, a foreground property and a background property. Both of these properties can be controlled using CSS styles. The following sections discuss both types of color properties.

Foreground colors

An element's foreground color is typically used on the visible portion of that element. In most cases, the visible foreground portion of an element is text, but there are instances where the foreground contains other, nontextual components. You can control the foreground color of an element using the CSS `color` property, which has the following format:

```
color:  <color_value>;
```

As with other properties that use color values, the value of the color property can be expressed using one of three methods:

- Predefined color keywords (such as blue, red, black, or green)
- Hexadecimal color values in #rrggbb form (#000000 for black, #FF0000 for red, #FF00FF for dark purple, and so on)
- An RGB value using the rgb( )function (rgb(100%,0%,0%) or rgb(255,0,0) for red)

For example, the following style defines a class of the paragraph element, which will be rendered with a red font because the foreground color is set to red via the color property:

```
p.redtext { color: red; }
```

Expanding on this example, the following paragraph, when used with the preceding style, will be rendered with red text:

```
<p class="redtext">This paragraph is important, and as such, appears
in red text. Other paragraphs in this section that are less
important, appear in standard black text.</p>
```

As with all style properties, you are not limited to element-level definitions. As shown in the following style definition, you can define a generic class that can be used with elements, spans, divisions, and more:

```
.redtext { color: red; }
```

Note

When defining an element's foreground color, you should pay attention to what that element's background color will be, avoiding dark foregrounds on dark backgrounds and light foregrounds on light backgrounds. However, matching foreground and background colors can have its uses, as discussed near the end of the "Background colors" section. ■

Keep in mind that user agent settings can affect the color of elements, as can the user's default local style sheet. If you don't explicitly define an element's color using appropriate styles, it might be otherwise chosen for you.

Background colors

An element's background color can be thought of as the color of the virtual page on which the element is rendered. For example, consider Figure 33-1, which shows two paragraphs: The first is rendered against the user agent's default background (in this case, white) and the second against a light-gray background.

Note

Saying that a document has a default color of white is incorrect. The document will have the color specified in the user agent's settings or in the user's default style sheet, if not otherwise instructed to change it. ■

FIGURE 33-1

The background color is the color that an object rests on when rendered.

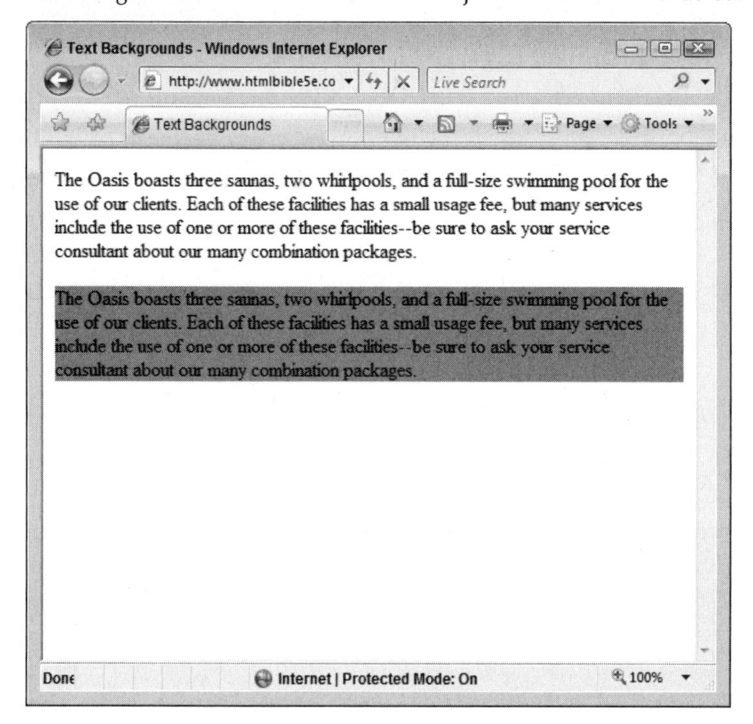

You can use the CSS `background-color` property to define a particular color that should be used for an element's background. The `background-color` property's syntax is similar to other element color properties:

```
background-color:  <color_value>
```

For example, you could use this property to define a navy-blue background for the entire document (or at least its body section):

```
body { background-color:  navy;
       color: white; }
```

This definition also sets a foreground color of white so the default text will be visible against the dark background.

Sometimes it can be advantageous to use similar foreground and background colors together. For example, on a forum that pertains to movie reviews, users may wish to publish spoilers — pieces of the plot that others may not wish to know prior to seeing the movie. On this type of site, a style can be defined such that the text cannot be viewed until it is selected in the user agent, as shown in Figure 33-2. You could define the style as follows:

```
<!DOCTYPE HTML PUBLIC "-//W3C//DTD HTML 4.01//EN"
   "http://www.w3.org/TR/html4/strict.dtd">
<html>
<head>
  <title>Spoiler Text</title>
  <style type="text/css">
    .spoiler { background-color: gray; color: gray; }
  </style>
</head>
<body>
<p>I was surprised by the ending of <i>Titanic</i>:
   <span class="spoiler">At the end of the movie, the boat sinks.
   </span></p>
</body>
</html>
```

FIGURE 33-2

A non-contrasting background has its uses.

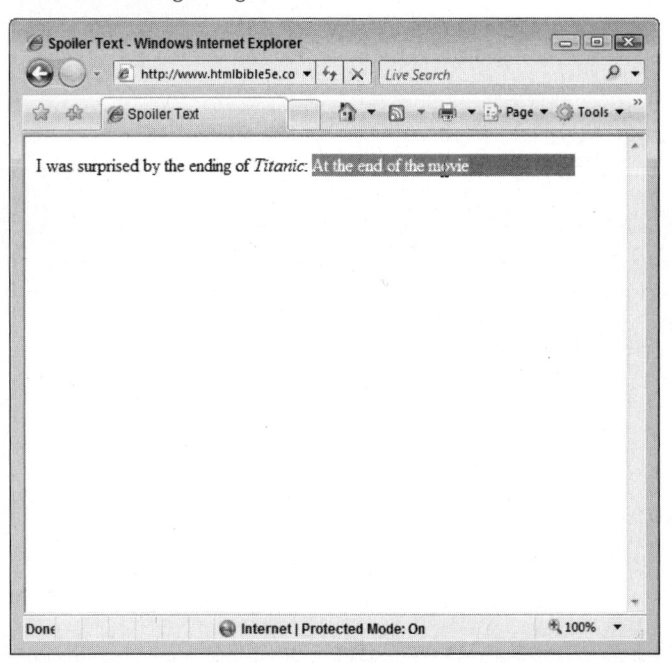

Note that an element's background extends to the end of its padding. If you want to enlarge the background of an element, expand its padding accordingly. For example, both paragraphs in Figure 33-3 have a lightly colored background. However, the second paragraph has had its padding expanded, as shown in the following code:

```
<!DOCTYPE HTML PUBLIC "-//W3C//DTD HTML 4.01//EN"
   "http://www.w3.org/TR/html4/strict.dtd">
<html>
<head>
  <title>Expanding Backgrounds</title>
  <style type="text/css">
    p { background-color: #CCCCCC; }
    p.larger-background { padding: 20px; }
  </style>
</head>
<body>
<p>The Oasis boasts three saunas, two whirlpools, and a full-size
swimming pool for the use of our clients. Each of these facilities
has a small usage fee, but many services include the use of one or
more of these facilities--be sure to ask your service consultant
about our many combination packages.</p>
<p class="larger-background">The Oasis boasts three saunas, two
whirlpools, and a full-size swimming pool for the use of our clients.
Each of these facilities has a small usage fee, but many services
include the use of one or more of these facilities--be sure to ask
your service consultant about our many combination packages.</p>
</body>
</html>
```

FIGURE 33-3

An object's background spans the size of its padding.

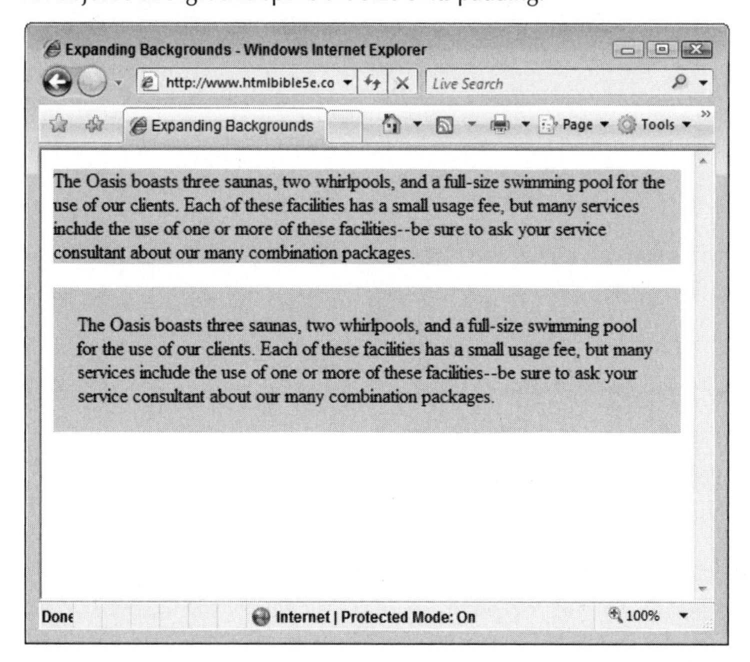

Background Images

In addition to solid colors, you can specify an image for an element's background. To do so, you use the background-image property. This property has the following syntax:

```
background-image: url("<url_to_image>");
```

For example, the following code produces the document rendered in Figure 33-4, where the paragraph is rendered over a light gradient image (gradient.gif):

```
<!DOCTYPE HTML PUBLIC "-//W3C//DTD HTML 4.01//EN"
   "http://www.w3.org/TR/html4/strict.dtd">
<html>
<head>
  <title>Background Images</title>
  <style type="text/css">
    p.gradient { background-image: url("gradient.gif");
                 padding: 20px; }
  </style>
</head>
<body>
<p class="gradient">The Oasis boasts three saunas, two whirlpools,
and a full-size swimming pool for the use of our clients. Each of
these facilities has a small usage fee, but many services include the
use of one or more of these facilities--be sure to ask your service
consultant about our many combination packages.</p>
<p>Background image:<br />
<img src="gradient.gif" alt="gradient" width="400"
  height="300" /></p>
</body>
</html>
```

Background images can be used for interesting effects, such as that shown in Figure 33-5, rendered from the following code:

```
<!DOCTYPE HTML PUBLIC "-//W3C//DTD HTML 4.01//EN"
   "http://www.w3.org/TR/html4/strict.dtd">
<html>
<head>
  <title>Text Frame</title>
  <style type="text/css">
    div.sightbox { height: 300px; width: 400px;
       background-image: url("sightframe.jpg");
       background-repeat: no-repeat; }
    div.sightbox p { font-size: small;
                     padding: 22px 120px 22px 25px; }
  </style>
</head>
<body>
<div class="sightbox">
```

```
 <p>Last week we were able to preview Foxfire II, the latest game
from Runaway Studios. FFII picks up where FFI left off, our hero
Colonel Cassius McQueen has just defeated the banshee colony. In a
stunning CG intro, we learn that the colony was not the only one
nesting on Earth and McQueen and company are again pressed into
service.<br/><br/>
 Although much of the flight engine has yet to be completed, one
level--a canyon flight--was close to being complete and we got a
preview of the game's nape of the earth flying.<br/><br/>
 Thanks to Runaway for the quick peek. We look forward to a full
preview in the not too distant future!</p>
 </div>
 <p>Background image:<br />
 <img src="sightframe.jpg" alt="sight frame" width="400"
   height="300" /></p>
 </body>
 </html>
```

FIGURE 33-4

Images such as this light gradient can also be used as backgrounds for objects.

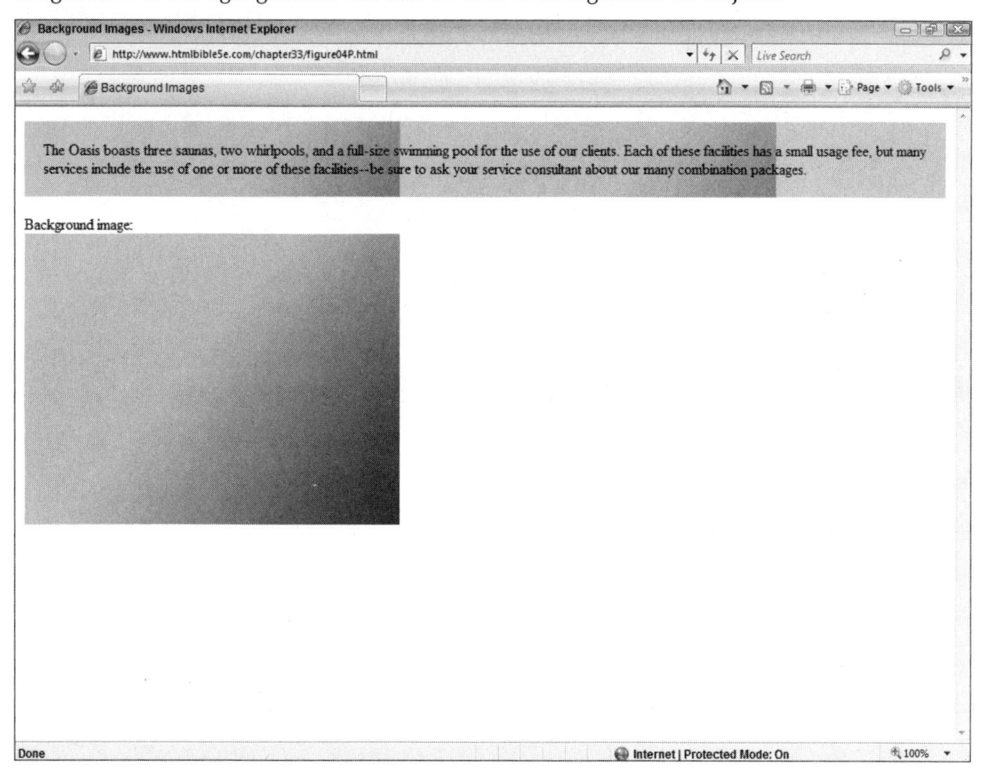

FIGURE 33-5

Background images can be used for interesting effects, such as frames around text.

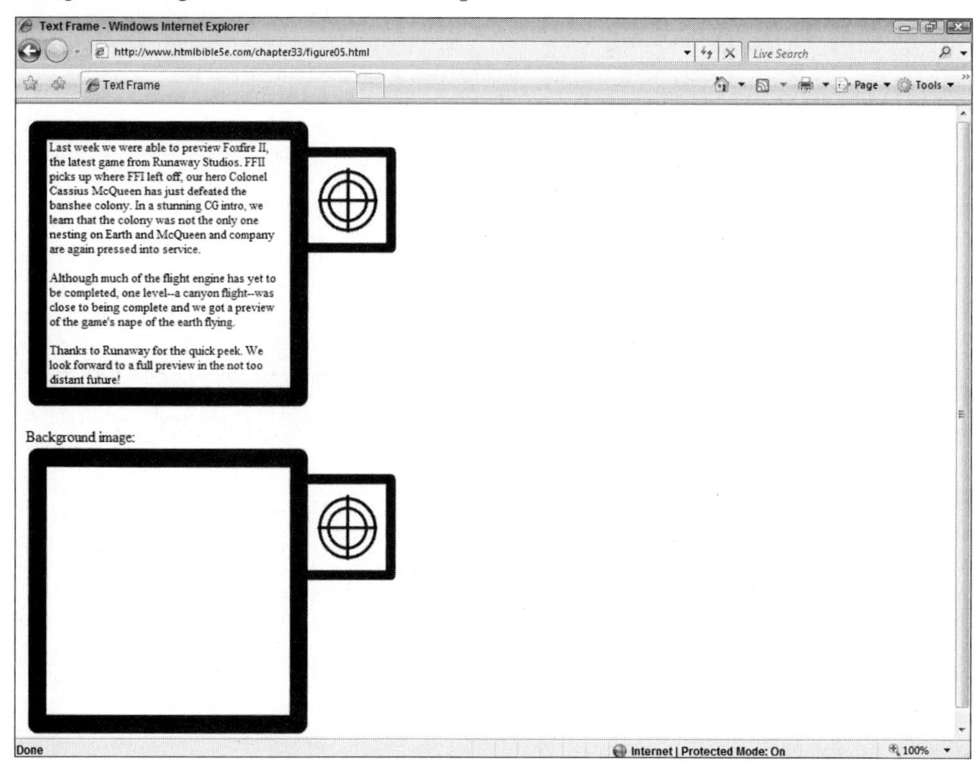

Note how the various sides of the paragraph were padded to ensure that the text appears in the correct position relative to the background frame without overfilling it.

Cross-Ref

Additional CSS formatting and display tips and tricks are covered in Chapter 41. ■

Repeating and scrolling images

Element background images tile themselves to fill the available space, as you saw in Figure 33-4 where the gradient tiles horizontally to span the width of the paragraph. You can control the scrolling and placement properties of a background image using the `background-repeat` and `background-attachment` properties.

The `background-repeat` property has the following syntax:

```
background-repeat: repeat | repeat-x | repeat-y | no-repeat;
```

The `background-attachment` property has the following format:

```
background-attachment: <i>scroll | fixed</i>;
```

Using the `background-repeat` property is straightforward — its values specify how the image repeats. For example, to repeat the crosshairs across the top of the paragraph, specify `repeat-x`, as shown in the following definition code and Figure 33-6:

```
div.sightfill { background-image: url("sight.gif");
                background-repeat: repeat-x;
                /* Border to clarity paragraph */
                border: thin solid black;
                padding: 10px; }
```

FIGURE 33-6

Images used as backgrounds can also be tiled vertically, horizontally, or both.

Specifying `repeat-y` would repeat the image vertically instead of horizontally. If you specify just `repeat`, the image tiles both horizontally and vertically. Specifying `no-repeat` will cause the image to be placed once only, not repeating in either dimension.

The `background-attachment` property specifies how the background image is attached to the element. Specifying `scroll` allows the image to scroll with the contents of the element, as shown by the second paragraph in Figure 33-7. Both paragraphs were rendered with the following paragraph definition — the second paragraph has been scrolled a bit, vertically shifting both text and image:

```
div.sightscroll { height: 220px; width: 520px;
                  /* Scroll the element's content */
                  overflow: scroll;
                 /* Define a background image and set
                   it to scroll */
                 background-image: url("sight.gif");
                 background-attachment: scroll;
                 /* Border for clarity only */
                 border: thin solid black;
                 padding: 10px; }
```

FIGURE 33-7

Background images can be fixed in place or set to scroll with an object (notice the images scrolling with the text in the second box).

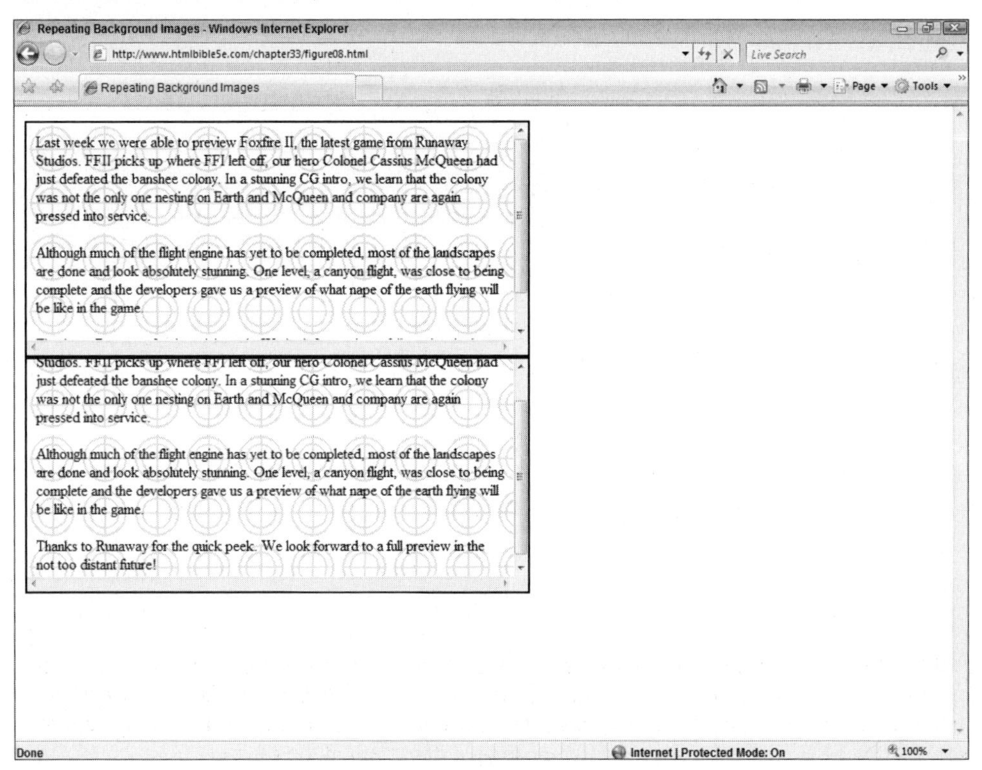

Specifying a value of `fixed` for the `background-attachment` property will fix the background image in place, causing it not to scroll if/when the element's content is scrolled. This value is particularly useful for images used as the background for entire documents for a watermark effect.

Note

Using the `overflow` property in the code for Figure 33-7 controls what happens when an element's content is larger than its containing box. The `scroll` value enables scroll bars on the element so users can scroll to see the entire content. The `overflow` property also supports the values `visible` (which causes the element to be displayed in its entirety, despite its containing box size) and `hidden` (which causes the portion of the element that overflows to be clipped and remain inaccessible to the user). ■

Positioning background images

You can use the `background-position` property to control where an element's background image is placed in relation to the element's containing box. The `background-position` property's syntax isn't as straightforward as some of the other properties. This property has three different forms for its values:

- Two percentages are used to specify where the upper-left corner of the image should be placed in relation to the element's padding area.
- Two lengths (in inches, centimeters, pixels, ems, and so on) specify where the upper-left corner of the image should be placed in relation to the element's padding area.
- Keywords specify absolute measures of the element's padding area. The supported keywords include `top`, `left`, `right`, `bottom`, and `center`.

No matter what format you use for the background-position values, the syntax for the definition is as follows:

```
background-position: <horizontal_value> <vertical_value>;
```

If only one value is given, it is used for the horizontal placement and the image is centered vertically. The first two formats can be mixed together (for example, `10px 25%`), but keywords cannot be mixed with other values (for example, `center 30%` is invalid).

To center a background image behind an element, you can use either of the following definitions:

```
background-position: center center;
background-position: 50% 50%;
```

If you want to specify an absolute position behind the element, you can do so as well:

```
background-position:  10px 10px;
```

Tip

You can combine the background image properties to achieve diverse effects. For example, you can use `background-position` to set an image to appear in the center of the element's padding, and specify `background-attachment: fixed` to keep it there. Furthermore, you could use `background-repeat` to repeat the same image horizontally or vertically, creating striping behind the element. ■

The background shortcut property

The `background` property is one of the more powerful shortcut properties, combining the `background-color`, `background-image`, `background-repeat`, `background-attachment`, and `background-position` properties in one property declaration. It has the following syntax:

```
background:  <background-color>  <background-image>
<background-repeat>  <background-attachment>  <background-position>
```

You can use this shortcut property, for example, to define a background image and its particulars all together:

```
background:  url('/images/joystickicon.jpg')  repeat-x  left center;
```

As with all shortcut properties, you should balance your use of it between convenience and readability. Generally speaking, it's easier to gather all information about an element from within one aggregated property, but longer property declarations require decoding of their own.

Summary

This chapter covered how CSS can affect the background and foreground of an element, employing colors and images. You learned how to change the text color of an element using the `color` property and how to use the `background` properties to change an element's background. The last chapters in this part of the book cover CSS formatting, generated and dynamic content, and how to define pages for printing.

CHAPTER 34

CSS Layouts

IN THIS CHAPTER

In the various chapters within this part, you have seen how dynamic documents can be when formatted with CSS. This chapter describes how you can position elements to create various page layouts using CSS properties.

Understanding CSS Positioning

There are several ways to position elements using CSS. Which method you use depends on what you want the element's position to be in reference to and how you want the element to affect other elements around it. The following sections cover the three main positioning models.

Note

It is important to include a valid DTD within documents using positioning. Without a valid DTD the browser might be prone to slipping into *quirks mode* and refuse to position your elements properly. For more information on quirks mode, see `www.quirksmode.org`. For more information on DTDs, see Chapter 1 of this book. ■

Static positioning

Static positioning is the standard positioning model — elements are rendered inline or within their respective blocks as normal. Figure 34-1 shows three paragraphs; the middle paragraph has the following styles applied to it:

```
width: 350px;
height: 200px;
border: 1pt solid black;
background-color: white;
padding: .5em;
position: static;
```

Note

Several styles have been inserted for consistency throughout the examples in this section. A border and background have been added to the element to enhance the visibility of the element's scope and position. The element also has two positioning properties (top and left), although they do not affect the static positioning model. ■

FIGURE 34-1

Static positioning is the normal positioning model, rendering elements where they should naturally be.

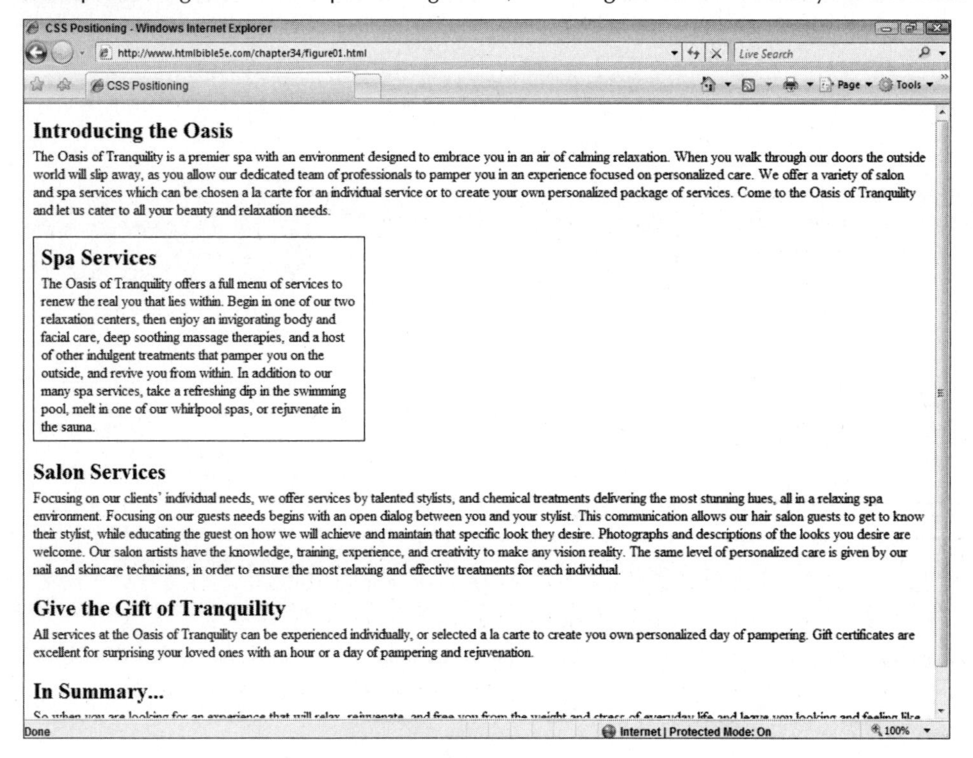

Relative positioning

Relative positioning is used to move an element from its normal position — where it would normally be rendered — to a new position. The new position is *relative* to the normal position of the element.

Figure 34-2 shows the second paragraph positioned using the relative positional model. The paragraph is positioned using the following styles (pay particular attention to the last three: `position`, `top`, and `left`):

```
width: 350px;
height: 200px;
```

```
border: 1pt solid black;
background-color: white;
padding: .5em;
position: relative;
top: 100px;
left: 100px;
```

FIGURE 34-2

Relatively positioned elements are positioned *relative* to the position they would otherwise occupy.

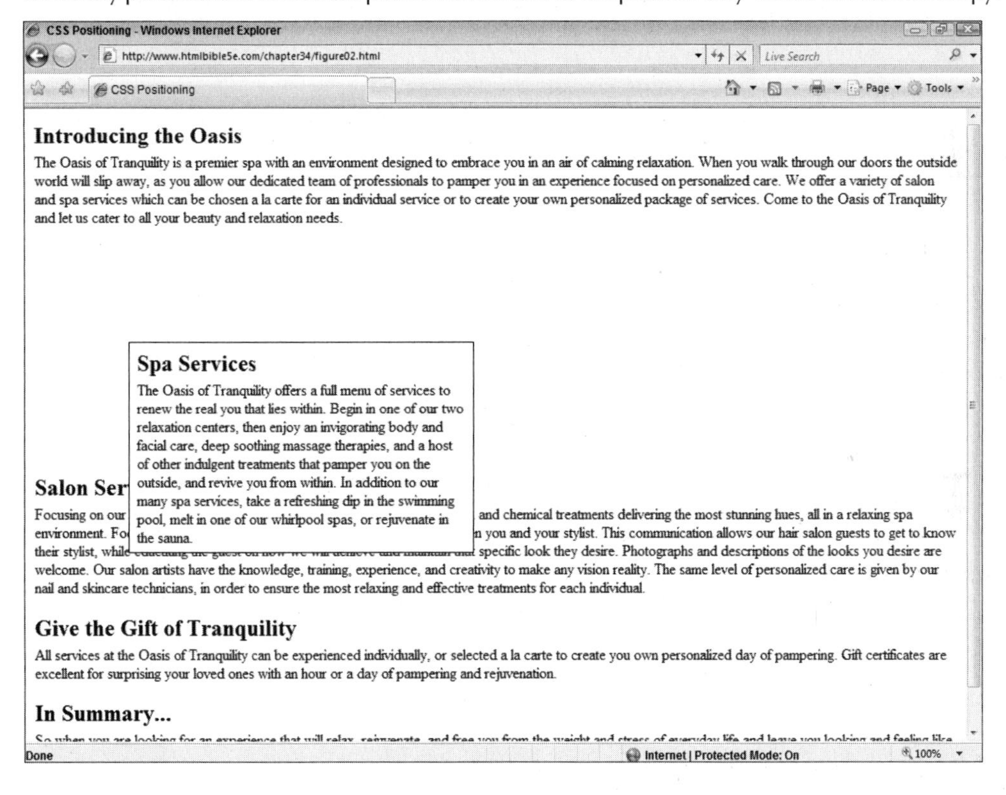

With relative positioning, you can use the side positioning properties (`top`, `left`, and so on) to position the element. Note the one major side-effect of using relative positioning: The space where the element would normally be positioned is left open, as though the element were positioned there.

Note

The size of the element is determined by the sizing properties (`width` or `height`), the positioning of the element's corners (via `top`, `left`, and so on), or by a combination of properties. ■

Absolute positioning

Elements using *absolute positioning* are placed in an absolute position, relative to the viewport instead of their normal position in the document. For example, the following styles are used to position the second paragraph in Figure 34-3:

```
width: 350px;
height: 200px;
border: 1pt solid black;
background-color: white;
padding: .5em;
position: absolute;
top: 30px;
left: 30px;
```

FIGURE 34-3

The absolute positioning model uses the user agent's viewport for positioning reference.

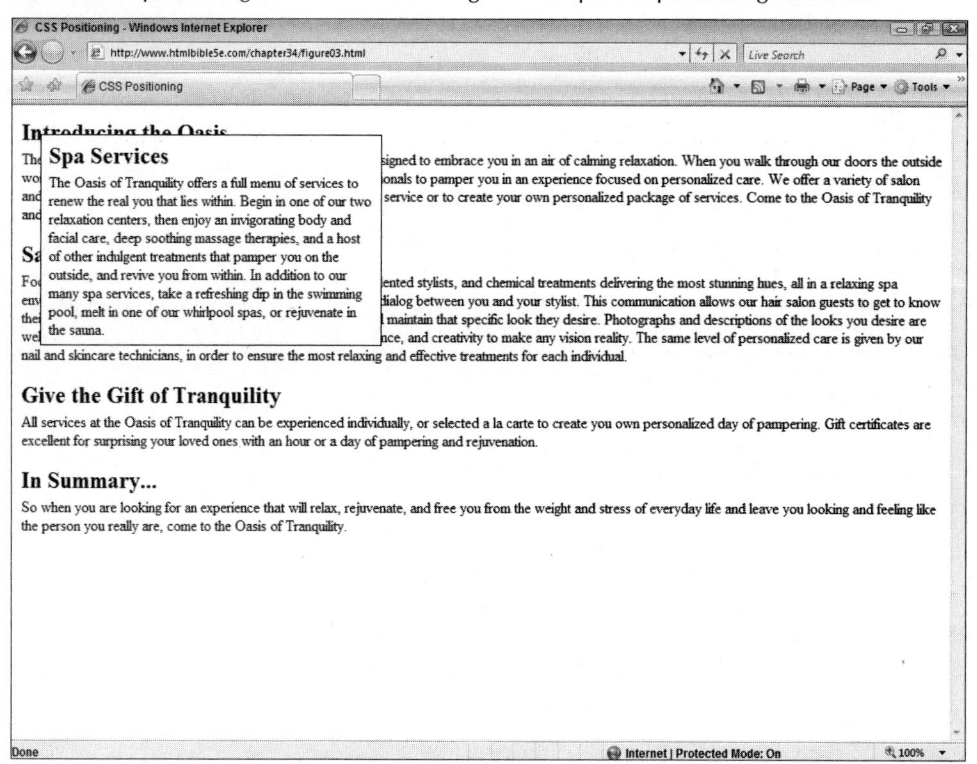

Note that the positioning properties are referenced against the viewport when using the absolute positioning model. The element in this example is positioned 30px from the top and 30px from the left of the viewport's edges.

Unlike the relative positioning model, absolute positioning does not leave space where the element would have been positioned. Neighboring elements position themselves as though the element were not present in the rendering stream.

Fixed positioning

Fixed positioning is similar to absolute positioning in that the element is positioned relative to the viewport. However, fixed positioning causes the element to be fixed in the viewport — it will not scroll when the document is scrolled; it maintains its position. The following code is used to position the second paragraph shown in Figures 34-4 and 34-5:

```
width: 350px;
height: 200px;
border: 1pt solid black;
background-color: white;
padding: .5em;
position: fixed;
top: 100px;
left: 100px;
```

FIGURE 34-4

Elements using the fixed positioning model are positioned relative to the viewport, much like absolute positioning.

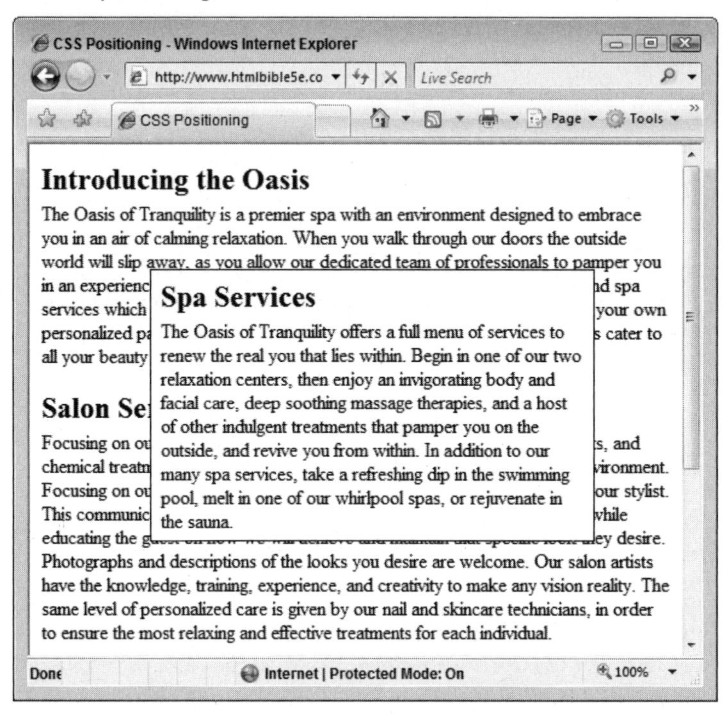

FIGURE 34-5

Elements using the fixed positioning model do not scroll within the viewport, as shown when this document scrolls (note the scroll bar's position compared to that in Figure 34-4).

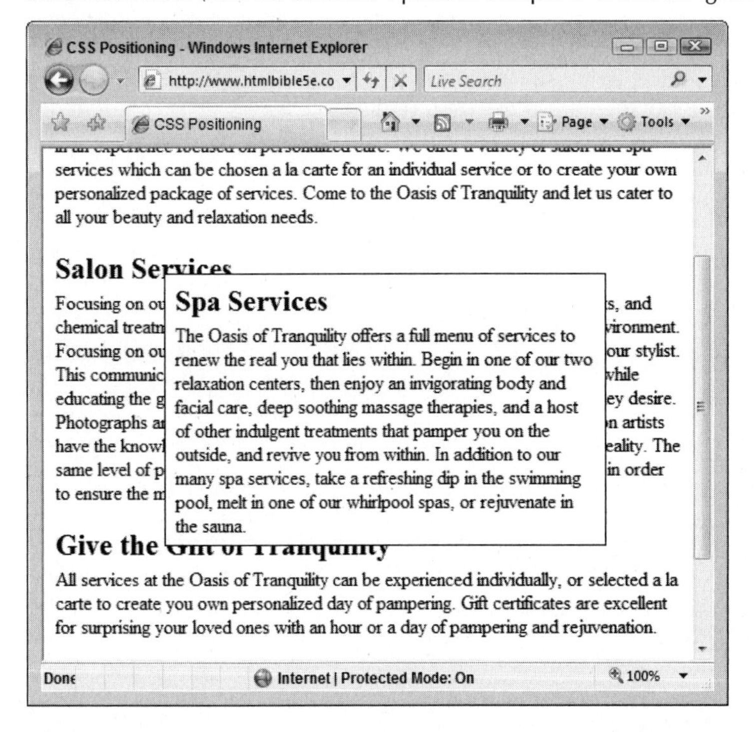

Note that when the document scrolls (refer to Figure 34-5) the fixed element stays put.

Note

Not all user agents support all the positioning models. In addition, some user agents change their support between versions — the positioning support in Internet Explorer 7 is different from that in Internet Explorer 6, for example. Before relying upon a particular model in your documents, you should test the documents in your target user agents. ■

Specifying the Element Position

Element positioning can be controlled by four positioning properties: `top`, `right`, `bottom`, and `left`. The effect of these properties on the element's position is largely driven by the type of positioning being used on the element.

The positioning properties have the following format:

```
<side>: <length> | <percentage> ;
```

The specified side of the element is positioned according to the value provided. If the value is a length, the value is applied to the reference point for the positioning model being used — the element's otherwise normal position if the relative model is used, the viewport if the absolute or fixed model is used. For example, consider the following code:

```
position: relative;
right: 25%;
```

These settings result in the element being shifted to the left by 25 percent of its width, as shown in Figure 34-6. This is because the user agent is told to position the right side of the element 25 percent of the element's width from where it should be.

FIGURE 34-6

A relative, 50% right value results in an element being shifted to the left by 50% of its width.

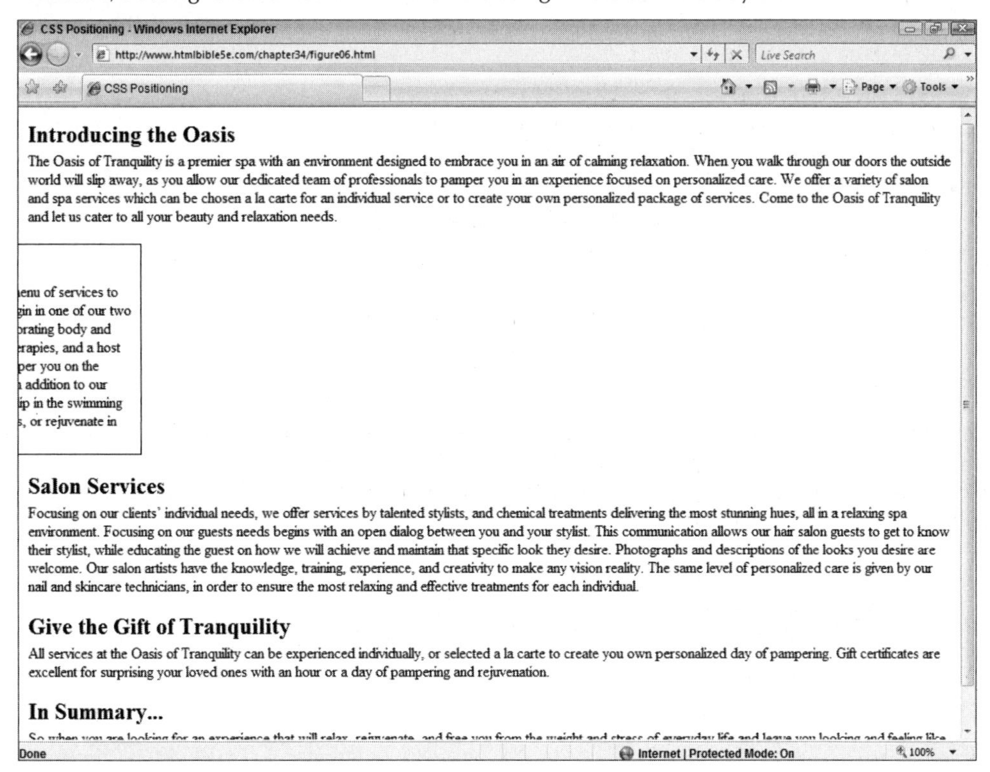

Note

This type of positioning can be confusing. For example, positioning an element *right* 50 percent means that it will be positioned 50 percent away from where it would have been on the right, which is the same as 50 percent toward the *left*. ■

However, if the following settings are used, the element is positioned with its left side in the horizontal center of the viewport, as shown in Figure 34-7:

```
position: absolute;
left: 50%;
```

FIGURE 34-7

An absolute, 50% left value results in an element being shifted such that its left side is in the middle of the viewport.

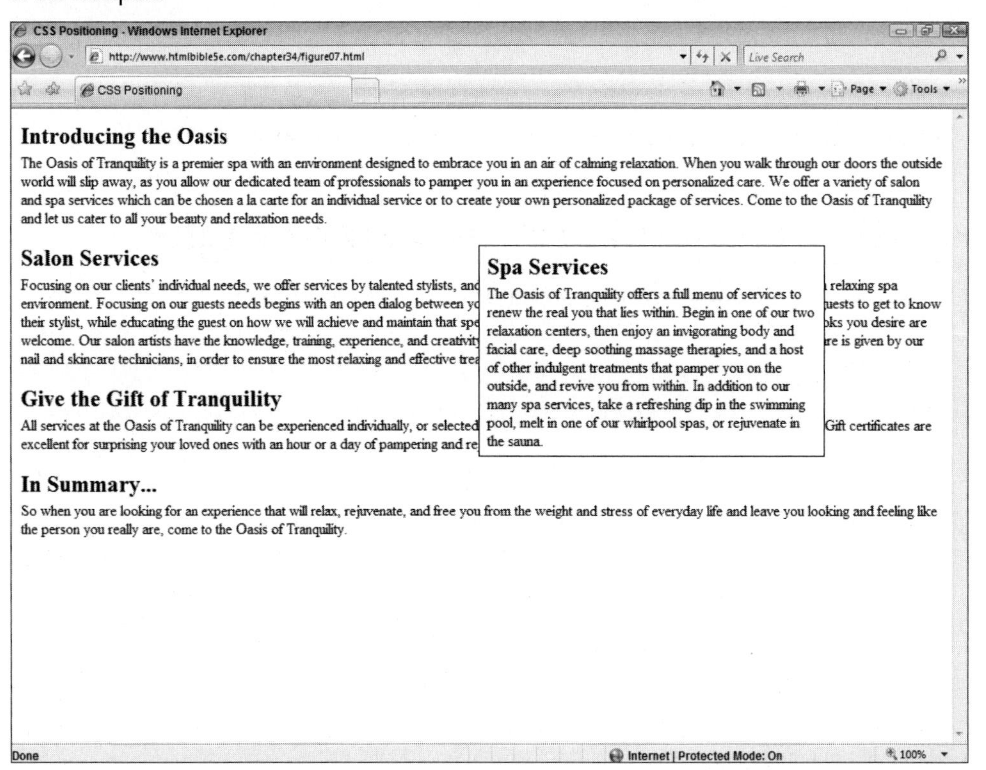

Here, the user agent references the positioning against the viewport (`absolute`), so the element's left side is positioned at the horizontal 50-percent mark of the viewport.

Note

Positioning alone can drive the element's size. For example, the following code will result in the element being scaled horizontally to 25 percent of the viewport, the left side positioned at the 25-percent horizontal mark, and the right at the 50-percent horizontal mark:

```
position: absolute;
left: 25%;
right: 50%;
```

Whichever property appears last in the definition has the most influence over the final size of the element. For example, the following definition will result in an element that has its left side positioned at the viewport's horizontal 25-percent mark, but is 300 pixels wide (despite the size of the viewport):

```
position: absolute;
left: 25%;
right: 50%;
width: 300px;
```

The `width` property overrides the `right` property because of the cascade effect of CSS. ■

Floating Elements to the Left or Right

Another method to position elements is to *float* them outside of the normal flow of elements. When elements are floated, they remove themselves from their normal position and float to the specified margin.

The `float` property is used to float elements. This property has the following format:

```
float: right | left | none;
```

If the property is set to `right`, the element is floated to the right margin. If the property is set to `left`, the element is floated to the left margin. If the property is set to `none`, the element maintains its normal position according to the rest of its formatting properties. If the element is floated to a margin, the other elements will wrap around the opposite side of the element. For instance, if an element is floated to the right margin, the other elements wrap on the left side of the element's bounding box.

Compare the image in Figure 34-8, which is not floated and appears in the normal flow of elements, with the same image floated to the right margin (via the style `float: right`) in Figure 34-9.

FIGURE 34-8

A nonfloated image is rendered where its tag appears.

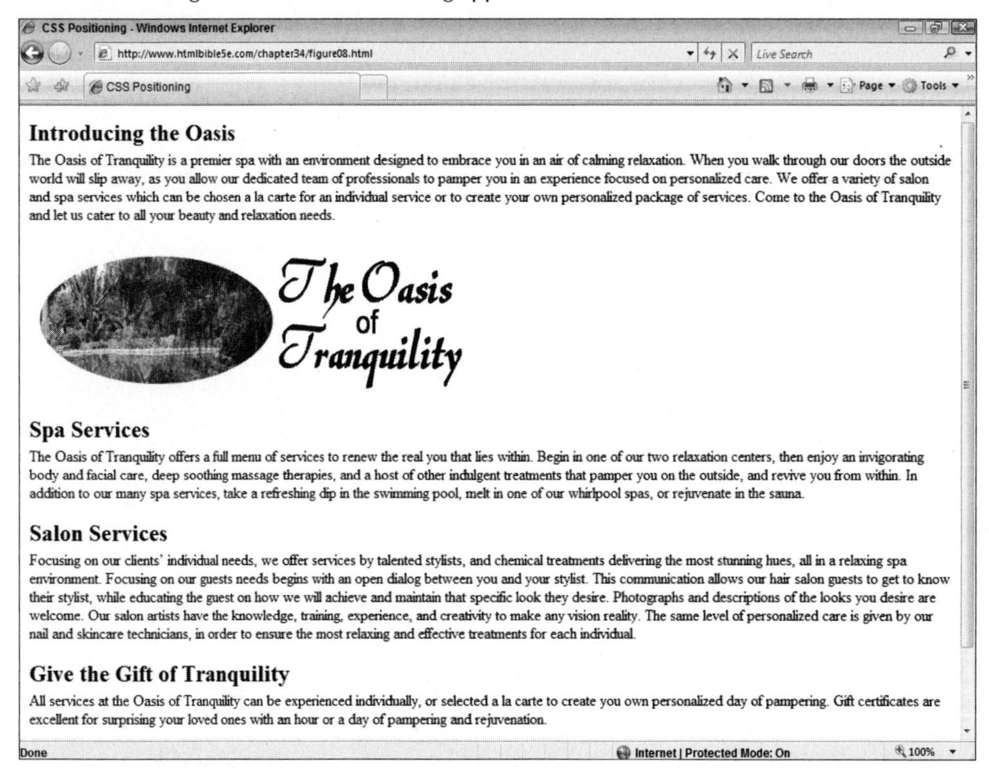

Cross-Ref

If you don't want elements to wrap around a floated element, you can use the `clear` property to keep the element away from floaters. See Chapter 30 for more information on the `clear` property. ■

The float property can also be used to effectively create parallel columns from elements. For example, consider the following code, whose output is shown in Figure 34-10:

```
<!DOCTYPE HTML PUBLIC "-//W3C//DTD HTML 4.01 Frameset//EN"
  "http://www.w3.org/TR/html4/frameset.dtd">
<html>
<head>
  <title>Parallel Floated Divs</title>
  <style type="text/css">
  div {
    border: 1pt solid black;
    padding: 10px;
```

```
        width: 200px;
        height: 400px;
        float: left;
    }
  </style>
</head>
<body>
<div id="1"><p>This is text for div 1</p></div>
<div id="2"><p>This is text for div 2</p></div>
<div id="3"><p>This is text for div 3</p></div>
</body>
</html>
```

FIGURE 34-9

An image that is floated is removed from the normal flow and is moved to the specified margin (in this case, the right margin). The other elements wrap on the exposed side of the element.

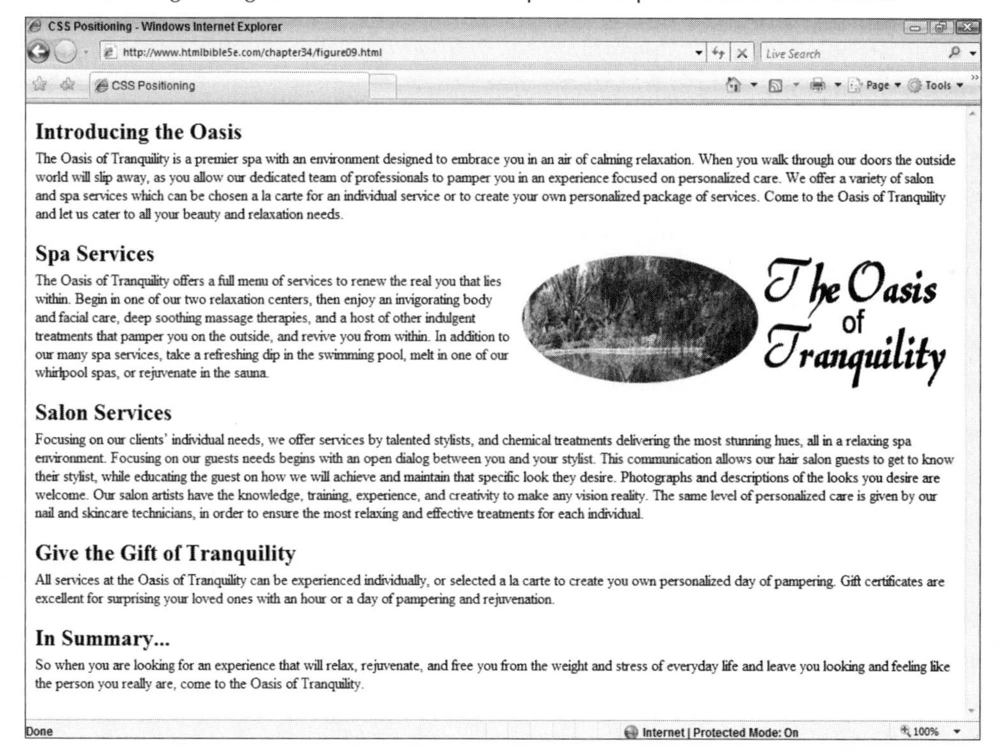

To create margins for the text within the columns, use the corresponding element's `padding` properties. Likewise, to increase the margins outside the columns — between the column and neighboring elements — use the corresponding element's `margin` properties.

FIGURE 34-10

Floated elements stacked against one another can be used for multiple, parallel columns.

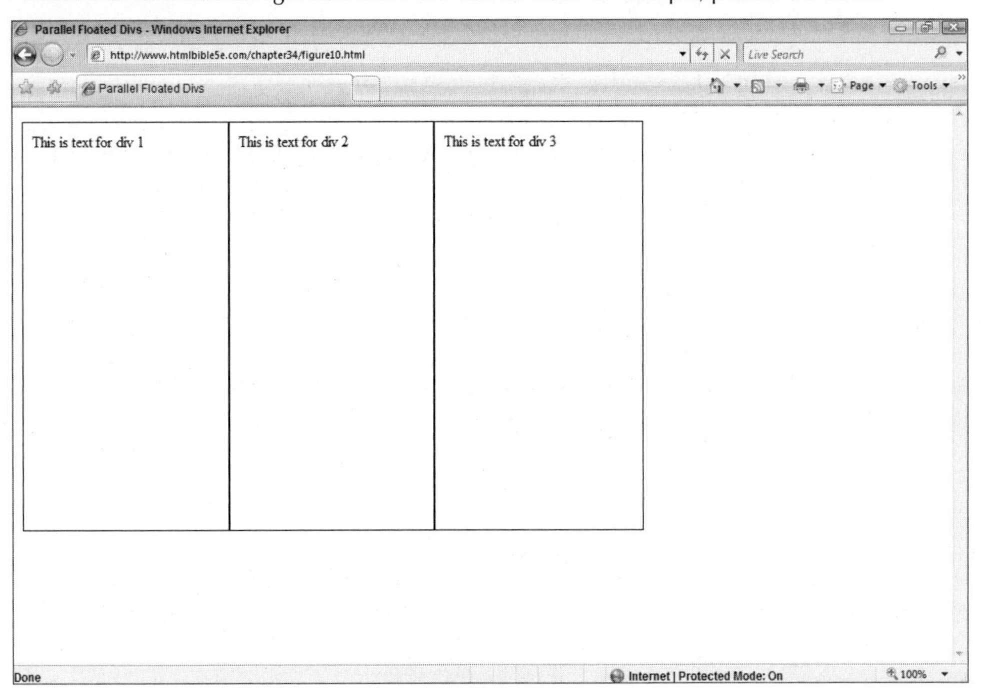

Defining an Element's Width and Height

There are multiple ways to affect an element's size. You have seen how other formatting can change an element's size; in the absence of explicit sizing instructions the user agent does its best to make everything fit. However, if you want to intervene and explicitly size an element, you can. The following sections show you how.

Specifying exact sizes

You can use the `width` and `height` properties to set the size of the element. For example, if you want a particular section of the document to be exactly 200 pixels wide, you can enclose the section in the following `<div>` tag:

```
<div style="width: 200px;"> ... </div>
```

Likewise, if you want a particular element to be a certain height, you can specify the height using the `height` property.

Note
Keep in mind that you can set size constraints — minimum and maximum sizes — as well as explicit sizes. See the next section for details on minimum and maximum sizes. ■

Specifying maximum and minimum sizes

There are properties to set maximum and minimum sizes for elements as well as explicit sizes. At times, you will want the user agent to be free to size elements by using the formatting surrounding the element, while still maintaining some constraint to ensure that an element will be displayed in its entirety, rather than be clipped or displayed in a sea of white space.

Note
Most user agents do not support min and max CSS settings. ■

You can use the following properties to constrain an element's size:

- `min-width`
- `max-width`
- `min-height`
- `max-height`

Each property takes a length or percentage value to limit the element's size. For example, to limit the element from shrinking to less than 200 pixels in height, you could use the following:

```
min-height: 200px;
```

Tip
All of the length and width properties accept values in any acceptable length format — pixels, ems, points, percentages, and so on. ■

Controlling element overflow

Whenever an element is sized independently of its content, there is a risk of the element becoming too small for its content. For example, consider the paragraphs in Figure 34-11. They are the same except that the second paragraph has had its containing box specified too small, causing the contents to fall outside of the border.

In this example, the user agent chose to display the rest of the element outside its bounding box. Other user agents may crop the element or refuse to display it at all.

If you want to control how the user agent handles mismatched elements and content sizes, use the `overflow` property. This property has the following format:

```
overflow: visible | hidden | scroll | auto;
```

FIGURE 34-11

An element that is mis-sized doesn't always handle its content properly.

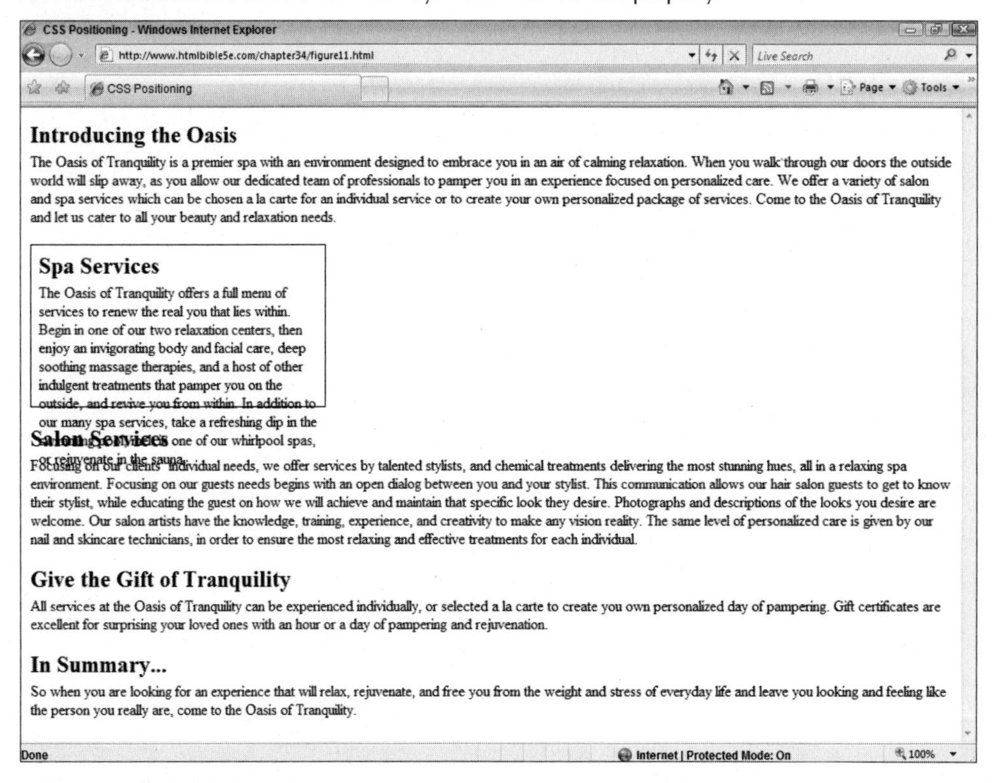

The values have the following effect:

- `visible` — The content is not clipped and is displayed outside of its bounding box, if necessary (refer to Figure 34-11).
- `hidden` — If the content is larger than its container, the content will be clipped. The clipped portion will not be visible, and the user will have no way to access it.
- `scroll` — If the content is larger than its container, the user agent should contain the content within the container but supply a mechanism for the user to access the rest of the content (usually through scroll bars).
- `auto` — The handling of element contents is left up to the user agent. Overflows, if they happen, are handled by the user agent's default overflow method.

Figure 34-12 shows the same paragraph shown in Figure 34-11, but with its `overflow` property set to `scroll`. The user agent obliges by providing scroll bars to access the rest of the element's content.

FIGURE 34-12

When the overflow property is set to scroll, the user agent supplies a mechanism (usually scroll bars) to view the entire content.

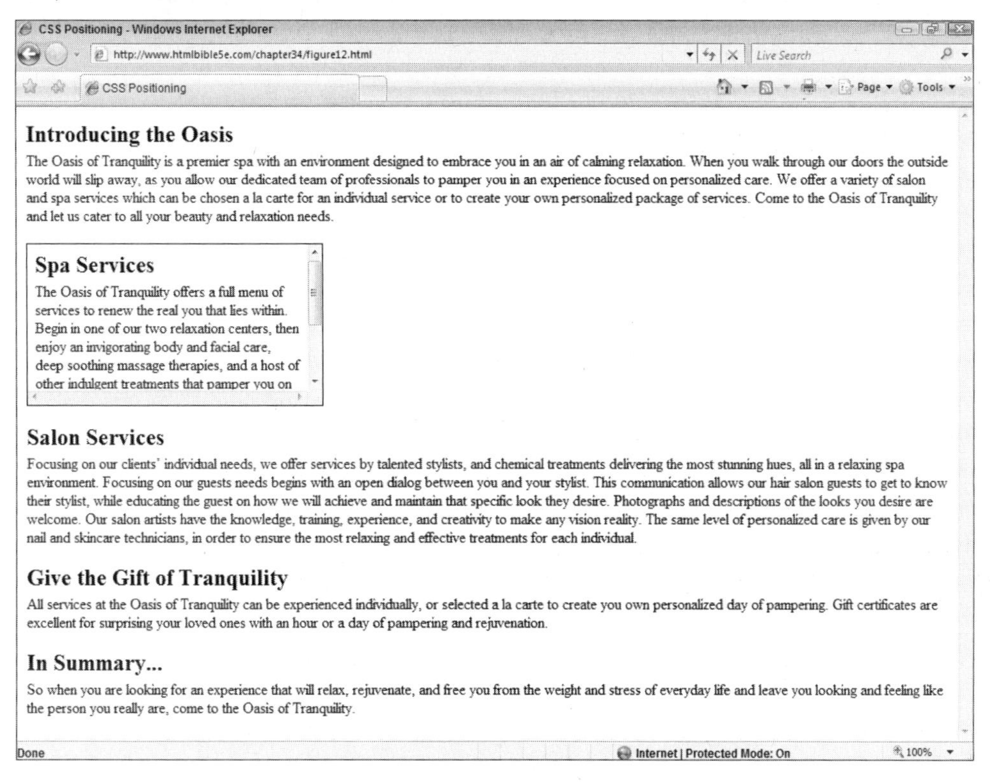

Stacking Elements in Layers

Using CSS positioning often causes elements to be stacked on top of one another. Usually, you can anticipate how the elements will stack and leave the user agent to its own devices regarding the final display of stacked elements. At times, however, you will want to explicitly specify how overlapping elements stack. To control the stacking of elements, you use the `z-index` property.

The `z-index` property has this format:

```
z-index:  value;
```

This property controls where elements should be positioned in the third dimension of the otherwise flat HTML media. Because the third dimension is typically referred to along a Z axis, this property is named accordingly (with a Z). You can think of the z-stack as papers stacked on a desktop, overlapping each other — some of the papers are covered by others.

The value of the z-index property controls where on the stack the element should be placed. The beginning reference (the document) is typically at index 0 (zero). Higher numbers place the element higher in the stack, as shown in the diagram in Figure 34-13.

FIGURE 34-13

The effect of the z-index property

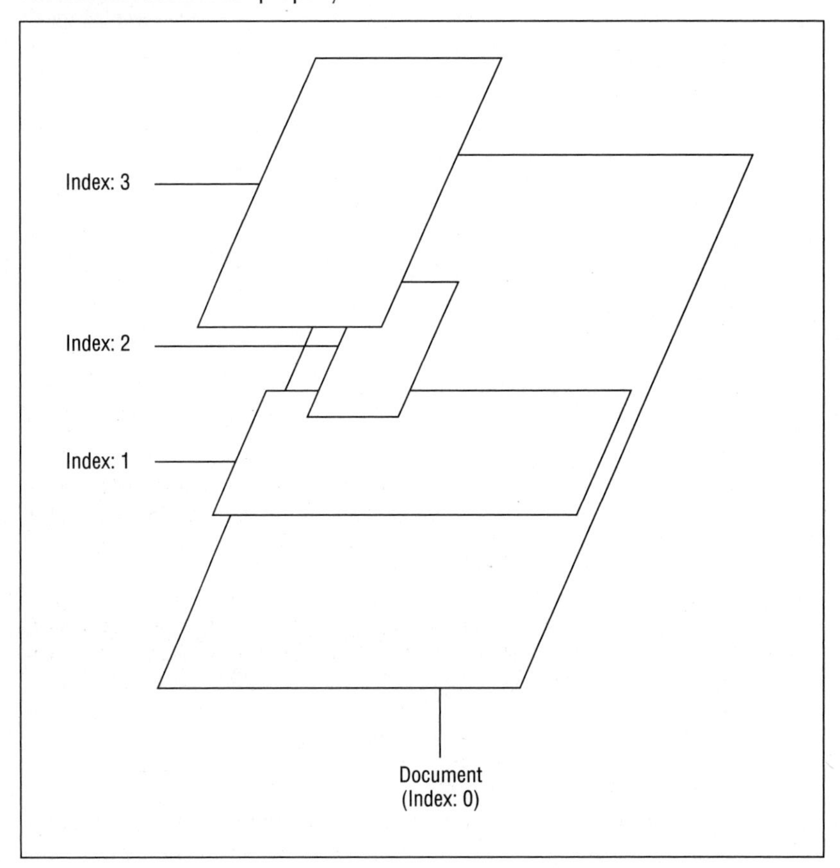

Figure 34-14 offers a practical example of z-index stacking. Each element is assigned a z-index, as shown in the following code:

```
<!DOCTYPE HTML PUBLIC "-//W3C//DTD HTML 4.01//EN"
  "http://www.w3.org/TR/html4/strict.dtd">
<html>
<head>
  <title>Z-index Stacking</title>
  <style type="text/css">
```

```
        .box1 { position: absolute;
                top: 25%;
                left: 25%;
                width: 200px;
                height: 200px;
                background-color: red;
                color: white;
                z-index: 200; }
        .box2 { width: 400px;
                height: 400px;
                background-color: yellow;
                z-index: 100; }
        .box3 { width: 400px;
                height: 100px;
                background-color: green;
                position: absolute;
                top: 20%;
                left: 10%;
                color: white;
                z-index: 150; }
    </style>
  </head>
  <body>
  <div class="box2">
  <p><b>Box 2:</b> Lorem ipsum dolor sit amet, consectetuer adipiscing
elit, sed diam nonummy nibh euismod tincidunt ut laoreet dolore magna
aliquam erat volutpat. Ut wisi enim ad minim veniam, quis nostrud
exerci tation ullamcorper suscipit lobortis nisl ut aliquip ex ea
commodo consequat. Duis autem vel eum iriure dolor in hendrerit in
vulputate velit esse molestie consequat, vel illum dolore eu feugiat
nulla facilisis at vero eros et accumsan et iusto odio dignissim qui
blandit praesent luptatum zzril delenit augue duis dolore te feugait
nulla facilisi.</p>
  <p class="box1"><b>Box 1:</b> This is text</p>
  <p>Ut wisi enim ad minim veniam, quis nostrud exerci tation
ullamcorper suscipit lobortis nisl ut aliquip ex ea commodo
consequat. Duis autem vel eum iriure dolor in hendrerit in vulputate
velit esse molestie consequat, vel illum dolore eu feugiat nulla
facilisis at vero eros et accumsan et iusto odio dignissim qui
blandit praesent luptatum zzril delenit augue duis dolore te feugait
nulla facilisi. Lorem ipsum dolor sit amet, consectetuer adipiscing
elit, sed diam nonummy nibh euismod tincidunt ut laoreet dolore
magna aliquam erat volutpat.</p>
  </div>
  <div class="box3">
    <p><b>Box 3:</b> This is text.</p>
  </div>
  </body>
  </html>
```

FIGURE 34-14

A sample of z-index stacking

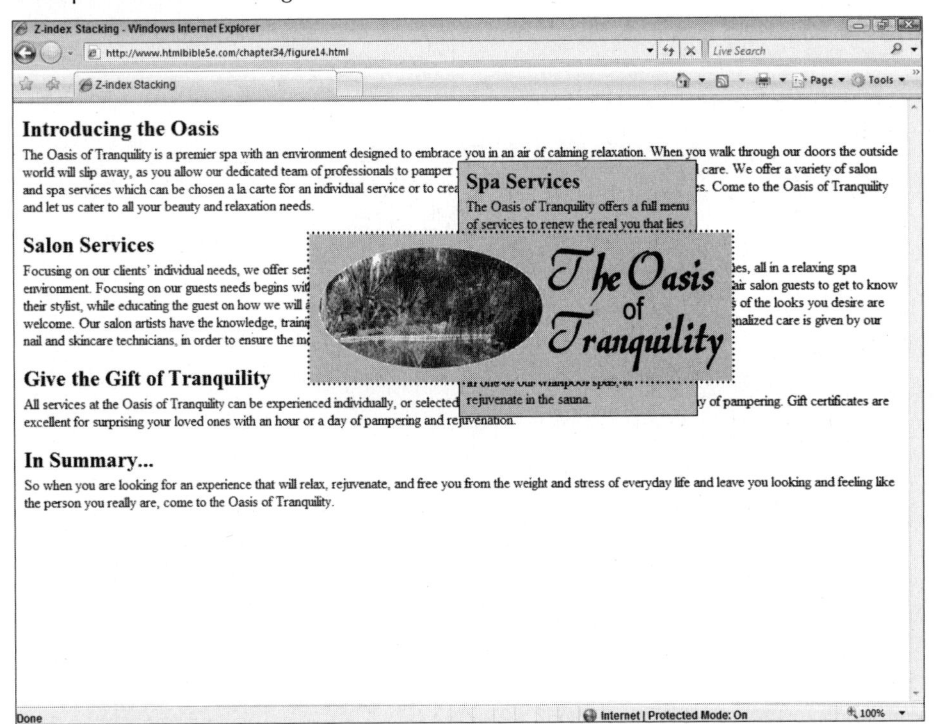

The code uses a mix of `div` and `p` elements for diversity. Because the index for `box1` is the highest (`200`), it is rendered on the top of the stack. The index for `box3` is the next highest (`150`), so it is rendered second to the top. The index for `box2` is the lowest (`100`), so it is rendered near the bottom. The document itself is recognized as being at 0, so its content and any other unspecified elements are rendered at the bottom of the stack.

If you change the `z-index` of `spa` to 300, it will then render over `logo`, as shown in Figure 34-15.

Tip

You can use many of the properties in this chapter for animation purposes. Using JavaScript, you can dynamically change an element's size, position, and/or index to animate it. For more information, see Chapters 16, 17, and 36. ■

FIGURE 34-15

Changing an element's z-index changes its position in the stack.

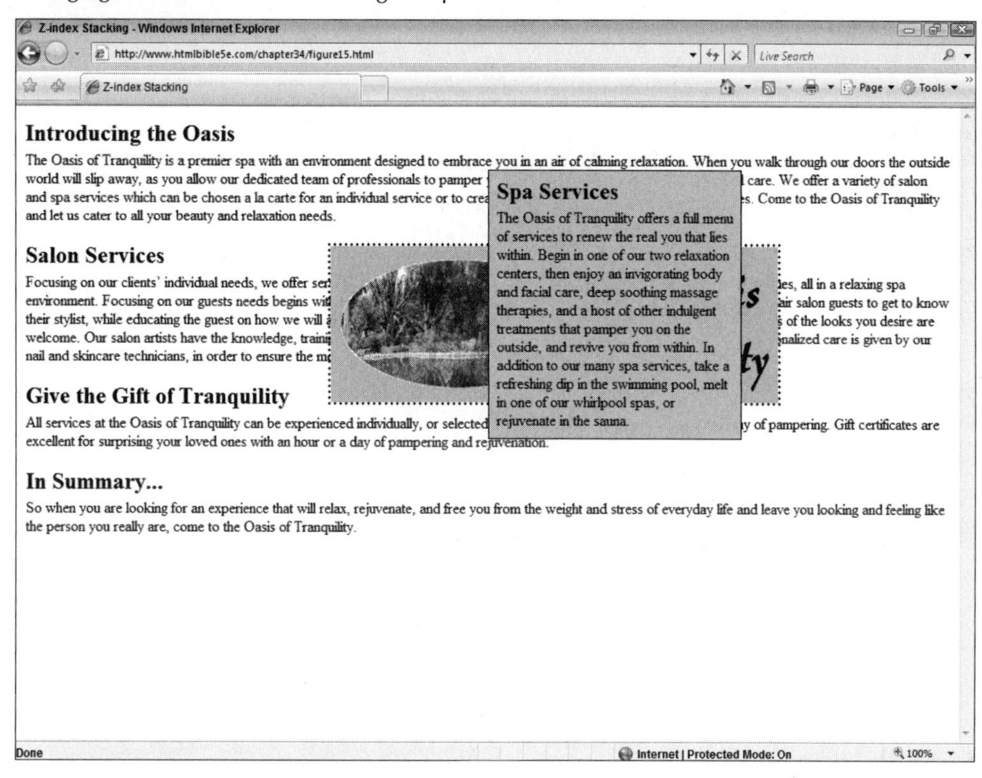

If you then change the `z-index` of `logo` to –200, it will render under the main body of the document (whose z-index is 0), as shown in Figure 34-16.

The effect shown in Figure 34-16 has several caveats:

- The user agent must support such layering.
- The user agent must support transparent backgrounds for the block to show through the document layer.
- The main document layer must not have a background that would otherwise obscure the visibility of the lower layers.

FIGURE 34-16

Items can have negative z-index values as well.

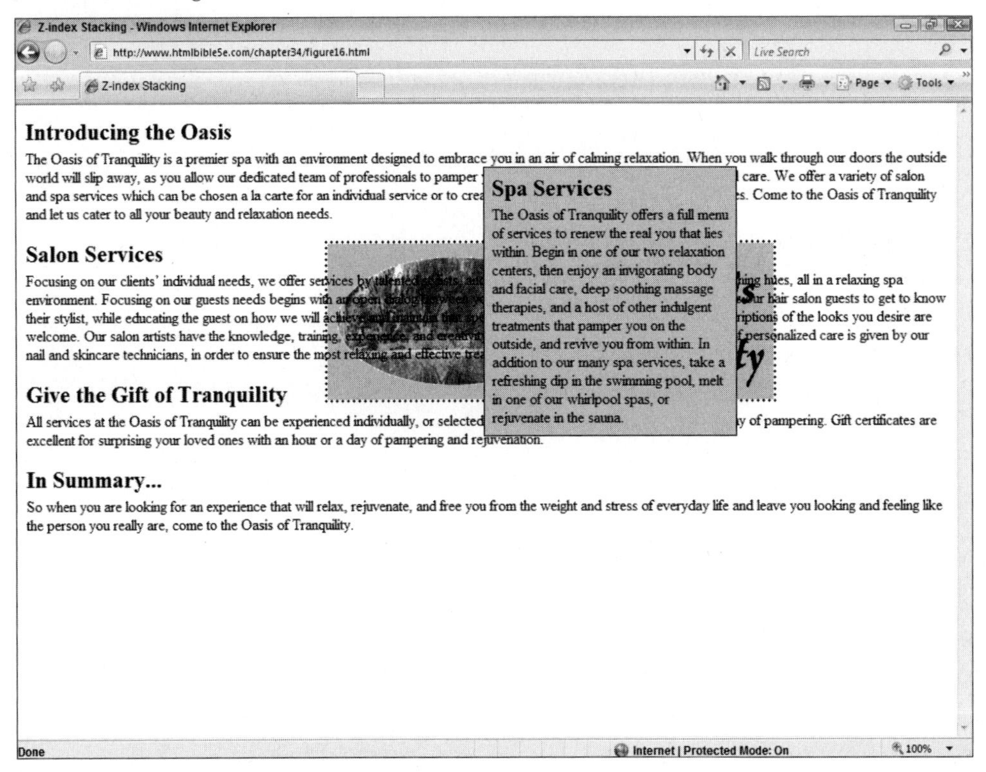

Controlling Element Visibility

You can use the `visibility` property to control whether an element is visible or not. The `visibility` property has the following format:

```
visibility: visible | hidden | collapse;
```

The `visible` and `hidden` values are fairly self-explanatory — set to `visible` (default), an element is rendered as normal; set to `hidden`, the element is still rendered but not displayed.

Note

Even though an element is hidden with `visibility`, set to `hidden` it will still affect the layout — that is, space for the element is still reserved in the layout. ■

The `collapse` value causes an element with rows or columns to collapse its borders. If the element does not have rows or columns, then this value is treated the same as `hidden`.

Cross-Ref

For more information on collapsing borders, see Chapter 30. ■

To truly hide an element, set its `display` property to `none`. An element styled this way will not be part of the render stream; it will be invisible and completely unknown within the user agent's rendering of the document's. However, the element will still be visible within the document's source.

Summary

This chapter covered the use of CSS to position elements, another one of the key concepts that really unlocks the power of CSS. If you master modifying the box model — padding, borders, and margins — and positioning, you have the power to create some truly amazing documents. The next few chapters wrap up the coverage of CSS with information on some of the more niche CSS topics.

CHAPTER

35

Pseudo-Elements and Generated Content

IN THIS CHAPTER

CSS works extremely well when you have concrete, single-state HTML elements to which to assign properties; but what happens when you want to assign certain properties to pieces of a document that aren't delimited by standard elements? In addition, there are times when it is convenient or necessary to automatically include generated content around elements. These out-of-bound cases are where CSS pseudo-elements come in handy.

This chapter introduces you to CSS pseudo-elements and generated content using CSS methods.

The Content Property

The CSS `content` property plays a key role in pseudo-elements, as it provides the actual content used by two pseudo-elements, `:before` and `:after`. The property itself is very simple and has the format

```
content: "<text>"
```

where `"<text>"` is the text that comprises the content. Note that the text must be plain text — no markup or other content needing parsing — and it must be enclosed in quotes. The text itself will inherit the attributes of its parent element.

The next section examines the particulars of using the `content` property with the `:before` and `:after` pseudo-elements, but use of the `content` property is not limited to those two elements. For example, the `content` property can be used to auto-generate content within any element. Consider the following code and the result shown in Figure 35-1 (the additional styles for the `div` are to enhance its visibility for the figure):

```
<!DOCTYPE HTML PUBLIC "-//W3C//DTD HTML 4.01//EN"
"http://www.w3.org/TR/html4/strict.dtd">
<html>
<head>
<title>The Content Property</title>
<style type="text/css">
div.text { padding: 20px;
border: thin solid black;
content: "Auto-generated text for the div";
}
</style>
</head>
<body>
<div class="text">
<p>This text will be replaced by the content property.</p>
</div>
</body>
</html>
```

FIGURE 35-1

The content property can supply auto-generated content for any textual element.

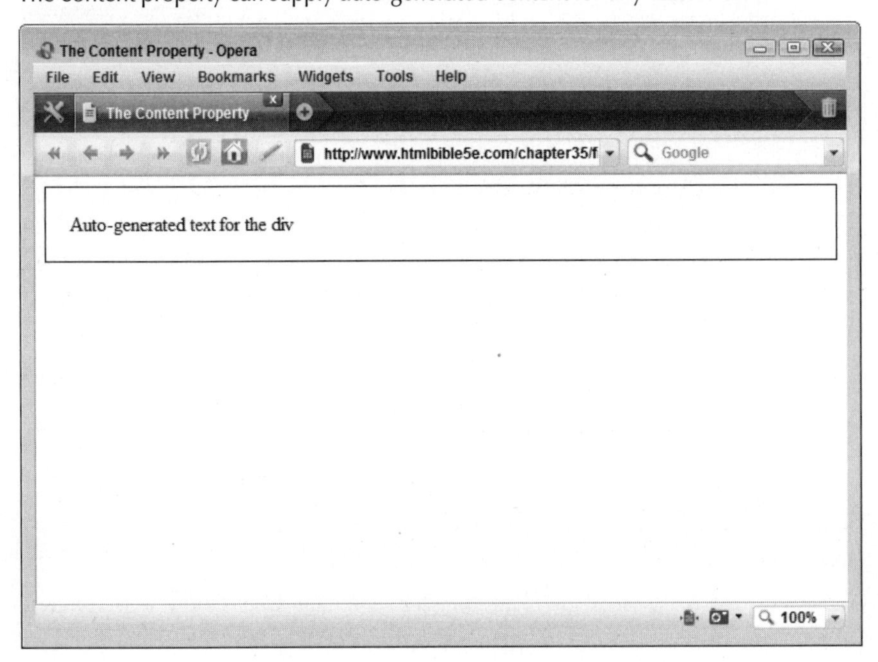

The `content` property can be used to insert content other than plain text, such as media delivered via the `url()` function. For example, the following property definition uses the `content` property to insert a `wav` sound effect:

```
content: url('media/sound.wav');
```

Note

Some applications of the `content` property are impractical and could be annoying to users. Still, it is worth noting the `content` property's capabilities for special applications. ■

It is important to note that the value of the `content` property replaces the contents of the `div`. This is true for any element that has a `content` property — whatever content is initially placed within the element will not be rendered in the user agent.

The `content` property can also be used to automate quotation marks by using a special `quotes` property to define the quote marks, and unique keywords to insert the marks. Quotations marks are covered later in this chapter.

Note

As of this writing, few browsers support using the `content` property or pseudo-elements. ■

Pseudo-Elements

CSS pseudo-elements enable you to assign properties to areas of a document that are not delimited by standard elements. Table 35-1 lists the available pseudo-elements and their scope — that is, the amount of a document they affect.

TABLE 35-1

Pseudo-Elements

Element	Scope
`:first-line`	The first line of an element's text — that is, text from the beginning of the element to the first line wrap, end of the paragraph, or line break.
`:first-letter`	The first letter of an element's text
`:before`	The space before an element. Commonly used to automatically place content before an element.
`:after`	The space after an element. Commonly used to automatically place content after an element.

Note that each element begins with a colon (:) because the identifiers are meant to be appended to the end of a selector, turning the elements that match that selector *into* pseudo-elements.

For example, consider the following two selectors, the first without and the second with an `:after` identifier:

```
/* selector (p) with no pseudo-element */
p  { color: white;
background-color: black;
padding: 10px;}
/* selector (p) with pseudo-element */
p:after  { color: white;
background-color: black;
padding: 10px;}
```

The pseudo-element identifier can be used with the most complex of selectors; simply append it to the last element of the selector, as in the following example:

```
div.sidebar p:after { ...}
```

Any paragraph that is a descendant of a `div`, with a class of `sidebar`, will have the `:after` pseudo-element applied.

Note

In CSS versions 1 and 2, both pseudo-elements and pseudo-classes began with a single colon (:). This will change in CSS3 — pseudo-elements will begin with two colons (::) to distinguish them from pseudo-classes. As of this writing, CSS3 is still under development, and adoption of its conventions is scarce. As such, we will stick with the CSS2 conventions. ■

The following sections detail the effects of the various pseudo-elements.

:first-line

The `:first-line` pseudo-element enables you to dynamically style the first line of an element. Of course, there are many things that can change the length of an element's first line, including a change in the size of the user agent's window, movement of elements within the document, or a subsequent change of the element's content.

If the element's text wrapping changes for any reason, the scope of the pseudo-element does as well. This effect can be seen in Figure 35-2, where two different-sized windows display the same paragraph using this style:

```
div:first-line  { text-decoration:  underline;}
```

:first-letter

The `:first-letter` pseudo-element enables you to style the first letter of an element. This ability is typically used for typographic effects such as drop caps, where the first letter of a section of text is printed in a larger or stylistic manner to offset it from the rest of the text. An example of this technique is provided with the following, whose output is shown in Figure 35-3:

```
<!DOCTYPE HTML PUBLIC "-//W3C//DTD HTML 4.01//EN"
"http://www.w3.org/TR/html4/strict.dtd">
```

```
<html>
<head>
<title>Drop Cap Effects</title>
<style type="text/css">
div.dropcap p:first-letter {
padding: 5px;
border: 1pt solid black;
font-size: 300%;
line-height: .8em;
margin-right: 10px;
float: left;
}
</style>
</head>
<body>
<div class="dropcap">
<p>Welcome to The Oasis of Tranquility, your source of day
spa services at hair salon prices. Come visit us for that
deep tissue or relaxing massage, facial, manicure, or
hair coloring you have been putting off.<br />
<br />
Our concept is simple{\emdash}to provide luxurious service
affordable to most consumers. So stop in and let our experts
please and pamper you today.</p>
</div>
</body>
</html>
```

FIGURE 35-2

The :first-line pseudo-element can be used to style the first line of an element — the styling is dynamic and changes if and when the first line changes.

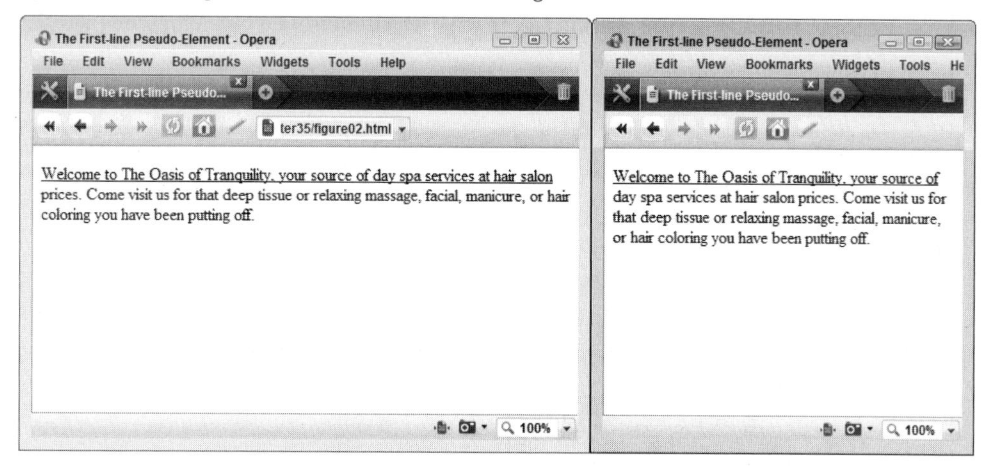

FIGURE 35-3

The :first-letter pseudo-element can create effective drop caps.

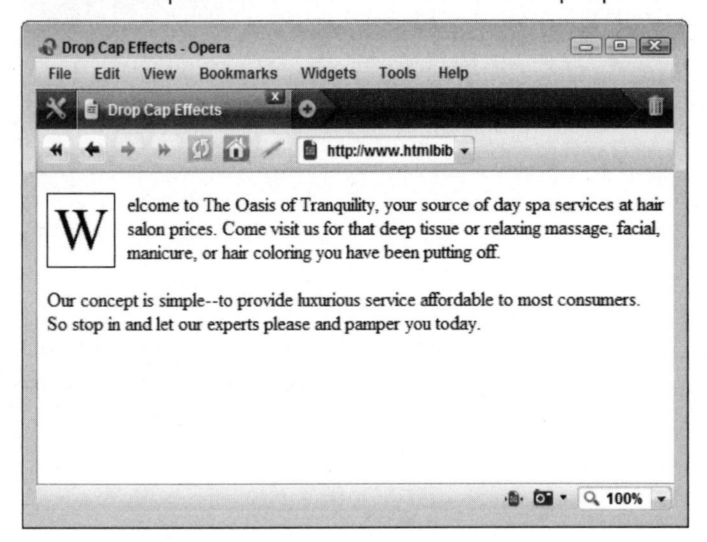

In the preceding example, a handful of additional properties help craft the drop-cap effect:

- The `padding` and `border` properties produce a thin border without crowding the letter.
- The `font-size` property sets the size of the letter to an appropriate size for a drop cap.
- The `line-height` property shortens the height of the box, giving it a more square profile.
- The `margin-right` property widens the space between the drop cap and the text to its right.
- The `float` property enables the drop cap to occupy the vertical space of several lines, instead of only the line on which it appears (the first line).

Tip

Combine the `:first-letter` and `:first-line` pseudo-elements to create a drop cap and first-line stylistic combo. ■

:before and :after

The `:before` and `:after` pseudo-elements enable you to specify text that will be automatically prepended or appended to an element. Both pseudo-elements have the same syntax; one simply controls the space before the element to which it is attached, and the other controls the space after the element to which it is attached.

For example, you could use a definition similar to the following to insert a colon after every `h1` element:

```
h1:after  {  content: ":";}
```

Likewise, you can use the `:before` pseudo-element to add content before an element. For example, you could add the word “Section” before all `h1` elements using a definition similar to the following:

```
h1:before  {  content: "Section";}
```

You can also use the `:before` and `:after` pseudo-elements to help automate quotation marks, as outlined in the next section.

Note

When using string values with the `content` property, be sure to enclose the string in quotes. If you need to include newlines in the text, use the \A placeholder. ■

Quotation Marks

You can use the auto-generation features of CSS to define and then automatically display quotation marks. First, you need to define the quotes, and then you can add them to appropriate elements.

The `quotes` property takes a list of arguments in string format to use for the open and close quotes at multiple levels. The various levels are designed to accommodate nested quotation marks. This property has the following form:

```
quotes: <open_first_level> <close_first_level>
<open_second_level> <close_second_level> $ $$\ldots$;
```

The standard definition for most English uses is as follows:

quotes: ‘“’ ‘”’ “‘” “’”;

This specifies a double-quote for the first level (open and closing) and a single-quote for the second level (open and closing). Note the use of the opposite quote type (single enclosing double and vice versa) within the definition.

Note

Most user agents do not support auto-generated content. ■

Once you define the quotes, you can use them along with the `:before` and `:after` pseudo-elements, as in the following example:

```
blockquote:before { content: open-quote;}
blockquote:after  { content: close-quote;}
```

The open-quote and close-quote words are shortcuts for the values stored in the quotes property. Technically, you can place just about anything in the content property, as it accepts string values. The next section shows how you can use the content property to create automatic counters.

Numbering Elements Automatically

One of the nicest features of using the content property with counters is the ability to automatically number elements. The advantage to using counters over standard lists is that counters are more flexible, enabling you to start at an arbitrary number, combine numbers (for example, 1.1), and so on.

Note

Most user agents do not support counters. ■

The counter object

A special object, counter, can be used to track a value, and can be incremented and reset by other style operations. The counter object has the following form when used with the content property:

```
content: counter(<char:Variable>counter_name}</char:Variable>);
```

This places the current value of the counter in the content object. For example, the following style definition will display "Chapter", the current value of the "chapter" counter, and a space at the beginning of each h1 element:

```
h1:before { content: "Chapter " counter(chapter) " ";}
```

Of course, it's of no use to always assign the same number to the :before pseudo-element. That's where the counter-increment and counter-reset objects come in, described in the next section.

Changing the counter value

The counter-increment property takes a counter object as an argument and increments its value by one. You can also increment the counter by other values by specifying the value to add to the counter. For example, to increment the chapter counter by 2, you would use this definition:

```
counter-increment: chapter 2;
```

Tip

You can increment several counters with the same property statement by specifying the additional counters after the first, separated by spaces. For example, the following definition will increment the chapter and section counters each by 2:

```
counter-increment: chapter 2 section 2;
```
■

You can also specify negative numbers to decrement the counter(s). For example, to decrement the `chapter` counter by 1, you can use the following:

```
counter-increment: chapter -1;
```

The other method for changing a counter's value is to use the `counter-reset` property. This property resets the counter to zero or, optionally, an arbitrary number specified with the property. The `counter-reset` property has the following format:

```
counter-reset: <char:Variable>{\it counter_name}</char:Variable>
[value];
```

For example, to reset the `chapter` counter to 1, you can use this definition:

```
counter-reset: chapter 1;
```

Tip

You can reset multiple counters with the same property by specifying all the counters on the same line, separated by spaces. ■

If a counter is used and incremented or reset in the same context (in the same definition), then the counter is first incremented or reset before being assigned to a property or otherwise used. This is important to keep in mind to ensure that the first use of the counter is the correct value.

A counter example: chapter and section numbers

Using counters, you can easily implement an auto-numbering scheme for chapters and sections. To implement this auto-numbering, use `h1` elements for chapter titles, and `h2` elements for sections. We will use two counters, chapter and section, respectively.

First, set up your chapter heading definition as follows:

```
h1:before {content: "Chapter " counter(chapter) ": ";
           counter-increment: chapter;
           counter-reset: section;}
```

This definition will display "Chapter *chapter_num*:" before the contents of each `h1` element. The `chapter` counter is incremented and the `section` counter is reset — both of these actions take place prior to the counter and text being assigned to the `content` property. Therefore, the following text would result in the output shown in Figure 35-4:

```
<h1>First Chapter Title</h1>
<h1>Second Chapter Title</h1>
<h1>Third Chapter Title</h1>
```

FIGURE 35-4

Auto-numbering h1 elements

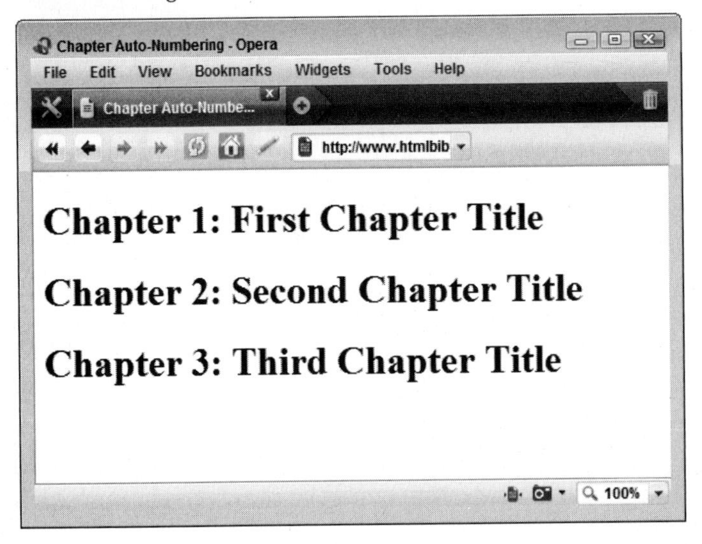

The next step is to set up the section numbering, which is similar to the chapter numbering but is applied to the `h2` elements (subheadings of `h1`):

```
h2:before {content: "Section " counter(chapter) "."
counter(section) ": ";
counter-increment: section;
h2 { text-indent: 20px;}
```

We also add `text-indent` to indent the subheads. Now the styles are complete. The final, following code results in the display shown in Figure 35-5:

```
<!DOCTYPE HTML PUBLIC "-//W3C//DTD HTML 4.01//EN"
  "http://www.w3.org/TR/html4/strict.dtd">
<html>
<head>
```

```
    <title>Chapter Auto-Number</title>
    <style type="text/css">
      h1:before {content: "Chapter " counter(chapter) ": ";
                 counter-increment: chapter;
                 counter-reset: section;}
      h2:before {content: "Section " counter(chapter) "."
                 counter(section) ": ";
                 counter-increment: section;}
      h2 { text-indent: 20px;}
    </style>
  </head>
  <body>
    <h1>First Chapter Title</h1>
      <h2>Section Name</h2>
      <h2>Section Name</h2>
    <h1>Second Chapter Title</h1>
      <h2>Section Name</h2>
    <h1>Third Chapter Title</h1>
  </body>
  </html>
```

FIGURE 35-5

The completed auto-numbering system numbers both chapters and sections.

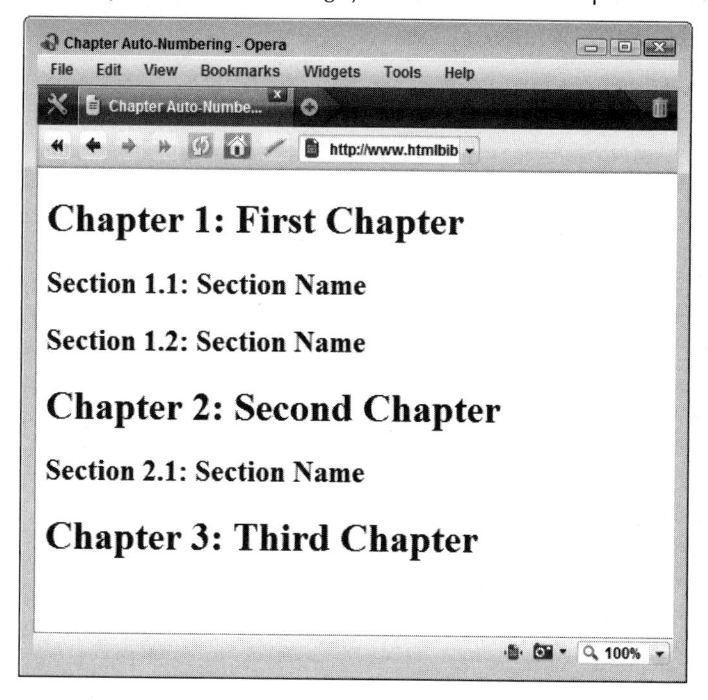

Tip

The counters should automatically start with a value of 0. In this example, that is ideal. However, if you need to start the counters at another value, you can attach resets to a higher tag (such as `<body id="c35-body-0001">`), as in the following example:

```
body:before {counter-reset: chapter 12 section 10;} ■
```

Custom list numbers

You can use a similar construct for custom list numbering. For example, consider the following code, which starts numbering the list at 20:

```
<!DOCTYPE HTML PUBLIC "-//W3C//DTD HTML 4.01//EN"
  "http://www.w3.org/TR/html4/strict.dtd">
<html>
<head>
  <title>List Custom Numbering</title>
  <style type="text/css">
    li:before {content: counter(list) ": ";
               counter-increment: list;}
  </style>
</head>
<body>
  <ol style="counter-reset: list 19;
       list-style-type:none;">
    <li>First item</li>
    <li>Second item</li>
    <li>Third item</li>
  </ol>
</body>
</html>
```

Note that the `<ol>` tag resets the counter to 19 because of the way the `counter-increment` works (it causes the counter to increment before it is used). So you must set the counter one lower than the first occurrence.

Tip

You can have multiple instances of the same counter in your documents, and they can all operate independently. The key is to limit each counter's scope: A counter's effective scope is within the element that initialized the counter with the first reset. In the example of lists, it is the `<ol>` tag. If you nested another `<ol>` tag within the first, it could have its own instance of the `list` counter, and they could operate independently of each other. ■

Summary

This chapter covered using pseudo-elements and generating content using CSS. Pseudo-elements enable you to select pieces of the document that aren't bound by traditional element boundaries, such as the first letter or first line of an element. Also introduced was the `content` property, which enables arbitrary pieces of text to be defined and then inserted via other CSS elements. Such a mechanism can automatically insert quotation marks or other desirable text. The last part of the chapter covered counters, which enable you to define and use an automatic numbering system, to auto-number elements (such as headers) or to custom number numbered lists. The next chapter expands on these concepts by introducing dynamic content.

CHAPTER

36

Dynamic HTML with CSS

IN THIS CHAPTER

Accessing CSS Properties with JavaScript

Useful CSS Manipulation

CSS can be a powerful tool for creating well-formatted documents. This chapter describes how you can change a CSS property in various user agents to lend a dynamic nature to documents. Here, you'll learn how to access CSS properties and script them to perform tasks, such as change text colors. You'll see that every CSS property can be changed programmatically.

You'll also find that some browsers, most notably Internet Explorer, feature CSS-like syntax for creating dynamic filtered effects such as drop shadows and blurs.

Accessing CSS Properties with JavaScript

Mozilla and Internet Explorer (IE) browsers make CSS1 element properties accessible from JavaScript through their Document Object Model (DOM). However, the Mozilla DOM and Internet Explorer DOM are different. They both implement parts of the W3C CSS2 standards, but they consistently cover different areas, so CSS2 JavaScript code on one browser may not work on other browsers. Note that the Gecko layout engine covers all of the properties in W3C CSS2 standards.

Generally, CSS properties are all accessed the same way, via reading values as properties and setting values via methods. To access the CSS properties in script, you use the property name, unless there's a hyphen in the name. In the case of hyphenated property names, delete the hyphen and uppercase the next letter. The rest of the property name remains in lowercase. For example,

```
font-size
```

becomes

```
fontSize
```

The property name is then appended to the object name/id with a style collection. For example, to access the `font-size` property of an object named `bigText`, you can use the following statement:

```
bigText.style.fontSize
```

In turn, that statement can be used to assign a value to the object's property. For example, the following JavaScript statement sets the `font-size` property of the element with an id of `bigText` to `xx-large`:

```
bigText.style.fontSize = "xx-large";
```

Consider the code in the following document. When the paragraph in the document is clicked, the `onClick` handler runs the `SuperSizeMe( )`JavaScript function, which sets the paragraph's `font-size` property to `xx-large` (effectively supersizing the paragraph). Figure 36-1 shows the paragraph before it is clicked, and Figure 36-2 shows the paragraph after it is clicked.

```
<!DOCTYPE HTML PUBLIC "-//W3C//DTD HTML 4.01//EN"
  "http://www.w3.org/TR/html4/strict.dtd">
<html>
<head>
  <title>Super Size Me</title>
  <style type="text/css">
    #bigText { font-size: medium;}
  </style>
  <script type="text/JavaScript">

    function SuperSizeMe(obj) {
      obj.style.fontSize = "xx-large";
}
  </script>
</head>
<body>
  <p id="bigText" onClick="SuperSizeMe(this);">Lorem ipsum dolor sit
  amet, consectetur adipisicing elit, sed do eiusmod tempor
  incididunt ut labore et dolore magna aliqua. Ut enim ad minim
  veniam, quis nostrud exercitation ullamco laboris nisi ut aliquip
  ex ea commodo consequat. Duis aute irure dolor in reprehenderit
  in voluptate velit esse cillum dolore eu fugiat nulla pariatur.
  Excepteur sint occaecat cupidatat non proident, sunt in culpa qui
  officia deserunt mollit anim id est laborum.</p>
</body>
</html>
```

It is important to take a moment and examine what the code actually is doing. You might think that the script accessing the style collection can therefore access the styles assigned to the element no matter the source of said styles. However, that is not the case — the style collection can only reference a local style embedded in the object's tag via the `script` attribute. As such, the following JavaScript statement would display a null value if run immediately after the preceding document was loaded into the user agent:

```
alert(document.getElementById('bigText').style.fontSize);
```

FIGURE 36-1

Before the text is clicked, it has a medium-size font.

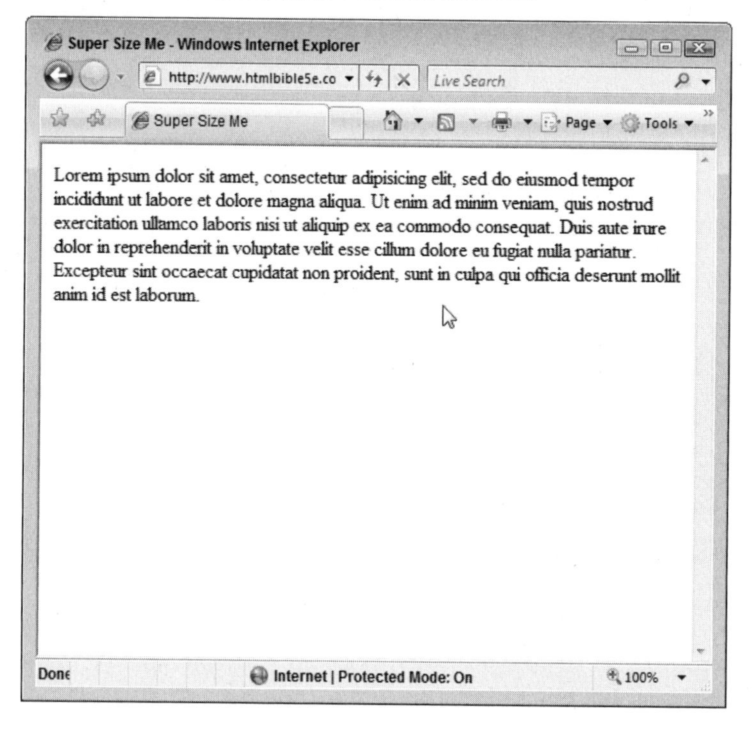

The `style.fontSize` property would be null because the `bigText` element does not contain a `style` attribute. How, then, does the preceding example work if it doesn't change the `medium` value of `font-size` set in the `<style>` section? The answer is that it doesn't need to change the values in the `<style>` section; it simply sets values in the element's `style` *attribute*, which has precedence over the styles in the `<style>` section.

Of course, if there were a value for an element's `style` attribute, the style collection could be used to determine it.

If you want to read the properties set in the `<style>` section, you must use one of two methods — one for IE browsers and another for Mozilla browsers. IE has an object property named `currentStyle`, while Mozilla browsers have a `window` objects property — specifically, `window.getComputedStyle`.

FIGURE 36-2

After the text is clicked, it now has an xx-large font.

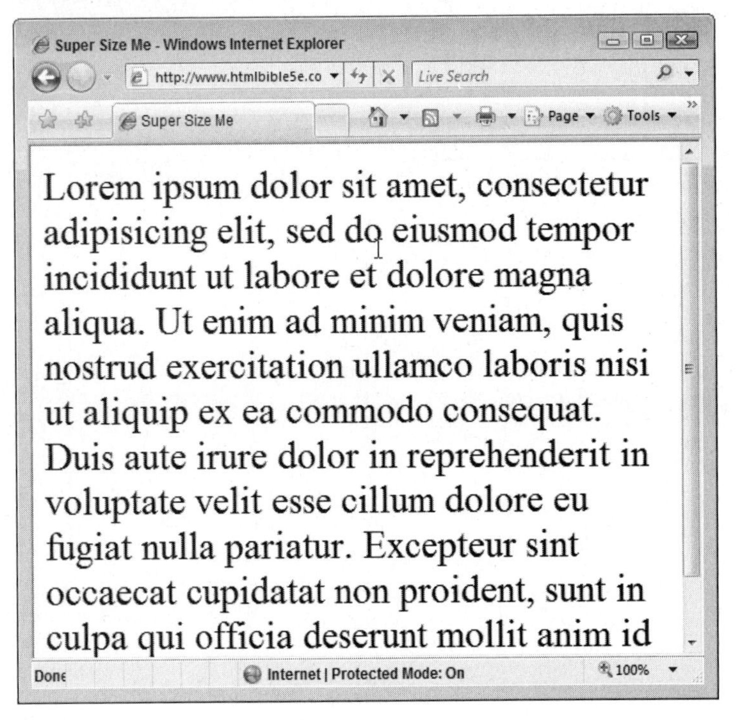

Use of the IE property is straightforward: Find the object via its `id` attribute and then use the property to return the style property's value, as in the following code.

```
obj = document.getElementById(id);
value = obj.currentStyle['fontSize'];
```

Note that the style property is given in the "omit hyphen" style — that is, `fontSize` instead of `font-size`.

The Mozilla method has an extra step because its property returns a collection that must be parsed for the desired property. The parsing is done via the `getPropertyValue( )`method, as shown here:

```
obj = document.getElementById(id);
objstyles = window.getComputedStyle(obj,null);
value = objstyles.getPropertyValue('font-size');
```

Notice that the Mozilla method uses the standard CSS name for properties, not the "omit hyphen" name. In either case, at the end of the code, the variable `value` would hold the value of the `font-size` property.

You could combine these methods into a single function by adding a bit of browser detection. The following listing shows a sample function that, given an object id and the "omit hyphen" and normal CSS property name, will return the value of the property:

```
// Return the value of CSS propName for element
//   with given id
function getStyleVal (id, propName) {
  // Can we do this at all? (getElementById available)
  if (obj = document.getElementById(id)) {
    // Is currentStyle available (IE)
    if (obj.currentStyle) {
      // Convert property name to IE format
      if (propName.indexOf("-") != -1) {
        hyp = propName.indexOf("-");
        propName = propName.substr(0,hyp) +
                   propName.charAt(hyp+1).toUpperCase() +
                   propName.substr(hyp+2);
}
      return obj.currentStyle[propName];
}
    // Is getComputedStyle available (Mozilla)
    if (window.getComputedStyle) {
        compStyle = window.getComputedStyle(obj,null);
        return compStyle.getPropertyValue(propName);
}
}   // End If obj=document.getElementById
  // Else return a blank string
  return "";
}
```

Note that the function checks whether the browser supports `document.getElementById` (it will if it is a modern browser) before doing anything. It then determines whether the IE or Mozilla method is available and acts accordingly to return the property value. Along the way, it also converts the property name, if necessary, to deal with IE's preferred format. Figures 36-3 and 36-4 show the function running in IE and Firefox, respectively, on a document that contains the following code:

```
  <style type="text/css">
    #bigText { font-size: medium;}
  </style>
...
<p id="bigText"
onClick="alert(getStyleVal('bigText','font-
size'));">Lorem ipsum dolor sit amet, consectetur
adipisicing elit, ...
```

When the paragraph text is clicked, a JavaScript alert box pops up and shows the value of the paragraph's `font-size` property.

FIGURE 36-3

The getStyleVal function is used to show the value of a paragraph's font-size property in Internet Explorer.

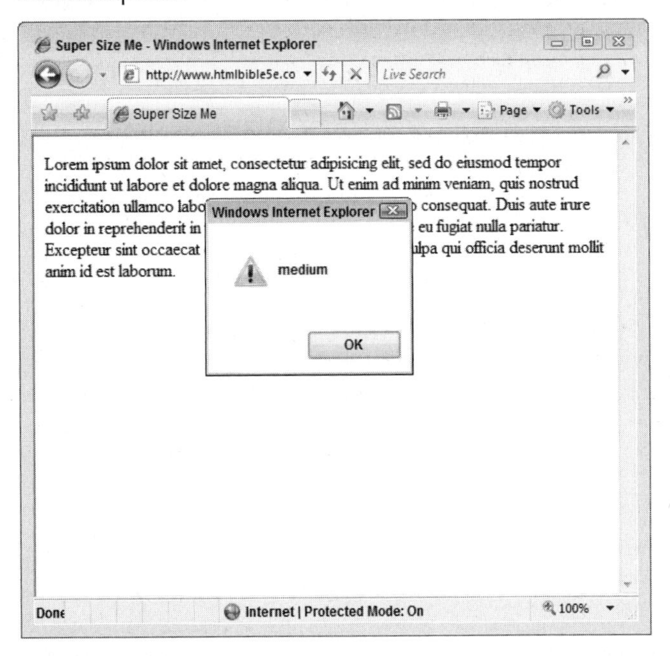

FIGURE 36-4

The getStyleVal function is used to show the value of a paragraph's font-size property in Firefox.

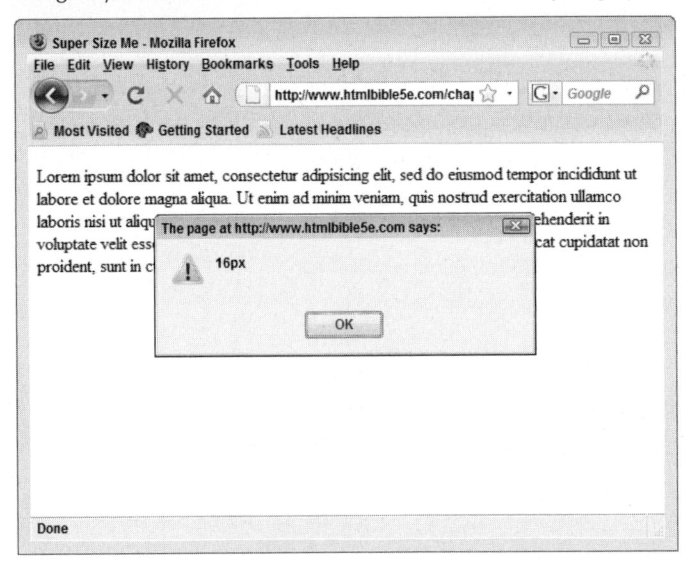

Note

Notice that the `getStyleVal` function returns an absolute font size, in points, when run in Firefox. Because of the nature of the functions to return the values, they may vary in format from the values used to set properties in the actual styles. For example, you might set a color to orange via a value like `#FFA500`, while the JavaScript function returns `orange`. Or, as in the example in the previous screen shots, the absolute font size is returned instead of the relative setting of `medium`. ■

Why, then, can't you use these two methods to also manipulate styles? Because these methods are read-only, you can retrieve the value of style properties using these methods, but you can't set properties with them. You can set the value of style properties directly, as shown in the beginning of this section.

Useful CSS Manipulation

Earlier examples showed how you can manipulate the font properties of elements in a document. Although such manipulations can be helpful, more involved manipulations of CSS using JavaScript can be even more useful. This section shows a few examples to get you started.

Hiding and showing text

With CSS and JavaScript, it is fairly trivial to alternately show and hide text. This can be used for a variety of purposes, such as drop-down menus or hiding text until a user decides to reveal it. For example, consider a list of questions and answers. A user of the site might not want to see the entire list of answers, but may want to selectively reveal a few. Using the CSS `display` property, you can write a script to enable this behavior.

Consider the following code, which hides the answer until any portion of the question is clicked. If the question is clicked a second time, the answer is again hidden. Figure 36-5 shows the answer in its hidden state, and Figure 36-6 shows the answer revealed after the "Q" is clicked.

```
<!DOCTYPE HTML PUBLIC "-//W3C//DTD HTML 4.01//EN"
  "http://www.w3.org/TR/html4/strict.dtd">
<html>
<head>
  <title>Hide and Seek Text</title>
  <style type="text/css">
    /* Initially hide all the questions */
    .hidenseek { display: none;}
    /* Question and answer display styles */
    .Q { font-size: xx-large;
         padding-bottom: 0;
         margin-bottom: 0;
         cursor: pointer;}
    .Qtext { margin-left: 20px;
             margin-top: 0;
             padding-top: 0;}
```

```
    .A { font-size: xx-large;
         padding-bottom: 0;
         margin-bottom: 0;
         clear: left;}
    .Atext { margin-left: 20px;
             margin-top: 0;
             padding-top: 0;}
  </style>
  <script type="text/JavaScript">
    // Alternately reveal or hide the element
    function hidenseek(id) {
      obj = document.getElementById(id);
      // If the style is blank, it hasn't been set yet
      //   and we can assume the element is hidden
      if ((obj.style.display == "") ||
          (obj.style.display == "none")) {
        obj.style.display = "block";
}       else {
        obj.style.display = "none";
}
}
  </script>
</head>
<body>
<div onClick="hidenseek('A1')"><p class="Q">Q:</p>
<p class="Qtext">What kind of equipment and peripherals do I need to
bring to the LAN event?</p>
</div>
<div id="A1" class="hidenseek">
<p class="A">A:</p>
<p class="Atext">You will need to bring the following (minimum)
items: your computer (minumum P4 with 1GB of RAM and a high-end
video card), a monitor (no larger than 19"), keyboard, mouse, a
surge protector, and a CAT-5 network cable at least 5' long. Do not
bring anything that is not listed herein, or attempt to bring and
use more than one computer.</p>
</div>
</body>
</html>
```

This example operates by using a JavaScript function that reads the value of an object's `display` property and sets the property to the opposite of its current value — revealing a hidden element or hiding a visible one. The function is called via an `onClick` handler attached to the `div` element that contains the question. The function call includes the `id` of the matching question so the function knows what element to act upon (in this case "A1").

As previously mentioned, you can use this technique for a variety of purposes. You simply hide the elements you wish to start hidden (using a value of `none` for the elements' display property) and use a function call — tied to buttons or other events — to show and optionally toggle the visibility of those elements.

FIGURE 36-5

The answer to the question starts out in a hidden state.

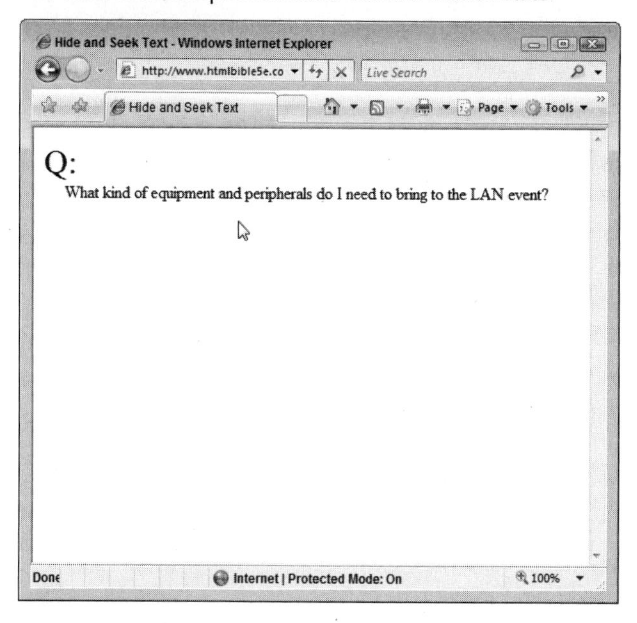

FIGURE 36-6

If the Q (or any part of the question text) is clicked, the answer is revealed. Clicking again hides the answer.

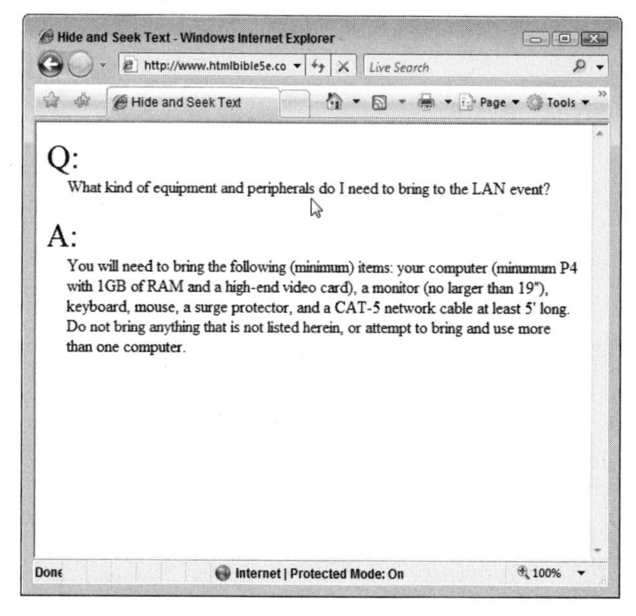

Picture zooming

Another common use for such CSS effects is to zoom images from thumbnails to their full size. This technique is used often in picture galleries and on other pages where showing a full-size image is desirable but prohibitive.

The technique is similar to the techniques already shown in this chapter — a JavaScript event triggers a script to change CSS properties of certain elements. In this case, the script changes the `display` property of an image thumbnail and a full-size image. A sample document with such a script is shown here:

```
<!DOCTYPE HTML PUBLIC "-//W3C//DTD HTML 4.01//EN"
  "http://www.w3.org/TR/html4/strict.dtd">
<html>
<head>
  <title>Picture Zoom</title>
  <style type="text/css">
    .zoom { display: none;
            float: left;}
    .thumb { display: block;
             float: left;}
    .text  { float: left;
             padding-left: 20px;}
  </style>
  <script type="text/JavaScript">
    function PicZoom(id) {
      pic = document.getElementById(id);
      thum = document.getElementById("T"+id);
      if ((pic.style.display == "") ||
        (pic.style.display == "none")) {
        pic.style.display = "block";
        thum.style.display = "none";
}       else {
        pic.style.display = "none";
        thum.style.display = "block";
}
}
  </script>
</head>
<body>
  <div id="1" class="zoom"><p><img src="ashley.jpg"
   width="428" height="568" alt="Ashley"
   onMouseOut="PicZoom(1);" /></p></div>
  <div id="T1" class="thumb"><p><img src="ashley-thumb.jpg"
   width="171" height="227" alt="Ashley"
   onMouseOver="PicZoom(1);" /></p></div>
  <div class="text" style="float:left;"><p>For the most wild, yet
   most homely narrative which I am about to pen, I neither expect
   nor solicit belief. Mad indeed would I be to expect it, in a case
   where my very senses reject their own evidence. Yet, mad am I
   not --and very surely do I not dream. But to-morrow I die, and
```

```
    to-day I would unburden my soul. My immediate purpose is to place
    before the world, plainly, succinctly, and without comment, a
    series of mere household events. In their consequences, these
    events have terrified --have tortured --have destroyed me. Yet I
    will not attempt to expound them. To me, they have presented
    little but Horror --to many they will seem less terrible than
    baroques. Hereafter, perhaps, some intellect may be found which
    will reduce my phantasm to the common-place --some intellect
    more calm, more logical, and far less excitable than my own,
    which will perceive, in the circumstances I detail with awe,
    nothing more than an ordinary succession of very natural causes
    and effects.
</p></div>
</body>
</html>
```

The images, thumbnail and full-size, are embedded in `div` elements for formatting and flexibility purposes. The thumbnail `div` initially has its `display` property set to `block` so it is visible. Conversely, the full-size image `div` initially has its `display` property set to `none` so it is not visible. The thumbnail `<img>` tag includes an `onMouseOver` event to call the `PicZoom( )`script when the mouse is placed over the image. The script reverses the `display` property of the thumbnail and full-size image `div` elements, making the full-size image visible and hiding the thumbnail. The mouse remains in position, now over the full-size image. When the mouse is moved off the image, an `onMouseOut` event in the full-size image tag calls the script again, setting the `display` properties back to their original settings to hide the full-size image and reveal the thumbnail.

This action can be seen in Figure 36-7, which shows the document in its beginning state, and in Figure 36-8, which shows the full-size image revealed, and the thumbnail hidden.

Note

As with most examples in this chapter, many methods can be used to create the image zoom effect. Some methods place both images on one large image and move the image around a "frame" to display one or the other, as necessary. Another method is to change the `src` attribute of the `<img>` tag so it displays the desired image. There are also complex, layered solutions, changing the `z-index` value of the concerned elements. Don't be afraid to play with your own solutions as well. ■

Menu buttons with rollovers

All the previous examples in this chapter use JavaScript to manipulate CSS to achieve various effects. So far, we have neglected the CSS anchor pseudo-classes, which can achieve similar effects.

The CSS anchor pseudo-classes are listed in Table 36-1.

The pseudo-classes are typically used to style elements as dynamic anchor elements. Using `:hover`, for example, you can dynamically change an element as the mouse passes over it — just like normal HTML anchors do.

For instance, the following document uses `:hover` to change the styling of anchors in table cells as the mouse passes over them. The effect, shown in Figure 36-9, is similar to dynamically styled menus driven by JavaScript.

FIGURE 36-7

The document begins with the thumbnail visible and the full-size image hidden.

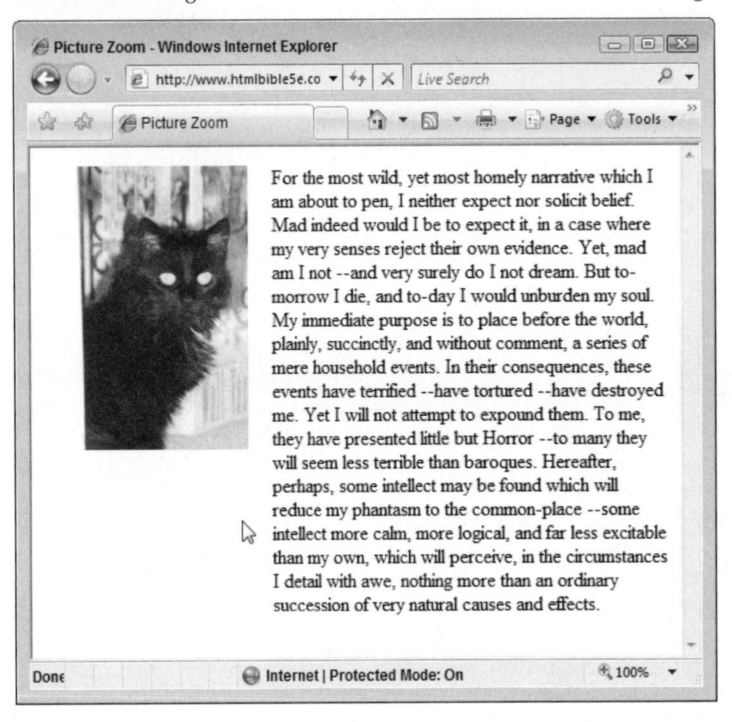


```
<!DOCTYPE HTML PUBLIC "-//W3C//DTD HTML 4.01//EN"
  "http://www.w3.org/TR/html4/strict.dtd">
<html>
<head>
  <title>Pseudo Class Menus</title>

  <style type="text/css">
    .nav tr td { border: 1pt solid black;}
    .menu { color: black;
            background-color: white;
            text-transform: none;
            text-decoration: none;}
    .menu:hover { color: white;
                  background-color: black;
                  text-transform: uppercase;
                  text-decoration: none;}
    .menucase { width: 100px;}
  </style>
</head>
<body>
<div class="menucase">
<table border="0" width=100%" class="nav">
```

```
    <tr><td><a class="menu" href="home.html">Home</a></td></tr>
    <tr><td><a class="menu" href="products.html">Products</a></td></tr>
    <tr><td><a class="menu" href="services.html">Services</a></td></tr>
    <tr><td><a class="menu" href="support.html">Support</a></td></tr>
    <tr><td><a class="menu" href="about.html">About</a></td></tr>
  </table>
  </div>
  </body>
  </html>
```

FIGURE 36-8

When the mouse is placed over the thumbnail image, the full-size image is revealed.

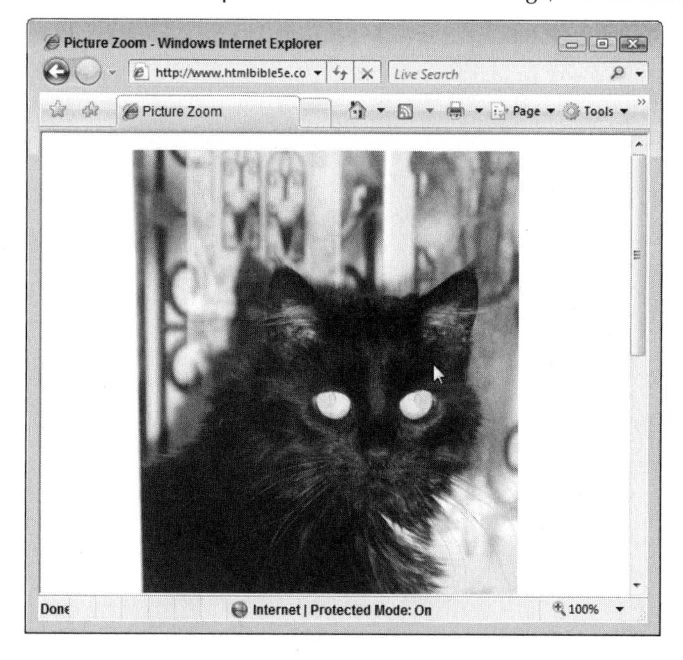

TABLE 36-1

CSS Anchor Pseudo-Classes

Pseudo-Class	Use/Effect
`:link`	Formats the element(s) matched in the attached selector as unvisited links
`:visited`	Formats the element(s) matched in the attached selector as visited links
`:hover`	Formats the element(s) matched in the attached selector when the mouse hovers over them
`:active`	Formats the element(s) matched in the attached selector as active links

FIGURE 36-9

The pseudo-classes can be used to create dynamic menus as you move the mouse over the menu items they highlight.

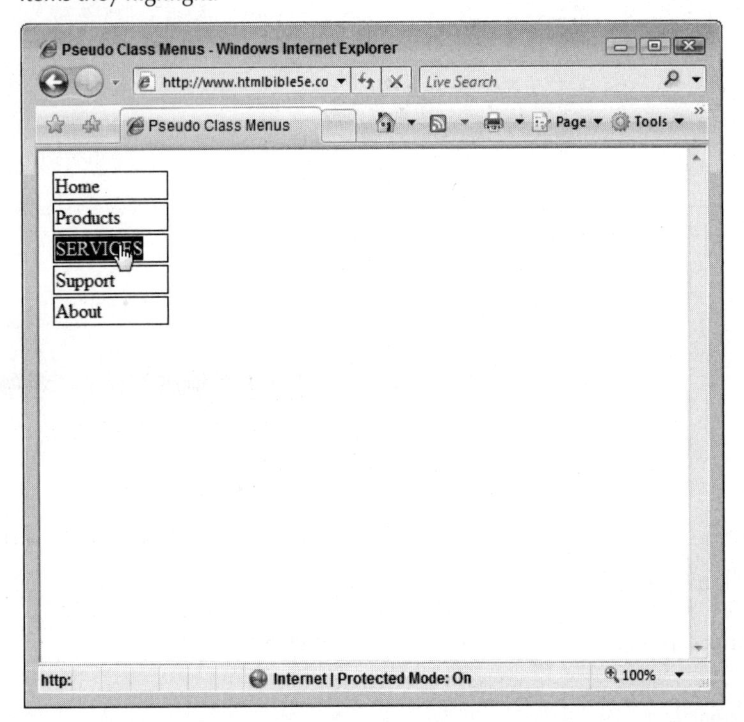

Note that although the technique of using pseudo-classes for such effects is very popular, it does disregard the best practice of separating behavior and presentation. This example is shown for completeness, but it is generally better to go the JavaScript route than CSS pseudo-classes for this type of effect.

Tip

Keep in mind that this technique can be used in conjunction with most elements. However, only the anchor tag can be formatted with the anchor pseudo-classes — use other elements to format the anchor tags within the document accordingly. ■

Summary

This chapter covered dynamic content and CSS. You learned how to use JavaScript to modify an element's underlying CSS for a variety of effects and how CSS pseudo-classes can be used to achieve dynamic effects. The next chapter covers how to use CSS to define pages for printing before we venture into niche CSS topics in the last part of the book (Chapters 38 through 41).

CHAPTER 37

Media Styles and Defining Documents for Printing

IN THIS CHAPTER

Understanding CSS Media Types

Setting Up Documents for Printing

Creating a Multimedia Document

The Web was originally designed to bring printed media to the computer screen. Paragraph elements, list elements, and tables were all designed to provide adequate vehicles for approximating documents normally found in print.

As times have changed, this situation has somewhat reversed. Now documents that originated on the Web are being formatted for the printed page. This phenomenon is especially true for such documents as e-commerce invoices, calendars and events, and documents of directions — whether they be do-it-yourself instructions or directions to a popular venue.

Of course, printed documents are not the only secondary destination for Web-originated documents; Web documents are also being made available to aural (speech only) devices, presentation and handheld devices, and low-resolution Web browsers (such as WebTV).

Thankfully, CSS has several mechanisms for formatting a document for these various media types. This chapter concentrates on the print media type, but many of the techniques discussed translate to other media types as well.

Understanding CSS Media Types

Table 37-1 lists the various media types supported in CSS.

Note

Because of the rapidly evolving deployment of Web documents to other media types, the preceding list (specified in CSS2) is not designed to be all-inclusive. The list is amended from time to time and will continue to grow as Web documents continue to be deployed in other formats. ■

TABLE 37-1

CSS Media Types

Media Type	Intended Destination/User Agent
`all`	Suitable for all devices
`aural`	Intended for speech-capable user agents and synthesizers
`Braille`	Intended for Braille tactile feedback devices
`embossed`	Intended for paged Braille printers
`handheld`	Intended for handheld devices (typically small screen, monochrome, limited bandwidth)
`print`	Intended for paged, opaque material and for documents viewed onscreen in print preview mode
`projection`	Intended for projected presentations, such as projectors or print to transparencies
`screen`	Intended primarily for color computer screens
`tty`	Intended for media using a fixed-pitch character grid, such as teletypes, terminals, or portable devices with limited display capabilities
`tv`	Intended for television-type devices (low resolution, color, limited-scrollability screens, with sound available)

Specifying media types

You have several ways to specify that a style, or group of styles, should be used only for a specific media type. The following sections detail each method.

Note

If no media type is specified in a document, the default of "all" is assumed and all user agents try to render the document according to its CSS code. If you intend your document to be displayed only on computer-type devices, ensure that you set all of your document's styles to the `screen` media type using the methods outlined in the next few sections. ■

Specifying one style's media type

The `@media` rule can be used to specify that a single style definition applies only to specific media type(s). This rule has the following syntax:

```
@media <media_type(s)> {  definition }
```

For example, to specify that a particular definition is to be used with print media only, you could use code similar to the following, which has been indented for legibility:

```
@media print {
              body  { background-color: white;
                      color: black;
                    }
              }
```

You might have noticed the mention of media types (plural) in the preceding definition of the `@media` rule. This is because you can specify several media types, each separated by a comma, in the `@media` definition. For example, you might choose to specify the same style for both print and handheld media, using code similar to the following:

```
@media print, handheld {
              body  { background-color: white;
                      color: black;
        }
 }
```

Specifying a group of styles' media type

The `@media` rule is not limited to specifying one style's media type; you can place as many styles as you like within the `@media` rule's brackets. For example, consider the following code, which specifies that two styles are meant for print media:

```
@media print {
              body  { background-color: white;
                      color: black;
        }
              .highlight { background-color: black;
                           color: white;
             }
 }
```

The style element (`style`) supports a media attribute that can be used to specify that all the styles encapsulated within the element are of a particular media type, or types. The `style` element has the following format:

```
<style type="text/css" media="<media_type(s)>">
... style definitions ...
</style>
```

Note that the `media` attribute can be used to specify a single media type or a comma-separated list of multiple types.

You can use either of these methods to specify the media for entire blocks of styles, and create multiple media blocks within the same `style` block. However, it is generally easier to create groups of media-specific styles in external files and use the `link` element to link each into your document. This technique is outlined in the next section.

Specifying an external style sheet's media type

If you choose to place your media-specific styles in an external file, you can use the link element (link) to attach one or more of the files into your document. The link element has the following syntax:

```
<link rel="stylesheet" href="<css_file>" type="text/css"
   media="<media_type>" />
```

For example, if you have a style sheet named printed.css that you intend to use as print media instructions for a document, you could use a link element similar to the following:

```
<link rel="stylesheet" href="printed.css" type="text/css"
   media="print" />
```

Note
The link element's href argument requires a full path to the specified CSS file. For example, if your CSS files are stored in a directory named "styles," you should specify something similar to styles/printed.css in the preceding example. ■

You can also use the CSS @import rule to specify an external style sheet. The @import rule has the following syntax:

```
@import url("<stylesheet>") <media_type>;
```

For example, the following code imports an external style sheet named printstyles.css and designates its media type as print:

```
@import url("printstyles.css") print;
```

Keep in mind that the @import rule is a CSS command and must appear within an appropriate style section within your document.

Setting Up Documents for Printing

Each media type has additional properties to help define aspects of its medium and how documents using that type should be handled and rendered; and covering all the media types is beyond the scope of this book. In addition to the screen media type, however, print media is the most frequently used media type for Web documents.

This section covers the properties and methods available for print media.

The page box formatting model

If you've ever worked with a desktop publishing platform using software such as Quark XPress, InDesign, or PageMaker, you're probably familiar with the concept of a page box, within which fits everything that must appear on a page. Even if you haven't worked with desktop publishing software, you've probably seen precursors to the HTML/CSS box formatting model in word-processing packages you've used.

When you work in a word-processing or desktop publishing environment, you work with finite page sizes and page margins. The CSS page box formatting model is an attempt to replicate this for browser-based media. The page box model is based on the CSS box model, as shown in Figure 37-1.

Figure 37-1 simply extends the familiar CSS box model to reveal two major areas:

- The **page area** contains all of a page's elements.
- The **margin area** surrounds the page area. When a page area size is specified, the margins, if any, are subtracted.

On top of the page box, the model is expanded still further to account for the difference between *continuous* media, as represented by a browser, and *paged* media, which consists of discrete and specific page entities. This expansion is represented by the visual formatting model, which allows transfer of the continuous media as seen in a Web browser to an actual sheet of paper or transparency.

Defining the page size with the @page rule

In CSS, you define your desired page size using the `@page` rule. The `@page` rule defines which pages should be bound to the definitions within the rule. You then use a `page` property within a style element or attribute to indicate to which page a specific element belongs.

Note

Unfortunately, browser support has still not caught up to this particular CSS rule, and support is largely nonexistent at this point. Microsoft actually does provide support for this rule, but only through the MSHTML component, which application developers use as a browser widget within their applications. Internet Explorer itself does not include support for this rule in its printing templates, which are used for print previewing and printing Web documents from the browser. ■

The following listing shows an example of `@page` use:

```
@page printed {
          size: 3in 3in;
 }
body, p {
          page: printed;
}
```

In this listing, a page named `printed` is defined. Then the body and paragraph elements are defined using `printed` as the value of the `page` property and should print according to the specifications outlined in the `@page` rule.

FIGURE 37-1

The CSS box model

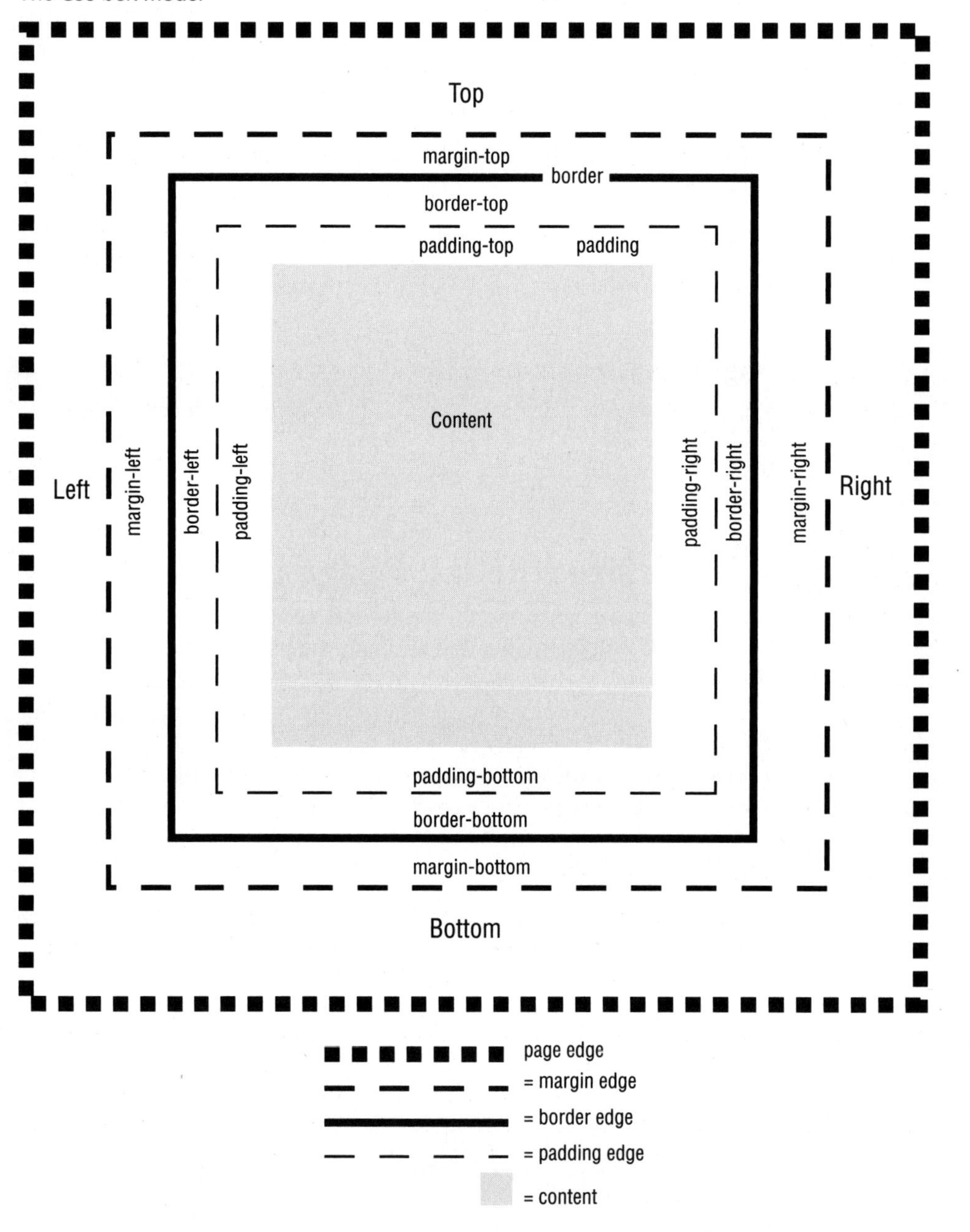

Note

The page name `printed` in the previous example is optional. If your document will use only one type of page, you can omit the page name, as in the following:

```
@page {
        size: 3in 3in;
}
```

Thereafter, any element defined as being print media will use the one, unnamed page definition. ■

In CSS2, you can use page selectors to name the first page, all left pages, all right pages, or a page with a specific name to which the rules apply. In the case of the previous listing, a named page called `printed` was used.

Setting up the page size with the size property

The actual dimensions of the page are defined using the `size` property, which consists of two values: one for the width and the other for the height. For example, the following definition sets up an 8½ by 11 inches page:

```
@page {
          size: 8.5in 11in;
     }
```

You can also use the following relative size values with the `size` property:

- `auto` — The default value set to whatever the target paper size is in the printer's settings.
- `landscape` — Rotates the page and swaps the two measures. In the previous example, the printed sheet would print at 11 inches wide by 8½ inches long.
- `portrait` — Overrides the targeted media's default settings to correspond with the dimensions you set in the `size` property.

Setting margins with the margin property

You should be careful when using margins because they are the outermost layer of a page. If you set the margins of a `body` element to three inches on either side, for example, be sure to adjust the width of the `body` element as well, or your page will not format properly.

However, in theory, you should be able to set margins for the printed page without worrying about the body text running off to one side of the browser when you neglect to set the width of the page's other elements. This is because margins can be set within the `@page` rule using the margin properties in CSS. You can set the page margins using the `margin` property in the same manner as you use it anywhere else, as shown here:

```
@page {
       size: 8.5in 11in;
       margin: .5in;
{
```

Cross-Ref

The CSS margin properties are covered in Chapter 32. ■

When they are set within the @page rule (currently supported by Opera only), the margin settings should be ignored when being viewed on the Web. However, as mentioned earlier, at the time of this writing, browser support for this feature is weak and results can be unpredictable.

Including crop and cross marks

If your document is destined for publication, it might be useful to include *crop marks* or *cross marks*. Crop marks look like plus signs (+) and are printed on the edge of page margins, showing a printer where to cut the page. Cross marks are other symbols printed near the edge of pages that enable printers to align numerous pages.

The marks property controls the printing of crop and cross marks and has the following syntax:

```
marks: <crop> | <cross> | <none> | <inherit> ;
```

Note

User agent support for the marks property is virtually nonexistent. ■

Controlling page breaks

In the event that your users may want to print your Web pages, you may want to avoid inappropriate page breaks. The three page-break properties can help better control page break behavior:

- page-break-before — Specifies how a page should break before a specific element, and on what side of the page the flow should resume
- page-break-after — Specifies how a page should break after a specific element, and on what side of the page the flow should resume
- page-break-inside — Tells the browser how to break a page from within a box element. Actual support for this property is limited to Opera. Neither Internet Explorer nor Netscape-based browsers support this property.

Using the page-break-before and page-break-after properties

The page-break-before and page-break-after properties specify how a page should break before or after a specific element, depending on which of the two properties you use, and on what side of the page the flow should resume. The CSS2 documentation provides some guidelines for page breaks:

- Page breaking should be avoided inside table elements, floating elements, and block elements with borders.
- Page breaking should occur as few times as possible. In other words, it's not a good idea to break a page with every paragraph.
- Pages that don't have explicit breaks should be approximately the same height.

Opera offers the best support for these properties. The Gecko browsers provide partial support, and support is all but missing from Internet Explorer. Table 37-2 lists the values that can be used with either the page-break-before or page-break-after property.

TABLE 37-2

Page-Break-Before/After Property Values

Value	Description
inherit	Specifies that the value should be inherited from the parent
auto	Allows the user agent (browser) to insert page breaks on an as-needed basis
avoid	Tells the user agent to avoid inserting page breaks before or after the current element
left	Forces one or two page breaks to create a blank left page
right	Forces one or two page breaks to create a blank right page
always	Tells the browser or user agent to always force a page break before or after the current element
'"'	This is not a value found in the spec but a value that can be used in Internet Explorer; it specifies that no property value should be used and, therefore, that no page break should be inserted before the current element.

Figure 37-2 shows the effects of a badly formatted page break. Notice how the heading remains on one page while its text flows to the next.

You can set the page-break-before or page-break-after property in a p element, for example, to force a page break before or after all p elements. You probably wouldn't want to actually do that, but you can create a class selector rule and apply the rule to the first or last paragraph of a page, depending on your needs, like this:

```
.pagebreak {
                page-break-before: always;
}
```

You can then use this class with elements, such as with specific h2 elements as shown in the following code, which fixes the odd page break shown earlier in Figure 37-2:

```
<h2 class="pagebreak">Spa Services</h2>
```

The fixed break is shown in Figure 37-3.

Note

Page breaks cannot be used within positioned elements. For example, if you have an absolutely positioned div element with a child p element, you cannot assign a page break to the p element. ■

FIGURE 37-2

A bad page break separates text from its heading.

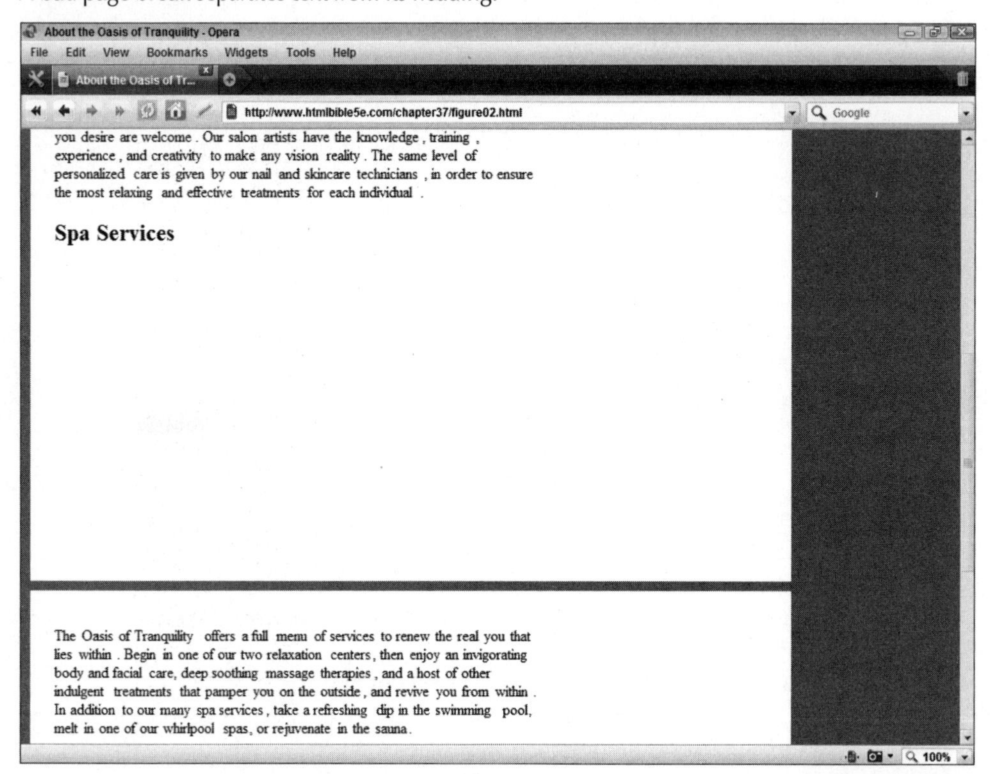

Using the page-break-inside property

You can also use a `page-break-inside` property to handle page breaks within elements (for example, if you have a very long `div` element). However, in practice, most browsers have little to no support for this property.

Handling widows and orphans

Widows and orphans are undesirable in typography, but CSS has provided an opportunity to reduce their impact. Widows and orphans refer to broken text, such as when a page break severs a paragraph, leaving one line from the paragraph on either side of the break. A *widow* is a spurious line at the top of a page, left over from the paragraph on the previous page. An *orphan* is similar, except it consists of a spurious line at the bottom of a page, where the remainder of the paragraph occurs on the next page. Again, it can be unsightly if a section or paragraph starts at the very end of a page and the page break results in a single line being left at the end of the previous page.

FIGURE 37-3

Adding a page break directive can indicate where a page should break, avoiding problems.

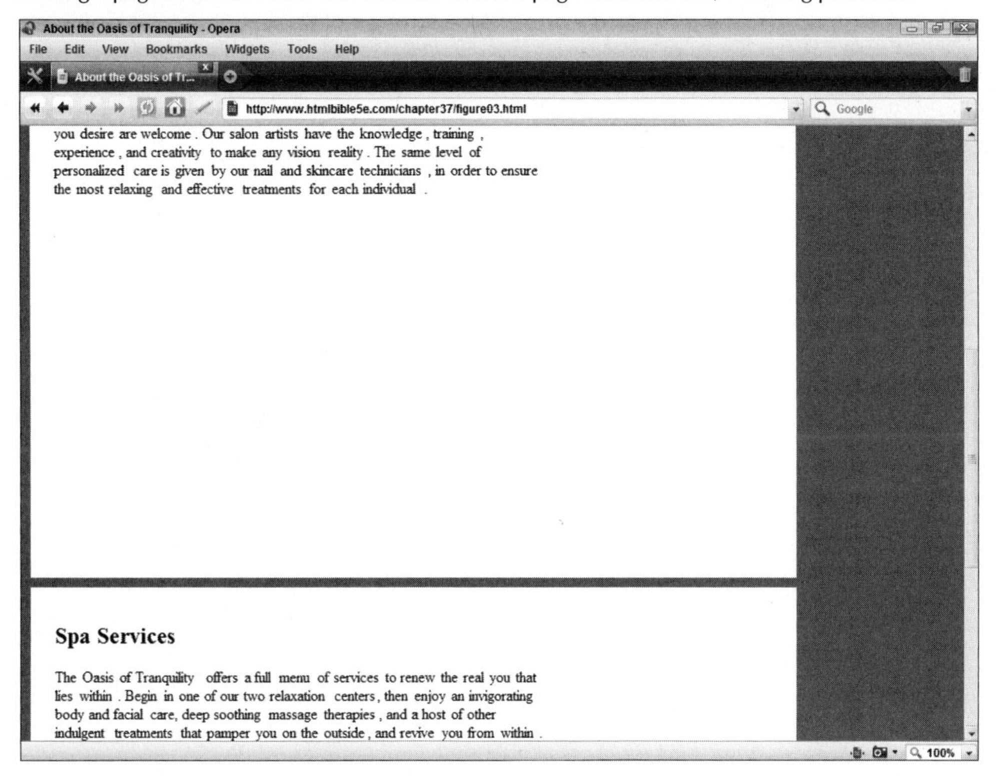

The two CSS properties relevant to widows and orphans, are conveniently named, respectively, `widow` and `orphan`.

Note

These two properties have virtually no support beyond the Opera browser. ■

Both of these properties have similar syntax:

```
widow: <integer or inherit>;
orphan: <integer or inherit>;
```

You name the property, and then supply the value, which can be either an integer or the explicit value `inherit`, the latter of which means that the element named in the style rule inherits the properties of its parent. The following sets a `p` element's widow to a minimum of three lines. This means that the bottom of the page must have a minimum of three lines when printing:

```
p { widow: 3; }
```

An integer value for either property specifies that the top (widow) or bottom (orphan) should have the given number of lines — if that is not possible, the entire element moves to the next page.

Preparing documents for double-sided printing

To set up pages for printing double-sided documents, you must account for different margins on each side of a page. One method to handle this would be to manually set margins for each element, anticipating on which side of the page each would appear. Thankfully, there is an easier way. You can use the pseudo-classes `:left` and `:right` to set the margins of each differently. For example, consider the following:

```
@page :left {
  margin-left: .5in;
  margin-right: .25in;
}
@page :right {
  margin-left: .25in;
  margin-right: .5in;
}
```

Note

Of course, like many advanced CSS features, user agent support for the `:left` and `:right` pseudo-classes is almost nonexistent. ■

You can also use the `:first` pseudo-class to specify different values for the first page of a document with code similar to the following:

```
@page {
        margin: 1in
}
@page :first {
        margin-top: 3in
}
```

The preceding code sets all the page margins to one inch, but the `:first` definition resets the top margin of the first page to three inches.

Creating a Multimedia Document

No doubt you have run across several documents on the Web that have corresponding "print friendly" versions. These documents tend to be informational in nature — recipes, maps and directions, do-it-yourself instructions, invoices, and so on. The screen media representations of the documents typically include all the usual elements — graphical headings, several advertisements, and colorful layouts — not entirely suitable for printing the key information embedded in the document.

As such, many of these documents include a print friendly link when displayed on the Web. Clicking that link displays a new page with the important information, but devoid of the superfluous elements and information. Sometimes the print friendly page includes additional information necessary, or information just simply nice to have.

Using CSS media descriptors and relying on the CSS cascade and inheritance properties, you can use one document for both the screen and print versions. An example of this concept follows.

The online (screen media) document

The following listing and Figure 37-4 show a typical online page with information (driving directions) that would be advantageous to print:

```
<!DOCTYPE HTML PUBLIC "-//W3C//DTD HTML 4.01//EN"
    "http://www.w3.org/TR/html4/strict.dtd">
    <html>
    <head>
    <!-- Breadcrumb and utility scripts -->
    <script type="text/JavaScript" src="/functions.js">
                     </script>
                     <style type="text/css">
  body { background-color: black; }
.main { width: 768px;
height: 1024px;
padding: 20px;
     text-align: center;
     background-color: #222222;
     background-image:url(/images/junglepool.jpg);
     background-position: center center;
     background-repeat: no-repeat;
border: 3pt #222222 solid; }
.breadcrumbs { font-size: small;
text-align: left;
padding-left: 10px;
background-color: #CCCCCC;
height: 1.5em; }
.heading { background-color: #CCCCCC;
text-align: left;
margin: 25px 0px; }
  /* Heading for printing - hide it for now */
.printheading { text-align: center;
margin-bottom: 50px;
display: none;
visibility: hidden; }
.content { text-align: left;
font-size: 9pt;
background-color: #CCCCCC;
margin: 15px;
    margin-bottom: 0px;
padding: 20px;  }
```

```
.center { text-align: center; }
.mleft { text-align: left; }
.mright { text-align: right; }
.mcenter { text-align: center; }
.footer {  margin-top: 25px;
font-size: small;
text-align: center;
background-color: #CCCCCC;
height: 1.5em; }
</style>
   <!-- Print friendly (print media) style sheet -->
   <link rel="stylesheet" href="/printstyles.css"
    type="text/css" media="print" />
  <title>Oasis of Tranquility - Directions</title>
  </head>
  <body>
  <div class="main">
         <div class="breadcrumbs">
              <script type="text/JavaScript">
                     breadcrumbs();
</script>
   </div>
   <div class="printheading">
        <h1>The Oasis of Tranquility</h1>
        </div>
        <div class="heading">
             <table border="0" width="100%">
  <tr>
  <td><img src="/images/OasisHeader.gif" width="475px"
  height="161" alt="The Oasis of Tranquility Header" /></td>
           <td>
           <table border="0">
                   <tr>
                   <td class="mleft"><a
                    href="services">Services</a></td>
  <td class="mright">
        <a href="facilities">Facilities</a>
            </td>
            </tr><tr>
            <td colspan="2" class="mcenter">
                      <a href="calendar-appointments">
  Calendar/Appointments</a>
  </td>
  </tr><tr>
  <td colspan="2" class="mcenter">
              <a href="consultants-staff">
                  Consultants/Staff</a>
                  </td>
                  </tr><tr>
                  <td class="mleft"><a
```

```
                    href="aboutus">About Us</a></td>
  <td class="mright">
        <a href="contact-directions">
            Contact/Directions</a>
            </td>
            </tr>
            </table>
            </td>
            </tr>
            </table>
            </div>
            <table border="0" width="95%">
                        <tr><td class="content">
  <h3>Directions from the International Airport</h3>
  <p>
  <ol>
  <li>Start out going NORTH on PENA BLVD. (0.2mi)</li>
  <li>Go STRAIGHT toward TERMINAL EAST. (2.0mi)</li>
  <li>Stay STRAIGHT to go onto PENA BLVD. (3.4mi)</li>
  <li>Take the E-470 TOLLWAY N exit- EXIT 6B-
  toward FORT COLLINS. (0.8mi)</li>
  <li>Merge onto E 470N (Portions toll). (14.7mi)</li>
  <li>Take the COLORADO BOULEVARD exit- EXIT 43. (0.4mi)</li>
  <li>Turn LEFT onto COLORADO BLVD. (4.2mi)</li>
  <li>Turn RIGHT onto E 120TH AVE / CO-128 W. (1.5mi)</li>
  <li>End at 1283 E 120th Ave - Denver, CO 80233-5728, US</li>
  </ol>
  </p>
  <p class="center" >
       <img src="/images/AirportMap.jpg" width="381" height="255"
  alt="Directions from airport" />
    </p>
    </td></tr>
    </table>
    <div class="footer">
          <p>
          <a href="services">Services</a>
<a href="facilities">Facilities</a>

<a href="calendar-appointments">Calendar/Appointments</a>

<a href="consultants-staff">Consultants/Staff</a>

<a href="aboutus">About Us</a>

<a href="contact-directions">Contact/Directions</a>
    </p>
    </div>
    </div> <!-- Main -->
    </body>
    </html>
```

FIGURE 37-4

Most Web pages contain many elements that are disadvantageous to print, such as headers, graphics, backgrounds, and special features.

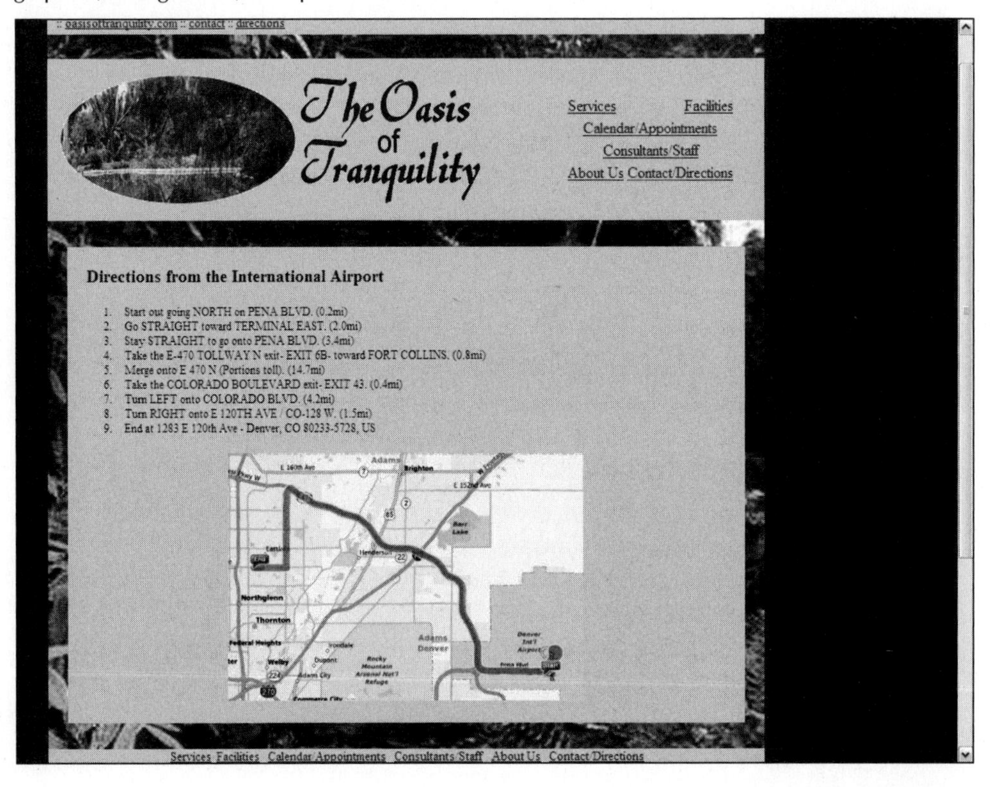

As you can see, a handful of superfluous elements on the page aren't only unnecessary to print, but are downright undesirable. Such elements include the following:

- Navigational aids
- Page background colors and graphics
- Graphical headers — image and stylistic text
- Footer navigation links

It is best to reformat or remove these elements from the printed page.

Reformatting the page

Because most of the elements are attached to styles, reformatting the page is fairly trivial. Using the CSS cascade and inheritance properties, you can create additional styles for print media. If the styles are added to the end of the style list, they will take precedence over the previous styles. However, when designated for print media, they will only come into play when printed.

For example, consider the following styles, created for all elements in the document that need different styles when printed. The code shows the styles created to modify elements for printing:

```
@page { size: 8.5in 11in;}
body { background-color: white;}
.main { border: none;
     background-color: white;
     background-image: none;}
.breadcrumbs { display: none;}
.heading { display: none;
           visibility: hidden;}
.heading-content { display: none;}
.printheading { display: block;
                visibility: visible;}
.content { background-color: white;}
.footer { display: none;
          visibility: hidden;}
```

As you can see, there isn't a one-to-one correlation between the styles in the original document and the print media styles, nor the properties of either. The print styles only need to include styles and individual properties needing changes. For example, the print styles concentrate on doing the following:

- Removing images
- Removing borders
- Removing backgrounds
- Hiding irrelevant elements (headers, footers, navigation elements)
- Making desirable print elements previously hidden visible

The last bullet in this list is important — you may have elements that you don't want to print, but which contain information you don't want to lose. In the example, I don't want to print the graphical header but would like to print the name of the website ("The Oasis of Tranquility"). To achieve this effect, I embed a special `div` in the document, give it a class of `printheader`, and use corresponding styles to hide it by default. The print styles then reverse the visibility, hiding the graphical header and revealing the plain text header.

The print styles are placed in a separate style document and linked into the main HTML document and to the end of the embedded styles using a `link` element, similar to the following:

```
<link rel="stylesheet" href="/printstyles.css"
type="text/css" media="print" />
```

Note

In this example, the styles are included in an external style sheet for manageability. They could also be embedded within the document using an `@media` rule. ■

It's important that the print media styles be included at the end of the style list to ensure that the style inheritance is correctly followed. You might have noticed that the styles embedded within the document are not coded for any particular media; this means they are valid for print media as well. If the print-specific styles did not appear at the end of the style list, the general styles could override them.

Tip

When creating media-specific styles for documents, it is generally a good idea to mark every group of styles for the media they should support. ■

Summary

This chapter covered how to use media styles to format a document for printing. You learned how to best define the page, adjust page breaks, and combine media types in one document. The next chapter wraps up Part III of the book, the core CSS coverage. The following part (Chapters 39 through 41) covers more niche CSS topics.

CHAPTER

38

The Future of CSS: CSS3

IN THIS CHAPTER

Modularity

Using CSS3 Properties Today

More Control over Selections

Revisiting the Brass Ring of CSS: Rounded Corners

For the development of Web content, Cascading Style Sheets (CSS) have become the inseparable sibling of HTML. Without CSS, designers cannot create elaborately designed documents; without HTML, designers cannot create any platform for documents.

Introduced in late 1996, CSS level 1 brought a whole new design perspective to the Web. Later, in mid-1998, CSS level 2 was responsible for a new dimension of Web content, positional element, a third dimension of elements, media types, and more. In 2005, CSS level 2.1 was released to fix existing bugs in CSS but did not provide any evolutionary changes to Web design.

CSS level 3, currently in development, promises another leap forward on the Web, introducing new properties and values that bring the current realm of the Web that much closer to printed medium. Although full coverage of the new version could fill a book of its own, this chapter provides an overview of some of the more globally anticipated features of CSS level 3.

Note

As mentioned, CSS3 is currently still in development. Because this chapter was written based on the current *draft* specification, it is likely that some of the material presented here will change. Visit the W3C working site to follow the development of this new version: `www.w3.org/Style/CSS/current-work#table`. ■

Just Better

Much of the work going into this new version of CSS is to make the specification more exacting, to better specify how dynamic elements should be dynamic and how static elements are static. Although CSS is thought of as being fairly mature, the fact that the CSS specification is only entering its fourth revision should be kept in mind — there is still plenty of room in the specification for alternate interpretations. A big part of the CSS2.1 specification was to close various holes and idiosyncrasies in CSS2. Look for CSS3 to continue this effort.

Note

In theory, a more exacting specification should mean more consistent support for the specification. After all, the specification should leave little doubt as to how the various properties should affect document elements. Unfortunately, the actual implementation of the CSS3 specification remains in the user agent vendor's hands — hands that have proven to take a few liberties with specification interpretation. ■

Modularity

CSS3 is being developed in a modular fashion, broken down into 26 distinct modules instead of the monolithic structure of CSS past. The modules and their descriptions are provided in the following table.

Module	Content/Purpose
Syntax/Grammar	A means to attach properties to a structured document
Selectors	Describes the selectors used to marry properties to document elements
Values and Units	Specifies how values and units are described and used
Value Assignment/ Cascade/Inheritance	Describes how various properties interact and how the core of CSS (cascade, inheritance, etc.) operates
Box Model/Vertical	Describes how the box model of CSS operates, causing element flow, floating elements, and providing a third dimension for elements
Positioning	Describes how elements are positioned differently from how they would normally appear in a document
Color/Gamma/Color Profiles	Describes the handling of color in CSS
Colors and Backgrounds	Describes how element foreground and background colors are handled
Line Box Model	Describes the format of the line element box model
Text	Describes the method of text handling in user agents
Fonts	Describes the method of font handling in user agents
Ruby	A draft describing methods of handling new styles of typographic traditions

Module	Content/Purpose
Generated Content/Markers	Describes of how content is generated and markers are displayed
Replaced Content	Describes the definition and handling of replaced content
Paged Media	Describes how documents should handle paged media — headers, footers, etc.
User Interface	Describes how the user interface should handle various states and elements
Web Fonts	Describes the use of fonts and better control over them
ACSS (Aural CSS)	Describes methods of making stylized content more accessible
Synchronized Multimedia Integration Language (SMIL)	Describes how to make CSS and SMIL work together to produce better multimedia
Tables	Describes how table content should be implemented via CSS
Columns	Describes how to use CSS to create flexible column layouts
Scalable Vector Graphics (SVG)	Describes methods that can be used to produce dynamic, scalable vector graphics
Math	Describes how to apply stylistic conventions to mathematic expressions
Behavioral Extensions to CSS (BECSS)	Describes methods to attach behaviors (rather than styles) to elements
Media Queries	Describes methods of dynamically determining what styles, from what source, should be applied

The reasoning behind breaking CSS into a modular structure is simple: It makes the project much easier to manage. As the popularity of CSS increases, so does the user's desire to extend the capabilities of the standard. Using a modular structure provides a more efficient way of extending features and capabilities while still being able to adequately manage the whole.

Using CSS3 Properties Today

For various reasons, some of the major user agents have implemented CSS3 properties, even though the specification isn't yet final. These user agents include the Firefox browser and browsers that rely upon the Webkit framework, such as Mac Safari.

To maintain compatibility with other browsers and older versions of CSS, these browsers implement CSS3 features by using unique property names. These property names use prefixes such as `-moz` and `-webkit`, making the property definitions unrecognizable to other browsers.

Unfortunately, support of CSS3 properties is sketchy at best, and the browsers are apt to use property names that only resemble the actual CSS properties.

For example, all modern user agents support the `border-<side>-color` property to CSS2.1 levels, whereas Firefox 3.1+ also supports the CSS3 level of this property, via the `-moz-border-<side>-colors` property. The CSS3 specification enables the Web author to use a range of colors in the `-moz-border-<side>-colors` definition to achieve unique results.

Cross-Ref

See the section "Revisiting the Brass Ring of CSS: Rounded Corners," later in this chapter for more information on border colors and CSS3. ■

To ensure that use of the browser-specific properties does not adversely affect documents, the properties should appear in the following order:

1. Standard CSS2.1 format
2. Browser-specific CSS3 format

This enables all browsers to pick up the CSS2.1 property, ensuring that the non-CSS3 browsers receive their property value(s), and then allows the CSS3-enabled browsers to receive their values, overwriting the CSS2.1 value.

For example, consider the border color example. If you wanted to infuse your documents with that CSS3 property for bottom borders, you should use definitions similar to the following:

```
div  { border-bottom-color: black; }
div  { -moz-border-bottom-colors: #F9F9F9 #AFAFAF
                                  #BFBFBF #CFCFCF
                                  #DFDFDF #EFEFEF
                                  #FFFFFF; }
```

These two definitions cover non-CSS3-enabled user agents as well as Firefox 3.1+ browsers that support the extended property. As a result, non-CSS3 user agents will use black borders for `div` elements while Firefox will use the extended definition resulting in the gradient.

Note

The website `www.css3.info/` is a good source of information on CSS level 3, including current browser support of its features. ■

More Control over Selections

Not surprisingly, CSS3's selector interface is much more robust than that of CSS2.1. The new selector formats provide the capability to select almost any element in a document. The new CSS3 selectors are summarized in the following table.

Selector Format	Selects ...
`E[foo^="bar"]`	an `E` element whose "`foo`" attribute value begins exactly with the string "`bar`"
`E[foo$="bar"]`	an `E` element whose "`foo`" attribute value ends exactly with the string "`bar`"
`E[foo*="bar"]`	an `E` element whose "`foo`" attribute value contains the substring "`bar`"
`E:root`	an `E` element, root of the document
`E:nth-child(n)`	an `E` element, the nth child of its parent
`E:nth-last-child(n)`	an `E` element, the nth child of its parent, counting from the last one
`E:nth-of-type(n)`	an `E` element, the nth sibling of its type
`E:nth-last-of-type(n)`	an `E` element, the nth sibling of its type, counting from the last one
`E:last-child`	an `E` element, last child of its parent
`E:first-of-type`	an `E` element, first sibling of its type
`E:last-of-type`	an `E` element, last sibling of its type
`E:only-child`	an `E` element, only child of its parent
`E:only-of-type`	an `E` element, only sibling of its type
`E:empty`	an `E` element that has no children (including text nodes)
`E:target`	an `E` element being the target of the referring URI
`E:checked`	a user interface element `E` which is checked (for instance a radio-button or checkbox)
`E:not(s)`	an `E` element that does not match simple selector `s`
`E ~ F`	an `F` element preceded by an `E` element

Revisiting the Brass Ring of CSS: Rounded Corners

As previously mentioned in this book, designers have been clamoring for the ability to provide rounded corners to elements. As of this writing, the number of ways to do this without pure CSS is numbered in the 50s. These methods use uniquely placed elements, special graphics, and other optical tricks to simulate rounded corners. CSS3 simplifies the matter by providing rounded corner properties for block elements. As of this writing, Firefox 3.1+ supports rounded corners. Besides rounded corners, Firefox also supports multiple-color borders, enabling designers to make document elements have a unique and 3D appearance. For example, consider the following code, and Figure 38-1, showing how the document renders in Firefox 3.5, thanks to the -moz properties:

```
<html>

<head>
<style type="text/css">

div { clear: both;
      width: 50%;
      padding: 10px;
      margin-bottom: 40px; }


#rounded { background-color: gray;
           border: 1px solid black;
           -moz-border-radius: 5px; }

#shadowed { background-color: white;
            border: 3px solid black;
            -moz-box-shadow: 5px 5px 5px #666;}


#colored { border-width: 8px;
           border-style: solid;
           -moz-border-bottom-colors: red yellow blue
                                      yellow green;}


#gradient { border-width: 8px;
            border-style: solid;
            -moz-border-bottom-colors: #F9F9F9 #AFAFAF
                                       #BFBFBF #CFCFCF
                                       #DFDFDF #EFEFEF
                                       #FFFFFF; }

#partial { border: 1px solid black;
           -moz-border-radius-topleft: 5px; }


</style>
</head>

<body>
<div id="rounded">Rounded corners</div>
<div id="partial">One corner rounded (top-left)</div>
<div id="shadowed">Drop shadow</div>
<div id="colored">Colored border</div>
```

```
<div id="gradient">Gradient border</div>
</body>
</html>
```

FIGURE 38-1

CSS level 3 enables much more control over the components of elements, such as borders.

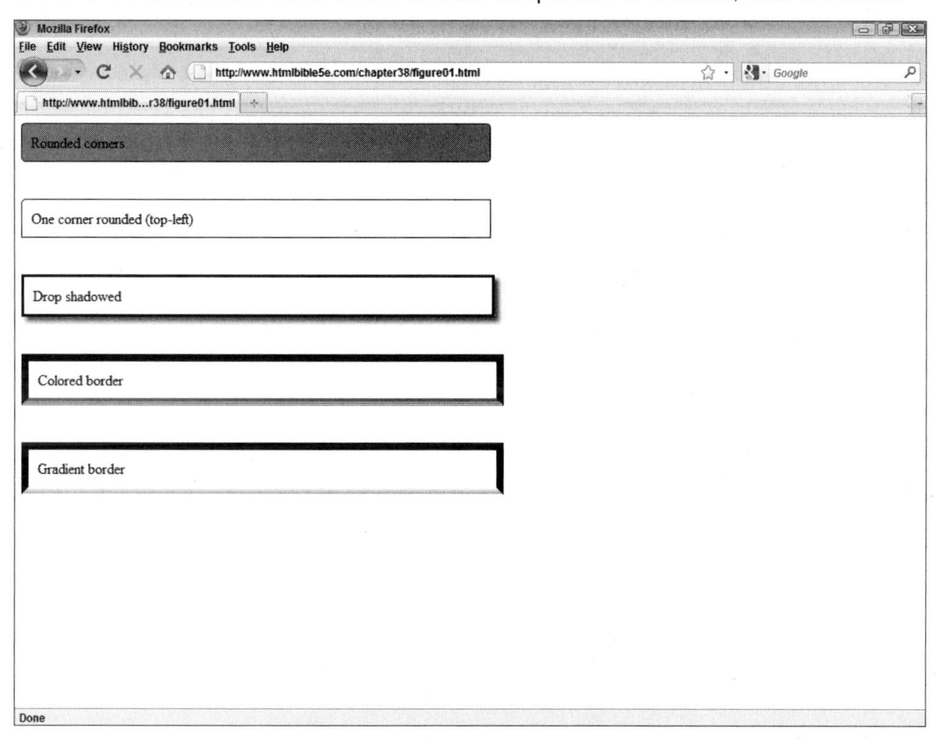

Note that the border color properties enable multiple colors to be defined. This allows borders to take on a rainbow effect or a 3D appearance if a smooth gradient of colors is specified. In addition, each side or corner of an element can be styled individually.

Summary

CSS level 3 has been in development since 1998. That has been plenty of time for the work group behind it to witness how the Web has matured and what is necessary to help revolutionize Web content.

Unfortunately, the CSS3 standard is still several years away from release; and even after the release, designers will have to wait for user agent adoption of the standards, and then user adoption of those new user agents. Nonetheless, it will be a welcome addition to the Web, providing a whole new generation of design possibilities.

Part IV

Additional CSS Tools

IN THIS PART

CHAPTER

39

User Interface Styles

In Part III of this book you learned how to use CSS to style and format almost every part of an HTML document. However, there are several additional, user agent-related elements you can affect with CSS. This chapter shows you how to use styles on user interface elements — the mouse pointer, system colors, and system fonts.

IN THIS CHAPTER

Changing the Cursor

User Interface Colors

User Interface Fonts

Changing the Cursor

The CSS `cursor` property enables you to specify what cursor type should be displayed when the cursor is over a specific element. This property is used like any other property, with a familiar format:

```
cursor: value;
```

The `cursor` property supports the values listed in Table 39-1.

The `uri` value takes the following familiar form:

```
url("uri_path_to_resource")
```

This value is unique in that it supports several values and can be followed by a default value if none of the `uri` resources can be found or used. For example, the following property definition defines two external pointer files that should be used, and a fallback default of `crosshair` if those two resources cannot be used for some reason:

```
cursor: url("angle.cur"), url("simple.cur"), crosshair;
```

Note

Many general graphic editing programs and several specific programs can be used to create custom cursors. Try searching Google for "create cursor file." ■

TABLE 39-1

Values for the Cursor Property

Value	Description
`auto`	The user agent displays an appropriate cursor for the current context.
`crosshair`	The cursor is set to the shape of a simple crosshair (resembling a narrow + sign).
`default`	The cursor is set to the platform's default cursor (typically an arrow).
`pointer`	The cursor is set to a shape that typically indicates a link (typically a pointing hand).
`move`	The cursor is set to a shape indicating that something can be moved (typically a four-pointed arrow).
`e-resize`, `ne-resize`, `nw-resize`, `n-resize`, `se-resize`, `sw-resize`, `s-resize`, or `w-resize`	The cursor is set to a shape indicating that something can be resized (typically a multi-headed arrow showing the direction(s) that an object can be sized). The leading letters refer to the edge of the sizable element that can be sized — `ne-resize`, for example, refers to an element's northeast (top-left corner) edge.
`text`	The cursor is set to a text edit/insert cursor (typically an I-beam cursor).
`wait`	The cursor is set to a shape that indicates the user should wait (typically an hourglass or clock image).
`progress`	The cursor is set to a shape that indicates the computer is in the process of doing an operation and the user might have to wait (typically an hourglass or clock).
`help`	The cursor is set to a shape indicating help is available, usually by clicking the object under the cursor. (The shape is typically a pointer with a question mark or a text balloon.)
`<uri>`	The cursor is set to a shape stored in an external cursor resource. This value supports multiple values in the form of a comma-separated list — if the first entry is unavailable, the second is used, and so forth.

Although CSS provides resize cursors for every side and corner of an element, they are not dynamic — as the cursor moves around the border of an element, the appropriate cursor will not automatically appear. You must assign the appropriate cursor to elements that can use the appropriate resize arrow.

Figure 39-1 shows how the default arrow cursor can be changed to a hand cursor (`pointer`) for the button, using the following code:

```
<image type="button" value="Button" style="cursor:pointer;" />
```

Tip

Just because you can change the cursor doesn't mean you should. Graphical user environments rely on consistency to increase user familiarity and comfort with their systems. If the cursor changes randomly in your pages, you risk confusing and alienating users. ■

FIGURE 39-1

A custom cursor

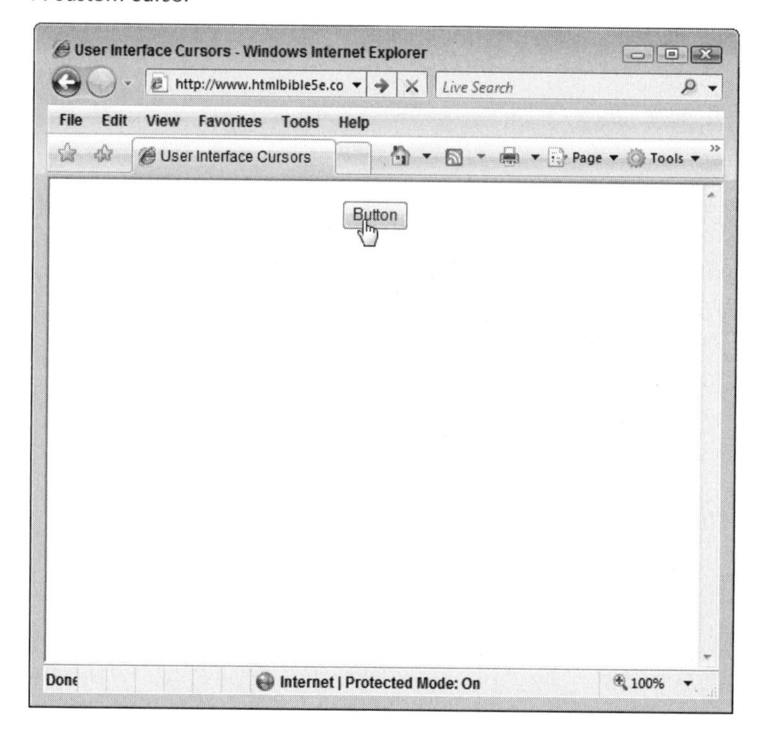

User Interface Colors

In addition to changing the cursor to system default cursors, you can also change your document's colors to match system colors. Table 39-2 lists the keyword values you can use with the `color` and `background-color` properties to match colors in your document to the current system colors.

TABLE 39-2

System Color Keywords

Keyword	Matches This System Color
ActiveBorder	The border of the current (active) window
ActiveCaption	The caption text of the current (active) window
AppWorkspace	The background color of a multiple-document interface (usually the background color of a document window)
Background	The background color (not image) of the desktop
ButtonFace	The face of button elements
ButtonHighlight	The dark shadow area on the edge of 3D button elements
ButtonShadow	The shadow area on the edge of 3D button elements
ButtonText	The text of button elements
CaptionText	The text in captions, size boxes, and scrollbar arrow boxes
GrayText	Gray (disabled) text
Highlight	Selected item(s)
HighlightText	The selected text
InactiveBorder	The border of an inactive window
InactiveCaption	The caption of an inactive window
InactiveCaptionText	The caption text of an inactive window
InfoBackground	The background for tooltips
InfoText	The text of tooltips
Menu	The background of menus
MenuText	The text of menus
Scrollbar	The "gray" area of scrollbars
ThreeDDarkShadow	The dark shadow for 3D elements
ThreeDFace	The face of 3D elements
ThreeDHighlight	The highlight color for 3D elements
ThreeDLightShadow	The light color shadow for 3D elements
ThreeDShadow	The dark color shadow for 3D elements
Window	The window background (for nondocument windows)
WindowFrame	The window frame
WindowText	The text in windows

These keywords can be used as you would any other color keyword, such as `blue`, `red`, or `green`. For example, to set up a paragraph to mimic system menus — background and text — you could use the following tag with its embedded styles:

```
<p style="background-color: Menu; color: MenuText">
```

FIGURE 39-2

A document with one system color scheme

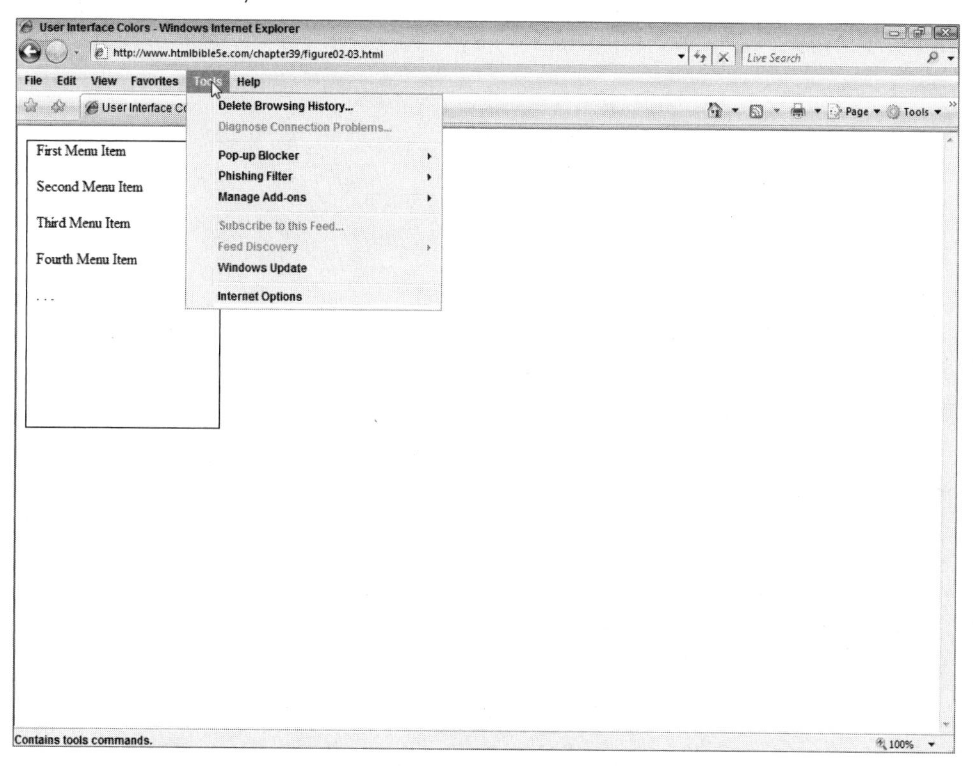

A big advantage to these keywords is that they are dynamic. As system colors change, so do the colors these keywords represent, so your document colors will match end users' colors even if they change. For an example of this effect, consider the following code and Figures 39-2 and 39-3, where the system color scheme changes between the figures (as referenced by the extended menu):

```
<!DOCTYPE HTML PUBLIC "-//W3C//DTD HTML 4.01//EN"
  "http://www.w3.org/TR/html4/strict.dtd">
<html>
<head>
  <title>User Interface Colors</title>
  <style type="text/css">
```

```
    div { padding: 0px 0px 0px 10px;
          border: 1pt solid black;
          width: 200px;
          height: 300px;
          background-color: Menu;}
    div p { color: MenuText;}
  </style>
</head>
<body>
<div>
   <p>First Menu Item</p>
   <p>Second Menu Item</p>
   <p>Third Menu Item</p>
   <p>Fourth Menu Item</p>
   <p>. . .</p>
</div>
</body>
</html>
```

FIGURE 39-3

The same document with another system color

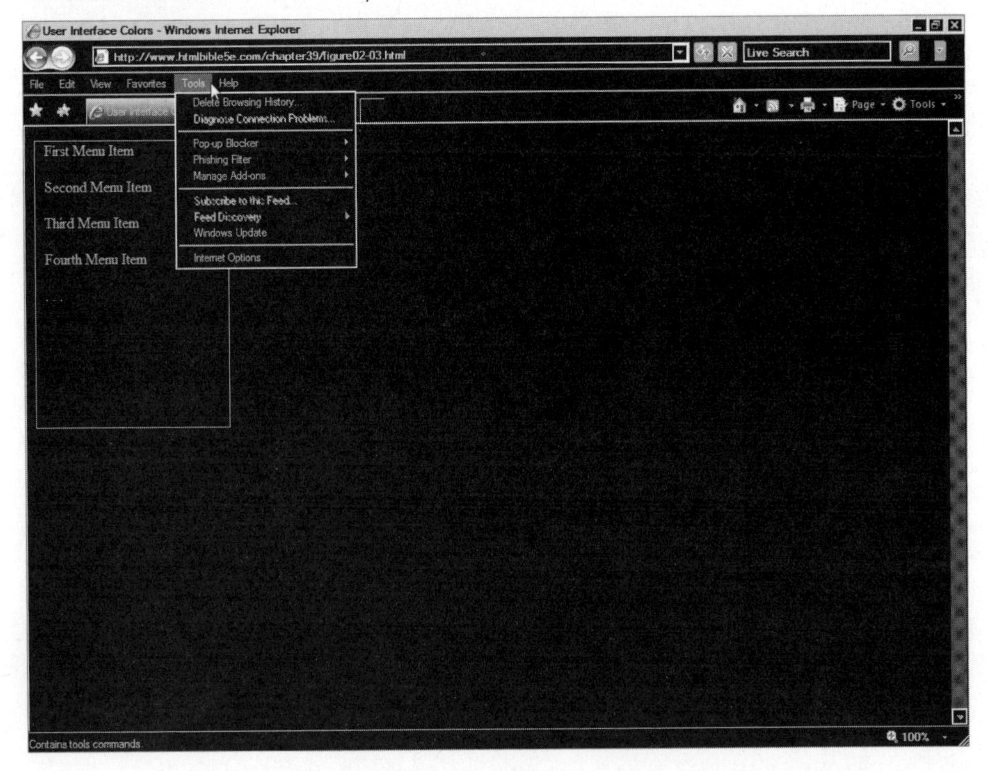

User Interface Fonts

CSS has a handful of interface font keywords that can be used similarly to the user interface color keywords to create documents that mesh with users' system interfaces. The interface font keywords set values of the `font` property. Table 39-3 lists the interface font keywords.

TABLE 39-3

Interface Font Keywords

Keyword	Matches This System Font
`caption`	Text on user interface elements
`icon`	Labels on icons
`menu`	Text in menus
`message-box`	Text in dialog boxes
`small-caption`	Text in small controls
`status-bar`	Text in window status bars

Like the color keywords, the font keywords are dynamic — the font they represent will change as the system fonts change.

Tip

Using the right combinations of user interface styles can give your document a look that's virtually indistinguishable from a user's system interface. Keep in mind that your document must still behave like a Web document if your audience approaches your document from a Web viewpoint. However, if your audience views your document as an application, infusing it with more of a computer interface design would be the better choice. In short, create a document and interface that will be familiar to your audience. ■

Summary

In this chapter you learned about the CSS user interface styles and how they can be used to customize a user agent's pointer, colors, and fonts. Using these styles you can easily change what the user interface of your document resembles. In the next chapter, you'll learn how to test and validate your CSS code.

Testing and Validating CSS

As you have seen in this book, HTML and CSS provide a yin and yang approach to the content and formatting of Web documents. As such, each depends on the other being complete, sturdy, and robust.

In Chapter 23 you saw the benefits of well-formed and validated HTML. This chapter explores the other piece of the equation — well-formed and validated CSS.

IN THIS CHAPTER

Testing Syntax As You Create Styles

The best and easiest method to ensure that your CSS is valid is to check its syntax as you create it. This means using a syntax highlighting, syntax checking, and text auto-insertion CSS editor for even the first draft of your styles.

Syntax highlighting involves using different colors for different portions of code. When editing CSS, for example, an editor might display the selector portion of a style in green, the braces in white, the properties in red, and the values in yellow. If a piece of the style is missing, the color of the previous element usually bleeds into the next section of the file. Using these visual cues, you can easily see the various pieces of the whole and recognize missing portions (such as a closing brace). These rudimentary editors also include features like auto-indenting of code to help keep your code tidy and easy to read. Figure 40-1 shows the popular Linux editor vim.

Syntax checking involves actively checking code as you type it and sometimes offering to auto-insert the next required piece for you. When editing CSS, for example, an editor might pop up a completion dialog box after you type a selector and its trailing space. The dialog box would contain an open brace ({) and perhaps a handful of selector symbols, such as a

FIGURE 40-1

Many text editors, like vim (shown here), offer syntax highlighting, automatic code indentation, and more.

```
body {
                margin:0px 0px 20px 0px;
                background-image: url("/images/spaimage.jpg");
                font-family:verdana, palatino,  georgia, arial, sans-serif;
                font-size:10pt;
                }

        blockquote { color:#0AAE02; }

        a img { border: none; }
        .picright  { float: right;
                        margin-left: 5px;  }

        .picleft  { float: left;
                      margin-right: 5px; }

        .quotethis { margin-right: 20px;
                          margin-left: 20px;
                          border-width: 1px 3px 3px 1px;
                          border-style: solid;
                          border-color: #0AAE02;
                          padding:5px;
                          font-style: italic; }
"styles.css" [noeol][dos] 346L, 10853C                    1,1          Top
```

FIGURE 40-2

A few specialty Web editors, such as Dreamweaver (shown here), offer syntax checking and text auto-completion.

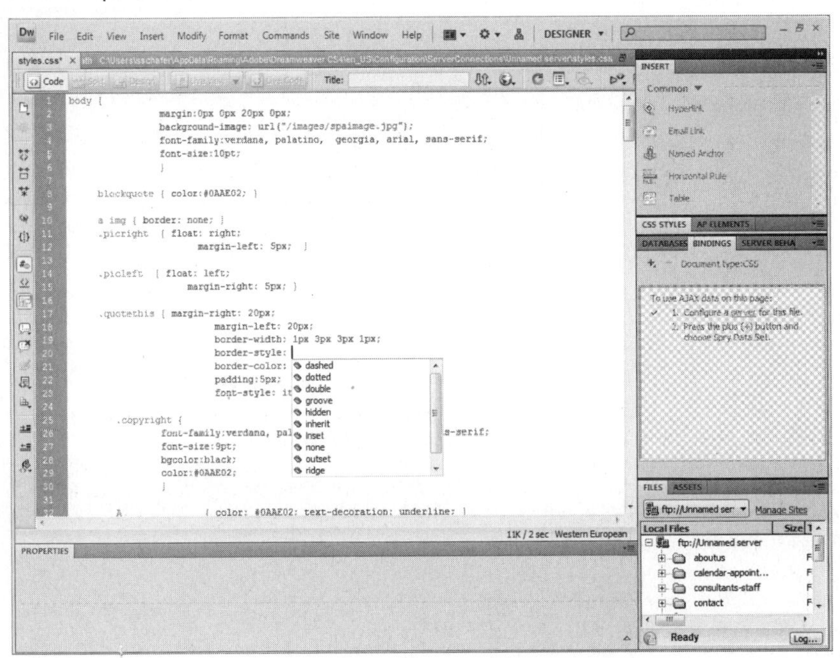

class indicator (.), a child separator (>), or an adjacent sibling separator (+). One keyboard stroke or mouse click can insert any of the suggested characters; and when a second character is necessary to complete a pair (as with braces), the second character is inserted as well. Savvy code editors know CSS properties and can offer to auto-insert them as well, reducing the chance of typing errors. Figure 40-2 shows a CSS file being edited in Dreamweaver, with Dreamweaver offering a dialog box of style properties that can be auto-inserted.

Using even the simplest editor with these features enables you to retain better control over your CSS documents as you edit them, helping to ensure that they begin, and stay, error-free.

A Word About Formatting

As you have probably noticed from examples in this book and other sources, you can format your CSS definitions in many ways. For example, consider the following definition, which adheres to CSS standards but is shown formatted three different ways:

```
h1 { font-size: 16px; margin: 0px; padding: 0px;
color: #0AAE02;}
h1 { font-size: 16px;
     margin: 0px;
     padding: 0px;
     color: #0AAE02;}
h1 {
  font-size: 16px;
  margin: 0px;
  padding: 0px;
  color: #0AAE02;
}
```

Each of the preceding examples is completely valid, although the last example seems to be preferred by experts such as the W3C. (It's the format the Jigsaw validation tool uses.)

When creating your styles, it is a good idea to pick a formatting style that you are comfortable with and use it exclusively. The routine will help you spot common errors, enabling you to write valid CSS out of the gate.

Validating CSS

Several tools are available for validating your CSS code — both online tools and applications. One of the best tools available is the W3C tool, code-named Jigsaw, which is available at `http://jigsaw.w3.org/css-validator/` and shown in Figure 40-3.

The tool enables you to provide your CSS via a URL or file upload, or by directly inputting your code into the tool. You can also tailor the types of warnings you receive, the CSS profile that should be used to check your code, and the intended medium for your styles (aural, print, screen, and so on).

One advantage of this tool is that it was developed and is maintained by the W3C, arguably the absolute authority for CSS.

FIGURE 40-3

The W3C Jigsaw tool provides in-depth validation for CSS files

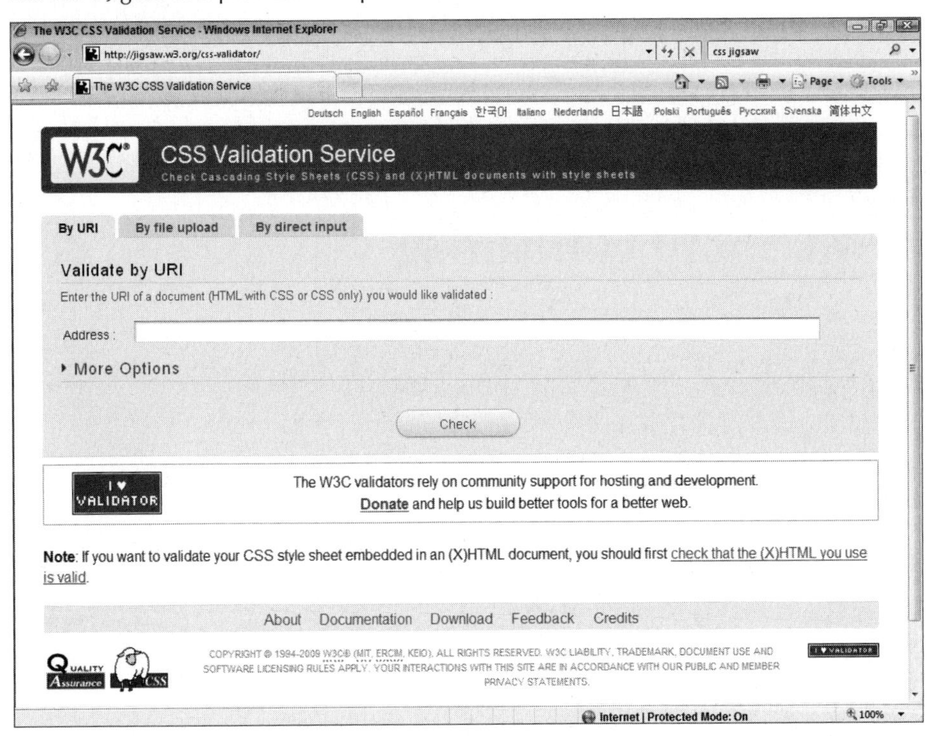

When your code is run through the tool, it will indicate any errors it finds and display the rest of your code in a particular format, as shown in Figure 40-4.

Firefox Add-ons for CSS Editing

As much as nature abhors a vacuum, Web developers abhor a lack of tools to edit Web code. To that end, many Firefox add-ons have been developed to aid in the creation and maintenance of CSS code. Piggybacking on the functionality of the Firefox browser, these tools provide very capable (and usually free) means of editing CSS.

One such tool is EditCSS, currently in pre-release version 0.3.7 (`https://addons.mozilla.org/en-US/firefox/addon/179`). Using a handful of editing features, EditCSS enables you to edit a currently loaded stylesheet.

Another tool is CSS Validator, currently in its third version (`https://addons.mozilla.org/en-US/firefox/addon/2289`). CSS Validator gives developers access to a handful of tools that can be used to correct validation errors it finds using its validation mode.

FIGURE 40-4

The Jigsaw tool both displays errors and formats the rest of your code.

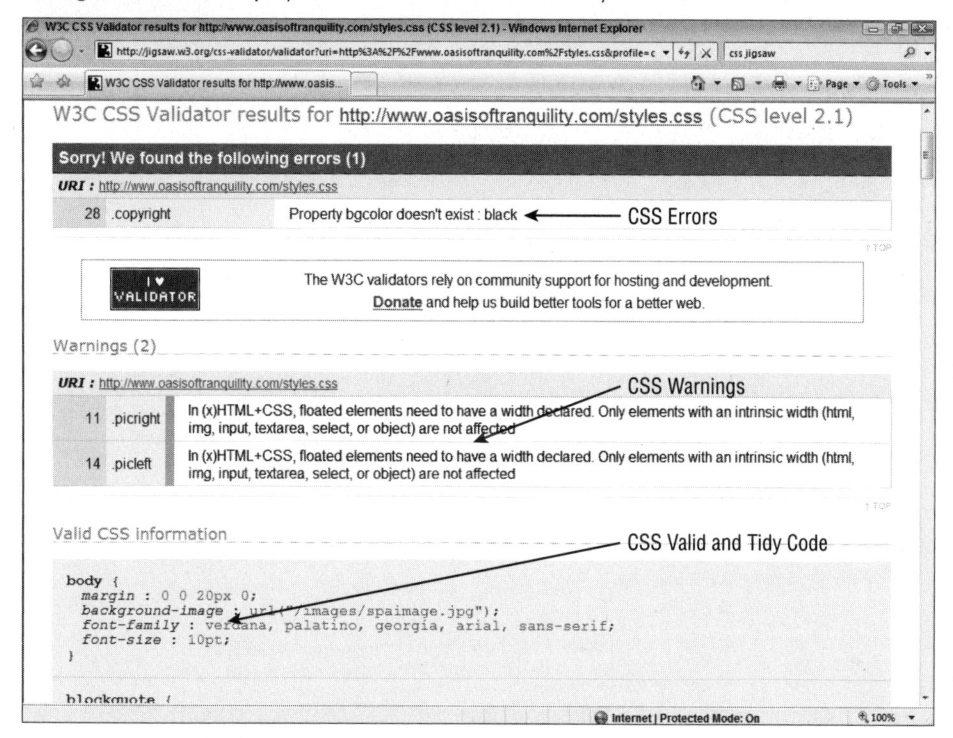

Other tools like Firebug, in version 1.4.2 (`https://addons.mozilla.org/en-US/firefox/addon/1843`), are geared more toward development than they are validation, but their ability to edit and manipulate styles provide some valuable insight during development.

Note

More plug-ins for Firefox are being developed every day. You are encouraged to visit the Firefox add-on site (`https://addons.mozilla.org/en-US/firefox/`) frequently to browse for additional tools. ■

Summary

Although CSS follows a very simple and strict format structure, it is still easy to incorrectly format a selector or improperly use a value keyword. This chapter presented a few ways you can double-check the formatting and validity of your CSS code, helping keep such errors to a minimum. The next chapter covers a handful of CSS tips and tricks you can use in your documents.

CHAPTER

CSS Tips and Tricks

IN THIS CHAPTER

Hanging Indents

Expanding Buttons

Pull Quotes

Tabbed Menus

Rounded Boxes

Flowing Elements

Flowing Text

Throughout this part, I've covered CSS from an elementary, technical standpoint. This chapter provides a handful of practical examples demonstrating how CSS can be used in unique yet useful ways.

Hanging Indents

The hanging indent, where all but the first line of a paragraph is indented, is a staple of the publishing world. As documentation on the Web becomes more reflective of the traditional printed page, the need for publishing conventions continues to grow.

For clarity, the following is an example of a hanging indent:

```
The Oasis of Tranquility offers a full menu of services
     to renew the real you that lies within. Begin
     in one of our two relaxation centers, then enjoy
     an invigorating body and facial care, deep soothing
     massage therapies, and a host of other indulgent
     treatments that pamper you on the outside, and
     revive you from within. In addition to our many
     spa services, take a refreshing dip in the swimming
     pool, melt in one of our whirlpool spas, or rejuvenate
     in the sauna.
```

Examining the list of indent, padding, margin, and alignment properties in CSS might give you quite a few ideas about how to accomplish this formatting. There is also the `:first-line` pseudo-element; despite its sketchy adoption in user agents, it might be the perfect solution.

However, the solution is quite simple: utilize the `text-indent` and `margin-left` properties, as shown in the following code and Figure 41-1:

```
<!DOCTYPE HTML PUBLIC "-//W3C//DTD HTML 4.01 Frameset//EN"
  "http://www.w3.org/TR/html4/frameset.dtd">
```

```
<html>
<head>
<title>A Hanging Indent</title>
<style type="text/css">
  p.hang { text-indent: -40px;
           margin-left: 40px;}
</style>
</head>
<body>
<p class="hang">The Oasis of Tranquility offers a full menu of
services to renew the real you that lies within. Begin in one of
our two relaxation centers, then enjoy an invigorating body and
facial care, deep soothing massage therapies, and a host of
other indulgent treatments that pamper you on the outside, and
revive you from within. In addition to our many spa services,
take a refreshing dip in the swimming pool, melt in one of our
whirlpool spas, or rejuvenate in the sauna.</p>
</body>
</html>
```

FIGURE 41-1

A hanging indent is relatively easy to achieve.

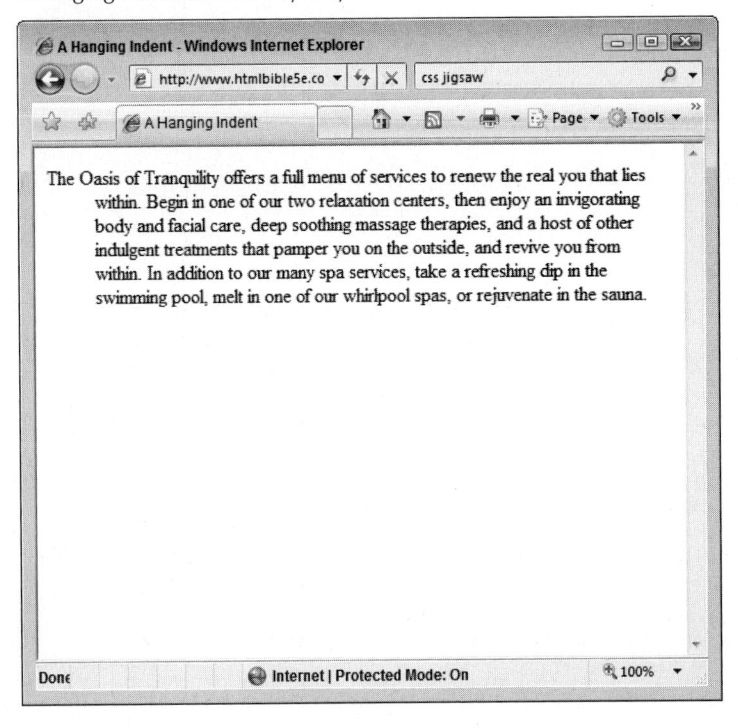

The trick is to set the paragraph's `text-indent` property to the exact negative of the `left-margin` property. The `text-indent` property controls the indentation of the first line of a block — our paragraph in this example. Setting this property to a negative value results in the first line escaping the overall margin.

Expanding Buttons

For many years, graphic images have been used as the background for buttons. However, for as many years these images suffered from a particular flaw: They didn't grow or shrink with the size of the text used for the button. An example of this is shown in Figure 41-2, where different-size captions are placed over the same button.

FIGURE 41-2

Small buttons with large type or large buttons with small type can look unprofessional.

Thankfully, several industrious souls have created methods for creating "shrink-wrapped" buttons, whereby the graphic acts like the plastic of the same name and wraps itself around the text it is given. The key to these buttons is a layered graphic approach, where one part of the button code contains the left half of the image and another part of the code contains the right. The result is a type of sliding door — like a set of glass patio doors — that slide together or apart, as necessary, to span the required gap.

Figure 41-3 shows a visual representation of how this concept works.

The key is that the right side of the button slides on top of the left, and the left side stops where the right side is placed. This keeps the extra length of the left side of the button from jutting out when the whole comes together.

Another image technique that has become popular for buttons is to place several images together in one background image and use the `background-position` property to slide the required image into place when it is needed. For example, it is a popular practice to place the inactive and active button graphics together in one image. The combined image is then placed as the button background such that only the inactive image is visible. When the button is activated, CSS rules cause the background graphic to shift and display the active image. Figure 41-4 illustrates this concept.

FIGURE 41-3

One approach to dynamically sized buttons is the "sliding door" approach–using two pieces of the button that can slide together or apart as necessary.

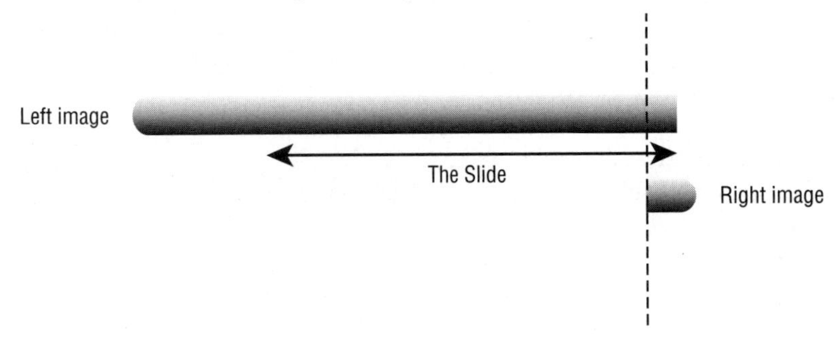

FIGURE 41-4

A popular technique to produce dynamic buttons is to place all the button graphics on a larger graphic and to use CSS positioning to expose the necessary graphic, as demonstrated in the figure below.

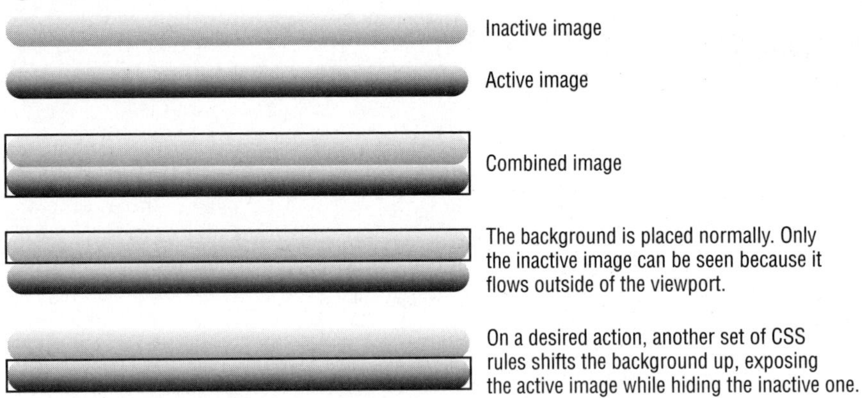

The following code illustrates the entire process by creating a handful of buttons, as shown in Figure 41-5. Note that the button graphics are displayed under the buttons to better illustrate how they look.

```
<!DOCTYPE HTML PUBLIC "-//W3C//DTD HTML 4.01 Frameset//EN"
  "http://www.w3.org/TR/html4/frameset.dtd">
```

```
<html>
<head>
<title>Shrinkwrapped Buttons</title>
<style type="text/css">
  a.button {
    background: transparent url('images/button_a.jpg')
          no-repeat scroll top right;
    color: black;
    display: block;
    float: left;
    font: 12px arial, sans-serif;
    height: 25x;
    margin-right: 6px;
    padding-right: 28px;     /* padding for the right image, */
    text-decoration: none;   /* should match the image width */
}
  a.button span {
    background: transparent url('images/button_span.jpg') no-repeat;
    display: block;
    line-height: 14px;
    padding: 5px 0 5px 20px;
}
  a.button:active {
    background-position: bottom right;
    color: #aaaaaa;
    outline: none; /* hide outline displayed by some user agents */
}
  a.button:active span {
    padding: 6px 0 4px 20px; /* move text a bit for effect */
    background-position: bottom left;
}
</style>
</head>
<body>
<div>
<a class="button" href="#" onclick="this.blur();">
<span>Home</span></a>
<a class="button" href="#" onclick="this.blur();">
<span>Products and Services</span></a>
<a class="button" href="#" onclick="this.blur();">
<span>Contact Us</span></a>
</div>
<hr style="clear: both;">
<table border="0" cellpadding="10px">
<tr>
  <td>button_span.jpg</td>
  <td><img src="images/button_span.jpg" width="372" height="50" />
  </td>
</tr>
<tr>
  <td>button_a.jpg</td>
```

```
  <td><img src="images/button_a.jpg" width="28" height="50" /></td>
</tr>
</table>
</body>
</html>
```

FIGURE 41-5

The finished buttons with two visual states and shrink-wrap capability

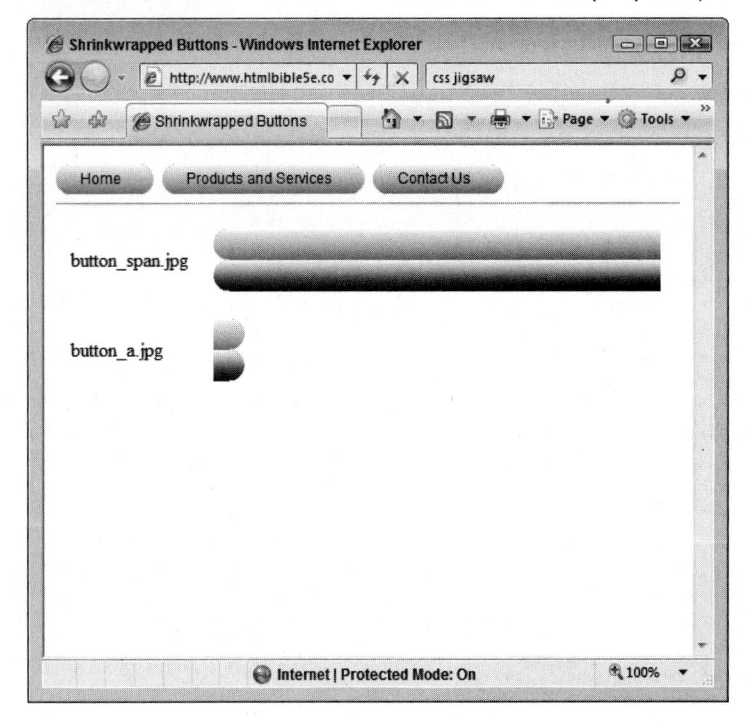

In this particular case, the `:active` link pseudo-class is used to trigger the button transformation. Unfortunately, this state is sticky in Internet Explorer, requiring the bit of JavaScript with each link to instantly set it back to inactive when clicked.

Pull Quotes

Although more prevalent in magazine publishing, pull quotes are another publishing convention that is now popular on the Web. Pull quotes are generally an edited excerpt of an article placed in larger type and outside the article's text. They are meant to draw attention to the article by offering little tidbits of content.

Although you are likely familiar with pull quotes, an example of a pull quote might resemble the following:

> " . . . his car and jacket were at the scene . . . "

Implementing a pull quote is simple: Place the appropriate text in a `div element`, make the text a bit larger than normal, and float the `div` to a margin. For example, consider the following code, whose results are shown in Figure 41-6:

```
<!DOCTYPE HTML PUBLIC "-//W3C//DTD HTML 4.01 Frameset//EN"
  "http://www.w3.org/TR/html4/frameset.dtd">
<html>
<head>
  <title>Pull Quotes</title>
    <style type="text/css">
        .pullquote {
            width: 150px;
            font-size:125%;
            line-height:140%;
            margin:10px;
            padding:10px;
            border: 1pt dotted black;
            float:right;
}
    </style>
<body>
<div id="intro"><div><h2>Introducing the Oasis</h2>
<p>The Oasis of Tranquility is a premier spa with an environment de-
signed to embrace you in an air of calming relaxation. When you walk
through our doors the outside world will slip away, as you allow our
dedicated team of professionals to pamper you in an experience
focused on personalized care. We offer a variety of salon and spa
services, which can be chosen a la carte for an individual service or
to create your own personalized package of services. Come to the
Oasis of Tranquility and let us cater to all your beauty and relaxa-
tion needs.</p></div></div>
<div class="pullquote"><p>...indulgent treatments that pamper you on
the outside, and revive you from within...</p></div>
<div id="spa"><h2>Spa Services</h2>
<p>The Oasis of Tranquility offers a full menu of services to renew
the real you that lies within. Begin in one of our two relaxation
centers, then enjoy an invigorating body and facial care, deep sooth-
ing massage therapies, and a host of other indulgent treatments that
pamper you on the outside, and revive you from within. In addition to
our many spa services, take a refreshing dip in the swimming pool,
melt in one of our whirlpool spas, or rejuvenate in the sauna.</p>
</div>
<div id="salon"><h2>Salon Services</h2>
<p>Focusing on our clients' individual needs, we offer services by
talented stylists, and chemical treatments delivering the most stun-
ning hues, all in a relaxing spa environment. Focusing on our guests'
needs begins with an open dialogue between you and your stylist. This
communication allows our hair salon guests to get to know their styl-
ist, while educating the guest on how we will achieve and maintain
that specific look they desire. Photographs and descriptions of the
looks you desire are welcome. Our salon artists have the knowledge,
```

```
training, experience, and creativity to make any vision reality. The
same level of personalized care is given by our nail and skincare
technicians, in order to ensure the most relaxing and effective
treatments for each individual.</p></div>
 <div id="gift"><h2>Give the Gift of Tranquility</h2>
 <p>All services at the Oasis of Tranquility can be experienced indi-
vidually, or selected a la carte to create your own personalized day
of pampering.  Gift certificates are excellent for surprising your
loved ones with an hour or a day of pampering and rejuvenation.</p>
</div>
 <div id="summary"><h2>In Summary...</h2>
 <p>So when you are looking for an experience that will relax, reju-
venate, and free you from the weight and stress of everyday life and
leave you looking and feeling like the person you really are, come to
the Oasis of Tranquility.</p></div>
 </body>
 </html>
```

FIGURE 41-6

The pull quote block can be as simple or as ornate as you wish.

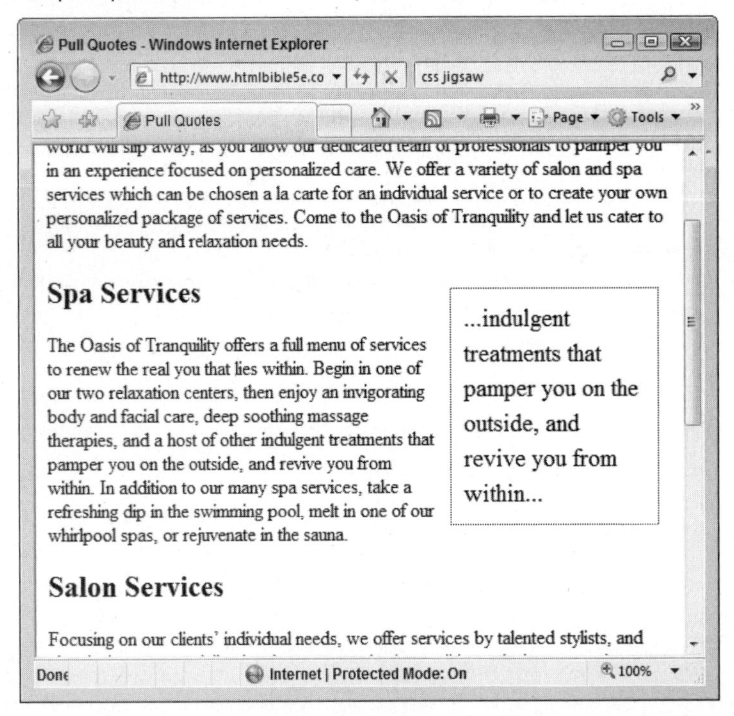

Of course, you can use additional CSS rules to style the pull quote block to your liking — inserting backgrounds, images, creative font effects, and so on.

Tabbed Menus

One trend in menu design is to create menus in tabular form — that is, menu items that look like the tabs at the top of paper files. This method of creating menus is popular for a couple of reasons:

- The structure more closely resembles the menus found in most computer applications.
- The structure is created from components that don't lose their visual meaning if the ornate styling is not present.

The importance of the first reason should be apparent — after years of cramming Web navigation into every nook and cranny on the page, we can start to emulate the rest of the computer world by putting distinct blocks across the top of a page.

The second reason makes more sense when you consider what most tabular menus are constructed of: unnumbered list elements. Because menus (and submenus) are just lists at heart, using list elements in their construction makes a lot of sense; and, of course, if a list is broken down into its base components due to the absence of fancy styles, it retains its meaning and hierarchy.

Of course, a list is meant to be vertical in orientation, so how do you get it to display horizontally? Using the `display` property and setting it to `inline` effectively takes a block element and makes it an inline one.

Figure 41-7 shows an example of a simple menu created from list elements.

The code that generates this menu is as follows:

```
<!DOCTYPE HTML PUBLIC "-//W3C//DTD HTML 4.01 Frameset//EN"
  "http://www.w3.org/TR/html4/frameset.dtd">
<html>
<head>
<title>Tabbed Menus</title>
<style type="text/css">
  li.menu   {
        display: inline;}
  li.menu a {
        background-image: url('images/tab.gif');
        width: 138px;
        text-align: center;
        border-bottom: 1pt black solid;
        float: left;}
  li.menu a:hover {
        background-image: url('images/tabhover.gif');
        font-weight: bold;}
  li.menu a.active {
        border-bottom: none;}
</style>
</head>
```

```
<body>
<p>
<ul>
  <li class="menu"><a href="#">One</a></li>
  <li class="menu"><a href="#">Two</a></li>
  <li class="menu"><a href="#" class="active">Three</a></li>
  <li class="menu"><a href="#">Four</a></li>
</ul>
</p>
</body>
</html>
```

FIGURE 41-7

List elements make excellent tabbed menus. Tab Three is active (note the line under the tab isn't visible) and tab One has changed color due to the mouse hovering over it.

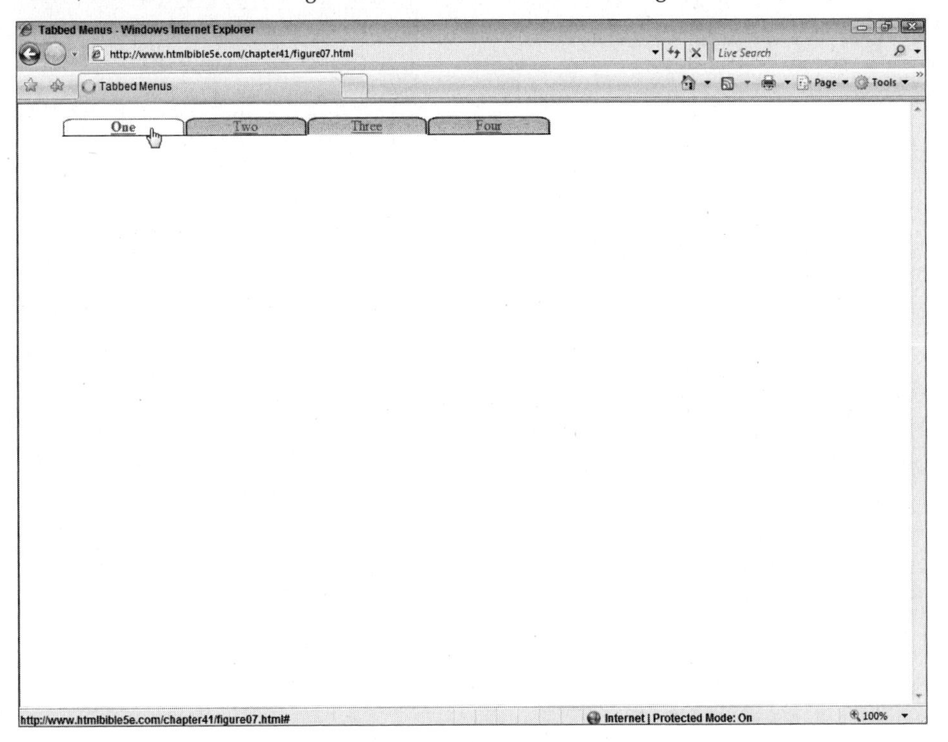

While the CSS is a bit complex, the HTML itself is very simple. The list elements handle the layout and some of the formatting, while their embedded anchors handle the actual navigation. A breakdown and explanation of the styles follow:

- All the `li` elements used in the menu have a class of `menu` to match the selectors that enable them.
- The first style simply sets each `li` element to be displayed inline so they display horizontally.

- The next style, selecting the anchor element under each list element, does most of the heavy lifting:
  - It sets a background image to that of a tab.
  - It sets the element's width to match the width of the background image.
  - It aligns the text to the center of the element.
  - It applies a border to the bottom of the element to give it the appearance of being behind the other elements.
  - Perhaps most important, it floats the element to the left to cause all the list elements to stack up against the element, or margin, to its left.
  - The hover style changes the tab's appearance when the mouse hovers over it. This is accomplished by making the font bold and changing the background image so the tab visually changes.
- The last style is applied only to a tab that has a class of `active`. This style removes the bottom border, making the tab appear as if it were on the top of the stack (hence, active).

Rounded Boxes

If there was ever a "brass ring" of CSS, it was elements with rounded corners. Text treatments of this type are fairly routine in the print world, but not in the boxy world of HTML.

Note

Several different techniques to achieve this result have been created over the years. The following code shows only one of the methods you can use. ■

To accomplish this effect, you create the four corners as images, placed using `div` elements, and fill the space in between with a matching background color. For example, consider the following code, and the annotated results shown in Figure 41-8:

```
<!DOCTYPE HTML PUBLIC "-//W3C//DTD HTML 4.01//EN"
   "http://www.w3.org/TR/html4/strict.dtd">
<html>
<head>
<title>Rounded Corner Content</title>
<style type="text/css">
  /* Main content div */
  .rounddiv {
    width: 250px;
    background-color: #E22000;
    color: #FFFFFF;
  }
  /* Paragraphs in rounded div get
     a default margin */
  .rounddiv p {
    margin: 0 10px;
  }
  /* Div for top corners */
  .roundtop {
    background: url('images/tr.jpg') no-repeat top right;
  }
  /* Div for bottom corners */
```

```
  .roundbottom {
    background: url('images/br.jpg') no-repeat top right;
  }
  /* Default settings for rounded corner images */
  img.corner {
     width: 17px;
     height: 17px;
     border: none;
     display: block !important;
  }
</style>
</head>
<body>
<div class="rounddiv">
   <div class="roundtop">
   <img src="images/tl.jpg" alt=""
   width="17" height="17" class="corner"
   style="display: none" />
   </div>
   <p>Lorem ipsum dolor sit amet, consectetur adipisicing
   elit, sed do eiusmod tempor incididunt ut labore et
   dolore magna aliqua. Ut enim ad minim veniam, quis
   nostrud exercitation ullamco laboris nisi ut aliquip
   ex ea commodo consequat. Duis aute irure dolor in
   reprehenderit in voluptate velit esse cillum dolore eu
   fugiat nulla pariatur. Excepteur sint occaecat cupidatat
   non proident, sunt in culpa qui officia deserunt mollit
   anim id est laborum.</p>
   <div class="roundbottom">
   <img src="images/bl.jpg" alt=""
   width="17" height="17" class="corner"
   style="display: none" />
   </div>
</div>
</body>
</html>
```

Note

Although `div` elements provide the most flexible and intuitive element to achieve rounded corners, it is possible to construct alternatives using other XHTML elements. ■

Note that the preceding code renders only the completed rounded-corner box shown on the left in Figure 41-8, not the exploded, annotated version on the right.

There are several caveats to this approach:

- The rounded image and the background of the `div` elements must match. You cannot use the same corner images with different color `div` elements.
- The rounded corners use a white background. While this is appropriate for documents that have a white background, it doesn't work well with documents that use a different color for their background, as shown in Figure 41-9.

FIGURE 41-8

The rounded-corner text box was once the brass ring of HTML formatting.

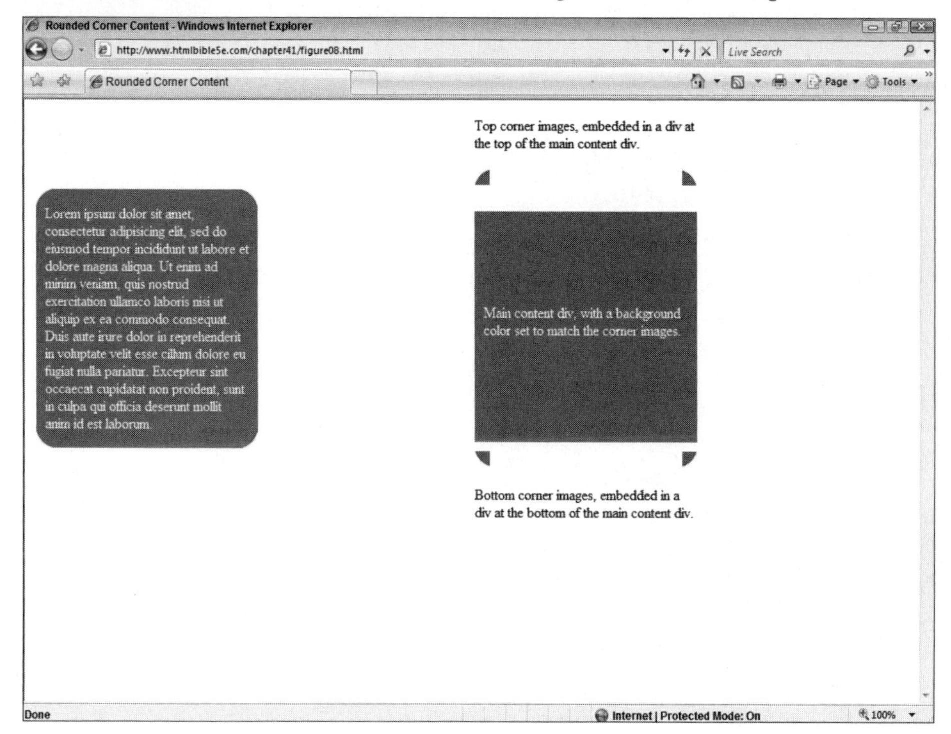

- The rounded corner element does not scale well — it is set for a fixed width of 20em, which is capable of handling most textual elements, but larger elements (such as tables) might cause issues within the confines of the rounded corner element.
- Most of these caveats have been overcome by other methods to achieve rounded corners. Of course, each method has its own set of caveats — the trick is to pick a method appropriate for your document.
- Currently, there are more methods to achieve rounded corners than can be reasonably counted. The following two sites provide many rounded corner methods:
  - Smileycat Web Design Blog — "CSS Rounded Corners 'Roundup'" at `www.smileycat.com/miaow/archives/000044.php`
  - CSS Juice — "25 Rounded Corners Techniques with CSS" at `www.cssjuice.com/25-rounded-corners-techniques-with-css/`

Tip

In the event that none of the techniques listed on these sites meet your requirements, use your favorite search engine to find more "CSS rounded corner" solutions. ■

FIGURE 41-9

Different background colors give the rounded corner trick away.

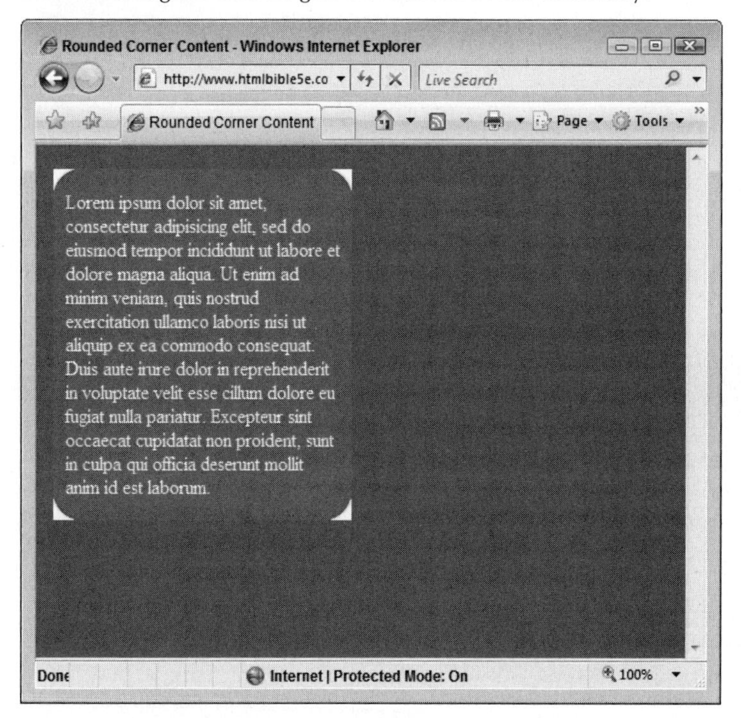

Flowing Elements

Some document designs can benefit from allowing certain elements on the page to "float." For example, compare Figure 41-10 and Figure 41-11. They show the same document in the same user agent, but the user agent's window has been narrowed in Figure 41-11.

Notice how the small boxes flow into rows that fit the document's width. As the document narrows, fewer elements can fit on each line. The last element(s) on the line are forced to the next line, accordingly. If the document widens, allowing more elements to fit on each line, element(s) from the next line move up a line to fill the gap. These types of document designs are used primarily in catalog or item lookup directories where the floating `div` size should remain constant but flow according to the document's width.

The design is remarkably easy to achieve. The general steps are listed here, followed by example code:

1. Create a container `div` element that is roughly the width of the user agent screen (width: 95%).
2. Set the top and right padding of the container to a suitable value — one that will provide the appropriate amount of space between the top and right edges of the container

and the interior div elements. For the best results, set both padding values to the same amount.

FIGURE 41-10

A directory or catalog of items can be represented by individual cells (*div* elements).

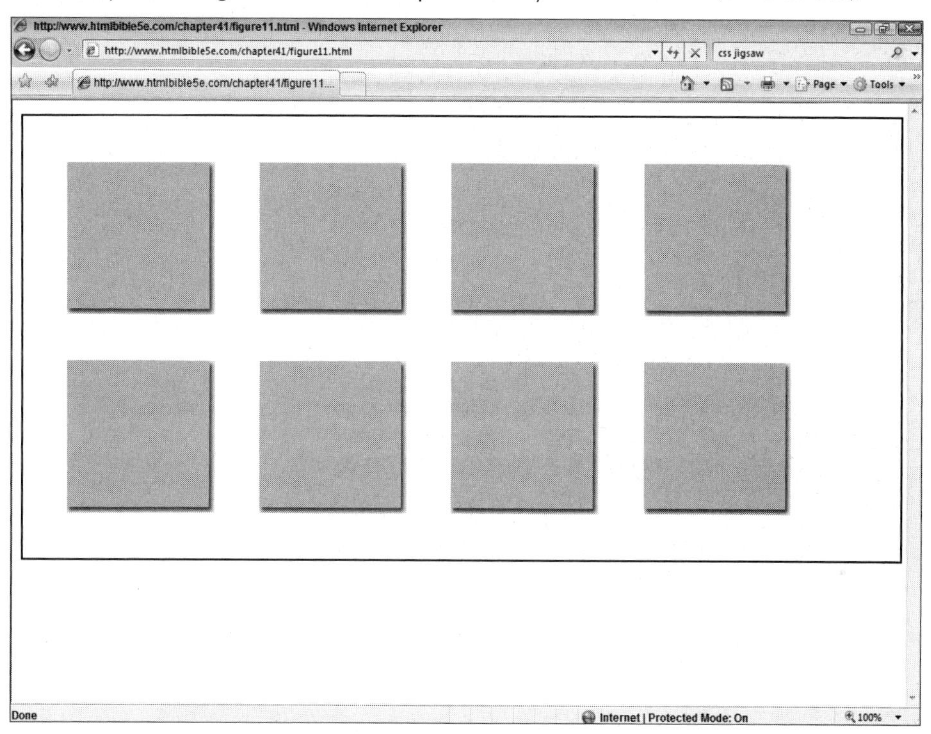

3. Place the required number of div elements (floaters) inside the container element.
4. Style the floating div elements any way you like (e.g., the drop shadow effect in Figure 41-11).
5. Set an explicit width and height for each floating element.
6. Set the right and bottom margins of the floating elements to the same value you used for the container's padding (step 2). The container's padding provides the space between the top row and rightmost column of floating elements. The floating element margins provide the space between floating element columns and rows.
7. Set all elements (container and float) to float to the left.

Note

All of the preceding formatting should be accomplished only via appropriate CSS styles. ■

FIGURE 41-11

If the container and elements are styled correctly, the elements will flow within the container and change their flow if the container changes shape.

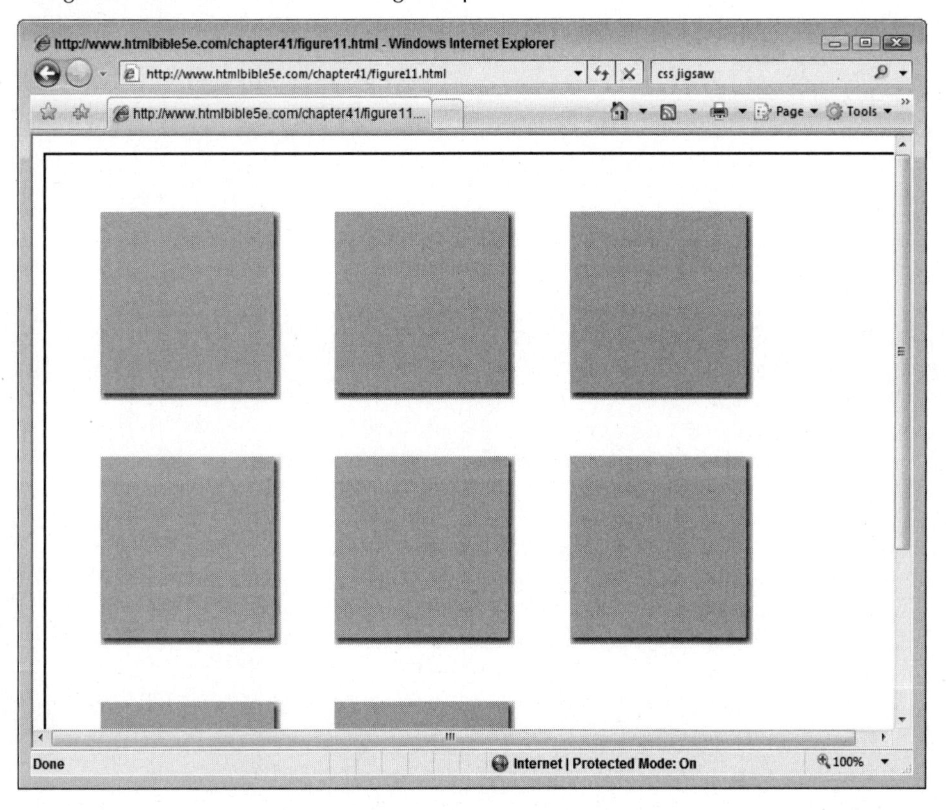


```
<!DOCTYPE html PUBLIC "-//W3C//DTD XHTML 1.0 Transitional//EN"
"http://www.w3.org/TR/xhtml1/DTD/xhtml1-transitional.dtd">
<html xmlns="http://www.w3.org/1999/xhtml">
<head>
<style type="text/css">
div.container {
    width: 90%;
    padding: 50px;
    float: left;
    border: 2px solid black;
    }

div.floating {
    background-image: url("images/thumbback.jpg");
    background-position: center;
    background-repeat: no-repeat;
    width: 165px;
    height: 165px;
```

```
    margin-right: 50px;
    margin-bottom: 50px;
    float: left;
    }

</style>

<body>

<div class="container">

<div class="floating"> </div>
<div class="floating"> </div>
<div class="floating"> </div>
<div class="floating"> </div>
<div class="floating"> </div>
<div class="floating"> </div>
<div class="floating"> </div>
<div class="floating"> </div>

</div>

</body>
</html>
```

Flowing Text

Another often sought after CSS formatting effect is the ability to flow text seamlessly around other elements. For example, Figure 41-12 shows text that flows around the curved image in the document.

This effect is achieved by placing several spacing `span` elements along the curve, forcing the text to flow accordingly. This is best illustrated by turning on the borders of the spacing `span` elements, as shown in Figure 41-13.

The following code can be used to accomplish the formatting shown in Figure 41-13:

```
<!DOCTYPE html PUBLIC "-//W3C//DTD XHTML 1.0 Transitional//EN"
"http://www.w3.org/TR/xhtml1/DTD/xhtml1-transitional.dtd">
<html xmlns="http://www.w3.org/1999/xhtml">
<head>
<style type="text/css">

   #wrapper {
           text-align: left;
           width: 600px;
           margin: 30px auto;
           border: 1px solid blue;
           padding: 15px 0px 5px 15px;
           background: url('images/circleRight.gif') no-repeat;
           background-position: right top;
           }
```

```
    .spacer {
            float: right;
            display: block;
            height: 15px;
            clear: right;
            margin-left: 10px;
            }

    #vspacer {
             width: 1px;
             height: 15px
             }


    #spacer01 { width: 70px; }
    #spacer02 { width: 85px; }
    #spacer03 { width: 100px; }
    #spacer04 { width: 115px; }
    #spacer05 { width: 130px; }
    #spacer06 { width: 140px; }
    #spacer07 { width: 140px; }
    #spacer08 { width: 130px; }
    #spacer09 { width: 115px; }
    #spacer10 { width: 100px; }
    #spacer11 { width: 85px; }
    #spacer12 { width: 70px; }
    #spacer13 { width: 60px; }
    #spacer14 { width: 60px; }

</style>

<body>

<div id="wrapper">
  <span id="spacer01" class="spacer"></span>
  <span id="spacer02" class="spacer"></span>
  <span id="spacer03" class="spacer"></span>
  <span id="spacer04" class="spacer"></span>
  <span id="spacer05" class="spacer"></span>
  <span id="spacer06" class="spacer"></span>
  <span id="spacer07" class="spacer"></span>
  <span id="spacer08" class="spacer"></span>
  <span id="spacer09" class="spacer"></span>
  <span id="spacer10" class="spacer"></span>
  <span id="spacer11" class="spacer"></span>
  <span id="spacer12" class="spacer"></span>
  <span id="spacer13" class="spacer"></span>
  <span id="spacer13" class="spacer"></span>
  <p>Lorem ipsum dolor sit amet, consectetuer adipiscing elit.
Nam venenatis  facilisis risus. Vestibulum lacus neque, scelerisque
ut, gravida sit amet, laoreet sed, sapien. Nunc tincidunt convallis
mauris. Proin  aliquam tristique ipsum. Pellentesque libero orci,
```

```
pharetra vel,  fringilla eu, pretium eget, enim. Quisque facilisis
tincidunt risus.  Mauris et elit. In hac habitasse platea dictumst.
Phasellus a dolor non  ligula laoreet aliquet. Vestibulum dolor.
Aliquam in sapien. Curabitur  pretium. Morbi vitae risus ut lectus
venenatis sagittis. Aliquam ut  sem. In a purus vel libero porttitor
suscipit. Duis odio leo,  pellentesque vitae, euismod ut, blandit sit
amet, urna. Nam suscipit  leo elementum elit. Donec dui. Etiam quam.
Morbi sodales, leo et semper  egestas, massa elit fermentum pede, non
scelerisque massa justo non  ante. Sed suscipit consequat tortor.
Duis at risus sit amet elit  faucibus facilisis. Vestibulum
lacinia. Vivamus rutrum interdum sem. Maecenas nisl risus, porta ac,
faucibus ac, euismod at, sem. Nulla tincidunt orci laoreet pede.
Morbi scelerisque erat vel nunc. Etiam a lectus vel diam congue
congue. Proin nec nibh. Nulla volutpat semper nisl.
</p>

</div>

</body>
</html>
```

FIGURE 41-12

Flowing text around objects and graphics is easy with CSS

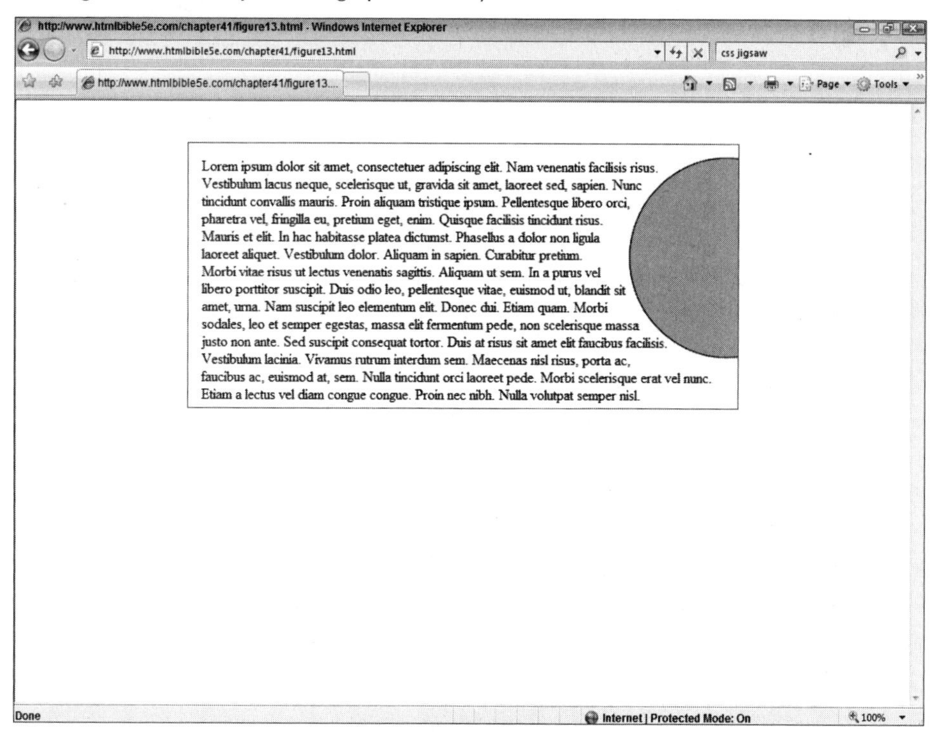

FIGURE 41-13

The invisible elements keep the text away from the edges of the graphic and simulate flowing text.

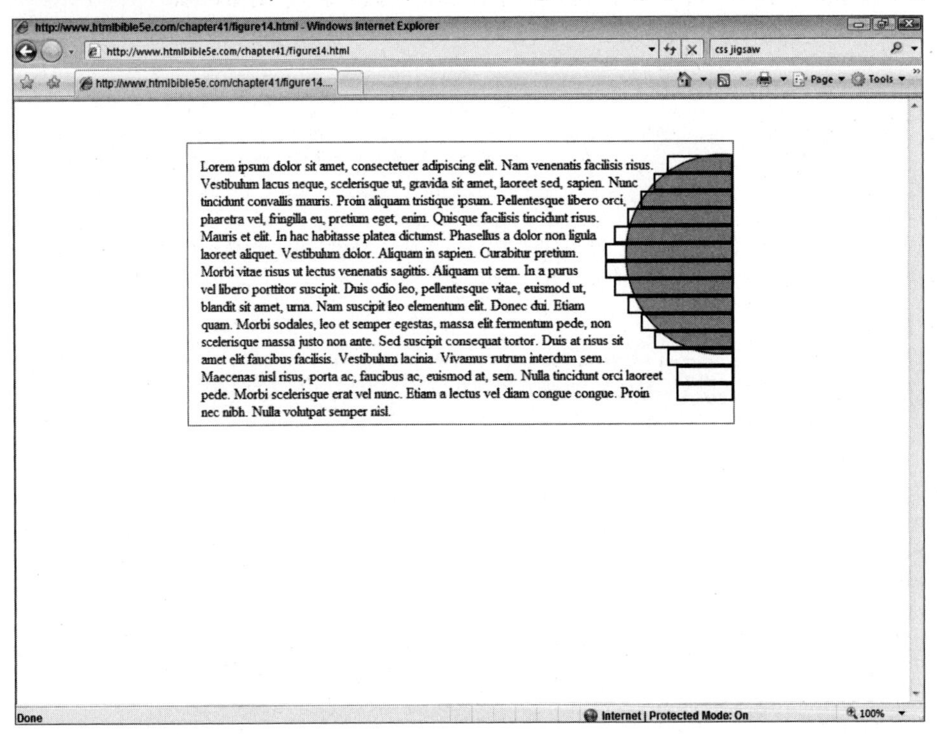

The CSS `vspacer id` definition (defined but not used in this example) can be used to start the spacing `span` elements lower on the page. For example, if the circle started 50 or so pixels lower in the document, the following CSS and XHMTL code would be used, with the `vspacer` placed before the other spacer `span` elements:

```
    #vspacer {
            width: 1px;
            height: 15px
            }
  ...
  <span id="vspacer" class="spacer"></span>
```

This would result in the horizontal spacers being pushed down in the document to better align with the circle.

Tip

This trick can be used to flow text around just about anything, even several images (or elements) in a document. The only limitation is where you can place the spacer elements to direct the text. ■

Summary

This chapter presented a handful of tips and tricks you can accomplish in your documents with the aid of CSS. You learned how to create hanging indents in your text, expandable buttons that can be used with almost any size of text, pull quotes, and tabular-style menus. You can create many more unique uses for CSS using these ideas as the basis.

APPENDIX

XHTML Element Quick Reference

IN THIS APPENDIX

Element Listings

Event Attributes

Other Common Attributes

This appendix provides a reference to XHTML 1.1 markup conventions and standards. As a result of its XML heritage, XHTML is much less forgiving than HTML has historically been (or, perhaps more accurately, than HTML browsers have been). You cannot omit closing tags or place an italic (`i`) element inside an anchor (`a`) element. Attribute values must be quoted, and minimized attributes are disallowed, which leads to odd constructs such as `<select multiple="multiple">`. The more strict conventions help ensure that your code is more standards-compliant and forward-looking.

Here are some tips to keep in mind when working with XHTML:

- XHTML documents must be well-formed (closing tags required, no overlapping tags allowed).
- Empty elements can be both opened and closed with one tag: `<img src="foo"/>`.
- All elements and tags must be in lowercase.
- Attribute values must be quoted (with either single or double quotes).
- Attributes cannot be minimized — that is, all attributes must have values. For example, the `textarea` element supports a `readonly` attribute. In HTML, the attribute had to be present only in the element, such as `<textarea readonly>`. In XHTML, however, the `readonly` attribute must have a value. When a value is not applicable, the name of the attribute is generally used, such as `<textarea readonly="readonly">`.

In the element listings that follow, the location within a document in which each element may reside is indicated through one of two mechanisms. If the element has a very limited number of valid parent elements, then those are listed. Otherwise, the placement is described as either "inline" or "block."

In turn, unless there are a limited number of valid children for a non-empty element, the content is documented as some combination of block, inline, or text.

If an element is listed as having a block placement, it may reside directly within any other element that is listed as having block contents (and nowhere else). Most block elements will render as such, and most inline elements will render inline, but that is not always true.

Note
For a list of the core, internationalization, and standard event attributes, see the end of this appendix. ■

Element Listings

The following section provides a list of all HTML elements.

Specify either the inclusion or terminating point of a hyperlink.

Context

Placement	Inline
Content	Inline and text

Attributes

Optional

```
accesskey="<character>"

charset="<character encoding>"

coords="<length, ... >"

href="<URL>"

hreflang="<language code>"

name="<anchor>"

onblur="<script>"

onfocus="<script>"

Rel="<linktype ... >"

Rev="<linktype ... >"
```

```
shape="rect|circle|poly|default"

tabindex="<number>"

type="<MIME type>"
```

Core, Internationalization, Standard events

Usage example

```
<p><a name="lincoln-anchor">Lincoln's</a>
<a href="http://en.wikipedia.org/wiki/Gettysburg_Address">Gettysburg
Address</a> has both been widely noted and long remembered.</p>
```

Using `<a>` as an anchor point with the `name` attribute is frequently seen with machine-generated HTML that includes a table of contents and/or an index.

<abbr>

Demarcate the enclosed text as an abbreviation.

Context

Placement	Inline
Content	Inline and text

Attributes

Optional
Core, Internationalization, Standard events

Usage example

```
<p>If you're old enough to remember using <abbr>Fla</abbr> to send
mail to Florida, you're getting up there.  Of course, if you're old
enough to remember sending letters at all&hellip;</p>
```

The W3C refers to acronyms such as HTTP as abbreviations, so the distinction between `abbr` and `acronym` elements seems to be pretty fuzzy.

<acronym>

Demarcate the enclosed text as an acronym.

Context

Placement	Inline
Content	Inline and text

Attributes

Optional
Core, Internationalization, Standard events

Usage example

```
<p>The <acronym title="World Wide Web Consortium">W3C</acronym> is
the organization responsible for guiding <acronym title="HyperText
Markup Language">HTML</acronym> and many related standards.</p>
```

When combined with the title attribute and CSS, this tag can be used to edify the reader. For example, if the preceding paragraph is combined with a stylesheet that indicates the browser should render acronyms as underlined or boxed, the browser will render the acronyms in a way that indicates the user can interact with them, and placing the mouse over one of them will display a tooltip (assuming a graphical Web browser).

<address>

Demarcate the enclosed content as the address of an individual or organization.

Context

Placement	Block
Content	Inline and text

Attributes

Optional
Core, Internationalization, Standard events

Usage example

```
<p>Sincerely, John Doe.</p>
<address>
  1234 Main St.<br />
  Springfield, U.S.  101010<br />
</address>
```

<area>

Describe the physical layout of an image map.

Context

Parent	map

Attributes

Required	Optional

`alt="<text>"`	`accesskey="<character>"`
	`coords="<length, ... >"`
	`href="<URL>"`
	`nohref="nohref"`
	`onblur="<script>"`
	`onfocus="<script>"`
	`shape="rect|circle|poly|default"`
	`tabindex="<number>"`
	Core, Internationalization, Standard events

Usage example

See `<map>`.

<b>

Indicate that the enclosed text should be rendered in a bold typeface.

Context

Placement	Inline
Content	Inline and text

Attributes

Optional
Core, Internationalization, Standard events

Usage example

```
<p>Do <b>not</b> press the red button!</p>
```

Whenever feasible, try describing the semantic meaning of the text instead of the rendering properties; for example, use <strong> instead of <b>. CSS is the most flexible mechanism for specifying the appropriate rendering for semantic content.

See also <em> and <strong>.

<base>

Define the original/desired location for the document.

Context

Parent	head

Attributes

Required
href="<URL>"

Usage example

```
<head>
  <base href="http://www.w3.org/TR/html401/index/elements.html"/>
  <title>Index of the HTML 4 Elements</title>
</head>
```

Used so that relative links within the document are evaluated with respect to the base location, rather than wherever they may currently reside.

<bdo>

Indicate that the enclosed text should be rendered in a specific direction (left to right or right to left) that may be different from its environment.

Context

Placement	Inline
Content	Inline and text

Attributes

Required	Optional

`dir="ltr|rtl"`	`lang="<language code>"`
	`xml:lang="<language code>"`
	Core, Standard events

Usage example

```
<p><bdo dir="rtl">Quite a dramatic cultural difference to read
text right to left.</bdo></p>
```

Internationalization is a complex issue; the directionality in which a language is rendered is just one of many issues to consider. Most Web content ignores the issue, assuming that most readers understand English, but it is unclear how long that assumption will hold true.

<big>

Indicate that the enclosed text should be rendered in a larger font.

Context

Placement	Inline
Content	Inline and text

Attributes

Optional
Core, Internationalization, Standard events

Usage example

```
<p>Last week I nearly caught a <big>really big</big> fish, but it
got away.</p>
```

CSS provides more flexible font resizing.

See also <small>.

<blockquote>

Enclose a long quotation.

Context

Placement	Block
Content	Block, inline, and text

Attributes

Optional
cite="<URL>"
Core, Internationalization, Standard events

Usage example

```
<blockquote cite="http://wikisource.org/wiki/Gettysburg_Address">
Four score and seven years ago our fathers brought forth on this
continent, a new nation, conceived in Liberty, and dedicated to the
proposition that all men are created equal.</blockquote>
```

This should not be used as a mechanism for indenting arbitrary text. Instead, use a `p` or `div` element with CSS.

See <q> for the inline equivalent to this tag.

<body>

All content visible on a Web page is contained within this tag.

Context

Parent	html
Content	Block, inline, and text

Attributes

Optional

onload="<script>"

onunload="<script>"

Core, Internationalization, Standard events

Usage example

```
<html>
  <head><title>Just another web page</title></head>
  <body><h1>Just another web page</h1>
...
  </body>
</html>
```

Once upon a time, the body tag was optional. This is no longer true.

Force a newline between text and/or inline elements.

Context

Placement	Inline

Attributes

Optional

Core

Usage example

```
<p>Down by the salley gardens my love and I did meet;<br/>
She passed the salley gardens with little snow-white feet.<br/>
She bid me take love easy, as the leaves grow on the tree;<br/>
But I, being young and foolish, with her would not agree.</p>
```

Use this tag sparingly. It should not be used as a substitute for paragraph tags.

See also `<pre>`.

<button>

Define a button in a form. Any content will be superimposed on the button.

Context

Placement	Inline
Content	Block, inline, and text

Attributes

Optional
`accesskey="<character>"`
`disabled="disabled"`
`name="<button name>"`
`onblur="<script>"`
`onfocus="<script>"`
`tabindex="<number>"`
`type="button|submit|reset"`
`value="<application value>"`
Core, Internationalization, Standard events

Usage example

```
<form action="/cgi-bin/post" method="post">
<p>...
<button value="submit"><img src="/images/submit.gif"/></button>
</p></form>
```

This is similar to the <input type='button'> element but allows content.

<caption>

Define a caption for a table.

Context

Parent	table
Content	Inline and text

Attributes

Optional
Core, Internationalization, Standard events

Usage example

See <table>.

Contrary to what one might expect, captions are not rendered in an emphasized typeface. Use CSS to place appropriate emphasis on the caption, such as a larger font or a bold typeface.

<cite>

Demarcate a source citation.

Context

Placement	Inline
Content	Inline and text

Attributes

Optional
Core, Internationalization, Standard events

Usage Example

```
<p>The population of Freedonia in 1803 was larger than that of
Malta. (<cite>Williams 1953, p. 42</cite>)</p>
```

<code>

Demarcate inline code snippets.

Context

Placement	Inline
Content	Inline and text

Attributes

Optional
Core, Internationalization, Standard events

Usage Example

```
<p>In Perl, iterating over a list can easily be achieved with
<code>foreach</code>: <code>foreach my $value (sort @keys) { ... }
</code>.</p>
```

For longer blocks of code, use the `pre` element.

<col>

Specify attributes for a full column in a table.

Context

Parents	`Colgroup` `table`

Attributes

Optional
`span="<number>"`
`width="<length (pixels, percentage, relative)>"`
Core, Internationalization, Standard events

Usage example

See <table>.

Support for this element is limited in some browsers.

<colgroup>

Group columns in a table for assigning attributes.

Context

Parent	`table`
Content	`col`

Attributes

Optional
`span="<number>"`
`width="<length (pixels, percentage, relative)>"`
Core, Internationalization, Standard events

Usage example

See <table>.

As with `col`, full support for this element is not widespread.

<dd>

Wrap the definition of a term in a definition list.

Context

Parent	`dl`
Content	Inline and text

Attributes

Optional
Core, Internationalization, Standard events

Usage example

See <dl>.

<del>

Demarcate content that has been deleted from a document.

Context

Placement	Anywhere inside body or its children
Content	Inline and text. Block permissible when not functioning as an inline.

Attributes

Optional
cite="<URL>"
datetime="<ISO Date/Time>"
Core, Internationalization, Standard events

Usage example

```
<p>Four score and seven years ago <del>when the British held sway
over these lands</del> our fathers brought forth, on this continent...
```

The inverse of this element is the ins element.

<dfn>

Indicate that a term is defined in this location.

Context

Placement	Inline
Content	Inline and text

Attributes

Optional
Core, Internationalization, Standard events

Usage example

```
<p><dfn>UNIX</dfn> is a widespread operating system that
originated at Bell Labs.</p>
```

This element is useful for machine-generated indices.

<div>

Enclose a block of content for structural or style purposes.

Context

Placement	Block
Content	Block, inline, and text

Attributes

Optional
Core, Internationalization, Standard events

Usage example

```
<div class="blockquote">With CSS, this block of text can be
rendered like a &lt;blockquote&gt;.</div>
```

The inline equivalent element is `span`.

<dl>

Enclose a list of terms and definitions.

Context

Placement	Block
Content	`dt` `dd`

Attributes

Optional
Core, Internationalization, Standard events

Usage example

```
<dl><dt>molecule</dt>
<dd><cite>Webster's Revised Unabridged Dictionary (1913)</cite>:
One of the very small invisible particles of which all matter is
supposed to consist.</dd>
</dl>
```

The `compact` attribute is not permitted in the Strict DTD. Use CSS instead.

<dt>

Wrap a term defined in a definition list.

Context

Parent	`dl`
Content	Inline and text

Attributes

Optional
Core, Internationalization, Standard events

Usage example

See `<dl>`.

<em>

Demarcate text that should be emphasized.

Context

Placement	Inline
Content	Inline and text

Attributes

Optional
Core, Internationalization, Standard events

Usage example

```
<p>There is <em>no</em> substitute for catsup.</p>
```

See also `<strong>`, `<i>`, and `<b>`.

<fieldset>

Wrap a group of related labels and controls in a form.

Context

Placement	Block
Content	First child: `legend`. Remainder: Block, inline, and text

Attributes

Optional
Core, Internationalization, Standard events

Usage example

See `<form>`.

This element is useful for accessibility purposes. See `<label>` for another form element that would enable you to provide better accessibility for those who are using a nonvisual mechanism to "view" a form.

<form>

Define a collection of controls used to gather and submit information to a Web application.

Context

Placement	Block
Content	Block (except nested form elements). Can also contain script.

Attributes

Required	Optional
action="<URL>"	accept-charset="<character encoding ... >" accept="<MIME type, ... >" enctype="<MIME type>" method="get|post" onreset="<script>" onsubmit="<script>" *Core, Internationalization, Standard events*

Usage example

```
<form action="https://www.example.com/cgi-bin/do-something.cgi"
onsubmit="validate()">
  <fieldset><legend>Shipping address</legend>
    <label>Name: <input type="text" name="name"/></label>
    <label>Street address: <input type="text" name="street"/>
    </label>
  </fieldset>
  <p>
    <input type="submit" value="Ship it!"/>
    <input type="reset" value="Oops, start over"/>
  </p>
</form>
```

Many HTML documents use inline elements such as <input> directly under a <form> tag, so the failure to use only block elements (not counting script) inside <form> is a common validation error when writing XHTML Strict DTD documents.

See also <input>, <button>, <textarea>, <select>, <label>, and <fieldset>.

<h1>, <h2>, <h3>, <h4>, <h5>, <h6>

Header tags provide some structure to a document.

Context

Placement	Block
Content	Inline and text

Attributes

Optional
Core, Internationalization, Standard events

Usage example

```
<body>
<h1>Analysis of the price of wheat in 17th century Freedonia</h1>
...
  <h2>Inflation between 1620 and 1640</h2>
...
    <h3>The great price spike of 1623</h3>
...
      <h4>Maltese shipping embargo: fact or political fiction?</h4>
...
  <h2>Price controls in the latter half of the century</h2>
```

If you are unhappy with the way different header tags are rendered, you can use CSS to correct the problem without changing the tags.

<head>

Wrap the important metadata for a document.

Context

Parent	`html`
Content	`base, link, meta, object, script, style, title`

Attributes

Optional
`profile="<URL>"` *Internationalization*

Usage example

```
<html>
  <head>
    <title>Freedonia through the ages</title>
    <meta name="author" content="John Q. Publique"/>
    <meta name="keywords" content="freedonia history europe"/>
    <style type="text/css"> ... </style>
  </head>
```

<hr>

Define the location for a horizontal rule in the document.

Context

Placement	Block

Attributes

Optional
Core, Internationalization, Standard events

Usage example

```
<p>...</p>
<hr/>
<h3>Constitutional crisis of 1901: Freedonia's last stand</h3>
```

Styling horizontal rules with CSS is challenging because of inconsistencies between browsers.

<html>

This is the master element for most XHTML documents.

Context

Content	head, body

Attributes

Optional
xmlns="<URI>" *Internationalization*

Usage example

```
<html>
  <head>
    <!-- Meta-data here -->
  </head>
  <body>
```

```
    <!-- Content here -->
  </body>
</html>
```

<i>

Indicate that the contained text should be rendered with italics.

Context

Placement	Inline
Content	Inline and text

Attributes

Optional
Core, Internationalization, Standard events

Usage example

```
<p><i>I thought they were finished,</i> she thought to herself.</p>
```

In many instances, the semantics behind the italics can be conveyed through elements such as `cite` or `em`, rather than using `i`.

<img>

Denote the location of an image to incorporate into the document.

Context

Placement	Inline

Attributes

Required	Optional

`alt="<text>"` `src="<URL>"`	`height="<length (pixels or percentage)>"`
	`ismap="ismap"`
	`longdesc="<URL>"`
	`name="<text>"`
	`usemap="<URL>"`
	`width="<length (pixels or percentage)>"`
	Core, Internationalization, Standard events

Usage example

```
<img alt="Sleeping polar bear"
  src="http://www.example.com/images/polarbear.jpg"/>
```

See also <object>.

<input>

Define a mechanism for form input.

Context

Placement	Inline

Attributes

Optional

```
accept="<MIME type, ... >"
accesskey="<character>"
alt="<short description>"
checked="checked"
disabled="disabled"
maxlength="<number>"
name="<input name>"
onblur="<script>"
onchange="<script>"
onfocus="<script>"
onselect="<script>"
readonly="readonly"
size="<length>"
src="<URL>"
tabindex="<number>"
```

```
type="<input type>"

usemap="<URL>"

value="<application value>"
```

Core, Internationalization, Standard events

Usage example

See <form>.

The valid type attributes: `text`, `password`, `checkbox`, `radio`, `submit`, `reset`, `file`, `hidden`, `image`, `button`.

See also <button>, <textarea>, <select>, <label>, and <fieldset>.

<ins>

Demarcate text and/or content that has been inserted into a document.

Context

Placement	Anywhere inside body
Content	Inline and text. Block permissible when not functioning as an inline character.

Attributes

Optional

```
cite="<URL>"

datetime="<ISO Date/Time>"
```

Core, Internationalization, Standard events

Usage example

```
<h2>Freedonia's Volcanoes</h2>
<ins><p>A new volcano erupted in 2003 along the northern coast..</p>
</ins>
```

See also <del>.

<kbd>

Indicate keyboard input.

Context

Placement	Inline
Content	Inline and text

Attributes

Optional
Core, Internationalization, Standard events

Usage example

```
<li>At the username prompt, type <kbd>einstein</kbd>.</li>
```

<label>

Associate explanatory text with a form input control.

Context

Placement	Inline
Content	Inline and text

Attributes

Optional
`accesskey="<character>"` `for="<IDREF>"`
`onblur="<script>"`
`onfocus="<script>"`
Core, Internationalization, Standard events

Usage example

See <form>.

This element can significantly add to the user-friendliness of a form, especially for accessibility purposes.

<legend>

Provide a caption for a set of form input controls.

Context

Parent	`fieldset`
Content	Inline and text

Attributes

Optional
`accesskey="<character>"`
Core, Internationalization, Standard events

Usage example

See `<form>`.

If used, this must be the first child of a `fieldset` element, with nothing but whitespace preceding it.

<li>

Wrap a list item for an ordered or unordered list.

Context

Parent	`ol ul`
Content	Block, inline, and text

Attributes

Optional
Core, Internationalization, Standard events

Usage example

See <ol>.

Vertical whitespace between list items will expand when including nested p elements. If p elements are necessary to separate paragraphs within a single list item, CSS can be used to shrink the vertical whitespace if desired.

<link>

Semantically associate related documents.

Context

Parent	head

Attributes

Optional
charset="<character encoding>"
href="<URL>"
hreflang="<language code>"
media="<media descriptor, ... >"
rel="<linktype ... >"
rev="<linktype ... >"
type="<MIME type>"
Core, Internationalization, Standard events

Usage example

```
<head>
  <link rel="start" href="introduction.html"/>
  <link rel="prev" href="chapter-21.html"/>
  <link rel="next" href="chapter-23.html"/>
  <title>Freedonia History: Chapter 22</title>
</head>
```

See www.w3.org/TR/html401/struct/links.html for a good overview of this element's usage. The DTD does not constrain the link types that can be used.

<map>

Define an image map for navigation.

Context

Placement	Block
Content	area, script, noscript, Block

Attributes

Required	Optional
id="<ID>"	class="<text>" name="<map name>" style="<CSS>" title="<text>" *Internationalization Standard events*

Usage example

```
<h3>Freedonia Regions</h3>
<div>
  <img src="/images/image-map.gif" usemap="map-links"/>
  <map id="map-links" name="map-links">
    <area alt="Northern provinces" shape="rectangle"
     coords="0,0,100,50"
          href="/regions/north.html"/>
    <area alt="Eastern provinces" shape="rectangle"
     coords="50,50,100,100"
          href="/regions/east.html"/>
  </map>
</div>
```

To maximize compatibility across browsers, specify both the id and name attributes.

<meta>

Describe metadata for the document.

Context

Parent	head

Attributes

Required	Optional

`content="<TEXT>"`	`http-equiv="<HTTP header>"`
	`id="<ID>"`
	`name="<metadata key>"`
	`scheme="<metadata scheme identifier>"`
	Internationalization

Usage example

See <head>.

The XHTML DTD does not constrain the values for the name attribute and there are many possible uses, including supplementary HTTP information and search engine hints regarding the document's content.

<noscript>

Offer alternative content for browsers that do not understand (or do not have enabled) the scripting language in use for the document.

Context

Placement	Block
Content	Block, inline, and text

Attributes

Optional
Core, Internationalization, Standard events

Usage example

See <script>.

Contrary to the example provided in the <script> section, <noscript> elements should not be used to nag the user about script support. They should be used only to convey information when the missing functionality is important.

<object>

Embed external content into the document.

Context

Placement	Inline
Content	First children (if used): `param`. Block, inline, and text

Attributes

Optional
`archive="<URL, ... >"`
`classid="<URL>"`
`codebase="<URL>"`
`codetype="<MIME type>"`
`data="<URL>"`
`declare="declare"`
`height="<length (pixels or percentage)>"`
`name="<object name>"`
`standby="<text>"`
`tabindex="<number>"`
`type="<MIME type>"`
`usemap="<URL>"`
`width="<length (pixels or percentage)>"`
Core, Internationalization, Standard events

Usage example

```
<object classid="clsid:8AD9C840-044E-11D1-B3E9-00805F499D93"
        height="400" width="600">
  <param name="code" value="Lifter"/>
  <param name="archive" value="Lifter.jar"/>
</object>
```

This element can be used to incorporate applications, images, and even other (X)HTML documents.

<ol>

Define an ordered list — that is, one that uses numbers or characters as sequence indicators.

Context

Placement	Block
Content	li

Attributes

Optional
Core, Internationalization, Standard events

Usage example

```
<ol style="list-style-type: lower-roman">
  <li>Register to vote</li>
  <li>Research candidates</li>
  <li>Vote on election day</li>
  <li>Complain about election results</li>
  <li>Rinse, repeat</li>
</ol>
```

There is no equivalent to the `caption` element in a table available for lists, but you can associate a header directly with the list by placing both inside a dedicated `div element`.

See also <ul>.

<optgroup>

Group form selection options into a hierarchical structure.

Context

Parent	select
Content	option

Attributes

Required	Optional
`label="<text>"`	`disabled="disabled"` *Core, Internationalization, Standard events*

Usage example

See `<select>`.

<option>

Define a form value to be selected from a list.

Context

Parents	`select, optgroup`
Content	Text

Attributes

Optional
`disabled="disabled"`
`label="<text>"`
`selected="selected"`
`value="<text sent to application>"`
Core, Internationalization, Standard events

Usage example

See `<select>`.

<p>

Demarcate the enclosed contents as a semantic paragraph.

Context

Placement	Block
Content	Inline and text

Attributes

Optional
Core, Internationalization, Standard events

Usage example

```
<p>It was a dark and stormy night.</p>
<p><i>No, that's a lousy way to start a book</i>, she thought to
herself, forcefully erasing the first sentence.</p>
```

If a block is desired but the contents are not a paragraph, then consider `div` elements instead, or `pre` elements for preformatted text.

<param>

Define values to be passed to a software object loaded into the document.

Context

Parent	`object`

Attributes

Optional
`id="<ID>"`
`name="<parameter name>"`
`type="<MIME type>"`
`value="<parameter value>"`
`valuetype="data|ref|object"`
Core, Internationalization, Standard events

Usage example

See <object>.

<pre>

Specify that the contents of this block should preserve the whitespace as written, instead of compressing multiple spaces into one and breaking lines as dictated by the width of the container.

Context

Placement	Block
Content	Inline and text. Disallowed: `img`, `object`, `big`, `small`

Attributes

Optional
Core, Internationalization, Standard events

Usage example

```
<pre style="font-family: serif">
Down by the salley gardens my love and I did meet;
She passed the salley gardens with little snow-white feet.
She bid me take love easy, as the leaves grow on the tree;
But I, being young and foolish, with her would not agree.</pre>
```

If preformatted text is desired but a monospaced font is not, CSS can be used to correct the presentation, as in the preceding example.

<q>

Demarcate text that should be quoted appropriately for the language encoding.

Context

Placement	Inline
Content	Inline and text

Attributes

Optional
`cite="<URL>"`
Core, Internationalization, Standard events

Usage example

```
<p>She said <q>Bite me,</q>, and Vlad took her literally.</p>
```

Internet Explorer is the only major browser that does not place quotes around the text as required by HTML 4.01 and XHTML 1.1.

<samp>

Indicate that the contents reflect sample output, such as from software.

Context

Placement	Inline
Content	Inline and text

Attributes

Optional
Core, Internationalization, Standard events

Usage example

```
<p>While working in the MacOS X Terminal, if you see <samp>command
not found</samp>, that means that you mistyped the command name.</p>
```

See also `<kbd>` and `<tt>`.

<script>

Define a script to be used within the document.

Context

Placement	Inline or inside <head>
Content	Text

Attributes

Required	Optional
type="<MIME type>"	charset="<character encoding>" defer="defer" id="<ID>" src="<URL>"

Usage example

```
<body onload="place_cursor(document.getElementById('searchbar'))">
  <script type="text/javascript">
    function place_cursor(o) {
      o.focus();
    }
  </script>
  <noscript>
    <p>This page best viewed with JavaScript enabled.</p>
  </noscript>
  <div>
    <form action="/actions/do-search">
      <input type="text" id="searchbar"/>
    </form>
  </div>
```

The script can be written into the document or defined outside the document and linked in via the src attribute.

<select>

Wrap a list of options in a form, creating a drop-down list.

Context

Placement	Inline
Content	optgroup, option

Attributes

Optional
`disabled="disabled"`
`multiple="multiple" name="<select name>"`
`onblur="<script>"`
`onchange="<script>"`
`onfocus="<script>"`
`size="<number>"`
`tabindex="<number>"`
Core, Internationalization, Standard events

Usage example

```
<select name="operating systems">
  <optgroup label="UNIX">
    <option label="HP-UX" value="HPUX">HP-UX</option>
    <option label="Solaris" value="Solaris">Solaris</option>
    <option label="MacOS X" value="Darwin" selected='selected'>
      MacOS X
    </option>
    <option label="Linux" value="Linux">Linux</option>
  </optgroup>
  <optgroup label="Macintosh">
    <option label="MacOS Classic (through v9)" value="MacOS">
      MacOS Classic (through v9)
    </option>
    <option label="MacOS X" value="Darwin">MacOS X</option>
  </optgroup>
  <optgroup label="Other">
    <option label="Windows" value="Windows">Windows</option>
    <option label="Amiga" value="Amiga">Amiga</option>
    <option label="Mainframe" value="mainframe">Mainframe</option>
  </optgroup>
</select>
```

In the absence of a `value` attribute, the contents of the `<option>` tag will be passed to the Web application. It is better to use `value` so that the appearance of the option can be changed without breaking the application.

<small>

Request that the enclosed contents be rendered with a smaller font.

Context

Placement	Inline
Content	Inline and text

Attributes

Optional
Core, Internationalization, Standard events

Usage example

```
<p>The oxonium ion is represented as
[H<small><sub>3</sub></small>O<small>]<sup>+</sup></small>.</p>
```

See also <big>.

<span>

Demarcate inline text for assigning attributes.

Context

Placement	Inline
Content	Inline and text

Attributes

Optional
Core, Internationalization, Standard events

Usage example

```
<p>You can use CSS <span style="font-variant: small-caps">to achieve
all sorts of interesting effects</span>.</p>
```

See also <div> for information on assigning attributes to a block.

<strong>

Demarcate text that should be rendered with strong emphasis.

Context

Placement	Inline
Content	Inline and text

Attributes

Optional
Core, Internationalization, Standard events

Usage example

```
<p>"There is <strong>no one</strong> better qualified to be dog
catcher than me," he reiterated.</p>
```

See also <em> and <b>.

<style>

Define style rules for the document.

Context

Parent	head
Content	Text

Attributes

Required	Optional
type="<MIME type>"	id="<ID>" media="<media descriptor, ... >" title="<text>" *Internationalization*

Usage example

```
<head>
  <style type="text/css">
    .booktitle { font-style: italic }
  </style>
</head>
```

```
<body>
  <p>The first book I read in college was
<span class="booktitle">Pride and Prejudice</span>.</p>
```

Linking an external stylesheet to the document is often preferable to achieve greater consistency across a site and limit the amount of spurious bandwidth usage. To do so, use <link>.

<sub>

Indicate text that should be rendered as a subscript.

Context

Placement	Inline
Content	Inline and text

Attributes

Optional
Core, Internationalization, Standard events

Usage example

See <small>.

<sup>

Indicate text that should be rendered as a superscript.

Context

Placement	Inline
Content	Inline and text

Attributes

Optional
Core, Internationalization, Standard events

Usage example

See <small>.

<table>

Define content to be presented in a tabular format.

Context

Placement	Block
Content	caption, col, colgroup, thead, tfoot, tbody, tr

Attributes

Optional
border="<pixel length>" cellpadding="<length (pixels or percentage)>" cellspacing="<length (pixels or percentage)>" frame="void|above|below|hsides|lhs|rhs|vsides|box|border" rules="none|groups|rows|cols|all" summary="<text>" width="<length (pixels or percentage)>" *Core, Internationalization, Standard events*

Usage example

```
<table>
  <caption>Freedonia National Debt: 1400-1800</caption>
  <col width="30%">
  <colgroup style="text-align: right">
    <col width="30%">
    <col width="30%">
  </colgroup>
  <thead>
    <tr><th>Decade</th><th>Debt (in Freds)</th><th>Percentage of GDP
    </th></tr>
  </thead>
  <tfoot>
    <tr><th>Decade</th><th>Debt (in Freds)</th><th>Percentage of GDP
    </th></tr>
  </tfoot>
  <tbody>
    <tr><th>1400-1410</th><td>3000</td><td>7%</td></tr>
    <tr><th>1410-1420</th><td>5000</td><td>8%</td></tr>
...
    <tr><th>1780-1790</th><td>425,000,000</td><td>10%</td></tr>
```

```
      <tr><th>1790-1800</th><td>500,000,000</td><td>10%</td></tr>
    </tbody>
  </table>
```

CSS provides for very granular control over table borders, both internal and external.

<tbody>

Define the main body of a table.

Context

Parent	`table`
Content	`tr`

Attributes

Optional
`align="left|center|right|justify|char"`
`char="<character>"`
`charoff="<length (pixels or percentage)>"`
`valign="top|middle|bottom|baseline"`
Core, Internationalization, Standard events

Usage example

See `<table>`.

<td>

Demarcate a data cell in a table.

Context

Parent	`tr`
Content	Block, inline, and text

Attributes

Optional
abbr="<text>"
align="left|center|right|justify|char"
axis="<category, ... >"
char="<character>"
charoff="<length (pixels or percentage)>"
colspan="<number>"
headers="<IDREFS>"
rowspan="<number>"
scope="row|col|rowgroup|colgroup"
valign="top|middle|bottom|baseline"
Core, Internationalization, Standard events

Usage example

See <table>.

<textarea>

Define a block for text input in a form.

Context

Placement	Inline
Content	Text

Attributes

Required	Optional
cols="<number>" rows="<number>"	accesskey="<character>" disabled="disabled" name="<textarea name>" onblur="<script>" onchange="<script>"

```
onfocus="<script>"
onselect="<script>"
readonly="readonly"
tabindex="<number>"
```

Core, Internationalization, Standard events

Usage example

```
<textarea name="address" cols='50' rows='5'>Please replace this
text with your billing address.</textarea>
```

For a single line of text input, use `<input type="text">` instead.

<tfoot>

Define the footer for a table.

Context

Parent	`table`
Content	`tr`

Attributes

Optional

`align="left|center|right|justify|char"`
`char="<character>"`
`charoff="<length (pixels or percentage)>"`
`valign="top|middle|bottom|baseline"`
Core, Internationalization, Standard events

Usage example

See `<table>`.

Defining footers and headers separately from the body for a table enables the browser to render them on each page for a long table.

<th>

Demarcate a data cell in a table that serves as a heading.

Context

Parent	`tr`
Content	Block, inline, and text

Attributes

Optional

`abbr="<text>"`

`align="left|center|right|justify|char"`

`axis="<category, ... >"`

`char="<character>"`

`charoff="<length (pixels or percentage)>"`

`colspan="<number>"`

`headers="<IDREFS>"`

`rowspan="<number>"`

`scope="row|col|rowgroup|colgroup"`

`valign="top|middle|bottom|baseline"`

Core, Internationalization, Standard events

Usage example

See `<table>`.

<thead>

Define the header for a table.

Context

Parent	`table`
Content	`tr`

Attributes

Optional

`align="left|center|right|justify|char"`
`char="<character>"`
`charoff="<length (pixels or percentage)>"`
`valign="top|middle|bottom|baseline"`
Core, Internationalization, Standard events

Usage example

See `<table>`.

<title>

Define the title for a document.

Context

Parent	`head`
Content	Text

Attributes

Optional
Internationalization

Usage example

```
<head>
  <title>Flora and Fauna of Freedonia</title>
</head>
```

A meaningful title is very useful when browsing search engine results.

<tr>

Define a row of data in a table.

Context

Parents	table, thead, tfoot>
Content	th, td

Attributes

Optional

```
align="left|center|right|justify|char"
char="<character>"
charoff="<length (pixels or percentage)>"
valign="top|middle|bottom|baseline"
```
Core, Internationalization, Standard events

Usage example

See <table>.

<tt>

Demarcate text that should be rendered in a monospace typeface.

Context

Placement	Inline
Content	Inline and text

Attributes

Optional

Core, Internationalization, Standard events

Usage example

```
<p>If you want to IM me, my username is <tt>frd42</tt>.</p>
```

Consider, instead, a semantic element such as samp, var, or kbd when appropriate.

<ul>

Define an unordered list.

Context

Placement	Block
Content	li

Attributes

Optional
Core, Internationalization, Standard events

Usage example

```
<div>
  <h3>Grocery list</h3>
  <ul style="list-style-type: square">
    <li>Milk</li>
    <li>Paper towels</li>
    <li>Salt</li>
  </ul>
</div>
```

<var>

Demarcate text as a variable name.

Context

Placement	Inline
Content	Inline and text

Attributes

Optional
Core, Internationalization, Standard events

Usage example

```
<p>Changing the environment variable <var>HOME</var> can have unex-
pected consequences.</p>
```

See also <kbd>, <samp>, and <tt>.

Event Attributes

This section lists those attributes relevant to providing script hooks for responding to events such as page loading and mouse movements.

Standard events

The standard event attributes are listed in the table that follows.

Attribute	Triggered By
onclick	Pointer button was clicked.
ondblclick	Pointer button was double-clicked.
onmousedown	Pointer button was pressed down.
onmouseup	Pointer button was released.
onmouseover	Pointer was moved into element.
onmousemove	Pointer was moved within element.
onmouseout	Pointer was moved away from element.
onkeypress	Key was pressed and released.
onkeydown	Key was pressed.
onkeyup	Key was released.

Other Events

The following table lists less common event attributes.

Attribute	Triggered By
onload	Document has been loaded.
onunload	Document has been removed.
onblur	Element lost focus.
onfocus	Element gained focus.
onreset	Form was reset.
onsubmit	Form was submitted.
onchange	Form element value changed.
onselect	Text in a form field has been selected.

Other Common Attributes

This section lists other attributes that are supported by most elements.

Core attributes

Attribute	Description
`id`	ID value unique to this document
`class`	Space-separated list of classes useful for selecting this element for style and other purposes
`style`	Local style information
`title`	Advisory title, typically rendered by a graphical browser when the pointer is over the element

Internationalization attributes

Attribute	Description
`lang`	Language code for this element's contents
`dir`	Direction (`ltr` or `rtl`) for the text

Common color codes

For a complete overview of color codes, see Chapter 12, "Colors and Images."

APPENDIX

B

HTML Special Characters Quick Reference

IN THIS APPENDIX

Essential Entities

En and Em Entities

Copyright, Trademark, and Registered Entities

Currency Entities

Quote Mark and Apostrophe Entities

Arrow Entities

Accented Character Entities

Greek Symbol Entities

Mathematical Symbol Entities

Miscellaneous Entities

This appendix lists the various *entities* — codes for inserting special characters in your documents — available in HTML. The listings are broken down by category of entity, and each table lists the character description, the decimal code, and the mnemonic code for each entity.

Cross-Ref

More information on character encodings and special characters can be found in Chapter 14. ■

Table B-1 lists the most common entities.

TABLE B-1

Essential Entities

Decimal Entity	Mnemonic Entity	Character
"	"	Double quote mark
&	&	Ampersand
<	<	Less than symbol
>	>	Greater than symbol
		Nonbreaking space

Table B-2 lists the entities for en and em elements.

TABLE B-2

En and Em Entities

Decimal Entity	Mnemonic Entity	Character
` `	` `	En space
` `	` `	Em space
`–`	`–`	En dash
`—`	`—`	Em dash

Table B-3 lists the entities pertinent to protection of intellectual property.

TABLE B-3

Copyright, Trademark, and Registered Entities

Decimal Entity	Mnemonic Entity	Character
`©`	`©`	Copyright symbol
`®`	`®`	Registered trademark symbol
`™`	`™`	Trademark symbol

Table B-4 lists many of the most common currency symbols.

TABLE B-4

Currency Entities

Decimal Entity	Mnemonic Entity	Character
`¢`	`¢`	Cent symbol
`£`	`£`	English pound
`¤`	`¤`	General currency
`¥`	`¥`	Japanese yen
`€`	`€`	European euro

Table B-5 lists the entities for real quotes.

TABLE B-5

Quote Mark and Apostrophe Entities

Decimal Entity	Mnemonic Entity	Character
`‘`	`‘`	Left/Opening single-quote
`’`	`’`	Right/Closing single-quote and apostrophe
`“`	`“`	Left/Opening double-quote
`”`	`”`	Right/Closing double-quote

Table B-6 lists the entities for a variety of arrow symbols.

TABLE B-6

Arrow Entities

Decimal Entity	Mnemonic Entity	Character
`←`	`←`	Left arrow
`↑`	`↑`	Up arrow
`→`	`→`	Right arrow
`↓`	`↓`	Down arrow
`↔`	`↔`	Left right arrow
`↵`	`↵`	Down arrow with corner leftwards
`⇐`	`⇐`	Left double arrow
`⇑`	`⇑`	Up double arrow
`⇒`	`⇒`	Right double arrow
`⇓`	`⇓`	Down double arrow
`⇔`	`⇔`	Left right double arrow

Table B-7 lists the accented character entities.

TABLE B-7

Accented Character Entities

Decimal Entity	Mnemonic Entity	Character
À	À	Latin capital letter A with grave
Á	Á	Latin capital letter A with acute
Â	Â	Latin capital letter A with circumflex
Ã	Ã	Latin capital letter A with tilde
Ä	Ä	Latin capital letter A with diaeresis
Å	Å	Latin capital letter A with ring above
Æ	Æ	Latin capital letter AE
Ç	Ç	Latin capital letter C with cedilla
È	È	Latin capital letter E with grave
É	É	Latin capital letter E with acute
Ê	Ê	Latin capital letter E with circumflex
Ë	Ë	Latin capital letter E with diaeresis
Ì	Ì	Latin capital letter I with grave
Í	Í	Latin capital letter I with acute
Î	Î	Latin capital letter I with circumflex
Ï	Ï	Latin capital letter I with diaeresis
Ð	Ð	Latin capital letter ETH
Ñ	Ñ	Latin capital letter N with tilde
Ò	Ò	Latin capital letter O with grave
Ó	Ó	Latin capital letter O with acute
Ô	Ô	Latin capital letter O with circumflex
Õ	Õ	Latin capital letter O with tilde
Ö	Ö	Latin capital letter O with diaeresis
Ø	Ø	Latin capital letter O with stroke
Ù	Ù	Latin capital letter U with grave
Ú	Ú	Latin capital letter U with acute
Û	Û	Latin capital letter U with circumflex

Decimal Entity	Mnemonic Entity	Character
Ü	Ü	Latin capital letter U with diaeresis
Ý	Ý	Latin capital letter Y with acute
Þ	Þ	Latin capital letter THORN
ß	ß	Latin small letter sharp s = ess-zed
à	à	Latin small letter a with grave
á	á	Latin small letter a with acute
â	â	Latin small letter a with circumflex
ã	ã	Latin small letter a with tilde
ä	ä	Latin small letter a with diaeresis
å	å	Latin small letter a with ring above
æ	æ	Latin small letter ae
ç	ç	Latin small letter c with cedilla
è	è	Latin small letter e with grave
é	é	Latin small letter e with acute
ê	ê	Latin small letter e with circumflex
ë	ë	Latin small letter e with diaeresis
ì	ì	Latin small letter i with grave
í	í	Latin small letter i with acute
î	î	Latin small letter i with circumflex
ï	ï	Latin small letter i with diaeresis
ð	ð	Latin small letter eth
ñ	ñ	Latin small letter n with tilde
ò	ò	Latin small letter o with grave
ó	ó	Latin small letter o with acute
ô	ô	Latin small letter o with circumflex
õ	õ	Latin small letter o with tilde
ö	ö	Latin small letter o with diaeresis
ø	ø	Latin small letter o with stroke
ù	ù	Latin small letter u with grave
ú	ú	Latin small letter u with acute

continued

TABLE B-7 *(continued)*

Decimal Entity	Mnemonic Entity	Character
û	û	Latin small letter u with circumflex
ü	ü	Latin small letter u with diaeresis
ý	ý	Latin small letter y with acute
þ	þ	Latin small letter thorn
ÿ	ÿ	Latin small letter y with diaeresis

Table B-8 lists various Greek symbol entities.

TABLE B-8

Greek Symbol Entities

Decimal Entity	Mnemonic Entity	Character
Α	Α	Greek capital letter alpha
Β	Β	Greek capital letter beta
Γ	Γ	Greek capital letter gamma
Δ	Δ	Greek capital letter delta
Ε	Ε	Greek capital letter epsilon
Ζ	Ζ	Greek capital letter zeta
Η	Η	Greek capital letter eta
Θ	Θ	Greek capital letter theta
Ι	Ι	Greek capital letter iota
Κ	Κ	Greek capital letter kappa
Λ	Λ	Greek capital letter lambda
Μ	Μ	Greek capital letter mu
Ν	Ν	Greek capital letter nu
Ξ	Ξ	Greek capital letter xi
Ο	Ο	Greek capital letter omicron
Π	Π	Greek capital letter pi
Ρ	Ρ	Greek capital letter rho
Σ	Σ	Greek capital letter sigma

Decimal Entity	Mnemonic Entity	Character
Τ	Τ	Greek capital letter tau
Υ	Υ	Greek capital letter upsilon
Φ	Φ	Greek capital letter phi
Χ	Χ	Greek capital letter chi
Ψ	Ψ	Greek capital letter psi
Ω	Ω	Greek capital letter omega
α	α	Greek small letter alpha
β	β	Greek small letter beta
γ	γ	Greek small letter gamma
δ	δ	Greek small letter delta
ε	ε	Greek small letter epsilon
ζ	ζ	Greek small letter zeta
η	η	Greek small letter eta
θ	θ	Greek small letter theta
ι	ι	Greek small letter iota
κ	κ	Greek small letter kappa
λ	λ	Greek small letter lambda
μ	μ	Greek small letter mu
ν	ν	Greek small letter nu
ξ	ξ	Greek small letter xi
ο	ο	Greek small letter omicron
π	π	Greek small letter pi
ρ	ρ	Greek small letter rho
ς	ς	Greek small letter final sigma
σ	σ	Greek small letter sigma
τ	τ	Greek small letter tau
υ	υ	Greek small letter upsilon
φ	φ	Greek small letter phi
χ	χ	Greek small letter chi
ψ	ψ	Greek small letter psi

continued

TABLE B-8 *(continued)*

Decimal Entity	Mnemonic Entity	Character
ω	ω	Greek small letter omega
ϑ	ϑ	Greek small letter theta symbol
ϒ	ϒ	Greek upsilon with hook symbol
ϖ	ϖ	Greek pi symbol

Table B-9 lists a variety of mathematical symbols.

TABLE B-9

Mathematical Symbol Entities

Decimal Entity	Mnemonic Entity	Character
×	×	Multiplication sign
÷	&division;	Division sign
∀	∀	For all
∂	∂	Partial differential
∃	∃	There exists
∅	∅	Empty set = null set = diameter
∇	∇	Nabla = backward difference
∈	∈	Element of
∉	∉	Not an element of
∋	∋	Contains as member
∏	∏	n-ary product = product sign
∑	∑	n-ary summation
−	−	Minus sign
∗	∗	Asterisk operator
√	√	Square root = radical sign
∝	∝	Proportional to
∞	∞	Infinity

Decimal Entity	Mnemonic Entity	Character
∠	∠	Angle
∧	∧	Logical and = wedge
∨	∨	Logical or = vee
∩	∩	Intersection = cap
∪	∪	Union = cup
∫	∫	Integral
∴	∴	Therefore
∼	∼	Tilde operator = varies with = similar to
≅	≅	Approximately equal to
≈	≈	Almost equal to = asymptotic to
≠	≠	Not equal to
≡	≡	Identical to
≤	≤	Less than or equal to
≥	≥	Greater than or equal to
⊂	⊂	Subset of
⊃	⊃	Superset of
⊄	⊄	Not a subset of
⊆	⊆	Subset of or equal to
⊇	⊇	Superset of or equal to
⊕	⊕	Circled plus = direct sum
⊗	⊗	Circled times = vector product
⊥	⊥	Up tack = orthogonal to = perpendicular
⋅	⋅	Dot operator
⌈	⌈	Left ceiling
⌉	⌉	Right ceiling
⌊	⌊	Left floor
⌋	⌋	Right floor
〈	⟨	Left-pointing angle bracket
〉	⟩	Right-pointing angle bracket

Table B-10 lists other miscellaneous entities.

TABLE B-10

Miscellaneous Entities

Decimal Entity	Mnemonic Entity	Character
¡	¡	Inverted exclamation mark
¦	¦	Broken bar = broken vertical bar
§	§	Section sign
¨	¨	Diaeresis = spacing diaeresis
ª	ª	Feminine ordinal indicator
«	«	Left-pointing double angle quotation mark = left pointing guillemet
¬	¬	Not sign
		Soft hyphen = discretionary hyphen
¯	¯	Macron = spacing macron = overline = APL overbar
°	°	Degree sign
±	±	Plus-minus sign = plus-or-minus sign
²	²	Superscript two = superscript digit two = squared
³	³	Superscript three = superscript digit three = cubed
´	´	Acute accent = spacing acute
µ	µ	Micro sign
¶	¶	Pilcrow sign = paragraph sign
·	·	Middle dot = Georgian comma = Greek middle dot
¸	¸	Cedilla = spacing cedilla
¹	¹	Superscript one = superscript digit one
º	º	Masculine ordinal indicator
»	»	Right-pointing double angle quotation mark = right pointing guillemet
¼	¼	Vulgar fraction one quarter = fraction one quarter
½	½	Vulgar fraction one half = fraction one half
¾	¾	Vulgar fraction three quarters = fraction three quarters
¿	¿	Inverted question mark = turned question mark
Œ	Œ	Latin capital ligature OE
œ	œ	Latin small ligature oe

Decimal Entity	Mnemonic Entity	Character
Š	Š	Latin capital letter S with caron
š	š	Latin small letter s with caron
Ÿ	Ÿ	Latin capital letter Y with diaeresis
ˆ	ˆ	Modifier letter circumflex accent
˜	˜	Small tilde
		Thin space
‌	‌	Zero width non-joiner
‍	‍	Zero width joiner
‎	‎	Left-to-right mark
‏	‏	Right-to-left mark
‚	‚	Single low-9 quotation mark
„	„	Double low-9 quotation mark
†	†	Dagger
‡	‡	Double dagger
‰	‰	Per mille sign
‹	‹	Single left-pointing angle quotation mark
›	›	Single right-pointing angle quotation mark

APPENDIX

CSS 2.1 Properties Quick Reference

IN THIS APPENDIX

This appendix follows CSS 2.1, which is a specification intended to represent the most commonly supported properties in modern browsers.

Note that aural stylesheet properties are not covered in this appendix because adequate coverage of their use and capabilities goes well beyond a quick reference. For information on aural properties and their use, visit The Alliance for Technology Access website at `www.ataccess.org`.

Unfortunately, solid support for many of the CSS properties is spotty, so testing on a wide variety of Web browsers is recommended. In addition, several websites provide extensive information on CSS support across the popular browsers.

Cross-Ref

For an overview of CSS selectors, see Appendix D. ■

Property Listings

In each table that follows, words under Supported values that are capitalized are placeholders for either a set of possible values or values drawn from a related property. Examples of placeholders include the following:

- **Length** — Number followed by a unit of measurement, such as "px" for pixel
- **Percentage** — Number followed by a percent sign
- **Integer** — Whole number

Inherited refers to whether a given property will be drawn from the element's parents if it is not explicitly provided.

Property List: Quick Reference

The following list provides an overview of the full list of CSS properties. Use this list as a reference to the assorted attributes listed within the appendix.

- Background
  - background-image
  - background-repeat
  - background-attachment
  - background-position
  - background-color
  - background
- List
  - list-style-type
  - list-style-position
  - list-style-image
  - list-style
- Generated content
  - content
  - quotes
  - counter-increment
  - counter-reset
- Font and text
  - text-align
  - text-decoration
  - text-indent
  - text-transform
  - color
  - font-family
  - font-size
  - font-style
  - font-variant
  - font-weight
  - font

- letter-spacing
- word-spacing
- white-space

Text direction

- unicode-bidi
- direction

Block

- margin-left, margin-right, margin-top, margin-bottom
- margin
- padding-left, padding-right, padding-top, padding-bottom
- padding
- clip
- overflow
- height, width
- max-height, max-width
- min-height, min-width
- line-height
- vertical-align

Positioning

- visibility
- display
- position
- float
- top, bottom, left, right
- z-index
- clear

Borders

- border-color, border-top-color, border-bottom-color, border-left-color, border-right-color
- border-style, border-top-style, border-bottom-style, border-left-style, border-right-style
- border-width, border-top-width, border-bottom-width, border-left-width, border-right-width
- border
- outline-color
- outline-style
- outline-width
- outline

- Table
  - table-layout
  - border-collapse
  - border-spacing
  - empty-cells
  - caption-side
- Printing
  - page-break-after, page-break-before
  - page-break-inside
  - orphans
  - widows
- Miscellaneous
  - cursor

Background

Listings of the background properties follow.

background-image

Place an image behind an element (typically the body of a document).

```
table { background-image: url("/images/draft.gif"); }
```

Supported values	`url()`, `none`, `inherit`
Default value	`none`
Inherited	No
Applies to	All

background-repeat

Define the background image behavior if it fails to fill its element.

```
table { background-repeat: none; }
```

Supported values	`repeat`, `repeat-x`, `repeat-y`, `no-repeat`, `inherit`
Default value	`repeat`
Inherited	No
Applies to	All

background-attachment

Specify whether the background image scrolls with the enclosing element.

```
table { background-attachment: fixed; }
```

Supported values	`scroll`, `fixed`, `inherit`
Default value	`scroll`
Inherited	No
Applies to	All
Note(s)	Browsers not required to support "fixed"

background-position

Declare the initial position of a background image.

```
table { background-position 25% 25%; }
```

Supported values	Percentage, Length, `top`, `center`, `bottom`, `left`, `right`, `inherit`
Default value	`0 0`
Inherited	No
Applies to	All
Note(s)	If two values are supplied, the first is a horizontal position and the second vertical. If one numeric value is supplied, it is treated as a horizontal position, and vertical will be 50 percent.

background-color

Define the background color for an element.

```
body { background-color: black; }
```

Supported values	Color, `transparent`, `inherit`
Default value	`transparent`
Inherited	No
Applies to	All

background

Consolidate background properties.

```
table { background: url("/images/draft.gif") none fixed 25% 25%; }
```

Supported values	Color, Image, Repeat, Attachment, Position, `inherit`
Default value	`transparent`, `none`, `repeat`, `scroll`, `0 0`
Inherited	No
Applies to	All

List

These properties apply to the rendering of lists. See also `counter-increment` and `counter-reset` in the section "Generated Content" later in this appendix.

list-style-type

Select the bullet markers for a list.

```
ul.nobullet { list-style-type: none; }
```

Supported values	`disc`, `circle`, `square`, `decimal`, `decimal-leading-zero`, `lower-roman`, `upper-roman`, `lower-greek`, `lower-latin`, `upper-latin`, `armenian`, `georgian`, `lower-alpha`, `upper-alpha`, `none`, `inherit`
Default value	`disc`
Inherited	Yes
Applies to	`li`

list-style-position

Indicate whether the list markers should be treated as internal to the box enclosing each list item.

```
ul.paragraphs { list-style-position: inside; }
```

Supported values	`inside`, `outside`, `inherit`
Default value	`outside`
Inherited	Yes
Applies to	`li`

list-style-image

Refer to an image to be used for bullet markers.

```
ul { list-style-image: url("/images/daggers.gif"); }
```

Supported values	`url()`, `none`, `inherit`
Default value	`none`
Inherited	Yes
Applies to	`li`

list-style

Consolidate list-style properties.

```
ul { list-style: circle outside url("/images/daggers.gif"); }
```

Supported values	Type Position Image, `inherit`
Default value	`disc outside none`
Inherited	Yes
Applies to	`li`
Note(s)	If both a type and an image are supplied, the list-style type will be used if the image cannot be retrieved.

Generated content

CSS provides for the insertion of new text in certain locations via the `content` property.

The other properties in this section affect the text inserted by the `content` property by modifying the open/close quotes or by impacting a named counter value. Many of these properties and methods are not widely supported.

content

Text to be displayed by autogeneration properties.

```
.quote:before { content: open-quote; }
.quote:after { content: close-quote; }
```

Supported values	`normal`, `String`, `url()`, `counter()`, `counters()`, `attr()`, `open-quote`, `close-quote`, `no-open-quote`, `no-close-quote`, `inherit`
Default value	Normal
Inherited	No
Applies to	`:before`, `:after` pseudo-elements

quotes

Define quotation marks for use with q elements and content properties.

```
body { quotes: "\00AB" "\00BB"; }
```

Supported values	String, none, inherit
Default value	Browser-defined
Inherited	Yes
Applies to	All

counter-increment

Indicate that the named counter should be incremented by one or the numeric value provided.

```
div.section { counter-increment: sectionheading; }
```

Supported values	Identifier Integer, none, inherit
Default value	none
Inherited	No
Applies to	All

counter-reset

Indicate that the named counter should be set back to zero or the numeric value provided.

```
div.section { counter-reset: sectionsubheading; }
```

Supported values	Identifier Integer, none, inherit
Default value	none
Inherited	No
Applies to	All

Font and text

These properties are used to specify the way in which text is rendered.

text-align

Specify the text alignment within the block.

```
pre.poem { text-align: center; }
```

Supported values	`center`, `left`, `right`, `justify`, `inherit`
Default value	`left` (but see Notes in this table)
Inherited	Yes
Applies to	Block elements, `td`, `th`, and form input fields
Note(s)	The default value is "correct" if `direction: rtl` is set.

text-decoration

Augment the text with underlining or similar properties.

```
p.annoying { text-decoration: line-through blink; }
```

Supported values	`none`, `underline`, `overline`, `line-through`, `blink`, `inherit`
Default value	`none`
Inherited	No
Applies to	All
Note(s)	Several decorations may be listed with whitespace separation.

text-indent

Specify the indentation for the first line in a block.

```
p { text-indent: 1em; }
```

Supported values	Length, Percentage, `inherit`
Default value	0
Inherited	Yes
Applies to	Block elements, `td`, `th`, and form input fields.

text-transform

Convert text to uppercase or lowercase.

```
span.customername { text-transform: uppercase; }
```

Supported values	`capitalize`, `uppercase`, `lowercase`, `none`, `inherit`
Default value	`none`
Inherited	Yes
Applies to	All

color

Define text color.

```
div.hardtoread { color: yellow; }
```

Supported values	Color, `inherit`
Default value	Browser-defined
Inherited	Yes
Applies to	All
Note(s)	Any borders in this scope will default to this color.

font-family

Define the desired typeface.

```
body { font-family: Garamond, serif; }
```

Supported values	Family (one or more comma-separated values), `inherit`
Default value	Browser-defined
Inherited	Yes
Applies to	All
Note(s)	Use quotes around font family names that include spaces. Be sure to provide generic families as alternatives should the browser not be able to locate the font you prefer.

font-size

Specify the type size.

```
caption { font-size: x-large; }
```

Supported values	Length, Percentage, `xx-large`, `x-large`, `large`, `medium`, `small`, `x-small`, `xx-small`, `larger`, `smaller`, `inherit`
Default value	`medium`
Inherited	Yes
Applies to	All

font-style

Render the enclosed text as italic, oblique, or normal.

```
.booktitle { font-style: italic; }
```

Supported values	`normal`, `italic`, `oblique`, `inherit`
Default value	`normal`
Inherited	Yes
Applies to	All

font-variant

Render the enclosed text as small capitals or normal.

```
span.manufacturername { font-variant: small-caps; }
```

Supported values	`normal`, `small-caps`, `inherit`
Default value	`normal`
Inherited	Yes
Applies to	All

font-weight

Specify the "boldness" of text.

```
caption { font-weight: 900; }
```

Supported values	`normal`, `bolder`, `bold`, `lighter`, `100`, `200`, `300`, `400`, `500`, `600`, `700`, `800`, `900`
Default value	`normal`
Inherited	Yes
Applies to	All
Note(s)	`normal` is equivalent to `400`; `bold` to `700`.

font

Consolidate font properties or specify system fonts.

```
h6 { font: menu; }
```

Supported values	`caption`, `icon`, `menu`, `message-box`, `small-caption`, `status-bar`, `inherit` (and see Note(s))
Default value	See `font-style`, `font-variant`, `font-weight`, `font-size`
Inherited	Yes
Applies to	All
Note(s)	The value can be one of the preceding or a combination of the other font properties with `line-height` thrown in to confuse things.

letter-spacing

Add to the spacing between letters.

```
blockquote { letter-spacing: 0.1em; }
```

Supported values	Length, `normal`, `inherit`
Default value	`normal`
Inherited	Yes
Applies to	All
Note(s)	The value may be negative.

word-spacing

Add to the spacing between words.

```
h2 { word-spacing: 1em; }
```

Supported values	Length, `normal`, `inherit`
Default value	`normal`
Inherited	Yes
Applies to	All

white-space

Specify the handling of whitespace, including line wrapping.

```
blockquote.poem { white-space: pre; }
```

Supported values	`normal`, `pre`, `nowrap`, `pre-wrap`, `pre-line`, `inherit`
Default value	`normal`
Inherited	Yes
Applies to	All

Text direction

These properties are required to deal with the problems arising from the fact that some languages read right to left while others read left to right.

unicode-bidi

This, combined with the `direction` property, handles the directionality of text for a document. This property is useful only when two languages of different directionality are present.

```
span.arabic { unicode-bidi: embed; direction: rtl; }
span.english { unicode-bidi: embed; direction: ltr; }
```

Supported values	`normal`, `embed`, `bidi-override`, `inherit`
Default value	`normal`
Inherited	No
Applies to	All

direction

Define the direction for the enclosed text.

```
p.english { direction: ltr; }
```

Supported values	ltr, rtl, inherit
Default value	ltr
Inherited	Yes
Applies to	All except for inline elements with unicode-bidi: normal

Block

The key differentiator between padding and margin: The padding is inside any border around a block, and the margin is outside that border.

margin-left, margin-right, margin-top, margin-bottom

Define the size of the margin on a given side of a block.

```
blockquote { margin-left: 10%; }
```

Supported values	Length, Percentage, auto
Default value	0
Inherited	No
Applies to	All except for table components (e.g., td, tfoot, tr)

margin

Consolidate margin widths.

```
p { margin: 1em 0 1em 0; }
```

Supported values	Length, Percentage, auto (up to four values defining up to the four sides)
Default value	0 0 0 0
Inherited	No
Applies to	All except for table components (that is, td, tfoot, tr)
Note(s)	Order of values: top, right, bottom, left.

padding-left, padding-right, padding-top, padding-bottom

Define the size of the padding on a given side of a block.

```
div.withborder { padding-top: 2%; }
```

Supported values	Length, Percentage, `inherit`
Default value	`0`
Inherited	No
Applies to	All excluding table components (but including `td`, `th`)

padding

Consolidate padding widths.

```
div.withborder { padding: 2% 0 0 0; }
```

Supported values	Length, Percentage, `inherit` (up to four values)
Default value	`0 0 0 0`
Inherited	No
Applies to	All excluding table components (but including `td` and `th`)
Note(s)	Order of values: `top`, `right`, `bottom`, `left`.

clip

Define a boundary for an element outside of which any presentation (text, border) should be clipped.

```
blockquote { clip: rect(5px, 20px, 20px, 5px); overflow: scroll; }
```

Supported values	Shape, `auto`, `inherit`
Default value	`auto`
Inherited	No
Applies to	Absolutely positioned elements
Note(s)	If overflow is `visible`, this has no effect. The only recognized shape is `rect()`.

overflow

Specify what happens when a block's content is larger than the clipping area.

```
blockquote { clip: rect(5px, 20px, 20px, 5px); overflow: scroll; }
```

Supported values	visible, hidden, scroll, auto, inherit
Default value	visible
Inherited	No
Applies to	Block elements, img, object, td, th

height, width

Specify the height or width of an element.

```
img.logo { height: 5cm; width: 5cm; }
```

Supported values	Length, Percentage, auto, inherit
Default value	auto
Inherited	No
Applies to	Block elements, img, object, and form input fields

max-height, max-width

Constrain element size.

```
table { max-width: 50%; }
```

Supported values	Length, Percentage, none, inherit
Default value	none
Inherited	No
Applies to	Block elements, img, object, and form input fields

min-height, min-width

Define a minimum element size.

```
textarea { min-width: 25%; }
```

Supported values	Length, Percentage, `inherit`
Default value	`0`
Inherited	No
Applies to	Block elements, `img`, `object`, and form input fields

line-height

Define line height. For block elements, this is the minimal line height; for inline, it is the specific height.

```
p { line-height: 150%; }
```

Supported values	Number, Length, Percentage, `normal`, `inherit`
Default value	`normal`
Inherited	Yes
Applies to	All
Note(s)	Unless an absolute measurement such as "cm" is used, this will be relative to the font size.

vertical-align

Define the vertical-alignment characteristics of this element relative to its line box (when `top` or `bottom` are specified) or its parent.

```
span.superscript { vertical-align: super; }
```

Supported values	Length, Percentage, `baseline`, `sub`, `super`, `top`, `text-top`, `middle`, `bottom`, `text-bottom`, `inherit`
Default value	`baseline`
Inherited	No
Applies to	Inline, `td`, `th`

Positioning

The preceding block properties specify the internal characteristics of the boxes that are used to lay out a page. The properties in this section can be used to describe the desired positions of those boxes.

visibility

Specify whether an element should be visible.

```
li.answer { visibility: hidden; }
```

Supported values	visible, hidden, collapse, inherit
Default value	visible
Inherited	Yes
Applies to	All
Note(s)	Unless display: none is set, the element will still occupy space, even if hidden.

display

Specify how an element should be presented.

```
.invisible { display: none; }
```

Supported values	none, inline, block, list-item, run-in, inline-block, table, inline-table, table-row-group, table-header-group, table-footer-group, table-row, table-column-group, table-column, table-cell, table-caption, inherit
Default value	inline
Inherited	No
Applies to	All
Note(s)	Other than removing objects from the document flow by setting display to none, this property is most valuable for defining the presentation of XML documents with no inherent style.

position

Specify the algorithm to be used for placing this element's containing box on the page.

```
div#menu { position: absolute; top: 3.8cm; left: 0;}
```

Supported values	`static, relative, absolute, fixed, inherit`
Default value	`static`
Inherited	No
Applies to	All

float

For elements that are not absolutely positioned, define their relationship to elements surrounding them.

```
div#logo { float: left; }
```

Supported values	`left, right, none, inherit`
Default value	`none`
Inherited	No
Applies to	All elements without `display: none`

top, bottom, left, right

For absolutely positioned elements, define the distance to the enclosing box's edges.

```
div#menu { position: absolute; top: 3.8cm; left: 0;}
```

Supported values	`Length, Percentage, auto, inherit`
Default value	`auto`
Inherited	No
Applies to	Positioned elements

z-index

Define stacking order for overlapping elements.

```
div#logo { z-index: 99; }
```

Supported values	`Integer`, `auto`, `inherit`
Default value	`auto`
Inherited	No
Applies to	Positioned elements
Note(s)	The higher the number, the higher on the stack.

clear

Specify which sides of an element's box may not be adjacent to a floating element.

```
h1 { clear: both; }
```

Supported values	`none`, `left`, `right`, `both`, `inherit`
Default value	`none`
Inherited	No
Applies to	Block elements
Note(s)	This element will be shifted to be below any floater.

Borders

These properties specify borders and outlines for the boxes used to lay out the page. Note that outlines are not widely supported.

border-color, border-top-color, border-bottom-color, border-left-color, border-right-color

Specify border colors.

```
div#logo { border-color: green; }
```

Supported values	`Color`, `transparent`, `inherit`
Default value	Element color property value
Inherited	No
Applies to	All

border-style, border-top-style, border-bottom-style, border-left-style, border-right-style

Specify the border design.

```
div#logo { border-style: groove; }
```

Supported values	none, hidden, dotted, dashed, solid, double, groove, ridge, inset, outset, inherit
Default value	none
Inherited	No
Applies to	All

border-width, border-top-width, border-bottom-width, border-left-width, border-right-width

Specify the border size.

```
div#logo { border-width: thin; }
```

Supported values	Length, thin, medium, thick, inherit
Default value	medium
Inherited	No
Applies to	All

border

Consolidate border properties.

```
div#logo { border: green groove thin; }
```

Supported values	Color Style Width, inherit
Default value	color, none, medium
Inherited	No
Applies to	All

outline-color

Specify outline color.

```
span.acronym { outline-color: blue; }
```

Supported values	Color, invert, inherit
Default value	invert
Inherited	No
Applies to	All

outline-style

Specify the outline style.

```
span.acronym { outline-style: dotted; }
```

Supported values	none, dotted, dashed, solid, double, groove, ridge, inset, outset, inherit
Default value	none
Inherited	No
Applies to	All

outline-width

Specify the outline width.

```
span.acronym { outline-width: thin; }
```

Supported values	Length, thin, medium, thick, inherit
Default value	medium
Inherited	No
Applies to	All

outline

Consolidate outline properties.

```
span.acronym { outline: blue dotted thin; }
```

Supported values	Color Style Width, `inherit`
Default value	`invert, none, medium`
Inherited	No
Applies to	All

Table

These properties specify how tables are rendered, primarily table borders.

table-layout

Specify a table layout algorithm. If `auto`, the table's contents will be scanned before generation to calculate the proper width of each column.

```
table.huge { table-layout: fixed; }
```

Supported values	`auto, fixed, inherit`
Default value	`auto`
Inherited	No
Applies to	`table`

border-collapse

Specify whether adjacent table cell borders should be consolidated.

```
table { border-collapse: collapse; }
```

Supported values	`collapse, separate, inherit`
Default value	`separate`
Inherited	Yes
Applies to	`table`

border-spacing

Define the space between internal table borders.

```
table { border-spacing: 2pt 4pt; }
```

Supported values	Length (1 or 2 values), `inherit`
Default value	`0`
Inherited	Yes
Applies to	`table`
Note(s)	If two values, the first is horizontal, the second vertical; otherwise, the value is applied to both dimensions.

empty-cells

Specify whether empty cells should be rendered with background and border.

```
table { empty-cells: hide; }
```

Supported values	`show`, `hide`, `inherit`
Default value	`show`
Inherited	Yes
Applies to	`td`, `th`

caption-side

Specify whether a caption is placed above or below its table.

```
table.figure { caption-side: bottom; }
```

Supported values	`top`, `bottom`, `inherit`
Default value	`top`
Inherited	Yes
Applies to	`caption`

Printing

These properties provide instructions to the user agent about how the page should be handled when printed. These can be used to help prevent inappropriate page breaks and otherwise format a printed page.

page-break-after, page-break-before

Specify whether a printed page break should occur before or after this block element.

```
h1 { page-break-after: avoid; }
```

Supported values	`auto, always, avoid, left, right, inherit`
Default value	`auto`
Inherited	No
Applies to	Block elements

page-break-inside

Specify a preference regarding page breaks internal to a block element.

```
table { page-break-inside: avoid; }
```

Supported values	`avoid, auto, inherit`
Default value	`auto`
Inherited	Yes
Applies to	Block elements

orphans

Define the minimum number of lines in a paragraph that must be left at the bottom of a page. Any fewer and the entire paragraph will wrap to the following page.

```
body { orphans: 3; }
```

Supported values	Integer, `inherit`
Default value	`2`
Inherited	Yes
Applies to	Block elements

widows

Define the minimum number of lines in a paragraph that must be available for the top of a page. Any fewer and the entire paragraph will wrap to that page.

```
body { widows: 4; }
```

Supported values	Integer, `inherit`
Default value	`2`
Inherited	Yes
Applies to	Block elements

Miscellaneous

The cursor property specifies what the user agent cursor should be when it is over the element to which the property is applied.

cursor

Define the type of cursor to be used when the mouse is over this element.

```
body.annoyuser { cursor: wait; }
```

Supported values	`auto`, `crosshair`, `default`, `pointer`, `move`, `nw-resize`, `n-resize`, `ne-resize`, `e-resize`, `se-resize`, `s-resize`, `sw-resize`, `w-resize`, `text`, `wait`, `help`, `progress`, `inherit`, `url()`
Default value	`auto`
Inherited	Yes (but see Note(s))
Applies to	All
Note(s)	The specification states that this is inherited, but browsers do not consistently do so. Use the `inherit` value if you want the parent's cursor to carry over to elements such as hyperlinks that would ordinarily have their own cursor type.

APPENDIX

CSS 2.1 Selectors Quick Reference

IN THIS APPENDIX

CSS selectors are specific patterns used to match elements that will have the corresponding properties applied to them. CSS has many different patterns to match many different aspects of elements — their name/type, class, ID, place in the document hierarchy, and more.

In addition to using a single pattern to match elements, you can also combine patterns to create more specific matches. For example, the following selector matches all h1 elements:

```
h1 { properties }
```

If you need more specificity, you can add a class selector as in the following example, which matches all h2 elements with a class of section:

```
h2.section  { properties }
```

You can take the selector even one step further by adding a descendant selector, as in the following example, which matches all h2 elements with a class of section that are also descendants of h1 elements:

```
h1 h2.section  { properties }
```

The following sections provide a quick reference into the various CSS selector patterns.

Basic Element Selectors

The basic element selectors are used to match specific elements by name (e.g., p, h1, and so on).

Syntax:

```
E { properties }
```

Matches all E elements.

Syntax:

```
* { properties }
```

Matches all elements.

Note

The universal selector (*) guarantees only a universal (all element) match if it is the sole criteria in the selector. If additional conditions are added, they too must be met to match elements. For example, the following selector will match elements with a class of `book` only:

```
*.book { properties }
```

However, because of the use of the universal selector, *all* elements with a class of `book` will be matched. ■

Syntax:

```
E, F, G { properties }
```

Matches all E, F, and G elements.

Note

The comma separator can be used to specify a variety of selector patterns for the same selector definition, not just element name selectors. ■

Descendant Selectors

Descendant selectors are used to match elements that are descendants of other, specific elements.

Syntax:

```
E F { properties }
```

Matches all F elements that are descendants of E elements.

Child Selectors

Child selectors are used to match elements that are children (direct descendants) of other, specific elements.

Syntax:

```
E > F { properties }
```

Matches all `F` elements that are children of `E` elements.

Note

Child selectors are very much like descendant selectors in scope in that they select elements that are descendants of a specific ancestor element. The distinction, however, is that children must be *direct descendants* of the specific ancestor element. That is, there can be no elements between the ancestor (parent) and descendant (child). ■

Adjacent Sibling Selectors

Adjacent sibling selectors are used to match the second of two elements that share the same parent.

Syntax:

```
E + F { properties }
```

Matches all `F` elements that have the same direct sibling relationship (share the same parent) as `E` elements. Note that the `E` element must immediately precede the `F` element in the document tree.

Class Selectors

Class selectors are used to match elements of a particular class (elements that have a particular value for their `class` attribute).

Syntax:

```
E.c { properties }
```

Matches all `E` elements that have a class of `c`.

Tip

You can also use the attribute selector method to select elements that have the class attribute set to a specific value or set to any value. See the "Attribute Selectors" section later in this appendix for more information. ■

ID Selectors

ID selectors are used to match elements of a particular ID (elements that have a particular value for their `ID` attribute).

Syntax:

```
E#i { properties }
```

Matches all E elements that have an ID of i.

Attribute Selectors

Attribute selectors are used to match elements that have a particular value for a particular attribute. The attribute selector has three different formats.

Syntax:

```
E[a] { properties }
```

Matches all E elements that have an attribute named a, no matter what the value.

```
E[a="v"]
```

Matches all E elements that have an attribute named a, with a value of v.

```
E[a~="v"]
```

Matches all E elements that have an attribute named a, with a space-separated list of values, one of which is v.

Tip

This selector method can also be used to match elements with a specific class using the format

```
E[class~="c"]
```

where c is the class value to match.

```
E[a|="v"]
```

Matches all E elements that have an attribute named a, with a hyphen-separated list of values, the first of which is v. ■

APPENDIX

Pseudo-Elements and Pseudo-Classes Quick Reference

IN THIS APPENDIX

Pseudo-Elements

Pseudo-Classes

CSS selectors are designed to match HTML elements that are in a static state. Occasionally, however, you will want to match pieces of a document that cannot be clearly delimited by HTML entities, or match elements that are in a particular phase of a dynamic state. For these purposes, pseudo-elements and pseudo-classes exist.

Pseudo-elements provide the means to match certain parts of a document that aren't delimited by standard elements — the first line or first letter of an element's content, for example.

Pseudo-classes provide the means to match elements that are in a certain state — being the first child of a parent element, having the mouse hovering over the element, and so on.

Both pseudo-elements and pseudo-classes have the same format: a colon followed by a keyword that is appended to the end of a selector. For example, the following selector will select the first line of all h1 elements:

```
h1:first-line { properties }
```

The following sections provide a quick reference for pseudo-elements and pseudo-classes.

Note

The pseudo-elements and pseudo-classes covered in this appendix are implemented in almost all modern browsers. Exceptions are the *before* and *after* pseudo-elements, which are not yet supported in Internet Explorer (as of version 7.0), and the *lang* pseudo-class, which is supported only in Internet Explorer for the Mac. The World Wide Web Consortium (W3C) has suggested many more pseudo-constructs for CSS level 3, which, as of this writing, is still in draft form. Pseudo-constructs are a powerful feature of CSS but should be tested on your target platform(s) before being implemented on a large scale. ■

Pseudo-Elements

Syntax:

```
E:first-line { properties }
```

Matches the first line of all E elements.

Syntax:

```
E:first-letter { properties }
```

Matches the first letter of all E elements.

Syntax:

```
E:before { properties } E:after { properties }
```

Matches the space immediately before (:before) and after (:after) all E elements.

Pseudo-Classes

Syntax:

```
E:first-child { properties }
```

Matches all E elements that are a first child of their parent element.

Syntax:

```
E:link { properties } E:visited { properties }
```

Matches all E elements that represent a link to another resource (:link) that has not been visited, or a link to another resource that has been previously visited (:visited).

Syntax:

```
E:active { properties } E:hover { properties } E:focus { properties }
```

Matches all E elements in an active state (:active) that are being hovered over by the mouse (:hover), or have the current focus (:focus).

Syntax:

```
E:lang(c)
```

Matches all E elements that are in language "c".

Index

A

Index

B

Index

E

F

G

H

I

J

K

L

M

N

O

P

Q

R

S

T

U

V

W

X

Y

Z

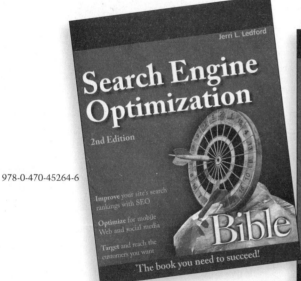